Peterson's

ULTIMATE ACT® TOOL KIT

2nd Edition

Mark Alan Stewart

PETERSON'S

A nelnet COMPANY

PETERSON'S
A nelnet COMPANY

About Peterson's, a Nelnet company

Peterson's (www.petersons.com) is a leading provider of education information and advice, with books and online resources focusing on education search, test preparation, and financial aid. Its Web site offers searchable databases and interactive tools for contacting educational institutions, online practice tests and instruction, and planning tools for securing financial aid. Peterson's serves 110 million education consumers annually.

For more information, contact Peterson's, 2000 Lenox Drive, Lawrenceville, NJ 08648; 800-338-3282; or find us on the World Wide Web at: www.petersons.com/about.

Editor: Wallie Walker Hammond; Production Editor: Linda Seghers; Manufacturing Manager: Ray Golaszewski; Composition Manager: Gary Rozmierski; CD Producer: Jason Kresge.

ISBN-13: 978-0-7689-2529-6
ISBN-10: 0-7689-2529-0

Printed in the United States of America

10 9 8 7 6 5 4 3 2 09 08 07

Second Edition

Petersons.com/publishing

Check out our Web site at www.petersons.com/publishing to see if there is any new information regarding the test and any revisions or corrections to the content of this book. We've made sure the information in this book is accurate and up-to-date; however, the test format or content may have changed since the time of publication.

Contents

PART V: THE SCIENCE TEST

PART VI: THREE PRACTICE ACTs

About This Tool Kit

Your Tools

Peterson's Ultimate ACT Tool Kit provides the complete package you need to score your personal best on the ACT and get into your top-choice college. Unlike any book previously published, this tool kit contains many features that used to be available *only* to those who purchased expensive test prep classes.

e-Tutoring

Use the CD to go online to register for one-on-one math help from a live expert whenever you need it. Tutoring is offered using an online whiteboard shared by you and the tutor, which allows you to communicate with one another in real time. However, if you prefer, you can submit your math question in writing instead and receive a written answer within 24 hours.

The free tutoring offered with this product is limited to 30 minutes, although you may purchase more time if you need it. A written response to a submitted question counts as 20 minutes. The tutoring service is available for six months from the date you register online.

This service is available 24 hours a day, seven days a week for most of the year. During the summer the service is available from 9 a.m. to 1 a.m. Eastern Standard Time. Due to low demand, the service is not available during several holiday periods, including Thanksgiving, Christmas, Easter, Labor Day, and Memorial Day.

Remember, to register for this service, you will need the CD that accompanies this book. You will also need to refer to this book to provide the access code when prompted.

Essay Scoring

The CD that accompanies this book allows you to write 1 practice test essay online and receive a score on it, which approximates your performance on the optional essay in the actual ACT. In addition to a score, you will also receive constructive feedback on your essay, including tips on how to improve your score.

With this tool kit, you get scoring for 1 practice test essay. If you wish, for a fee, you may obtain scoring information and feedback for additional practice essays you write online.

To register for the essay-scoring service you need the CD that accompanies this book. In addition, you will need to refer to this book to provide the access code when prompted.

Note: The scoring of the 1 essay is offered *free* to purchasers of the *Ultimate ACT Took Kit, 2nd edition.*

The CD

There are 3 full-length practice tests for the ACT on the CD-ROM that accompanies this book. These tests, along with the 3 full-length practice tests in this book, provide a total of 6 simulated tests you can incorporate into your test prep plan. Since the actual ACT is a paper-and-pencil test, be sure to go through at least one of the tests printed in this book. (The CD version will automatically time your test and compute your score.)

The Flash Cards

Vocabulary flash cards are bound into the back of this book. Separate these at the perforations to create a deck of 216 ACT vocabulary flashcards to help you expand your vocabulary. While no questions on the ACT will specifically ask you to provide definitions of any words, building a better vocabulary will improve your performance on the ACT, especially the Reading Test.

Give Us Your Feedback

Peterson's publishes a full line of resources to help guide you through the college admission process. Peterson's publications can be found at your local bookstore, library, and high school guidance office, and you can access us online at www.petersons.com.

We welcome any comments or suggestions you may have about this publication and invite you to complete our online survey at www.petersons.com/booksurvey. Or you can fill out the survey at the back of this book, tear it out, and mail it to us at:

Publishing Department
Peterson's, a Nelnet company
2000 Lenox Drive
Lawrenceville, NJ 08648

Your feedback will help us make your educational dreams possible.

Introduction

About This Book

Peterson's Ultimate ACT Tool Kit provides the complete package you need to score your personal best on the ACT and gain admission to your top-choice colleges. This book contains six parts:

Part I: Overview of the ACT

Part I focuses on the "big picture." Here you'll learn about the overall structure of the four ACT multiple-choice tests and what each test covers. You'll also examine the directions for each of the four multiple-choice tests and see what typical test questions look like. Then, you'll learn strategies for ACT preparation as well as general test-taking strategies.

Parts II–V: Study Guides for the Multiple-Choice Tests

This book's ACT study guides for the four ACT multiple-choice tests are unique in that you have the opportunity to study each part of the exam and then you can *Take It to the Next* Level—a section in each chapter covering advanced topics and concepts you may encounter on the ACT. Both "levels" cover all four test sections and all of the general question types, and both contain lots of example questions, which reinforce what you learn along the way. The unique two-level feature will help you tailor your ACT prep to your individual needs.

ACT Study Guide, "Basics"

The first section of each study guide chapter covers the basic skills and concepts every ACT test-taker needs to know. For each of the four ACT tests, this first "level" walks you, step-by-step, through sample questions and then reveals the fundamental strategies that will help you attain a solid score on the ACT.

ACT Study Guide, "Take It to the Next Level"

Take It to the Next Level concentrates on the tougher stuff. For each of the four ACT tests, *Take It to the Next Level* briefly reviews the basic strategies and key concepts from the basics—just to make sure you're up to speed. When you "take it to the next level," however, you won't dwell on basics. Instead, you'll focus on advanced concepts and on challenging and complex question types.

Should You Take It to the Next Level?

You should start with the basic instruction if either of the following describes you:

- You're an ACT "newbie" who's just beginning your ACT prep.
- The college you want to attend doesn't require especially high ACT scores for admission.

You can go directly to the Next Level if you're a repeat ACT test taker whose scores were high the first time around, but your ACT goals are even higher. Of course, regardless of your goals for the ACT and for college admission, you can always work through both levels. In fact, that's what we recommend to any student with enough time before exam day.

Study Guide for the Writing Test

In Chapter 6, you'll learn the essentials about the Writing Test, as well as the skills you need to produce a high-scoring ACT writing sample.

Note

Although the ACT Writing Test is optional, one or more of the colleges you're applying to might want, or even require, the Writing Test scores to help evaluate prospective students.

Part VI: Three Practice ACTs

In Part VI, you'll find three full-length, practice ACTs. Each one covers all four multiple-choice tests and includes a mix of easy, moderate, and difficult questions. To accurately measure your performance on the practice tests, be sure to adhere strictly to their time limits.

You can take all three practice ACTs after completing your self-study. Or, you can take one practice ACT beforehand as a diagnostic tool. If your scores show that you rank above the 80th percentile on a test, you can skip over the basics to *Take It to the Next Level* for that test; otherwise, start at the "basic" level. Then, after you've completed your self-study, take the remaining two practice ACTs to measure your improvement.

About the Sidebars in This Book

Throughout this book you'll encounter four different iconic symbols. (Flip through this book, and you'll see oodles of each one.) Here's what these symbols are and what they mean:

Alert!

This sidebar warns you about a common blunder or testing trap, trick, or ploy that might trip you up during the test if you're not careful.

Note

This sidebar signals information that, although isn't a "need-to-know" fact, you might find interesting and that rounds out your knowledge of the topic at hand.

Tip

This sidebar signals a tip, strategy, or fine point related to the topic or example at hand.

X-Ref

This sidebar signals a reference to a concept or other information located elsewhere in the book.

PART

I

Overview of the ACT

Chapter 1

The ACT—In a Nutshell

What Is the ACT?

The ACT is a battery of standardized tests used by colleges and universities to help them decide which applicants to admit. Other tests—most notably, the SAT—also serve this purpose. However, almost all colleges accept ACT scores, and many colleges require them for admission. Every year, more than 2 million high school students sit for the ACT, which is given five times each year at locations throughout the United States and Canada, as well as many other countries.

The ACT is designed by a nonprofit organization called ACT, Inc. This organization also administers the test, processes test scores, and provides the scores to colleges and universities. The design of the ACT is based on a standard high school curriculum—in other words, it measures the skills that college-bound high school students learn every day.

There are two ways to register for the ACT:

- Via the official ACT Web site (www.act.org)
- By filling out the paper forms included in the official ACT registration packet

You can probably obtain the registration packet from your high school guidance office. You can also obtain the packet directly from ACT. To request the packet and other registration information from ACT, write or call:

ACT Registration
P.O. Box 414
Iowa City, IA 52243-0414
319-337-1270 (Mon.–Fri. 8 a.m.–8 p.m., Central Time)

Your ACT prep begins with an overview of the four multiple-choice ACT tests. In this chapter, you'll:

- learn about the overall structure of the four multiple-choice tests and what each test covers.
- examine the directions for each of the four multiple-choice tests.
- see what typical test questions look like.

- learn how the ACT is scored and how to interpret your scores.
- learn strategies for ACT preparation.
- learn general ACT test-taking strategies.

X-Ref

This overview covers the traditional ACT, which consists of four multiple-choice sections, but not the optional ACT Writing Test. You'll learn all about this optional test in Chapter 6.

The Four ACT Multiple-Choice Tests

The ACT includes four distinct multiple-choice tests, each test with its own focus. The order in which the four tests are presented is always the same:

1. English Test (75 questions, 45 minutes)
2. Mathematics Test (60 questions, 60 minutes)
3. Reading Test (40 questions, 35 minutes)
4. Science Test (40 questions, 35 minutes)

The total testing time for the entire ACT is 2 hours 55 minutes—not counting brief breaks between sections (and not including the optional Writing Test). But, as you can see, the total number of questions per test, as well as time limit, varies among the four tests.

The English Test (75 questions, 45 minutes)

The *English Test* is designed to measure your ability to recognize effective, and ineffective, writing and to remedy specific writing problems. For this test, you'll need a firm grasp of the conventions of Standard Written English and of so-called "rhetorical" skills (the appropriate and effective expression and organization of ideas). The number of ACT questions that cover each of various writing skills, or elements, is always about the same. Here's the breakdown along with a brief description of each element (numbers are approximate):

Elements of usage and mechanics:

Punctuation (10 questions)

Grammar and Usage (12 questions)

Sentence Structure (18 questions)

Elements relating to rhetorical skills:

Strategy (12 questions)

Organization (11 questions)

Style (12 questions)

Questions of the various types are interspersed and based on 5 discrete writing passages, each accompanied by 15 questions. So, the structure of the English Test is as follows:

Passage 1 (15 questions, some from each element)

Passage 2 (15 questions, some from each element)

Passage 3 (15 questions, some from each element)

Passage 4 (15 questions, some from each element)

Passage 5 (15 questions, some from each element)

The Mathematics Test (60 questions, 60 minutes)

The *Mathematics Test* is designed to measure your understanding of basic concepts in the math areas typically covered up through early 12th grade. These include the six areas listed on the following page. The number of ACT questions that cover each area is always about the same. Here's the breakdown, along with a brief description of each area (numbers are approximate):

Pre-Algebra (14 questions):

Applying the four basic arithmetic operations

Fractions, percent, ratio, and proportion

Decimal numbers, place value, and scientific notation

Integers, number signs, and ordering numbers by value

Prime numbers, factors, and divisibility

Basic descriptive statistics (mean, median, mode)

Counting techniques (permutations and combinations) and basic probability

Interpretation of graphical data (charts and graphs)

Matrices

Elementary Algebra (10 questions):

Solving systems of linear equations by substitution

Simplifying and factoring algebraic expressions

Properties of exponents and roots

Solving factorable quadratic equations

Intermediate Algebra (9 questions):

Applying the quadratic formula

Complex numbers

Algebraic problems involving inequalities and absolute value

Functions, including inverse and logarithmic functions

Progressions and patterns (of a series of numbers or other terms)

Coordinate Geometry (9 questions):

Defining and graphing points and lines on the coordinate plane

Distance and midpoint formulas

Equations of curved figures ("conic sections") and their graphs

Plane Geometry (14 questions):

Properties and relationships involving parallel and perpendicular lines

Properties of triangles, quadrilaterals, and other polygons

The Pythagorean Theorem and special properties of right, isosceles, and equilateral triangles

Properties of a circle

Applications involving three-dimensional figures (including cubes, other rectangular solids, and right cylinders)

Trigonometry (4 questions):

Definitions and properties of trigonometric functions

Trigonometric identities

Solving trigonometric equations

Applying trigonometric functions to right triangles

Graphing trigonometric functions

The Reading Test (40 questions, 35 minutes)

The *Reading Test* is designed to measure your ability to understand what a reading passage states and to draw reasonable inferences from it. The test is organized into four reading passages, each one accompanied by 10 questions. Each passage is drawn from one of four broad categories listed below (passage types can appear in any order on the test):

Social Studies passage (10 questions)

Natural Science passage (10 questions)

Humanities passage (10 questions)

Prose Fiction passage (10 questions)

What you'll encounter in ACT reading passages is similar to what you'll find in college texts for freshmen—in terms of both subject matter and reading level. Here are just some of the specific academic areas under each of the four broad categories listed above and that are fair game for an ACT reading passage (these are not comprehensive lists):

Social Studies: history, economics, sociology, political science, psychology

Natural Science: astronomy, biology, geology, physics, technology

Humanities: art, film, language, literary criticism, philosophy

Prose Fiction: short stories and excerpts from short stories and novels

The test-makers don't specify particular question "types" for the Reading Test. However, analysis of previously administered Reading Tests reveals that the following types of questions are the most common:

- *Simple recall* questions, which test whether you remember what you read
- *Recap* questions, which test your understanding of a large portion of the passage or of the passage as a whole
- *Restatement* questions, which test your understanding of specific ideas the author is trying to convey
- *Inference* questions, which test your ability to recognize what the passage implies, or infers, but does not come right out and state explicitly

Note

These four aren't the only question types you might encounter on the Reading Test, but they're by far the most common ones.

The Science Test (40 questions, 35 minutes)

The *Science Test* is designed to measure your ability to interpret, analyze, and evaluate scientific information from various fields, such as biology, chemistry, the earth/space sciences, and physics. You don't need advanced knowledge of any specific field to handle the science questions. However, knowledge of the basics covered in introductory high school coursework *might* be needed to handle a few questions.

The test is organized into seven "sets" of scientific information, each one accompanied by several questions. Each of the seven sets is cast in one of three formats, listed here along with the approximate number of total questions in each format:

Data Representation (15 questions). This format presents scientific information in textual as well as visual forms such as graphs, scatter plots, and tables. Data Representation questions gauge your ability to read, interpret, and draw conclusions from the graphical data.

Research Summaries (18 questions). This format provides an account of one or more scientific experiments. Research Summary questions test your ability to understand or critique the design of the experiment(s) and to interpret their results.

Conflicting Viewpoints (7 questions). This format presents two or more conflicting hypotheses or viewpoints, each based on the same premises or data. Conflicting Viewpoints questions measure your ability to understand, compare, and evaluate the hypotheses or viewpoints.

Here's the breakdown of a typical Science Test. Keep in mind that this is only one possibility; the sequence of sets by format and the number of questions per any set can vary. Notice that the Research Summary format can also accommodate graphical data and questions about interpreting that data:

Set 1—Data Representation (5 questions)

Set 2—Research Summaries, including data representation (6 questions)

Set 3—Research Summaries (6 questions)

Set 4—Data Representation (5 questions)

Set 5—Conflicting Viewpoints (7 questions)

Set 6—Research Summaries, including data representation (6 questions)

Your ACT Scores and Subscores

The ACT testing service produces a dizzying array of scores for each ACT test-taker—well over a dozen altogether. How can this be, given that the ACT contains only four multiple-choice tests? In this section, you'll learn the answer to this question.

Your Scores for Each Test and Your "Composite" Score

For each of the four multiple-choice tests—English, Math, Reading, and Science—the testing service will generate three scores for the test *as a whole*:

1. **Raw Score.** This score is simply the number of questions you answer correctly; that is, one point for each correct answer.
2. **Scale score.** The scoring system converts each raw score to scale score from 1 to 36. These are the scores that are reported to you and to the schools you've designated to receive them. The main reason for converting raw scores to scale scores is to adjust for slight variations in overall difficulty level from test to test. Scale scores compare your performance with everyone else who has taken the test—whether this year, last year, or ten years ago. In theory, the skill level required to score, for example, a 30 today is the same as it ever was and ever will be.
3. **Percentile score ("rank").** Based on your scale score, the scoring system then determines your percentile score (or "rank"). Percentile scores range from 0 to 99 and tell you how your ACT performance compared with that of all other test-takers. A percentile score of 60, for example, means that out of every 100 test-takers, you performed better than 60 (but worse than 39). Your percentile scores are provided to you—on your score report—but not to the schools. (All the schools have to go on are your scale scores.)

The testing system will also generate your *composite* scale score and, based on it, your percentile rank. Your composite score is simply the average of your four scale scores.

Note

The five scale scores just described are the ones that colleges are most interested in; these are the scores the schools use to compare you with other applicants.

Benchmark ACT Scores

The following four tables show how raw scores, scale scores, and percentile scores correlate to one another. You can use these tables to figure out how many questions on a test you need to answer correctly to attain a certain scale score or percentile rank. For example, the table for the English Test shows you that if your goal is to rank in the 70th percentile on that test, you must attain a scale score of 23 by answering 54 of the 75 questions correctly.

Alert!

These tables include percentile benchmarks only for the 50th percentile rank and higher. Also, note that score conversions are approximate, based on several previously administered ACTs. Conversions for your particular test might differ slightly. So, use this table just to "get a feel" for how raw scores translate into scale and percentile scores.

English Test

Raw Score (out of 75)	Scale Score (1–36)	Percentile Rank
72	33	99
64	28	90
59	25	80
54	23	70
49	21	60
46	20	50

Mathematics Test

Raw Score (out of 60)	Scale Score (1–36)	Percentile Rank
57	32	99
50	28	90
44	25	80
40	23	70
36	21	60
31	19	50

Note

Did you notice that, for the Mathematics Test, raw scores as a percentage of the total number of questions convert to higher scale scores than they do for the other three tests? That's because math questions each include five answer choices, compared with four for the other tests. Simply put, more choices result in more incorrect answers.

Reading Test

Raw Score (out of 40)	Scale Score (1–36)	Percentile Rank
38	35	99
34	30	90
31	26	80
29	24	70
26	22	60
24	21	50

Science Test

Raw Score (out of 40)	Scale Score (1–36)	Percentile Rank
38	32	99
34	27	90
31	25	80
29	23	70
25	21	60
23	20	50

Your ACT "Subscores"

For specific areas covered by the English, Mathematics, and Reading Tests, the scoring system will also generate raw, scale, and percentile *subscores.* (Each scale subscore ranges from 1 to 18.) Here are the various subscore areas for these three tests (there are no subscore areas for the Science Test):

Test	Subscore Areas
English	Usage/Mechanics Rhetorical Skills
Mathematics	Pre-Algebra/Elementary Algebra Intermediate Algebra/Coordinate Geometry Plane Geometry/Trigonometry
Reading	Social Studies/Sciences Arts/Literature
Science	(No Subscore Areas)

Subscores are also reported to the schools. So if you're weak in geometry, you can't hide this fact behind higher subscores in the other areas of the Math Test. The lesson is clear: You'd better be prepared for every area of each test.

Eight Awesome Tips for ACT Prep

Regardless of what books, software, or other ACT prep resources you're using, certain time-tested strategies for ACT prep never go out of style. To stay on the straight-and-narrow path to your first-choice college, be sure to heed the following sage advice.

1. Focus on Improving Your Weakest Skills

In gearing up for the ACT, many test-takers make the mistake of focusing on their strengths while neglecting their weaknesses. They tell themselves: "I can't handle this tough stuff right now; so I'll either face it later or skip it altogether and hope to make some lucky guesses on the exam." But, you can't hide any of your individual ACT scores from college admissions officials. So, don't spin your ACT prep wheels by spending more time than you need on any one of the ACT tests or by rehashing what you already know. Instead, devote more time to improving on your weaknesses than basking in your strengths.

2. Keep Practice Scores in Perspective

If you're like most ACT test-takers, you've set your sights on two or three particular colleges or universities as your top choices, and you have a good idea what ACT scores you'll need for a strong chance of getting into those schools. So, perhaps you've set a goal for your ACT scores. That's understandable. But don't psyche yourself out by obsessing over your practice-test scores. Gloating over high scores can lead to complacency and overconfidence, while brooding over low scores can result in discouragement and self-doubt. Either way, you're sabotaging yourself. The bottom line: Try to concern yourself not with test scores themselves but rather with what you can constructively do between now and exam day to improve these scores.

3. Practice under Exam Conditions

You can sit back and read all the lessons in this book, understand all that you've read, yet still end up scoring far lower on the ACT than you're capable of. When it comes to ACT prep, there's simply no substitute for "putting yourself to the test" by taking practice questions under simulated testing conditions. Here are some specific tips for simulating real exam conditions while attempting the Practice Tests in Part VI of this book. Follow these suggestions, and you'll feel more comfortable during the real test:

- Find a quiet spot that simulates the ACT testing environment, a place where you can hide from friends and other distractions. (A library study carrel is a good choice; your comfy chair in your TV room at home is not.)
- If possible, always use the same spot for ACT practice, and only for this purpose.

- Take practice questions at the same time of the day—ideally during the same time that you'll sit for the real ACT.
- Always allow more than enough time to take at least two ACT tests (for example, one English Test and one Reading Test) in one session—without interruption.

4. Maintain the Right "ACTitude"

It's important to maintain a positive attitude about the ACT, of course. But, it's also important to keep your self-confidence from swelling to the point that you become complacent and over-confident. Think you can just "wing it" on the ACT and still manage to crush the competition? Think again. Even if you're an "A" student who raises curves at your school, there are thousands of others like you out there who are taking the ACT very, very seriously and who would be more than happy to bump you down the ACT-scoring curve. Enough said?

5. Be Realistic in Your Expectations of Yourself

You'd love perfect ACT scores, wouldn't you? And each time the test is administered, at least a few test-takers do score a "straight 36" across all four tests. Will you be next to do so? Probably not. Your innate fallibility, not to mention the statistical odds, are stacked heavily against your fulfilling this ACT fantasy. So relax, follow a sensible study and practice schedule, and have faith that on exam day you'll perform just about as well as you can reasonably expect. Surrender whatever stubborn insistence on ACT perfection you're harboring, and, paradoxically, you'll probably score higher as a result.

6. Be Realistic about How Much Help Others Can Provide

Many test-takers "ask" for disappointing ACT scores by relying entirely on the "sage" advice of experts or the so-called "secrets" revealed only after you've paid a hefty price for an ACT-prep course. Be realistic about the benefits you can garner from this book—or from any ACT product or service. It's ultimately up to you to make the ACT prep effort you need to perform your personal best on exam day.

7. Take Steps to Minimize ACT Anxiety

Perhaps you've never had a serious problem with test anxiety. But this doesn't mean you're immune, especially considering how much more important the ACT is than any one high school exam. If you're like most ACT test-takers, you've put a lot of pressure on yourself to score high on the ACT. So, don't be surprised if you start feeling anxious during your practice tests and as exam day draws near.

Test anxiety, whether before or during a test, can only hurt your performance. So, it's a good idea to try to keep a lid on it (although don't expect to eliminate it entirely). If you're starting to feel the heat, try the following anxiety-busting techniques:

- After taking one or two timed practice tests, if the running clock still interferes with your concentration or makes you anxious, condition yourself by practicing individual questions under a strict one-minute limit per question. Don't spend any more or less than one minute on any question. Use a minute-timer with an alarm. Spend 20 minutes each day (20 questions) for a week on this exercise.

- Join (or form) a group of test-takers to openly discuss your anxieties. Invite suggestions from your peers about how to reduce yours. Try taking practice questions in front of the group; your peers might notice some manifestation of your anxiety—a certain posture, a nervous habit, or tension in specific muscles—that you don't. Then make a conscious then the underlying cause (test anxiety) will subside.
- Before taking practice tests, try simple relaxation techniques: stretching, quieting your thoughts, deep breathing, or whatever else works for you. Some people find a quick burst of vigorous exercise to be highly effective.
- Reward yourself for good behavior. For example, if you're easily distracted during your practice tests, promise yourself a pizza if you can get through an entire test section without looking up from the paper.

You'll be anxious about the ACT only if you're actually thinking about it. So, during the weeks that you're gearing up for the test, keep yourself preoccupied and busy with your other, regular activities. Try not to discuss the ACT with others except during planned study sessions or classes.

8. Know When You've Peaked

Preparing for the ACT is a bit like training for an athletic event. You need to familiarize yourself with the event, learn to be comfortable with it, and build up your skill and endurance. At some point—hopefully around exam day—your motivation, interest, and performance will peak. Sure, it takes *some* time and effort to get comfortable with the exam; to correct poor test-taking habits; to bone up on whatever math, grammar, and science you might have forgotten; to develop an instinct for recognizing wrong-answer choices; and to find your optimal pace. But there's a point beyond which additional study and practice confer little or no additional benefit. Don't drag out the process by starting several months in advance or by postponing the ACT to give yourself more time than you really need for preparation.

Chapter 2

Example Questions and Test-Taking Strategies

In this chapter, you'll take a quick glance at the directions for each of the four multiple-choice tests along with two typical questions—one a bit easier than average, the other a bit tougher than average. You can use these sample questions as a diagnostic tool to help determine which section of the study guide (basic or *Take It to the Next Level*) is more appropriate for you. You'll also learn general test-taking strategies that apply to all four multiple-choice tests.

The English Test

Here are test directions that are essentially what you'll see at the beginning of the ACT English Test:

Directions: This test consists of six passages in which particular words or phrases are underlined and numbered. Alongside the passage, you will see alternative words and phrases that could be substituted for the underlined part. Select the alternative that expresses the idea most clearly and correctly or that best fits the style and tone of the entire passage. If the original version is best, select "No Change."

The test also includes questions about entire paragraphs and the passage as a whole. These questions are identified by a number in a box.

After you select the correct answer for each question, on your answer sheet, mark the oval corresponding to the correct answer.

The following is a brief excerpt from a sample English passage (the entire passage would be much longer than this excerpt).

Regeneration: A Natural Miracle

Urodeles, a kind of vertebrate that include (1) such small, lizard-like creatures as newts and salamanders, have an enviable ability few other animals enjoy. They can regenerate arms, legs, and other body parts injured or destroyed by accidents or by those who prey on them. (2)

Now, attempt two ACT-style questions (along with explanations) about this passage. Just like every ACT English question, these ask you to choose the correct answer from the four choices—labeled either **A**, **B**, **C**, and **D** or **F**, **G**, **H**, and **J**. This first one is pretty easy; the rule of grammar that is the question's focus is a simple one, and the best answer is easy to distinguish from the others. Only a small percentage of test-takers would answer this question incorrectly.

1. A. NO CHANGE
B. includes
C. comprise
D. numbers

The correct answer is B. The only reasonable choices are **A** and **B**. Neither choice **C** nor **D** makes any sense in context. The subject of the verb "include" is the pronoun "that," which can be either singular or plural. To tell which it is, refer back to its antecedent, which is "kind." Since "kind" is singular, so is "that." Hence, the singular verb "includes" is needed.

Now, try a more difficult English question. To analyze it, you need to make a close judgment call between the best and "runner up" choice. What's more, this question involves not only a rule of grammar but also two separate rhetorical issues. A much higher percentage of test-takers would respond incorrectly to this question than the preceding one.

2. F. NO CHANGE
G. by animals who prey on them
H. predatory animals
J. these vertebrates' predators

The correct answer is H. The original version suffers from one minor problem: It isn't clear what noun the indefinite pronoun "those" refers to. The three alternatives, **G**, **H**, and **J**, each remedy this problem. Of these three choices, **J** is easiest to eliminate because it is awkward and confusing. **G** and **H** are both clear in meaning and grammatically correct. (The preposition "by" is optional; you can achieve proper parallelism between the two phrases separated by the word "or" either with or without this word.) Of these two remaining choices, **H** is the more concise one and is therefore preferable to **G**.

The Mathematics Test

Here are directions that are essentially what you'll see at the beginning of the Mathematics Test:

Directions: Solve each problem; then, on your answer sheet, mark the oval corresponding to the correct answer.

Be careful not to spend too much time on any one question. Instead, solve as many problems as possible, and then use the remaining time to return to those questions you were unable to answer at first.

You may use a calculator on any problem in this test. However, some problems can best be solved without use of a calculator.

Note: Unless otherwise stated, you can assume that:

1. Diagrams that accompany problems are *not* necessarily drawn to scale.
2. All figures lie in the same plane.
3. The word "line" refers to a straight line (and lines that appear straight are straight).
4. The word "average" refers to arithmetic mean.

Every ACT math question will ask you to solve a mathematical problem, choosing the correct answer from the five choices—labeled either **A, B, C, D,** and **E** or **F, G, H, J,** and **K.** Here are two sample questions, along with explanations. This first problem is easy to understand, and no formulas or tricky math is needed to solve it. Most test-takers would answer this question correctly. Go ahead and attempt it now.

Village A's population, which is currently 6,800, is decreasing at a rate of 120 each year. Village B's population, which is currently 4,200, is increasing at a rate of 80 each year. At these rates, in how many years will the population of the two villages be equal?

A. 9
B. 11
C. 13
D. 14
E. 16

The correct answer is C. One way to solve this problem is to subtract 120 from A's population while adding 80 to B's population—again and again until the two are equal—keeping track of the number of times you perform these simultaneous operations. (You'll find that number to be 13.) But there's a faster way to solve the problem that also helps you avoid computation errors. The difference between the two populations is currently 2,600 (6,800 − 4,200). Each year, that gap closes by 200 (120 + 80). So you can simply divide 2,600 by 200 to determine the number of years for the gap to close completely. That's easy math: 2,600 ÷ 200 = 13.

Now, here's a more difficult math question. To handle it, you need to understand rules involving exponents and their effect on the size and sign (positive or negative) of fractional numbers. Most test-takers would respond incorrectly to this question. Go ahead and try it.

If, $-27 = \left(-\frac{1}{3}\right)^k$ what is the value of k?

F. -9

G. -3

H. $-\frac{1}{3}$

J. $\frac{1}{3}$

K. 3

The correct answer is G. This question is asking you to determine the power that $-\frac{1}{3}$ must be raised to in order to obtain -27. First, look at the numbers in the question. Note that $-27 = (-3)^3$. That's a good clue that the answer to the question must involve the number -3. If the number we were raising to the power of k were -3, then the value of k would be 3. But, the number we're raising to the power k is $-\frac{1}{3}$, which is the *reciprocal* of -3. (By definition, the product of a number and its reciprocal is 1.) So, you need to apply the rule that a negative exponent reciprocates its base. In other words, raising a base number to a negative power is the same as raising the base number's reciprocal to the power's absolute value. Therefore:

$$\left(-\frac{1}{3}\right)^{-3} = (-3)^3$$

As you can see, that value of k is -3.

The Reading Test

The directions for the Reading Test are similar to these:

Directions: This test consists of four passages, each followed by several questions. Read each passage and select the best answer for each question following the passage. Then, on your answer sheet, mark the oval corresponding to the best answer.

Here's a sample reading passage, which is typical of an ACT passage, except that it is much shorter than the ones you'll find on the test.

Note

On the test, the general subject category will immediately precede each Reading passage, just as with the one here.

Passage I

Social Science

A legendary island in the Atlantic Ocean beyond the Pillars of Hercules was first mentioned by Plato in the *Timaeus*. Atlantis was a fabulously beautiful and prosperous land, the seat of an empire nine thousand years before Solon. Its inhabitants overran part of Europe and Africa, Athens alone being able to defy them. Because of the impiety of its people, the island was destroyed by an earthquake and inundation. The legend may have existed before Plato and may have sprung from the concept of Homer's *Elysium*. Much speculation that such an island once actually existed has spawned various historical theories, one of which is that pre-Columbian civilizations in America were established by colonists from the lost island.

Now answer two ACT-style questions (along with explanations) about this passage. Just like every ACT reading question, these ask you to choose the correct answer from the four choices—labeled either **A**, **B**, **C**, and **D** or **F**, **G**, **H**, and **J**. This first one is pretty easy; the best answer is easy to distinguish from the others. Most test-takers would answer this question correctly.

The main purpose of the passage is to:

A. discuss the legend of Atlantis and its possible origins.
B. make the point that enduring legends are often rooted in classical literature.
C. refute the claim that Atlantis actually existed.
D. compare Plato's description of Atlantis with Homer's.

The correct answer is A. The passage's "main purpose" must encompass all of the ideas presented in the passage without referring to ideas outside the passage. A fits the bill, since the passage describes Atlantis and its inhabitants, explains its demise, then discusses the possibility either that it originated in Homer's *Elysium* or that it actually existed. **B** generalizes information from the passage, which provides no support for the point in **B**. **C** is wrong because it is too narrow and because the passage makes no attempt to refute the claim to which **C** refers. **D** is wrong because the passage makes no such comparison—nor does it indicate how either Plato or Homer described Atlantis.

Here's a more difficult reading question. To analyze it, you need to recall different bits of information scattered throughout the passage and infer what the passage does not explicitly state. A high percentage of test-takers would respond incorrectly to this question. Go ahead and attempt this question.

Which of the following statements finds the LEAST support from the passage?

F. The people of Atlantis were imperialistic and warring.
G. Resistance by the Athenians contributed to the demise of Atlantis.
H. Solon eventually replaced Atlantis as the seat of Atlantis' former empire.
J. The inhabitants of Atlantis were disrespectful of their gods.

The correct answer is G. Although the passage does indicate that Athens successfully resisted incursions by the people of Atlantis, nothing in the passage supports the claim that this resistance helped cause the demise of Atlantis. F and J both find strong, explicit support in the passage, which states that Atlantis' inhabitants overran other countries and that they were an "impious" people. H is not supported so strongly by the passage as the other wrong answer choices. However, it is reasonable to infer H from the statement that Atlantis was "the seat of an empire nine thousand years before Solon."

The Science Test

Here are test directions that are essentially what you'll see at the beginning of the Science Test:

Directions: This test consists of seven passages, each followed by several questions. Read each passage and select the best answer for each question following the passage. Then, on your answer sheet, mark the oval corresponding to the best answer. You may NOT use a calculator on this test.

Here's a sample science passage along with two graphs, which is typical of an ACT passage. Read the passage before looking at the two questions that follow it.

In small communities, infectious organisms such as *Varicella-zoster* virus, which causes chickenpox, occasionally become extinct. The threshold at which such extinctions occur is known as the *critical community size*. Extinctions are followed by a period in which there are no infections until the virus is reintroduced from an outside source.

Researchers collected data on these extinctions, or *fadeouts*, in various communities before a fadeout was defined as a period of three or more weeks in which there were no new reported cases of the infection. They then attempted to develop computer models of the patterns of fadeouts seen, using information about the dynamics of the infection. The first of the following two figures shows the real data on chickenpox versus the data generated by two different computer models. The second figure demonstrates the different assumptions made by the two models concerning the duration of the *infectious period* (the period in which an individual can transmit the infection to another individual). This was the only difference between the two models.

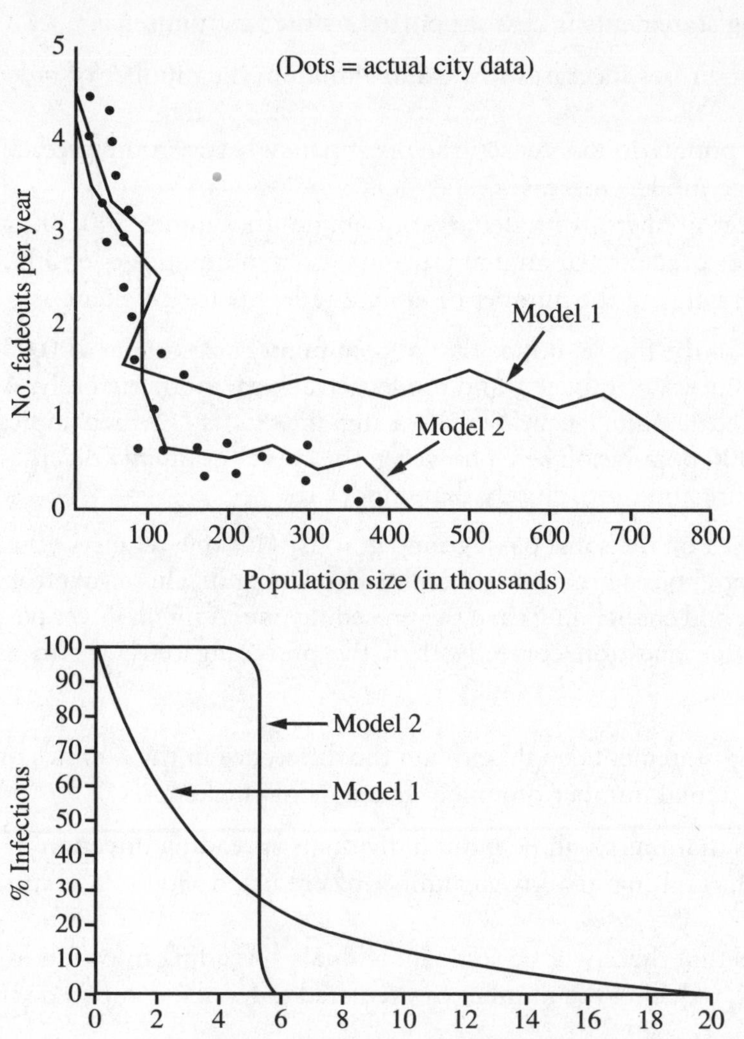

Here are two ACT-style questions (along with explanations) based on the passage and the two graphs. Just like every ACT science question, these ask you to choose the correct answer from the four choices—labeled either **A, B, C,** and **D** or **F, G, H,** and **J**. This first one is relatively easy. To answer it, you need to analyze only one of the two graphs. What's more, the analysis involves little more than a cursory visual inspection of the two curves as compared to the scatter plot (the pattern of dots). Most test-takers would answer this question correctly. Go ahead and attempt the following question.

Which of the following statements is best supported by the first figure?

A. As the number of viruses increases toward one million, the number of fadeouts per year declines.
B. As a community population increases, the discrepancy between the predictive abilities of the two models increases.
C. Model 1 is a better predictor of fadeouts for communities under 300,000, while model 2 is a better predictor of annual fadeouts for communities over 300,000.
D. Both models overestimate the number of annual fadeouts for chickenpox.

The correct answer is B. In the figure, notice that at community sizes under 100,000 (the left end of the graph), the two curves of model 1 and model 2 track each other closely. Also notice that the two models are both quite accurate in tracing the "dots," which indicate actual fadeouts. Beyond the 100,000 population level, however, the curves gradually diverge—model 2 tracking actual fadeouts more and more closely than model 1.

Here's another question based on the same passage and graphs. This one requires you to analyze both graphs, and the answer choices are more difficult to understand. These two features make this question more complex and challenging than the preceding one. A much lower percentage of test-takers would answer this question correctly than the preceding one. Try to answer the question now.

Which of the following statements might explain the difference in the abilities of models 1 and 2 to predict the actual number of annual fadeouts of chickenpox?

F. Model 2 predicts that there will be more individuals spreading infection in the early infectious period, resulting in a lower number of predicted fadeouts, compared with model 1.
G. Model 1 predicts that there will be some individuals spreading infection in the late infectious period, reducing the number of predicted fadeouts, compared with model 2.
H. Model 2 predicts that there will be a longer infectious period in larger communities, increasing the number of predicted fadeouts, compared with model 2.
J. Model 2 predicts a more constant rate of movement from an infectious to a noninfectious status.

The correct answer is F. To answer this question, you need to consider data from both graphs. Only choice **F** fits the information in both graphs: Model 2 does in fact predict a greater number of people spreading infection early in the infectious period, and it also predicts a smaller number of fadeouts than does model 1.

Top 10 ACT Test-Taking Strategies

Here are some basic test-taking strategies that apply to all four multiple-choice ACT tests (except for tip 10, which applies only to the Mathematics Test). What you'll find here is common sense advice for guessing, pacing yourself, and tracking your answers during these four tests. Even if you've read about these strategies elsewhere, it's a good idea to reinforce them in your mind.

X-Ref

The strategies here apply to the four multiple-choice tests. In Part IV, you'll review strategies for the optional ACT Writing Test.

1. Know Your Optimal Pace

Each of your four multiple-choice tests—English, Mathematics, Reading, and Science—will be scored on a curve, based on the number of questions you answer correctly. While the sharpest test-takers might be capable of tackling nearly every available question within a test's time limit, most test-takers score their best by skipping some of the tougher questions.

The following tables will help you determine your optimal strategy, which depends on your aptitude or ambition for each ACT test. Referring to each table, determine the percentage of all other test-takers you hope to beat (your "percentile rank"), then note the approximate number of questions you need to answer correctly to attain your goal. As a rule of thumb, you should plan to randomly answer about *half* the number of questions that you can answer incorrectly and still attain your percentile goal. (Keep in mind: Your goal might be higher for one test than for another, depending on where your natural abilities lie.)

English Test (75 questions, 45 minutes)
To rank in the 99th percentile, you need 72 correct answers. Randomly answer 1 question. To rank in the 90th percentile, you need 64 correct answers. Randomly answer 4 questions. To rank in the 80th percentile, you need 59 correct answers. Randomly answer 7 questions. To rank in the 70th percentile, you need 54 correct answers. Randomly answer 9 questions. To rank in the 60th percentile, you need 49 correct answers. Randomly answer 12 questions. To rank in the 50th percentile, you need 46 correct answers. Randomly answer 14 questions.

Mathematics Test (60 questions, 60 minutes)
To rank in the 99th percentile, you need 57 correct answers. Randomly answer 1 question. To rank in the 90th percentile, you need 50 correct answers. Randomly answer 5 questions. To rank in the 80th percentile, you need 44 correct answers. Randomly answer 8 questions. To rank in the 70th percentile, you need 40 correct answers. Randomly answer 10 questions. To rank in the 60th percentile, you need 36 correct answers. Randomly answer 12 questions. To rank in the 50th percentile, you need 31 correct answers. Randomly answer 15 questions.

Reading Test (40 questions, 35 minutes)
To rank in the 99th percentile, you need 38 correct answers. Randomly answer 1 question.
To rank in the 90th percentile, you need 34 correct answers. Randomly answer 3 questions.
To rank in the 80th percentile, you need 31 correct answers. Randomly answer 4 questions.
To rank in the 70th percentile, you need 29 correct answers. Randomly answer 5 questions.
To rank in the 60th percentile, you need 26 correct answers. Randomly answer 7 questions.
To rank in the 50th percentile, you need 24 correct answers. Randomly answer 8 questions.
Science Test (40 questions, 35 minutes)
To rank in the 99th percentile, you need 38 correct answers. Randomly answer 1 question.
To rank in the 90th percentile, you need 34 correct answers. Randomly answer 3 questions.
To rank in the 80th percentile, you need 31 correct answers. Randomly answer 4 questions.
To rank in the 70th percentile, you need 29 correct answers. Randomly answer 5 questions.
To rank in the 60th percentile, you need 25 correct answers. Randomly answer 7 questions.
To rank in the 50th percentile, you need 23 correct answers. Randomly answer 8 questions.

X-Ref

The scale scores that correspond to the percentile rankings and raw scores in the preceding tables are shown in the four tables you saw in Chapter 1 (page 12).

2. "Educated" Guesswork Can Boost Your Score

The ACT scoring system won't penalize you for incorrect responses. So, if you can eliminate just *one* incorrect choice, you're better off when making a random guess among the remaining choices. Of course, the more choices you can eliminate, the better your odds. But the point is that you should always try to eliminate at least one choice before answering each question.

Note

On the SAT (that other standardized test for college admission), a fractional point is deducted for each incorrect response. The purpose of the penalty is to eliminate the statistical advantage of random guesswork. But the ACT doesn't follow suit, although neither scoring system is inherently fairer than the other.

3. If You're Not Sure What the Correct Answer Is, Don't Dwell on It . . . Move on

If you can't figure out the correct answer, don't obsess over it. People under pressure are especially prone to this tendency. Your time is better spent on questions you haven't considered yet. Even if you've answered every other question, get away from the one that's stumping you and check your work on others you weren't sure about—or, if you're taking the Math Test, go back and check your calculations.

4. Start with the Types of Questions You Can Answer Most Quickly

It makes sense to attack the easier questions first, just in case you run out of time. After all, every question is worth the same: one point. Since easier questions require less time than tougher ones, try to identify and answer the questions that are easier for you (without sacrificing accuracy) before handling the tougher ones.

5. Use a Watch to Keep Yourself on Track

To make sure you stay at your proper pace, keep track of the time. There will probably be a clock in the testing room, but bring a watch anyway.

Tip

Try using a watch with hands. At the start of each timed section, set the minute hand to either "3" (for the 45-minute English Test) or "5" (for the 35-minute Reading or Science Test). During any test, you know your time has elapsed when "the clock strikes 12." A quick glance at your watch will tell you how much time remains—and whether you need to pick up the pace.

6. Mark Your Answers in Groups

It's easy to lose your place when you move back and forth from the test booklet to the answer sheet after each question. Finding your place again eats up time. So, instead, try marking answers in groups. For example, if you're working with a set of 10 Reading questions, all based on the same passage, answer each question in the group, and circle your answer choices in the test booklet. Then, after you've finished all 10 questions, transfer your 10 answers to the answer sheet. This way, you're making only one trip to the answer sheet to fill in those ovals.

Alert!

The Math Test is the only one where questions don't come in groups. But does this mean you should abandon this strategy for the Math Test? No. Just answer a certain number of math questions (perhaps five) at a time before transcribing your answers to the answer sheet.

7. Circle Your Answers in Your Test Booklet

In addition to filling in your answer sheet, *always* circle your answer choices in your test booklet (but don't circle any other choice). Why? What if you skip a certain question but forget to skip it on your answer sheet? Or, what if you select choice **B** but inadvertently fill in choice **C** on your answer sheet? (Either could happen to any test-taker.) Circling answers in your test booklet will ensure that you can track the error and make the changes, if needed.

8. Mark Questions You Want to Come Back to

On any test section, there are bound to be at least a few questions of which you're not 100 percent sure of your answer. Mark these questions (for example, with a large question mark) so you can return to them later if you have time. You might even make shorthand notes to remind yourself later why you're unsure of your answer and why a certain other choice might be the correct one.

9. Don't Leave Any Question Unanswered on Your Answer Sheet

Remember, you are not penalized for incorrect responses on the ACT. So, if you must make a random guess, be sure to darken one of the answer choices for that question. You've got nothing to lose, and your odds of earning credit for the question will improve infinitely—from 0 to either 20 or 25 percent.

Note

Each English, Reading, and Science question includes four answer choices—so your odds of making a correct random guess are 25 percent. Each Math question includes five answer choices, so your odds of making a correct random guess are 20 percent on the Math Test.

10. Use a Calculator Sparingly during the Math Test

According to the testing service, ACT test-takers who use a calculator during the test generally score slightly higher than those who don't. This fact should not surprise you. After all, using a calculator can help ensure the accuracy of any calculation. To make sure your calculator turns out to be your ACT ally rather than your nemesis, follow these points of advice:

1. Use your calculator to check your work, not as a crutch. No ACT math question *requires* the use of a calculator. (The ACT is designed as a *reasoning* test, not a number-crunching drill.) So try to perform every computation using your brain.Then, use your calculator to verify the answers you're not 100 percent comfortable with.
2. Use a calculator during practice testing. Get a feel for the calculations you're comfortable performing without it and the ones you think you'd better check with the calculator—just to be safe.
3. Memorize the three computational tables in this book, so you won't need to resort to your calculator so often.

The English Test

Chapter

3

Strategies for the English Test

In this chapter, you'll:

- Take a close look at the format of the English Test and at what the test covers (and doesn't cover)
- Learn a step-by-step approach to handling an ACT English question set
- Learn success keys for the ACT English Test

The English Test Is Really an "Editing" Test

The ACT English Test is essentially an editing exercise. You're given 5 passages altogether. Each passage contains a number of grammatical mistakes, stylistic weaknesses, errors in punctuation, lapses in reasoning, and other writing flaws. Your job is to detect those flaws and pick alternative ways of writing and organizing the passage so as to correct the flaws without introducing any new ones. In other words, during the English Test, you're essentially pretending that you're a writer who is about to revise the rough draft of a piece of work you're writing.

In Chapter 1, you saw a basic breakdown of the general areas that the English Test covers. You saw that the test questions fall into two broad categories: "Usage/Mechanics" and "Rhetorical Skills." Now, let's look at the breakdown again along with detailed lists of what the different areas include. (The number of questions indicated for each category are approximate.)

Note

The word *rhetoric* means "the art of effective writing and speaking." Accordingly, on the ACT English Test, questions in the Rhetorical Skills category don't test you on correctness in grammar and word usage. Instead, they ask you essentially how to express ideas "artfully"—in other words, in a clear, logical, graceful, and concise manner that is appropriate in style and tone.

"Usage/Mechanics" Test Questions

Usage/Mechanics refers to the degree to which a sentence obeys the rules of English grammar and usage. Forty of the 75 questions cover Usage/Mechanics, and one of your two subscores for the test will be based on your responses to these 40 questions, which cover the three broad categories described below.

Punctuation (10 questions). A question in this category might test you on a punctuation mark either at the end of a sentence or somewhere within a sentence. Fair game includes the use of the period, comma, colon, semicolon, and the so-called "em" dash. The test's emphasis is on the use of these marks to achieve sentence sense and clarity. Also tested is the use of apostrophes (to indicate either the possessive case or a contraction). The test does *not* cover the use of quotation marks.

Grammar and Usage (12 questions). This broad category covers a lot of ground, including: (1) *agreement* between two different grammatical elements of a sentence, such as the sentence's subject and verb, a pronoun and its antecedent (the noun to which it refers), or a modifying phrase (such as a prepositional phrase or a so-called "appositive") and whatever it modifies; (2) *forms and cases* of particular parts of speech, including verbs, pronouns, adjectives, and adverbs; and (3) *idioms*—words and phrases that are correct simply due to their widespread use.

Sentence Structure (18 questions). These questions test you on the relationships between different parts of a sentence and on how to arrange the grammatical elements of a sentence so that the meaning of the sentence is clear and unambiguous. Specific issues covered include *parallelism* between elements that are grammatically equivalent, *placement of modifiers* vis-à-vis the words they modify, and *shifts* in voice (passive or active) and tense (present, past, and so on).

Note

An *idiom* is a word or phrase that has become proper and acceptable simply due to extensive, common use among people who speak and write English. (A correct *idiom* is said to be *idiomatic.*) You'll be seeing this word many times throughout the English Test chapters in this book, so make sure you remember what it means.

"Rhetorical Skills" Test Questions

"Rhetorical Skills" cover the overall organization of the passage (Which topic logically belongs first? Which belongs last?), transitions from topic to topic, decisions about what to include and what to omit from the passage, and stylistic choices. Thirty-five of the 75 questions cover Rhetorical Skills, and one of your two subscores for the test will be based on your responses to these 35 questions. The test-makers list three broad categories under the Rhetorical Skills rubric, as listed and described below.

Strategy (12 questions). A "strategy" question might involve adding or deleting a sentence that provides a *transition* from one sentence (or paragraph) to another or that provides *support* for certain ideas in the passage. In handling any strategy question, your job is to evaluate a proposed addition, deletion, or revision (usually, you'll choose the best among four options) in terms of its effect on the passage's purpose or on how well it serves to communicate the passage's ideas.

Organization (11 questions). A question of this type deals with the *sequence of ideas* in the passage. These questions typically take one of two forms. In one form, you're asked to select the best sequence of sentences within a paragraph. In the other, you must select the best sequence of paragraphs for the passage as a whole. For either type, your job is to determine the sequence that makes for the most logical and cohesive passage.

Style (12 questions). This is a catch all category that embraces stylistic problems such as wordiness, awkwardness, ambiguity, and redundancy, as well as the "appropriate" tone and choice of words for the passage.

Note

No question type is inherently easier than another. Whatever the skill, the test-makers can devise test questions ranging from easiest to most challenging.

What's Not Covered

Very subtle stylistic or aesthetic considerations are not tested on the ACT, nor are rules of grammar and usage that are disputed or changing. Also excluded are slang, colloquialisms, technical jargon, geographic or ethnic dialects, archaic language (like Shakespeare's), and creative or experimental language (like James Joyce's).

The "Weird" Format of the ACT English Test

The ACT English Test consists of 5 distinct passages, each one accompanied by 15 questions based on it. The English Test looks nothing like any other test you've taken in school. To master it, you first need to understand its unique format. Here are the test's key features you should know about:

- Each passage will be titled—to help you get an idea about the passage's topic. But you don't need any specific knowledge of a passage's topic to handle the questions.
- Each passage appears in the left-hand column of the test booklet's pages, while the questions corresponding to the passage appear next to it, in a right-hand column. This feature makes it easier for you to glance back and forth between a question and the portion of the passage that's relevant to it.
- Most questions are based on brief underlined portions of the passage. The underlined portion might be a single word, a brief phrase, or possibly, an entire sentence. These questions are generally Usage/Mechanics questions that deal with grammar, sentence structure, usage, style, and such "mechanical" details as punctuation. (Numbers beneath the underlined portions correspond to question numbers.)
- Some questions (usually 2–4) in each set are marked by boxed numbers appearing in various places in the passage—between sentences, at the end of paragraphs, or at the end of the entire passage. These questions deal with larger questions of writing strategy and

organization—for example, the sequence of a paragraph's sentences, transitions from one sentence (or paragraph) to another, or the effect of adding or deleting certain material.

- The final question in a set of 15 might involve the passage as a whole; the test will tell you if it does. This type of question usually (but not always) asks about the best sequence for the passage's paragraphs. If a question involves the sequence of the passage's paragraphs, then the paragraphs will be numbered. The same is true if any question refers to one or more specific paragraphs by number (for example, "In Paragraph 3 . . ."). Otherwise, the passage's paragraphs won't be numbered.

If a question involves the sequence of sentences in a certain paragraph, then the sentences will be numbered as follows: (1) *First sentence.* (2) *Second sentence.* (3) *Third sentence . . .*

The following ACT-style passage and set of 15 questions illustrate these features. Go ahead and take a quick glance at the passage and questions now (but, don't read the passage or answer any questions yet).

X-Ref

Later in this chapter, we'll walk you through all 15 questions in this set and show you how to handle each one.

In Search of Life on Mars

[1]

A major goal of the Viking spacecraft missions of the late 1980s were to determine whether [1] the soil of Mars is dead, like the soil of the moon, or teeming with microscopic life, like the soils of Earth. Soil samples brought into the Viking lander were sent to three separate biological laboratories to be tested in different ways for indications of the presence of living things. [2]

[2]

[3] First, it was assumed that life on Mars would be like life on Earth; which is [4] based on the element carbon and thriving by chemically transforming carbon compounds. Second, on Earth, although there are many large life-forms (like human beings and pine trees), there are

also small ones (like bacteria)—and the small ones are far more abundant, thousands or millions of them being 5 in every gram of soil. To have the best possible chance of detecting life, an instrument should look for the most abundant kind of life. The lander's laboratories, therefore, were designed to detect carbon-based Martian microbes living in the soil—more specifically, to nourish any life in the Martian soil and to detect with sensitive instruments the chemical activity of the organisms. 6

[3]

One characteristic of earthly plants is to transform 7 carbon dioxide in the air into the compounds that make them up. Accordingly, one Viking experiment, called the carbon assimilation test, added radioactive carbon dioxide to the atmosphere above the soil sample, then flooded the sample 8 with simulated Martian sunlight.

[4]

(1) Living organisms on Earth give off gases. (2) The gas exchange test, another experiment on each lander was 9 designed to detect this kind of activity. (3) Plants give off oxygen, animals give off carbon dioxide, and water is exhaled by both. 10 (4) Nutrients and water were added to the soil, and the chemical composition of the gas above the soil was continuously analyzed 11 for changes that might indicate life. [12]

[5]

Unfortunately, neither this one nor 13 the other Viking experiment uncovered clear indications of Martian life-forms. More recently, during a 2003–04 mission, NASA landed two rovers on the Martian surface. [14] However, the rovers found no conclusive evidence of life on Mars, primitive or otherwise. Nevertheless, our the search for life on Mars will undoubtedly continue during the twenty-first century.

1. A. NO CHANGE
   B. was the determination of whether
   C. was to determine whether
   D. was determining if

2. F. NO CHANGE
   G. the existence of life
   H. indications that living things exist there
   J. the presence of living things indicating life

3. Which of the following sentences, if added to the beginning of Paragraph 2, would most smoothly and logically lead into the paragraph?

   A. This was a challenging scientific assignment in two respects.
   B. The tests were based on two underlying ideas.
   C. For two reasons, the Viking scientists were uncertain how to proceed.
   D. There were two main objectives being pursued in these experiments.

4. F. NO CHANGE
   G. Earth, that is
   H. Earth—
   J. Earth, which is

5. A. NO CHANGE
   B. containing thousands or millions of them
   C. with thousands or millions of them
   D. numbering in the thousands or millions

6. F. NO CHANGE
   G. and to detect the chemical activity of the organisms with sensitive instruments
   H. and using sensitive instruments, to detect the chemical activity of the organisms
   J. as well as to, with sensitive instruments, detect the organisms' chemical activity

7. A. NO CHANGE
   B. the transformation of
   C. that of transforming
   D. that they transform

8. F. NO CHANGE
   G. flooded it
   H. had it flooded
   J. had the sample flooded

9. A. NO CHANGE
   B. lander, was
   C. lander were
   D. lander,

10. F. NO CHANGE
    G. both exhale water
    H. water is exhaled by both plants and animal
    J. both of them exhale water

11. A. NO CHANGE
    B. under continuous analysis
    C. continuous analyzed
    D. being continuously analyzed

12. Which of the following is the most logical order for the sentences in Paragraph 4?

F. NO CHANGE
G. 2, 4, 1, 3
H. 4, 1, 2, 3
J. 2, 1, 3, 4

13. A. NO CHANGE
B. neither this or
C. neither this experiment nor
D. neither this nor

14. Which of the following sentences, if inserted at this point, would be most logical and relevant?

F. This recent mission, although expensive, was far safer and less costly than a manned mission to Mars would have been.
G. Except for one brief period of time, both rovers maintained continual communication with NASA's team of engineers here on Earth.
H. NASA used two rovers so that, if one failed, the other rover could still explore the Martian surface.
J. For a period of about sixty days, each of the two rovers explored the Martian terrain immediately around it.

Question 15 poses a question about the passage as a whole.

15. The writer is considering adding the following sentence to the passage:

Since the 1980s, the U.S. space agency NASA has carried out three series of unmanned missions to Mars.

What would be the best place to insert this sentence, considering the passage's overall organization and flow of information?

A. At the beginning of Paragraph 1
B. At the end of Paragraph 1
C. At the beginning of Paragraph 5
D. At the end of Paragraph 5

The ACT English Test—Your 6-Step Game Plan

Most ACT test-takers answer English questions simply in the order that the test presents them. The 6-step approach you'll learn in this section is quite different, and much more effective. It involves previewing the passage, then answering certain types of questions first, others second, and still others third. Here are six basic steps for handling each of the five passages and question sets on the ACT English Test:

Step 1: Read the entire passage straight through.

Step 2: Answer the "whole passage" questions (if any).

Step 3: Answer the "boxed-number" questions.

Step 4: Answer the questions about the passage's underlined portions.

Step 5: Check the clock; if you have time, look again at questions that gave you trouble.

Step 6: On your answer sheet, mark your selections for all 15 questions in the set.

In the following pages, you'll learn what each step involves, and you'll apply the steps to the ACT-style passage and set of 15 questions from pages 35–36.

Step 1: Read the entire passage straight through.

When you tackle the English Test, you should approach it as if you're a writer who is about to revise the rough draft of a piece of work you're writing. Naturally, to do this, before you begin it helps to have a general sense of the overall meaning and purpose of the passage. It's especially important because, as you'll see, some of the test questions turn on the meaning of a given sentence or paragraph as well as its grammatical form. So, begin work on a particular passage by reading it quickly from beginning to end, looking for its general theme, its style and tone, and the basic sequence of ideas. The passages are generally short (300 to 400 words), so 30–40 seconds should be ample time for this task.

Alert!

Immediately preceding at least one of the five passages on the test, expect to see the following statement:

The following paragraphs may or may not be arranged in the best possible order. The last question will ask you to choose the most effective order for the paragraphs as numbered.

If you see this statement, keep it in mind as you read the passage straight through; pay close attention to the main topic of each paragraph and whether the paragraphs flow logically from one to the next. Think about which paragraph makes the best introduction, and which makes the best conclusion. Then, proceed to Step 2.

Let's apply Step 1 to the Mars passage on pages 33–34. (It's important not to get hung up on the underlined portions—to try and fix any errors—right now.):

There's no statement preceding the passage that states that the paragraphs might not be presented in their best sequence. (See Alert! on the previous page.) So as we begin reading, we don't need to think about whether each paragraph makes sense where it is in relation to the others.

Paragraph 1:

This paragraph, along with the title of the passage, tells us that the passage as a whole is about the space program's efforts to detect life on Mars. So far, it looks like the passage will be concerned mainly with describing the different kinds of tests performed on soil brought back to Earth by the Viking lander.

Paragraph 2:

The boxed number 3 tells us that a sentence might need to be added to the beginning of Paragraph 2—to help us anticipate what the paragraph is about. But let's not worry about that right now. Instead, let's just try to get the basic gist of Paragraph 2 based on what's there. Paragraph 2 explains how the researchers designed the instruments to perform these tests. The basic idea is that they were to look for very small carbon-based microbes, under the assumption that life on Mars is carbon-based, just like life on Earth.

Paragraph 3:

This paragraph describes one particular test. That's all we need to understand during this initial reading.

Paragraph 4:

The parenthesized numbers preceding this paragraph's sentences tell us to expect a test question about the best sequence for these sentences. So, they're not necessarily in proper order. But, don't try to rearrange the sentences now. Instead, just try to get the gist of Paragraph 4. It describes a second test performed on the soil samples—which makes sense based on what we know from Paragraphs 2 and 3.

Paragraph 5:

This paragraph tells us that the results of the two tests (described in Paragraphs 3 and 4) were inconclusive—as were the results of tests performed during a more recent mission to Mars—but that scientists will probably continue their search in the future. The boxed number 14 suggests that it may be helpful to add a sentence here; but don't worry about it right now. You got the gist of Paragraph 5, which is all you need during Step 1.

Now, take a few seconds to recap the flow of information from paragraph to paragraph. Then, move on to Step 2.

Step 2: Answer the "whole passage" questions (if any).

Most question sets will include at least one question that asks about the passage as a whole. (These questions are always the last ones in a set.) These questions can be especially time-consuming if you need to *re*read the entire passage to answer the question. Yet that's exactly what many test-takers end up doing when facing a "whole passage" question.

You should take a different approach: After you read the entire passage straight through (Step 1), check for a question involving the whole passage. If you see one, handle it *immediately*—before going back to tackle questions dealing with specific parts of the passage—while you're focusing on the big picture (read: the whole passage). That way, you won't need to reread the entire passage again just to answer this one question.

The Mars question set included one whole-passage question: 15. Let's answer it now. Here's question 15 again:

15. The writer is considering adding the following sentence to the passage:

Since the 1980s, the U.S. space agency NASA has carried out three series of unmanned missions to Mars.

What would be the place to insert this sentence, considering the passage's overall organization and flow of information?

A. At the beginning of Paragraph 1
B. At the end of Paragraph 1
C. At the beginning of Paragraph 5
D. At the end of Paragraph 5

Step 1 prepared you well for this question. As you read the passage with your eye on the structure of ideas, you should have noticed that the passage began rather abruptly with a discussion of the Viking missions and that, in the final paragraph, the discussion turned, however briefly, from the Viking missions to the more recent mission. An effective passage would tie together the introductory paragraph and the concluding one—by letting the reader know at the outset, at the beginning of Paragraph 1, what the reader might expect from the passage as a whole—including the final paragraph. So the correct answer is probably **A**. Before circling **A** in your test booklet, however, read the additional sentence to yourself, then read from the beginning of the original passage. Does one sentence flow logically and smoothly to the next? Yes, it does. Select choice **A**, then move on to Step 3. (Question 15 was a bit easier than average.)

Step 3: Answer the "boxed-number" questions.

For each passage, at least two or three of the 15 questions will be marked by boxed numbers appearing somewhere in the passage. These "box" questions generally involve transitions from one sentence or paragraph to another. Tackle these questions now, while you're still focused on the "big picture"—the flow of ideas from paragraph to paragraph.

Let's apply Step 3 to the Mars question set, which includes three boxed-number items. Here's each one again, in turn, along with an analysis.

3. Which of the following sentences, if added to the beginning of Paragraph 2, would most smoothly and logically lead into the paragraph?

A. This was a challenging scientific assignment in two respects.
B. The tests were based on two underlying ideas.
C. For two reasons, the Viking scientists were uncertain how to proceed.
D. There were two main objectives being pursued in these experiments.

Paragraph 2 is devoted to explaining the two underlying assumptions, or "ideas," that guided the scientists who designed the Viking experiments and those ideas influenced the laboratories' design. Choice **B** sets this up accurately and clearly. In contrast, each of the three other options would only mislead the reader as to what's coming in Paragraph 2. Circle choice **B** in your test booklet, then go on to the next boxed-number question: 12. (Question 3 would be considered average in difficulty.)

12. Which of the following is the most logical order for the sentences in Paragraph 4?

F. NO CHANGE
G. 2, 4, 1, 3
H. 4, 1, 2, 3
J. 2, 1, 3, 4

During Step 1, you should have noticed that the preceding paragraph [3] discussed one experiment, while this paragraph [4] clearly discusses another. Understanding the main topic of each paragraph is the key to getting off on the right foot with question 12. Of the four sentences, 2 is the smoothest, most logical way to make the transition from Paragraph 3 to 4. The viable options are thus narrowed to choices G and J. Immediately following sentence 2 (which should come first in the paragraph), it is logical to expect a description of the experiment, *then* perhaps an explanation of its rationale. Sentence 4 provides the description, while sentences 1 and 3 provide the rationale. This sequence (4, 1, 3) is precisely what choice **G** indicates.

Before moving on to another question, read all four sentences in the order specified by choice **G**. Do the ideas flow smoothly? Does the paragraph make sense as a whole? Yes, indeed it does! Circle **G** in your test booklet, then move on to the next boxed-number question: 14. (Question 12 would be considered average in difficulty.)

14. Which of the following sentences, if inserted at this point, would be most logical and relevant?

- **F.** This recent mission, although expensive, was far safer and less costly than a manned mission to Mars would have been.
- **G.** Except for one brief period of time, both rovers maintained continual communication with NASA's team of engineers here on Earth.
- **H.** NASA used two rovers so that, if one failed, the other rover could still explore the Martian surface.
- **J.** For a period of about sixty days, each of the two rovers explored the Martian terrain immediately around it.

First of all, the connecting sentence must relate directly to what precedes and follows it. On this basis, you can easily eliminate choice **F**; nowhere in the paragraph, or even in the entire passage, does the writer talk about the expense involved in exploring Mars, let alone weigh the advantages of unmanned missions versus manned missions. You can also eliminate choice **H**. It makes little sense to digress from the central topic—the search for life on Mars—just to explain why two rovers were used.

That leaves choices **G** and **J**. Each one seems a good fit, but choice **J** connects to the next sentence more effectively. Notice the key word *However* in that sentence. With choice **J**, the writer is telling us that *even though* the rovers performed their duties as expected, they found no conclusive evidence of life on Mars. It makes sense to evaluate the success or failure of the mission in terms of the passage's central topic—the search for life on Mars.

Once again, Step 1, during which we identified the passage's central theme and main ideas, helped us zero-in on the correct answer—in this case, choice **J**. Circle **J** in your test booklet. (Question 14 would be considered a bit more challenging than the average English Test question.)

You're now done answering the boxed-number questions. If you're the least bit unsure about any of your selections so far, earmark those questions to return to during Step 5, if you have time. Then, move ahead to Step 4.

Step 4: Answer the questions about the passage's underlined portions.

After completing Steps 1–3, you should be left with about 10 or 11 unanswered questions—the ones involving the underlined portions of the passage. Most of these questions will focus on the Usage/Mechanics subscore area (grammar, punctuation, sentence structure), although a few might involve either strategy or style (part of the Rhetorical Skills subscore area).

Don't worry if it seems you've already spent a lot of time with the passage; answering the questions involving the underlined portions should go much more quickly than answering the other question types.

Let's apply Step 4 to the set of questions about the Mars passage. The passage contains 11 underlined portions; let's take them in order, beginning with question 1. (The passage is on pages 33–34.)

X-Ref

As you read the analysis of each question, you'll encounter a variety of grammatical terms. Don't worry if you're not familiar with them all; you'll learn them during the next chapter.

1. **A.** NO CHANGE
B. was the determination of whether
C. was to determine whether
D. was determining if

Question 1 is a grammar question and is average in difficulty. The subject of the verb is *goal*, so the verb should be singular—*was* rather than *were*. [Eliminate the original version, **A.**] Notice that the sentence intends to provide two alternatives (*whether . . . or . . .*). The word *whether* conveys this intent more clearly than the word *if*. [Eliminate choice **D.**] That leaves choices **B** and **C.** Although *the determination of* and *to determine* in this context are both acceptable, *the determination of* is wordier and a bit awkward. Hence, **C** is the best choice; circle it in your test booklet, then move on to question 2.

2. **F.** NO CHANGE
G. the existence of life
H. indications that living things exist there
J. the presence of living things indicating life

Question 2, which focuses on style, is average in difficulty. The original version is perfectly fine. Although it's possible to create a more concise and less awkward version (e.g., *indications of life on Mars*), none of the alternatives listed provide such a version. **G** results in the idiomatically improper *tested . . . for the existence of life*, which is also a bit nonsensical. **H** is the runner-up choice; it is grammatically correct, and contains no idiom or word-usage problems. However, **H** suffers from a so-called *vague pronoun reference*. Given the sentence's structure, it isn't clear what the pronoun *there* refers to. In all likelihood, it refers to Mars. But since Mars had not been mentioned since early in the previous sentence, the writer should either clarify the reference by replacing *there* with its antecedent *on Mars* or simply omit the pronoun, as in the original, and best, version. **J** is redundant; the writer should choose either *the presence of living things* or *indicating life*, but not both, because they say essentially the same thing. Circle choice **F** in your test booklet.

Question 3 was a boxed-number question, which we answered during Step 3. Let's move ahead to question 4.

4. **F.** NO CHANGE
G. Earth, that is
H. Earth—
J. Earth, which is

Question 4 deals with punctuation and is easier than average. The semicolon in the original version is wrong, since what follows the semicolon can't stand alone as a sentence. Fixing this problem requires changing the punctuation mark. If the word *thriving* (later in the sentence) were replaced by either *which thrives* or *thrives*, then **J** would be the best choice. But you're stuck with *thriving*, which is a *gerund* (a verb transformed into a noun by adding *ing*). Mixing a gerund with a regular verb within the same grammatical construct (in this case, mixing *which is based* and *which is . . . thriving*) is considered improper, and it sounds wrong. Choice **H** fixes this problem by omitting *which is*. Read the original sentence aloud, then read it aloud using choice **H** instead. Notice that **H** *sounds* better. Notice also that **H** uses an *em* dash (—), a mark used to signal a phrase that elucidates or describes what precedes it. Since the second part of the sentence describes *life on Earth*, the use of the *em* dash here is appropriate and effective. Hence, choice **H** provides the best alternative to the original version. Circle **H** in your test booklet.

In question 4, notice choices **G** and **J** differ in only one respect: "that" versus "which." Although both choices were incorrect because of the same punctuation problem, the test-makers could have designed question 4 to test you instead on word usage—specifically, when to use "that" or "which" in a particular sentence.

5. **A.** NO CHANGE
B. containing thousands or millions of them
C. with thousands or millions of them
D. numbering in the thousands or millions

Question 5 is the second question that focuses on style; this one is more challenging than average. The underlined portion contains the superfluous word *being*, which can and should be omitted. Although deleting *being* is the only revision that's needed, none of the answer choices provides this option. Of the three alternatives, **D** is the clearest and most idiomatic—that is, the most normal-sounding to a person with a well-developed "ear" for the language. Given the phrase that **D** provides, an even more effective sentence might also replace *in every gram* with *per gram*, in order to avoid the successive use of the preposition *in*. But this would be a subtle refinement in style only, and question 5 doesn't provide this option anyway. Besides, your job is to look not for the *ideal* version but rather the best among four. Choice **B** is wrong because it's unclear who or what "contains" the thousands or millions of life-forms mentioned. Similarly, choice **C** is wrong because it's unclear who or what the preposition *with* describes, or modifies. Circle **D** in your test booklet.

6. **F.** NO CHANGE
G. and to detect the chemical activity of the organisms with sensitive instruments
H. and, using sensitive instruments, to detect the chemical activity of the organisms
J. as well as to, with sensitive instruments, detect the organisms' chemical activity

Question 6 focuses on sentence structure and is more challenging than average. This underlined portion is about as lengthy as you'll find on the ACT English Test. Although it's grammatically correct and contains no idiom or usage errors, notice that the modifying phrase *with sensitive instruments* separates the verb *detect* from its direct object *chemical activity*. While there's nothing wrong with doing this, you can make the sentence a bit clearer by joining these two elements, which calls for restructuring (rearranging) the underlined portion. Choice **H** provides a good way to do it. This choice not only joins the verb and its direct object, but it also sets apart the modifying phrase with commas. This additional technique makes for an even clearer sentence. Choice **G** also fixes the original version's problem, but in the process **G** misplaces *with sensitive instruments* at the end, so that it's unclear what or whom the phrase describes. Choice **J** separates, or splits, the infinitive *to detect*. The result is not only grammatically incorrect but also clumsy in the way it sounds, or "reads" (a huge clue that it's not the best version). Circle **H** in your test booklet.

Whenever you see a lengthy underlined portion, chances are that, just like question 6, the question at hand will focus on the structure of that part. In other words, your job will be to determine the most effective arrangement of elements within the underlined portion.

7. **A.** NO CHANGE
B. the transformation of
C. that of transforming
D. that they transform

Question 7, another grammar question, is more challenging than average. In the sentence, the verb *is* anticipates what's called a *subject complement*—something that complements or completes the meaning of the sentence's subject. Since the sentence is telling you about what the subject ("characteristic") *is* rather than what it *does*, the infinitive *to transform* clearly does not logically match the subject. Hence, the original version cannot be the best of the four options. Each of the three alternatives [Choices **B**, **C**, and **D**] fix this problem. [Choice **B** provides a noun, while **C** and **D** each provides a *noun clause*; all three indicate what the subject "is."] Among the three, however, choice **D** is the most idiomatic (normal-sounding). Circle **D** in your test booklet.

8. F. NO CHANGE
G. flooded it
H. had it flooded
J. had the sample flooded

Question 8 is the second one that focuses on sentence structure; this one is average in difficulty. The underlined phrase is parallel in construction to *added radioactive carbon dioxide*. Repeating *the sample* here is necessary in order to make clear that it is the soil sample, rather than the atmosphere, that was flooded. Choice **G** is more concise than the original version, and it contains no parallelism problem, either. However, the use of the pronoun *it* in place of *soil sample* leaves it unclear as to what *it* refers. (Is "it" the soil sample or the atmosphere?) As for choices **H** and **J**, neither one is parallel in its construction to *added radioactive carbon dioxide*. The original version is the best one, so circle choice **F** in your test booklet.

In question 8, choices **H** and **J** both employ what's called the *passive voice*—in which the subject is *acted upon*. Although the passive voice is acceptable in Standard Written English, the writer should not mix it with the active voice, especially in the same sentence.

9. A. NO CHANGE
B. lander, was
C. lander were
D. lander,

Question 9 is the second one in this set focusing on punctuation; this one is also a bit easier than average. Try reading the sentence aloud without pausing as you read the underlined portion (*lander was*). Confusing, isn't it? Now read the sentence again, this time pausing between the two words. Aha! The sentence now makes sense. Notice that the phrase *another experiment on each lander* describes what immediately precedes it (*the gas exchange test*). In grammatical parlance, the phrase is called an *appositive*, a parenthetical phrase that should be set off by commas so the sentence makes sense—which means placing a comma before *and after* the phrase, as choice **B** provides. Choice **C** is wrong not only because it omits the comma that's needed but also because its verb *were*, which should be used only with a plural subject, is inconsistent with the singular subject *test*. Choice **D** results in what's called a "sentence fragment" (an incomplete sentence)—a serious grammatical error. Circle choice **B** in your test booklet.

10. F. NO CHANGE
G. both exhale water
H. water is exhaled by both plants and animals
J. both of them exhale water

Question 10, which deals with sentence structure, is average in difficulty. In each of the first two clauses of the sentence, the writer employs what's called the active voice, which means that the subject is what acts. (In the two clauses, the writer describes plants and animals as acting.) But, in the final clause, the writer shifts to the so-called passive voice, in which the subject (*water*) is acted upon (by *both*). This needless shift in voice is confusing, and it sounds awkward. You can easily eliminate choice **H** because it does not fix the problem. Although choices **G** and **J** both fix the problem by recasting the underlined portion in the active voice, choice **G** is the most concise one and therefore the better choice. Circle **G** in your test booklet.

11. A. NO CHANGE
B. under continuous analysis
C. continuous analyzed
D. being continuously analyzed

Question 11 is a grammar question that is easier than average. Adverbs, which are used to describe adjective and verbs, should generally end in *-ly*. In the underlined portion, the writer has used the adverb *continuously* properly, to describe the verb *analyzed*. Choice **C** is the easiest choice to eliminate—it uses the adjective *continuous* where the adverb *continuously* is needed. Choices **B** and **D** are both grammatically correct, but they're awkward and wordy—especially compared with the original version. The original version is the best one, so circle choice **A** in your test booklet.

Question 12 was a boxed-number question, which we answered during Step 3. So, let's move ahead to question 13.

13. A. NO CHANGE
B. neither this or
C. neither this experiment nor
D. neither this nor

Question 13 is a style question and is a bit tougher than average. The correlative *neither . . . nor . . .* is the correct idiom. However, the word *one* has no clear antecedent, and it can be safely omitted [as in choice **D**] without the need to replace it with *experiment* [as in choice **C**]. As for choice **B**, *neither . . . or . . .* is an improper idiom. Choice **D** is the best alternative, so circle **D** in your test booklet.

We've now answered all 15 questions in the set. It's time to move on to Step 5.

Note

The 15 questions we just tackled, as a group, were very typical of what you'll see on the ACT:

- 11 questions involved underlined portions (most covered Usage/Mechanics).
- 3 questions involved boxed numbers (covering Strategy and Organization).
- 1 question (the final one) involved the passage as a whole (it was an Organization question).
- Some questions were quite easy, while others were more challenging.

Step 5: Check the clock; if you have time, look again at questions that gave you trouble.

Check the time remaining for the English Test. Remember: Your goal is to devote 9 minutes, on average, to each passage and accompanying question set. If you're ahead of schedule, go back and look again at the questions you weren't sure about. Otherwise, move on to Step 6.

Tip

During Step 5, check your selections for the questions dealing with underlined portions. Unless you selected "NO CHANGE" (either choice **A** or **F**) for at least two of these questions, then you probably "overcorrected" the passage. Go back and look for underlined portions that you might needlessly have found fault with.

Step 6: On your answer sheet, mark your selections for all 15 questions in the set.

During a question set, don't interrupt your brainwork to fill in your answer sheet. Wait until after answering all the questions, then fill in the corresponding ovals on the answer sheet. After Step 6, if you're still uncertain about the correct answer to certain questions, earmark them in your test booklet. You can come back to them if you have enough time remaining after answering all 45 questions.

Success Keys for the ACT English Test

So far in this chapter, the chief test-taking strategy you've learned for the English Test is the 6-step game plan. In reading the explanations for the 15 questions, you picked up other valuable Tips and strategies as well. Now, let's review what you've learned.

X-Ref

To illustrate each success key, we'll refer to specific questions based on the Mars passage; the passage and question set are on pages 33–36.

Answer Some Question Types before Others

This first success key is the heart of the 6-step game plan. As you read each passage the first time, focus on the passage as a whole and how its ideas connect from one paragraph to the next. While you're in this mode, answer "whole passage" questions, and then answer "boxed" questions (which cover whole paragraphs and transitions between paragraphs). *Then*, switch to Grammar/Usage mode, and answer the questions dealing with the passage's underlined portions.

Questions 3, 12, 14, 15: In the question set about the Mars passage, we answered question 15 (a whole-passage question) first, then we answered questions 3, 12, and 14 (boxed-number question).

Use Your English Instincts to "Listen" for Sentences That Don't Sound Right

As you know, most questions involve underlined phrases and test your ability to apply the rules of English grammar and usage correctly to those phrases. However, these questions will also reward test-takers who have developed a good "feel," or "instinct," for the language. So, when you read a sentence containing underlining, *listen*—as if you were reading aloud—for anything that sounds awkward, confusing, odd, or just plain weird. If you're certain that you've heard something wrong, but you're not sure why it's wrong other than that it sounds wrong, don't worry about it. Eliminate the first answer choice ("No Change") and look for a better alternative. In short, trust your instincts and your ear.

Question 4

As you read the underlined portion for the first time, you probably guessed that what was needed there was a comma instead of a semicolon. Since choice G fixed that error, you might have selected it as the correct choice. But if you did, you were wrong! To catch the error in G, you needed to read the entire sentence with the alternative that G provides, *listening* carefully for something awkward, for any "clunkers." Assuming you have good English instincts, the phrase that G provides, together with the word *thriving*, should have sounded wrong to you.

Don't Rely Exclusively on Your Ear, and Apply the Rules of Standard Written English

On the English Test, you won't need to explain grammar errors, and you won't need to know grammar terminology. In other words, you won't score any points for knowing exactly *why* a wrong answer choice is wrong, technically speaking. But, does this mean that it's pointless to study (or review) the rules of grammar, and that you should rely exclusively on your ear for English? Not at all. Your ear for correct English might suffice for handling the easiest English questions. But for others, your ear might tell you that a certain incorrect answer sounds right.

Question 5

In handling this question, perhaps your ear betrayed you, and choice C sounded more "correct" than choice D. If so, you're not alone. Question 5 would fall squarely into the "tough" category because many, many people commit just the kind of error that C exemplifies. It's for questions like this one that a solid knowledge of the rules and conventions of Standard Written English can save your ACT hide!

X-Ref

Your English language instincts, and hence your ACT English Test scores, can be greatly enhanced by knowing the specific rules that linguists and grammarians have devised to explain how sentences are normally constructed. In the next chapter, you'll review the rules that are tested most frequently on the ACT.

Apply the Four Basic Principles for Error-Spotting in ACT Sentences

These four basic principles can help you zero in on the grammar and stylistic errors most often appearing in ACT passages—a useful supplement and aid to your instinctive "ear" for what's right and wrong in English. When in doubt about where the error is located in a sentence containing an underlined word or phrase, follow these four steps in the sequence indicated. If there's an error, you'll probably uncover it through the following process.

1. *Find the Verb, then Its Subject*

Check subject-verb agreement, correct tense, and proper verb formation.

Question 1

The underlined portion creates a subject-verb agreement error.

2. *Examine All Pronouns*

Make sure each has a clear antecedent with which it agrees in person and number.

Question 8

In choice G, the antecedent of the pronoun *it* is unclear.

3. *Look for Wobbling of the Sentence Structure*

Make sure modifiers are attached to what they modify, parallel ideas are grammatically parallel, and comparisons are clear and logical.

Question 4

Choice J corrected a punctuation problem but failed to correct the improper grammatical parallel between *which is based* . . . and *[which is] thriving* . . .

Question 6

The underlined portion "detaches" a verb from its direct object, so you should look for a better option among the choices.

Question 7

The verb *is* sets up a subject complement, which must logically match the sentence's subject. (In the original version, it does not.)

Question 8

Choices H and J mix the passive and active voices.

4. Listen for Awkwardness, Wordiness, and Incorrect use of Idioms

Question 5

The underlined portion contains the superfluous word *being*, which can and should be omitted.

Question 7

Although grammatically correct, neither choice **B** nor **C** is idiomatic.

Question 13

Choice **C** is too wordy to be a viable option, even though it is grammatically and idiomatically correct.

X-Ref

If any of the rules mentioned here, or the terms used, seem unfamiliar, don't worry—they're all clearly explained in the next chapter.

Try to Predict What the Correct Answer Will Look Like *before* Scanning the Choices

Assume you've "heard" an error in an underlined phrase. To tackle the question about that phrase, first consider how you'd correct the error *if you had written the sentence*. Do this before looking at any of the answer choices. Try rephrasing the faulty part of the sentence in your mind, figuring out what word or punctuation mark you'd eliminate, change, move, or add, and imagine how the improved phrase or clause would read.

This step is an important one, but one that average test-takers skip. By correcting the error before checking the answer choices, you'll more quickly zero in on the correct choice and you'll be far less confused and tempted by wrong answer choices.

Questions 1–15

In the question set about the Mars passage, you can apply this strategy to any question dealing with an underlined portion. If you didn't, go back now and reconsider each question in turn, without looking at the answer choices. You'll see that, in every case, you can predict, or rephrase, how the best version might "read."

Never Select an Answer Choice Merely Because It Corrects All Errors in an Underlined Portion

Scanning the answer choices to eliminate those that fail to correct the error in an underlined portion might leave you with more than one possible option. If so, read them all carefully. Although each corrects the original error, you'll generally find that the incorrect options each introduce some new error, whereas the correct answer doesn't. Be sure to "listen" for these new errors so you can zero in on the best answer choice.

Question 1

Choice **D** corrects the subject-verb agreement error but creates a new problem by using the word *if* instead of *whether*.

Question 5

Choices **B** and **C** both fix the problem with the underlined portion, but both also introduce a new problem: The modifying phrase that the choice provides lacks a clear antecedent.

Question 6

Choices **G** and **J** both restructure the underlined portion to fix the problem with it, but each also introduces a similar new problem.

Alert!

Introducing a new problem is probably the test-makers' very favorite wrong-answer ploy, and you saw many examples earlier in this chapter.

Look Around the Underlining for Important Clues

The average test-taker assumes that focusing just on the underlined portion will suffice to handle the question at hand. But as the preceding set illustrates, to handle nearly any of these questions, you also need to look at what precedes and follows the underlined portion. At the very least, you should read the entire sentence that contains the underlining.

Question 1

Questions like this one, which cover subject-verb agreement problems, generally turn on a single word appearing somewhere before or after the underlined portion. (In this case, that word is the singular subject *goal* near the beginning of the sentence.)

Question 4

To get this question correct, you needed to notice not just the punctuation problem but also the single word *thriving* (later in the sentence), which was the key to homing in on the correct choice.

Question 9

Even if you had read the sentence's entire second clause (following the comma), you would not have spotted the problem here. The clause sounds like a perfectly correct independent clause. To notice the punctuation problem, you needed to read the whole sentence.

Be Careful Not to "Over-Correct"

On each of the four ACT tests (including the English Test), the test-makers will give you roughly equal numbers of each correct answer choice. What this means is that for the questions that include "NO CHANGE" as the first answer choice, the correct answer will in fact be "NO

CHANGE" (the first choice, either **A** or **F**) in about *one out of four* questions. Of course, this choice usually means that the original sentence contains no errors or other problems—that it's perfectly correct as written and in no need of revision.

Many test-takers tend to "over-correct" and find errors where none exist. To avoid this tendency, keep in mind that if you read a sentence that sounds perfectly okay, *it probably is*. This doesn't mean you shouldn't look at the three alternative options for a better one, especially one that's more concise. But be careful not to violate your initial instinct that the original version was perfectly fine—just for the sake of improvement.

Question 2

The original underlined portion could probably stand improvement, as the analysis indicates. But that doesn't mean that "NO CHANGE" **F** is an incorrect answer. As it turns out, the original version, imperfect as it may be, is nevertheless the best of the four choices listed. Test-takers who tend to over-correct would probably reject **F**; and they'd be wrong.

Tip

A good way to make sure you didn't over-correct is to count your **A** and **F** selections (NO CHANGE) for questions dealing with underlined questions, and then adjust if the count is too high or too low. If you count no **A** or **F** selections, you were probably overly critical, and found errors where none actually exist. On the other hand, if you've found too many—say, six or more—you may be too forgiving, overlooking errors you should be spotting. Adjust accordingly.

Choose the Shortest Answer—But Only If All Else Is Equal!

Occasionally, you'll find that eliminating all the answers that contain errors does not narrow your options to a single choice. You may find that two (or rarely three) answer choices all appear completely correct and equally clear, graceful, and unambiguous.

When this happens, choose whichever answer is shortest. Generally speaking, the test-makers regard a concise, tightly worded sentence as more stylistically effective than a wordy, loosely structured one. Therefore, when all other factors appear equal, the shortest sentence is the one that the test-makers are most likely to consider correct.

Question 1

Choices **B** and **C** are both grammatically and idiomatically correct. But, **C** has a "tighter" structure and is more concise than **B**, so it's a better choice.

Question 8

Choices **F** and **G** are both grammatically and idiomatically correct. Although **G** is more concise, it suffers from a pronoun reference problem. Hence, in this case, "all else" is *not* equal!

Chapter 4

Review of Standard Written English

In the first section, you'll review most of the rules of grammar, sentence structure, and style that the ACT English Test covers. Specifically, you'll learn to recognize and fix simple errors and other problems involving the following testing areas:

- *Punctuation*
  The comma and the apostrophe (the two most frequently tested punctuation marks)
- *Grammar*
  Choice of adjectives, adverbs, and pronouns, as well as pronoun-antecedent and subject-verb agreement
- *Sentence Structure*
  Incomplete and run-on sentences and parallelism between a sentence's structural elements
- *Style*
  Redundancy, the use of superfluous words and phrases, general wordiness, and awkwardness

Alert!

Immersing yourself in the rules of English grammar and the guidelines for effective written expression (as you're about to do) will help you not only on the ACT English Test but also on the optional ACT Writing Test. So pay close attention; if you plan to take the Writing Test, your efforts here will be doubly rewarded on exam day!

Punctuation

Test questions that focus on punctuation account for about 10 of the 75 questions on the ACT English Test. Most of these questions deal with the uses and misuses of the comma and the apostrophe (for possessives and contractions). In this chapter, you'll review the rules and guidelines for using these two marks, and you'll find out how the test-makers design test items focusing on them.

Uses and Misuses of Commas

A comma indicates a pause that should correspond to a pause in the logic of the sentence. The commas make it clear to the reader that the logic of the sentence is being (temporarily) interrupted. The ACT tests four different uses (and misuses) of the comma. Pay particular attention to the last one listed below, which the ACT covers more frequently than the others:

- Overuse of the comma, resulting in the splitting of a grammatical unit
- Too few commas, resulting in a confusing sentence
- Commas used to separate a list of three or more items
- Commas used in pairs to set appositives (parenthetical phrases)

Commas That Split a Grammatical Unit

Commas should not needlessly separate parts of the sentence that "want" to be together, such as the subject and verb:

> **incorrect:** Former secretary of state Henry Kissinger, is the author of several books on the history of diplomacy.

The verb *is* should not be separated by a comma from its subject *Henry Kissinger* (unless a parenthetical phrase intervenes between them—not the case here).

Similarly, no comma should come between the verb and a subject complement that may follow it:

> **incorrect:** The nineteenth-century explorers Lewis and Clark may be, two of America's most-admired historical figures.

In the same way, a preposition should not be separated from its object by a comma:

> **incorrect:** As the storm continued, pieces of driftwood as well as, large quantities of sand were blown up onto the front porch.

The preposition *as well as* needs to remain connected to its object, the phrase *large quantities of sand.*

When commas are overused on the ACT, it will usually be in sentences like these examples, where the commas jarringly separate parts of the sentence that seem to "want" to be together. These abuses are generally pretty easy to spot.

Commas for Sentence Sense

A tougher task is deciding whether a sentence uses too *few* commas, a problem that can easily confuse the reader. Here's the guideline: A sentence should use the minimum number of commas needed for a reader to understand the intended meaning of the sentence.

> **too few commas:** Enzyme catalysis takes place in living systems and as it is not a laboratory procedure is therefore subject to cellular controls.

> **better:** Enzyme catalysis takes place in living systems, and as it is not a laboratory procedure is therefore subject to cellular controls.

also acceptable: Enzyme catalysis takes place in living systems, and, as it is not a laboratory procedure, is therefore subject to cellular controls.

There are two special situations that you should look for in ACT sentences: commas used to separate items in a list, and commas used to set off parenthetical phrases. You'll look at both types of situations immediately ahead.

Commas for Lists of Three or More Items

When three or more words, phrases, or clauses are presented in sequence, they should be separated by commas. Here are examples of each:

commas separating a list of words: The Galapagos Islands boast some of the world's most unusual plants, birds, mammals, reptiles, and fish.

commas separating a list of phrases: We looked for the missing gloves under the sofa, in the closet, and behind the dresser, but we never found them.

commas separating a list of clauses: The plot of the movie was a familiar one: boy meets girl, boy loses girl, mutant from outer space devours both.

Notice two things about how these lists are crafted. First, you normally insert the word *and* before the final item in the series ("plants, birds, mammals, reptiles, and fish"). Second, the last comma (the one after reptiles in this example) is optional. Sometimes called the serial comma, it may be included or omitted according to taste. (The ACT test-makers have no special preference, and there's no "right" or "wrong" about it on the exam.) The other commas, however, are not optional; they must be used.

Commas for Setting off Appositives (Parenthetical Phrases)

Wherever a commonly used parenthetical phrase such as *for example*, *that is*, or *first of all* appears, it should be separated from the rest of the sentence by commas (or, if the phrase appears at the beginning of a sentence, by one comma). These phrases are easy enough for any test-taker to spot.

Another type of parenthetical phrase is an *appositive*, which names or describes a noun. It, too, should be set off by commas. In the next example, "the great left-handed Dodger pitcher" is an appositive:

Sandy Koufax, the great left-handed Dodger pitcher, was the guest of honor at this year's sports club banquet.

Sometimes a parenthetical phrase may be quite long:

I was surprised to learn that Paula, my cousin Frank's former girlfriend and a well-known local artist, had decided to move to Santa Fe.

You can probably see how the ten words enclosed by commas interrupt the main flow of the sentence. If you're unsure, try this test: Read the sentence without the phrase. If it still makes grammatical sense and the meaning is basically the same, then the phrase is parenthetical and should be set off by commas. This example passes the test—the interrupting words (*my cousin Frank's former girlfriend and a well-known local artist*) should be surrounded by commas.

Now try applying the test you just learned about to an ACT-style sentence, which actually involves two separate appositive issues.

Note

The following example incorporates two similar issues into the same paragraph in order to help illustrate the concept you just learned. On the actual test, don't expect one paragraph to test you twice on the same concept.

During the 1980s when their funds dried up [1] the Girls Choir of Harlem temporarily disbanded. In 1989, however the [2] choir reassembled.

1. Which of the alternatives provides the most effective punctuation for the underlined portion?

A. NO CHANGE
B. Place a comma before and after the underlined portion.
C. Place a comma before, but not after, the underlined portion.
D. Place a comma after, but not before, the underlined portion.

The correct answer is B. The sentence makes perfect grammatical and logical sense without the underlined portion. This is a good indication that the portion is an appositive, which should be set off by a pair of commas. Without a comma after *dried up*, the sentence nonsensically suggests that the Girls Choir became *dried up*! Thus, neither choice **A** nor **C** can be correct. A comma is also needed immediately after *1980s* for clarity.

2. F. NO CHANGE
G. In 1989 however, the
H. In 1989, however, the
J. In 1989 however the

The correct answer is H. If you omit the word *however*, the sentence makes perfect grammatical and logical sense: *In 1989, the choir reassembled.* That's your clue that you should set off *however* by commas.

The Apostrophe (for Possessives and Contractions)

The apostrophe is used for two purposes in English, both frequently tested on the ACT. A *possessive* is used to indicate ownership or some other close connection between a noun or pronoun and what follows it ("Susan's car," "the company's employees"). Form the possessive as follows:

- For a singular noun, add *'s* (*the dog's paw* or *James's necktie*).
- For a plural noun ending in *s*, just add an apostrophe (*the Wangs' apartment* or *the birds' feathers*).

- For a plural noun that does not end in *s*, add *'s*, (*the children's teacher* or *the cattle's hooves*).
- The possessive pronouns *his*, *hers*, *its*, *ours*, *yours*, and *theirs* contain no apostrophes.
- The other use of an apostrophe is in a *contraction*, a word made up of two or more words from which letters have been omitted for easier pronunciation.

Note

Contractions are *not* generally considered "incorrect" or "slangy"; they're perfectly acceptable in all but the most formal writing.

The apostrophe is usually (but not always!) inserted in place of the letters omitted. If in doubt, mentally "expand" the contraction to determine which letters have been left out; this is often a useful guide to where the apostrophe belongs.

we've got to go = *we have* got to go

I'd rather not = *I would* rather not

she won't mind = she *will not* mind

it's your turn = *it is* your turn

you're welcome = *you are* welcome

Proper use of the apostrophe in a contraction is basically a matter of correct spelling.

Grammatical Errors Involving Parts of Speech

Test items focusing on the rules of grammar account for about 12 of the 75 questions on the ACT English Test. Next in this chapter, you'll examine the most basic kinds of grammatical errors that appear in ACT English passages. These are the ones that, for most test-takers, are easiest to recognize and most straightforward to fix. In addition to learning how to fix these problems, you'll see how the ACT might test you on each one. Here are the kinds of errors we'll cover in the pages ahead:

- Error in choice between adjective and adverb
- Error in choice of adjective for comparisons
- Error in choice of personal pronoun
- Error in pronoun-antecedent agreement
- Error in subject-verb agreement

X-Ref

If you go on to *Take It to the Next Level*, you'll learn the rules for so-called "relative" pronouns and for subject-verb agreement involving compound subjects.

Error in Choice Between Adjective and Adverb

Adjectives describe nouns, while *adverbs* describe verbs, adjectives, and other adverbs. Adverbs generally end with *-ly*, while adjectives don't. Look for adjectives incorrectly used as adverbs (and vice versa).

incorrect: The movie ended *sudden*.

correct: The movie ended *suddenly*.(The adverb *suddenly* describes the verb *ended*.)

Although adverbs generally end with *-ly*, some adverbs don't. Also, if you're dealing with two adverbs in a row, sometimes the *-ly* is dropped from the second adverb. There are no hard-and-fast rules here. Trust your ear as to what sounds correct.

incorrect: Risk-takers drive *fastly*, play *hardly*, and arrive *lately* for their appointments.

correct: Risk-takers drive *fast*, play *hard*, and arrive *late* for their appointments.

incorrect: The Canadian skater jumps *particularly highly*.

correct: The Canadian skater jumps *particularly high*.

Also keep in mind that adjectives, not adverbs, should be used to describe verbs involving the senses (sight, taste, smell, hearing, touch).

incorrect: Dinner tasted *deliciously*.

incorrect: Dinner tasted *awful* delicious.

correct: Dinner tasted *awfully* delicious.

(The adjective *delicious* is used to describe the verb *tasted*, while the adverb *awfully* is used to describe *delicious*.)Even if an adjective or adverb is used correctly in the grammatical sense, there might still be room for improvement, as in the next item.

A recent report from the Department of Energy suggests that, over the next two decades, demand for crude oil will increase <u>at an alarming and quick rate</u>.

A. NO CHANGE
B. at a rate that is alarming and quick
C. at an alarmingly quick rate
D. alarmingly quickly

The correct answer is C. In the original version, the adjectives *alarming* and *quick* both describe *rate* (a noun). Hence, this version is grammatically correct. But it would make more sense for *alarming* to describe the adjective *quick*, as choices **C** and **D** provide. So you can eliminate **A** and **B**. This is where the question becomes tricky. In choice **D**, the use of two adverbs in the phrase *increase alarmingly quickly* is technically correct—but doesn't **D** sound a bit awkward, especially compared with choice **C**? Even though **D** is more concise, **C** supplies a clearer, more graceful expression of the idea.

Alert!

Look carefully at adjectives and adverbs, *especially when they appear in pairs*—as in the sample question above! And remember: The most concise answer choice is not necessarily the best one. It might obscure the sentence's meaning, or it might make for a phrase that sounds a bit clumsy—as in choice **D** above.

Error in Choice of Adjective for Comparisons

As you read an ACT sentence, pay close attention to any adjective ending in *-er*, *-ier*, *-est*, and *-iest*. Adjectives ending in *-er* and *-ier* should be used to compare *two* things, while adjectives ending in *-est* and *-iest* should be used in dealing with three or more things.

Comparative Form (two things)	Superlative Form (three or more things)
brighter	brightest
greater	greatest
fewer	fewest
lesser	least
more	most
better	best

incorrect: Frank is less intelligent than the other four students.

correct: Frank is the *least* intelligent among the *five* students.

correct: Frank is *less* intelligent than *any* of the other four students. (The word *any* is singular, so the comparative form is proper.)

Another way of making a comparison is to precede the adjective with a word such as *more*, *less*, *most*, or *least*. But if both methods are used together, the sentence is incorrect.

incorrect: Francis is *more healthier* than Greg.

correct: Francis is *healthier* than Greg.

Now look at an ACT-style item involving the rules we just covered.

The more busy the trading floor at the stock exchange, the less likely that large institutional investors can influence the direction of price by initiating large leveraged transactions.

A. NO CHANGE
B. The busier is the
C. As a result of a busier
D. The busiest the

The correct answer is A. The original version correctly uses *more* preceding the adjective *busy*. It is idiomatic to say *The more . . . , the less . . .* (Although replacing the underlined portion with *The busier the* would also be grammatically correct and idiomatic, this option is not available among the answer choices.) Choice **B** is wrong because *The busier is the* is not idiomatic. Choice **C** is wrong because the result, while it might look like a complete sentence, is actually not. Choice **D** is wrong because it uses the superlative *busiest* where the comparative *busier* is appropriate.

When the ACT tests you on an idiomatic phrase that's unfamiliar to you, use process of elimination to determine whether the phrase is proper. In the preceding question, for example, you can rule out choices **C** and **D** because they result in grammatical errors.

Error in Choice of Personal Pronoun

Personal pronouns are words such as *they*, *me*, *his*, and *itself*—words that refer to specific people, places, and things. Pronouns take different forms, called "cases," depending on how they're used in a sentence. Just for the record, you'll find all the various cases in the following table.

	Subjective Case	Possessive Case	Objective Case	Objective Case—Reflexive
first-person singular	I	my, mine	me	myself
first-person plural	we	our, ours	us	ourselves
second-person singular	you	your, yours	you	yourself
second-person plural	you	your, yours	you	yourselves
third-person singular	he, she, it	his, her, hers, its	him, her, it	himself, herself, itself
third-person plural	they	their, theirs	them	themselves

You can generally trust your ear when it comes to detecting personal-pronoun errors. In some cases, however, your ear can betray you, so make sure you are "tuned in" to the following uses of pronouns.

incorrect: Either him or Trevor *would be* the best spokesperson for our group.

incorrect: The best spokesperson for our group *would be* either him or Trevor.

correct: Either Trevor or *he would be* the best spokesperson for our group.

correct: The best spokesperson for our group *would be* either *he* or Trevor.

(Any form of the verb *to be* is followed by a subject pronoun, such as *he*.)

incorrect: One can't help admiring *them* cooperating with one another.

correct: One can't help admiring *their cooperating* with one another.

(The *possessive* form is used when the pronoun is part of a "noun clause," such as *their cooperating*.)

incorrect: In striving to understand others, we also learn more about *us*.

correct: In striving to understand others, *we* also learn more about *ourselves*.

(A *reflexive* pronoun is used to refer to the sentence's subject.)

> **Alert!**
>
> What appears to be a reflexive pronoun may not even be a real word! Here's a list of "non-words," any of which might masquerade as a reflexive pronoun in an ACT sentence: *ourself*, *our own selves*, *theirselves*, *theirself*, *themself*, *their own self*, and *their own selves*.

Now look at *two* ways in which one of these tricky pronoun-case issues might rear its ugly head in an ACT sentence:

Despite his admiring of [1] the great jazz musicians that preceded him, John Coltrane opposed them trivializing [2] the style of music he so loved.

1. A. NO CHANGE
   B. him admiring
   C. that he admired
   D. his admiration of

The correct answer is D. Although the noun clause *his admiring* is perfectly acceptable here, the word *of* should be omitted. (*His admiring of* is not idiomatic.) None of the alternative choices provides *his admiring*. However, choice **D** provides an appropriate, idiomatic substitute. Choice **B** is wrong because it improperly uses the object-case *him*—in a noun clause. Choice **C** is not idiomatic. (A proper idiom here would be *Despite the fact that he admired*.)

2. F. NO CHANGE
   G. their trivializing
   H. these musicians trivializing
   J. trivializing

The correct answer is G. Choice **G** corrects the improper use of *them*, replacing it with the possessive *their*, which properly precedes the gerund *trivializing*. Choice **H** fails to correct the problem; instead, it simply substitutes the noun for the object-case pronoun. Choice **J** omits any reference to the musicians who preceded Coltrane, leaving you with no idea as to who was trivializing.

Note

In the preceding example, the sentence contained two underlined portions involving *the same kind* of grammar issue. But don't expect this on the real ACT.

Error in Pronoun-Antecedent Agreement

An *antecedent* is simply the noun to which a pronoun refers. In ACT sentences, make sure that pronouns agree in *number* (singular or plural) with their antecedents.

singular: Studying other artists actually helps a young *painter* develop *his* or *her* own style.

plural: Studying other artists actually helps young *painters* develop *their* own style.

Singular pronouns are generally used in referring to antecedents such as *each*, *either*, *neither*, and *one*.

correct: *Neither* of the two countries imposes an income tax on *its* citizens.

correct: *One* cannot be too kind to *oneself*.

If a pronoun and its antecedent are far apart, it can be especially easy to overlook an agreement problem, as in this ACT-style example.

Neither a brilliant movie script nor a generous budget can garner critical acclaim without a good director to make the most of them.

A. NO CHANGE
B. it
C. that
D. those things

The correct answer is B. The antecedent of *them* (a plural pronoun) is *script* or *budget* (singular). One way to remedy the disagreement is to replace *them* with *it*, as in choice **B**. Since the antecedent and pronoun are so far apart, another solution is to replace the pronoun with its antecedent—for example, with *that script or budget*. Choice **D** comes close, but it's too imprecise and vague.

Error in Subject-Verb Agreement

A verb should always "agree" in number—either singular or plural—with its subject. A singular subject takes a singular verb, while a plural subject takes a plural verb:

correct (singular): The *parade was* spectacular.

correct (singular): Both *parades were* spectacular.

correct (plural): The parade *and* the pageant *were* spectacular.

Don't be fooled by any words or phrases that might separate the verb from its subject. In each sentence below, the singular verb *was* agrees with its subject, the singular noun *parade*:

correct: The *parade* of cars *was* spectacular.

correct: The *parade* of cars and horses *was* spectacular.

An intervening clause set off by commas can serve an especially effective "smokescreen" for a subject-verb agreement error. Pay careful attention to what comes immediately before and after the intervening clause. Reading the sentence without the clause often reveals a subject-verb agreement error.

incorrect: John, as well as his sister, *were* absent from school yesterday.

correct: *John*, as well as his sister, *was* absent from school yesterday.

Here's how this type of subject-verb agreement error might show up in an ACT-style sentence. Notice that the sentence contains not just one, but *two* prepositional phrases between the subject and verb.

Grade-school instruction in ethical and social values, particularly the values of respect and tolerance, are required for any democracy to thrive.

A. NO CHANGE
B. values of respect and of tolerance, are
C. value of respect, together with tolerance, is
D. values of respect and tolerance, is

The correct answer is D. In the original sentence, the subject of the plural verb *are* is the singular noun *instruction*. The correct answer choice must correct this subject-verb agreement problem. Also, the second *of* in the underlined phrase should be deleted because its use results in an awkward and nonsensical clause, which seems to suggest that *of tolerance* is a value. Choice **B** fails to correct the problem. Choices **C** and **D** both correct the problem by changing *are* to *is*. However, choice **C** creates two new problems. First, using the word *value* instead of *values* distorts the meaning of the underlined phrase. Respect and tolerance are not referred to in **B** as values. However, the original sentence, considered as a whole, clearly intends to refer to respect and tolerance as examples of ethical and social *values*. Second, the phrase *together with tolerance* (set off by commas) adds an unnecessary clause and results in a sentence that is wordy and awkward. Choice **D** is clearer and more concise.

Alert!

Keep a keen eye out for ACT sentences that separate verbs from their subjects.

Problems Involving a Sentence's Structural Elements

Now, let's move ahead to the broad testing area of *sentence structure*, which accounts for about 18 of the 75 questions on the ACT English Test. Here are the specific kinds of structural problems we'll cover in this chapter:

- Sentence fragments (incomplete sentences)
- Two main clauses connected improperly
- Faulty parallelism involving lists, or "strings"
- Faulty parallelism involving correlatives

X-Ref

If you go on to the *Take It to the Next Level*, you'll learn to recognize and fix other problems with sentence construction, including improper *shifts* in verb tense, in voice, and in mood. You'll also learn to rearrange parts of a sentence that are assembled in a confusing or awkward way.

Sentence Fragments (Incomplete Sentences)

It was probably your fifth- or sixth-grade teacher who first informed you that a sentence must include both a subject and a predicate. Well, your teacher was right, and the ACT is here to remind you. Grammarians call incomplete sentences "sentence fragments."

fragment: Expensive private colleges, generally out of financial reach for most families with college-aged children.

fragment: Without question, responsibility for building and maintaining safe bridges.

On the ACT, you probably won't have any trouble recognizing a sentence fragment. However, an especially long fragment might escape your detection if you're not paying close attention. Here's an ACT-style example.

> One cannot deny that, even after the initial flurry of the feminist movement subsided, Congresswoman Bella Abzug, undeniably her female constituency's truest voice, as well as its most public advocate.

A. NO CHANGE
B. who was her constituency's
C. and also its
D. was also its

The correct answer is D. With the phrase that D provides, the sentence can be distilled down to this: *One cannot deny that Bella Abzug was its [the feminist movement's] most public advocate.* Adding the verb *was* is the key to transforming the original fragment into a complete sentence. None of the other options provides the necessary verb to establish a predicate for the would-be sentence.

If you're not sure whether you're looking at a complete sentence, ask yourself two questions: What's the subject? Where's the verb that establishes a predicate?

Two Main Clauses Connected Improperly

A *main clause* is any clause that can stand alone as a complete sentence. There's nothing wrong with combining two main clauses into one sentence—as long as the clauses are properly connected. On the ACT, look for any of these three flaws:

1. No punctuation between main clauses
2. A comma between main clauses, but no connecting word, such as *and*, *or*, *but*, *yet*, *for*, *so* (this problem is called a *comma splice*)
3. A confusing or inappropriate connecting word

incorrect:

Dan ran out of luck Mike continued to win.

Dan ran out of luck, Mike continued to win.

Dan ran out of luck, or Mike continued to win.

correct:

Dan ran out of luck, *but* Mike continued to win.

Dan ran out of luck, *while* Mike continued to win.

Dan ran out of luck, *yet* Mike continued to win.

Here's an ACT-style item that focuses on the connection between two main clauses.

The Aleutian Islands of Alaska include many islands near the populated mainland, the majority of them are uninhabited by humans.

A. NO CHANGE
B. mainland but
C. mainland, yet
D. mainland; the

The correct answer is C. In the original sentence, notice that as you read *the majority of them*, there's still no hint of the comma-splice problem that exists. The transition from one clause to the other seems smooth and logical. It isn't until you get to the next word (*are*) that the splice becomes apparent. (In fact, without *are*, the sentence would be perfectly fine.) Notice also that choice **C** adds the connecting word *yet*, which gives the sentence a reasonable meaning by underscoring the contrast between the mainland (which is populated) and the unpopulated nearby islands. Choice **B** also adds an appropriate connecting word. But **B** creates a new problem by omitting the comma, which should remain here to make clear that the writer is conveying two distinct ideas. Although choice **D** solves the comma-splice problem by replacing the comma with a semicolon, the resulting sentence is rhetorically ineffective.

Faulty Parallelism Involving Lists, or "Strings"

Sentence elements that are grammatically equal should be constructed similarly; otherwise, the result will be what is referred to as *faulty parallelism*. For instance, whenever you see a list, or "string," of items in a sentence, look for inconsistent or mixed use of the following:

- Prepositions (such as *in*, *with,* or *on*)
- Gerunds (verbs with an *-ing* added to the end)
- Infinitives (plural verb preceded by *to*)
- Articles (such as *a* and *the*)

faulty: Flight 82 travels first to Boise, then to Denver, then Salt Lake City. (*to* precedes only the first two of the three cities in this list.)

parallel: Flight 82 travels first to Boise, then Denver, then Salt Lake City.

parallel: Flight 82 travel first to Boise, then to Denver, then to Salt Lake City.

faulty: Being understaffed, lack of funding, and being outpaced by competitors soon resulted in the fledgling company's going out of business. (Only two of the three listed items begin with the gerund *being*.)

parallel: Understaffed, underfunded, and outpaced by competitors, the fledgling company soon went out of business.

parallel: As a result of understaffing, insufficient funding, and outpacing on the part of its competitors, the fledgling company soon went out of business.

faulty: Among *the* mountains, *the* sea, and desert, we humans have yet to fully explore only the sea.

parallel: Among *the* mountains, sea, and desert, we humans have yet to fully explore only the sea.

parallel: Among *the* mountains, *the* sea, and *the* desert, we humans have yet to fully explore only the sea.

Now, look at an ACT-style item involving lists and faulty parallelism.

Long before the abolition of slavery, many freed indentured servants were able to acquire property, interact with people of other races, <u>and to maintain</u> their freedom.

A. NO CHANGE
B. as well as to
C. and maintain
D. as well as maintaining

The correct answer is C. In the original version, the second item does *not* repeat the preposition *to*, but the third (underlined) item does. Choice **C** corrects this faulty parallelism. Choice **B** does not. Choice **D** improperly mixes the use of a prepositional phrase (beginning with *to*) with a construction that instead uses a gerund (*maintaining*).

Alert!

Just because all items in a string are parallel, don't assume that the string is problem-free! Repeating the same preposition, article, or other modifier before each item in a string can sometimes result in an awkward and unnecessary wordy sentence. In other instances, repeating the modifier may be necessary to achieve clarity.

awkward: Some pachyderms can go for days at a time without water or without food or without sleep.

better: Some pachyderms can go for days at a time without water, food, or sleep.

unclear: Going for broke and broke usually carry identical consequences.

clear: Going for broke and going broke usually carry identical consequences.

Faulty Parallelism Involving Correlatives

You just saw how items in a list can suffer from faulty parallelism. Now look at how this grammatical error shows up in what are called *correlatives*. Here are the most commonly used correlatives:

- either . . . or . . .
- neither . . . nor . . .
- both . . . and . . .
- not only . . . but also . . .

Whenever you spot a correlative in a sentence, make sure that the element immediately following the first correlative term is parallel in construction to the element following the second term.

faulty: Those wishing to participate should *either* contact us by telephone *or* should send e-mail to us.

parallel (but repetitive): Those wishing to participate *either should* contact us by telephone *or should* send e-mail to us.

parallel: Those wishing to participate should *either* contact us by telephone *or* send e-mail to us.

Now, look at how faulty parallelism in a correlative might appear in an ACT sentence.

Species diversity in the Amazon basin results not from climate stability, as once believed, but rather climate disturbances.

A. NO CHANGE
B. also from
C. instead
D. rather from

The correct answer is D. The idiomatic correlative in this sentence is *not . . . but rather . . .* In the original sentence, *from* follows the first correlative term, but not the second. Choice **D** corrects the faulty parallelism (*from* appears in each correlative term). Although choice **B** also corrects the faulty parallelism, it uses the nonsensical (and improper) correlative *not . . . but also*. (The idiom is *not only . . . but also*, which in any event would completely alter the sentence's meaning.)

Redundancy, Wordiness, and Awkwardness

The ACT English Test also covers certain issues of writing "style." Test items focusing on style account for about 12 of the test's 75 questions and test you on your skill at recognizing and fixing the following types of problems:

- Redundancy (repeating the same idea)
- Wordiness (using more words than needed to make the point)
- Awkwardness (using clumsy, confusing, or overly complicated wording)

Alert!

Always be on the lookout for problems of wordiness, awkwardness, and redundancy—not just in the underlined portion but also in the alternative versions.

Redundant Words and Phrases

Look for words and phrases that express the same essential idea twice. This syndrome is known as "redundancy." In many cases, correcting the problem is as simple as omitting one of the redundant phrases.

redundant: *The reason that* we stopped for the night was *because* we were sleepy.

redundant: *Because* we were sleepy, we *therefore* stopped for the night.

better: We stopped for the night because we were sleepy.

redundant: The *underlying* motive *behind* his seemingly generous offer was old-fashioned greed.

better: The motive behind his seemingly generous offer was old-fashioned greed.

better: The underlying motive for his seemingly generous offer was old-fashioned greed.

redundant: One of the fossils is twenty thousand years old *in age*.

better: One of the fossils is twenty thousand years old.

redundant: The German Oktoberfest takes place *each October of every year*.

better: The German Oktoberfest takes place *every October*.

redundant: *At the same time* that lightning struck, we *simultaneously* lost our electric power.

better: At the same time that lightning struck, we lost our electric power.

redundant: *Both* unemployment *as well as* interest rates can affect stock prices.

better: Both unemployment levels and interest rates can affect stock prices.

better: Unemployment levels as well as interest rates can affect stock prices.

redundant: Not only does dinner smell good, but it *also* tastes good *too*.

better: Not only does dinner smell good, but it tastes good too.

On the ACT, be on the lookout for sentences that have the following "themes" and keywords. Redundancies are most likely to spring up in these kinds of sentences:

- Words establishing cause-and-effect (*because*, *since*, *if*, *then*, *therefore*)
- References to time (*age*, *years*, *hours*, *days*)
- Words used in conjunctions (*both*, *as well*, *too*, *also*)

Now, look at an ACT-style item that raises the issue of redundancy.

Due to the harmful side effects associated with using certain diet pills, the Food and Drug Administration often refuses to approve these drugs <u>on this basis.</u>

A. NO CHANGE
B. based on this difference
C. for this reason
D. OMIT the underlined portion.

The correct answer is D. In the original sentence, *due to* and *on this basis* serve the same function: to express that the FDA's refusal was based on the side effects. (The redundancy is easy to miss since one phrase begins the sentence while the other phrase ends it.) Of the three alternatives, only choice D corrects the problem, simply by omitting *on this basis*.

The answer choice "OMIT the underlined portion" is often the correct choice for a question that tests you on redundancy. So, when you see this choice [usually choice D], be sure to look around the sentence for an idea that expresses the same idea as the underlined portion.

Superfluous (Unnecessary) Words

You just took a look at one variety of unnecessary verbiage: redundancy. Now, look at some other kinds of sentences in which certain words can simply be omitted without affecting the meaning or effectiveness of the original sentence. Remember: Briefer is better!

Each sentence in the first group below contains an *ellipsis*: a word or phrase that can be omitted because it is clearly implied. (In the incorrect version, the ellipsis is italicized.)

superfluous: The warmer the weather *is*, the more crowded the beach *is*.

concise: The warmer the weather, the more crowded the beach.

superfluous: He looks exactly like Francis *looks*.

concise: He looks exactly like Francis.

superfluous: That shirt is the ugliest *shirt that* I have ever seen.

concise: That shirt is the ugliest I have ever seen.

Each sentence in the next group includes a superfluous preposition. (In the incorrect version, the preposition is italicized.)

superfluous: The other children couldn't help *from* laughing at the girl with mismatched shoes.

concise: The other children couldn't help laughing at the girl with mismatched shoes.

superfluous: One prominent futurist predicts a nuclear holocaust by the year *of* 2020.

concise: One prominent futurist predicts a nuclear holocaust by the year 2020.

superfluous: They made the discovery *in* around December of last year.

concise: They made the discovery around December of last year.

superfluous: The waiter brought half *of* a loaf of bread to the table.

concise: The waiter brought half a loaf of bread to the table.

Superfluous words can also appear in a series of parallel clauses. Both versions of the next sentence use proper parallelism, but briefer is better—as long as the meaning of the sentence is clear.

superfluous: My three goals in life are to be healthy, *to be* wealthy, and *to be* wise.

concise: My three goals in life are to be healthy, wealthy, and wise.

Before you decide that certain words are superfluous and can be omitted, be sure that omitting them won't distort the meaning of the sentence. Here's an ACT-style item that focuses on this problem.

Some varieties of parrots live as long as one hundred years.

- **A.** NO CHANGE
- **B.** one hundred years
- **C.** to be one hundred years old in age
- **D.** as long as the age of one hundred years

The correct answer is A. Choice B is obviously more concise, but omitting *as long as* unfairly implies that the varieties to which the writer refers never live less than one hundred years. Choice C suffers from this problem as well; what's more, it creates a redundancy: The word *old* expresses the same idea as *in age.* (One or the other, but not both, should be used.) Choice D provides an illogical phrase—its grammatical construction implies that *one hundred years* is an *age.*

Wordy and Awkward Phrases

Because a sentence is grammatically acceptable, you shouldn't assume that there is no room for improvement. You've already seen that unnecessary words can sometimes be omitted, thereby improving an ACT sentence. Now, look at some phrases that can be *replaced* with clearer, more concise ones.

wordy: Failure can *some of the time* serve as a prelude to success.

concise: Failure can *sometimes* serve as a prelude to success.

wordy: *As a result of Greg's being* a compulsive overeater, *it is not likely that he will* live past the age of 50.

concise: *Because Greg is* a compulsive overeater, *he is unlikely* to live past the age of 50.

wordy: Before the mother eats, she feeds *each and every one* of her offspring.

concise: Before the mother eats, she feeds *each* of her offspring.

wordy: There are fewer buffalo on the plains today than *there ever were* before.

concise: There are fewer buffalo on the plains today than *ever* before.

wordy: Discipline is crucial to *the attainment of* one's objectives.

concise: Discipline is crucial to *attaining* one's objectives.

wordy: Her husband was waiting for her on the platform *at the time of the train's arrival.*

concise: Her husband was waiting for her on the platform *when the train arrived.*

awkward: Calcification *is when* (or *is where*) calcium deposits form around a bone.

concise: Calcification *occurs when* calcium deposits form around a bone.

awkward: *There are* eight cats in the house, *of which* only two have been fed.

concise: Of the eight cats in the house, only two have been fed.

awkward: The wind poses a serious threat to the old tree, and *so does* the snow.

concise: The wind and snow both pose a serious threat to the old tree.

Now take a look at a wordy *and* awkward ACT-style sentence.

> In order to avoid confusion between oral medications, <u>different pills' coatings should have different colors, and pills should be different in shape and size.</u>
>
> A. NO CHANGE
> B. pills should differ in color as well as in shape and size
> C. pills should be able to be distinguished by their color, shape and size
> D. different pills should have different colors, different shapes, and different sizes

The correct answer is B. There are several problems with the original sentence. The first is that *different pills' coatings* is very awkward. Second, the word *coatings* is probably superfluous here; *color* suffices to make the point. Third, *have different colors* is awkward (*differ in color* would be better). Fourth, the phrase *be different* is ambiguous (different from what?). Finally, a parallel series including color, shape, and size would be more concise and less awkward than the construction used in the sentence. Choice **B** corrects all these problems. In choice **C**, the phrase *be able to be distinguished* is wordy and very awkward; the phrase *be distinguishable* would be better. Choice **D** repeats the word *different* (*different colors, shapes, and sizes* is less repetitive).

Note

The wordy and awkward phrases that the ACT can throw at you are limited in variety only by the collective imagination of the test-makers. So the phrases we've provided here are just a small sampling.

Take It to the Next Level

At this level, you'll review additional errors and other problems with punctuation, grammar, sentence structure, and sentence sense and "rhetorical" skills—problems that aren't so easy to detect and trickier to fix. Here's a preview:

- *Punctuation:* You'll examine the uses and misuses of the colon and semicolon.
- *Grammar:* You'll recognize and fix challenging grammatical problems involving relative pronouns and subject-verb agreement.
- *Sentence structure:* You'll learn to recognize and fix improper mixing and shifting of tense, voice, and mood, and to revise sentences whose structure makes them ambiguous, confusing, or nonsensical.

You'll also examine how the English Test covers the proper use of idioms and other words and phrases.

Note

We'll apply the principles you learned to ACT-style questions that would be considered at least average in difficulty. (Many will be more challenging than average.)

Punctuation

Questions about punctuation account for about 13 percent of the total number of questions on the ACT English Test. Simpler punctuation questions usually test on the use of commas and apostrophes. Here, you'll examine the guidelines for using two additional, and especially tricky, punctuation marks:

- The colon
- The semicolon

You'll also find out how a sentence in an ACT passage might test you on these marks.

The Colon and the Semicolon

Many ACT test-takers are uncertain as to how the proper uses of the colon (:) and the semicolon (;) differ. To ensure that you're not among those many, keep in mind the following guidelines and examples.

Use the colon to introduce either a list or a restatement.

Here's an example of a colon used to introduce a list:

> For my term paper, I decided to write about the Beatles' last three albums: *The White Album*, *Abbey Road*, and *Let It Be*.

Notice that the colon alerts the reader that a list specifying whatever has just been referred to is immediately ahead.

Alert!

Usually, if an introductory word precedes the list and leads directly into it, you should omit the colon. Thus, if the sentence reads like the following, you do not need a colon: For my term paper, I decided to write about several of the Beatles' albums, including *The White Album*, *Abbey Road*, and *Let It Be*.

Here's an example of using a colon to introduce a restatement:

> Barbara was named valedictorian for one reason: her exceptional academic achievement.

What follows the colon "restates" what precedes it; the words "her exceptional academic achievement" name the "one reason" mentioned before the colon.

Here's a handy rule of thumb for testing whether a colon is appropriate in a given sentence. If either the phrase *that is* or the word *namely* could be inserted at the same spot as the colon, instead of it, then a colon is probably correct.

Use a semicolon to connect two independent clauses.

You can use a comma followed by a connecting word such as *and*, *but*, or *although* to connect one independent clause (which can stand alone as a complete sentence) to another independent clause. Of course, your choice of word should help convey the idea of the sentence. You can also use a semicolon (;) to connect two independent clauses, as long as the ideas are closely related, as in this sentence:

> In third-world countries, the need for trained workers is partially met by the Peace Corps; without this organization, public health problems in many developing countries would be far worse than they are.

Now, look at an ACT-style example that tests you on both the colon and semicolon:

Adams was initially drawn into the slavery question not by the controversy over slavery <u>itself; but</u> by the so-called "gag rule" used by the South to stifle debates in the Senate concerning slavery.

- **A.** NO CHANGE
- **B.** itself. Instead,
- **C.** itself, but
- **D.** itself: but

The correct answer is C. The semicolon in the middle of this sentence is wrong because it doesn't connect two independent clauses. The first part of the sentence (from *Adams* through *itself*) is an independent clause—it could stand alone as a sentence. However, the rest of the sentence couldn't stand alone as a sentence; it lacks a subject and verb (and therefore isn't even a proper clause). So the semicolon should be replaced by a comma. The result of choice **B** is a sentence fragment following the period. As for choice **D**, a colon is improper because what follows is neither a list nor a restatement.

Note

In the preceding example, what if you were to omit a punctuation mark altogether between *itself* and *but* in the original sentence? For the purpose of conveying the sentence's ideas, this option would not be quite so effective as inserting a comma. But it would come very close—too close for the ACT. That's why it's not listed as an answer choice.

Use a semicolon to separate lengthy items in a list or series.

In the following sentence, for example, semicolons are used instead of commas so that you can easily tell where one item leaves off and the next one starts.

> Houses made of natural materials such as straw, adobe, or cob are more energy efficient than conventional houses; they are often less expensive to construct, in terms of materials as well as labor; and, if constructed properly, they are more durable and less susceptible to natural threats such as earthquakes and strong winds.

Grammatical Errors Involving Parts of Speech

The first section of this chapter covered grammatical errors involving parts of speech that are most basic and that the ACT covers most frequently. Here at *Take It to the Next Level*, you'll focus on the trickiest, yet test-worthy, rules of grammar involving pronoun choice and subject-verb agreement:

- Error in choice of *relative* pronoun
- Error in agreement between a *pronoun* or *compound* subject and verb

Error in Choice of Relative Pronoun

The English language includes only the following handful of *relative* pronouns: *which*, *who*, *that*, *whose*, *whichever*, *whoever*, and *whomever*. Don't worry about what the term "relative pronoun" means. Instead, just remember the following rules about when to use each one.

1. Use *which* to refer to things.
2. Use either *who* or *that* to refer to people.

incorrect: Amanda, *which* was the third performer, was the best of the group.

correct: Amanda, *who* was the third performer, was the best of the group.

correct: The first employee *that* fails to meet his or her sales quota will be fired.

correct: The first employee *who* fails to meet his or her sales quota will be fired.

3. Whether you should use *which* or *that* depends on what the sentence is supposed to mean. *Which* should be used with restrictive clauses and is *always* preceeded by a comma.

 one meaning: The third page, *which* had been earmarked, contained several typographical errors.

 different meaning: The third page *that* had been earmarked contained several typographical errors.

 (The first sentence merely describes the third page as earmarked. The second sentence also suggests that the page containing the errors was the third earmarked page.)

4. Whether you should use *who* (*whoever*) or *whom* (*whomever*) depends on the grammatical function of the person (or people) being referred to. Confused? Don't worry; just take a look at the sample sentences here, and you shouldn't have any trouble deciding between *who* and *whom* on the ACT.

 incorrect: It was the chairman *whom* initiated the bill.

 correct: It was the chairman *who* initiated the bill.

 incorrect: First aid will be available to *whomever* requires it.

 correct: First aid will be available to *whoever* requires it.

 incorrect: The team members from East High, *who* the judges were highly impressed with, won the debate.

 correct: The team members from East High, with *whom* the judges were highly impressed, won the debate.

On the ACT, to make sure that *who (whoever)* and *whom (whomever)* are being used correctly, try substituting a regular pronoun, then rearrange the clause (if necessary) to form a simple sentence. If a subject-case pronoun works, then *who* (*whoever*) is the right choice. On the other hand, if an object-case pronoun works, then *whom* (*whomever*) is the right choice. Here's how it works with the above sentences:

- It was the chairman *whom* initiated the bill.

 He initiated the bill.

 (*He* is a subject-case pronoun, so *whom* should be replaced with *who*.)

- First aid will be available to *whomever* requires it.

 She requires it.

 (*She* is a subject-case pronoun, so *whomever* should be replaced with *whoever*.)

- The team members from East High, *who* the judges were highly impressed with, won the debate.

  The judges were impressed with *them*.

  (*Them* is an object-case pronoun, so *who* should be replaced by *whom*.)

Now, look at an ACT-style item that focuses on the use of a relative pronoun.

An art critic's primary task is elucidation, which is not easily separable from a second task: evaluation.

A. NO CHANGE
B. a task which is
C. that is
D. OMIT the underlined portion.

The correct answer is A. The relative pronoun *which* clearly describes elucidation, as opposed to describing a certain type or form of elucidation. Hence, choice **A** is correct, and choice **C** is incorrect. Choice **B** commits the reverse error: It uses *which* where *that* is called for—to describe a specific type of task. Choice **D** leaves it a bit unclear as to what is "not easily separable." Hence, although choice **D** makes for the most concise version, the original version is preferable.

First use you ear to ferret out correct answers and rule out others. But if more than one option *sounds* okay, compare those choices *first* for clarity and grammar correctness, *then* for conciseness.

Error in Subject-Verb Agreement (Pronoun and Compound Subjects)

Determining whether a sentence's subject is singular or plural isn't always as simple as you might think. You can easily determine whether a personal pronoun such as *he*, *they*, and *its* is singular or plural. But other pronouns are not so easily identified as either singular or plural. Here are two lists, along with some sample sentences, to help you keep these pronouns straight in your mind:

Singular Pronouns

anyone, anything, anybody

each

either, neither

every, everyone, everything, everybody

nobody, no one, nothing

what, whatever

who, whom, whoever, whomever

correct: *Every* possible cause *has* been investigated.

correct: *Each* one of the children here *speaks* fluent French.

correct: *Neither* of the pens *has* any ink remaining in *it*.

correct: *Whatever* he's doing *is* very effective.

correct: *Everything* she touches *turns* to gold.

Even when they refer to a "compound" subject joined by *and*, the pronouns listed above remain *singular*.

correct: *Each adult and child* here *speaks* fluent French.

correct: *Every* possible *cause and suspect was* investigated.

Plural Pronouns

both

few

many

several

some

others

correct: *Few* would *argue* with that line of reasoning.

correct: *Many claim* to have encountered alien beings.

correct: *Some thrive* on commotion, while *others need* quiet.

It's especially easy to overlook a subject-verb agreement problem in a sentence involving a compound subject (multiple subjects joined by connectors such as the word *and* or the word *or*). If joined by *and*, a compound subject is usually plural (and takes a plural verb). But if joined by *or*, *either . . . or*, or *neither . . . nor*, compound subjects are usually singular.

plural: The chorus *and* the introduction *need* improvement.

singular: *Either* the chorus *or* the introduction *needs* improvement.

singular: *Neither* the chorus *nor* the introduction *needs* improvement.

But, what if one subject is singular and another one is plural? Which form should the verb take? Here's the rule: Look to see which subject is *nearer* to the verb; the verb should agree with that subject.

plural: Either the rhythm or the *lyrics need* improvement.

singular: Either the lyrics or the *rhythm needs* improvement.

In some cases, you can't tell whether a subject is singular or plural without looking at how it's used in the sentence. This is true of so-called *collective* nouns and nouns of *quantity*. These "special animals" might call for either a singular verb or a plural verb, depending on whether the noun is used in a singular or plural sense.

correct: Four years *is* too long to wait. (*four years* used in singular sense)

correct: Four years can *pass* by quickly. (*four years* used in plural sense)

correct: The majority *favors* the Republican candidate. (*majority* used in singular sense)

correct: The majority of the voters here *favor* the Republican candidate. (*majority* used in plural sense)

Here's an ACT-style item involving a "compound" subject. What makes this one tricky is that even a good ear for English might mislead to an incorrect answer choice.

Neither the result of the first experiment nor that of the second were what the researchers had expected.

A. NO CHANGE
B. was what
C. was that which
D. resulted in what

The correct answer is B. In the original version, the plural verb *were* does not agree in number with its singular subject *neither result*. Choice **B** remedies this problem. So does choice **C**; but the phrase that **C** supplies is not idiomatic. Choice **D** creates a redundancy ("the result . . . resulted in").

Use your ear for English as your first weapon against the ACT English Test—but, just to be safe, use your knowledge of English grammar as a backup.

Problems Involving Tense, Voice, and Mood

You've arrived at what some grammarians would consider the inner sanctum of Standard Written English: tense, voice, and mood. These three concepts are among the trickiest that ACT Sentence Correction covers. In this section, you'll focus on the following types of problems involving these three concepts (notice the similarities):

- Error in verb tense, and shifting or mixing of tenses in a confusing manner
- Awkward use of either the active or passive voice, and needless mixing of the two voices
- Improper use of the subjunctive mood, and needless mixing of the subjunctive mood and one of the tenses

Error in Verb Tense and Improper Tense Shifting and Mixing

Tense refers to how a verb's form indicates the *time frame* (past, present, or future) of the sentence's action. You won't need to know the names of the tenses for the ACT, of course. But, here they are anyway (all six of them), in case you're interested. Notice that we've used the singular form of the confusing verb *to have* in order to illustrate how verb form differs among different tenses. All of these sentences are correct.

simple present: He *has* enough money to buy a new car.

simple past: He *had* enough money after he was paid to buy a new car.

simple future: He *will have* enough money after he is paid to buy a new car.

present perfect: He *has had* enough food but *has* continued to eat anyway.

past perfect: He *had had* enough food but *had* kept eating anyway.

future perfect: He *will have had* enough food once he *has* finished eating the dessert.

With many verbs, the same form is used for all tenses, except that *-ed* is added for the past tenses—as in *walk*, *walked*. However, other verbs use distinctive forms for different tenses—as in *see*, *saw*, *seen*. Use your ear to determine whether the form sounds correct.

incorrect: The pilot seen the mountain but was flying too low to avoid a collision.

correct: The pilot *saw* the mountain but was flying too low to avoid a collision.

An incorrect sentence might needlessly *mix* tenses or *shift* tense from one time frame to another in a confusing manner.

incorrect: If it rains tomorrow, we cancel our plans.

correct: If it rains tomorrow, we *will cancel* our plans.

incorrect: When Bill arrived, Sal still did not begin to unload the truck.

correct: When Bill arrived, Sal still *had not begun* to unload the truck.

Our warning about mixing and shifting tenses also applies to sentences like these:

incorrect: *To go* to war is *to have traveled* to hell.

correct: *To go* to war is *to go* to hell.

correct: *To have gone* to war is *to have traveled* to hell.

incorrect: *Seeing* the obstacle *would have allowed* him to alter his course.

correct: *Having seen* the obstacle *would have allowed* him to alter his course.

correct: *Seeing* the obstacle *would allow* him to alter his course.

Note

By the way, verbs preceded by *to* (for example, *to go*) are called *infinitives*, and verbs turned into nouns by tacking an *-ing* to the end (for example, *seeing*) are called *gerunds*. Of course, you don't need to know that for the ACT.

Now, look at how a tense-shift problem might appear in an ACT-style sentence.

> Companies that have failed to make cost-of-living adjustments in their workers' salaries cannot attract or retain competent employees.
>
> A. NO CHANGE
> B. were not able to
> C. will be unable to
> D. could not

The correct answer is C. The original sentence mixes the past perfect tense (*have failed*) with the present tense (*cannot*). Compare this sentence with one that uses *fails* instead of *have failed*. The revised version makes much better sense, doesn't it? Of course, you're stuck with *have failed* for this question. And, matching tenses by changing *cannot* to either *have been unable to* or *have not* is not among the listed options. But choice C, which provides a shift to future tense, also makes sense: The first clause describes an event occurring in the past up to the present, while the second clause anticipates future events. This forward movement in time frame is understandable and logical in context. Choices B and D each provide a past-tense verb form, which illogically reverses the time frame—back to the past from the present perfect.

Inappropriate Voice and Improper Shifts in Voice

In a sentence expressed in the *active voice*, the subject "acts upon" an object. Conversely, in a sentence expressed in the passive voice, the subject "is acted upon" by an object. The passive voice can sound a bit awkward, so the active voice is generally preferred.

passive (awkward): The book was read by the student.

active (better): The student read the book.

passive (awkward): Repetitive tasks are performed tirelessly by computers.

active (better): Computers perform repetitive tasks tirelessly.

Mixing the active and passive voices results in an even more awkward sentence.

mixed (awkward): Although the house was built by Gary, Kevin built the garage.

passive (less awkward): Although the house was built by Gary, the garage was built by Kevin.

active (best): Although Gary built the house, Kevin built the garage.

Although the active voice is usually less awkward than the passive voice, sometimes the passive voice is appropriate for emphasis or impact.

active (less effective): Yesterday, a car hit me.

passive (more effective): Yesterday, I was hit by a car.

passive (more effective): Sunrise over the Tetons *is surpassed* in beauty only *by* the sun itself.

active (less effective): Only the sun itself *surpasses* the Tetons in beauty.

Take It to the Next Level

Typically, to avoid an awkward shift in voice, what's needed is to restructure an entire sentence. So, on the ACT, if you see an entire sentence underlined, be sure to check for a needless voice shift (either in the original version or among the alternatives), as in the following example:

The recent increase in the number of fish caught by commercial vessels can be explained largely by improved sonar technology. Less stringent quotas have also contributed to the trend.

A. NO CHANGE
B. Largely explaining the recent increase in the number of fish caught by commercial vessels is improved sonar technology.
C. Improved sonar technology largely explains the recent increase in the number of fish caught by commercial vessels.
D. Largely, improved sonar technology explains the recent increase in the number of fish that commercial vessels catch.

The correct answer is A. The original version is cast entirely in the passive voice *(caught by* and *explained largely by)*. Although in the next sentence there is a shift to the active voice, the shift is not awkward, and it does not obscure the idea that the writer seeks to convey. The sentence that choice **B** provides mixes voices and is a bit confusing. The sentence in choice **C** is a bit clearer than the one in **B**, but it also mixes voices. As for choice **D**, the position of *largely* is awkward and confusing. What's more, because of the sentence's structure, the reader expects the writer to list something else that improved sonar technology—rather than something else that explains the increase in the number of fish caught.

Alert!

Keep in mind that both the active and passive voices are grammatically proper. So, don't eliminate an answer choice merely because it uses the passive voice. Check the answer choices for consistency in voice.

Error in Using the Subjunctive Mood

The *subjunctive mood* should be used to express a *wish* or a *contrary-to-fact* condition. These sentences should include words such as *if*, *had*, *were*, and *should*.

incorrect: I wish it was earlier.

correct: I wish it *were* earlier.

incorrect: Suppose he speeds up suddenly.

correct: Suppose he *were* to speed up suddenly.

incorrect: If the college lowers its tuition, I would probably enroll.

correct: *Should* the college lower its tuition, I *would* probably enroll.

correct: *If* the college *were* to lower its tuition, I *would* probably enroll.

incorrect: Had he driven slower, he will recognize the landmarks from now on.

correct: *Had* he driven slower, he *would* recognize the landmarks from now on.

correct: *If* he *had* driven slower, he *would* recognize the landmarks from now on.

Tip

The subjunctive mood can be tricky because it uses its own idiomatic verb forms and because you can't always trust your ear when it comes to catching an error. Just remember: If the sentence uses a regular verb tense (past, present, future, etc.) to express a wish or contrary-to-fact condition, then it is grammatically incorrect, even if the subjunctive verb form is also used. Look, for example, at the *incorrect* sample sentences above.

- I wish it was earlier. (*It was earlier* uses past tense.)
- Suppose he speeds up suddenly. (*He speeds up suddenly* uses present tense.)
- If the college lowers its tuition, I would probably enroll. (The first clause uses present tense, while the second clause uses subjunctive form.)
- Had he driven slower, he will recognize the landmarks from now on. (The first clause uses subjunctive form, while the second clause uses future tense.)

The subjunctive mood is also used in clauses of recommendation, request, suggestion, or demand. These clauses should include the word *that*:

incorrect: Ann suggested we should go to the Chinese restaurant.

correct: Ann *suggested that* we go to the Chinese restaurant.

incorrect: I insist you be quiet.

correct: I *insist that* you be quiet.

incorrect: The supervisor preferred all workers wear uniforms from now on.

correct: The supervisor *preferred that* all workers wear uniforms from now on.

Now look at an ACT-style sentence designed to test you on the use of the subjunctive mood.

The Environmental Protection Agency would be overburdened by its detection and enforcement duties <u>in the case it fully implemented</u> all of its own regulations.

A. NO CHANGE
B. in case it was to implement
C. were it to fully implement
D. if it implements fully

The correct answer is C. The sentence clearly intends to express a hypothetical or contrary-to-fact situation; yet the underlined phrase does not use the subjunctive *were*. Choice **C** corrects the problem. Choice **B** incorrectly uses *was* instead of the subjunctive *were*. Choice **D** incorrectly uses the present tense.

Sentence Structure and Sense

Sentence structure refers to how the parts of a sentence fit together as a whole. You know a sentence is poorly structured when its ideas are confusing, vague, ambiguous, or nonsensical—or even when its structure seems to place undue emphasis (or de-emphasis) on certain ideas.

Problems involving sentence structure can be challenging to fix because there are no hard-and-fast rules of grammar to tell you what the best solution is. And since there are many acceptable ways to make any statement, the distinction between a highly effective structure and a less effective one can be subtle.

Here are the specific types of structural problems you'll examine in this section:

- Improper placement of modifiers
- Confusing pronoun references
- Dangling modifier errors
- Improper splitting of a grammatical unit
- Too many subordinate clauses in a row
- Omitting a necessary word

Improper Placement of Modifiers

A *modifier* is a word or phrase that describes, restricts, or qualifies another word or phrase. Modifying phrases are typically set off with commas, and many such phrases begin with a relative pronoun (*which*, *who*, *that*, *whose*, *whom*). Modifiers should generally be placed as close as possible to the word(s) they modify. Positioning a modifier in the wrong place can result in a confusing or even nonsensical sentence.

misplaced: His death shocked the entire family, which occurred quite suddenly.

better: His death, which occurred quite suddenly, shocked the entire family.

misplaced: Nearly dead, the police finally found the victim.

better: The police finally found the victim, who was nearly dead.

unclear: Bill punched Carl while wearing a mouth protector.

clear: While wearing a mouth protector, Bill punched Carl.

Modifiers such as *almost*, *nearly*, *hardly*, *just*, and *only* should immediately precede the word(s) they modify, even if the sentence sounds correct with the parts separated. For example:

misplaced: Their one-year-old child *almost* weighs *forty pounds*.

better: Their one-year-old child weighs *almost forty pounds*.

Note the position of *only* in the following sentences:

clear: *Only the assistant* was able to detect obvious errors.

unclear: The assistant was *only* able to detect obvious errors.

unclear: The assistant was able to *only* detect *obvious errors.*

clear: The assistant was able to detect *only obvious errors.*

Now look at an ACT-style item involving a misplaced modifier.

Exercising contributes frequently to a sense of well being as well as to longevity.

A. NO CHANGE
B. Exercising frequently contributes
C. Frequently exercising contributes
D. Frequent exercise contributes

The correct answer is D. In the original sentence, *frequently* is probably intended to describe (modify) *exercising* (frequent exercise). But separating these words makes it appear that *frequently* describes *contributing*, which doesn't make sense in the overall context of the sentence. Choice **D** corrects the problems. With **D**, it is clear that what is frequent is *exercise* (rather than *contributing*). Choice **C** also clears up the confusion as to whether *frequently* describes *exercising* or *contributes*. But in **C**, an adverb is used incorrectly to describe a gerund (*exercising*). Adverbs must be used to describe only verbs, adjectives, and other adverbs.

Alert!

The general rule about placing modifiers near the words they modify applies *most* of the time. In some cases, however, trying to place a modifier near the words it modifies actually confuses the meaning of the sentence, as with the modifier *without his glasses* in the sentences below.

unclear: Nathan can read the newspaper and *shave without his glasses*. (It is unclear whether *without his glasses* refers only to *shave* or to both *shave* and *read the newspaper*)

unclear: *Without his glasses, Nathan* can read the newspaper and can shave. (This sentence implies that these are the only two tasks Nathan can perform without his glasses.)

clear: *Even without his glasses*, Nathan can read the newspaper and shave.

So, don't apply the rule mechanically. Instead, check to see whether the sentence as a whole makes sense.

Confusing Pronoun References

A pronoun (e.g., *she*, *him*, *their*, *its*) is a "shorthand" way of referring to an identifiable noun—person(s), place(s), or thing(s). Nouns to which pronouns refer are called *antecedents*. Make sure every pronoun in a sentence has a clear antecedent!

unclear: Minutes before Kevin's meeting with Paul, *his* wife called with the bad news. (Whose wife called—Kevin's or Paul's?)

clear: *Kevin's* wife called with the bad news minutes before *his* meeting with Paul.

clear: Minutes before Kevin's meeting with Paul, *Kevin's* wife called with the bad news.

Pronoun reference errors are usually corrected in one of two ways:

1. By placing the noun and pronoun as near as possible to each other, without other nouns coming between them (as in the second sentence of the preceeding sentences)
2. By replacing the pronoun with its antecedent (as in the third of the preceeding sentences)

Also look for the vague use of *it*, *you*, *that*, or *one*—without clear reference to a particular antecedent.

vague: When one dives in without looking ahead, *you* never know what will happen. (Does *you* refer to the diver or to the broader *one*?)

clear: *One* never knows what will happen when *one* dives in without looking ahead.

clear: When *you* dive in without looking ahead, *you* never know what will happen.

vague: When the planets are out of alignment, *it* can be disastrous. (*It* does not refer to any noun.)

clear: Disaster can occur when the planets are out of alignment.

Here's an ACT-style item involving a pronoun-reference issue.

E-mail accounts administered by employers belong to the employers, <u>and they</u> can be seized and used as evidence against employees.

A. NO CHANGE
B. so they
C. and so e-mails
D. but

The correct answer is C. In the original version, the antecedent of *they* is separated from its intended antecedent *accounts* by two occurrences of *employers*. Choice **C** makes the reference as unambiguous as possible by replacing the pronoun *they* with its antecedent. Also, adding the word *so* enhances the sentence's rhetorical effectiveness—by making it clearer that e-mails can be used as evidence *because* they belong to the employer. Choice **B** fails to correct the ambiguous pronoun reference. Choice **D** is wrong for two reasons. First, the connecting word *but* misleads the reader to think that an opposing idea is ahead. Second, by omitting the pronoun *they*, **D** creates a dependent clause that need not be preceded by a comma.

When you see a pronoun in an ACT sentence, ask yourself: "To what noun does this pronoun refer?" If the answer is the least bit unclear, you can rule out that version of the sentence as the best choice.

Dangling Modifier Errors

A *dangling modifier* is a modifier that doesn't refer to any particular word(s) in the sentence. The best way to correct a dangling-modifier problem is to reconstruct the sentence.

dangling: *Set by an arsonist*, firefighters were unable to save the burning building. (This sentence makes no reference to whatever was set by an arsonist.)

better: Firefighters were unable to save the burning building from *the fire set by an arsonist*.

Despite the rule against dangling modifiers, certain dangling modifiers are acceptable because they're idiomatic.

acceptable: *Judging* from the number of violent crimes committed every year, our nation is doomed. (The sentence makes no reference to whomever is judging; but it is acceptable anyway.)

acceptable: *Considering* that star's great distance from Earth, its brightness is amazing. (This sentence makes no reference to whomever is considering; but it is acceptable anyway.)

If you encounter a dangling modifier in an ACT sentence that you've heard many, many times from well-educated people, then it's probably one of those idiomatic exceptions to the prohibition against dangling modifiers.

Now, look at an ACT-style sentence that contains a dangling modifier.

By imposing price restrictions on oil suppliers, these suppliers will be forced to lower production costs.

A. NO CHANGE
B. Imposing price restrictions
C. If price restrictions are imposed
D. In the event of price restrictions

The correct answer is C. The original sentence includes a dangling modifier. The sentence makes no reference to whomever (or whatever) is imposing the price restrictions. Choice **C** corrects the problem by reconstructing the underlined portion using the passive voice. (Also notice the consistency in voice now between the two clauses *are imposed* and *will be forced*.) Choice **B** lacks the preposition needed for the original version to make grammatical sense as a complete sentence. (An additional revision would be needed as well: *Imposing price restrictions on oil suppliers would force these suppliers . . . .*) Choice **D** corrects the dangling modifier problem, but it lacks a verb and is unnecessarily wordy—especially compared with choice **B**.

Improper Splitting of a Grammatical Unit

Splitting apart clauses or phrases (by inserting another clause between them) often results in an awkward and confusing sentence.

split: The value of the dollar *is not*, relative to other currencies, *rising* universally.

better: The value of the dollar *is not rising* universally relative to other currencies.

split: The government's goal this year *is to provide* for its poorest residents *an economic safety net.*

split: *The government's goal* is to provide an economic safety net *this year* for its poorest residents.

better: The government's goal this year is to provide an economic safety net for its poorest residents.

In ACT sentences, look especially closely for *split infinitives*. An infinitive is the plural form of an "action" verb, preceded by the word "to." If *to* is separated from its corresponding verb, then you're dealing with a "split infinitive" and a sentence that is grammatically incorrect!

improper (split): The executive was compelled *to*, by greed and ambition, *work* more and more hours each day.

correct: The executive was compelled by greed and ambition *to work* more and more hours each day.

improper (split): Meteorologists have been known *to* inaccurately *predict* snowstorms.

correct: Meteorologists have been known *to predict* snowstorms inaccurately.

Now, look at an ACT-style sentence with a split personality.

Typographer Lucian Bernhard was influenced, <u>perhaps to a greater extent than any of his contemporaries</u>, by Toulouse-Lautrec's emphasis on large, unharmonious lettering.

Which of the following is the best editorial proposal for the preceding sentence, disregarding punctuation and capitalization?

A. NO CHANGE
B. Move the underlined portion to the beginning of the sentence.
C. Move the underlined portion to the end of the sentence.
D. OMIT the underlined portion.

The correct answer is B. The original sentence awkwardly splits the main clause with an intervening subordinate one (set off by commas). Choice **B** keeps the main clause intact. Choice C creates a pronoun reference problem: It unclear as to whom the pronoun *his* refers—Bernhard or Toulouse-Lautrec.

Whenever you see a clause set off by commas in the middle of the sentence, check the words immediately before and after the clause. If keeping those words together would sound better to your ear or would more effectively convey the sentence's main point, then the sentence (answer choice) is wrong, and you can safely eliminate it!

Too Many Subordinate Clauses in a Row

A *subordinate clause* is one that does not stand on its own as a complete sentence. Stringing together two or more subordinate clauses can result in an awkward and confusing sentence.

awkward: Barbara's academic major is history, *which* is a very popular course of study among liberal arts students, *who* are also contributing to the popularity of political science as a major.

better: Barbara's academic major is history, which along with political science is a very popular course of study among liberal arts students.

Now, look at an ACT-style sentence that suffers from this sort of error.

By relying unduly on anecdotal evidence, which often conflicts with more reliable data, including data from direct observation and measurement, scientists risk losing credibility among their peers.

Which of the following is the best suggestion for the underlined portion, disregarding changes in punctuation and capitalization?

A. NO CHANGE
B. Move the underlined portion to the beginning of the sentence.
C. Reposition the underlined portion between *evidence* and *which* (immediately following the first comma).
D. Reposition the underlined portion between *data* and *including* (immediately following the second comma).

The correct answer is B. The original sentence strings together three dependent clauses—all of which precede the main clause, which is underlined. Since only the first clause modifies the main clause, it makes sense to move the main clause to the beginning of the sentence. Although choices C and D break the long string of dependent clauses, each choice results in a more serious problem. Choice C makes it appear that the antecedent of *which* is *peers*. (But the intended antecedent of *which* is *anecdotal evidence*.) Similarly, proposal D makes it appear that *data* is a type of *peer*, which makes no sense.

Note

Subordination of a dependent clause to a main clause can be achieved through the use of:

- Words modifying relative pronouns: *which*, *who*, *that*.
- Words establishing time relationship: *before*, *after*, *as*, *since*.
- Words establishing a causal relationship: *because*, *since*.
- Words of admission or concession: *although*, *though*, *despite*.
- Words indicating place: *where*, *wherever*.
- Words of condition: *if*, *unless*.

Omitting a Necessary Word

Excluding a necessary word can obscure or confuse the meaning of the sentence. In the underlined portions, check especially for the omission of key "little" words—prepositions, pronouns, conjunctives, and especially the word *that*.

omission: The newscaster announced the voting results were incorrect. (What did the newscaster announce: the results or the fact that the results were incorrect?)

clearer: The newscaster announced *that* the voting results were incorrect.

Look out especially for an omission that results in an illogical comparison, as in the following sentences. It can easily slip past you if you're not paying close attention.

illogical: The color of the blouse is different from the skirt.

logical: The color of the blouse is different from *that* of the skirt.

illogical: China's population is greater than any country in the world.

(This sentence draws an illogical comparison between a population and a country and illogically suggests that China is not a country.)

logical: China's population is greater than *that of* any *other* country in the world.

In many cases, the word *that* is optional. For example, here's a sentence that makes sense either with or without it: *Some evolutionary theorists believe [that] humans began to walk in an upright posture mainly because they needed to reach tree branches to obtain food.*

Omission problems are not limited to prepositions, connecting words, and pronouns like the word *that*. If an ACT sentence simply doesn't make sense, check the alternatives to the underlined portion for any word that's missing from the original version and that turns utter nonsense into perfect sense.

Harnessing the power of nature has resulted in our control over it rather than to it.

A. NO CHANGE
B. us controlling instead of submitting
C. control over it by us, not
D. our controlling it rather than submitting

The correct answer is D. The structure of the underlined portion implies a contrast between *our control over it* and *our control to it*. The latter phrase makes no sense; clearly, something is missing at the end of the underlined portion. Choices **B** and **D** both inject the word *submitting*, which makes sense in context. However, choice **B** uses the wrong pronoun form; the possessive form (*our*) should be used instead of *us* preceding a gerund (*controlling*). Also, by omitting the word *it* (as in *controlling it*), choice **B** supplies the nonsensical *controlling . . . to it.*

As you've just seen, one little word can make all the difference! Your mind can easily trick you by filling in a key word that is not actually there. The moral here is: Read every ACT sentence that contains underlining slowly and carefully!

Chapter 5

Rhetorical Skills, Idioms, and Usage

In this chapter, you'll:

- Learn how to handle the most common forms of strategy and organization questions—which contribute to the test's Rhetorical Skills subscore area
- Review idiom and word usage issues that are frequently covered on the ACT

Rhetorical Skills

The first of this chapter's two main parts deals exclusively with the English Test's "Rhetorical Skills" subscore area, which encompasses three broad issues: style, strategy, and organization. In the following pages, you'll learn how ACT questions cover the goals of essay-writing listed below, and you'll learn how to handle these questions.

Style

- Achieving appropriate rhetorical emphasis within sentences

Strategy

- Creating logical transitions from one idea to another within each paragraph
- Creating effective transitions between paragraphs
- Inserting relevant and appropriate supporting material

Organization

- Establishing the most logical sequence of sentences within each paragraph
- Establishing the most logical sequence of paragraphs
- Ensuring that the essay's beginning and ending tie together and clearly convey the essay's overall theme

Rhetorical Imbalance between Sentence Parts

An effective sentence gets its point across by placing appropriate emphasis on its different parts. If you're dealing with two equally important ideas, they should be separated as two distinct "main clauses," and they should be similar in length (to suggest equal importance).

unbalanced: Julie and Sandy were the first two volunteers for the fund-raising drive, *and* they are twins.

balanced: Julie and Sandy, *who* are twins, were the first two volunteers for the fund-raising drive.

commingled (confusing): Julie and Sandy, *who* are twins, are volunteers.

separated (balanced): Julie and Sandy are twins, *and* they are volunteers.

On the other hand, if you're dealing with only one main idea, be sure that it receives greater emphasis (as a main clause) than the other ideas in the sentence.

equal emphasis (confusing): Jose and Victor were identical twins, *and* they had completely different ambitions.

emphasis on second clause (better): *Although* Jose and Victor were identical twins, they had completely different ambitions.

Here's an ACT-style example of a rhetorically-challenged sentence.

> Treating bodily disorders by noninvasive methods is generally painless, and these methods are less likely than those of conventional Western medicine to result in permanent healing.
>
> A. NO CHANGE
> B. although these methods
> C. even though these methods
> D. methods which

The correct answer is B. Notice that the original sentence contains two main clauses, connected by *and*. Two problems should have occurred to you as you read the sentence: (1) the connector *and* is inappropriate to contrast differing methods of treatment (it fails to get the point across), and (2) the second clause expresses the more important point but does not receive greater emphasis than the first clause. Choice **B** corrects both problems by transforming the second clause into a subordinate one—by replacing *and* with *although*. Choice **C** corrects the first problem, but it places the rhetorical emphasis on the wrong clause (the first one). Choice **D** results in a confusing, even nonsensical, sentence.

Paragraph Structure (Sentence Sequence)

One type of organization item you'll encounter at least once or twice on the ACT English Test is the paragraph structure question, in which you're asked to select the best sequence of sentences within a certain paragraph. When you see a paragraph whose sentences are numbered, you know the paragraph is the subject of such a question.

Certain words used in the paragraph might provide clues for determining the best sentence sequence. For example, words such as *however*, *but*, *yet*, and *nevertheless* signal a contrast, contrariness, or opposition to the idea in what should be the preceding sentence. And, words such as *clearly*, *therefore*, *thus*, and *hence* signal a conclusion, which should follow the sentences that contain the evidence upon which the conclusion is based.

The overall theme of the paragraph can provide an additional clue. The sentences might discuss past events that occurred in a chronological order. If so, it probably makes sense to sequence them that way. Here's an example of what a paragraph structure question might look like in the context of an ACT-style paragraph involving chronological events.

> *(1)* The immigration laws ultimately led to a quote system based on the number of individuals of each national origin reported in the 1989 census. *(2)* The United States, which was founded mainly by people who had emigrated from northern Europe, had an essentially open-door immigration policy for the first 100 years of its existence. *(3)* But starting in the 1880s and continuing through the 1920s, Congress passed a series of restrictive immigration laws. *(4)* The door to freedom hadn't exactly been slammed shut, but it was now open only to the "right" sort of people.

Which of the following sequences will make the paragraph most logical?

A. 4, 3, 1, 2
B. 2, 3, 1, 4
C. 1, 3, 2, 4
D. 2, 3, 4, 1

The correct answer is B. Sentence 2 describes American immigration policy during the early years of the country's history, while the other sentences describe how that policy later changed. So, it makes sense to put sentence 2 first. Now, glance at the four answer choices. Only answers **B** and **D** are possible. Read the paragraph in both sequences and you'll probably be able to tell that choice **B** provides the better sequence.

For a paragraph that makes a claim and backs it up with reasons and/or supporting evidence, it generally makes sense to state the claim either *before* or *after* all the supporting sentences. Here's a good ACT-style example (this one is tougher than the previous one):

> *(1)* Yet perhaps one of the reasons that alternative medicine is booming today is precisely because in an era in which medical procedures and antibiotics are prescribed at the drop of a hat, people have become less trusting of medical science. *(2)* When anecdotal evidence of its successes is trotted out, doctors routinely put it down to the placebo effect. *(3)* The medical profession has traditionally scoffed at the claims of alternative medicine.
> *(4)* Clearly, drugs and technology, as valuable as they are, do not hold all the keys to good health.

Which of the following sequences will make the paragraph most logical?

A. NO CHANGE
B. 2, 4, 1, 3
C. 4, 1, 3, 2
D. 3, 2, 1, 4

The correct answer is D. Notice that sentence 4 makes the claim about which the other sentences provide supporting detail. So, it makes sense that sentence 4 should come either first or last, and you can at least rule out choice **B**. Next, notice that sentence 2 elucidates (provides illustrative detail about) the more general point in sentence 3. Accordingly, one should come immediately after the other, but their order should be reversed. Now you can narrow down the possibilities to choices **C** and **D**. The word *Yet* in sentence 1 indicates the sentence's contrasting nature. By placing it after sentences 3 and 2, it counters the position of the medical establishment and serves as a bridge to sentence 4—the conclusion that medical science does not hold all the keys to good health.

If you're stymied as to the best sequence of sentences for a paragraph structure question, look for a sentence that provides the broadest assertion, which will probably be the paragraph's overall topic. Try placing that sentence first, then see if the others fall into place. If not, try placing it last.

Transitions between Sentences

One type of strategy question focuses on the transition between one sentence and the next one within the same paragraph. If a complete sentence is called for, the item will be indicated by a boxed number (inserted at the transition point). If all that's needed is a single word or brief phrase, then the first word or two of the second sentence will be underlined.

Your job is to pick the word or phrase that most logically links what comes before the insertion point with what comes after—the one that provides the most natural and sensible flow of ideas from one sentence to the next. To see how to accomplish this task, take a look at two ACT-style examples, and read the analysis that follows each one. To handle this first example, you need to consider only two sentences.

The polar ice cap's high-pressure system controls the cold, relatively stable climate of Mount Vinson, the highest peak in Antarctica. Since Vinson is located in an arctic climate, snowstorms and terrific wind gusts are always possible.

A. NO CHANGE
B. However, since
C. Because
D. Also, since

The correct answer is B. The first sentence tells us that Mount Vinson's climate is stable, while the second sentence provides opposing, contrary information. A transition word is needed to signal that opposing ideas are being presented. The word *however* does the trick. Choice **C** is a red herring; the problem with the underlined portion has nothing to do with the word *since*. (Either *since* or *because* would be perfectly correct and appropriate here.) Choice **D** provides the wrong transition; *also* signals similar ideas, not contrasting ones.

The next example involves three sentences altogether and is a bit tougher than the previous one. To determine the best transition to the third sentence, you should consider *both* of the others together.

> Undoubtedly, the most significant revolution in modern art was the invention of the purely abstract painting in the 1930s. Pablo Picasso is generally regarded as the quintessential modern artist. Thus, in all of Picasso's long and varied career, he never painted any significant abstract picture.

A. NO CHANGE
B. Furthermore
C. So
D. Nonetheless

The correct answer is D. The underlined word *Thus* implies that what follows is a logical result of what comes before. But, this connection makes no sense in the context of the paragraph. The first two sentences tell us that abstract painting was the great revolution of the twentieth-century and that Picasso was a revolutionary twentieth-century artist. The fact that Picasso never made an abstract painting doesn't follow as a logical result; it's a surprising contradiction—not at all what we would reasonably expect. You can also rule out choice **C**, because the word *So* has essentially the same meaning as *Thus*. As for choice **B**, the word *Furthermore* suggests that what follows elaborates on or adds to what has been said previously. That's not a logical connection between the paragraph's first two sentences and the last one. The correct answer, of course, is **D**. *Nonetheless* fits the sense of surprise or contradiction we felt when we read the last sentence; it links that sentence appropriately and logically to the two preceding sentences.

Tip: An appropriate transition word provides a logical link between ideas. A transition word (or phrase) should steer the reader in the right direction—for example, by signaling a conclusion, an opposing or contradictory idea, or an elaboration. It's like a good signpost that correctly signals the direction in which the next sentence is headed.

Transitions between Paragraphs

Another type of strategy question focuses on the transition between two paragraphs. In most cases, the item will be indicated by a boxed number—inserted at either the end of the first paragraph or at the beginning of the second.

Your task is to pick the sentence that most logically links the two paragraphs—the one that provides the most natural and sensible flow of ideas from one paragraph to the next. To handle these questions, think of the ideal transition sentence as a *bridge* whose ideas touch those of both paragraphs. To see what we mean by this, consider the following two paragraphs, along with question 1. (In the second paragraph, item 2 involves the transition between two sentences, the question type you examined in the preceding section. As a review, go ahead and attempt item 2 as well.)

[1]

When asked to imagine an ideal life, many people immediately think of the life of a prince or princess. The benefits of such a life include servants waiting to attend to your every need, a magnificent dwelling, and expensive jewelry and clothes. [1]

[2]

Perched on the Mediterranean Riviera and blessed with 300 sunny days a year, Monaco seems like a truly wonderful place in which to be royal. The tiny but wealthy country is currently ruled by Prince Rainer III. His family name is Grimaldi, and one or another of his relatives has ruled Monaco for hundreds of years. Also, (2) the Grimaldi family is the oldest ruling family in Europe.

1. The writer wants to end Paragraph 1 with a sentence that provides an effective transition to Paragraph 2. Which of the following sentences best accomplishes this objective?
   - A. When asked for the name of a member of royalty, many people think of one of the members of the British royal family, but few people think of Prince Ranier of Monaco.
   - B. For other people, the fantasy might involve a simpler life, but one which is lived in a beautiful setting where one is in close touch with the best that nature offers.
   - C. Of all the countries in the world ruled by a monarchy, the small land of Monaco is perhaps the one that brings that fantasy most to mind.
   - D. Because of its lenient tax policies, the country of Monaco has long been both a haven and a playground for the rich and famous.

The correct answer is C. Paragraph 1 describes a fantasy: the ideal life of a prince or princess. Paragraph 2 begins by describing the idyllic setting and climate of the monarchy of Monaco. The most effective transition between the two paragraphs is one that ties together the ideal—the fantasy—with Monaco. Choice **C** supplies just the link we're looking for. Choice **A** introduces the topic of Paragraph 2, but it fails to tie it to the fantasy discussed in Paragraph 1. Choice **B** is the runner-up, and it's what makes this question more challenging than average. It elaborates on the ideal life described earlier in Paragraph 1, and it does mention geographic setting—as does the first sentence of Paragraph 2. However, the "simpler life" in which one is in "close touch" with nature doesn't relate to Monaco, at least not as Paragraph 2 describes it. For this reason, choice **B** doesn't provide so smooth a transition as choice **C**. As for choice **D**, although it does mention Monaco, the topic of Paragraph 2, it provides a poor transition because it digresses from the fantasy described in Paragraph 1.

2. A. NO CHANGE
B. In fact,
C. Without a doubt,
D. OMIT the underlined portion (begin the sentence with *The Grimaldi family*).

The correct answer is B. The connecting word *also* does not provide an effective or natural link between the preceding sentence to one that begins with this underlined word. Although the link is not illogical, choice **B** provides a more rhetorically effective alternative. The phrase *In fact* provides a signal that what follows emphasizes or underscores the preceding idea—giving it additional credence. Choice **C** supplies a phrase that would be more appropriate to signal a conclusion. As for choice **D**, without a connecting word, the transition between the two sentences seems awkward and stilted. Some sort of link is clearly needed, so you can rule out choice **D**.

When faced with a paragraph transition question, look for a sentence that provides a *bridge* whose ideas connect directly to what immediately precedes and what immediately follows it.

Adding Supporting Sentences

Another type of strategy item you're sure to encounter on the English Test is the type that proposes the insertion of a sentence or general discussion somewhere in the essay—not to provide a transition, but rather to provide additional, supporting information. Although these test items come in several varieties, the following three variations appear most frequently:

- You decide which of four proposed sentences fits best at a particular point in the essay.
- You evaluate a proposal to insert a given sentence (or paragraph) at a particular point in the essay. (You decide whether or not it fits, and why.)
- You determine the best place in the essay to insert a particular sentence or an additional area of discussion.

Regardless of which variety you're dealing with, to handle this question type, you need to understand the structure of ideas—how the ideas flow from one to the next—for at least one entire paragraph, and possibly for the entire essay. Here's a good example of the first type listed above. The analysis that follows it will illustrate how to handle this type of question.

> In November of each year, bottles of *Beaujolais Nouveau*, a French wine, are sent to shops and restaurants all over the world, an event heralded by colorful banners that, in many languages, read: "The *Beaujolais Nouveau* has arrived!" Whenever I see one of these banners, I'm reminded of the month I spent harvesting grapes in the *Beaujolais* region of France. [1] Every day at the crack of dawn, the grape pickers piled into a wagon and rode out to the fields. In order to complete the harvest quickly, the vineyard's owner had hired workers from many countries. Although everyone spoke some French, the conversation that traveled through the morning air was mostly a jumble of languages.

The writer is thinking of inserting a sentence here to provide supporting details about the topic under discussion in this paragraph. For the sake of relevance and unity, which of the following proposed sentences would be most effective?

A. I worked alongside people not just from France, but also from Algiers, Morocco, Poland, and Bulgaria.
B. I was still a teenager at the time, and I could perform manual labor tirelessly from dawn to dusk
C. Although other parts of France are renowned for particular foods, others, such as the *Beaujolais* region, are known for their wine.
D. The *Beaujolais* region is located south of Macon and north of Lyon and, like many regions of France, has a wonderfully temperate climate.

The correct answer is B. The sentence in choice **B** provides new and specific information relating to what the writer was reminded of (see the preceding sentence) as well as to the fact that the workers started at the crack of dawn (see the next sentence). Choice **A** is relevant to the paragraph, but it belongs after the next sentence. Choice **C** is the easiest one to eliminate; it digresses from the paragraph's topic, which has nothing to do with special foods of other regions of France. Choice **D** is probably the second-best choice. In the preceding sentence, the writer first mentions the *Beaujolais* region, so the reader may be wondering where it's located. However, the region's location and climate do not relate directly to the grape-harvesting discussion that follows, whereas the sentence in choice **B** does.

Note

In the preceding example, notice that no additional sentence is needed in the paragraph; the discussion flows smoothly and logically from the sentences preceding the insertion point to those that follow it. So, you're *not* dealing with transition questions like the ones you examined earlier in this chapter.

Theme and Structure of the Essay as a Whole

For some Rhetorical Skills items, you'll need to see the "big picture"—the essay as a whole, rather than one or two sentences or paragraphs. Whole-essay questions are always the last ones in a question set. In one type of whole-essay question, your job is to determine the best (read: most logical) sequence for the essay's paragraphs. (You saw an example of this question type in Part I, Chapter 2, and you'll encounter more examples during the practice tests in Part VI of this book.)

In another type of whole-essay question, your job is to pick the most effective final sentence for the essay among four alternatives. How can you know which one is best? Well, it should flow logically and smoothly from the sentences that immediately precede it, of course. But, it should also tie together the entire essay—in other words, recall or reflect the essay's overall theme. It's this feature that often makes the difference between the best concluding sentence and the runner-up choice.

Whole-essay questions aren't limited to the two types just described. A whole-essay question might ask whether the essay fulfills a specified assignment, and why (or why not). Or, it might ask you to identify the best description of the essay's overall structure or theme. Other variations are possible as well.

To be ready for any whole-essay question, our best advice is to read the essay straight through before tackling any questions at all. As you do so, focus on the essay's overall structure, theme, and flow of ideas. Then, answer the whole-essay questions (if any) first, while you're focused on the big picture.

Usage and Idioms

The ACT English Test also covers *word usage* and *idioms*. Usage errors involve using the wrong word to express the intended idea. Idioms are particular phrases that are either proper or improper simply based upon whether they have become acceptable over time—through repeated and common use.

In many instances, you'll recognize improper word usage or an improper idiom (or, more correctly, a phrase that is "not idiomatic") simply because the word or phrase doesn't *sound* right. But that doesn't mean you should trust your ear entirely when it comes to the ACT. Although it's impossible to predict what specific usage and idiom issues will pop up on the ACT, you should still prepare for the trickiest ones and the ones that appear most frequently on the test. The guidelines for using the groups of words and phrases listed below will help you.

Alert!

The English language contains more idioms and usage issues than you can shake a thesaurus at. So, don't expect the words and phrases covered in the following pages to be the only ones you'll encounter in ACT idiom and usage questions. The test-makers don't design the ACT English Test to be that predictable.

more greater fewer less

Words describing and comparing size, number, and quantity are often misused. Distinguish words used to describe *degree* or *amount* (weight, size, etc.) from those used to describe *number* (quantity).

- *More* salt is used in the stew recipe than in the soup recipe.
- The *amount* of salt used in the stew recipe is *greater* (not *more*) than that used in the soup recipe.
- The *number* (not *amount*) of people in Smallville is *smaller* (not *fewer*) than the number of people in Bigville.
- *Fewer* (not *less*) people reside in Smallville than in Bigville.

such

The word *such* can be used as an alternative to *of these* or *of those*, but using it this way can sometimes sound awkward.

proper: Good liars may appear successful, but most *such* people are usually miserable inside.

awkward: A good liar may appear successful, but *such a person* is usually miserable inside.

to be as being as

Neither *as* or *as being* is a proper substitute for the infinitive *to be*.

proper (but confusing): Many people consider Lincoln America's greatest president.

proper (and clearer): Many people consider Lincoln *to be* America's greatest president.

improper: Many people consider Lincoln *as* America's greatest president.

improper: Many people consider Lincoln *as being* America's greatest president.

former latter

Use *former* to refer to the first of two items in a sequence, and use *latter* to refer to the second of the two items. Do not use either term, however, to compare *three or more* items.

improper: Graphic arts, music theory, and literature all interested Gwen, but among these course of study only the *latter* was offered at the local college.

proper: Graphic arts and music theory both interested Gwen, but the latter course of study was not offered at the local college.

because since as a result of as so being that (awkward)

All of these terms can be used to express a cause-and-effect relationship; however, they are not interchangeable.

unclear: *Since* the prankster set off the alarm, the school has been evacuated. (Does *since* mean "because" or "after"?)

clear (but wordy): *As a result of* the prankster's setting off the alarm, the school has been evacuated.

clear: *Because* the prankster set off the alarm, the school has been evacuated.

unclear: The prankster has been expelled from school *since* he set of the alarm. (Does *since* mean "because" or "after"?)

unclear: *Since* the prankster set off the alarm, he has been expelled from school. (Does *since* mean "because" or "after"?)

clear: The prankster was expelled from school *since* (or *because*) he refused to stop setting off the alarm.

unclear: The school was evacuated, *as* the prankster set off the alarm. (Does *as* mean "because" or "at the same time that"?)

acceptable: The prankster was expelled from school, *as* (or *since*) he could not resist setting off the alarm.

proper (but awkward): *Being that* the prankster is about to set off the alarm, the school will probably be evacuated.

better: The prankster is about to set off the alarm, *so* the school will probably be evacuated.

although despite (the fact that) in spite of (the fact that)

All of these terms can be used to express the same idea, but only the last two are interchangeable.

improper: *Despite* (or *in spite of*) *the fact of* her parents' financial assistance, she was unable to pay her credit card bill.

proper (but wordy): *Despite* (or *in spite of*) *the fact that* her parents assisted her financially, she was unable to pay her credit card bill.

proper (concise): *Despite* (or *in spite of*) her parents' financial assistance, she was unable to pay her credit card bill.

proper (concise): *Although* her parents assisted her financially, she was unable to pay her credit card bill.

to do so

The word *so*, like the word *such*, can serve as shorthand for a word (or words) appearing earlier in the sentence (an antecedent). But it should be used in this way only as part of the idiom *to do so*.

awkward and unclear: The House of Representatives quickly passed the bill, but the Senate failed *to so pass it*.

proper: The House of Representatives quickly passed the bill, but the Senate failed *to do so*.

nevertheless nonetheless anyway

Nevertheless and *nonetheless* have the same meaning, but they differ in terms of where they are generally placed for greatest impact. *Anyway* is a more concise alternative to either one.

- Stan suffered a painful injury when he fell off his horse, but he *nevertheless* kept riding.
- Stan suffered a painful injury when he fell off his horse, but he kept riding *nonetheless.*
- Stan suffered a painful injury when he fell off his horse, but he kept riding *anyway.*

alike whether . . . or

Either of these terms can be used to place two items on equal footing.

- Humans should dignify all living things, flora and fauna *alike.*
- Humans should dignify each living thing, *whether it be* flora *or* fauna.
- *Whether* flora *or* fauna, any living thing should be accorded dignity as such.

even

Besides its more obvious meaning ("equal" or "tied"), *even* can be used as a modifier for rhetorical emphasis. But, its placement can be crucial to the meaning of the sentence.

- Canada is *even* larger than the United States. (Canada is being compared with other countries).
- *Even* Canada is larger than the United States. (The United States is being compared with other countries).

if whether whether or not

The words *if* and *whether* can be used interchangeably; *whether or not* carries a distinct meaning.

proper: Nobody knows *if* (or *whether*) Kurt survived the war.

proper: Nobody knows *whether or not* Kurt survived the war.

improper: Nobody knows *whether* Kurt survived the war.

proper: *Whether or not* Kurt survived the war, his family will continue to celebrate his birthday.

as of as for as with as in

Each of these idiomatic phrases carries its own distinct meaning.

- *As of* yesterday, the leader still had not transmitted any news about his expedition.
- *As for* the youngest climber, he quit about half way up.
- *As with* mountain climbers, some politicians don't quit until they reach the summit.
- *As in* mountain climbing, in politics only the fittest reach the summit.

as opposed to

Use *as opposed to* when expressing a preference, but don't use *prefer* in the same sentence.

- The chef decided to fry the fish *as opposed to* broiling it.
- I like fried fish *as opposed to* broiled fish.
- The chef preferred frying the fish *to* (not *as opposed to*) broiling it.

regarding in regard to as regards with respect to respecting concerning as to about

All of these terms are proper and have essentially the same meaning. In the proceeding sentence, any of the terms could be used. In the second sentence, any of the terms but *as to* and *about* would be appropriate.

- Richard consulted his accountant *as to* the income-tax consequences of the sale.
- *In regard to* (not *as to* or *about*) the first issue, neither candidate is in favor of a tax increase for the middle class.

Do not confuse the proper idioms to the left with the following improper ones:

in regards to
with regards to
as regarding
as respecting
in respect of

while although

While or *although* can both be used to subordinate one idea to another. However, *while* is appropriate only when describing concurrent events or conditions (occurring at the same time).

- *Although* (or *while*) the mortality rate from car accidents last year was high, the death rate from cancer was much higher.
- *Although* (not *while*) last year's mortality rates appear very high, one must keep in mind that the rates have decreased steadily over the last decade.

such as like

Use *such as* to give examples. Use *like* to express similarity between two things.

- Mold can grow in many places, *such as* (not *like*) bathrooms, forests, and petri dishes.
- The mold growing in the bathroom looked very much *like* the mold I've seen in the forest.

which under which in which by which of which

The proper phrase depends on the point you wish to make.

- Einstein originated the theory of relativity, *which* holds that time is a relative concept.
- Einstein originated the theory of relativity, *under which* time is a relative concept.

- Einstein's theories emerged during the same century *in which* his theories were first confirmed empirically.
- Most people have heard of Einstein's theory of relativity, *by which* a clock traveling through space will become out of sync with a stationary clock.
- Einstein's theory of relativity fascinates today's scientists, only a few *of which* ever met Einstein personally.

based on based upon on the basis of

All three phrases are proper idioms, but only the first two are interchangeable in all instances.

- *Based upon* (or *based on* or *on the basis of*) the stock's past performance, I don't think I should sell it.
- My opinion about this stock is *based upon/on* (not *on the basis of*) its past performance.

by by means of by way of

Which phrase is proper depends on how it is used in the sentence.

- The hikers reached the valley *by* taking the main trail.
- The hikers reached the valley *by way of* the main trail.
- The hikers reached the valley *by means of* horseback.

account for on account of take into account

Which phrase is proper depends on how it is used in the sentence.

- The scout leader could not *account for* the missing child.
- The scout leader was reprimanded *on account of* his losing the child.
- The results of the scout leader's roll call failed to *take into account* the missing child.

among between

Use *among* for three or more items. Use *between* for two items.

- *Among* the many celebrities at the gala, she was dressed most flamboyantly.
- He was *between* a rock and a hard place.

like as as if as though

Use *as though* or *as if* (not *like*) for the subjunctive mood. Use *as* (not *like*) for a simile. Use *like* to make an analogy between two different things.

improper: He looked *like* he was about to cry.

proper: He looked *as though* he were about to cry.

proper: He looked *as if* he were about to cry.

improper: The television news reporter spoke about the election *like* a nonpartisan journalist should.

proper: The television news reporter spoke about the election *as* a nonpartisan journalist should.

improper: The prisoner behaved *as* a caged animal.

proper: The prisoner behaved *like* a caged animal.

differ different

The proper preposition to use with each of these words depends on the context.

improper: Smith and Adams *differ about* their positions on the issues.

improper: Smith and Adams *differ from each other on* their positions on the issues.

proper: Smith and Adams *differ on* their positions on the issues.

proper: The positions of Smith and Adams *differ from* those of all other candidates.

proper: Smith and Adams *differ with* each other as to who the better candidate is.

proper: The candidates *differ in* party membership but not in ideology.

improper: Smith's position on the issue is *different than* that of Adams.

proper: Smith's position on the issue is *different from* that of Adams.

proper: The candidates are *different in* party membership but not in ideology.

In each of the following sentence groups, the proper preposition depends on the context.

It is not always easy to *distinguish* good art *from* (not *with* or *and*) bad art.

The university *distinguished* the alumnus *with* an honorary doctoral degree.

Fluffy the cat can be *distinguished by* her unique markings.

The two analysts *agreed with* each other.

The two analysts *agreed to* examine the numbers further.

The two analysts *agreed on* (not *about*) only one conclusion.

No reasonable jury could *concur in* (not *about*) finding the defendant guilty.

The jury members have decided to *concur with* one another regarding the defendant's guilt.

Susan's former boyfriend plans to *interfere with* (not *in*) the wedding reception.

Susan's former boyfriend *interfered in* (not *by*) spiking the punch at the wedding reception.

The Cougars will *prevail over* (not *against*) the Panthers in the upcoming game.

The Cougars' coach must *prevail on* his team to play more aggressively during the second half of the game.

The contract *provides for* mandatory arbitration in the event of a dispute.
The contract *provides that* the parties must arbitrate any dispute.

The cave *provided* shelter for the bears.
The mother bear *provided for* her cubs.

Gary was *disappointed in* his son.
Gary was *disappointed with* (not *in* or *by*) his son's test results.

The runner grew *impatient with* (not *about* or *at*) the slow pace of the race.
Sprinters are often *impatient in* (not *with* or *about*) waiting for the final lap of longer races.

Doug will surely *die from* excessive smoking.
Doug will surely *die of* pneumonia.

John *confided in* his older brother.
John *confided to* his older brother that he stole the bicycle.

Each of the following phrases illustrates the proper (and improper) use of particular prepositions.

alarmed *at* (not *about*) the news
apologize *for* (not *about*) a mistake
aside from (not *outside of*) one particular instance
could *have* (not *of*) won the game
ignorant *of* (not *about*) the facts
independent *of* (not *from*) parental assistance
insist *on* (not *in*) a course of action
oblivious *of* (not *about* or *to*) the time
preferable *to* (not *than* or *over*) the other choice
price/cost *of* (not *for*) a shirt
required *of* (not *from*) all students
rich *in* (not *with*) resources
short *of* (not *on*) cash
succeed *in* (not *with*) an attempt
superior *to* (not *over*) the alternatives
within (not *inside of*) a few minutes

Chapter 6

The ACT Writing Test

In this chapter, you'll learn all about the ACT Writing Test and how to write an effective ACT essay—one that will earn you a better-than-average ACT Writing Test score of at least 4 on the 0–6 scale. Specifically, you'll learn:

- How the test is designed, what skills are tested, and what kind of questions to expect on the test
- How ACT essays are evaluated and scored
- A step-by-step approach to brainstorming, organizing, composing, and proofreading your essay, all within the test's 30-minute time limit
- Success keys to a high score on the Writing Test
- Useful tips for using the kind of language and writing style that will make a distinctly positive impression

The ACT Writing Test—In a Nutshell

As of February 2005, you have the option of sitting for a 30-minute Writing Test in addition to the four multiple-choice ACT tests. The Writing Test is given *last*—after the other four tests. If you opt to take the Writing Test, add 30 minutes to your total ACT testing time. When you register for the ACT, you'll indicate whether you want to take the Writing Test by checking the appropriate box on the registration form.

Note

The testing service charges an additional fee for the Writing Test. For details on registration procedures, including current fee amounts, consult the testing service's Web site (www.act.org).

Why Has a Writing Test Been Added to the ACT?

For the purposes of comparing admission applicants and for placing new students at appropriate course levels, colleges and universities are becoming increasingly interested in gauging the writing skills of admission applicants *directly*—rather than relying just on their ACT English Test scores and their grades in high school English classes. The ACT test-makers have added the optional Writing Test in response to this growing interest.

The ACT Writing Test and the ACT English Test cover much of the same ground. They both test on grammar, sentence structure, usage and idiom, and rhetorical effectiveness. So, if you're well prepared for the English Test, then you've got a head start on gearing up for the Writing Test.

Should You Opt to Take the Writing Test?

Few colleges or universities require ACT Writing Test scores *yet*, although the number is expected to increase steadily. By the time you apply for college admission, one or more of the schools that interest you might very well require Writing Test scores—in which case you should opt to take the test, of course.

It's also possible that one or more schools on your application list will say that, although they don't require Writing Test scores, they'll *consider* these scores in making admissions and placement decisions. In this case, if you're confident that you'd score high on the Writing Test, you should opt to take it. On the other hand, if your writing skills are weak, even after a conscientious effort to improve them by practicing what you'll learn in this chapter, then you should probably opt out of the Writing Test.

Alert!

Don't even think about basing your decision of which colleges you'll apply to (and which ones you won't) on whether a college requires ACT Writing Test scores. If you doubt the wisdom of our advice here, consult your high school career counselor, who will no doubt agree wholeheartedly with us.

Ground Rules for the ACT Writing Test

- Your time limit is 30 minutes.
- You'll write *one* essay responding to *one* essay question, or "prompt." (You will *not* be able to choose among prompts.)
- You'll produce a handwritten essay in your test booklet using a black-ink pen provided by the testing administrator. (No erasers or white-out are permitted.)
- Scratch paper for making notes and outlines is provided.

Note

The testing service will provide photocopies of your essay to the people who read and score your essay. Black-ink pens are issued in order to ensure high-quality copies. (By the way, you can take the pen with you as a souvenir!)

What an ACT Essay Question ("Prompt") Looks Like

The ACT Writing Test prompt consists of two parts. The first part is a paragraph-length description of a specific issue of interest to many high school students, along with two alternative viewpoints on the issue. The final sentence of this paragraph will ask for your opinion on the issue. Here's an ACT-style prompt, which contains all the same elements as the prompt you'll encounter on the actual test:

Essay Prompt No. 1

An increasing number of high schools are teaching classes in ethical and social values. Some people, especially parents, object to this trend because they think that it is not the appropriate role of school teachers to provide instruction in any areas other than academic subjects—math, science, English, and so forth. Other people support the trend because they think it just as important for young people to learn and apply values such as honesty, fairness, respect, and tolerance as to learn any particular academic subject. In your opinion, should high schools be responsible not only for teaching academic subjects and skills but also for teaching ethical and social values?

Alert!

The test-makers have compiled a large pool of essay topics, which vary widely. Any topic in their pool might show up on your test. So, although the prompt on your ACT Writing Test *might* involve an issue similar to the issue presented in the example here, the overwhelming odds are that it won't.

The second part of the Writing Test prompt is a brief paragraph of instructions and guidelines for writing your essay. Regardless of the specific issue, the instructions and guidelines are *always* the same and are essentially as follows:

Directions: Write an essay in which you take a position on this issue. Be sure to support your position with reasons and examples. In your essay, you may discuss either one of the two viewpoints described above, or you may present a different viewpoint on the issue.

Skills Tested and Scoring Criteria

The ACT Writing Test is designed to gauge your communication, analytical, and writing skills. Readers evaluate and score Writing Test essays based on five criteria, which include your ability to:

1. Recognize the complexities of an issue and adopt and articulate a position on it.
2. Develop and support your position using sound reasons and relevant examples.
3. Sustain a focused discussion on an issue.
4. Organize and present your ideas in logical groups and in a logical sequence, and to connect your ideas together using transitional devices effectively.
5. Communicate clearly and effectively, as demonstrated by language (word choice, usage, and use of idioms), writing mechanics (grammar, spelling, and punctuation), sentence structure, and overall writing style.

> **Note**
> Some of the abilities that the Writing Test gauges, especially skills 4 and 5 listed here, are similar to those the ACT English Test measures. In this way, the Writing Test is a supplement to the English Test.

What's Not Tested

In evaluating and scoring your essay, ACT readers focus only on the scoring criteria you just read about. Many test-takers will try to impress the readers in ways that the readers really don't care about—which is a big waste of time and effort. Other test-takers will be too concerned about saying the "right thing" and not concerned enough about how they say it. To avoid these strategic blunders, here's what you need to keep in mind:

- **There is no "correct" answer.** First and foremost, remember that there is no "best" response or "correct" position on any issue. As the test instructions suggest, it's perfectly acceptable to develop an essay in which you support one of the two perspectives described in the prompt; or, you can develop a response based on your own perspective. What's important is how effectively you present and support your position, not what your position is.
- **Special knowledge about the topic at hand won't matter.** The ACT Writing Test is a *skills* test. So, you don't need any special knowledge of the topic presented in order to produce a high-scoring essay. Besides, the Writing Test topics are not technical in nature. So, though you'll need to know something about the subject, common everyday knowledge will suffice.
- **The Writing Test is not a vocabulary exercise.** You won't score points with the readers by using obscure or so-called "big" words—the kinds of words you may have memorized for the SAT. When it comes to vocabulary, all that matters to the readers is that whatever words you use make sense in context. (Word choice and usage are included in the official scoring criteria.)
- **The Writing Test is not a creative writing exercise.** Some test-takers will make the mistake of using an unconventional essay structure or style in order to impress the reader with their originality. This is, simply put, a bad idea. The ACT is not the place to experiment with imagery, to display wit or humor, or to prove to the reader that you have "Hemingway potential." Impress the reader with strong organization, reasoning, and communication skills—not with your astounding creativity.
- **Occasional, minor gaffes will not hurt your score.** In evaluating your essay, the readers will focus mainly on the big picture: your ideas, how you've organized them, and the overall quality of your writing. They'll overlook the occasional punctuation gaffe, awkward sentence, or misspelled word. But don't get the wrong idea. Frequent problems, even the little ones, can add up to make a distinctively negative impression that might hurt your score. So, don't ignore mechanical details altogether.

Note

During the test, you'll use only a pen, and you can't erase or white-out what you've written. So, if you need to correct a mistake or rewrite a sentence, you'll strike through or cross out your mistake.

How ACT Essays Are Scored

For evaluation and scoring of ACT essays, the test-makers hire special "readers"—most of whom are high school English teachers. In evaluating your essay, readers apply a *holistic* scoring approach, meaning that they evaluate your essay based on the overall quality of your writing. In other words, instead of awarding separate subscores for the five different scoring criteria (listed on page 109), the reader will consider how effective your essay is *as a whole*—accounting for all these factors.

Two different readers will read and evaluate your essay. Each reader will award a single score on a scale of 0–6 in whole-point intervals (6 is highest). If the scores awarded by the two readers differ by more than one point, then a third reader will read and score your essay. Your final score is the average of the scores awarded by the readers, rounded to the nearest half point. (Averages falling midway between half-point intervals are rounded *up*.) Each reader evaluates your writing independently of other readers, and no reader is informed of other readers' scores for your essay.

Here are two examples showing how the scoring system works:

Example 1

6	Score awarded by Reader A
5	Score awarded by Reader B
5.5	Your final ACT Writing Test score

Example 2

5	Score awarded by Reader A
3	Score awarded by Reader B
3	Score awarded by Reader C
3.5	Your final ACT Writing Test score

Notice in Example 2 that a third reader evaluated the essay because the scores awarded by Readers A and B differed by more than one point, and that the average of the three scores $\left(3\frac{2}{3}\right)$ has been rounded to the nearest half point (3.5).

What Kinds of Topics to Expect on the Test

The test-makers have not revealed their official pool of Writing Test prompts; all they've said is that these prompts are designed to focus on issues that are relevant and of general interest to high school students. Here's a diverse list of issues that the prompts in the official pool might involve:

- Which is more important: teamwork or individual initiative?
- Should high school students hold part-time jobs?
- Is the violence frequently portrayed in today's movies a bad influence on today's teenagers?

- Which is more important in school: learning job-related skills or receiving a "well-rounded" education?
- Is computerized instruction a good substitute for live instruction by human teachers?
- Which is more key to individual success: innate talent or perseverance and effort?
- Should all high school students spend at least one term studying abroad?
- In our society, does television do more harm than good, or vice versa?
- Should businesses be allowed to advertise their products on high school campuses?
- Should it be illegal to use a cell phone while driving?
- Is it fair for school administrators to censor articles written by students for their school newspapers?
- Should consumers be required to pay for music they download from the Internet?
- Which is fairer in assessing a student's academic performance: a pass/fail system or a letter-grade system?
- Should high school students be required to wear uniforms or conform to a dress code?
- Which do we learn more from studying: history or current events?
- Will digital books and the World Wide Web make printed books obsolete?
- Should high school administrators attempt to identify "gifted" students and provide advanced classes for them?
- Should the voting age be lowered from 18 to 16?
- On balance, do high-tech gadgets save us time in our daily lives or do they rob us of time?

As you've no doubt concluded based on the preceding list, whatever issue you face on the test, in all likelihood you'll have some familiarity with it—enough to write a brief essay on it. So, you don't need to worry that you might draw a complete "blank."

Alert!

The preceding list covers only some of the many, and diverse, topics that the prompts in the official pool might deal with. Although the prompt on your test might involve an issue similar to one of those in our list, don't be the least bit surprised if it doesn't.

The ACT Writing Test—Your 7-Step Game Plan

For a high-scoring ACT essay, you need to accomplish these four basic tasks:

1. Recognize and deal with the complexities and implications of the issue.
2. Organize, develop, and express your ideas in a coherent and persuasive manner.
3. Support your ideas with sound reasons and relevant examples.

4. Demonstrate adequate control of the elements of Standard Written English (grammar, syntax, and usage).

The 30 minutes you're allowed to write your essay isn't much time. So, you need to use the time wisely. This does *not* mean using every one of your 30 minutes to scribble like mad. You should spend some time upfront thinking about what you should write and how you should organize your ideas. And you should save some time at the end to proofread your essay. Here's a 7-step game plan to help you budget your time so you can accomplish all four tasks listed above within your 30-minute time limit (suggested times are parenthesized):

Step 1: Brainstorm and make notes (3 min.).

Step 2: Review your notes and decide on a viewpoint (1 min.).

Step 3: Organize your ideas into a logical sequence (1 min.).

Step 4: Compose a brief introductory paragraph (2 min.).

Step 5: Compose the body of your response (20 min.).

Step 6: Compose a brief concluding or summary paragraph (2 min.).

Step 7: Proofread for mechanical and language errors (1 min.).

Notice that, by following the suggested times for each step, you'll spend about 5 minutes planning your essay, 24 minutes writing it, and 1 minute proofreading it.

Note

These suggested time limits for each step are merely guidelines, not hard-and-fast rules. As you practice composing your own essays under timed conditions at www.petersons.com/actessayedge, start with these guidelines, then adjust to a pace that works best for you.

In the following pages, you'll walk through each step in turn, applying them to the ACT-style essay prompt you read earlier. Here it is again:

Essay Prompt No. 1

An increasing number of high schools are teaching classes in ethical and social values. Some people, especially parents, object to this trend because they think that it is not the appropriate role of school teachers to provide instruction in any areas other than academic subjects—math, science, English, and so forth. Other people support the trend because they think it just as important for young people to learn and apply values such as honesty, fairness, respect, and tolerance as to learn any particular academic subject. In your opinion, should high schools be responsible not only for teaching academic subjects and skills but also for teaching ethical and social values?

Directions: Write an essay in which you take a position on this issue. Be sure to support your position with reasons and examples. In your essay, you may discuss either one of the two viewpoints described above, or you may present a different viewpoint on the issue.

Step 1: Brainstorm and make notes.

Your first step in developing your essay is to brainstorm ideas that are relevant to the topic. Try to think of some reasons and examples supporting not just one but *both* of the viewpoints presented. To conjure up ideas for your essay, you can draw on any of the following:

- Classroom discussions
- Books, articles, and other writings
- Your own experiences
- Stories people have told you
- Current events

As you think of ideas, don't commit to a position on the issue, and don't try to filter out what you think might be unconvincing reasons or weak examples. Just let all your ideas flow onto your scratch paper, in no particular order. (You can sort through them during steps 2 and 3.) Here's what a test-taker's notes on Prompt No. 1 might look like after a few minutes of brainstorming:

Whose values?
- Amish
- suburbanites
- yuppies
- Southern Baptists

pluralism
schools need focus
sex education
classroom cooperation vs. competition
teachers set examples—indirectly
drugs & violence

Notice that the first several lines reflect one train of thought (If schools were to teach ethical values, whose values would they teach?) while the other notes reflect other random ideas. The notes are somewhat of a hodgepodge, but that's okay. The point of brainstorming is just to generate a bunch of ideas—the raw material for your issue essay. Let your ideas flow freely, and you'll have plenty of fodder for that essay.

Step 2: Review your notes, and decide on a viewpoint.

Decide which of the two viewpoints presented in the prompt you're going to adopt and defend, at least to a greater extent than the other. Your notes from Step 1 should help you decide. Review the ideas you jotted down, and then ask yourself which of the two positions you can make a stronger case for. It's perfectly acceptable to agree entirely with one viewpoint while disagreeing entirely with the other. But, it's also okay to adopt your own perspective—for example, by taking a "middle-of-the-road" position in which you agree partly with each of the two viewpoints.

Alert!

Remember: There is no "correct" viewpoint or position. So, don't waste time debating over what your viewpoint should be. Just go with the flow—choose whichever viewpoint seems easiest or most natural for you to defend.

Then, pick the three or four ideas from your notes that best support your viewpoint. These should be ideas that you think make sense, that support your viewpoint reasonably well, and that you know enough about to write at least a few sentences on. Put a checkmark next to those ideas to signify that these are the ones you're certain you want to use in your essay. If there aren't enough ideas, take one or two of the ideas you like and elaborate on them. Think of related ideas, add details or examples, and use these to fill out your list.

Step 3: Organize your ideas into a logical sequence.

Next, decide on a sequence for the ideas. The best sequence might be obvious. One idea may lead logically to another. If there's no obvious sequence, one good approach is to decide which two ideas you like best—the two you consider most convincing or that you happen to know the most about and can develop most fully—and earmark these ideas to discuss *first* and *last* (in either order) in the body of your essay. Then, sequence the remaining ideas in any order, but *between* your two best ideas. Why sequence your ideas this way? The most emphatic and memorable parts of any essay are its beginning and end. It makes sense that your best material should go there, where it will have the greatest possible impact on the reader.

Once you've decided on a sequence for your ideas, number them accordingly in your notes. Here's an example of how a test-taker might turn the notes based on Prompt No. 1 into a simple outline:

2. ✓ Whose values?
   - Amish
   - suburbanites
   - yuppies
   - Southern Baptists

1. ✓ pluralism

3. ✓ schools need focus
   - sex education
   - classroom cooperation vs. competition
   - teachers set examples-indirectly
   - drugs & violence

4. ✓ U.S. Schools lag

Notice that this test-taker has decided to favor the first of the two viewpoints presented—that schools should teach academics only, and not ethical values. The first three points in his notes all fit nicely into an argument for this viewpoint. He also thought of a fourth idea that might make a good ending—that U.S. schools lag behind most other countries in academic standards, and so time must not be taken away from teaching academic subjects to teach ethics. So, he made a note of that idea, and checked it off as well.

He decided to start with the idea that America is pluralistic, which means that many diverse cultures and value systems are represented. From this idea, it makes sense to ask, "Whose values would be taught in schools?" and use the examples listed. This leads nicely to the point about focusing on academics and, finally, the argument about how U.S. students lag behind others.

Step 4: Compose a brief introductory paragraph.

Now that you've spent about 5 minutes planning your essay, it's time to compose it. You'll begin with a brief introductory paragraph, in which you should accomplish the following:

- Demonstrate that you understand the issue that the prompt raises, and its implications.
- Let the reader know that you have a clear viewpoint on the issue.
- Anticipate the ideas you intend to present in your essay's body paragraphs.

You can probably accomplish all three tasks in two or three sentences. In your introductory paragraph, don't go into detail about your reasoning, and don't provide specific examples. This is what your essay's body paragraphs are for. Also, don't begin your introductory paragraph by repeating what the prompt states. Instead, show the reader from the very first sentence that you're thinking for yourself.

Here's a good introductory paragraph for Prompt No. 1:

Introductory Paragraph (Prompt No. 1)

The issue presented here is by no means clear-cut; learning academic skills and ethics are both important in order for a young person to mature into a productive member of society. In my view, however, any high school in a pluralistic nation such as the United States should limit what it teaches to academic subjects, leaving it to parents and churches to teach ethical and social values. To do otherwise is to invite trouble, for several reasons.

Step 5: Compose the body of your essay.

During Step 4, your chief ambition is to get your main points—and supporting reasons and examples—from your brain and your scratch paper into your test booklet! Here's what you need to keep in mind as you compose your body paragraphs:

- Be sure the first sentence of each paragraph begins a distinct train of thought and clearly conveys to the reader the essence of the paragraph.
- Arrange your paragraphs so that your essay flows logically and persuasively from one point to the next. Try to stick to your outline, but be flexible.
- Try to devote at least two, but no more than three or four, sentences to each main point in your outline.

- Don't worry if you don't have time to include every single point from your outline. The readers understand that the test's time constraint prevents most test-takers from covering every point they want to make.
- Don't stray from the issue at hand, or even from the points you seek to make. Be sure to stay well focused on both.

Now here are the body paragraphs of a response to Prompt No. 1 (these body paragraphs are based on our notes from Step 3):

4-Paragraph Body (Prompt No. 1)

If our schools are to teach values, the most important question to answer is: Whose values would they teach? Not all ethical values are the same. For example, the Amish have a way of life that stresses simplicity and austerity; they shun modern conveniences and even such activities as dancing. By contrast, the typical young urban family—"yuppies," as they're often called—enjoys buying the latest electronic gadgets and going on expensive vacations. Either group might be offended by the values of the other.

True, Amish and yuppie children aren't likely to attend the same schools; but what about children from Jewish and fundamentalist Christian households? These two religious groups may live in the same town or neighborhood, and either one might very well be incensed if the other group's moral teachings were imposed on them.

The only way to avoid the inevitable conflicts that teaching ethics would bring to our schools is by allowing teachers to focus on what they're paid to do: teach academics. We send children to school to learn math, English, history, and science. How would our parents feel if we came home ignorant about geometry but indoctrinated with someone else's religious or ethical ideas? I'd feel outraged if I were the parent.

Besides, recent statistics show that high school students in the U.S. have fallen behind those in most other developed nations in academic achievement. In light of this fact, it would seem foolish for high schools to divert classroom time from teaching academics to teaching "morality." Without a solid academic background, young adults will have trouble later competing with immigrants for the best jobs in the highest-paying fields.

Notice the following features of these body paragraphs, which show that the test-taker tried to stick to his outline, while at the same time remaining flexible as new ideas for content or organization occurred to him:

- Point 2 in the outline ("Whose values?") became the basis for *two* paragraphs (the second and third ones), not just one.
- After writing about the Amish and yuppies, the test-taker seemed to realize that the contrast between them, while illustrating the point, was a bit exaggerated. Rather than replacing the entire paragraph with a more realistic pairing, which would have meant substantial time wasted, the test-taker *added* the third paragraph to provide a more down-to-earth pairing.
- The suburbanites got left out of the essay altogether, possibly because they seemed unnecessary. (Or, perhaps the test-taker realized that he was running short on time.)

Step 6: Compose a brief concluding or summary paragraph.

Unless your essay has a clear end, the reader might think you didn't finish in time. That's not the impression you want to make; so, be sure to make time to wrap up your discussion. Convey the main thrust of your essay in a clear, concise, and forceful way. Two or three sentences should suffice. If an especially insightful concluding point occurs to you, the final sentence of your essay is a good place for it.

Here's a brief but effective concluding paragraph for the response to Prompt No. 1. Notice that it assures the reader that the test-taker has organized his time well and finished the writing task. Also, notice that this brief summary does not introduce any new reasons or examples; it's just a quick recapitulation:

Final Paragraph (Prompt No. 1)

Ironically, what is most ethical for our schools to do in the interest of educating our children is to avoid becoming entangled in ethical issues. Stick to academics, and let families and clergy teach morality in their own way and on their own time.

From beginning to end (including the introductory, body, and concluding paragraphs), the preceding sample essay runs just under 400 words in length. So, it's not especially lengthy. Nor is it a literary masterpiece. Nevertheless, it expresses a clear viewpoint, it's smartly organized, it employs relevant reasons and examples, and it's crisp and effective in style. In short, it contains all the elements of a better-than-average ACT essay.

Step 7: Proofread for mechanical and language errors.

Save the last minute or so to proofread your essay from start to finish for mechanical problems that you can quickly and easily fix, such as errors in spelling, punctuation, diction (word choice and usage), and idiom. Since you're required to write your ACT essay in pen, you can't erase what you write. But you can strike-through (cross out) words and phrases and replace them by writing just above or below your strike-through. Just make sure that your corrections are clear and legible.

Alert!

Avoid making major revisions or rewriting significant portions of your essay. By striking and replacing entire sentences or paragraphs, you'll leave the reader with the impression that you have difficulty organizing your ideas. What's more, your essay will look sloppy, which can leave a negative impression on the reader.

Writing Style

Your writing style, your diction (word choice and usage), the structure of your sentences, and your use of transitional and rhetorical devices can all significantly influence the reader and affect your ACT Writing Test score. To ensure yourself a high score, strive for writing that is:

- Appropriate in tone and voice for academic writing at the college freshman level
- Clear and concise (easy to understand, and direct rather than wordy or verbose)

- Varied in sentence length and structure (to add interest and variety as well as to demonstrate maturity in writing style)
- Correct in diction (word choice and usage) and idiom
- Easy to follow, using transitional devices effectively
- Persuasive in style, using language and rhetorical devices effectively

All of this is easier said than done, of course. Don't worry if you're not a natural when it comes to writing the kind of prose that's appropriate for the ACT. You *can* improve your writing for your exam, even if your time is short. Start by reading the suggestions and guidelines in the following pages. But, keep in mind: Improvement in writing comes mainly with practice.

Overall Tone and Voice

In general, you should try to maintain a somewhat formal tone throughout your essay. An essay that comes across as conversational is probably a bit too informal for the ACT. Here are some specific guidelines:

- The overall tone should be critical, but don't try to overstate your position by using extreme or harsh language. Don't attempt to elicit a visceral or emotional response from the reader. Appeal instead to the reader's intellect.
- When it comes to your main points, a very direct, even forceful voice is perfectly acceptable. Just don't overdo it.
- You might also wish to refer to yourself from time to time. Self-references—singular as well as plural—are perfectly acceptable, though optional. Just be consistent; for example, be sure not to mix phrases such as *I disagree with* . . . or *In my view* . . . with phrases such as *We cannot assume that* . . . .
- Although the occasional self-reference is perfectly okay, don't get too personal. In citing examples to support your ideas, don't dwell exclusively on your personal experiences. And, *never* apologize to the reader or make excuses for your essay.
- Don't try to make your point with "cutesy" or humorous remarks. Avoid puns, double-meanings, plays on words, and other forms of humor. Not that ACT readers don't have a sense of humor; it's just that they leave it at the door when they go to work for the testing service. (That sentence exhibits just the sort of "humor" you should avoid in your ACT essay.)
- Sarcasm is entirely inappropriate for your ACT essay. Besides, the reader might not realize that you're being sarcastic, in which case your remark might confuse the reader, who might award a lower score as a result.

Clear and Concise Writing

With enough words, anyone can make the point; but, it requires skill and effort to make your point with concise phrases. Before you commit to paper any sentence you have in mind, ask yourself whether it seems a bit clumsy or too long, and whether you can express the same idea more concisely and clearly.

Although punctuation is probably the least important aspect of your ACT essay, too few or too many commas might interfere with the reader's ability to understand a sentence, at which point punctuation becomes important. Too few commas might confuse the reader, while too many can unduly interrupt the sentence's flow. Here's the guideline: Use the minimum number of commas needed to ensure that the reader will understand your point.

Sentence Length and Variety

Sentences that vary in length make for a more interesting and persuasive essay. For rhetorical emphasis, try using an abrupt short sentence for a crucial point, either before or after longer sentences that elucidate that point. For additional variety, use a semicolon to transform two sentences involving the same train of thought into one; and use the word "and" to connect your two independent clauses (just as in this sentence).

Sentences that essentially repeat (verbatim) throughout your essay demonstrate immature, even lazy writing. Try to avoid using so-called "template" sentences over and over—especially for the first (or last) sentence of each body paragraph.

Alert!

Be especially careful not to repeat complete sentences from the essay prompt. Trust us: This gaffe is a huge turn-off for ACT readers! If you must express an idea that's essentially the same as one in the prompt, paraphrase in a way that shows that reader you understand the idea and can express it just as well in your own words.

Effective Use of Language

To score high with your essay, you'll need to convince the readers that you possess a solid command of the English language—in other words, that you can use the language correctly, clearly, and persuasively in writing. By all means, show the reader that you possess the vocabulary of a broadly educated individual, and that you know how to use it. But, keep the following warnings in mind:

- Don't overuse SAT-style words just to make an impression. Doing so will only serve to warn the reader that you're trying to mask poor content with window dressing.
- Avoid obscure or archaic words that few readers are likely to know. The readers will not take time while reading essays to consult their unabridged dictionaries.
- Avoid colloquialisms (slang and vernacular). Otherwise, instead of hitting a home run with your essay, your essay will turn out lousy, and you'll be out of luck and need to snake your way into college. (Did you catch the *four* colloquialisms in the preceding sentence?)

In evaluating your ACT essay, the readers also take into account your *diction*—your choice of words as well as the manner in which a word is used. When you commit an error in diction, you might be confusing one word with another because the two words look or sound similar. Or, you might be using a word that isn't the best one to convey the idea you have in mind.

ACT readers also take into account your use of idioms. An *idiom* is a distinctive (*idio*syncratic) phrase that is either proper or improper simply based upon whether it has become acceptable over time—through repeated and common use. For example, here's a sentence that contains an idiomatic prepositional phrase as well as another idiom:

> This viewpoint *flies in the face of* my own personal experience, and *in any event* runs contrary to common sense.

The English language contains more idiomatic expressions than you can shake a thesaurus at, and the number of possible diction errors isn't even limited only to the number of entries in a good English dictionary. Although it is impossible in these pages to provide an adequate diction or idiom review, here are some guidelines to keep you on the straight and narrow when it comes to these aspects of your writing:

- If you're the least bit unsure about the meaning of a word you're thinking of using in your essay, don't use it. Why risk committing a diction blunder just to impress the reader with an erudite vocabulary? (And if you're not sure what "erudite" means, either find out or don't use it in your essay!)
- If a phrase sounds wrong to your ear, change it until it sounds correct to you.
- The fewer words you use, the less likely you'll commit an error in diction or idiom. So, when in doubt, go with a relatively brief phrase that you still think conveys your point.

Rhetorical Devices

Certain kinds of words and phrases can be especially useful in rhetorical writing, where you're trying to argue for one viewpoint over another or otherwise persuade the reader. Here's a reference list of useful rhetorical words and phrases, categorized by function.

- Use phrases such as these to subordinate an idea:

  although it might appear that, at first glance it would seem/appear that, admittedly

- Use phrases such as these to argue for a position, thesis, or viewpoint:

  promotes, facilitates, provides a strong impetus, serves to, directly, furthers, accomplishes, achieves, demonstrates, suggests, indicates

- Use phrases such as these to refute, rebut, or counter a position, theory, or viewpoint:

  however, closer scrutiny reveals, upon closer inspection/examination, a more thorough analysis, in reality, actually, when viewed more closely, when viewed from another perspective, further observation shows

- Use phrases such as these to point out problems with a position, theory, or viewpoint:

  however, nevertheless, yet, still, despite, of course, serious drawbacks, problematic, countervailing factors

- Use phrases such as these to argue against a position or viewpoint:

  works against, undermines, thwarts, defeats, runs contrary to, fails to achieve/promote/accomplish, is inconsistent with, impedes

- Use phrases such as these to argue that the merits of one position outweigh those of another:

    on balance, on the whole, all things considered, in the final analysis

Alert!

Many test-takers try to mask weak ideas by relying too much on rhetorical words and phrases such as *undeniably*, *absolutely*, and *without a doubt*, which by themselves mean absolutely nothing. Avoid using this kind of empty rhetoric in your ACT essay.

You can also use punctuation for rhetorical emphasis. To emphasize a particular idea, you can end a sentence with an exclamation mark instead of a period. Also, you can emphasize a particular word by underlining it. (In handwriting, underlining serves as a substitute for italics.) But use these two rhetorical devices *very* sparingly; one of each in your essay is plenty! (Notice the use of both devices in the preceding sentence.)

As we mentioned earlier, for rhetorical emphasis you can use an abrupt short sentence for a crucial point, either before or after longer sentences that elucidate that point. Sentences that pose questions can be a useful rhetorical device. Like short, abrupt sentences, rhetorical questions can help persuade the reader—or at least help to make your point. They can be quite effective. They also add interest and variety. Yet, how many test-takers think to incorporate them into their essays? Not many. (By the way, we just posed a rhetorical question.) Just be sure to provide an answer to your question. And don't overdo it; one rhetorical question per essay is plenty.

Connecting Your Ideas Together

Your essay will not earn a high score unless your ideas flow naturally from one to the next, so the reader can easily follow your train of thought. To connect your ideas, develop your own arsenal of transition devices—words and phrases that serve as bridges between ideas, helping to convey your line of reasoning to the reader.

Each transition device should help the reader see the logic and structure of your ideas. For example, some lead your reader forward and imply the building of an idea or thought, while others prompt the reader to compare ideas or draw conclusions from the preceding thoughts. Here's a reference list that includes many of those devices—by functional category.

To signal addition:

and, again, and then, besides, equally important, finally, further, furthermore, nor, too, next, lastly, what's more

To connect ideas:

furthermore; additionally; in addition; also; first, second, . . . ; moreover; most important/significantly; consequently; simultaneously; concurrently; next; finally

To signal comparison or contrast:

but, although, conversely, in contrast, on the other hand, whereas, but, except, by comparison, where, compared to, weighed against, vis-à-vis, while, meanwhile

To signal proof:

because, for, since, for the same reason, obviously, evidently, furthermore, moreover, besides, indeed, in fact, in addition, in any case, that is

To signal exception:

yet, still, however, nevertheless, in spite of, despite, of course, occasionally, sometimes, in rare instances, infrequently

To signal sequence (chronological, logical, or rhetorical):

first, second(ly), third(ly), . . .; next; then; now; at this point; after; in turn; subsequently; finally; consequently; previously; beforehand; simultaneously; concurrently

To signal examples:

for example, for instance, perhaps, consider, take the case of . . . , to demonstrate, to illustrate, as an illustration, one possible scenario, in this case, in another case, on this occasion, in this situation

To signal your reasoning from premise to conclusion:

therefore, thus, hence, accordingly, as a result, it follows that, in turn

Use these phrases for your concluding or summary paragraph:

in sum, in the final analysis, in brief, summing up, in conclusion, to conclude, to recapitulate, in essence, in a nutshell

Success Keys for Writing an ACT Essay

Here's our very best advice for writing ACT essays—in bite-sized pieces. Some of these tips reiterate suggestions made earlier in this chapter—suggestions that are well worth reiterating. Others are new here.

Adopt a Viewpoint . . . *ANY* Viewpoint

It's perfectly acceptable to strongly agree or disagree with an issue statement. Don't worry that your position may appear somewhat "right-wing" or "left-wing." Just be sure to provide sound reasons and relevant examples to justify your viewpoint. It's also perfectly okay to take a "middle ground" position in which you agree *partly* with each of the two viewpoints presented (and disagree partly with each one). Again, just be sure to justify your middle-ground position with sound reasons and relevant examples.

Appeal to Reason, Not Emotion

Avoid inflammatory statements, and don't preach or proselytize. Approach the ACT essay as an intellectual exercise in which you dispassionately argue for a certain viewpoint. Do not use it as a forum for sharing your personal belief system. It's perfectly appropriate to criticize particular behavior, policies, or viewpoints; but, refrain from either condemning or extolling based on personal moral grounds. Also avoid demagoguery (appeal to prejudice or emotion) and jingoism (excessive patriotism).

Spare the Reader Rote Facts and Technical Details

The issue essay is not like a game of *Jeopardy!* or *Trivial Pursuit*. You will not score points simply by recounting statistics, compiling long lists, or conjuring up little-known facts. And, don't try to impress the reader with your technical knowledge of any particular subject. That's what your GPA and high school transcripts are for.

Don't Dwell on One Point; but Don't Try to Cover Everything Either

Avoid harping on one particular reason that you believe is the most convincing one, or on one example that you know a lot about or that best illustrates your point. Instead, try to cover as many points in your outline as you have time for, devoting no more than one paragraph to each one.

At the same time, if you try to cover everything you can think of about the issue at hand, you're likely to become frustrated, and you might even panic as the testing clock ticks away your 30 minutes. The readers understand your time constraints. So, don't worry if you're forced to leave the secondary and minor points on your scratch paper. Stick to your outline, ration your time, and you'll be fine.

Keep It Simple; the Reader Will Reward You for It

Don't make the Writing Test more difficult than it needs to be for you to attain a solid score. Keep you sentences clear and simple. Use a simple, straightforward structure for your essay. Avoid using "fancy" words just to impress the reader. Don't waste time ruminating over how you can come across as ultra-brilliant, mega-insightful, or super-eloquent.

Look Organized and in Control of the Task

Use every tool at your disposal to show the reader that you can write well under pressure. Use logical paragraph breaks—one after your introduction, one between each of your main points, and one before your concluding paragraph. Be sure to present your main points in a logical, easy-to-follow sequence. Your essay's "bookends"—the introductory and concluding paragraph—are especially key to looking organized and in control. First of all, make sure they're there! Then, make sure they're consistent with each other, and that they reveal your viewpoint and recap your reasons for your viewpoint.

It's Quality, Not Quantity, That Counts

The only limitations on your essay's length are the space provided in your test booklet and the 30-minute time limit. But, do the readers prefer brief or longer essays? Well, it all depends on the essay's quality. A lengthy essay that's articulate and that includes many insightful ideas that are well supported by examples will score higher than a briefer essay that lacks substance. On the other hand, an essay that's concise and to the point can be more effective than a long-winded, rambling one.

Don't worry about the word length of your essay. ACT readers don't count words. As long as you incorporate into your essay all the suggested elements you learned about in this chapter, you don't need to worry about your essay's length. Just keep in mind that it's quality, not quantity, that counts.

Don't Lose Sight of Your Primary Objectives

The official scoring criteria for the essay boil down to broad criteria listed on page 109. Never lose sight of them during the 30-minute Writing Test. After brainstorming and outlining your ideas, but before you start writing, ask yourself:

- *Do I have a clear viewpoint on the issue?*
- *Can I support my viewpoint with sound reasons and relevant examples?*
- *Do I have in mind a clear, logical structure for presenting my ideas?*

Once you can confidently answer "Yes" to each question, start composing your essay. Along the way, continue to ask yourself:

- *Am I linking my ideas with transitional devices that help these ideas flow smoothly and logically from one to the next?*
- *Are my sentences easy to understand, without undue awkwardness, repetitiveness, or wordiness?*

Then, once you finish your draft, ask yourself:

- *Does my finished product exemplify good grammar, diction (word choice and usage), spelling, and punctuation?*

If you can answer "Yes" to all of these questions, rest assured that you've produced a solid, high-scoring ACT essay.

The Mathematics Test

Chapter

7

Strategies for the Mathematics Test

In this chapter, you'll learn:

- A step-by-step approach to handling any ACT math question
- Success keys for tackling ACT math questions
- To *Take It to the Next Level*

Success in ACT Math Requires Knowledge *and* Skill

To handle ACT math questions, there's no doubt that you'll need to be well versed in the fundamental rules of arithmetic, algebra, and geometry. And, your knowledge of these basics is, to a large extent, what's being tested.

But, the test-makers are just as interested, if not more interested, in gauging your mental agility, flexibility, creativity, and efficiency when it comes to solving math problems. More specifically, they design ACT math questions to help them answer questions such as these:

- Can you manipulate numbers with a certain end result already in mind?
- Can you see the dynamic relationships between numbers as you apply operations to them?
- Can you visualize geometric shapes and relationships between shapes?
- Can you devise unconventional solutions to conventional quantitative problems?
- Can you solve problems efficiently, by recognizing the easiest, quickest, or most reliable route to a solution?

This chapter will help give you the skills you need to answer "yes" to these questions. What follows might strike you as a series of "tips," "shortcuts," or "secrets" for ACT math. But you shouldn't think this way. The skills you'll learn here are intrinsic to the test; along with your knowledge of substantive rules of math, they're precisely what ACT math questions are designed to measure.

The ACT Mathematics Test—Your 5-Step Game Plan

The first task in this chapter is to learn the five basic steps for handling any ACT math question. You'll apply these steps to the following three sample questions.

Sample Questions

Question 1 involves *changes in percent*. Notice that the question is a word problem (it involves a real-world situation). Expect to see quite a few word problems on the ACT Mathematics Test.

1. If Susan drinks 10% of the juice from a 16-ounce bottle immediately before lunch and 20% of the remaining amount with lunch, approximately how many ounces of juice are left to drink after lunch?

A. 4.8
B. 5.5
C. 11.2
D. 11.5
E. 13.0

This next question involves the concept of *simple average*.

2. The average of 6 numbers is 19. When one of those numbers is taken away, the average of the remaining 5 numbers is 21. What number was taken away?

F. 2
G. 8
H. 9
J. 11
K. 20

Here's a somewhat more difficult math question. This one involves the concept of *proportion*.

3. If p pencils cost $2q$ dollars, how many pencils can you buy for c cents? [Note: 1 dollar = 100 cents]

A. $\frac{pc}{2q}$
B. $\frac{pc}{200q}$
C. $\frac{50pc}{q}$
D. $\frac{2pq}{c}$
E. $200pcq$

Note

Notice that instead of performing a numerical computation, your task in question 3 is to *express a computational process* in terms of letters. Expressions such as these are known as *literal expressions*, and they can be perplexing! On the ACT, you'll probably find at least five of them among your 60 math questions.

The 5-Step Plan

Here's the 5-step approach that will help you to handle these three, or any other, math questions. Just a few pages ahead, we'll apply this approach to our three sample math questions.

Step 1: Size up the question.

Read the question, then pause for a moment to ask yourself:

- What specific subject area is being covered?
- What rules and formulas are likely to come into play?
- How complex is this question? (How many steps are involved in solving it? Does it require setting up equations, or does it require merely a few quick calculations?)
- Do I have a clue, off the top of my head, how I would begin solving this problem?

Determine how much time you're willing to spend on the problem, if any. Recognizing a "toughie" when you see it may save you valuable time; if you don't have a clue, take a guess, earmark the question to come back to if you have time later, and then move on.

Step 2: Size up the answer choices.

Before you attempt to solve the problem at hand, examine the answer choices. They can provide helpful clues about how to proceed in solving the problem and about what sort of solution you should be aiming for. Pay particular attention to the following:

- *Form*
  Are the answer choices expressed as percentages, fractions, or decimals? Ounces or pounds? Minutes or hours? If the answer choices are expressed as equations, are all variables together on one side of the equation? As you work through the problem, convert numbers and expressions to the same form as the answer choices.
- *Size*
  Are the answer choices extremely small numbers? Numbers between 1 and 10? Larger numbers? Negative or positive numbers? Do the answer choices vary widely in value, or are their values clustered closely around an average? If all answer choices are tightly clustered in value, you can probably disregard decimal points and extraneous zeros in performing calculations. At the same time, however, you should be more careful about rounding off your figures where answer choices do not vary widely. Wide variation in value suggests that you can easily eliminate answer choices that don't correspond to the general size of numbers suggested by the question.
- *Other distinctive properties and characteristics*
  Are the answer choices integers? Do they all include a variable? Do one or more include radicals (roots)? Exponents? Is there a particular term, expression, or number that they have in common?

Step 3: Look for a shortcut to the answer.

Before plunging headlong into a problem, ask yourself if there's a quick, intuitive way to get to the correct answer. If the solution is a numerical value, perhaps only one answer choice is in the right ballpark. Also, some questions can be solved *intuitively*, without resorting to equations and calculations. (You'll see how when we apply this step to our sample questions.)

Step 4: Set up the problem and solve it.

If your intuition fails you, grab your pencil, roll up your sleeves, and do whatever computations, algebra, or other procedures are needed to solve the problem at hand. Simple problems may require just a few quick calculations, while complex algebra and geometry questions may require setting up one or more equations.

Step 5: Verify your response before moving on.

After solving the problem, if your solution does *not* appear among the answer choices, go back and check your work. (You obviously made at least one mistake.) If your solution *does* appear among the choices, don't celebrate quite yet. Although there's a good chance your answer is correct, it's possible your answer is wrong, and that the test-maker anticipated your error by including a "sucker bait" answer choice—just for you and other test-takers who made the same mistake. (We'll look at some "sucker-bait" answer choices a few pages later.) So, check the question to verify that your response corresponds to what the question calls for—in terms of size, expression, units of measure, and so forth. If it does, and you're confident that your work was careful and accurate, don't spend any more time checking your work. Confirm your response and move on to the next question.

Applying the 5-Step Plan

It's time to go back to the three sample questions you looked at earlier. Let's walk through them—one at a time—using the 5-step game plan you just learned.

Question 1

Question 1 is a relatively easy question. Approximately 75% of test-takers respond correctly to questions like it. Here's the question again:

1. If Susan drinks 10% of the juice from a 16-ounce bottle immediately before lunch and 20% of the remaining amount with lunch, approximately how many ounces of juice are left to drink after lunch?

A. 4.8
B. 5.5
C. 11.2
D. 11.5
E. 13.0

Step 1: This problem involves the concept of *percent*—more specifically, *percent decrease*. The question is asking you to perform two computations in sequence. (The result of the first computation is used to perform the second one.) Percent questions tend to be relatively simple. All that is involved here is a 2-step computation.

Step 2: The five answer choices in this question provide two useful clues:

- Notice that they range in value from 4.8 to 13.0. That's a wide spectrum, isn't it? But what general size should we be looking for in a correct answer to this question? Without crunching any numbers, it's clear that most of the juice will still remain in the bottle, even after lunch. So, you're looking for a value much closer to 13 than to 4. Eliminate choices **A** and **B**.
- Notice that each answer choice is carried to exactly one decimal place, and that the question asks for an *approximate* value. These two features are clues that you can probably round off your calculations to the nearest "tenth" as you go.

Step 3: You already eliminated choices **A** and **B** in Step 1. But if you're on your toes, you can eliminate all but the correct answer without resorting to precise calculations. Look at the question from a broader perspective. If you subtract 10% from a number, then 20% from the result, that adds up to *a bit less* than a 30% decrease from the original number. 30% of 16 ounces is 4.8 ounces. So, the solution must be a number that is a bit larger than 11.2 (16 − 4.8). Answer choice **D**, 11.5, is the only choice that fits the bill!

Alert!

Many ACT math questions are designed to reward you for recognizing easier, more intuitive ways of narrowing down the choices to the correct answer. Don't skip over Step 3. It's well worth your time to look for a shortcut to the correct answer choice.

Step 4: If your intuition fails you, go ahead and crunch the numbers. First, determine 10% of 16, then subtract that number from 16:

$16 \times 0.1 = 1.6$

$16 - 1.6 = 14.4$

Susan now has 14.4 ounces of juice. Now, perform the second step. Determine 20% of 14.4, then subtract that number from 14.4:

$14.4 \times 0.2 = 2.88$

Round off 2.88 to the nearest tenth: 2.9

$14.4 - 2.9 = 11.5$

Step 5: The decimal number 11.5 is indeed among the answer choices. Before moving on, however, ask yourself whether your solution makes sense—in this case, whether the size of our number (11.5) "fits" what the question asks for. If you performed Step 2, you should already realize that 11.5 is in the right ballpark. If you're confident that your calculations were careful and accurate, confirm your response, choice **D**, and move on to the next question.

Question 2

Question 2 is a bit tougher than average. Approximately 60% of test-takers respond correctly to questions like it. Here's the question again:

2. The average of 6 numbers is 19. When one of those numbers is taken away, the average of the remaining 5 numbers is 21. What number was taken away?

F. 2
G. 8
H. 9
J. 11
K. 20

Step 1: This problem involves the concept of *arithmetic mean* (simple average). To handle this question, you need to be familiar with the formula for calculating the average of a series of numbers. But, notice that the question does not ask for the average, but rather for one of the numbers in the series. This curveball makes the question a bit tougher than most ACT problems involving the concept of simple average.

Step 2: Take a quick look at the answer choices for clues. Notice that the middle three are clustered together in value. So, take a closer look at the two extreme choices: **F** and **K**. Choice **F** would be the correct answer to the question: "What is the difference between 19 and 21?" But this question is asking something entirely different, so you can probably rule out **F** as a "sucker bait" answer choice. **K** might also be a sucker-bait choice, since 20 is simply 19 + 21 divided by 2. If this solution strikes you as too simple, you've got good instincts! The correct answer is probably either **G**, **H**, or **J**. If you're pressed for time, guess one of these, and move on to the next question. Otherwise, go to Step 3.

Alert!

In complex questions, don't look for easy solutions. Problems involving algebraic formulas generally aren't solved simply by adding (or subtracting) a few numbers. Your instinct should tell you to reject easy answers to these kinds of problems.

Step 3: If you're on your "intuitive toes," you might recognize a shortcut to the answer here. You can solve this problem quickly by simply comparing the two *sums*. Before the sixth number is taken away, the sum of the numbers is 114 (6×19). After taking away the sixth number, the sum of the remaining numbers is 105 (5×21). The difference between the two sums is 9, which must be the value of the number taken away.

Step 4: Lacking a burst of intuition (Step 3), you can solve this problem in a conventional (and slower) manner. The formula for arithmetic mean (simple average) can be expressed this way:

$$AM = \frac{\text{sum of terms in the set}}{\text{number of terms in the set}}$$

In the question, you started with six terms. Let a through f equal those six terms:

$$19 = \frac{a + b + c + d + e + f}{6}$$

$$114 = a + b + c + d + e + f$$

$$f = 114 - (a + b + c + d + e)$$

Letting f = the number taken away, here's the arithmetic-mean formula, applied to the remaining five numbers:

$$21 = \frac{a + b + c + d + e}{5}$$

$$105 = a + b + c + d + e$$

Substitute 105 for $(a + b + c + d + e)$ in the first equation:

$$f = 114 - 105$$

$$f = 9$$

The correct answer is H.

Step 5: If you have time, check to make sure you got the formula right, and check your calculations. Also make sure you didn't inadvertently switch the numbers 19 and 21 in your equations. (It's remarkably easy to commit this careless error under time pressure!) If you're satisfied that your analysis is accurate, confirm your answer and move on to the next question.

Question 3

Question 3 is a challenging question. Approximately 40% of test-takers respond correctly to questions like it. Here's the question again:

3. If p pencils cost $2q$ dollars, how many pencils can you buy for c cents? [Note: 1 dollar = 100 cents]

A. $\frac{pc}{2q}$

B. $\frac{pc}{200q}$

C. $\frac{50pc}{q}$

D. $\frac{2pq}{c}$

E. $200pcq$

Step 1: The first step is to recognize that this question involves a *literal expression.* Although it probably won't be too time-consuming, it may be a bit confusing. You should also recognize that the key to this question is the concept of *proportion.* It might be appropriate to set up an equation to solve for c. Along the way, expect to convert dollars into cents.

Step 2: The five answer choices provide a couple useful clues:

- Notice that each answer choice includes all three letters (p, q, and c). So, the solution you're shooting for must also include all three letters.
- Notice that every answer choice but (E) is a fraction. So, anticipate building a fraction to solve the problem algebraically.

Step 3: Is there any way to answer this question besides setting up an algebraic equation? You bet! In fact, there are two ways. One is to use easy numbers for the three variables—for example, $p = 2$, $q = 1$, and $c = 100$. These simple numbers make the question easy to work with: "If 2 pencils cost 2 dollars, how many pencils can you buy for 100 cents?" Obviously, the answer to this question is 1. So, plug in the numbers into each answer choice to see which choice provides an expression that equals 1. Only choice **B** fits the bill: $\frac{(2)(100)}{(200)(1)} = 1$.

Another way to shortcut the algebra is to apply some intuition to this question. If you strip away the pencils, p's, q's and c's, in a very general sense the question is asking:

"If you can by an item for a dollar, how many can you buy for one *cent*?"

Since one cent (a penny) is $\frac{1}{100}$ of a dollar, you can buy $\frac{1}{100}$ of one item for a cent. So, you're probably looking for a fractional answer with a large number in the denominator—something on the order of 100 (as opposed to a number such as 2, 3, or 6). Answer choice **B** is the only choice that appears to be in the right ballpark. As it turns out, choice **B** is indeed the correct answer.

Step 4: You can also answer the question in a conventional manner, using algebra. (This is easier said than done.) Here's how to approach it:

Express $2q$ dollars as $200q$ cents (1 dollar = 100 cents).

Let x equal the number of pencils you can buy for c cents.

Think about the problem "verbally," then set up an equation and solve for x:

"p pencils is to $200q$ cents as x pencils is to c cents."

"The ratio of p to $200q$ is the same as the ratio of x to c" (in other words, the two ratios are proportionate).

$$\frac{p}{200q} = \frac{x}{c}$$

$$\frac{pc}{200q} = x$$

Note

Don't worry if you didn't fully understand the way we set up and solved the equation here. You'll learn more about how to handle ACT proportion questions in a later chapter.

Step 5: Our solution, $\frac{pc}{200q}$, is indeed among the answer choices. If you arrived at this solution using the conventional algebraic approach (Step 4), you can verify your solution by substituting simple numbers for the three variables (as we did in Step 3). Or, if you arrived at your solution by plugging in numbers, you can check your work by plugging in a different set of numbers, or by thinking about the problem conceptually (as in Step 3). Once you're confident you've chosen the correct expression among the five choices, move on to the next question. The correct answer is indeed **B**.

Success Keys for the ACT Mathematics Test

Here are some basic tips you should follow for any type of ACT math question. Apply these "keys" to the ACT-style math tests in Part VI of this book, and then review them again just before test day.

Narrow Down Answer Choices Upfront by Sizing Up the Question

If the question asks for a number value, you can probably narrow down the answer choices by estimating the size and type of number you're looking for. Use your common sense and real-world experience to formulate a ballpark estimate for word problems.

Question 1

You can narrow down answer choices by looking at the problem from a common sense viewpoint. The five answer choices in this question provide some useful clues. Notice that they range in value from 4.8 to 13.0. That's a wide spectrum, isn't it? But what general size should you be looking for in a correct answer to this question? Without crunching any numbers, it's clear that most of the juice will still remain in the bottle, even after lunch. So, you're looking for a value much closer to 13 than to 4. Therefore, you can safely eliminate choices **A** and **B**.

Common Sense Can Sometimes Reveal the Right Answer

In many questions, you can eliminate all but the correct answer without resorting to precise calculations.

Question 1

Look at the question from a broader perspective. If you subtract 10% from a number, then 20% from the result, that adds up to *a bit less* than a 30% decrease from the original number. 30% of 16 ounces is 4.8 ounces. So, the solution must be a number that is a bit larger than 11.2 (16 − 4.8). Choice **D**, 11.5, is the only choice that fits the bill!

Question 3

Notice that c is a much larger number than either p or q. Only a fraction with c in the numerator and a large number in the denominator (or vice versa) is likely to yield a quotient you're looking for. With this in mind, choice **B** jumps off the paper as the likely choice!

Scan the Answer Choices for Clues to Solving the Problem

Scan the answer choices to see what all or most of them have in common—such as radical signs, exponents, factorable expressions, or fractions. Then, try to formulate a solution that looks like the answer choices.

Question 3

Notice that each answer choice includes all three letters (p, q, and c). So, the solution you're aiming for must also include all three letters. Also, notice that every answer but choice (E) is a *fraction*. So, anticipate building a fraction to solve the problem.

Don't Be Reeled in by Too-Obvious, "Sucker-Bait" Answer Choices

The test-makers will intentionally tempt, or "bait," you with wrong-answer choices that result from making common errors in calculation and in setting up and solving equations. Don't assume that your response is correct just because your solution appears among the five answer choices! Rely instead on your sense for whether you understood what the question calls for and performed the calculations and other steps carefully and accurately.

Question 1

In this question, each of the four incorrect choices is "sucker bait":

A. 4.8	You performed the wrong calculation: 30% of 16 ounces = 4.8 ounces
B. 5.5	This is the number of ounces Susan drank. (The question asks for the amount remaining.)
C. 11.2	You performed the wrong calculation: 30% of 16 ounces = 4.8 ounces 16 − 4.8 = 11.2
D. 11.5	This is the correct answer.
E. 13.0	You confused percentages with raw numbers, erroneously converting 30% (10% + 20%) into 3.0: 16 − 3.0 = 13.0

Question 2

This question contains two "sucker bait" answer choices:

F. 2	This would be the correct answer to the question: "What is the difference between 19 and 21?" But this question is asking something entirely different.
K. 20	20 is simply 19 + 21 divided by 2. If this solution strikes you as too simple, you've got good instincts!

Don't Do More Work Than Needed to Get to the Answer

If the question asks for an approximation, that's a huge clue that precise calculations aren't necessary.

Question 1

Notice that each answer choice is carried to exactly one decimal place, and that the question asks for an approximate value. These two features are clues that you can probably round off your calculations to the nearest tenth as you go.

Look for Shortcuts to Conventional Ways of Solving Problems

The adage "There's more than one way to skin a cat" applies to many ACT math questions.

Question 2

You can solve this problem quickly by simply comparing the two *sums*. Before the sixth number is taken away, the sum of the numbers is 114 (6 × 19). After taking away the sixth number, the sum of the remaining numbers is 105 (5 × 21). The difference between the two sums is 9, which must be the value of the number taken away.

Know When to Plug in Numbers for Variables

If the answer choices contain variables (like x and y), the question might be a good candidate for the "plug-in" strategy. Pick simple numbers (so the math is easy), and substitute them for the variables. You'll definitely need your pencil for this strategy.

Question 3

This question was a perfect candidate for the plug-in strategy. Instead of trying to figure out how to set up and solve an algebraic equation, in Step 3 we used easy numbers for the three variables, then plugged those numbers into each answer choice to see which choice worked.

Know When to Work Backward from Numerical Answer Choices

If a math question asks for a number value, and if you draw a blank as far as how to set up and solve the problem, don't panic. You might be able to work backward by testing each answer choice. This might take a bit of time, but if you test the answer choices in random order, the statistical odds are that you'll only need to test three choices to find the correct one.

Question 2

You already learned that comparing the two sums is the quickest shortcut to the answer. But, if this strategy didn't occur to you, working backward from the answer choices would be the next quickest method. After the sixth number is taken away, the sum of the five remaining numbers is $21 \times 5 = 105$. So, to test an answer choice, add this sum to the number provided in the choice, dividing the new sum by 6. If the result is 19, you've found the correct choice. Here's how to do the math for choice C, which is the correct answer choice:

$$\frac{105 + 9}{6} = \frac{114}{6} = 19$$

Tip

ACT math questions always list numerical answer choices in order of value—either ascending or descending. So, if you use the strategy of working backward, start with the median value: choice **C**. If **C** turns out to be incorrect, then figure out whether you need a larger value or a smaller value. This way you'll narrow down the viable choices to two: either **A** and **B** or **C** and **D**. Of course, you might also be able to eliminate an answer choice right away by sizing up the question (a previous strategy). Doing so would make your job even quicker!

Always Check Your Work

Here are three suggestions for doing so:

1. Do a reality check. Ask yourself whether your solution makes sense for what the question asks. (This check is especially appropriate for word problems.)
2. For questions where you solve algebraic equations, plug your solution into the equation(s) to make sure it works.
3. Confirm your calculations (except for the simplest no-brainers) with your calculator. It's amazingly easy to accidentally push the wrong button on the keypad.

Alert!

Checking your calculations is especially crucial for questions asking for an approximation. Why? If your solution doesn't precisely match one of the five answer choices, you might conclude that you should just pick the choice that's closest to your solution—a big mistake if you miscalculated!

Question 1

A reality check on this question will tell you that answer choice C, 11.5, seems about right, but that most of the other choices aren't.

Read the Question One Last Time before Moving On

Among ACT test-takers, simple carelessness in reading a math question is by far the most likely cause of an incorrect answer. So, even if your solution is among the choices, and you're confident that your calculations are accurate, don't move on quite yet. Read the question again. Make sure you answered the precise question asked. For example, does the question ask for:

Arithmetic mean or median?

A circumference or an area?

A sum or a difference?

A perimeter or a length of one side only?

An aggregate rate or a single rate?

Total time or average time?

Also check to make sure you:

- Used the same numbers provided in the question
- Didn't inadvertently switch any numbers or other expressions
- Didn't use raw numbers where percentages were provided, or vice-versa

Question 1

The question asked for the amount of juice remaining, not the amount Susan drank. Also, a careless test-taker might subtract 10 ounces instead of 10%.

Question 2

A careless test-taker might inadvertently switch the numbers 19 and 21.

Question 3

The question asks for an answer in cents, not dollars.

Take It to the Next Level

At this level, you'll:

- Apply to some more challenging math questions some of the success keys you learned at the first level
- Learn additional success keys that apply to certain types of math questions, and apply these keys to example questions

You'll also explore further some of the strategies listed above—applying them to ACT-style questions that are a bit more challenging. You'll also learn some additional strategies that apply to certain types of ACT math questions.

Strategies for Success

Scan the Answer Choices for Clues to Solving the Problem

Scan the answer choices to see what all or most of them have in common—such as radical signs, exponents, factorable expressions, or fractions. Then, try to formulate a solution that looks like the answer choices.

If $a \neq 0$ or 1, then $\dfrac{\frac{1}{a}}{2 - \frac{2}{a}} =$

A. $\dfrac{1}{2a - 2}$

B. $\dfrac{2}{a - 2}$

C. $\dfrac{1}{a - 2}$

D. $\dfrac{1}{a}$

E. $\dfrac{2}{2a - 1}$

The correct answer is A. Notice what all the answer choices have in common: Each one is a fraction in which the denominator contains the variable *a*. And, there are no fractions in either the numerator or the denominator. That's a clue that your job is to manipulate the expression given in the question so that the result includes these features. First, place the denominator's two terms over the common denominator *a*. Then cancel *a* from the denominators of both the numerator fraction and the denominator fraction (this is a shortcut to multiplying the numerator fraction by the reciprocal of the denominator fraction):

$$\frac{\frac{1}{a}}{2-\frac{2}{a}}=\frac{\frac{1}{a}}{\frac{2a-2}{a}}=\frac{1}{2a-2}$$

Use Common-Sense "Guesstimates" to Narrow the Field—But Know the Limits of This Strategy

If the question asks for a numerical value, you can probably narrow down the answer choices by estimating the size and type of number you're looking for. Use your common sense and real-world experience to formulate a ballpark estimate for word problems. But, keep in mind: Don't expect to eliminate all answer choices but the correct one by common sense alone.

A spinner containing seven equal regions numbered 1 through 7 is spun two times in a row. What is the probability that the first spin yields an odd number and the second spin yields an even number?

F. $\frac{2}{7}$

G. $\frac{12}{49}$

H. $\frac{5}{14}$

J. $\frac{1}{2}$

K. $\frac{4}{7}$

The correct answer is G. This problem involves the concept of probability. Common sense about basic probability should tell you that, with odds of *close to* 50% of spinning the desired type of number on each of the two spins, the odds of spinning such a number twice in a row should be less than 50%. So, you can eliminate choices J and (K). Your odds of answering the question correctly are now 1 in 3. But, notice that the remaining choices—F, G, and H—are closely grouped in value. Also notice that, in each of these remaining choices, the denominator contains the sort of number you could end up with when you apply a mathematical operation to the numbers given in the question.

Conclusion: You've probably reached the limits of applying common sense, and you'll need to solve the problem mathematically to zero in on the correct choice. Here's how to do it. There are four odd numbers (1, 3, 5, and 7) and three even numbers (2, 4, and 6) on the spinner. So, the chances of yielding an odd number with the first spin are 4 in 7, or $\frac{4}{7}$. The chances of yielding an even number with the second spin are 3 in 7, or $\frac{3}{7}$. To determine the probability of both events occurring, combine the two individual probabilities by multiplication:

$$\frac{4}{7} \times \frac{3}{7} = \frac{12}{49}$$

Alert!

Notice the "sucker-bait" answer choice in this question. Choice J provides the simple average of the two individual probabilities: $\frac{4}{7}$ and $\frac{3}{7}$. Aside from the fact that $\frac{1}{2}$, or 50%, is too high a probability from a common-sense viewpoint, $\frac{1}{2}$ should strike you as too easy a solution to what appears to be a complex problem.

Know When to Plug in Numbers for Variables

If the answer choices contain variables (like x and y), the question might be a good candidate for the "plug-in" strategy. Pick simple numbers (so the math is easy), and substitute them for the variables. You'll definitely need your pencil for this strategy.

If a train travels $r + 2$ miles in h hours, which of the following represents the number of miles the train travels in 1 hour 30 minutes?

A. $\frac{3r + 6}{2h}$

B. $\frac{3r}{h + 2}$

C. $\frac{r + 2}{h + 3}$

D. $\frac{r}{h + 6}$

E. $\frac{3}{2}(r + 2)$

The correct answer is A. This is an algebraic word problem involving rate of motion (speed). You can solve this problem either conventionally or by using the plug-in strategy.

The conventional way: Notice that all of the answer choices contain fractions. This is a clue that you should try to create a fraction as you solve the problem. Here's how to do it. Given that the train travels $r + 2$ miles in h hours, you can express its rate in miles per hour as $\frac{r+2}{h}$. In $\frac{3}{2}$ hours, the train would travel $\frac{3}{2}$ this distance:

$$\left(\frac{3}{2}\right)\left(\frac{r+2}{h}\right) = \frac{3r+6}{2h}$$

The plug-in strategy: Let $r = 8$ and $h = 1$. Given these values, the train travels 10 miles $(8 + 2)$ in 1 hour. So, obviously, in $1\frac{1}{2}$ hours the train will travel 15 miles. Start plugging these r and h values into the answer choices. You won't need to go any further than choice **A**:

$$\frac{3r+6}{2h} = \frac{3(8)+6}{2(1)} = \frac{30}{2}, \text{ or } 15$$

Even if you had no clue how to handle this question, you could at least eliminate choice (E) out of hand. It omits h! Common sense should tell you that the correct answer must include both r and h.

Know When to Work Backward from Numerical Answer Choices

If a question asks for a number value, and if you draw a blank as far as how to set up and solve the problem, don't panic. You might be able to work backward by testing the answer choices, each one in turn.

A ball is dropped 192 inches above level ground, and after the third bounce, it rises to a height of 24 inches. If the height to which the ball rises after each bounce is always the same fraction of the height reached on its previous bounce, what is this fraction?

F. $\frac{2}{3}$

G. $\frac{1}{2}$

H. $\frac{1}{3}$

J. $\frac{1}{4}$

K. $\frac{1}{8}$

The correct answer is G. The fastest route to a solution is to plug in an answer. Try choice **H**, and see what happens. If the ball bounces up $\frac{1}{3}$ as high as it started, then after the first bounce it will rise up $\frac{1}{3}$ as high as 192 inches, or 64 inches. After a second bounce, it will rise $\frac{1}{3}$ as high, or about 21 inches. But, the problem states that the ball rises to 24 inches after the *third* bounce. Obviously, if the ball rises less than that after two bounces, it'll be way too low after three. So, choice **H** cannot be the correct answer.

We can see that the ball must be bouncing higher than one third of the way; so, the correct answer must be a larger fraction, meaning either choice **F** or choice **G**. You've already narrowed your odds to 50%. Try plugging in choice **G**, and you'll see that it works: $\frac{1}{2}$ of 192 is 96; $\frac{1}{2}$ of 96 is 48; and $\frac{1}{2}$ of 48 is 24.

Although it would be possible to develop a formula to answer the question, doing so would be senseless, considering how quickly and easily you can work backward from the answer choices.

Know When Not to Work Backward from Numerical Answer Choices

Working backward from numerical answer choices works well when the numbers are easy, and when few calculations are required, as in the preceding question. In other cases, applying algebra might be a better way.

How many pounds of nuts selling for 70 cents per pound must be mixed with 30 pounds of nuts selling at 90 cents per pound to make a mixture that sells for 85 cents per pound?

A. 10
B. 12
C. 15
D. 20
E. 24

The correct answer is A. Is the easiest route to the solution to test the answer choices? Let's see. First of all, calculate the total cost of 30 pounds of nuts at 90 cents per pound: $30 \times 0.90 =$ \$27. Now, start with choice **C**: 15 pounds of nuts at 70 cents per pound costs \$10.50. The total cost of this mixture is \$37.50, and the total weight is 45 pounds. Now you'll need to perform some long division. The average weight of the mixture turns out to be between 83 and 84 cents—too low for the 85-cent average given in the question. So, you can at least eliminate choice **C**.

You should realize by now that testing the answer choices might not be the most efficient way to tackle this question. Besides, there are ample opportunities for calculation errors. Instead, try solving this problem algebraically—by writing and solving a system of equations. Here's how to do it. The cost (in cents) of the nuts selling for 70 cents per pound can be expressed as $70x$, letting x equal the number that you're asked to determine. You then add this cost to the cost of

Take It to the Next Level

the more expensive nuts ($30 \times 90 = 2{,}700$) to obtain the total cost of the mixture, which you can express as $85(x + 30)$. You can state this algebraically and solve for x as follows:

$$70x + 2700 = 85(x + 30)$$
$$70x + 2700 = 85x + 2550$$
$$150 = 15x$$
$$10 = x$$

10 pounds of 70-cent-per-pound nuts must be added in order to make a mixture that sells for 85 cents per pound.

Avoid Heavy Lifting; Look for the Easiest Route to the Answer

If the question asks for an approximation, then you know that precise calculations won't be necessary, and you can safely "round off" the numbers as you go. But, even in other questions, you can sometimes eliminate all but the correct answer without resorting to precise calculations.

What is the difference between the sum of all positive even integers less than 102 and the sum of all positive odd integers less than 102?

F. 0
G. 1
H. 50
J. 51
K. 101

The correct answer is J. To see the pattern, compare the initial terms of each sequence:

even integers: {2,4,6, . . . ,100}

odd integers: {1,3,5, . . . , 99,101}

Notice that, for each successive term, the odd integer is one less than the corresponding even integer. There are a total of 50 corresponding integers, so the difference between the sums of all these corresponding integers is 50. But, the odd-integer sequence includes one additional integer: 101. So, the difference is $(-50 + 101)$, or 51.

If a Geometry Problem Provides a Figure, Mine It for Clues

Most geometry problems are accompanied by figures. They're there for a reason! The pieces of information a figure provides can lead you, step-by-step, to the answer.

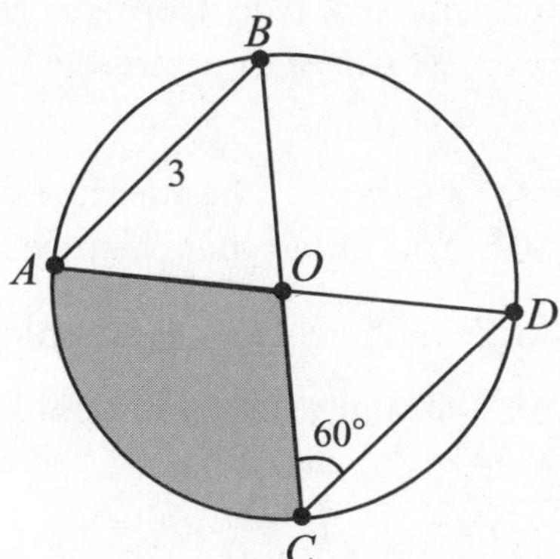

If O is the center of the circle in the figure above, what is the area of the shaded region, expressed in square units?

A. $\frac{3}{2}\pi$

B. 2π

C. $\frac{5}{2}\pi$

D. $\frac{8}{3}\pi$

E. 3π

The correct answer is E. This question asks for the area of a portion of the circle defined by a central angle. To answer the question, you'll need to determine the area of the entire circle as well as what percent (portion) of that area is shaded. This multi-step question is as complex as any you might encounter on the ACT. But, there's no need to panic; just start with what you know, then move step-by-step toward the answer. Mine the figure for a piece of information that might provide a starting point. ΔOCD is your first "stepping stone." Here are the steps to the answer:

1. You know that $\overline{OC}$ and $\overline{OD}$ are congruent (equal in length) because each one is the circle's radius. In any triangle, angles opposite congruent sides are also congruent (the same size, or degree measure). Thus, $\angle ODC$ must measure 60°—just like $\angle OCD$.
2. For any triangle, the sum of the measures of all three interior angles is 180°. Thus, $\angle COD$ measures 60°, just like the other two angles.
3. Vertical angles created by two intersecting lines are congruent. Thus, $\angle AOB$ also measures 60°.

Take It to the Next Level

4. By the same reasoning as in steps 1 and 2, each angle of ΔABO measures 60°. Notice that the length of $\overline{AB}$ is given as 3. Accordingly, the length of each and every side of both triangles is 3.
5. Since this length (3) is also the circle's radius (the distance from its center to its circumference), you can determine the circle's area. The area of any circle is πr^2, where r is the circle's radius. Thus, the area of the circle is 9π.
6. Now determine what portion of the circle's area is shaded. The measures of the four angles formed at the circle's center (O) total 360°. You know that the measures of two of these angles account for 120°, or $\frac{1}{3}$ of those 360°. $\angle AOC$ is supplementary to $\angle DOC$; that is, the two angles combine to form a straight line, and so their measures total 180°. Thus, $\angle AOC$ measures 120°.
7. 120° is $\frac{1}{3}$ of 360°. Thus, the shaded portion accounts for $\frac{1}{3}$ the circle's area, or 3π.

Tip

If you look at the 60° angle in the figure, you might recognize right away that both triangles are equilateral and, extended out to their arcs, form two "pie slices," each one $\frac{1}{6}$ the size of the whole "pie" (the circle). What's left are two big slices, each of which is twice the size of a small slice. So, the shaded area must account for $\frac{1}{3}$ the circle's area. With this intuition, the problem is reduced to the simple mechanics of calculating the circle's area, then dividing it by 3.

If a Geometry Problem Doesn't Provide a Figure, Sketch One

A geometry problem that does not provide a diagram might cry out for one. That's your cue to take pencil to scratch paper and draw one for yourself.

A rancher uses 64 feet of fencing to create a rectangular horse corral. If the ratio of the corral's length to width is 3:1, which of the following most closely approximates the minimum length of additional fencing needed to divide the rectangular corral into three triangular corrals, one of which is exactly twice the area of the other two?

F. 48 feet
G. 41 feet
H. 36 feet
J. 29 feet
K. 24 feet

The correct answer is J. Your first step is to determine the dimensions of the rectangular corral. Given a 3:1 length-to-width ratio, you can solve for the width (w) of the field using the perimeter formula:

$$2(3w) + 2(w) = 64$$
$$8w = 64$$
$$w = 8$$

Accordingly, the length of the rectangular corral is 24 feet. Next, determine how the rancher must configure the additional fencing to meet the stated criteria. This calls for a bit of sketching to help you visualize the dimensions. One possible configuration creates three triangular corrals with the desired ratios:

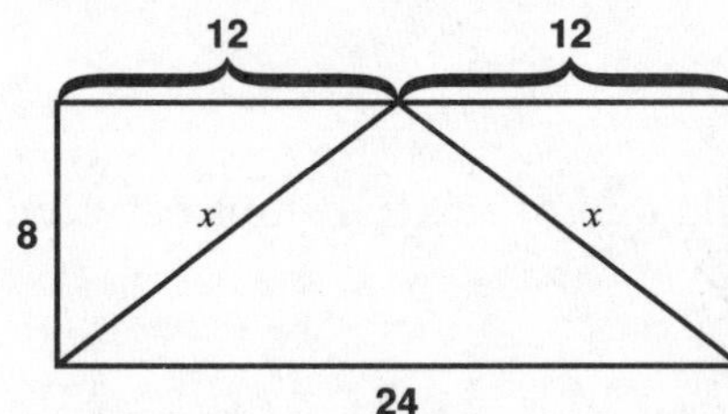

You can calculate each length (using the Pythagorean theorem). Or, you can also use logic and visualization. Here's how. As a rectangle becomes flatter ("less square"), the shorter length approaches zero (0), at which point the minimum amount of fencing needed in this configuration would decrease, approaching the length of the longer side.

Your final step is to calculate the amount of fencing required by the above figure, applying the Pythagorean theorem (let x = either length of cross-fencing):

$$8^2 + 12^2 = x^2$$
$$64 + 144 = x^2$$
$$208 = x^2$$
$$x = \sqrt{208} \approx 14.4$$

Thus, a minimum of approximately 28.8 feet of fencing is needed. Choice J approximates this solution.

Since the question asks for an approximation, it's a safe bet that estimating $\sqrt{208}$ to the nearest integer will suffice. If you learned your "times table," you know that $14 \times 14 = 196$, and $15 \times 15 = 225$. So, $\sqrt{208}$ must be between 14 and 15. That's close enough to zero in on choice J, which provides twice that estimate, as the best answer choice.

Chapter 8

Number Forms, Relationships, and Sets

In this chapter, you'll focus on various forms of numbers and of relationships between numbers. Specifically, you'll learn how to:

- Combine fractions using the four basic operations
- Combine decimal numbers by multiplication and division
- Compare numbers in percentage terms
- Compare percent changes with number changes
- Convert percents, fractions, and decimal numbers from one form to another
- Determine ratios between quantities and determining quantities from ratios
- Set up equivalent ratios (proportions)

Then, you'll explore the following topics, all of which involve sets (defined groups) of numbers or other objects:

- Simple average and median (two ways that a set of numbers can be measured as a whole)
- Arithmetic series (the pattern from one number to the next in a linear sequence of numbers)
- Permutations (the possibilities for arranging a set of objects)
- Combinations (the possibilities for selecting groups of objects from a set)
- Probability (the statistical chances of a certain event, permutation, or combination occurring)
- Matrices (operations on rectangular arrays of numbers)
- *Take It to the Next Level*

Alert!

Although this chapter is the most basic of all the math reviews in this book, don't think for a minute that you should skip this chapter. The skills covered here are basic building blocks for other types of questions, the ones you'll encounter in the chapters to follow.

Percent, Fraction, and Decimal Conversions

Any real number can be expressed as a fraction, a percent, or a decimal number. For instance, $\frac{2}{10}$, 20 percent, and 0.2 are different forms of the same quantity, or value. ACT math questions often require you to convert one form to another as part of solving the problem at hand. You should know how to make any conversion quickly and confidently.

For percent-to-decimal conversions, move the decimal point two places to the *left* (and drop the percent sign). For decimal-to-percent conversions, move the decimal point two places to the *right* (and add the percent sign).

$9.5\% = 0.095$

$0.004 = 0.4\%$

For percent-to-fraction conversions, *divide* by 100 (and drop the percent sign). For fraction-to-percent conversions, *multiply* by 100 (and add the percent sign). Percents greater than 100 convert to numbers greater than 1.

$$810\% = \frac{810}{100} = \frac{81}{10} = 8\frac{1}{10}$$

$$\frac{3}{8} = \frac{300}{8}\% = \frac{75}{2}\% = 37\frac{1}{2}\%$$

Alert!

Percents greater than 100 or less than 1 (such as 457% and 0.067%, respectively) can be confusing, because it's a bit harder to grasp the size of these numbers. To guard against conversion errors, keep in mind the general size of the number you're dealing with. For example, think of 0.09% as just under 0.1%, which is one-tenth of a percent, or a thousandth (a pretty small number). Think of $\frac{0.4}{5}$ as just under $\frac{0.5}{5}$, which is obviously $\frac{1}{10}$, or 10%. Think of 668% as more than 6 times a complete 100% or between 6 and 7.

To convert a fraction to a decimal number, simply divide numerator by denominator, using long division or your calculator. A fraction-to-decimal conversion might result in a precise value, an approximation with a repeating pattern, or an approximation with no repeating pattern:

$\frac{5}{8} = 0.625$	The equivalent decimal number is precise after three decimal places.
$\frac{5}{9} \approx 0.555$	The equivalent decimal number can only be approximated (the digit 5 repeats indefinitely).
$\frac{5}{7} \approx 0.714$	The equivalent decimal number can only be approximated (there is no repeating pattern by carrying the calculation to additional decimal places).

Certain fraction-decimal-percent equivalents show up on the ACT more often than others. The numbers in the following tables are the test-makers' favorites because they reward test-takers who recognize quick ways to deal with numbers. Memorize these conversions, so that they're second nature to you on exam day.

Percent	Decimal	Fraction
50%	0.5	$\frac{1}{2}$
25%	0.25	$\frac{1}{4}$
75%	0.75	$\frac{3}{4}$
10%	0.1	$\frac{1}{10}$
30%	0.3	$\frac{3}{10}$
70%	0.7	$\frac{7}{10}$
90%	0.9	$\frac{9}{10}$
$33\frac{1}{3}\%$	$0.33\frac{1}{3}$	$\frac{1}{3}$
$66\frac{2}{3}\%$	$0.66\frac{2}{3}$	$\frac{2}{3}$

Percent	Decimal	Fraction
$16\frac{2}{3}\%$	$0.16\frac{2}{3}$	$\frac{1}{6}$
$83\frac{1}{3}\%$	$0.83\frac{1}{3}$	$\frac{5}{6}$
20%	0.2	$\frac{1}{5}$
40%	0.4	$\frac{2}{5}$
60%	0.6	$\frac{3}{5}$
80%	0.8	$\frac{4}{5}$
$12\frac{1}{2}\%$	0.125	$\frac{1}{8}$
$37\frac{1}{2}\%$	0.375	$\frac{3}{8}$
$62\frac{1}{2}\%$	0.625	$\frac{5}{8}$
$87\frac{1}{2}\%$	0.875	$\frac{7}{8}$

Simplifying and Combining Fractions

An ACT question might ask you to combine fractions using one or more of the four basic operations (addition, subtraction, multiplication, and division). The rules for combining fractions by addition and subtraction are very different from the ones for multiplication and division.

Addition and Subtraction, and the LCD

To combine fractions by addition or subtraction, the fractions *must* have a common denominator. If they already do, simply add (or subtract) numerators. If they don't, you'll need to find one. You can always multiply all of the denominators together to find a common denominator, but it might be a big number that's clumsy to work with. Instead, try to find the *least (or lowest) common denominator* (LCD) by working your way up in multiples of the largest of the denominators given. For denominators of 6, 3, and 5, for instance, try out successive multiples of 6 (6, 12, 18, 24, . . .), and you'll hit the LCD when you get to 30.

$\frac{5}{3} - \frac{5}{6} + \frac{5}{2} =$

A. $\frac{15}{1}$

B. $\frac{5}{2}$

C. $\frac{15}{6}$

D. $\frac{10}{3}$

E. $\frac{15}{3}$

The correct answer is D. To find the LCD, try out successive multiples of 6 until you come across one that is also a multiple of both 3 and 2. The LCD is 6. Multiply each numerator by the same number by which you would multiply the fraction's denominator to give you the LCD of 6. Place the three products over this common denominator. Then, combine the numbers in the numerator. (Pay close attention to the subtraction sign!) Finally, simplify to lowest terms:

$$\frac{5}{3} - \frac{5}{6} + \frac{5}{2} = \frac{(5)(2) - (5)(1) + (5)(3)}{6} = \frac{10 - 5 + 15}{6}, \text{ or } \frac{10}{3}$$

Multiplication and Division

To multiply fractions, first multiply the numerators, and then multiply the denominators. The denominators need not be the same. To divide one fraction by another, multiply by the reciprocal of the divisor (the number after the division sign).

Multiplication	Division
$\frac{1}{2} \times \frac{5}{3} \times \frac{1}{7} = \frac{(1)(5)(1)}{(2)(3)(7)} = \frac{5}{42}$	$\frac{\frac{2}{5}}{\frac{3}{4}} = \frac{2}{5} \times \frac{4}{3} = \frac{(2)(4)}{(5)(3)} = \frac{8}{15}$

To simplify the multiplication or division, cancel factors common to a numerator and a denominator before combining fractions. It's okay to cancel across fractions. Take, for instance, the operation $\frac{3}{4} \times \frac{4}{9} \times \frac{3}{2}$. Looking just at the first two fractions, you can factor out 4 and 3, so the operation simplifies to $\frac{1}{1} \times \frac{1}{3} \times \frac{3}{2}$. Now, looking just at the second and third fractions, you can factor out 3, and the operation becomes even simpler: $\frac{1}{1} \times \frac{1}{1} \times \frac{1}{2} = \frac{1}{2}$.

Apply the same rules in the same way to variables (letters) as to numbers.

$\frac{2}{a} \times \frac{b}{4} \times \frac{a}{5} \times \frac{8}{c} =$

F. $\frac{ab}{4c}$

G. $\frac{10b}{9c}$

H. $\frac{8}{5}$

J. $\frac{16b}{5ac}$

K. $\frac{4b}{5c}$

The correct answer is K. Since you're dealing only with multiplication, look for factors and variables (letters) in any numerator that are the same as those in any denominator. Canceling common factors leaves $\frac{2}{1} \times \frac{b}{1} \times \frac{1}{5} \times \frac{2}{c}$. Combine numerators, then combine denominators, which gives you $\frac{4b}{5c}$.

Mixed Numbers and Multiple Operations

A *mixed number* consists of a whole number along with a simple fraction—for example, the number $4\frac{2}{3}$. Before combining fractions, you might need to convert the mixed number to simple fractions. To do so, follow these three steps:

1. Multiply the denominator of the fraction by the whole number.
2. Add the product to the numerator of the fraction.
3. Place the sum over the denominator of the fraction.

For example, here's how to convert the mixed number $4\frac{2}{3}$ to a simple fraction:

$$4\frac{2}{3} = \frac{(3)(4) + 2}{3} = \frac{14}{3}.$$

To perform multiple operations, always perform multiplication and division before you perform addition and subtraction.

$$\frac{4\frac{1}{2}}{1\frac{1}{8}} - 3\frac{2}{3} =$$

A. $\frac{1}{3}$

B. $\frac{3}{8}$

C. $\frac{11}{6}$

D. $\frac{17}{6}$

E. $\frac{11}{2}$

The correct answer is A. First, convert all mixed numbers to fractions. Then, eliminate the complex fraction by multiplying the numerator fraction by the reciprocal of the denominator fraction (cancel across fractions before multiplying):

$$\frac{\frac{9}{2}}{\frac{9}{8}} - \frac{11}{3} = \left(\frac{9}{2}\right)\left(\frac{8}{9}\right) - \frac{11}{3} = \left(\frac{1}{1}\right)\left(\frac{4}{1}\right) - \frac{11}{3} = \frac{4}{1} - \frac{11}{3}$$

Then, express each fraction using the common denominator 3, then subtract:

$$\frac{4}{1} - \frac{11}{3} = \frac{12 - 11}{3} = \frac{1}{3}$$

Place Value and Operations with Decimal Numbers

Place value refers to the specific value of a digit in a decimal number. For example, in the decimal number 682.793:

The digit 6 is in the "hundreds" place.

The digit 8 is in the "tens" place.

The digit 2 is in the "ones" place.

The digit 7 is in the "tenths" place.

The digit 9 is in the "hundredths" place.

The digit 3 is in the "thousandths" place.

So, you can express 682.793 as follows:

$$600 + 80 + 2 + \frac{7}{10} + \frac{9}{100} + \frac{3}{1{,}000}.$$

To approximate, or round off, a decimal number, round any digit less than 5 down to 0, and round any digit greater than 5 up to 0 (adding one digit to the place value to the left). So, for 682.793:

The value of 682.793, to the nearest hundredth, is 682.79.

The value of 682.793, to the nearest tenth, is 682.8.

The value of 682.793, to the nearest whole number, is 683.

The value of 682.793, to the nearest ten, is 680.

The value of 682.793, to the nearest hundred, is 700.

To combine decimal numbers by either multiplication or division, you can use your calculator, of course. But, you should always check your calculator-work with your brain-work.

Multiplying decimal numbers. The number of decimal places (digits to the right of the decimal point) in a product should be the same as the total number of decimal places in the numbers you multiply. So, to multiply decimal numbers quickly:

1. Multiply, but ignore the decimal points.
2. Count the total number of decimal places among the numbers you multiplied.
3. Include that number of decimal places in your product.

Here are two simple examples:

(23.6)(0.07)	3 decimal places altogether
(236)(7) = 1652	Decimals temporarily ignored
(23.6)(0.07) = 1.652	Decimal point inserted

(0.01)(0.02)(0.03)	6 decimal places altogether
(1)(2)(3) = 6	Decimals temporarily ignored
(0.01)(0.02)(0.03) = 0.000006	Decimal point inserted

Dividing decimal numbers. When you divide (or compute a fraction), you can move the decimal point in both numbers by the same number of places either to the left or right without altering the quotient (value of the fraction). Here are three related examples:

$$11.4 \div 0.3 = \frac{11.4}{0.3} = \frac{114}{3} = 38$$

$$1.14 \div 3 = \frac{1.14}{3} = \frac{114}{300} = 0.38$$

$$114 \div 0.03 = \frac{114}{0.03} = \frac{11{,}400}{3} = 3{,}800$$

Eliminate decimal points from fractions, as well as from percents, to help you see the general size of the quantity you're dealing with.

ACT questions involving place value and decimal numbers usually require a bit more from you than just identifying a place value or moving around a decimal point. Typically, they require you to combine decimal numbers with fractions or percents. Although your calculator might help you make certain calculations along the way, the best way to solve these problems is by doing some brain-work as well.

Which of the following is nearest in value to $\frac{1}{3} \times 0.3 \times \frac{1}{30} \times 0.03$?

F. $\frac{99}{10{,}000}$

G. $\frac{33}{10{,}000}$

H. $\frac{99}{100{,}000}$

J. $\frac{33}{100{,}000}$

K. $\frac{99}{1{,}000{,}000}$

The correct answer is K. There are several ways to convert and combine the four numbers provided in the question. Here's one method: First, combine the two fractions: $\frac{1}{3} \times \frac{1}{30} = \frac{1}{90} \approx 0.011$. Then, combine the two decimal numbers: $0.3 \times 0.03 = 0.009$. Finally, combine the two products $0.011 \times 0.009 \approx 0.000099$. Each answer choice expresses a fraction, so you need to convert 0.000099 to a fraction by carefully counting place values. The final digit is in the "millionth" place. Choice (K) provides the fractional equivalent of this number.

Simple Problems Involving Percent

On the ACT, a simple problem involving percent might ask you to perform any one of these four tasks:

1. Find a % of a %.
2. Find a % of a number.
3. Find a number when a % is given.
4. Find what % one number is of another.

The following examples show you how to handle these four different tasks (task 4 is a bit trickier than the others):

1. Find a % of a %.	*What is 2% of 2%?* Convert 2% to 0.02, and then multiply: $0.02 \times 0.02 = 0.0004$, or 0.04%
2. Find a % of a number.	*What is 35% of 65?* Convert 35% to 0.35, and then multiply: $0.35 \times 65 = 22.75$
3. Find a number when a % is given.	*7 is 14% of what number?* Translate the question into an algebraic equation, writing the % as either a fraction or decimal: $7 = 14\% \text{ of } x$ $7 = 0.14x$ $x = \frac{7}{0.14} = \frac{1}{0.02} = \frac{100}{2} = 50$
4. Find what % one number is of another.	*90 is what % of 1,500?* Set up an equation to solve for the percent: $\frac{90}{1{,}500} = \frac{x}{100}$ $1{,}500x = 9{,}000$ $15x = 90$ $x = \frac{90}{15}$, or 6

Percent Increase and Decrease

The concept of percent change is one of the test-makers' favorites. Here's the key to answering questions involving this concept: Percent change always relates to the value *before* the change. Here are two simple illustrations:

10 increased by what percent is 12?	12 decreased by what percent is 10?
1. The amount of the increase is 2.	1. The amount of the decrease is 2.
2. Compare the change (2) to the original number (10).	2. Compare the change (2) to the original number (12).
3. The change in percent is $\frac{2}{10}$, or 20%.	3. The change is $\frac{2}{12}$, or $\frac{1}{6}$, or approximately 16.6% (Did you remember from the conversion table on page 152 that $\frac{1}{6} = 16\frac{2}{3}\%$?

Notice that the percent increase from 10 to 12 (20%) is not the same as the percent decrease from 12 to 10 ($16\frac{2}{3}\%$). That's because the original number (before the change) is different in the two questions.

A typical ACT percent-change problem will involve a story—about a type of quantity such as tax, profit or discount, or weight—in which you need to calculate successive changes in percent:

- An increase, then a decrease (or vice versa)
- Multiple increases or decreases

Whatever the variation, just take the problem one step at a time, and you'll have no trouble handling it.

A stereo system originally priced at $500 is discounted by 10%, then by another 10%. If a 20% tax is added to the purchase price, how much would a customer buying the system at its lowest price pay for it, including tax, to the nearest dollar?

A. $512
B. $500
C. $486
D. $480
E. $413

The correct answer is C. After the first 10% discount, the price was $450 ($500 minus 10% of $500). After the second discount, which is calculated based on the $450 price; the price of the stereo is $405 ($450 minus 10% of $450). A 20% tax on $405 is $81. Thus, the customer has paid $405 + $81 = $486.

A percent-change problem might also involve an accompanying chart or graph, which provides the numbers needed for the calculation.

Based on the graph below, the average low price of Holden Software stock for the two-year period 1993–1994 was approximately what percent lower than its average high price for the two-year period 1996–1997?

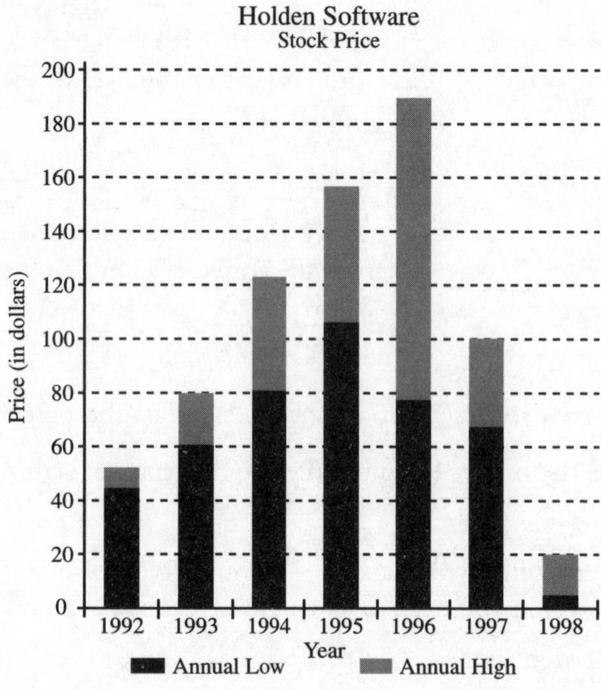

F. 25
G. 37
H. 45
J. 52
K. 75

The correct answer is J. Average *low* prices (represented by black bars) for 1993 and 1994 were \$60 and \$80, respectively, which yield an average of \$70 for the two-year period. Average *high* prices (represented by gray bars) for 1996 and 1997 were approximately \$190 and \$100, respectively, which yield an average of \$145. The percent decrease from \$145 to \$70 is just over 50%. The only viable answer choice is J.

If a question based on a bar graph, line graph, or pie chart asks for an approximation, the test-makers are telling you that it's okay to round off numbers you glean from the chart or graph. For example, in the preceding question, a rough estimate of \$145 for the high 1996–1997 average was close enough to determine the correct answer choice.

Ratios and Proportion

A *ratio* expresses proportion or comparative size—the size of one quantity *relative to* the size of another. As with fractions, you can reduce ratios to lowest terms by canceling common factors. For example, given a class of 28 students—12 freshmen and 16 sophomores:

- The ratio of freshmen to sophomores is 12:16, or 3:4.
- The ratio of freshmen to the total number of students is 12:28, or 3:7.
- The ratio of sophomores to the total number of students is 16:28, or 4:7.

Finding a Ratio

An ACT question might ask you to determine a ratio based on given quantities. This is the easiest type of ACT ratio question.

A class of 56 students contains only freshmen and sophomores. If 21 of the students are sophomores, what is the ratio between the number of freshmen and the number of sophomores in the class?

A. 2:1
B. 7:4
C. 5:3
D. 5:7
E. 3:5

The correct answer is C. Since 21 of 56 students are sophomores, 35 must be freshmen. The ratio of freshmen to sophomores is 35:21. To reduce the ratio to lowest terms, divide both numbers by 7, giving you a ratio of 5:3.

Determining Quantities from a Ratio (Part-to-Whole Analysis)

You can think of any ratio as parts adding up to a whole. For example, in the ratio 5:6, 5 parts + 6 parts = 11 parts (the whole). If the actual total quantity were 22, you'd multiply each element by 2: 10 parts + 12 parts = 22 parts (the whole). Notice that the ratios are the same: 5:6 is the same ratio as 10:12.

You might be able to solve an ACT ratio question using this part-to-whole approach.

A class of students contains only freshmen and sophomores. If 18 of the students are sophomores, and if the ratio between the number of freshmen and the number of sophomores in the class is 5:3, how many students altogether are in the class?

F. 30
G. 36
H. 40
J. 48
K. 56

The correct answer is J. Using a part-to-whole analysis, look first at the ratio and the sum of its parts: 5 (freshman) + 3 (sophomores) = 8 (total students). These aren't the actual quantities, but they're proportionate to those quantities. Given 18 sophomores altogether, sophomores account for 3 parts—each part containing 6 students. Accordingly, the total number of students must be $6 \times 8 = 48$.

Determining Quantities from a Ratio (Setting Up a Proportion)

Since you can express any ratio as a fraction, you can set two equivalent, or proportionate, ratios equal to each other, as fractions. So, the ratio 16:28 is proportionate to the ratio 4:7 because $\frac{16}{28} = \frac{4}{7}$. If one of the four terms is missing from the equation (the proportion), you can solve for the missing term using algebra. So, if the ratio 3:4 is proportionate to 4:x, you can solve for x in the equation $\frac{3}{4} = \frac{4}{x}$. Using the *cross-product* method, equate product of numerator and denominator across the equation:

$$(3)(x) = (4)(4)$$

$$3x = 16$$

$$x = \frac{16}{3}, \text{ or } 5\frac{1}{3}$$

Or, since the numbers are simple, shortcut the algebra by asking yourself what number you multiply the first numerator (3) by for a result that equals the other numerator (4):

$3 \times \frac{4}{3} = 4$ (a no-brainer calculation)

So, you maintain proportion (equal ratios) by also multiplying the first denominator (4) by: $4 \times \frac{4}{3} = \frac{16}{3}$ (another no-brainer calculation)

Even if the quantities in a question strike you as decidedly "unround," it's a good bet that doing the math will be easier than you might think at first.

If 3 miles are equivalent to 4.83 kilometers, then 11.27 kilometers are equivalent to how many miles?

A. 16.1
B. 8.4
C. 7.0
D. 5.9
E. 1.76

The correct answer is C. The question essentially asks: "3 is to 4.83 as *what* is to 11.27?" Set up a proportion, then solve for x by the cross-product method:

$$\frac{3}{4.83} = \frac{x}{11.27}$$
$$(4.83)(x) = (3)(11.27)$$
$$x = \frac{(3)(11.27)}{4.83}$$
$$x = \frac{33.81}{4.83}, \text{ or } 7$$

Notice that, despite all the intimidating decimal numbers, the solution turns out to be a nice tidy number: 7. That's typical of the ACT.

Simple Average (Arithmetic Mean)

For any set of terms, the *arithmetic mean* (*AM*), also called the *simple average*, is the sum of the terms $(a + b + c + \ldots)$ divided by the number of terms (n) in the set.

$$AM = \frac{(a + b + c + \ldots)}{n}$$

For example, here's how to calculate the average of the six terms {8, −4, 8, 3, 2, 7}:

$$AM = \frac{(8 - 4 + 8 + 3 + 2 + 7)}{6} = \frac{24}{6}, \text{ or } 4$$

Note

The *median* is the middle term in value if the set contains an odd number of terms, or the arithmetic mean (average) of the two middle terms if the set contains an even number of terms. So, the median of the set of six measurements {8, −4, 8, 3, 2, 7} is 5, which is the average of 3 and 7—the two middle measurements in the set ordered in this way: {−4, 2, 3, 7, 8, 8}.

In finding a simple average, be sure the numbers being added are all of the same form or in terms of the same units.

What is the average of $\frac{1}{5}$, 25%, and 0.09?

F. 0.18

G. 20%

H. $\frac{1}{4}$

J. 0.32

K. $\frac{1}{3}$

The correct answer is F. Since the answer choices are not all expressed in the same form, first convert numbers into whichever form you think would be easiest to work with when you add the numbers together. In this case, the easiest form to work with is probably the decimal-number form. So, convert the first two numbers into decimal form, and then find the sum of the three numbers: $0.20 + 0.25 + 0.09 = 0.54$. Finally, divide by 3 to find the average: $0.54 \div 3 = 0.18$.

To find a missing number when the average of all the numbers in a set is given, plug into the arithmetic-mean formula all the numbers you know, which include the average, the sum of the other numbers, and the number of terms. Then, use algebra to find the missing number. Or, you can try out each answer choice, in turn, as the missing number until you find one that results in the average that's given.

The average of five numbers is 26. Four of the numbers are −12, 90, −26, and 10. What is the fifth number?

A. 84
B. 68
C. 44
D. 42
E. 16

The correct answer is B. To solve the problem algebraically, let x = the missing number. Set up the arithmetic-mean formula, then solve for x:

$$26 = \frac{(90 + 10 - 12 - 26) + x}{5}$$

$$26 = \frac{62 + x}{5}$$

$$130 = 62 + x$$

$$68 = x$$

Or, you can try out each answer choice, in turn. Start with the middle value, 44, choice **C**. The sum of 44 and the other four numbers is 106. Dividing this sum by 5 gives you 21.2, a number smaller than the average of 26 that you're aiming for. So, you know the fifth number is greater than 44—and that leaves choices **A** and **B** as the only two viable ones. Try out the number 68, choice **B**, and you'll obtain the average of 26.

If the numbers are easy to work with, you might be able to determine a missing term, given the simple average of a set of numbers, without resorting to algebra, by simply applying a dose of logic.

If the average of six consecutive multiples of 4 is 22, what is the largest of these integers?

A. 22
B. 24
C. 26
D. 28
E. 32

The correct answer is E. You can answer this question with common sense—no algebra is required. Consecutive multiples of 4 are 4, 8, 12, 16, . . . Given that the average of six such numbers is 22, the two middle terms (the third and fourth terms) must be 20 and 24. (Their average is 22.) Accordingly, the fifth term is 28, and the sixth, and largest term, is 32.

Arithmetic Series

In an *arithmetic series* of numbers, there is a constant (unchanging) difference between successive numbers in the series. In other words, all numbers in an arithmetic series are evenly spaced apart. All of the following are examples of an arithmetic series:

- Successive integers
- Successive even integers
- Successive odd integers
- Successive multiples of the same number
- Successive integers ending in the same digit

On the ACT, questions involving an arithmetic series might ask for the average or the sum of a series. When the numbers to be averaged form an arithmetic (evenly spaced) series, the average is simply the middle number (or the average of the two middle numbers if the number of terms is even). In other words, the mean and median of the set of numbers are the same. So, faced with calculating the average of a long series of evenly spaced integers, you can shortcut the addition.

What is the average of the first 20 positive integers?

F. $7\frac{1}{2}$

G. 10

H. $10\frac{1}{2}$

J. 15

K. 20

The correct answer is H. Since the terms are evenly spaced, the average is halfway between the 10th and 11th terms, which happen to be the integers 10 and 11. So, the average is $10\frac{1}{2}$. (This number is also the median.) If you take the average of the first term (1) and the last term (20), you get the same result: $\frac{1+20}{2} = \frac{21}{2}$, or $10\frac{1}{2}$.

Finding the sum (rather than the average) of an arithmetic (evenly spaced) series of numbers requires only one additional step: multiplying the average (which is also the median) by the number of terms in the series. The trickiest aspect of this type of question is determining the number of terms in the series.

What is the sum of all odd integers between 10 and 40?

A. 450
B. 400
C. 375
D. 325
E. 250

The correct answer is C. The average of the described numbers is 25, halfway between 10 and 40 (in other words, half the sum of 10 and 40). The number of terms in the series is 15. (The first term is 11, and the last term is 39.) The sum of the described series of integers $= 25 \times 15 = 375$.

Alert!

When calculating the average or sum of a series of evenly spaced numbers, be careful when counting the number of terms in the series. For instance, the number of positive *odd* integers less than 50 is 25, but the number of positive *even* integers less than 50 is only 24.

Permutations

A *permutation* is an arrangement of objects in which their order (sequence) is important. Each arrangement of the letters A, B, C, and D, for example, is a different permutation of the four letters. There are two different ways to determine the number of permutations for a group of objects.

1. List all the permutations, using a methodical process to make sure you don't overlook any. For the letters A, B, C, and D, start with A in the first position, then list all possibilities for the second position, along with all possibilities for the third and fourth positions (you'll discover six permutations):

A *B* C D A *B* D C	A *C* B D A *C* D B	A *D* B C A *D* C B

Placing B in the first position would also result in 6 permutations. The same applies to either C or D in the first position. So, the total number of permutations is $6 \times 4 = 24$.

2. Use the following formula (let n = the number of objects), and limit the number of terms to the counting numbers, or positive integers:

$$\text{Number of permutations} = n(n - 1)(n - 2)(n - 3) \ldots$$

The number of permutations can be expressed as $n!$ ("n factorial"). Using the factorial formula is much easier than compiling a list of permutations. For example, try applying the formula to the letters A, B, C, and D:

$$4! = 4(4 - 1)(4 - 2)(4 - 3) = 4 \times 3 \times 2 \times 1 = 24$$

Five tokens—one red, one blue, one green, and two white—are arranged in a row, one next to another. If the two white tokens are next to each other, how many arrangements according to color are possible?

F. 12
G. 16
H. 20
J. 24
K. 30

The correct answer is J. The two white tokens might be in positions 1 and 2, 2 and 3, 3 and 4, or 4 and 5. For each of these four possibilities, there are 6 possible color arrangements (3!) for the other three tokens (which all differ in color). Thus, the total number of possible arrangements is 4×6, or 24.

You can shortcut common factorial calculations by memorizing them: 3! = 6, 4! = 24, and 5! = 120.

Combinations

A *combination* is a group of certain objects selected from a larger set. The order of objects in the group is not important. You can determine the total number of possible combinations by listing the possible groups in a methodical manner. For instance, to determine the number of possible three-letter groups among the letters A, B, C, D, and E, work methodically, starting with A as a group member paired with B, then C, then D, then E. Be sure not to repeat combinations (repetitions are indicated in parentheses here):

A, B, C	(A, C, B)	(A, D, B)	(A, E, B)
A, B, D	A, C, D	(A, D, C)	(A, E, C)
A, B, E	A, C, E	A, D, E	(A, E, D)

Perform the same task assuming B is in the group, then assuming C is in the group (all combinations not listed here repeat what's already listed):

B, C, D	C, D, E
B, C, E	
B, D, E	

So, the total number of combinations is 10.

How many two-digit numbers can be formed from the digits 1 through 9, if no digit appears twice in a number?

F. 162
G. 144
H. 81
J. 72
K. 36

The correct answer is J. Each digit can be paired with any of the other 8 digits. To avoid double-counting, account for the possible pairs as follows: 1 and 2–9 (8 pairs), 2 and 3–9 (7 pairs), 3 and 4–9 (6 pairs), and so forth. The total number of distinct pairs is $8 + 7 + 6 + 5 + 4 + 3 + 2 + 1 = 36$. Since the digits in each pair can appear in either order, the total number of possible two-digit numbers is 2×36, or 72.

Probability

Probability refers to the statistical chances, or "odds," of an event occurring (or not occurring). By definition, probability ranges from 0 to 1. (Probability is never negative, and it's never greater than 1.) Here's the basic formula for determining probability:

$$\text{Probability} = \frac{\text{number of ways the event can occur}}{\text{total number of possible occurrences}}$$

If you randomly select one candy from a jar containing two cherry candies, two licorice candies, and one peppermint candy, what is the probability of selecting a cherry candy?

A. $\frac{1}{6}$
B. $\frac{1}{5}$
C. $\frac{1}{3}$
D. $\frac{2}{5}$
E. $\frac{3}{5}$

The correct answer is D. There are two ways among five possible occurrences that a cherry candy will be selected. Thus, the probability of selecting a cherry candy is $\frac{2}{5}$.

To calculate the probability of an event NOT occurring, just *subtract* the probability of the event occurring *from 1*. So, referring to the preceding question, the probability of NOT selecting a cherry candy is $\frac{3}{5}$. (Subtract $\frac{2}{5}$ from 1.)

Matrices

A *matrix* is a rectangular array of numbers. To multiply a matrix A by a *scalar* (number) k, multiply every entry in A by k. For example:

$$3\begin{bmatrix} 2 & 6 \\ 3 & -1 \end{bmatrix} = \begin{bmatrix} 6 & 18 \\ 9 & -3 \end{bmatrix}$$

Matrices with the same "shape" (the same number of rows and columns) can be added or subtracted simply by adding or subtracting entries in their positions. For example:

If $A = \begin{bmatrix} 2 & 6 \\ 3 & -1 \end{bmatrix}$ and $B = \begin{bmatrix} 4 & 0 \\ 2 & 1 \end{bmatrix}$, then $A + B = \begin{bmatrix} 6 & 6 \\ 5 & 0 \end{bmatrix}$

If $P = \begin{bmatrix} 8 & 3 & -1 \\ -2 & 2 & 7 \end{bmatrix}$ and $Q = \begin{bmatrix} -1 & 3 & 8 \\ 7 & 2 & -2 \end{bmatrix}$, then $P - Q =$

F. $\begin{bmatrix} 9 & 0 & -9 \\ -9 & 0 & 9 \end{bmatrix}$

G. $\begin{bmatrix} 7 & 0 & 7 \\ 5 & 0 & 5 \end{bmatrix}$

H. $\begin{bmatrix} -9 & 0 & 9 \\ 9 & 0 & -9 \end{bmatrix}$

J. $\begin{bmatrix} 9 & 0 & 7 \\ 5 & 0 & 9 \end{bmatrix}$

K. $\begin{bmatrix} 9 & 6 & -9 \\ -9 & 6 & 7 \end{bmatrix}$

The correct answer is F. Subtracting each entry in matrix Q from each corresponding entry in matrix P results in the matrix provided in choice **F.**

Take It to the Next Level

At this level, you'll first focus on the following specific applications of fractions, percents, decimals, ratios, and proportion (with special emphasis on how the test-makers incorporate algebraic features into ACT questions covering these concepts):

- Scientific notation
- Altering fractions and ratios
- Ratios involving more than two quantities
- Proportion problems with variables

Then, you'll explore how the test-makers design tougher-than-average ACT questions involving the following topics (the first section of this chapter covered the basics about all but the second topic listed here):

- Simple average and median (two ways that a set of numbers can be measured as a whole)
- Geometric series (the pattern from one number to the next in an exponential sequence of numbers)
- Permutations (the possibilities for arranging a set of objects)
- Combinations (the possibilities for selecting groups of objects from a set)
- Probability (the statistical chances of a certain event, permutation, or combination occurring)
- Matrices (operations on rectangular arrays of numbers)

Scientific Notation

To express a decimal number in *scientific notation*, place the decimal point after the number's first digit, then multiply that number by 10 raised to the number (power) of places you shifted the point. A negative exponent signifies a fractional number x ($-1 < x < 1$). To illustrate, here's a list of related decimal numbers and their equivalents in scientific notation:

$837{,}000 = 8.37 \times 10^5$ (decimal point shifts 5 places to the left)
$8{,}370 = 8.37 \times 10^3$ (decimal point shifts 3 places to the left)
$83.7 = 8.37 \times 10^1$ (decimal point shifts 1 place to the left)
$8.37 = 8.37 \times 10^0$ (decimal point unchanged in position)
$0.837 = 8.37 \times 10^{-1}$ (decimal point shifts 1 place to the right)
$0.0837 = 8.37 \times 10^{-2}$ (decimal point shifts 2 places to the right)
$0.000837 = 8.37 \times 10^{-4}$ (decimal point shifts 4 places to the right)

An easier ACT question might ask you to simply convert a number from one form to the other. A more challenging question might require you to combine numbers given in scientific notation by either multiplication or division. To handle this type of question, just remember these two rules:

1. To multiply, apply *addition* to exponents:	*Examples:* $(5 \times 10^5)(4 \times 10^4) = 20 \times 10^{(5+4)}$ $= 20 \times 10^9$ $= 2 \times 10^{10}$, or 20,000,000,000 $(5 \times 10^{-5})(4 \times 10^4) = 20 \times 10^{(-5+4)}$ $= 20 \times 10^{-1}$ $= 2 \times 10^0$, or 2
2. To divide, apply *subtraction* to exponents:	*Examples:* $(5 \times 10^5) \div (4 \times 10^4) = 1.25 \times 10^{(5-4)}$ $= 1.25 \times 10^1$, or 12.5 $(5 \times 10^{-5}) \div (4 \times 10^{-4}) = 1.25 \times 10^{(-5-[-4])}$ $= 1.25 \times 10^{-1}$, or 0.125

A computer can process data at the rate of 3.9×10^8 bits per second. How many bits can the computer process in .0006 seconds?

A. 2.34×10^{12}
B. 6.5×10^5
C. 2.34×10^5
D. 6.5×10^4
E. 2.34×10^4

Take It to the Next Level

The correct answer is C. First, express 0.0006 in scientific notation: 6.0×10^{-4}. Then, set up a proportion of two equal fractions and cross-multiply to solve for x:

$$\frac{3.9 \times 10^8}{1} = \frac{x}{6.0 \times 10^{-4}}$$

$$\begin{aligned} x &= (3.9 \times 10^8)(6.0 \times 10^{-4}) \\ &= (3.9)(6) \times 10^{(8-4)} \\ &= 23.4 \times 10^4 \\ &= 2.34 \times 10^5 \end{aligned}$$

Altering Fractions and Ratios

An average test-taker might assume that *adding* the same *positive* quantity to a fraction's numerator (p) and to its denominator (q) leaves the fraction's value $\left(\frac{p}{q}\right)$ unchanged. But, this is true *if and only if* the original numerator and denominator were equal to each other. Otherwise, the fraction's value will change. Remember three rules that apply to any positive numbers x, p, and q (the first one is the no-brainer you just read):

If $p = q$, then $\frac{p}{q} = \frac{p+x}{q+x}$ (The fraction's value remains unchanged, and is always 1.)

If $p > q$, then $\frac{p}{q} > \frac{p+x}{q+x}$ (The fraction's value will *decrease*.)

If $p < q$, then $\frac{p}{q} < \frac{p+x}{q+x}$ (The fraction's value will *increase*.)

An ACT question might ask you to alter a ratio, by adding or subtracting from one (or both) terms in the ratio. The rules for altering ratios are the same as for altered fractions. In either case, set up a proportion, and solve algebraically for the unknown term.

A drawer contains exactly half as many white shirts as blue shirts. If four more shirts of each color are added to the drawer, the ratio of blue to white shirts would be 8:5. How many blue shirts does the drawer contain?

F. 9
G. 10
H. 11
J. 12
K. 14

The correct answer is J. Represent the original ratio of white to blue shirts by the fraction $\frac{x}{2x}$, where x is the number of white shirts, then add 4 to both the numerator and denominator. Set this fraction equal to $\frac{5}{8}$ (the ratio after adding shirts). Cross-multiply to solve for x:

$$\frac{x+4}{2x+4} = \frac{5}{8}$$
$$8x + 32 = 10x + 20$$
$$12 = 2x$$
$$x = 6$$

The original denominator is $2x$, or 12.

When you add (or subtract) the same number from both numerator and denominator of a fraction—or from each term in a ratio—you alter the fraction or ratio, unless the original ratio was 1:1 (in which case the ratio goes unchanged).

Ratios Involving More than Two Quantities

You approach ratio problems involving three or more quantities the same way as for those involving only two quantities. The only difference is that there are more "parts" that make up the "whole."

Three lottery winners—*X*, *Y*, and *Z*—are sharing a lottery jackpot. *X*'s share is $\frac{1}{5}$ of *Y*'s share and $\frac{1}{7}$ of *Z*'s share. If the total jackpot is \$195,000, what is the dollar amount of *Z*'s share?

A. \$15,000
B. \$35,000
C. \$75,000
D. \$105,000
E. \$115,000

The correct answer is D. At first glance, this problem doesn't appear to involve ratios. (Where's the colon?) But it does. The ratio of *X*'s share to *Y*'s share is 1:5, and the ratio of *X*'s share to *Z*'s share is 1:7. So, you can set up the following triple ratio:

$$X : Y : Z = 1 : 5 : 7$$

X's winnings account for 1 of 13 equal parts (1 + 5 + 7) of the total jackpot. $\frac{1}{13}$ of \$195,000 is \$15,000. Accordingly, *Y*'s share is 5 times that amount, or \$75,000, and *Z*'s share is 7 times that amount, or \$105,000.

Proportion Problems with Variables

An ACT proportion question might use *letters* instead of numbers to focus on the process rather than the result. You can solve these problems algebraically or by using the plug-in strategy.

A candy store sells candy only in half-pound boxes. At c cents per box, which of the following is the cost of a ounces of candy? (1 pound = 16 ounces)

F. $\frac{c}{a}$

G. $\frac{a}{16c}$

H. ac

J. $\frac{ac}{8}$

K. $\frac{8c}{a}$

The correct answer is J. This question is asking: "c cents is to one box as *how many cents* are to a ounces?" Set up a proportion, letting x equal the cost of a ounces. Because the question asks for the cost of *ounces*, convert 1 box to 8 ounces (a half pound). Use the cross-product method to solve quickly:

$$\frac{c}{8} = \frac{x}{a}$$

$$8x = ca$$

$$x = \frac{ca}{8}$$

You can also use the plug-in strategy for this question—either instead of algebra or, better yet, to check the answer you chose using algebra. Pick easy numbers to work with, such as 100 for c and 8 for a. At 100 cents per 8-ounce box, 8 ounces of candy costs 100 cents. Plug in your numbers for a and c into each answer choice. Only choice J gives you the number 100 you're looking for.

Average

For any set of terms, the *arithmetic mean* (*AM*), also called the *simple average*, is the sum of the terms ($a + b + c + \ldots$) divided by the number of terms (n) in the set.

$$AM = \frac{(a + b + c + \ldots)}{n}$$

On the ACT, easier questions involving simple average might ask you to add numbers together and divide a sum. A tougher question might ask you to perform one or both of these tasks (both of which involve algebra):

- Find the value of a number that changes an average from one number to another.
- Express simple average in terms of variables instead of just numbers.

When an additional number is added to a set and the average of the numbers in the set changes as a result, you can determine the value of the number that's added by applying the arithmetic-mean formula twice.

The average of three numbers is −4. If a fourth number is added, the average of all four numbers is −1. What is the fourth number?

A. 16
B. 10
C. 8
D. 2
E. −10

The correct answer is C. To solve the problem algebraically, first determine the sum of the three original numbers by the arithmetic-mean formula:

$$-4 = \frac{a + b + c}{3}$$

$$-12 = a + b + c$$

Then, apply the formula again accounting for the additional (fourth) number. The new average is −1, the sum of the other three numbers is −12, and the number of terms is 4. Solve for the missing number (x):

$$-1 = \frac{-12 + x}{4}$$

$$-4 = -12 + x$$

$$8 = x$$

You approach arithmetic-mean problems that involve *variables* instead of (or in addition to) numbers in the same way as those involving only numbers. Just plug-in the information you're given to the arithmetic-mean formula, and then solve the problem algebraically.

If A is the average of P, Q, and another number, which of the following represents the missing number?

F. $3A - P - Q$

G. $\frac{1}{3}(A + P + Q)$

H. $3A - P + Q$

J. $A - P + Q$

K. $3A + P - Q$

The correct answer is F. Let x = the missing number. Solve for x by the arithmetic-mean formula:

$$A = \frac{P + Q + x}{3}$$

$$3A = P + Q + x$$

$$3A - P - Q = x$$

Should you try using the plug-in strategy to solve this problem, testing each answer choice by substituting simple numbers for P, Q, and A? No; it's too complex. So, you'll need to be flexible. Try using shortcuts wherever you can, but recognize their limitations.

Geometric Sequence

In a *geometric sequence* of numbers, each term is a constant multiple of the preceding one; in other words, the ratio between any term and the next one is constant. The multiple (or ratio) might be obvious by examining the sequence—for example:

In the geometric sequence 2, 4, 8, 16, . . . , you can easily determine that the constant multiple is 2 (and the ratio of each term to the next is 1:2).

In the geometric sequence 1, −3, 9, −27, . . . , you can easily determine that the constant multiple is −3 (and the ratio of each term to the next is 1:−3).

Once you know the multiple (or ratio), you can answer any question asking for an unknown term—or for either the sum or the average of certain terms.

In a geometric sequence, each term is a constant multiple of the preceding one. If the third and fourth numbers in the sequence are 8 and −16, respectively, what is the first term in the sequence?

A. −32

B. −4

C. 2

D. 4

E. 64

The correct answer is C. The constant multiple is -2. But, since you need to work backward from the third term (8), apply the *reciprocal* of that multiple twice. The second term is $(8)\left(-\frac{1}{2}\right) = -4$. The first term is $(-4)\left(-\frac{1}{2}\right) = 2$.

In a geometric series, each term is a constant multiple of the preceding one. What is the sum of the first four numbers in a geometric series whose second number is 4 and whose third number is 6?

F. $22\frac{1}{2}$

G. $21\frac{2}{3}$

H. 20

J. 19

K. 16

The correct answer is G. The constant multiple is $\frac{3}{2}$. In other words, the ratio of each term to the next is 3:2. Since the second term is 4, the first term is $4 \times \frac{2}{3} = \frac{8}{3}$. Since the third term is 6, the fourth term is $6 \times \frac{3}{2} = \frac{18}{2}$, or 9. The sum of the four terms $= \frac{8}{3} + 4 + 6 + 9 = 21\frac{2}{3}$.

Alert!

You can't calculate the average of terms in a geometric series simply by averaging the first and last term in the series. That's because the progression is geometric, not arithmetic. Instead, you need to add up the terms, then divide by the number of terms.

You can also solve geometric series problems by applying a special formula. But, you'll need to memorize it, because the test won't provide it. In the following formula, r = the constant multiple (or the ratio between each term and the preceding one), a = the first term in the series, n = the position number for any particular term in the series, and T = the particular term itself:

$$ar^{(n-1)} = T$$

You can solve for any of the formula's variables, as long as you know the values for the other three. Here are two examples:

If $a = 3$ and $r = 2$, then the third term $= (3)(2)^2 = 12$, and the sixth term $= (3)(2)^5 = (3)(32) = 96$.

If the sixth term is $-\frac{1}{16}$ and the constant ratio is $\frac{1}{2}$, then the first term $(a) = -2$:

$$a\left(\frac{1}{2}\right)^5 = -\frac{1}{16}$$

$$a\left(\frac{1}{32}\right) = -\frac{1}{16}$$

$$a = \left(-\frac{1}{16}\right)(32) = -2$$

The algebra is simple enough, but you need to know the formula, of course.

In a geometric series, each term is a constant multiple of the preceding one. If the first three terms in a geometric series are -2, x, and -8, which of the following could be the sixth term in the series?

A. -32
B. -16
C. 16
D. 32
E. 64

The correct answer is E. Since all pairs of successive terms must have the same ratio, $\frac{x}{-2} = \frac{-8}{x}$. By the cross-product method, $x^2 = 16$, and hence $x = \pm 4$. Applying the formula you just learned, for $+4$, the ratio would be $\frac{-8}{4} = -2$. The sixth term would be $(-2)(-2)^5 = 64$. For -4, the ratio would be $\frac{-8}{-4} = 2$. The sixth term would be $(-2)(2)^5 = -64$.

Permutations

A *permutation* is an arrangement of objects in which their order (sequence) is important. Each arrangement of the letters A, B, C, and D, for example, is a different permutation of the four letters. There are two different ways to determine the number of permutations for a group of distinct objects.

1. List all the permutations, using a methodical process to make sure you don't overlook any.
2. Use the following formula (let n = the number of objects), and limit the number of terms to the counting numbers, or positive integers:

   Number of permutations $= n(n-1)(n-2)(n-3)\ldots$

   For example, the number of arrangements (permutations) of the four letters A, B, C, and D is $4! = 4 \times 3 \times 2 \times 1 = 24$.

To handle a tougher permutation question, you might need to calculate multiple permutations, then add them together—applying a dose of logic along the way.

Five children—2 boys and 3 girls—are standing in a single-file line. If the first in line is a girl, how many different arrangements of the 5 children are possible?

F. 72
G. 45
H. 36
J. 20
K. 16

The correct answer is F. Label the 5 children B1, B2, G1, G2, and G3. If G1 is first in line, with the other 4 children in any order, the number of permutations is 4!, or 24. The same applies to either G2 or G3 in the first position. So, the total number of permutations is $4! + 4! + 4! = 72$.

Combinations

A *combination* is a group of certain objects selected from a larger set. The order of objects in the group is not important. You can determine the total number of possible combinations by listing the possible groups in a methodical manner. On the ACT, a simple combination question will involve the selection of one or more objects from *one* larger set. A more complex combination question might require you to determine the number of combinations involving *two or more* sets of objects.

From a group of 3 violinists and 4 pianists, a judge must select 2 violinists and 2 pianists to perform at a music recital. How many different combinations of musicians might perform at the recital?

A. 9
B. 12
C. 18
D. 24
E. 30

The correct answer is C. The judge must select 2 of 3 violinists, for a total of 3 possible combinations. The judge must select 2 of 4 pianists, for a total of 6 possible combinations. For each pair of violinists, there are 6 possible pairs of pianists. Thus, the total number of 4-musician combinations is $6 \times 3 = 18$.

A combination question might also incorporate a permutation feature, making it even more challenging.

From a group of 3 singers and 3 comedians, a show organizer must select 2 singers and 2 comedians to appear one after another in a show. How many different ways can the organizer arrange performers for the show?

F. 72
G. 90
H. 136
J. 180
K. 216

The correct answer is K. The organizer must select 2 of 3 singers, for a total of 3 possible combinations. Similarly, the judge must select 2 of 3 comedians, for a total of 3 possible combinations. For each pair of singers, there are 3 possible pairs of comedians. Thus, the total number of 4-performer combinations is 3×3, or 9. The 4 performers can appear in any order in the show. So, for each 4-performer combination are 24 permutations (4!, or $4 \times 3 \times 2 \times 1$). The total number of possible arrangements, then, is 24×9, or 216.

Probability

Here's the basic formula for determining the probability of an event occurring:

$$\text{Probability} = \frac{\text{number of ways the event can occur}}{\text{total number of possible occurences}}$$

For example, a standard deck of 52 playing cards contains 12 face cards. The probability of selecting a face card from a standard deck is $\frac{12}{52}$, or $\frac{3}{13}$. On the ACT, a tougher probability question will involve this basic formula, but will also add a complication of some kind. It might require you to determine any of the following:

- Certain missing facts needed for a given probability
- Probabilities involving two (or more) *independent* events
- Probabilities involving an event that is *dependent* on another event

Alert!

Think twice before you try to "intuit" the answer for these three types of probability questions. Probabilities involving complex scenarios such as these are often higher or lower than you might expect.

Missing Facts Needed for a Given Probability

In this question type, instead of calculating probability, you determine what missing number is needed for a given probability. Don't panic; just plug what you know into the basic formula, and solve for the missing number.

A piggy bank contains a certain number of coins, of which 53 are dimes and 19 are nickels. The remainder of the coins in the bank are quarters. If the probability of selecting a quarter from this bank is $\frac{1}{4}$, how many quarters does the bank contain?

F. 30
G. 27
H. 24
J. 21
K. 16

The correct answer is H. On its face, this question looks complicated, but it's really not. Just plug in what you know into the probability formula. Let x = the number of quarters in the bank (this is the numerator of the formula's fraction), and let $x + 72$ = the total number of coins (the fraction's denominator). Then solve for x (use the cross-product method to clear fractions):

$$\frac{1}{4} = \frac{x}{x + 72}$$

$$x + 72 = 4x$$

$$72 = 3x$$

$$24 = x$$

Probability Involving Two (or More) Independent Events

Two events are "independent" if neither event affects the probability that the other will occur. (You'll look at dependent events soon.) On the ACT, look for either of these scenarios involving independent events:

- The random selection of one object from *each of two or more groups*
- The random selection of one object from a group, then *replacing* it and selecting again (as in a "second round" or "another turn" of a game)

In either scenario, the simplest calculation involves finding the probability of two events BOTH occurring. All you need to do is MULTIPLY together their individual probabilities:

(probability of event 1 occurring) × (probability of event 2 occurring) = (probability of both events occurring)

For example, assume that you randomly select one letter from each of two sets: {A, B} and {C, D, E}. The probability of selecting A and C = $\frac{1}{2} \times \frac{1}{3}$, or $\frac{1}{6}$.

To calculate the probability that two events will *not both* occur, *subtract from 1* the probability of both events occurring. To determine the probability that *three* events will all occur, just multiply the third event's probability by the other two.

If one student is chosen randomly out of a group of seven students, then one student is again chosen randomly from the same group of seven, what is the probability that two different students will be chosen?

A. $\frac{36}{49}$

B. $\frac{6}{7}$

C. $\frac{19}{21}$

D. $\frac{13}{14}$

E. $\frac{48}{49}$

The correct answer is B. You must first calculate the chances of picking *the same student twice*. There are 7 ways of picking the same student twice. Numbering the students 1, 2, 3, 4, 5, 6, 7 we could have 11, 22, 33, 44, 55, 66, 77. Thus, $\frac{7}{49} = \frac{1}{7}$ = probability of selecting some student twice. The probability of not selecting some student twice (ie, selecting 2 students) = $1 - \frac{1}{7} = \frac{6}{7}$.

Alert!

In one selection, the probability of *not* selecting a certain student from the group of seven is $\frac{6}{7}$ (the probability of selecting the student, subtracted from 1). But, does this mean that the probability of not selecting the same student twice $= \frac{6}{7} \times \frac{6}{7} = \frac{36}{49}$? No! Make sure you understand the difference.

Probability Involving a Dependent Event

Two distinct events might be related in that one event affects the probability of the other one occurring—for example, randomly selecting one object from a group, then selecting a second object from the same group *without replacing* the first selection. Removing one object from the group *increases the odds* of selecting any particular object from those that remain.

You handle this type of problem as you would any other probability problem: Calculate individual probabilities, and then combine them.

In a random selection of 2 people from a group of 5—A, B, C, D, and E—what is the probability of selecting A and B?

F. $\frac{2}{5}$

G. $\frac{1}{5}$

H. $\frac{1}{10}$

J. $\frac{1}{15}$

K. $\frac{1}{20}$

The correct answer is H. You need to consider each of the two selections separately. In the first selection, the probability of selecting either A or B is $\frac{2}{5}$. But the probability of selecting the second of the two is $\frac{1}{4}$—because after the first selection only four people remain from whom to select. Since the question asks for the odds of selecting both A and B (as opposed to either one), multiply the two individual probabilities:.

$$\frac{2}{5} \times \frac{1}{4} = \frac{2}{20} = \frac{1}{10}$$

You can also approach a question such as this one as a *combination* problem. For this question, here are all the possibilities: AB, AC, AD, AE, BC, BD, BE, CD, CE, DE

There are 10 possible combinations, so the probability of selecting A and B is 1 in 10.

Alert!

Strategies such as plugging-in numbers, working backwards, and even sizing up the answer choices, don't work for most probability questions (including the preceding one).

Matrices

A *matrix* is a rectangular array of numbers. Matrices with the same "shape" (the same number of rows and columns) can be added or subtracted simply by adding or subtracting entries in their positions. To multiply a matrix A by a *scalar* (number) k, multiply every entry in A by k.

Each of the three operations just described is pretty easy. Combining matrices by multiplication is much trickier, however. To form the product of two matrices, you first need to know how to form the product of a single-row matrix and a single-column matrix. The product, RC, of row-matrix R and column-matrix C can be defined only if the number of entries in each is the same. When this occurs, product RC is the sum of the products of each corresponding pair of entries. For example:

$$\text{If } R = [\,1\ 2\ 3\,] \text{ and } C = \begin{bmatrix} 4 \\ 5 \\ 6 \end{bmatrix}, \text{ then } RC = [(1)(4) + (2)(5) + (3)(6)] = [32]$$

As long as the number of rows in one matrix equals either the number of rows *or* the number of columns in another matrix, you can define the product of the two matrices. (Otherwise, you can't.) To form a product matrix, determine the product of each row in one matrix and each column in the other matrix. Enter each product in the position in the product matrix that corresponds to the row and column you combined for the entry. For instance, the product of row 2 of matrix A and Column 1 of matrix B will be the entry for row 2, Column 1 of matrix AB. A moderately difficult ACT matrix question might test you on this very procedure.

If $A = \begin{bmatrix} 2 & 6 \\ 3 & -1 \end{bmatrix}$ and $B = \begin{bmatrix} 4 & 3 & -2 \\ 2 & 1 & 5 \end{bmatrix}$,
then the entry in the second row, third column of AB =

A. 20
B. 11
C. 1
D. −1
E. −11

The correct answer is E. To solve the problem, find the product of the second row of A and the third column of B: $(3)(-2) + (-1)(5) = -11$.

To combine matrices by addition (or subtraction), you add (or subtract) corresponding entries. But, to multiply one matrix by another, you do *not* simply multiply together corresponding entries—even if the two matrices have the same "shape" (the same number of rows and columns).

Chapter

9

Number Theory and Algebra

In this section of the chapter, first you'll broaden your arithmetical horizons by dealing with numbers in more abstract, theoretical settings. You'll examine the following topics:

- The concept of absolute value
- Number signs and integers—and what happens to them when you apply the four basic operations
- Factors, multiples, divisibility, prime numbers, and the "prime factorization" method
- The rules for combining exponential numbers (base numbers and "powers") using the four basic operations
- The rules for combining terms under radical signs (roots) using the four basic operations
- The rules for simplifying terms containing radical signs

Then, you'll review the following basic algebra skills:

- Solving a linear equation in one variable
- Solving a system of two equations in two variables—by substitution and by addition-subtraction
- Recognizing unsolvable equations when you see them
- Handling algebraic inequalities

Basic Properties of Numbers

Let's review the basics about integers, number signs (positive and negative), and prime numbers. First, make sure you're up to speed on the following definitions, which you'll need to know for this chapter as well as for the ACT:

Absolute value (of a real number)
The number's distance from zero (the origin) on the real number line. The absolute value of x

is indicated as $|x|$. (The absolute value of a negative number can be less than, equal to, or greater than a positive number. It equals the positive number resulting from the removal of the minus sign. For example, $|-4| = 4$.)

Integer
Any non-fraction number on the number line: $\{\ldots -3, -2, -1, 0, 1, 2, 3, \ldots\}$. Except for the number zero (0), every integer is either positive or negative and either even or odd. *Note:* 0 is an even integer.

Factor (of an integer *n*)
Any integer that you can multiply by another integer for a product of n.

Prime number
Any positive integer that has only two positive factors: 1 and the number itself. In other words, a prime number is not divisible by (a multiple of) any positive integer other than itself and 1.

Note

The factors of any integer n include 1 as well as n itself. Zero (0) and 1 are not considered prime numbers; 2 is the first prime number.

Number Signs and the Four Basic Operations

The four basic operations are addition, subtraction, multiplication, and division. Be sure you know the sign of a number that results from combining numbers using these operations. Here's a table that includes all the possibilities (a "?" indicates that the sign depends on which number is greater):

Addition	Subtraction	Multiplication	Division
$(+) + (+) = +$	$(+) - (-) = (+)$	$(+) \times (+) = +$	$(+) \div (+) = +$
$(-) + (-) = -$	$(-) - (+) = (-)$	$(+) \times (-) = -$	$(+) \div (-) = -$
$(+) + (-) = ?$	$(+) - (+) = ?$	$(-) \times (+) = -$	$(-) \div (+) = -$
$(-) + (+) = ?$	$(-) - (-) = ?$	$(-) \times (-) = +$	$(-) \div (-) = +$

ACT problems involving combining numbers by addition or subtraction usually incorporate the concept of absolute value, as well as the rule for subtracting negative numbers.

$|-2 - 3| - |2 - 3| =$

A. -2
B. -1
C. 0
D. 1
E. 4

The correct answer is E. $|-2 - 3| = |-5| = 5$, and $|2 - 3| = |-1| = 1$. Performing subtraction: $5 - 1 = 4$.

Because multiplication (or division) involving two negative terms always results in a positive number:

- Multiplication or division involving any *even* number of negative terms gives you a positive number.
- Multiplication or division involving any *odd* number of negative terms gives you a negative number.

A number M is the product of three negative numbers, and the number N is the product of two negative numbers and one positive number. Which of the following holds true for all possible values of M and N?

I. $M \times N < 0$
II. $M - N < 0$
III. $N + M < 0$

F. I only
G. II only
H. I and II only
J. II and III only
K. I, II, and III

The correct answer is H. The product of three negative numbers is always a negative number. (M is a negative number.) The product of two negative numbers is always a positive number, and the product of two positive numbers is always a positive number. (N is a positive number.) Thus, the product of M and N must be a negative number; (I) is always true. Subtracting a positive number N from a negative number M always results in a negative number less than M; (II) is always true. However, whether (III) is true depends on the values of M and M. If $|N| > |M|$, then $N + M > 0$, but if $|N| < |M|$, then $N + M < 0$.

Integers and the Four Basic Operations

When you combine integers using a basic operation, whether the result is an odd integer, an even integer, or a non-integer, depends on the numbers you combined. Here's a table that summarizes all the possibilities:

Addition and Subtraction	Multiplication and Division
integer ± integer = integer even integer ± even integer = even integer even integer ± odd integer = odd integer odd integer ± odd integer = even integer	integer × integer = integer integer ÷ non-zero integer = integer, but only if the numerator is divisible by the denominator (if the result is a quotient with no remainder) odd integer × odd integer = odd integer even integer × non-zero integer = even integer even integer ÷ 2 = integer odd integer ÷ 2 = non-integer

ACT questions that test you on the preceding rules sometimes look like algebra problems, but they're really not. Just apply the appropriate rule or, if you're not sure of the rule, plug in simple numbers to zero in on the correct answer.

If P is an odd integer, and if Q is an even integer, which of the following expressions CANNOT represent an even integer?

A. $3P - Q$
B. $3P \times Q$
C. $2Q \times P$
D. $3Q - 2P$
E. $3P \times 3Q$

The correct answer is A. Since 3 and P are both odd integers, their product ($3P$) must also be an odd integer. Subtracting an even integer (Q) from an odd integer results in an odd integer in all cases.

Factors, Multiples, and Divisibility

Figuring out whether one number (f) is a factor of another (n) is no big deal. Just divide n by f. If the quotient is an integer, then f is a factor of n (and n is divisible by f). If the quotient is not an integer, then f is not a factor of n, and you'll end up with a *remainder* after dividing. For example, 2 is a factor of 8 because $8 \div 2 = 4$, which is an integer. On the other hand, 3 is not a factor of 8 because $8 \div 3 = \frac{8}{3}$, or $2\frac{2}{3}$, which is a non-integer. (The remainder is $\frac{2}{3}$.)

Remember these basic rules about factors, which are based on the definition of the term "factor":

1. Any integer is a factor of itself.
2. 1 and -1 are factors of all integers (except 0).
3. The integer zero has no factors and is not a factor of any integer.
4. A positive integer's largest factor (other than itself) will never be greater than one half the value of the integer.

On the "flip side" of factors are multiples. If f is a factor of n, then n is a multiple of f. For example, 8 is a multiple of 2 for the same reason that 2 is a factor of 8—because $8 \div 2 = 4$, which is an integer.

As you can see, factors, multiples, and divisibility are simply different aspects of the same concept. So, an ACT question about factoring is also about multiples and divisibility.

If $n > 6$, and if n is a multiple of 6, which of the following is always a factor of n?

F. $n - 6$

G. $n + 6$

H. $\frac{n}{3}$

J. $\frac{n}{2} + 3$

K. $\frac{n}{2} + 6$

The correct answer is H. Since 3 is a factor of 6, 3 is also a factor of any positive-number multiple of 6. Thus, if you divide any multiple of 6 by 3, the quotient will be an integer. In other words, 3 will be a factor of that number (n). As for the incorrect choices, $n - 6$, choice **F**, is a factor of n only if $n = 12$. $n + 6$, choice **G**, can never be a factor of n because $n + 6$ is greater than n. With choice **J**, you always end up with a remainder of 3. You can eliminate choices **J** and **K** because the largest factor of any positive number (other than the number itself) is half the number, which in this case is $\frac{n}{2}$.

Although the plug-in strategy works for the preceding question, you should try out more than one sample value for n. If $n = 12$, choices F, H, and K all are viable. But, try out the number 18, and choice H is the only factor of n. (To be on the safe side, you should try out at least one additional sample value as well, such as 24.)

Prime Numbers and Prime Factorization

A *prime number* is a positive integer that is divisible by (a multiple of) only two positive integers: itself and 1. Just for the record, here are all the prime numbers less than 50:

2 3 5 7

11 13 17 19

23 29

31 37

41 43 47

Determining all the factors of large integers can be tricky; it's easy to overlook some factors. To find all factors of a large number, use a method called *prime factorization*. Divide the number by each prime number in turn, starting with 2 and working up from there (2,3,5,7,11, . . .), then try to find factors for the quotients as well, using the same method. Test prime numbers up to the point where your quotient is no greater than the largest factor you've already found. For example, here's how you apply prime factorization to the number 110 (prime-number quotients are shown in *italics*):

$110 \div 2 = 55$, and $55 = 5 \times 11$

$110 \div 3 =$ non-integer

$110 \div 5 = 22$, and $22 = 2 \times 11$
$110 \div 7 =$ non-integer
$110 \div 11$ (already covered)

The prime factor quotients are 2, 5, and 11, and their product is 110. (That's no coincidence.) *The product of all prime-number quotients will equal your original number.* A number's prime factorization refers to all its prime factors multiplied together.

Note

To find all other *positive* factors of a number, combine any two or more prime factors by multiplication.

Which of the following is a prime factorization of 144?

A. $2^4 \times 3^2$
B. 4×3^3
C. $2^3 \times 12$
D. $2^2 \times 3 \times 5$
E. $2 \times 3^2 \times 4$

The correct answer is A. Divide 144 by its smallest possible prime factor, which is 2. Continue to divide the result by 2, and you ultimately obtain a prime-number quotient:

$144 \div 2 = 72 \div 2 = 36 \div 2 = 18 \div 2 = 9 \div 3 = 3.$

Exponents (Powers)

An *exponent*, or *power*, refers to the number of times that a number (referred to as the *base* number) is multiplied by itself, plus 1. In the number 2^3, the base number is 2 and the exponent is 3. To calculate the value of 2^3, you multiply 2 by itself twice: $2^3 = 2 \times 2 \times 2 = 8$.

On the ACT, questions involving exponents usually require you to combine two or more terms that contain exponents. To do so, you need to know some basic rules. Can you combine base numbers—using addition, subtraction, multiplication, or division—*before* applying exponents to the numbers? The answer depends on which operation you're performing.

Combining Exponents by Addition or Subtraction

When you add or subtract terms, you cannot combine base numbers or exponents. It's as simple as that.

$a^x + b^x \neq (a + b)^x$

$a^x - b^x \neq (a - b)^x$

If you don't believe it, try plugging in a few easy numbers. Notice that you get a different result depending on which you do first: Combine base numbers or apply each exponent to its base number:

$(3 + 4)^2 = 7^2 = 49$

$3^2 + 4^2 = 9 + 16 = 25$

If $x = -2$, then $x^5 - x^2 - x =$

F. 26
G. 4
H. −34
J. −58
K. −70

The correct answer is H. You cannot combine exponents here, even though the base number is the same in all three terms. Instead, you need to apply each exponent, in turn, to the base number, then subtract:

$x^5 - x^2 - x = (-2)^5 - (-2)^2 - (-2) = -32 - 4 + 2 = -34$

Combining Exponents by Multiplication or Division

It's a whole different story for multiplication and division. First, remember these two simple rules:

1. You can combine base numbers first, but only if the exponents are the same:

   $a^x \times b^x = (ab)^x$

   $\frac{a^x}{b^x} = \left(\frac{a}{b}\right)^x$

2. You can combine exponents first, but only if the base numbers are the same. When multiplying these terms, add the exponents. When dividing them, subtract the denominator exponent from the numerator exponent:

   $a^x \times a^y = a^{(x + y)}$

   $\frac{a^x}{a^y} = a^{(x - y)}$

When the same base number (or term) appears in both the numerator and denominator of a fraction, you can factor out, or cancel, the number of powers common to both.

Which of the following is a simplified version of $\frac{x^2y^3}{x^3y^2}$?

A. $\frac{y}{x}$

B. $\frac{x}{y}$

C. $\frac{1}{xy}$

D. 1

E. x^5y^5

The correct answer is A. The simplest approach to this problem is to factor out x^2 and y^2 from the numerator and denominator. This leaves you with y^1 in the numerator and x^1 in the denominator.

Additional Rules for Exponents

To cover all your bases, also keep in mind these three additional rules for exponents:

1. When raising an exponential number to a power, multiply exponents:

   $(a^x)^y = a^{xy}$

2. Any number other than zero (0) raised to the power of 0 (zero) equals 1:

   $a^0 = 1$ $[a \neq 0]$

3. Raising a base number to a negative exponent is equivalent to 1 divided by the base number raised to the exponent's absolute value:

   $$a^{-x} = \frac{1}{a^x}$$

The preceding three rules are all fair game for the ACT. In fact, an ACT question might require you to apply more than one of these rules.

$(2^3)^2 \times 4^{-3} =$

F. 16

G. 1

H. $\frac{2}{3}$

J. $\frac{1}{2}$

K. $\frac{1}{8}$

The correct answer is G.

$$(2^3)^2 \times 4^{-3} = 2^{(2)(3)} \times \frac{1}{4^3} = \frac{2^6}{4^3} = \frac{2^6}{2^6} = 1$$

Exponents You Should Know

For the ACT, memorize the exponential values in the following table. You'll be glad you did, since these are the ones that you're most likely to see on the exam.

Power & Corresponding Value

Base	2	3	4	5	6	7	8
2	4	8	16	32	64	128	256
3	9	27	81	243			
4	16	64	256				
5	25	125	625				
6	36	216					

Roots and Radicals

On the flip side of exponents and powers are roots and radicals. The *square root* of a number n is a number that you "square" (multiply it by itself, or raise to the power of 2), to obtain n.

$2 = \sqrt{4}$ (the square root of 4) because 2×2 (or 2^2) $= 4$

The *cube root* of a number n is a number that you raise to the power of 3 (multiply by itself twice) to obtain n. You determine higher roots (for example, the "fourth root") in the same way. Except for square roots, the radical sign will indicate the root to be taken.

$2 = \sqrt[3]{8}$ (the cube root of 8) because $2 \times 2 \times 2$ (or 2^3) $= 8$

$2 = \sqrt[4]{16}$ (the fourth root of 16) because $2 \times 2 \times 2 \times 2$ (or 2^4) $= 16$

For the ACT, you should know the rules for simplifying and for combining radical expressions.

Simplifying Radicals

On the ACT, always look for the possibility of simplifying radicals by moving what's under the radical sign to the outside of the sign. Check inside your square-root radicals for "perfect squares": factors that are squares of nice tidy numbers or other terms. The same advice applies to "perfect cubes," and so on.

$\sqrt{4a^2} = 2a$	4 and a^2 are both perfect squares; remove them from under the radical sign, and change each one to its square root.
$\sqrt{8a^3} = \sqrt{(4)(2)a^3}$ $= 2a\sqrt{2a}$	8 and a^3 are both perfect cubes, which contain perfect-square factors; remove the perfect squares from under the radical sign, and change each one to its square root.

You can simplify radical expressions containing fractions in the same way. Just be sure that what's in the denominator under the radical sign stays in the denominator when you remove it from under the radical sign.

$$\sqrt{\frac{20x}{x^3}} = \sqrt{\frac{(4)(5)}{x^2}} = \frac{2\sqrt{5}}{x}$$

$$\sqrt[3]{\frac{3}{8}} = \sqrt[3]{\frac{3}{2^3}} = \frac{1}{2}\sqrt[3]{3}$$

$$\sqrt{\frac{28a^6b^4}{36a^4b^6}} =$$

A. $\frac{a}{b}\sqrt{\frac{a}{2b}}$

B. $\frac{a}{2b}\sqrt{\frac{a}{b}}$

C. $\frac{a}{3b}\sqrt{7}$

D. $\frac{a^2}{3b^2}\sqrt{2}$

E. $\frac{2a}{3b}$

The correct answer is C. Cancel a^4 and b^4 from the numerator and denominator of the fraction. Also, factor out 4 from 28 and 36. Then, remove perfect squares from under the radical sign:

$$\sqrt{\frac{28a^6b^4}{36a^4b^6}} = \sqrt{\frac{7a^2}{9b^2}} = \frac{a\sqrt{7}}{3b}, \text{ or } \frac{a}{3b}\sqrt{7}$$

Combining Radical Terms

The rules for combining terms that include radicals are quite similar to those for exponents. Keep the following two rules in mind; one applies to addition and subtraction, while the other applies to multiplication and division.

Addition and subtraction: If a term under a radical is being added to or subtracted from a term under a different radical, you cannot combine the two terms under the same radical.

$$\sqrt{x} + \sqrt{y} \neq \sqrt{x + y}$$

$$\sqrt{x} - \sqrt{y} \neq \sqrt{x - y}$$

$$\sqrt{x} + \sqrt{x} = 2\sqrt{x}, \text{ not } \sqrt{2x}$$

On the ACT, if you're asked to combine radical terms by adding or subtracting, chances are you'll also need to simplify radical expressions along the way.

$\sqrt{24} - \sqrt{16} - \sqrt{6} =$

F. $\sqrt{6} - 4$

G. $4 - 2\sqrt{2}$

H. 2

J. $\sqrt{6}$

K. $2\sqrt{2}$

The correct answer is F. Although the numbers under the three radicals combine to equal 2, you cannot combine terms this way. Instead, simplify the first two terms, then combine the first and third terms:

$$\sqrt{24} - \sqrt{16} - \sqrt{6} = 2\sqrt{6} - 4 - \sqrt{6} = \sqrt{6} - 4.$$

Multiplication and division: Terms under different radicals can be combined under a common radical if one term is multiplied or divided by the other, but only if the radical is the same.

$$\sqrt{x}\sqrt{x} = \left(\sqrt{x}\right)^2, \text{ or } x$$

$$\frac{\sqrt{x}}{\sqrt{y}} = \sqrt{\frac{x}{y}}$$

$\sqrt[3]{x}\sqrt{x} =$? (you cannot combine, simplify $\sqrt[3]{x}\sqrt{x} = x^{\frac{1}{3}} \bullet x^{\frac{1}{2}} = x^{\frac{5}{6}}$)

$\left(2\sqrt{2a}\right)^2 =$

A. $16a$

B. $8a^2$

C. $8a$

D. $4a^2$

E. $4a$

The correct answer is C. Square each of the two terms, 2 and $\sqrt{2a}$, separately. Then, combine their squares by multiplication:

$$\left(2\sqrt{2a}\right)^2 = 2^2 \times \left(\sqrt{2a}\right)^2 = 4 \times 2a = 8a.$$

Roots You Should Know

For the ACT, memorize the roots in the following table. If you encounter one of these radical terms on the exam, chances are you'll need to know its equivalent integer to answer the question.

In the table, notice that positive numbers have two square roots, one positive and one negative. Also, notice that positive numbers have only one cube root, a positive number, while negative numbers have only one cube root, a negative number.

Square roots of "perfect square" integers	Cube roots of "perfect cube" integers (positive and negative)
$\sqrt{121} = \pm 11$	$\sqrt[3]{(-)8} = (-)2$
$\sqrt{144} = \pm 12$	$\sqrt[3]{(-)27} = (-)3$
$\sqrt{169} = \pm 13$	$\sqrt[3]{(-)64} = (-)4$
$\sqrt{196} = \pm 14$	$\sqrt[3]{(-)125} = (-)5$
$\sqrt{225} = \pm 15$	$\sqrt[3]{(-)216} = (-)6$
$\sqrt{256} = \pm 16$	$\sqrt[3]{(-)343} = (-)7$
	$\sqrt[3]{(-)512} = (-)8$
	$\sqrt[3]{(-)729} = (-)9$
	$\sqrt[3]{(-)1000} = (-)10$

Linear Equations with One Variable

Algebraic expressions are usually used to form equations, which set two expressions equal to each other. Most equations you'll see on the ACT are *linear* equations, in which the variables don't come with exponents. To solve any linear equation containing one variable, your goal is always the same: Isolate the unknown (variable) on one side of the equation. To accomplish this, you may need to perform one or more of the following operations on both sides, depending on the equation:

1. Add or subtract the same term from both sides.
2. Multiply or divide by the same term by both sides.
3. Clear fractions by cross-multiplication.
4. Clear radicals by raising both sides to the same power (exponent).

Performing any of these operations on *both* sides does not change the equality; it merely restates the equation in a different form.

Alert!

Whatever operation you perform on one side of an equation you must also perform on the other side; otherwise, the two sides won't be equal!

Let's take a look at each of these four operations to see when and how to use each one.

1. Add or subtract the same term from both sides of the equation.

To solve for x, you may need to either add or subtract a term from both sides of an equation—or do both.

If $2x - 6 = x - 9$, then $x =$

F. -9
G. -6
H. -3
J. 2
K. 6

The correct answer is H. First, put both x-terms on the left side of the equation by subtracting x from both sides; then combine x-terms:

$$2x - 6 - x = x - 9 - x$$

$$x - 6 = -9$$

Next, isolate x by adding 6 to both sides:

$$x - 6 + 6 = -9 + 6$$

$$x = -3$$

2. Multiply or divide both sides of the equation by the same non-zero term.

To solve for x, you may need to either multiply or divide a term from both sides of an equation. Or, you may need to multiply *and* divide.

If $12 = \frac{11}{x} - \frac{3}{x}$, then $x =$

A. $\frac{3}{11}$

B. $\frac{1}{2}$

C. $\frac{2}{3}$

D. $\frac{11}{12}$

E. $\frac{11}{3}$

The correct answer is C. First, combine the x-terms: $12 = \frac{8}{x}$. Next, clear the fraction by multiplying both sides by x:

$$12x = 8$$

Finally, isolate x (strip it of its coefficient 12) by dividing both sides by 12:

$$x = \frac{8}{12}, \text{ or } \frac{2}{3}$$

3. If each side of the equation is a fraction, your best bet is to cross-multiply.

Where the original equation equates two fractions, use cross-multiplication to eliminate the fractions. Multiply the numerator from one side of the equation by the denominator from the other side. Set the product equal to the product of the other numerator and denominator. (In effect, cross-multiplication is a shortcut method of multiplying both sides of the equation by both denominators.)

If $\frac{7a}{8} = \frac{a+1}{3}$ then $a =$

F. 15

G. $\frac{7}{3}$

H. 2

J. $\frac{7}{8}$

K. $\frac{8}{13}$

The correct answer is K. First, cross-multiply as we've described:

$$(3)(7a) = (8)(a + 1)$$

Next, combine terms (distribute 8 to both *a* and 1):

$$21a = 8a + 8$$

Next, isolate *a*-terms on one side by subtracting 8*a* from both sides; then combine the *a*-terms:

$$21a - 8a = 8a + 8 - 8a$$
$$13a = 8$$

Finally, isolate *a* by dividing both sides by its coefficient 13:

$$\frac{13a}{13} = \frac{8}{13}$$
$$a = \frac{8}{13}$$

4. Square both sides of the equation to eliminate radical signs.

Where the variable is under a square-root radical sign, remove the radical sign by squaring both sides of the equation. (Use a similar technique for cube roots and other roots.)

If $3\sqrt{2x} = 2$, then $x =$

A. $\frac{1}{18}$

B. $\frac{2}{9}$

C. $\frac{1}{3}$

D. $\frac{5}{4}$

E. 3

The correct answer is B. First, clear the radical sign by squaring all terms:

$$(3^2)(\sqrt{2x})^2 = 2^2$$
$$(9)(2x) = 4$$
$$18x = 4$$

Next, isolate *x* by dividing both sides by 18:

$$x = \frac{4}{18}, \text{ or } \frac{2}{9}$$

Alert!

Look out when you square both sides of an equation! In some instances, doing so will reveal that you're really dealing with a quadratic equation—perhaps with more than one solution. Don't panic; you'll learn all about quadratic equations a bit later.

Linear Equations in Two Variables

What we've covered up to this point is pretty basic stuff. If you haven't quite caught on, you should probably stop here and consult a basic algebra workbook for more practice. On the other hand, if you're with us so far, let's forge ahead and add another variable. Here's a simple example:

$$x + 3 = y + 1$$

Quick . . . what's the value of x? It depends on the value of y, doesn't it? Similarly, the value of y depends on the value of x. Without more information about either x or y, you're stuck; well, not completely. You can express x in terms of y, and you can express y in terms of x:

$$x = y - 2$$

$$y = x + 2$$

Let's look at one more:

$$4x - 9 = \frac{3}{2}y$$

Solve for x in terms of y:

$$4x = \frac{3}{2}y + 9$$

$$x = \frac{3}{8}y + \frac{9}{4}$$

Solve for y in terms of x:

$$\frac{4x - 9}{\frac{3}{2}} = y$$

$$\frac{2}{3}(4x - 9) = y$$

$$\frac{8}{3}x - 6 = y$$

To determine numerical values of x and y, you need a system of two linear equations with the same two variables. Given this system, there are two different methods for finding the values of the two variables:

1. The *substitution* method
2. The *addition-subtraction* method

Next, we'll apply each method to determine the values of two variables in a two-equation system.

Note

You can't solve one equation if it contains two unknowns (variables). You either need to know the value of one of the variables, or you need a second equation.

The Substitution Method

To solve a system of two equations using the substitution method, follow these steps (we'll use x and y here):

1. In *either* equation isolate one variable (x) on one side.
2. Substitute the expression that equals x in place of x in the other equation.
3. Solve that equation for y.
4. Now that you know the value of y, plug it into *either* equation to find the value of x.

If $\frac{2}{5}p + q = 3q - 10$, and if $q = 10 - p$, then $\frac{p}{q} =$

F. $\frac{5}{7}$

G. $\frac{3}{2}$

H. $\frac{5}{3}$

J. $\frac{25}{6}$

K. $\frac{35}{6}$

The correct answer is F. Don't let the fact that the question asks for $\frac{p}{q}$ (rather than simply p or q) throw you. Because you're given two linear equations with two unknowns, you know that you can first solve for p and q, then divide p by q. First things first: Combine the q-terms in the first equation:

$$\frac{2}{5}p = 2q - 10$$

Next, substitute $(10 - p)$ for q (from the second equation) in the first equation:

$$\frac{2}{5}p = 2(10 - p) - 10$$

$$\frac{2}{5}p = (20 - 2p) - 10$$

$$\frac{2}{5}p = 10 - 2p$$

Move the p-terms to the same side, then isolate p:

$$\frac{2}{5}p + 2p = 10$$

$$\frac{12}{5}p = 10$$

$$p = \left(\frac{5}{12}\right)(10)$$

$$p = \frac{25}{6}$$

Substitute $\frac{25}{6}$ for p in either equation to find q (we'll use the second equation):

$$q = 10 - \frac{25}{6}$$

$$q = \frac{60}{6} - \frac{25}{6}$$

$$q = \frac{35}{6}$$

The question asks for $\frac{p}{q}$, so do the division:

$$\frac{p}{q} = \frac{\frac{25}{6}}{\frac{35}{6}} = \frac{25}{35}, \text{ or } \frac{5}{7}$$

The Addition-Subtraction Method

Another way to solve for two unknowns in a system of two equations is with the addition-subtraction method. Here are the steps:

1. Make the coefficient of *either* variable the same in both equations (you can disregard the sign) by multiplying every term in one of the equations.
2. Make sure the equations list the same variables in the same order.
3. Place one equation above the other.
4. Add the two equations (work down to a sum for each term), or subtract one equation from the other, to eliminate one variable.
5. You can repeat steps 1–3 to solve for the other variable.

If $3x + 4y = -8$, and if $x - 2y = \frac{1}{2}$, then $x =$

A. 9

B. $\frac{14}{5}$

C. $\frac{1}{3}$

D. $-\frac{7}{5}$

E. -12

The correct answer is D. To solve for x, you want to eliminate y. You can multiply each term in the second equation by 2, then add the equations:

$$\begin{array}{r} 3x + 4y = -8 \\ \underline{2x - 4y = 1} \\ 5x + 0y = -7 \\ x = -\frac{7}{5} \end{array}$$

Since the question asked only for the value of x, stop here. If the question had asked for both x and y (or for y only), you could have multiplied both sides of the second equation by 3, then subtracted the second equation from the first:

$$\begin{array}{r} 3x + 4y = -8 \\ \underline{3x - 6y = \frac{3}{2}} \\ 0x + 10y = -9\frac{1}{2} \\ 10y = \frac{-19}{2} \\ y = -\frac{19}{20} \end{array}$$

Note

If a question requires you to find values of both unknowns, you can combine the two methods. For example, after using addition-subtraction to solve for x in the last question, you can then substitute $-\frac{7}{5}$, the value of x, into either equation to find y.

Which Method Should You Use?

Which method, substitution or addition-subtraction, you should use depends on what the equations look like to begin with. To see what we mean, look again at the system:

$$p + q = 3q - 10$$
$$q = 10 - p$$

Notice that the second equation is already set up nicely for the substitution method. This system is an ideal candidate for the substitution method. But, you could use addition-subtraction instead; you'd just have to rearrange the terms in both the equations first:

$$p - 2q = -10$$
$$p + q = 10$$

Now, look again at the following system:

$$3x + 4y = -8$$
$$x - 2y = \frac{1}{2}$$

Notice that the x-term and y-term already line up nicely here. Also, notice that it's easy to match the coefficients of either x or y: Multiply both sides of the second equation by either 3 or 2. This system is an ideal candidate for addition-subtraction. To appreciate this point, try using substitution instead. You'll discover that it takes far more number crunching.

To solve a system of two linear equations in two variables, use addition-subtraction if you can quickly and easily eliminate one of the variables. Otherwise, use substitution.

Linear Equations That Can't Be Solved

Never assume that one linear equation with one variable is solvable. If you can reduce the equation to $0 = 0$, then you can't solve it. In other words, the value of the variable could be any real number.

If $-1 < x < 1$, and if $3x - 3 - 4x = x - 7 - 2x + 4$, then how many real numbers does the solution set for x contain?

F. 0
G. 1
H. 2
J. 3
K. Infinitely many

The correct answer is K. All terms on both sides cancel out:

$$3x - 3 - 4x = x - 7 - 2x + 4$$
$$-x - 3 = -x - 3$$
$$0 = 0$$

Thus, x could equal any real number between -1 and 1 (not just the integer 0).

In some cases, what appears to be a system of two equations in two variables might actually be the same equation expressed in two different ways. In other words, what you're really dealing with are two equivalent equations, which you cannot solve.

If $2b = 60 - 2a$, and $a + b = 30$, then what is the value of a?

A. -10
B. -2
C. 10
D. 12
E. It cannot be determined from the information given.

The correct answer is E. An unwary test-taker might assume that the values of both a and b can be determined with both equations together, because they appear at first glance to provide a system of two linear equations with two unknowns. Not so! You can easily manipulate the first equation so that it is identical to the second:

$$2b = 60 - 2a$$
$$2b = 2(30 - a)$$
$$b = 30 - a$$
$$a + b = 30$$

As you can see, the equation $2b = 60 - 2a$ is identical to the equation $a + b = 30$. Thus, a and b could each be any real number. You can't solve one equation in two unknowns, so the correct answer must be **E**.

Whenever you encounter a question that calls for solving one or more linear equations, and answer choice **E** provides something other than a numerical answer, stop in your tracks before taking pencil to paper. Size up the equation to see whether it's one of the two unsolvable animals you learned about here. If so, the correct answer will be **E**.

Solving Algebraic Inequalities

You can solve algebraic inequalities in the same manner as equations. Isolate the variable on one side of the equation, factoring and canceling wherever possible. However, one important rule distinguishes inequalities from equations: Whenever you multiply or divide by a negative number, you must reverse the inequality symbol. Simply put: If $a > b$, then $-a < -b$.

$12 - 4x < 8$	original inequality
$-4x < -4$	12 subtracted from each side; inequality unchanged
$x > 1$	both sides divided by -4; inequality reversed

Here are some general rules for dealing with algebraic inequalities. Study them until they're second nature to you, because you'll put them to good use on the ACT.

1. Adding or subtracting unequal quantities to (or from) equal quantities:

   If $a > b$, then $c + a > c + b$

   If $a > b$, then $c - a < c - b$

2. Adding unequal quantities to unequal quantities:

   If $a > b$, and if $c > d$, then $a + c > b + d$

3. Comparing three unequal quantities:

   If $a > b$, and if $b > c$, then $a > c$

4. Combining the same *positive* quantity with unequal quantities by multiplication or division:

   If $a > b$, and if $x > 0$, then $xa > xb$

   If $a > b$, and if $x > 0$, then $\frac{a}{x} > \frac{b}{x}$

   If $a > b$, and if $x > 0$, then $\frac{x}{a} < \frac{x}{b}$

5. Combining the same *negative* quantity with unequal quantities by multiplication or division:

   If $a > b$, and if $x < 0$, then $xa < xb$

   If $a > b$, and if $x < 0$, then $\frac{a}{x} < \frac{b}{x}$

   If $a > b$, and if $x < 0$, then $\frac{x}{a} > \frac{x}{b}$

If $a > b$, and if $c > d$, then which of the following inequalities holds true in all cases?

F. $a - b > c - d$
G. $a - c > b - d$
H. $c + d < a - b$
J. $a - c < b + d$
K. $b + d < a + c$

The correct answer is K. Inequality questions can be a bit confusing, can't they? In this problem, you need to remember that if unequal quantities (c and d) are added to unequal quantities of the same order (a and b), the result is an inequality in the same order. This rule is essentially what answer choice **K** says.

Alert!

When handling inequality problems, you might think that by simply plugging in some sample numbers, you can zero in on the correct answer. Be careful! The wrong answers might look right, depending on the values you use for the different variables.

Take It to the Next Level

This next section focuses on the following advanced topics involving number theory and algebra:

- The impact of exponents and radicals on the size and sign of numbers
- Functions and the relationship between inverse functions, especially between exponential and logarithmic functions
- Factoring quadratic expressions
- Finding the roots of quadratic equations by factoring
- Finding the roots of quadratic equations by applying the quadratic formula
- Factoring nonlinear equations in two variables
- Algebraic expressions and problem-solving involving certain types of word problems, including weighted average, interest on investment, and rate

Exponents and the Real Number Line

Raising base numbers to powers can have surprising effects on the size and/or sign—negative vs. positive—of the base number. You need to consider four separate regions of the real number line:

1. Values greater than 1 (to the right of 1 on the number line)
2. Values less than -1 (to the left of -1 on the number line)
3. Fractional values between 0 and 1
4. Fractional values between -1 and 0

The table below indicates the impact of positive-integer exponent (x) on base number (n) for each region.

$n > 1$	n raised to any power: $n^x > 1$ (the greater the exponent, the greater the value of n^x)
$n < -1$	n raised to even power: $n^x > 1$ (the greater the exponent, the greater the value of n^x) n raised to odd power: $n^x < 1$ (the greater the exponent, the smaller the value of n^x)
$0 < n < 1$	n raised to any power: $0 < n^x < n < 1$ (the greater the exponent, the smaller the value of n^x)
$-1 < n < 0$	n raised to even power: $0 < n^x < 1$ (the greater the exponent, the smaller the value of n^x, approaching 0 on the number line) n raised to odd power: $-1 < n^x < 0$ (the greater the exponent, the greater the value of n^x, approaching 0 on the number line)

The preceding set of rules are easy enough to understand. But, when you apply them to an ACT question, it can be surprisingly easy to confuse yourself, especially if the question is designed to create confusion.

If $-1 < x < 0$, which of the following must be true?

I. $x < x^2$
II. $x^2 < x^3$
III. $x < x^3$

A. I only
B. II only
C. I and II only
D. I and III only
E. I, II, and III

The correct answer is D. The key to analyzing each equation is that raising x to successively higher powers moves the value of x closer to zero (0) on the number line.

(I) must be true. Since x is given as a negative number, x^2 must be positive and thus greater than x.

(II) cannot be true. Since x is given as a negative number, x^2 must be positive, while x^3 must be negative. Thus x^2 is greater than x^3.

(III) must be true. Both x^3 and x are negative fractions between 0 and -1, but x^3 is closer to zero (0) on the number line—that is, greater than x.

Take It to the Next Level

Roots and the Real Number Line

As with exponents, the root of a number can bear a surprising relationship to the size and/or sign (negative vs. positive) of the number (another of the test-makers' favorite areas). Here are four rules you should remember:

1. If $n > 1$, then $1 < \sqrt[3]{n} < \sqrt{n} < n$ (the greater the root, the lower the value). However, if n lies between 0 and 1, then $n < \sqrt{n} < \sqrt[3]{n} < 1$ (the greater the root, the greater the value).

$n = 64$	$n = \frac{1}{64}$
$1 < \sqrt[3]{64} < \sqrt{64} < 64$	$\frac{1}{64} < \sqrt{\frac{1}{64}} < \sqrt[3]{\frac{1}{64}} < 1$
$1 < 4 < 8 < 64$	$\frac{1}{64} < \frac{1}{8} < \frac{1}{4} < 1$

2. Every negative number has exactly one cube root, and that root is a negative number. The same holds true for all other odd-numbered roots of negative numbers.

$\sqrt[3]{-27} = -3$	$\sqrt[5]{-32} = -2$
$(-3)(-3)(-3) = -27$	$(-2)(-2)(-2)(-2)(-2) = -32$

3. Every positive number has two square roots: a negative number and a positive number (with the same absolute value). The same holds true for all other even-numbered roots of positive numbers.

$$\sqrt{16} = \pm 4$$
$$\sqrt[4]{81} = \pm 3$$

4. Every positive number has only one *cube* root, and that root is always a positive number. The same holds true for all other odd-numbered roots of positive numbers.

Note

The square root (or other even-number root) of any negative number is an imaginary number, not a real number. That's why the preceding rules don't cover these roots.

Which of the following inequalities, if true, is sufficient alone to show that $\sqrt[3]{x} < \sqrt[5]{x}$?

F. $-1 < x < 0$
G. $x > 1$
H. $|x| < -1$
J. $|x| > 1$
K. $x < -1$

The correct answer is K. If $x < -1$, then applying a higher root yields a *smaller negative* value—further to the left on the real number line.

Functions

In a *function* (or *functional relationship*), the value of one variable depends upon the value of, or is "a function of," another variable. In mathematics, the relationship is expressed in the form $y = f(x)$—where y is a function of x. To find the value of the function for any value x, simply substitute the x-value for x wherever it appears in the function. For instance, suppose that $f(x) = x^2 + 3x - 4$. Here's how you'd find $f(2 + a)$:

$$\begin{aligned} f(2 + a) &= (2 + a)^2 + 3(2 + a) - 4 \\ &= 4 + 4a + a^2 + 6 + 3a - 4 \\ &= a^2 + 7a + 6 \end{aligned}$$

On the ACT, it's unlikely that you'll encounter a function question as simple as the preceding example. On the simplest function questions, your task will probably be one of the following two:

1. Apply the same function twice. For example:

   If $f(x) = x + 1$, then

   $$\frac{1}{f(x)} \times f\left(\frac{1}{x}\right) = \left(\frac{1}{x+1}\right)\left(\frac{1+x}{x}\right) = \frac{1}{x}$$

2. Apply two different functions, where one function is a function of the other. For example:

   If $f(x) = x^2$ and $g(x) = x + 3$, then to find $g(f(x))$, substitute $f(x)$ for x in the function $g(x) = x + 3$: $g(f(x)) = f(x) + 3$. Then substitute x^2 for $f(x)$: $g(f(x)) = x^2 + 3$.

As you can see, easier function questions amount to little more than an exercise in substitution.

Note

In mathematical terms, a function g that is a function of f can be written either as $(f \bullet g)(x)$ or $f(g(x))$.

Take It to the Next Level

A more challenging function question might involve an inverse function, in which $f(g(x)) = g(f(x)) = x$. Inverse functions are so named because they "undo" each other. That is, for any value x, calculating $f(x)$ and substituting the result into $g(x)$ brings you right back to the value of x, where you started. Given a function $f(x)$, determine its inverse function by solving for $g(x)$.

Which of the following is the inverse function, $g(x)$, for $f(x) = \frac{2x}{x+4}$?

A. $g(x) = \frac{4x}{x-2}$

B. $g(x) = \frac{4x}{2-x}$

C. $g(x) = \frac{4x+4}{2x}$

D. $g(x) = \frac{-2x}{x+4}$

E. $g(x) = \frac{4x}{x+2}$

The correct answer is B. To find the inverse function, write y for $f(x)$, then interchange x and y in the original equation:

$y = \frac{2x}{x+4}$ becomes $x = \frac{2y}{y+4}$

Then solve for y in terms of x:

$$x = \frac{2y}{y+4}$$
$$(y+4)x = 2y$$
$$xy + 4x = 2y$$
$$4x = 2y - xy$$
$$4x = y(2-x)$$
$$\frac{4x}{2-x} = y$$

In another tough type of function question, your job is to determine a certain function that is expressed in terms of another function. As in easier questions involving two functions, one of which is a function of the other, substitute the *dependent* function for the variable in the *independent* function.

If $f(x) = x^2$ and $f(g(x)) = \frac{1}{x^2 + 1}$, then $g(x)$ could be which of the following?

F. $\frac{1}{x + 1}$

G. $\sqrt{x} + 1$

H. $\frac{1}{\sqrt{x^2 + 1}}$

J. $\frac{1}{x}$

K. $\frac{1}{x^2}$

The correct answer is H. In $f(x) = x^2$, substitute $g(x)$ for x: $f(g(x)) = [g(x)]^2 = \frac{1}{x^2 + 1}$. Accordingly, $g(x) = \pm \frac{1}{\sqrt{x^2 + 1}}$. The positive value is the one that's listed as choice H.

Exponential and Logarithmic Functions

Among the most important, and test-worthy, examples of two inverse functions is the relation between an *exponential* and a *logarithmic* function. By definition, each one is the inverse of the other. Stated in mathematical terms, for any constant $b > 0$ and $\neq 1$:

The exponential function $f(x) = b^x$ is the inverse of the logarithmic function $g(x) = \log_b x$. Or, put another way: $y = b^x$ is equivalent to $x = \log_b y$.

For example, $125 = 5^3$ is equivalent to $3 = \log_5 125$. In the logarithmic function $g(x) = \log_b x$, the variable x is the logarithm, and b is the base of the logarithm.

Alert!

If no base number is given, then the base number is understood to be 10.

An easier ACT question might provide a logarithmic function, then simply ask for its equivalent exponential function. For example:

If $\log_x 125 = 3$, then $x = 5$. (The function $\log_x 125 = 3$ is equivalent to $x^3 = 125$. Hence, $x = \sqrt[3]{125} = 5$.)

If $\log_x y = z$, *then, in terms of* x *and* z, $y = x^z$. *(The function* $\log_x y = z$ *is equivalent to* $y = x^z$.*)*

To toughen up questions like these just a bit, the test-makers might resort to negative or fractional exponents, as in these two examples:

If $\log_{\frac{1}{2}}x = -4$, then $x = 16$. (Given $\log_{\frac{1}{2}}x = -4$, $x = \left(\frac{1}{2}\right)^{-4} = 2^4 = 16$.)

If $x = \log_4\sqrt{64}$, then $x = \frac{3}{2}$. (The function $x = \log_4\sqrt{64}$ is equivalent to $4^x = \sqrt{64} = \sqrt{4^3} = 4^{\frac{3}{2}}$.)

A more challenging ACT question might require you to apply one or more of the following basic properties of algorithms. Notice that each one follows from (is equivalent to) one of the laws of exponents:

Logarithm property	Equivalent law of exponents
1. $\log_b xy = \log_b x + \log_b y$	1. $b^x b^y = b^{(x+y)}$
2. $\log_b \frac{x}{y} = \log_b x - \log_b y$	2. $\frac{b^x}{b^y} = b^{(x-y)}$
3. $\log_b 1 - \log_b x = \log_b \frac{1}{x}$	3. $b^{-x} = \frac{1}{b^x}$
4. $y\log_b x = \log_b x^y$	4. $(b^x)^y = b^{xy}$
5. $\log_b 1 = 0$	5. $b^0 = 1$

A test question might ask you to express an exponential function as its equivalent logarithmic function (or vice versa) *and* apply one or more of the properties of logarithms.

If $b^x = 5$ and $b^y = 2$, then $\log_b 20 =$

A. $x + 2y$
B. $x - 2y$
C. $xy + 10$
D. $5x + 2y$
E. $2x + 5y$

The correct answer is A. First, express $b^x = 5$ and $b^y = 2$ in their equivalent logarithmic form: $\log_b 5 = x$ and $\log_b 2 = y$. You can express $\log_b 20$ as $\log_b(2^2)(5)$, which in turn you can express as $\log_b 2^2 + \log_b 5$—applying logarithm property 2. Now apply property 4: $\log_b 2^2 = 2\log_b 2$. Substituting x for $\log_b 5$ and y for $\log_b 2$ gives you $x + 2y$, choice A.

The test-makers aren't interested in your ability to look up information in logarithm tables. What they're interested in is your understanding of the relation between exponential and logarithmic functions and of the properties of logarithms. So, you won't find any logarithm tables on the ACT, or in this book.

Factorable Quadratic Expressions in One Variable

A *quadratic expression* includes a "squared" variable, such as x^2. An equation is quadratic if you can express it in this general form: $ax^2 + bx + c = 0$, where:

x is the variable

a, b, and c are constants (numbers)

$a \neq 0$

b can equal 0

c can equal 0

Here are four examples (notice that the b-term and c-term are not essential; in other words, either b or c, or both, can equal zero):

Quadratic equation	Same equation, but in the form: $ax^2 + bx + c = 0$
$2w^2 = 16$	$2w^2 - 16 = 0$ *(no* b*-term)*
$x^2 = 3x$	$x^2 - 3x = 0$ *(no* c*-term)*
$3y = 4 - y^2$	$y^2 + 3y - 4 = 0$
$7z = 2z^2 - 15$	$2z^2 - 7z - 15 = 0$

Every quadratic equation has exactly two solutions, called *roots*. (But, the two roots might be the same.) On the ACT, you can often find the two roots by *factoring*. To solve any factorable quadratic equation, follow these three steps:

1. Put the equation into the standard form: $ax^2 + bx + c = 0$.
2. Factor the terms on the left side of the equation into two linear expressions (with no exponents).
3. Set each linear expression (root) equal to zero and solve for the variable in each one.

Take It to the Next Level

Factoring Simple Quadratic Expressions

Some quadratic expressions are easier to factor than others. If either of the two constants b or c is zero, factoring requires no sweat. In fact, in some cases, no factoring is needed at all—as in the following:

A quadratic with no c term	A quadratic with no b term
$2x^2 = x$	$2x^2 - 4 = 0$
$2x^2 - x = 0$	$2(x^2 - 2) = 0$
$x(2x - 1) = 0$	$x^2 - 2 = 0$
$x = 0, 2x - 1 = 0$	$x^2 = 2$
$x = 0, \frac{1}{2}$	$x = \sqrt{2}, -\sqrt{2}$

Alert!

When dealing with a quadratic equation, your first step is usually to put it into the general form $ax^2 + bx + c = 0$. But, keep in mind: The only essential term is ax^2.

Factoring Quadratic Trinomials

A trinomial is simply an algebraic expression that contains three terms. If a quadratic expression contains all three terms of the standard form $ax^2 + bx + c$, then factoring becomes a bit trickier. You need to apply the FOIL method, in which you add together these terms:

F the product of the *first* terms of the two binomials

(O) the product of the *outer* terms of the two binomials

(I) the product of the *inner* terms of the two binomials

(L) the product of the *last* (second) terms of the two binomials

Note the following relationships:

F is the first term (ax^2) of the quadratic expression.

(O + I) is the second term (bx) of the quadratic expression.

(L) is the third term (c) of the quadratic expression.

You'll find that the two factors will be two binomials. The ACT might ask you to recognize one or both of these binomial factors.

Which of the following is a factor of $x^2 - x - 6$?

F. $(x + 6)$
G. $(x - 3)$
H. $(x + 1)$
J. $(x - 2)$
K. $(x + 3)$

The correct answer is G. Notice that x^2 has no coefficient. This makes the process of factoring into two binomials easier. Set up two binomial shells: $(x \quad)(x \quad)$. The product of the two missing second terms (the "L" term under the FOIL method) is −6. The possible integral pairs that result in this product are (1,−6), (−1,6), (2,−3,), and (−2,3). Notice that the second term in the trinomial is $-x$. This means that the sum of the two integers whose product is −6 must be −1. The pair (2,−3) fits the bill. Thus, the trinomial is equivalent to the product of the two binomials $(x + 2)$ and $(x - 3)$.

To check your work, multiply the two binomials, using the FOIL method:

$$\begin{aligned}(x + 2)(x - 3) &= x^2 - 3x + 2x - 6\\ &= x^2 - x - 6\end{aligned}$$

If the preceding question had asked you to determine the roots of the equation $x^2 - x - 6 = 0$, you'd simply set each of the binomial factors equal to 0 (zero), then solve for x in each one. The solution set (the two possible values of x) includes the roots −2 and 3.

How many different values of x does the solution set for the equation $4x^2 = 4x - 1$ contain?

A. None
B. One
C. Two
D. Four
E. Infinitely many

The correct answer is B. First, express the equation in standard form: $4x^2 - 4x + 1 = 0$. Notice that the c-term is 1. The only two integral pairs that result in this product are (1, 1) and (−1, −1). Since the b-term ($-4x$) is negative, the integral pair whose product is 1 must be (−1, −1). Set up a binomial shell:

(? − 1)(? − 1)

Notice that the a-term contains the coefficient 4. The possible integral pairs that result in this product are (1, 4), (2, 2), (−1, −4), and (−2, −2). A bit of trial-and-error reveals that only the pair (2, 2) works. Thus, in factored form, the equation becomes $(2x - 1)(2x - 1) = 0$. To check your work, multiply the two binomials, using the FOIL method:

$$\begin{aligned}(2x - 1)(2x - 1) &= 4x^2 - 2x - 2x + 1\\ &= 4x^2 - 4x + 1\end{aligned}$$

Take It to the Next Level

Since the two binomial factors are the same, the two roots of the equation are the same. In other words, x has only one possible value. (Although you don't need to find the value of x in order to answer the question, solve for x in the equation $2x - 1 = 0$; $x = \frac{1}{2}$.)

Stealth Quadratic Equations

Some equations that appear linear (variables include no exponents) may actually be quadratic. For the ACT, there are two situations you need to be on the lookout for:

1. The same variable inside a radical also appears outside:

$$\begin{aligned} \sqrt{x} &= 5x \\ (\sqrt{x})^2 &= (5x)^2 \\ x &= 25x^2 \\ 25x^2 - x &= 0 \end{aligned}$$

2. The same variable that appears in the denominator of a fraction also appears elsewhere in the equation:

$$\begin{aligned} \frac{2}{x} &= 3 - x \\ 2 &= x(3 - x) \\ 2 &= 3x - x^2 \\ x^2 - 3x + 2 &= 0 \end{aligned}$$

In both scenarios, you're dealing with a quadratic (nonlinear) equation in one variable. So, in either equation, there are two roots. (Both equations are factorable, so go ahead and find their roots.) The solutions for example 1 are 0 and $\frac{1}{25}$; the solutions for example 2 are 1 and 2.

The Quadratic Formula and Complex Numbers

For some quadratic equations, although rational roots exist, they're difficult to find. For example, $12x^2 + x - 6 = 0$ can be solved by factoring, but the factors are not easy to see:

$$12x^2 + x - 6 = (3x - 2)(4x + 3)$$

Faced with a quadratic equation that's difficult to factor, you can always use the quadratic formula, which states that, for any equation of the form $ax^2 + bx + c = 0$:

$$x = \frac{-b \pm \sqrt{b^2 - 4ac}}{2a}$$

In the equation $12x^2 + x - 6 = 0$, for example, $a = 12$, $b = 1$, and $c = -6$. Plugging these values into the quadratic formula, you'll find that the two roots are $\frac{2}{3}$ and $-\frac{3}{4}$.

Some quadratic equations have no rational roots (solutions). Referring to the quadratic formula, if $\sqrt{b^2 - 4ac}$ turns out to be a negative number, then its square root will be *imaginary*, and hence so will the roots of the quadratic equation at hand. In general, if N is a positive number, then $\sqrt{-N}$ is written as $i\sqrt{N}$. For example, $\sqrt{-4} = i\sqrt{4} = 2i$ and $\sqrt{-3} = i\sqrt{3}$. So, if the ACT asks you to find the root of a quadratic equation, and some of the answer choices are expressed in terms of i, that's a clue that the equation's roots might very well include an imaginary number.

Which of the following is a root of the equation $x^2 = 4x - 5$?

F. $4 - i$
G. $2 - i$
H. $2 + 2i$
J. $3i$
K. $2 - 2i$

The correct answer is G. First, express the equation in the quadratic form $ax^2 + bx + c = 0$:

$$x^2 - 4x + 5 = 0$$

In this equation, $a = 1$, $b = -4$, and $c = 5$. Apply the quadratic formula, using these values:

$$x = \frac{-(-4) \pm \sqrt{(-4)^2 - 4(1)(5)}}{2(1)}$$

$$= \frac{4 \pm \sqrt{16 - 20}}{2}$$

$$= \frac{4 \pm \sqrt{-4}}{2}$$

$$= \frac{4 \pm 2i}{2}$$

$$= 2 \pm i$$

The two roots are $2 + i$ and $2 - i$, choice G.

Tip

Numbers of the form $a + bi$, where a and b are both real numbers and $i = \sqrt{-1}$, are called *complex numbers*—hence, the heading for this section. Whenever you perform arithmetic with complex numbers, treat i as any other variable, unless i is raised to an even power, in which case you replace the term with a real number. For example, you'd replace i^2 with -1 and i^4 with 1.

Nonlinear Equations in Two Variables

In the world of math, solving nonlinear equations in two or more variables can be *very* complicated, even for bona-fide mathematicians. But on the ACT, all you need to remember are these three general forms:

Sum of two variables, squared: $(x + y)^2 = x^2 + 2xy + y^2$

Difference of two variables, squared: $(x - y)^2 = x^2 - 2xy + y^2$

Difference of two squares: $x^2 - y^2 = (x + y)(x - y)$

You can verify these equations using the FOIL method:

$(x + y)^2 = (x + y)(x + y)$ $= x^2 + xy + xy + y^2$ $= x^2 + 2xy + y^2$	$(x - y)^2 = (x - y)(x - y)$ $= x^2 - xy - xy + y^2$ $= x^2 - 2xy + y^2$	$(x + y)(x - y) = x^2 + xy - xy - y^2$ $= x^2 - y^2$

For the ACT, memorize the three equations listed here. When you see one form on the exam, it's a sure bet that your task is to convert it to the other form.

If $x^2 - y^2 = 100$, and if $x + y = 2$, then $x - y =$

A. 200
B. 50
C. 20
D. 10
E. −2

The correct answer is B. If you're on the lookout for the difference of two squares, you can handle this question with no sweat. Use the third equation you just learned, substituting 2 for $(x + y)$, then solving for $(x - y)$:

$$x^2 - y^2 = (x + y)(x - y)$$
$$100 = (x + y)(x - y)$$
$$100 = (2)(x - y)$$
$$50 = (x - y)$$

What about working backward from the answer choices to solve this problem? Go ahead and try it. You don't get very far, do you? There are two lessons here: (1) You usually can't solve quadratics using a shortcut, and (2) always look for one of the three common quadratic forms; if you see it, convert it to its equivalent form to answer the question as quickly and easily as possible.

Weighted Average Problems

You solve *weighted average* problems using the arithmetic mean (simple average) formula, except you give the set's terms different weights. For example, if a final exam score of 90 receives *twice* the weight of each of two mid-term exam scores 75 and 85, think of the final-exam score as *two* scores of 90—and the total number of scores as 4 rather than 3:

$$WA = \frac{75 + 85 + (2)(90)}{4} = \frac{340}{4} = 85$$

Similarly, when some numbers among terms might appear more often than others, you must give them the appropriate "weight" before computing an average.

> During an 8-hour trip, Brigitte drove 3 hours at 55 miles per hour and 5 hours at 65 miles per hour. What was her average rate, in miles per hour, for the entire trip?
>
> F. 58.5
> G. 60
> H. 61.25
> J. 62.5
> K. 66.2

The correct answer is H. Determine the total miles driven: (3)(55) + (5)(65) = 490. To determine the average over the entire trip, divide this total by 8, which is the number of total hours: $\frac{490}{8} = 61.25$.

A tougher weighted-average problem might provide the weighted average and ask for one of the terms, or require conversions from one unit of measurement to another—or both.

> A certain olive orchard produces 315 gallons of oil annually, on average, during four consecutive years. How many gallons of oil must the orchard produce annually, on average, during the next six years, if oil production for the entire ten-year period is to meet a goal of 378 gallons per year?
>
> A. 468
> B. 420
> C. 396
> D. 285
> E. 240

Take It to the Next Level

The correct answer is B. In the weighted-average formula, 315 annual gallons receives a weight of 4, while the average annual number of gallons for the next six years (x) receives a weight of 6:

$$378 = \frac{1{,}260 + 6x}{10}$$

$$3{,}780 = 1{,}260 + 6x$$

$$3{,}780 - 1{,}260 = 6x$$

$$420 = x$$

This solution (420) is the average number of gallons needed per year, on average, during the next six years.

To guard against calculation errors, check your answer by sizing up the question. Generally, how big a number are you looking for? Notice that the stated goal is a bit greater than the annual average production over the first four years. So you're looking for an answer that is greater than the goal—a number somewhat greater than 378 gallons per year. You can eliminate choices D and E out of hand. The number 420 fits the bill.

Investment Problems

ACT *investment* problems involve interest earned (at a certain percentage rate) on money over a certain time period (usually a year). To calculate interest earned, multiply the original amount of money by the interest rate:

amount of money $\times$ interest rate = amount of interest on money

For example, if you deposit \$1,000 in a savings account that earns 5% interest annually, the total amount in the account after one year will be \$1,000 + 0.05(\$1,000) = \$1,000 + \$50 = \$1,050.

ACT investment questions usually involve more than simply calculating interest earned on a given principal amount at a given rate. They usually call for you to set up and solve an algebraic equation. When handling these problems, it's best to eliminate percent signs.

Gary wishes to have \$2,970 in a savings account at the end of the year. How much must Gary deposit in his account at the start of the year if the account pays him 8% interest per year?

F. \$2,575
G. \$2,680
H. \$2,732
J. \$2,750
K. \$3,208

The correct answer is J. Letting x equal the original amount deposited, set up the following equation: $x + 0.08x = 2{,}970$. Combining terms on the left side of the equation: $1.08x = 2{,}970$. Now, solve for x by dividing both sides by 1.08:

$$x = \frac{2{,}970}{1.08} = 2{,}750$$

Thus, Gary must invest $2,750 at the start of the year to end with $2,970.

Problems Involving Rate

A *rate* is a fraction that expresses a quantity per unit of time. For example, the rate of travel is expressed this way:

$$\text{rate of travel} = \frac{\text{distance}}{\text{time}}$$

Similarly, the rate at which a machine produces a certain product is expressed this way:

$$\text{rate of production} = \frac{\text{number of units produced}}{\text{time}}$$

An ACT rate question will usually provide two of the three terms, and then ask you for the value of the third term. A rate question might also require you to convert a number from one unit of measurement to another.

If a printer can print pages at a rate of 15 pages per minute, how many pages can it print in $2\frac{1}{2}$ hours?

A. 1,375
B. 1,500
C. 1,750
D. 2,250
E. 2,500

The correct answer is D. Apply the following formula:

$$\text{rate} = \frac{\text{numbr of pages}}{\text{time}}$$

The rate is given as 15 minutes, so convert the time ($2\frac{1}{2}$ hours) to 150 minutes. Determine the number of pages by applying the formula to these numbers:

$$15 = \frac{\text{number of pages}}{150}$$

$$(15)(150) = \text{number of pages}$$

$$2{,}250 = \text{number of pages}$$

Take It to the Next Level

Chapter

10

Geometry and Trigonometry

In this chapter, first you'll review the fundamentals involving plane geometry, which include:

- Relationships among angles formed by intersecting lines
- Characteristics of any triangle
- Characteristics of special right triangles
- The Pythagorean theorem
- Characteristics of squares, rectangles, and parallelograms
- Characteristics of circles

Then, you'll learn the basics for handling ACT questions involving the standard (x,y) coordinate plane. Here are the specific topics covered:

- The characteristics of the (x,y) coordinate plane
- Defining and plotting points and lines on the plane
- Applying the midpoint and distance formulas

Next, you'll review trigonometric functions involving the sides and angles of right triangles.

And last, you'll learn to *Take It to the Next Level.*

Note

If you haven't learned any trigonometry in high school, don't panic. As you'll discover later in this chapter, basic right-angle trigonometry is not difficult to understand or to apply to the ACT. In addition, there will be few trig questions on the test.

Lines and Angles

Lines and line segments are the basic building blocks for most ACT geometry problems. An ACT geometry question might involve nothing more than intersecting lines and the angles they form. To handle the question, just remember four basic rules about angles formed by intersecting lines:

1. Vertical angles (angles across the vertex from each other and formed by the same two lines) are equal in degree measure, or *congruent* (≅).
2. If adjacent angles combine to form a straight line, their degree measures total 180. In fact, a straight line is actually a 180° angle.
3. If two lines are perpendicular (⊥) to each other, they intersect at right (90°) angles.
4. The sum of the measures of all angles where two or more lines intersect at the same point is 360° (regardless of how many angles are involved).

Note

The symbol (≅) symbolizes that two geometric features are *congruent*, which means that they are identical. The equation $\overline{AB} \cong \overline{CD}$ means that line segment AB is congruent (equal in length) to line segment $\overline{CD}$. The two equations $\angle A \cong \angle B$ and $m\angle A = m\angle B$ are two different ways of symbolizing the same relationship: the angle whose vertex is at point A is congruent (equal in degree measure) to the angle whose vertex is at point B. (The letter m symbolizes degree measure.)

Angles Formed by Intersecting Lines

When two or more lines intersect at the same point, they form a "wheel-spoke" pattern with a "hub." On the ACT, wheel-spoke questions require you to apply one or more of the preceding four rules.

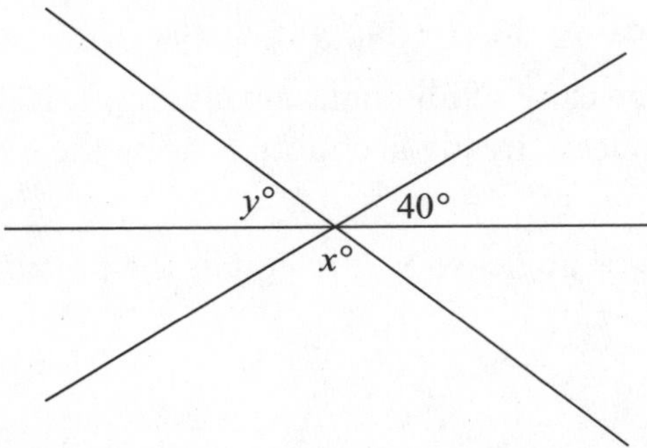

The figure above shows three intersecting lines. What is the value of $x + y$?

A. 150
B. 140
C. 130
D. 80
E. 50

The correct answer is B. The angle vertical to the one indicated as 40° must also measure 40°. That 40° angle, together with the angles whose measures are $x°$ and $y°$, combine to form a straight (180°) line. In other words, $40 + x + y = 180$. Thus, $x + y = 140$.

A slightly tougher wheel-spoke question might focus on overlapping angles, and require you to apply rule 1 (about vertical angles) to determine the amount of the overlap. Look at this next wheel-spoke figure:

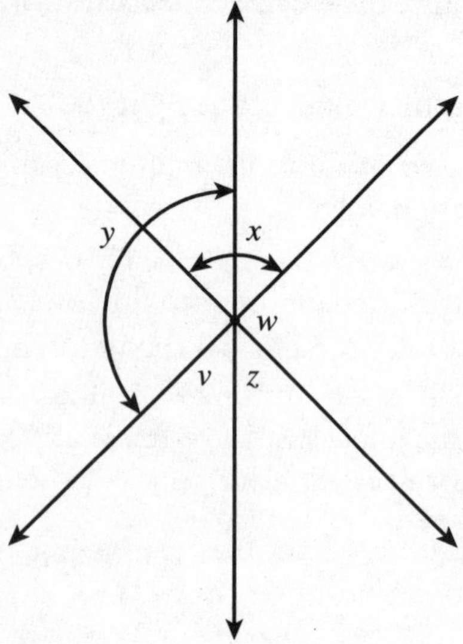

An ACT question about the preceding figure might test your ability to recognize one of the following relationships:

$x + y - z = 180$	$x + y$ exceeds 180 by the amount of the overlap, which equals z, the angle vertical to the overlapping angle.
$x + y + v + w = 360$	The sum of the measure of all angles, excluding z, is 360°; z is excluded because it is already accounted for by the overlap of x and y.
$y - w = z$	w equals its vertical angle, so $y - w$ equals the portion of y vertical to angle z.

Parallel Lines and Transversals

ACT problems involving parallel lines also involve at least one transversal, which is a line that intersects each of two (or more) lines. Look at this next figure, in which $l_1 \parallel l_2$ and $l_3 \parallel l_4$:

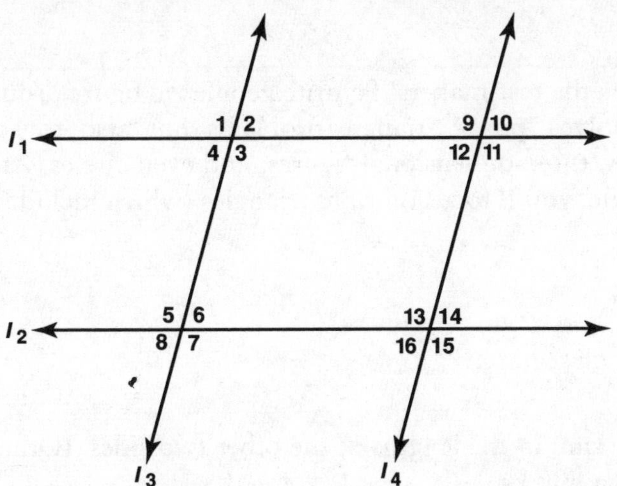

The upper-left "cluster" of angles 1, 2, 3, and 4 matches each of the three other clusters. In other words:

All the odd-numbered angles are congruent to one another. All the even-numbered angles are congruent to one another. So, if you know the measure of just one angle, you can determine the measure of all 16 angles!

In the figure below, lines P and Q are parallel to each other. If $\angle x$ measures 75°, what is the measure of $\angle y$?

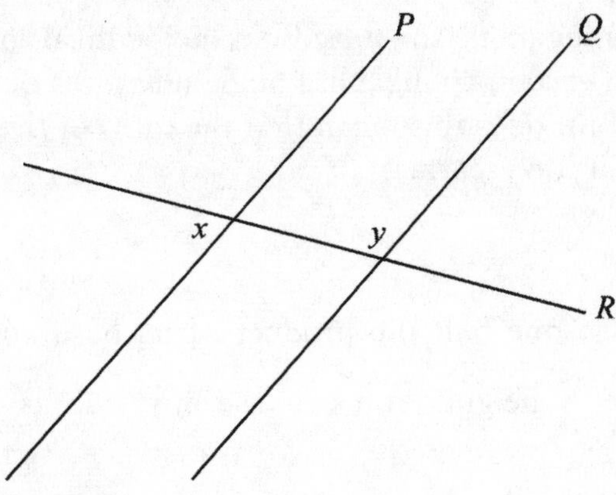

F. 75°
G. 85°
H. 95°
J. 105°
K. 115°

The correct answer is J. The angle "cluster" where lines *P* and *R* intersect corresponds to the cluster where lines *Q* and *R* intersect. Thus, $\angle x$ and $\angle y$ are supplementary (their measures add up to 180°). Given that $\angle x$ measures 75°, $\angle y$ must measure 105°.

Triangles

The *triangle* (a three-sided polygon) is the test-makers' favorite geometric figure. You'll need to understand triangles not only to solve "pure" triangle problems but also to solve some problems involving four-sided figures, three-dimensional figures, and even circles. After a brief review of the properties of any triangle, you'll focus on right triangles (which include one right, or 90°, angle).

Properties of All Triangles

Here are four properties that all triangles share:

1. *Length of the sides.*
   Each side is shorter than the sum of the lengths of the other two sides. (Otherwise, the triangle would collapse into a line.)
2. *Angle measures.*
   The measures of the three angles total 180°, and each angle is smaller than the sum of the other two. (Otherwise, the triangle would collapse into a line.)
3. *Angles and opposite sides.*
   Comparative angle sizes correspond to the comparative lengths of the sides opposite those angles. For example, a triangle's largest angle is opposite its longest side. (The sides opposite two congruent angles are also congruent.)

Alert!

Don't take this rule too far! The ratio among angle sizes need not be identical to the ratio among lengths of sides! For example, if a certain triangle has angle measures of 30°, 60°, and 90°, the ratio of the angles is 1:2:3. But, does this mean that the ratio of the opposite sides is also 1:2:3? No, it doesn't, as you'll soon learn.

4. *Area.*
   The area of any triangle is equal to one half the product of its base and its height (or "altitude"): Area $= \frac{1}{2} \times$ base $\times$ height. You can use any side as the base to calculate area.

Do not equate altitude (height) with any particular side. Instead, imagine the base on flat ground, and drop a plumb line straight down from the top peak of the triangle to define height or altitude. The only type of triangle in which the altitude equals the length of one side is the *right* triangle—as you'll see next.

Right Triangles and the Pythagorean Theorem

In a right triangle, one angle measures 90° (and, of course, each of the other two angles measures less than 90°). The *Pythagorean theorem* expresses the relationship among the sides of any right triangle. In the following expression of the theorem, a and b are the two *legs* (the two shortest sides) that form the right angle, and c is the *hypotenuse* (the longest side, opposite the right angle):

$$a^2 + b^2 = c^2$$

For any right triangle, if you know the length of two sides, you can determine the length of the third side by applying the theorem. For example:

If the two shortest sides (the legs) of a right triangle are 2 and 3 units long, then the length of the triangle's third side (the hypotenuse) is $\sqrt{13}$ units: $2^2 + 3^2 = \left(\sqrt{13}\right)^2$.

If a right triangle's longest side (hypotenuse) is 10 units long and another side (one of the legs) is 5 units long, then the third side is $5\sqrt{3}$ units long: $a^2 + 5^2 = 10^2$; $a^2 = 75$; $a = \sqrt{75}$, or $\sqrt{(25)(3)} = 5\sqrt{3}$.

Pythagorean Side Triplets

A Pythagorean side triplet is a specific ratio among the sides of a triangle that satisfies the Pythagorean theorem. In each of the following triplets, the first two numbers represent the comparative lengths of the two legs, whereas the third—and largest—number represents the comparative length of the hypotenuse (on the ACT, the first four appear far more frequently than the last two):

$1{:}1{:}\sqrt{2}$	$1^2 + 1^2 = \left(\sqrt{2}\right)^2$
$1{:}\sqrt{3}{:}2$	$1^2 + \left(\sqrt{3}\right)^2 = 2^2$
3:4:5	$3^2 + 4^2 = 5^2$
5:12:13	$5^2 + 12^2 = 13^2$
8:15:17	$8^2 + 15^2 = 17^2$
7:24:25	$7^2 + 24^2 = 25^2$

Each triplet above is expressed as a *ratio* because it represents a proportion among the triangle's sides. All right triangles with sides having the same proportion, or ratio, have the same shape. For example, a right triangle with sides of 5, 12, and 13 is smaller but exactly the same shape (proportion) as a triangle with sides of 15, 36, and 39.

Two boats leave the same dock at the same time, one traveling due east at 10 miles per hour and the other due north at 24 miles per hour. How many miles apart are the boats after three hours?

A. 68
B. 78
C. 88
D. 98
E. 110

The correct answer is B. The distance between the two boats after three hours forms the hypotenuse of a triangle in which the legs are the two boats' respective paths. The ratio of one leg to the other is 10:24, or 5:12. So, you know you're dealing with a 5:12:13 triangle. The slower boat traveled 30 miles (10 mph $\times$ 3 hours). 30 corresponds to the number 5 in the 5:12:13 ratio, so the multiple is 6 ($5 \times 6 = 30$). Thus, 5:12:13 = 30:72:78.

To save valuable time on ACT right-triangle problems, learn to recognize given numbers (lengths of triangle sides) as multiples of Pythagorean triplets.

Pythagorean Angle Triplets

In two (and only two) of the unique triangles identified in the preceding section as Pythagorean side triplets, all degree measures are *integers*:

1. The corresponding angles opposite the sides of a $1:1:\sqrt{2}$ triangle are 45°, 45°, and 90°.
2. The corresponding angles opposite the sides of a $1:\sqrt{3}:2$ triangle are 30°, 60°, and 90°.

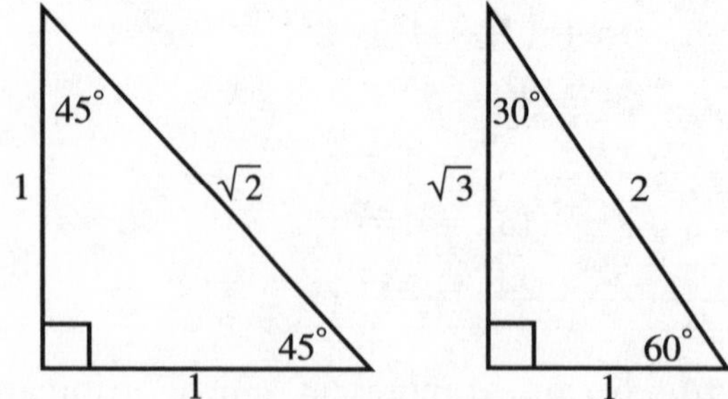

If you know that the triangle is a right triangle (one angle measures 90°) and that one of the other angles is 45°, then given the length of any side you can determine the unknown lengths. For example:

- If one leg is 5 units long, then the other leg must also be 5 units long, while the hypotenuse must be $5\sqrt{2}$ units long.

- If the hypotenuse (the longest side) is 10 units long, then each leg must be $5\sqrt{2}$ units long. (Divide hypotenuse by $\sqrt{2}$: $\frac{10}{\sqrt{2}} = \frac{10\sqrt{2}}{2} = 5\sqrt{2}$.)

Similarly, if you know that the triangle is a right triangle (one angle measures 90°) and that one of the other angles is either 30° or 60°, then given the length of any side you can determine the unknown lengths. For example:

- If the shortest leg (opposite the 30° angle) is 3 units long, then the other leg (opposite the 60° angle) must be $3\sqrt{3}$ units long, and the hypotenuse must be 6 units long (3×2).
- If the longer leg (opposite the 60° angle) is 4 units long, then the shorter leg (opposite the 30° angle) must be $\frac{4\sqrt{3}}{3}$ units long (divide by $\sqrt{3}$: $\frac{4}{\sqrt{3}} = \frac{4\sqrt{3}}{3}$), while the hypotenuse must be $\frac{8\sqrt{3}}{3}$ (twice as long as the shorter leg).
- If the hypotenuse is 10 units long, then the shorter leg (opposite the 30° angle) must be 5 units long, while the longer leg (opposite the 60° angle) must be $5\sqrt{3}$ units long (the length of the shorter leg multiplied by $\sqrt{3}$).

In the figure below, $\overline{AC}$ is 5 units long, $m\angle ADC = 90°$, $m\angle ABD = 45°$, and $m\angle DAC = 60°$. How many units long is $\overline{BD}$?

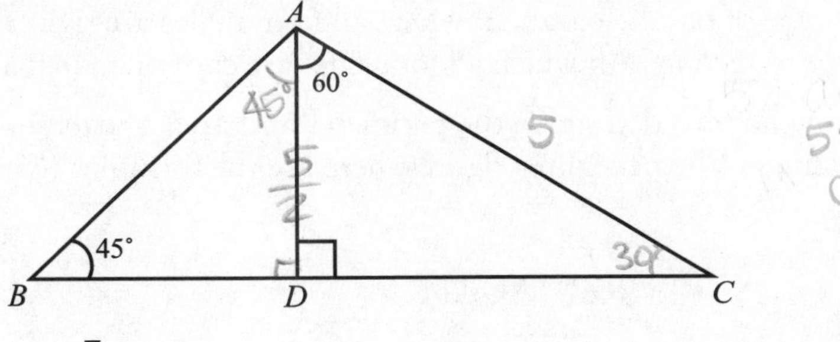

F. $\frac{7}{3}$

G. $2\sqrt{2}$

H. $\frac{5}{2}$

J. $\frac{3\sqrt{2}}{2}$

K. $\frac{7}{2}$

The correct answer is H. To find the length of $\overline{BD}$, you first need to find $\overline{AD}$. Notice that ΔADC is a 30°-60°-90° triangle. The ratio among its sides is $1:\sqrt{3}:2$. Given that $\overline{AC}$ is 5 units long, $\overline{AD}$ must be $\frac{5}{2}$ units long. (The ratio 1:2 is equivalent to the ratio $\frac{5}{2}$:5.) Next, notice that ΔABD is a 45°-45°-90° triangle. The ratio among its sides is $1:1:\sqrt{2}$. You know that $\overline{AD}$ is $\frac{5}{2}$ units long. Thus, $\overline{BD}$ must also be $\frac{5}{2}$ units long.

X-Ref

A 45°-45°-90° triangle is a special type of *isosceles* triangle—a triangle with two congruent sides. If you advance to *Take It to the Next Level*, you'll look closer at this type of triangle, as well as another special type: the *equilateral* triangle (a triangle whose three sides are all congruent).

Rectangles, Squares, and Parallelograms

Rectangles, squares, and parallelograms are types of *quadrilaterals* (four-sided geometric figures). Here are the characteristics that apply to all rectangles, squares, and parallelograms:

- The sum of the measures of all four interior angles is 360°.
- Opposite sides are parallel.
- Opposite sides are congruent (equal in length).
- Opposite angles are congruent (equal in degree measure).
- Adjacent angles are supplementary (their measures total 180°).
- A rectangle is a special type of parallelogram in which all four angles are right angles (90°). A square is a special type of rectangle in which all four sides are congruent (equal in length).

For the ACT, you should know how to determine the perimeter and area of each of these three types of quadrilaterals. Referring to the next three figures, here are the formulas (l = length and w = width):

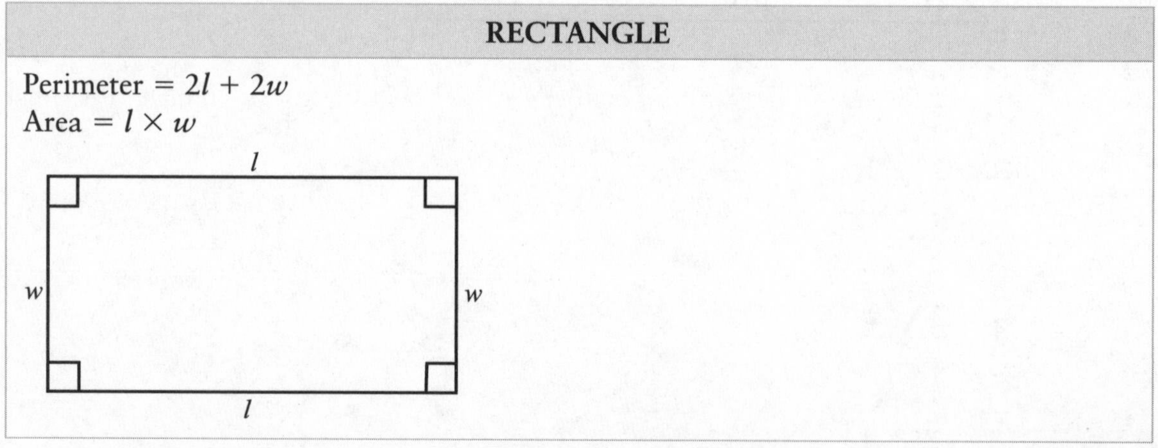

SQUARE

Perimeter = $4s$ [s = side]
Area = s^2

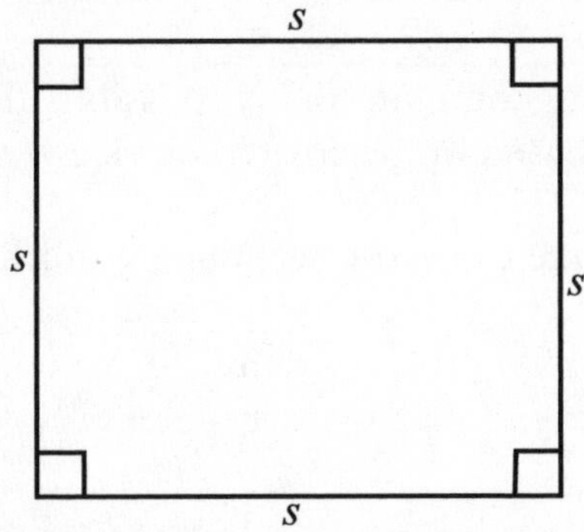

PARALLELOGRAM

Perimeter = $2l + 2w$
Area = base (b) × altitude (a)

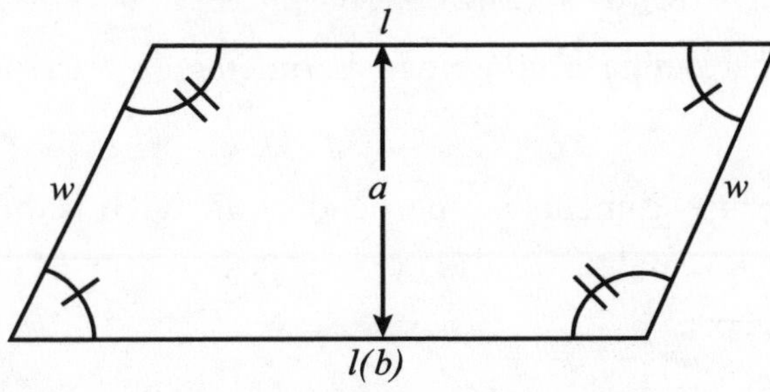

ACT questions involving squares come in many varieties. For example, you might need to determine an area based on a perimeter, or you might need to do just the opposite—find a perimeter based on a given area. For example:

The area of a square with a perimeter of 8 is 4. ($s = 8 \div 4 = 2$; $s^2 = 4$)

The perimeter of a square with an area of 8 is $8\sqrt{2}$. ($s = \sqrt{8}$; $4s = 4 \times 2\sqrt{2}$)

Or, you might need to determine a change in area resulting from a change in perimeter (or vice versa).

If a square's sides are each increased by 50%, by what percent does the square's area increase?

A. 200%
B. 150%
C. 125%
D. 100%
E. 75%

The correct answer is C. Letting s = the length of each side before the increase, area = s^2. Let $\frac{3}{2}s$ = the length of each side after the increase, the new area = $\left(\frac{3}{2}s\right)^2 = \frac{9}{4}s^2$. The increase from s^2 to $\frac{9}{4}s^2$ is $\frac{5}{4}$, or 125%.

ACT questions involving non-square rectangles also come in many possible flavors. For example, a question might ask you to determine area based on perimeter, or vice versa.

The length of a rectangle with an area of 12 is three times the rectangle's width. What is the perimeter of the rectangle?

F. 10
G. 12
H. 14
J. 16
K. 20

The correct answer is J. The ratio of length to width is 3:1. The ratio 6:2 is equivalent, and 6 × 2 = 12 (the area). Thus, the perimeter = (2)(6) + (2)(2) = 16.

Or, a question might require you to determine a combined perimeter or area of adjoining rectangles.

In the figure below, all intersecting line segments are perpendicular. What is the area of the shaded region, in square units?

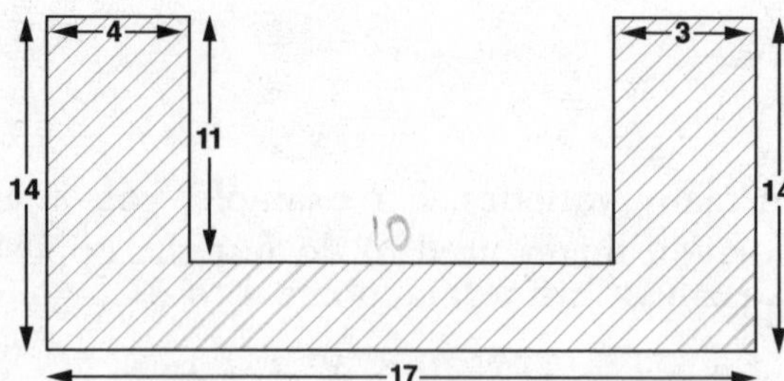

A. 84
B. 118
C. 128
D. 139
E. 238

The correct answer is C. The figure provides the perimeters you need to calculate the area. One way to find the area of the shaded region is to consider it as what remains when a rectangular shape is cut out of a larger rectangle. The area of the entire figure without the "cut-out" is 14 × 17 = 238. The "cut-out" rectangle has a length of 11, and its width is equal to 17 − 4 − 3 = 10. Thus, the area of the cut-out is 11 × 10 = 110. Accordingly, the area of the shaded region is 238 − 110 = 128.

Another way to solve the problem is to partition the shaded region into three smaller rectangles, as shown in this figure, and sum up the area of each. Thus, $14 \times 4 = 56$; $10 \times 3 = 30$; $14 \times 3 = 42$; and $56 + 30 + 42 = 128$.

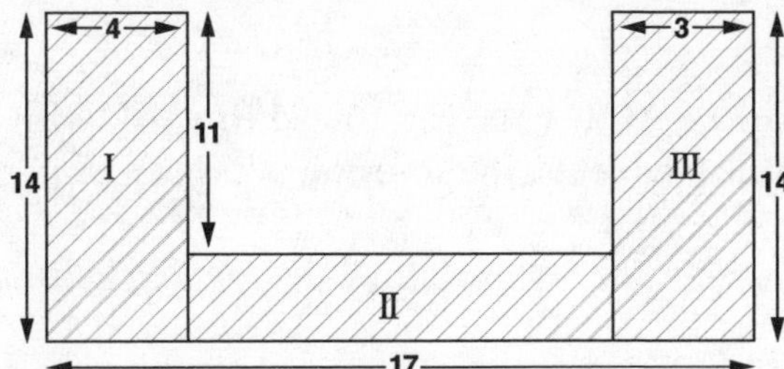

An ACT question about a non-rectangular parallelogram might focus on angle measures. These questions are easy to answer. In any parallelogram, opposite angles are congruent, and adjacent angles are supplementary. (Their measures total 180°.) So, if one of a parallelogram's angles measures 65°, then the opposite angle must also measure 65°, while the two other angles each measure 115°.

A more difficult question about a non-rectangular parallelogram might focus on area. To determine the parallelogram's altitude, you might need to apply the Pythagorean theorem (or one of the side or angle triplets).

In the quadrilateral *ABCD*, $\overline{AB} \parallel \overline{CD}$ and $\overline{AD} \parallel \overline{BC}$. If $\overline{BC}$ is 4 units long and $\overline{CD}$ is 2 units long and $m\angle B = 45°$, what is the area of quadrilateral *ABCD*?

F. $6\sqrt{2}$
G. 8
H. 6
J. $4\sqrt{2}$
K. 4

The correct answer is J. Since *ABCD* is a parallelogram, its area = base (4) × altitude. To determine altitude (*a*), draw a vertical line segment connecting point *A* to $\overline{BC}$, which creates a 45°-45°-90° triangle. The ratio of the triangle's hypotenuse to each leg is $\sqrt{2}:1$. The hypotenuse $AB = 2$. Thus, the altitude (*a*) of *ABCD* is $\frac{2}{\sqrt{2}}$, or $\sqrt{2}$. Accordingly, the area of $ABCD = (4)(\sqrt{2})$, or $4\sqrt{2}$.

Circles

For the ACT, you'll need to know the following basic terminology involving circles:

circumference: the distance around the circle (its "perimeter")

radius: the distance from a circle's center to any point on the circle's circumference

diameter: the greatest distance from one point to another on the circle's circumference (twice the length of the radius)

chord: a line segment connecting two points on the circle's circumference (a circle's longest possible chord is its diameter, passing through the circle's center)

You'll also need to apply the two basic formulas involving circles (r = radius, d = diameter):

Circumference = $2\pi r$, or πd

Area = πr^2

Note

The value of π is approximately 3.14. For the ACT, you won't need to work with a value for π any more precise. In fact, in most circle problems, the solution is expressed in terms of π rather than numerically.

With the two formulas, all you need is one value—area, circumference, diameter, or radius—and you can determine all the others. For example:

Given a circle with a diameter of 6:

radius = 3

circumference = $(2)(\pi)(3) = 6\pi$

area = $\pi(3)^2 = 9\pi$

If a circle's circumference is 10 centimeters long, what is the area of the circle, in square centimeters?

A. 12.5

B. 3π

C. 10

D. $\frac{25}{\pi}$

E. $\frac{5\pi}{2}$

The correct answer is D. First, determine the circle's radius. Applying the circumference formula $C = 2\pi r$, solve for r:

$$10 = 2\pi r$$

$$\frac{5}{\pi} = r$$

Then, apply the area formula, with $\frac{5}{\pi}$ as the value of r:

$$A = \pi\left(\frac{5}{\pi}\right)^2 = \frac{25}{\pi}$$

X-Ref

ACT circle problems might involve other types of geometric figures as well—such as triangles, squares and non-square rectangles, and tangent lines. If you advance to *Take It to the Next Level*, you'll learn how to handle these kinds of problems.

Coordinate Signs and the Four Quadrants

ACT *coordinate geometry* questions involve the rectangular *coordinate plane* (or *xy*-plane) defined by two axes—a horizontal *x-axis* and a vertical *y-axis*. You can define any point on the coordinate plane by using two coordinates: an *x-coordinate* and a *y-coordinate*. A point's *x*-coordinate is its horizontal position on the plane, and its *y*-coordinate is its vertical position on the plane. You denote the coordinates of a point with (x,y), where x is the point's *x*-coordinate and y is the point's *y*-coordinate.

The center of the coordinate plane—the intersection of the x and y axes—is called the *origin*. The coordinates of the origin are (0,0). Any point along the *x*-axis has a *y*-coordinate of 0 $(x,0)$, and any point along the *y*-axis has an *x*-coordinate of 0 $(0,y)$. The coordinate signs (positive or negative) of points lying in the four quadrants I–IV in this next figure are as follows:

Quadrant I (+,+)

Quadrant II (−,+)

Quadrant III (−,−)

Quadrant IV (+,−)

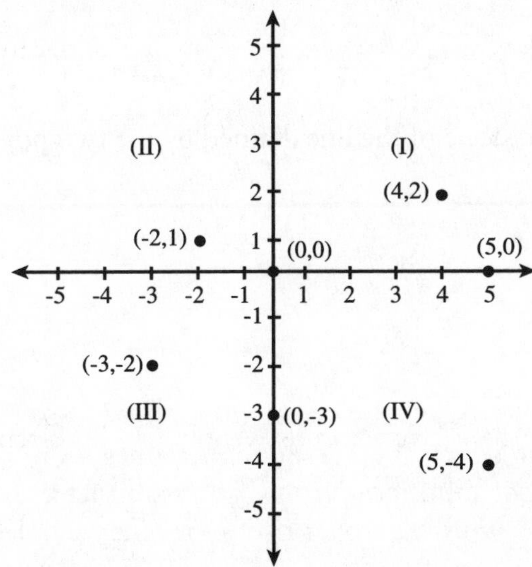

Note

Notice that we've plotted seven different points on this plane. Each point has its own unique coordinates. Before you read on, make sure you understand why each point is identified (by two coordinates) as it is.

Defining a Line on the Coordinate Plane

You can define any line on the coordinate plane by the equation: $y = mx + b$

In this equation:

- The variable m is the slope of the line.
- The variable b is the line's y-intercept (where the line crosses the y axis).
- The variables x and y are the coordinates of any point on the line. Any (x,y) pair defining a point on the line can substitute for the variables x and y.

Determining a line's *slope* is often crucial to solving ACT coordinate geometry problems. Think of the slope of a line as a fraction in which the numerator indicates the vertical change from one point to another on the line (moving left to right) corresponding to a given horizontal change, which the fraction's denominator indicates. The common term used for this fraction is "rise-over-run."

You can determine the slope of a line from any two pairs of (x,y) coordinates. In general, if (x_1,y_1) and (x_2,y_2) lie on the same line, calculate the line's slope as follows (notice that you can subtract either pair from the other):

$$\text{slope } (m) = \frac{y_2 - y_1}{x_2 - x_1} \text{ or } \frac{y_1 - y_2}{x_1 - x_2}$$

For example, here are two ways to calculate the slope of the line defined by the two points $P(2,1)$ and $Q(-3,4)$:

$$\text{slope } (m) = \frac{4 - 1}{-3 - 2} = \frac{3}{-5}$$

$$\text{slope } (m) = \frac{1 - 4}{2 - (-3)} = \frac{-3}{5}$$

Alert!

In applying the preceding formula, be sure to subtract corresponding values! For example, a careless test-taker calculating the slope might subtract y_1 from y_2 but subtract x_2 from x_1. Also, be sure to calculate "rise-over-run," *not* "run-over-rise"—another careless, but common, error.

An ACT question might ask you to identify the slope of a line defined by a given equation, in which case you simply put the equation in the standard form $y = mx + b$, then identify the m-term. Or, it might ask you to determine the equation of a line, or just the line's slope (m) or y-intercept (b), given the coordinates of two points on the line.

In the standard (x,y) coordinate plane, at what point along the vertical axis (the y-axis) does the line passing through points $(5,-2)$ and $(3,4)$ intersect that axis?

F. -8

G. $-\frac{5}{2}$

H. 3

J. 7

K. 13

The correct answer is K. The question asks for the line's y-intercept (the value of b in the general equation $y = mx + b$). First, determine the line's slope:

$$\text{slope } (m) = \frac{y_2 - y_1}{x_2 - x_1} = \frac{4 - (-2)}{3 - 5} = \frac{6}{-2} = -3$$

In the general equation $(y = mx + b)$, $m = -3$. To find the value of b, substitute either (x,y) value pair for x and y, then solve for b. Substituting the (x,y) pair $(3,4)$:

$$\begin{aligned} y &= -3x + b \\ 4 &= -3(3) + b \\ 4 &= -9 + b \\ 13 &= b \end{aligned}$$

To determine the point at which two nonparallel lines intersect on the coordinate plane, first determine the equation for each line. Then, solve for x and y by either substitution or addition-subtraction.

In the standard xy-coordinate plane, the xy-pairs $(0,2)$ and $(2,0)$ define a line, and the xy-pairs $(-2,-1)$ and $(2,1)$ define another line. At which of the following points do the two lines intersect?

A. $\left(\frac{4}{3},\frac{2}{3}\right)$

B. $\left(\frac{4}{3},\frac{4}{3}\right)$

C. $\left(-\frac{1}{2},\frac{3}{2}\right)$

D. $\left(\frac{3}{4},-\frac{2}{3}\right)$

E. $\left(-\frac{3}{4},-\frac{2}{3}\right)$

The correct answer is A. For each line, formulate its equation by determining slope (m), then y-intercept (b). For the pairs (0,2) and (2,0):

$$y = \left(\frac{0-2}{2-0}\right)x + b \text{ (slope } = -1)$$

$$0 = -2 + b$$

$$2 = b$$

The equation for the line is $y = -x + 2$. For the pairs $(-2,-1)$ and (2,1):

$$y = \left(\frac{1-(-1)}{2-(-2)}\right)x + b \left(\text{slope } = \frac{1}{2}\right)$$

$$1 = \frac{1}{2}(2) + b$$

$$0 = b$$

The equation for the line is $y = \frac{1}{2}x$. To find the point of intersection, solve for x and y by substitution. For example:

$$\frac{1}{2}x = -x + 2$$

$$\frac{3}{2}x = 2$$

$$x = \frac{4}{3}$$

$$y = \frac{2}{3}$$

The point of intersection is defined by the coordinate pair $\left(\frac{4}{3}, \frac{2}{3}\right)$.

Graphing a Line on the Coordinate Plane

You can graph a line on the coordinate plane if you know the coordinates of any two points on the line. Just plot the two points, and then draw a line connecting them. You can also graph a line from one point on the line, if you also know either the line's slope or its y-intercept.

An ACT question might ask you to recognize the value of a line's slope (m) based on a graph of the line. If the graph identifies the precise coordinates of two points, you can determine the line's precise slope (and the entire equation of the line). Even without any precise coordinates, you can still estimate the line's slope based on its appearance.

Lines that slope* upward *from left to right:

- A line sloping *upward* from left to right has a positive slope (m).
- A line with a slope of 1 slopes upward from left to right at a 45° angle in relation to the x-axis.
- A line with a fractional slope between 0 and 1 slopes upward from left to right but at less than a 45° angle in relation to the x-axis.
- A line with a slope greater than 1 slopes upward from left to right at more than a 45° angle in relation to the x-axis.

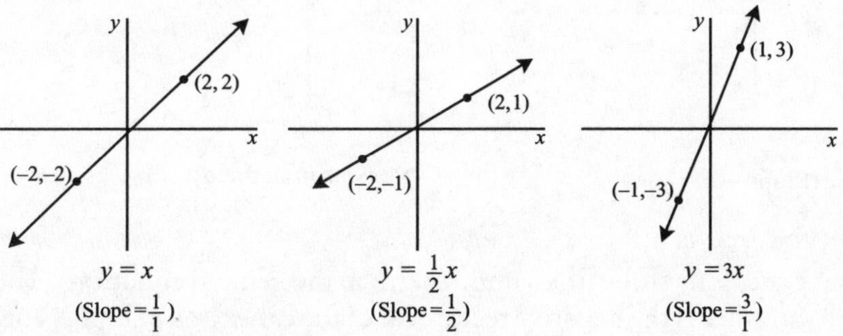

Lines that slope* downward *from left to right:

- A line sloping *downward* from left to right has a negative slope (m).
- A line with a slope of -1 slopes downward from left to right at a 45° angle in relation to the x-axis.
- A line with a fractional slope between 0 and -1 slopes downward from left to right but at less than a 45° angle in relation to the x-axis.
- A line with a slope less than -1 (for example, -2) slopes downward from left to right at more than a 45° angle in relation to the x-axis.

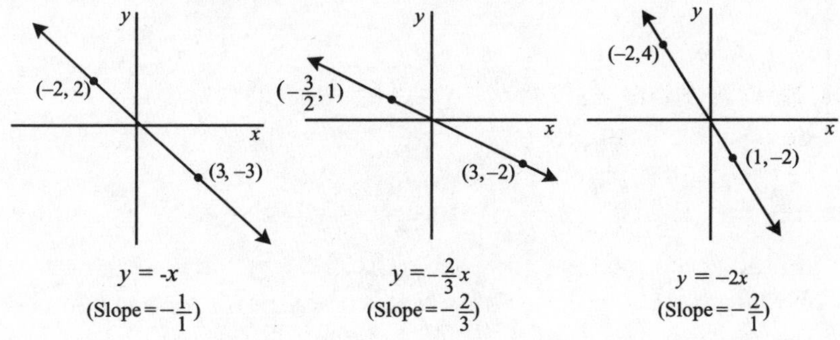

Horizontal and vertical lines:

- A *horizontal* line has a slope of zero ($m = 0, mx = 0$).
- A *vertical* line has either an undefined or an indeterminate slope (the fraction's denominator is 0), so the m-term in the equation is ignored.

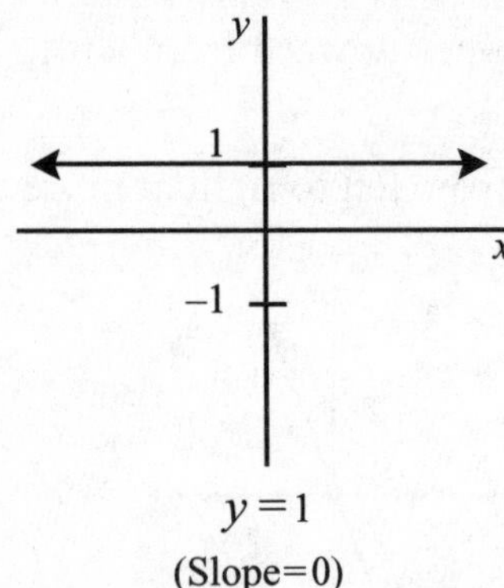

$y=1$
(Slope=0)

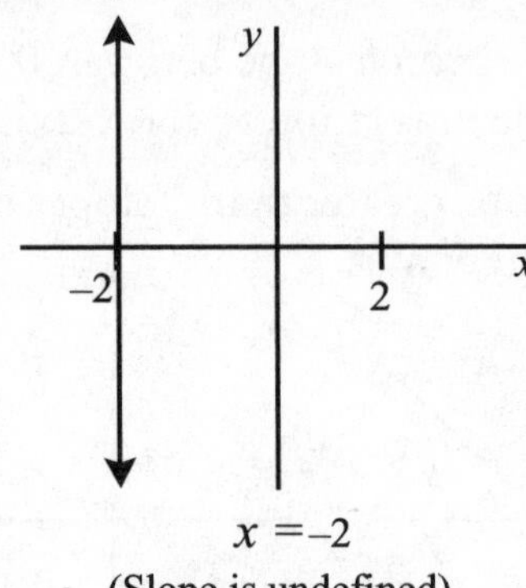

$x=-2$
(Slope is undefined)

Tip

Parallel lines have the same slope (the same m-term in the general equation). The slope of a line perpendicular to another is the negative reciprocal of the other line's slope. (The product of the two slopes is -1.) For example, a line with slope $\frac{3}{2}$ is perpendicular to a line with slope. $-\frac{2}{3}$

If the two axes in the standard (x,y) coordinate plane below are on the same scale, which of the following could be the equation of line P?

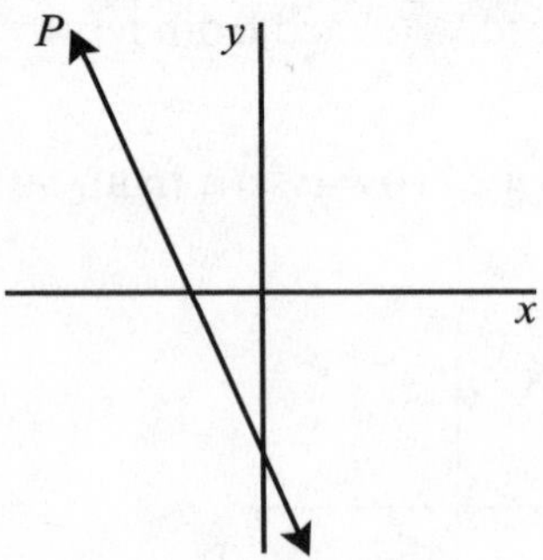

F. $y = \frac{2}{5}x - \frac{5}{2}$

G. $y = -\frac{5}{2}x + \frac{5}{2}$

H. $y = \frac{5}{2}x - \frac{5}{2}$

J. $y = \frac{2}{5}x + \frac{2}{5}$

K. $y = -\frac{5}{2}x - \frac{5}{2}$

The correct answer is K. Notice that line P slopes downward from left to right at an angle greater than 45°. Thus, the line's slope (m in the equation $y = mx + b$) < -1. Also notice that line P crosses the y-axis at a negative y-value (that is, below the x-axis). That is, the line's y-intercept (b in the equation $y = mx + b$) is negative. Only choice **K** provides an equation that meets both conditions.

The Midpoint and Distance Formulas

To be ready for ACT coordinate geometry, you'll need to know these two formulas. To find the coordinates of the midpoint of a line segment, simply average the two endpoints' x-values and y-values:

$$x_M = \frac{x_1 + x_2}{2} \text{ and } y_M = \frac{y_1 + y_2}{2}$$

For example, the midpoint between $(-3,1)$ and $(2,4) = \left(\frac{-3+2}{2}, \frac{1+4}{2}\right)$, or $\left(-\frac{1}{2}, \frac{5}{2}\right)$.

An ACT question might simply ask you to find the midpoint between two given points. Or, it might provide the midpoint and one endpoint, and then ask you to determine the other point.

In the standard xy-coordinate plane, the point $M(-1,3)$ is the midpoint of line segment whose endpoints are $A(2,-4)$ and B. What are the xy-coordinates of point B?

A. $(-1,-2)$
B. $(-3,8)$
C. $(8,-4)$
D. $(5,12)$
E. $(-4,10)$

The correct answer is E. Apply the midpoint formula to find the x-coordinate of point B:

$$-1 = \frac{x + 2}{2}$$
$$-2 = x + 2$$
$$-4 = x$$

Apply the midpoint formula to find the y-coordinate of point B:

$$3 = \frac{y - 4}{2}$$
$$6 = y - 4$$
$$10 = y$$

To find the *distance* between two points that have the same x-coordinate (or y-coordinate), simply compute the difference between the two y-values (or x-values). Otherwise, the line segment is neither vertical nor horizontal, and you'll need to apply the *distance formula*, which is actually the Pythagorean theorem, in thin disguise (it measures the length of a right triangle's hypotenuse):

$$d = \sqrt{(x_1 - x_2)^2 + (y_1 - y_2)^2}$$

For example, the distance between (−3,1) and (2,4)

$$= \sqrt{(-3 - 2)^2 + (1 - 4)^2} = \sqrt{25 + 9} = \sqrt{34}.$$

Alert!

In the distance formula, it doesn't matter which of the two points (x_1,y_1) signifies, or which point (x_2,y_2) signifies. But whichever pair you choose as (x_1,y_1), be sure not to inadvertently switch x_1 with x_2, or y_1 with y_2.

An ACT question might ask for the distance between two defined points (as in the previous example). Or, it might provide the distance, and then ask for the value of a missing coordinate—in which case you solve for the missing *x*-value or *y*-value in the formula.

In a more complex question, the distance between two points might be key to determining the area, perimeter, or other characteristic of a geometric figure such as a triangle, rectangle, or circle.

In the standard (*xy*) coordinate plane, a circle has center (2,−1), and the point (−3,3) lies along the circle's circumference. What is the area of the circle, expressed in square coordinate units?

F. 36π

G. $\frac{81\pi}{2}$

H. 41π

J. 48π

K. 57π

The correct answer is H. The circle's radius is the distance between its center (2,−1) and any point along its circumference, including (−3,3). Hence, you can find *r* by applying the distance formula:

$$\sqrt{(-3 - 2)^2 + (3 - (-1))^2} = \sqrt{25 + 16} = \sqrt{41}$$

The area of the circle $= \pi\left(\sqrt{41}\right)^2 = 41\pi$.

Right-Triangle Trigonometry

Right-triangle trigonometry involves the ratios between sides of right triangles and the angle measures that correspond to these ratios. Refer to the following right triangle, in which the sides opposite angles *A*, *B*, and *C* are labeled *a*, *b*, and *c*, respectively (*A* and *B* are the two acute angles):

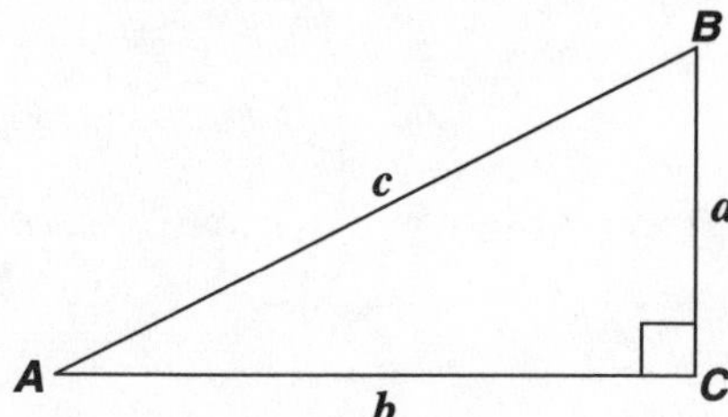

Referring to ΔABC, here's how you would express and define the six trigonometric functions sine, cosine, tangent, cotangent, secant, and cosecant for angle *A* (notice that the functions in the right column are reciprocals of the functions in the left column):

$\sin A = \frac{a}{c}$	$\csc A = \frac{c}{a}$
$\cos A = \frac{b}{c}$	$\sec A = \frac{c}{b}$
$\tan A = \frac{a}{b}$	$\cot A = \frac{b}{a}$

The six functions for angle *B* would be expressed and defined similarly. The sine, cosine, and tangent functions are by far the most important, so be sure to memorize these three general definitions (for the ACT, these three functions should be second-nature to you):

$$\text{sine} = \frac{\text{opposite}}{\text{hypotenuse}}$$

$$\text{cosine} = \frac{\text{adjacent}}{\text{hypotenuse}}$$

$$\text{tangent} = \frac{\text{opposite}}{\text{adjacent}}$$

An ACT question might provide the lengths of a right triangle's two legs and ask you for the sine, cosine, or tangent of one of a triangle's two acute angles. Just apply the preceding definitions and you won't have any trouble with the question.

In the figure below, $\cos x =$

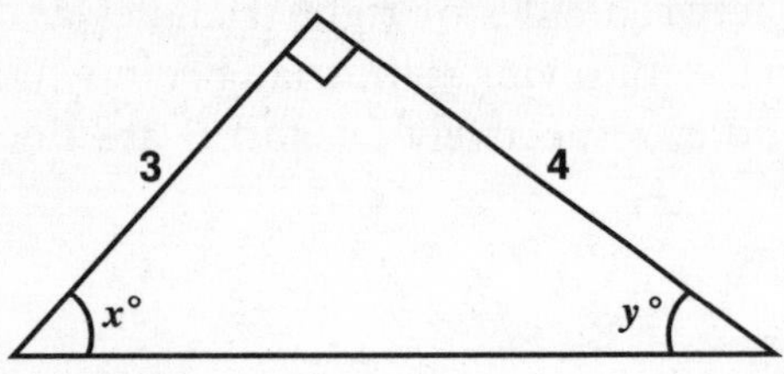

A. $\frac{2}{5}$

B. $\frac{3}{5}$

C. $\frac{3}{4}$

D. $\frac{4}{5}$

E. $\frac{4}{3}$

The correct answer is B. You should recognize the Pythagorean side triplet 3:4:5 and, accordingly, that the length of the hypotenuse is 5. Hence, $\cos x = \frac{3}{5}$.

Just for the record, referring to the figure in the preceding question, $\tan x = \frac{4}{3}$, $\sin x = \frac{4}{5}$, $\tan y = \frac{3}{4}$, $\sin y = \frac{3}{5}$. You can easily obtain values for the other functions (cotangent, secant, and cosecant) from the ones listed here.

To spice up questions like these, the test-makers might use numbers that don't correspond neatly to a Pythagorean triplet. Or, they might ask you to combine two different functions by one of the four basic operations. For instance, referring again to the figure in the preceding question:

$$(\tan x)(\tan y) = \left(\frac{4}{3}\right)\left(\frac{3}{4}\right) = 1$$

$$\sin x - \sin y = \frac{4}{5} - \frac{3}{5} = \frac{1}{5}$$

$$\sin y \div \cos y = \frac{3}{5} \div \frac{4}{5} = \frac{3}{4}$$

Many other combinations are possible, but they all involve a similar drill: Determine the value of two functions, then combine them.

For the ACT, you should know the definitions of the six basic trigonometric functions relating to the sides of a right triangle—sine, cosine, tangent, cotangent, secant, and cosecant. You should also keep in mind the following trigonometric *identities* (of the four, the first one will probably be the most useful for the ACT):

$$\text{tangent} = \frac{\text{sine}}{\text{cosine}}$$

$$\text{cotangent} = \frac{1}{\text{tangent}}$$

$$\text{cosecant} = \frac{1}{\text{sine}}$$

$$\text{secant} = \frac{1}{\text{cosine}}$$

The relationships among the sine, cosine, and tangent functions result in the following additional observations for a triangle with acute angles A and B:

- By definition, $\tan A \times \tan B = 1$.
- For all right triangles, $\sin A = \cos B$ (and $\sin B = \cos A$). For all other triangles, $\sin A \neq \cos B$ (and $\sin B \neq \cos A$).
- In a right isosceles triangle (in which A and B each measures 45°), $\sin A = \sin B = \cos A = \cos B = \frac{\sqrt{2}}{2}$.

The preceding identities and other relationships between functions can serve as shortcuts to the solution to an ACT problem that otherwise might elude you.

> If $\sin A = x$, which of the following expressions is equal to x at all points for which it is defined?
>
> **F.** $1 - \cos A$
> **G.** $(\cot A)(\cos A)$
> **H.** $(\tan A)(\cos A)$
> **J.** $\cos A - 1$
> **K.** $\sec A \div \tan A$

The correct answer is H. Applying the tangent identity $\tan A = \frac{\sin A}{\cos A}$ to choice **H**:

$$(\tan A)(\cos A) = \left(\frac{\sin A}{\cos A}\right)(\cos A) = \sin A$$

The acute angles of the Pythagorean triplets 45°-45°-90° and 30°-60°-90° are especially test-worthy when it comes to right-triangle trigonometry questions. That's because the values of these angles' functions are easy to express using the theorem. For the ACT, you should memorize the sine, cosine, and tangent functions of the 30°, 45°, and 60° angles of a right triangle:

$\sin 30° = \frac{1}{2}$	$\sin 45° = \frac{\sqrt{2}}{2}$	$\sin 60° = \frac{\sqrt{3}}{2}$
$\cos 30° = \frac{\sqrt{3}}{2}$	$\cos 45° = \frac{\sqrt{2}}{2}$	$\cos 60° = \frac{1}{2}$
$\tan 30° = \frac{\sqrt{3}}{3}$	$\tan 45° = 1$	$\tan 60° = \sqrt{3}$

Another type of question involving right-triangle trigonometry provides one angle measure and one side length, then asks for another side length *in terms of* one of the trigonometry functions. These questions are often cast as word problems.

A 50-foot wire is attached to the top of a vertical electric pole and is anchored on the ground. If the wire rises in a straight line at a 70° angle for the ground, what is the height of the pole, in linear feet?

A. $50\sin 70°$
B. $50\cos 70°$
C. $50\tan 70°$
D. $\frac{\cos 70°}{50}$
E. $\frac{50}{\cos 70°}$

The correct answer is A. As shown in the diagram below, the height of the pole (x) is opposite the 70° angle, and the triangle's hypotenuse (length of the wire) is 50. Since sine = opposite divided by hypotenuse:

$$\frac{x}{50} = \sin 70°$$

$$x = 50\sin 70°$$

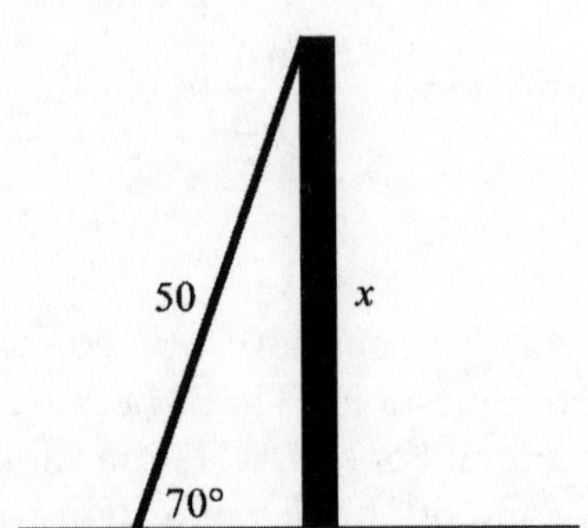

To further complicate this type of question, the test-makers might require you to work with two separate triangles that share one common vertex. Or, they might require you to construct a right triangle from a *non*-right triangle.

In the figure below, $m\angle ABC = 130°$. What is the unit area of ΔABC?

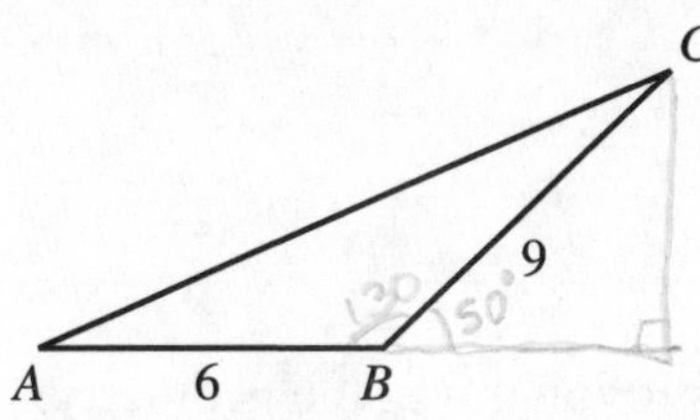

F. $27\sin 50°$

G. $27\cos 50°$

H. $\frac{27}{\sin 50°}$

J. $54\cos 50°$

K. $54\sin 50°$

The correct answer is F. Dropping a perpendicular from C down to the extension of $\overline{AB}$ (see the diagram below), you can see that $m\angle CBD = 50°$ and hence that $\sin 50° = \frac{h}{9}$ (the triangle's altitude h divided by its hypotenuse). Thus, $h = 9\sin 50°$. Now that you know the base and height of ΔABC, you can determine its area: $\frac{1}{2}(6)(9\sin 50°) = 27\sin 50°$.

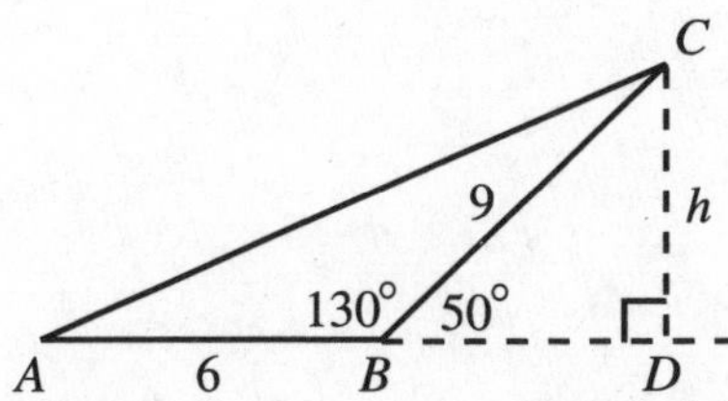

Note

On the ACT, you won't find any trigonometric tables, which list angle measures and their corresponding trigonometry function values. The question might provide the angles measure you need. More likely, however, you'll express solutions to problems like the two preceding ones *in terms of* trigonometric functions.

Take It to the Next Level

At this level, you'll review the following advanced topics involving plane geometry:

- Characteristics of isosceles and equilateral triangles
- The properties of polygons having more than four sides
- Relationships created by combining a circle with another geometric figure (such as a triangle, square, or another circle)
- Relationships between arcs and other features of circles
- Relationships between circles and tangent lines
- Properties of cubes and other rectangular solids
- Equations of conic sections (circles and ellipses) and of parabolas and hyperbolas and their corresponding graphs on the (x,y) plane.

Isosceles Triangles

An *isosceles* triangle has the following special properties:

1. Two of the sides are congruent (equal in length).
2. The two angles opposite the two congruent sides are congruent (equal in size, or degree measure).

If you know any two angle measures of a triangle, you can determine whether the triangle is isosceles.

In the figure below, $\overline{BC}$ is 6 units long, m$\angle A$ = 70°, and m$\angle B$ = 40°. How many units long is $\overline{AB}$?

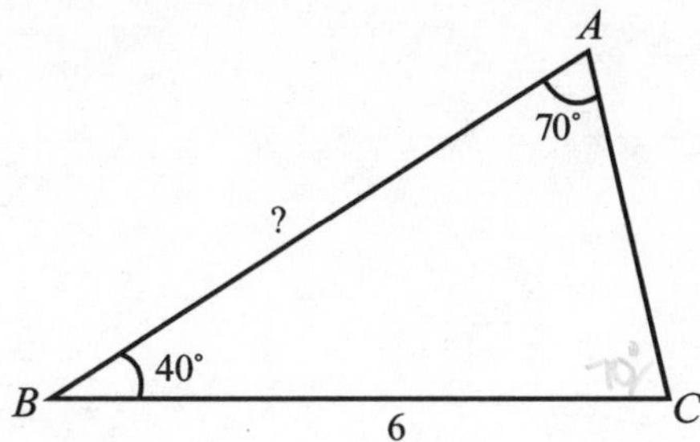

A. 5
B. 6
C. 7
D. $5\sqrt{25}$
E. It cannot be determined from the information given.

The correct answer is B. Since m$\angle A$ and $\angle B$ add up to 110°, m$\angle C$ = 70° (70 + 110 = 180), and you know the triangle is isosceles. What's more, since m$\angle A$ = m$\angle C$, $\overline{AB} \cong \overline{BC}$. Given that $\overline{BC}$ is 6 units long, $\overline{AB}$ must also be 6 units long.

In any isosceles triangle, the line bisecting the angle connecting the two congruent sides divides the triangle into two congruent right triangles. So, if you know the lengths of all three sides of an isosceles triangle, you can determine the area of the triangle by applying the Pythagorean theorem.

Two sides of a triangle are each 8 units long, and the third side is 6 units long. What is the area of the triangle, expressed in square units?

F. 14
G. $12\sqrt{3}$
H. 18
J. 22
K. $3\sqrt{55}$

The correct answer is K. Bisect the angle connecting the two congruent sides ($\overline{BC}$ and $\overline{AC}$ in ΔABC in the next figure). The bisecting line is the triangle's height (h), and $\overline{AB}$ is its base, which is 6 units long.

Take It to the Next Level

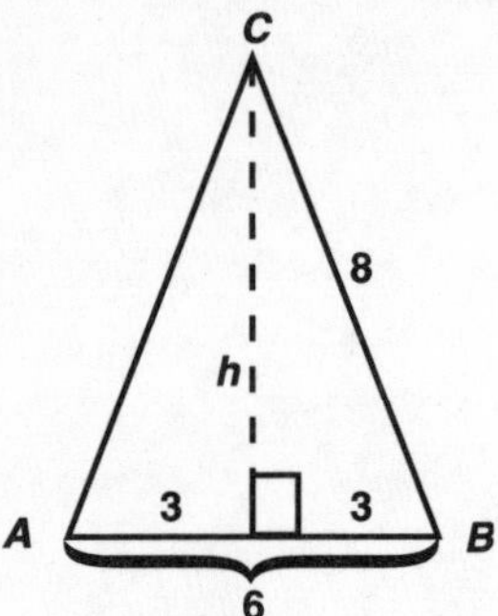

You can determine the triangle's height (h) by applying the Pythagorean theorem:

$$3^2 + h^2 = 8^2$$
$$h^2 = 64 - 9$$
$$h^2 = 55$$
$$h = \sqrt{55}$$

A triangle's area is half the product of its base and height. Thus, the area of ΔABC = $\frac{1}{2}(6)\sqrt{55} = 3\sqrt{55}$.

Equilateral Triangles

An equilateral triangle has the following three properties:

1. All three sides are congruent (equal in length).
2. The measure of each angle is 60°.
3. Area = $\frac{s^2\sqrt{3}}{4}$ (s = any side)

Any line bisecting one of the 60° angles divides an equilateral triangle into two right triangles with angle measures of 30°, 60°, and 90°; in other words, into two $1:\sqrt{3}:2$ triangles, as shown in the right-hand triangle in the next figure. (Remember that Pythagorean angle triplet?)

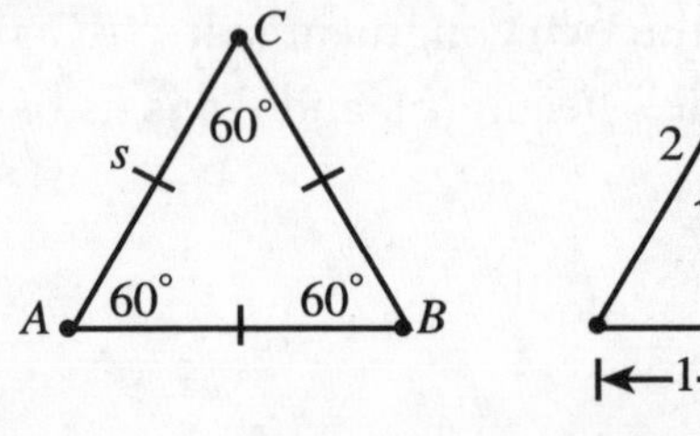

In the left-hand triangle, if $s = 2$, the area of the triangle = $\sqrt{3}$. To confirm this formula, bisect the triangle into two 30°-60°-90° $(1:\sqrt{3}:2)$ triangles (as in the right-hand triangle in the preceding figure). The area of this equilateral triangle is $\frac{1}{2}(2)\sqrt{3}$, or $\sqrt{3}$. The area of each smaller right triangle is $\frac{\sqrt{3}}{2}$.

X-Ref

On the ACT, equilateral triangles usually appear in problems involving *circles*. You'll look at this type of problem later in this level.

Polygons

Polygons include all plane figures formed only by straight lines. The first level focused on only two types of polygons: three-sided ones (triangles) and four-sided ones (quadrilaterals). Now, take a quick look at the key characteristics of all polygons. First, remember these two reciprocal rules:

1. If all angles of a polygon are congruent (the same size), then all sides are congruent (equal in length).
2. If all sides of a polygon are congruent (the same size), then all angles are congruent (equal in size, or degree measure).

Note

A polygon in which all sides are congruent and all angles are congruent is called a *regular* polygon. But, for the ACT, you don't need to know the terminology, just the principle.

You can use the following formula to determine the sum of all interior angles of *any* polygon whose angles each measure less than 180° (n = number of sides):

$(n - 2)(180°)$ = sum of interior angles

For *regular* polygons, the average angle size is also the size of every angle. But, for any polygon (except for those with an angle exceeding 180°), you can find the average angle size by dividing the sum of the angles by the number of sides. One way to shortcut the math is to memorize the angle sums and averages for polygons with three to eight sides:

3 sides: $(3 - 2)(180°) = 180° \div 3 = 60°$

4 sides: $(4 - 2)(180°) = 360° \div 4 = 90°$

5 sides: $(5 - 2)(180°) = 540° \div 5 = 108°$

6 sides: $(6 - 2)(180°) = 720° \div 6 = 120°$

7 sides: $(7 - 2)(180°) = 900° \div 7 \approx 129°$

8 sides: $(8 - 2)(180°) = 1080° \div 8 = 135°$

If all five sides of a pentagon are congruent, what is the measure of each of the pentagon's interior angles?

A. 90°
B. 108°
C. 112°
D. 120°
E. It cannot be determined from the information given.

The correct answer is B. The polygon is a regular pentagon (five-sided polygon). Each interior angle measures 108°.

Advanced Circle Problems

ACT circle problems sometimes involve other geometric figures as well, so they're inherently tougher than average. The most common such "hybrids" involve triangles, squares, and other circles. In the next sections, you'll learn all you need to know to handle any hybrid problem.

Arcs and Degree Measures of a Circle

An *arc* is a segment of a circle's circumference. A *minor arc* is the shortest arc connecting two points on a circle's circumference. For example, in the next figure, minor arc *AB* is the one formed by the 60° angle from the circle's center (O).

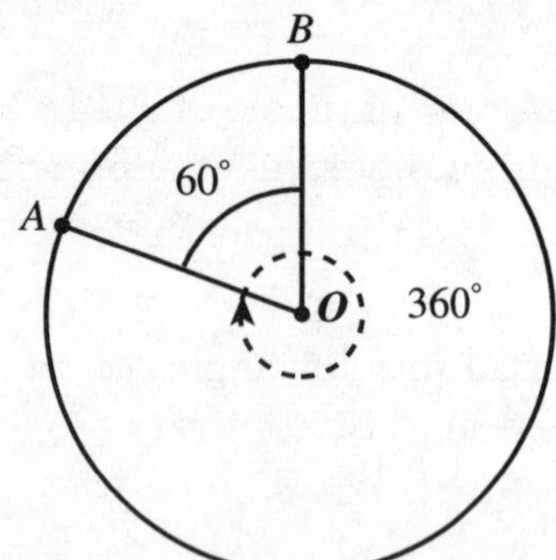

A circle, by definition, contains a total of 360°. The length of an arc relative to the circle's circumference is directly proportionate to the arc's degree measure as a fraction of the circle's total degree measure of 360°. For example, in the preceding figure, minor arc *AB* accounts for $\frac{60}{360}$, or $\frac{1}{6}$, of the circle's circumference.

> **Note**
>
> An arc of a circle can be defined either as a length (a portion of the circle's circumference) or as a degree measure.

Given that point O is the center of the circle, if m$\angle OAB$ = 70° and the circumference is 9, what is the length of minor arc AB?

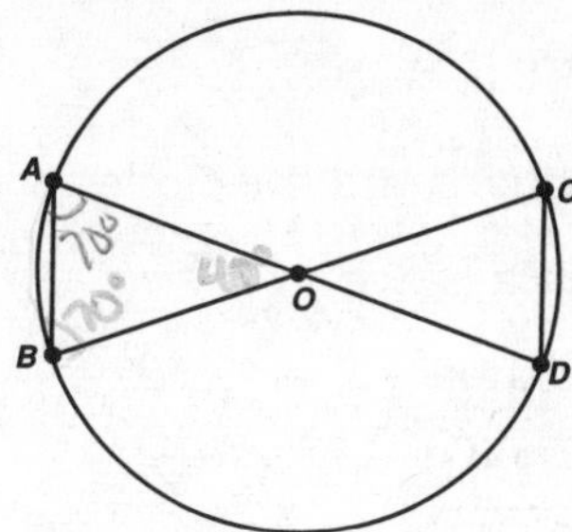

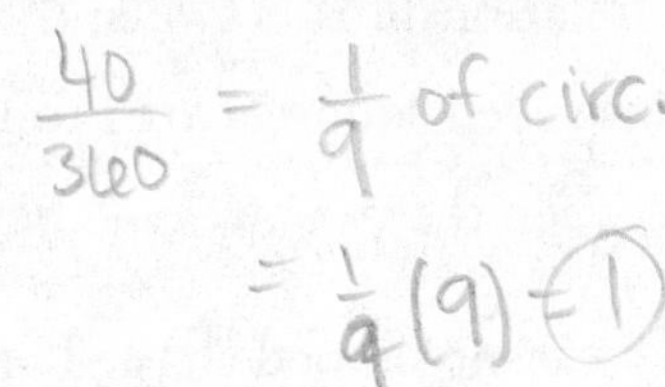

F. $\frac{1}{9}$

G. $\frac{2}{9}$

H. 1

J. $\frac{9}{7}$

K. 2

The correct answer is H. Since $\triangle AOB$ is isoceles, m$\angle OBA$ = 70°. Then $\angle AOB$ = 180° − 70° − 70° = 40°. This means that minor arc AB must account for $\frac{40}{360} = \frac{1}{9}$ of the entire circumference. Thus, its length = $\left(\frac{1}{9}\right)(9) = 1$.

Circles and Inscribed Polygons

A polygon is *inscribed* in a circle if each vertex of the polygon lies on the circle's circumference. The next figure shows an inscribed square. The square is partitioned into four congruent triangles, each with one vertex at the circle's center (O).

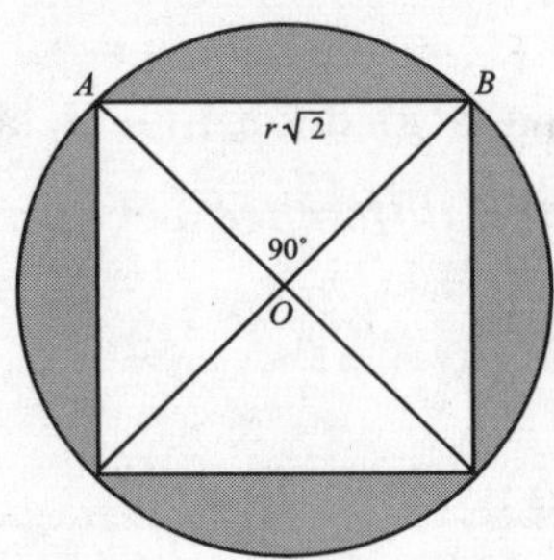

Look at any one of the four congruent triangles—for example, ΔABO. Notice that ΔABO is a *right* triangle with the 90° angle at the circle's center. The length of each of the triangle's two legs ($\overline{AO}$ and $\overline{BO}$) equals the circle's radius (r). Accordingly, ΔABO is a right isosceles triangle,

$m\angle OAB = m\angle OBA = 45°$, and $AB = r\sqrt{2}$. (The ratio of the triangle's sides is $1:1:\sqrt{2}$.) Since $\overline{AB}$ is also the side of the square, the area of a square inscribed in a circle is $\left(r\sqrt{2}\right)^2$, or $2r^2$. (The area of ΔABO is $\frac{r^2}{2}$, one fourth the area of the square.)

You can also determine relationships between the inscribed square and the circle:

- The ratio of the inscribed square's area to the circle's area is $2:\pi$.
- The *difference* between the two areas—the total shaded area—is $\pi r^2 - 2r^2$.
- The area of each crescent-shaped shaded area is $\frac{(\pi r^2 - 2r^2)}{4}$.

The next figure shows a circle with an inscribed regular hexagon. (In a regular polygon, all sides are congruent.) The hexagon is partitioned into six congruent triangles, each with one vertex at the circle's center (O).

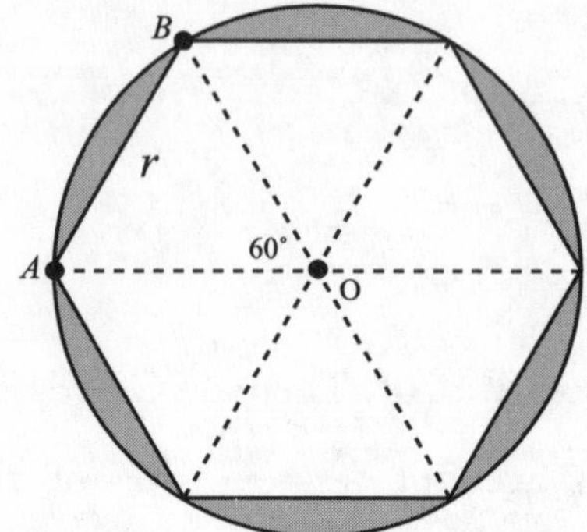

Look at any one of the six congruent triangles—for example, ΔABO. Since all six triangles are congruent, $m\angle AOB = 60°$ (one sixth of 360°). You can see that the length of $\overline{AO}$ and $\overline{BO}$ each equals the circle's radius (r). Accordingly, $m\angle OAB = m\angle OBA = 60°$, ΔABO is an equilateral triangle, and the length of $\overline{AB} = r$.

Applying the area formula for equilateral triangles: Area of $\Delta ABO = \frac{r^2\sqrt{3}}{4}$. The area of the hexagon is six times the area of ΔABO, or $\frac{3r^2\sqrt{3}}{2}$. You can also determine relationships between the inscribed hexagon and the circle. For example, the *difference* between the two areas—the total shaded area—is $\pi r^2 - \frac{3r^2\sqrt{3}}{2}$.

The figure below shows a square that is touching to each of two circles at four points. If the diameter of the large circle is 10, what is the diameter of the smaller circle?

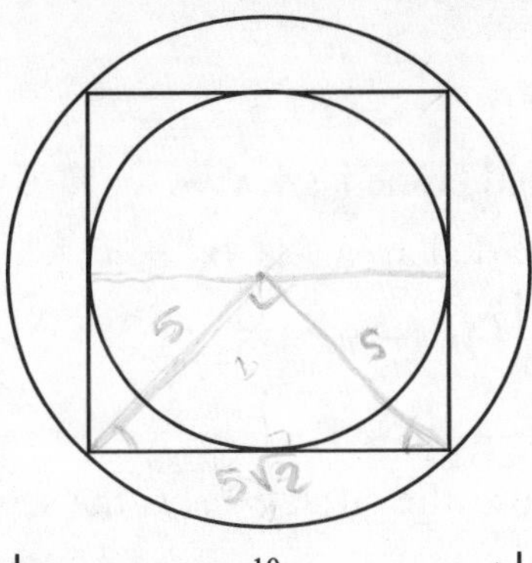

A. $\frac{5\sqrt{3}}{2}$

B. 5

C. 2π

D. $5\sqrt{2}$

E. 7.5

The correct answer is D. The square's diagonal is equal in length to the large circle's diameter, which is 10. This diagonal is the hypotenuse of a triangle whose legs are two sides of the square. The triangle is a right isosceles, with sides in the ratio $1:1:\sqrt{2}$. The length of each side of the square $= \frac{10}{\sqrt{2}}$, or $5\sqrt{2}$. This length is also the diameter of the small circle.

Tangents and Inscribed Circles

A circle is *tangent* to a line (or line segment) if they intersect at one and only one point (called the *point of tangency*). Here's the key rule to remember about tangents: A line that is tangent to a circle is *always* perpendicular to the line passing through the circle's center and the point of tangency.

The next figure shows a circle with center O inscribed by a square. Point P is one of four points of tangency. By definition, $\overline{OP} \perp \overline{AB}$.

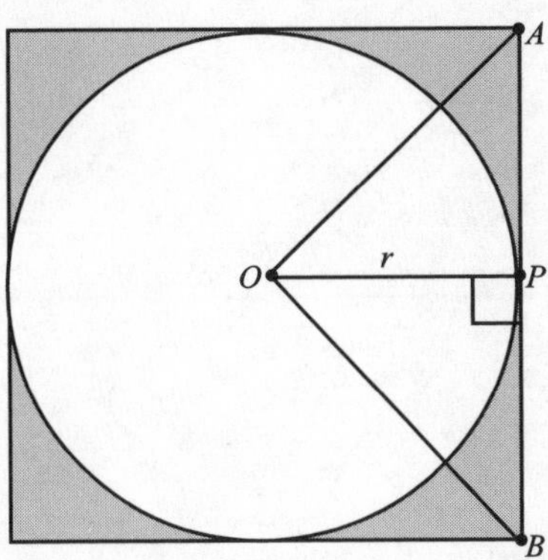

Also, notice the following relationships between the circle in the preceding figure and the inscribing square (r = radius):

- Each side of the square is $2r$ in length.
- The square's area is $(2r)^2$, or $4r^2$.
- The ratio of the square's area to that of the inscribed circle is: $4:\pi$.
- The *difference* between the two areas—the total shaded area—is $4r^2 - \pi r^2$.
- The area of each separate (smaller) shaded area is $\frac{1}{4}(4r^2 - \pi r^2)$.

For *any* regular polygon (including squares) that inscribes a circle:

- The point of tangency between each line segment and the circle *bisects* the segment.
- Connecting each vertex to the circle's center creates an array of congruent angles, arcs, and triangles.

For example, the left-hand figure below shows a regular pentagon, and the right-hand figure shows a regular hexagon. Each polygon inscribes a circle. In each figure, the shaded region is one of five (or six) identical ones.

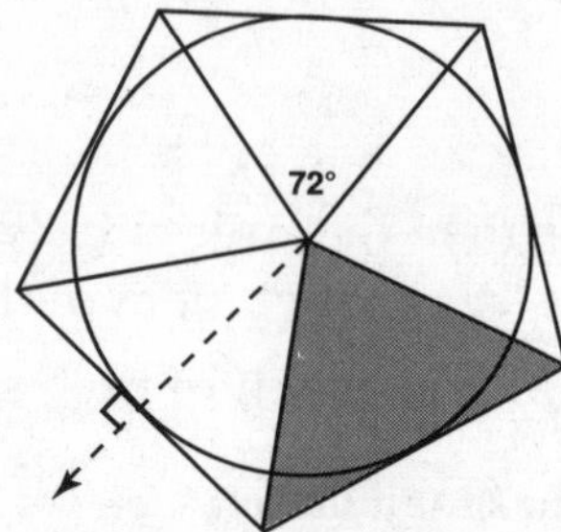

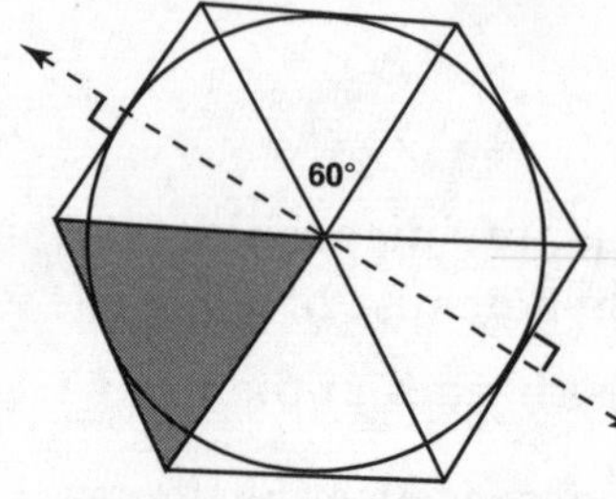

In the figure below, a circle with center O is tangent to $\overline{AB}$ at point D and tangent to $\overline{AC}$ at point C. If $m\angle BAC = 40°$, then $x =$

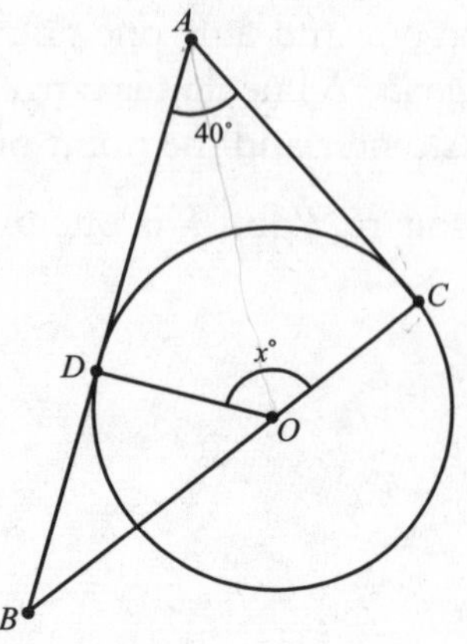

F. 140
G. 145
H 150
J. 155
K. It cannot be determined from the information given.

The correct answer is F. Since $\overline{AC}$ is tangent to the circle, $\overline{AC} \perp \overline{BC}$. Accordingly, ΔABC is a right triangle, and $m\angle B = 50°$. Similarly, $\overline{AB} \perp \overline{DO}$, ΔDBO is a right triangle, and $m\angle DOB = 40°$. $\angle DOC$ (the angle in question) is supplementary to $\angle DOB$. Thus, $m\angle DOC = 140°$ ($x = 140$).

Comparing Circles

On the ACT, questions asking you to compare circles come in two varieties. You either:

- Calculate the *difference* between radii, circumferences, or areas, or
- Determine *ratios* involving the two circles and their radii, circumference, or areas.

To calculate a *difference* between the radii, circumferences, or areas, just calculate each area or circumference, then subtract. And if the question asks you for a difference between proportionate *segments* of the two circles, first find the difference between the circular areas, then calculate the fractional portion. No sweat.

To handle questions involving *ratios*, you need to understand that the relationship between a circle's radius or circumference and its area is *exponential*, not linear (because $A = \pi r^2$). For example, if one circle's radius is *twice* that of another, the ratio of the circles' areas is 1:4($\pi r^2:\pi(2r)^2$). If the larger circle's radius is *three* times that of the smaller circle, the ratio is 1:9 [$\pi r^2:\pi(3r)^2$]. A 1:4 ratio between radii results in a 1:16 area ratio (and so forth).

The same proportions apply if you compare circumferences and areas. If the circumference ratio is 2:1, then the area ratio is 4:1. If the circumference ratio is 4:1, then the area ratio is 16:1.

In the figure below, point O lies at the center of both circles. If $\overline{OP} = 6$ and $\overline{PQ} = 2$, what is the ratio of the area of the smaller circle to the area of the larger circle?

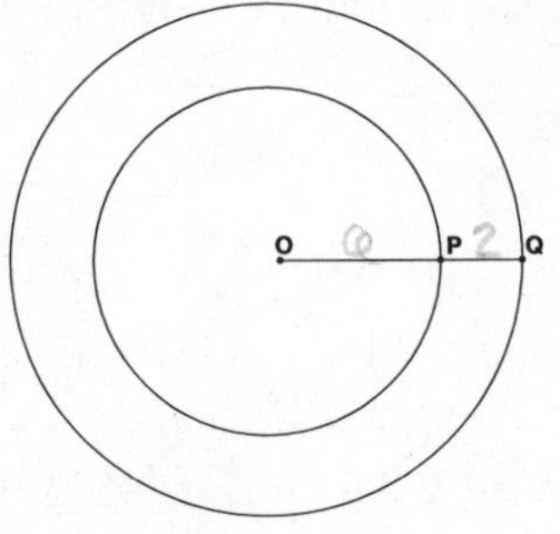

A. $\frac{5}{8}$

B. $\frac{9}{16}$

C. $\frac{1}{2}$

D. $\frac{7}{16}$

E. $\frac{3}{8}$

The correct answer is B. The ratio of the small circle's radius to that of the large circle is 6:8, or 3:4. Since area = πr^2, the area ratio is $\pi(3)^2$: $\pi(4)^2$, or 9:16.

Cubes and Other Rectangular Solids

ACT questions involving *rectangular solids* always involve one or both of two basic formulas (l = length, w = width, h = height):

Volume = lwh

Surface Area = $2lw + 2wh + 2lh = 2(lw + wh + lh)$

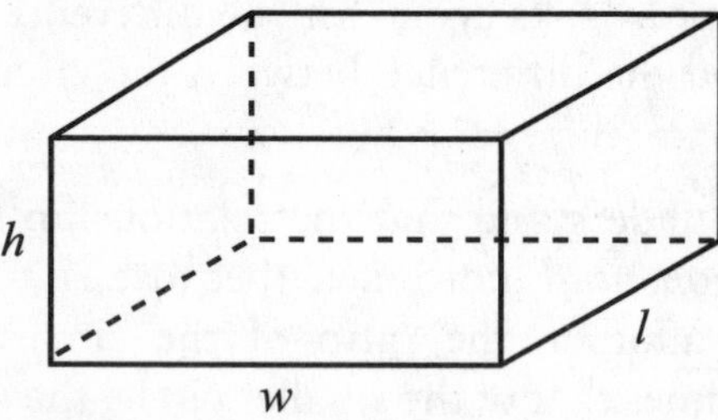

For *cubes*, the volume and surface-area formulas are even simpler than for other rectangular solids (let s = any edge):

Volume = s^3 , or $s = \sqrt[3]{\text{Volume}}$

Surface Area = $6s^2$

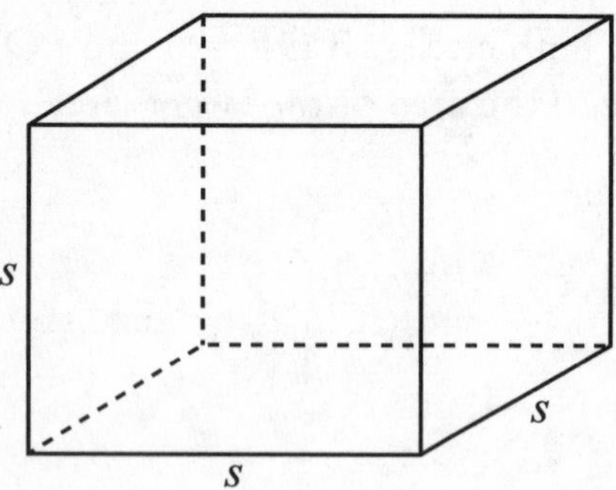

An ACT question might require you to apply any one of the formulas. Plug what you know into the formula, then solve for whatever characteristic the question asks for. Or, a question might require you to deal with the formulas for both surface area and volume.

A closed rectangular box with a square base is 5 inches in height. If the volume of the box is 45 square inches, what is the box's surface area, in square inches?

F. 45
G. 75
H. 78
J. 81
K. 90

The correct answer is H. First, determine the dimensions of the square base. The box's height is given as 5. Accordingly, the box's volume (45) = $5lw$, and $lw = 9$. Since the base is square, the base is 3 inches long on each side. Now you can calculate the total surface area: $2lw + 2wh + 2lw = (2)(9) + (2)(15) + (2)(15) = 78$.

A variation on the preceding question might ask the number of smaller boxes you could fit, or "pack," into the box that the question describes. For instance, the number of cube-shaped boxes, each one 1.5 inches on a side, that you could pack into the $3\times3\times5$ box is 12 (3 levels of 4 cubes, with a half-inch space left at the top of the box).

A test question involving a cube might focus on the *ratios* among the cube's linear, square, and cubic measurements.

> If the volume of one cube is 8 times greater than that of another, what is the ratio of the area of one square face of the larger cube to that of the smaller cube?
>
> A. 16:1
> B. 12:1
> C. 8:1
> D. 4:1
> E. 2:1

The correct answer is D. The ratio of the two volumes is 8:1. Thus, the linear ratio of the cubes' edges is the cube root of this ratio: $\sqrt[3]{8}$, or 2:1. The area ratio is the square of the linear ratio, or 4:1.

Equations and Graphs of Circles

In the standard (x,y) coordinate plane, the equation for a circle whose radius is r and whose center is at the origin (shown in the left-hand figure below) is $x^2 + y^2 = r^2$. The graph of this general equation is shown in the left-hand figure below. Similarly, the equation for a circle whose radius is r and whose center is at (h,k) — shown in the right-hand figure—is $(x - h)^2 + (y - k)^2 = r^2$.

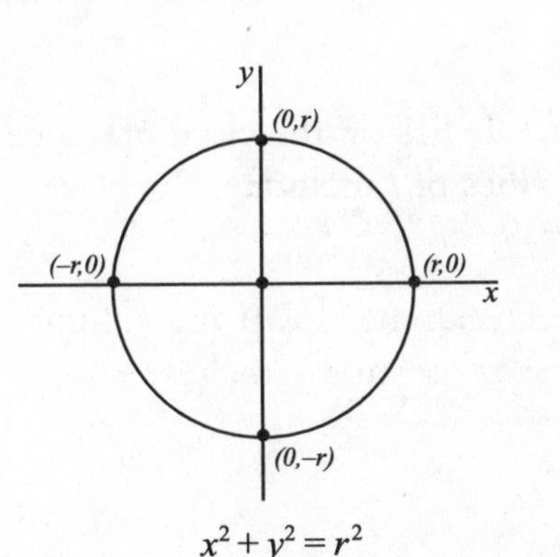

$x^2 + y^2 = r^2$

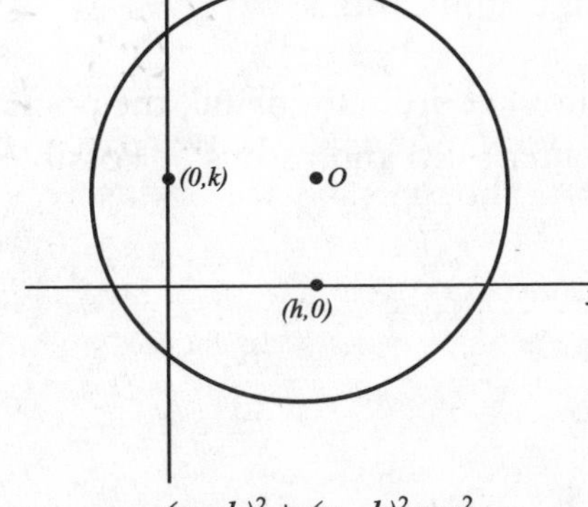

$(x - h)^2 + (y - k)^2 = r^2$

An ACT question might provide the equation of a certain circle and ask you to identify the circle's center or its radius (or its diameter, circumference, or area). For example, given the equation $(x - 3)^2 + (y + 3)^2 = 25$, you can easily determine by the general equation that the circle's center is at the point $(3,-3)$ and that the circle's radius is 5. Conversely, a question might provide the coordinates of a circle's center and its radius, then ask you to identify the equation of the circle. For example, the equation of a circle with center $(-2,-4)$ and radius 4 is $(x + 2)^2 + (y + 4)^2 = 16$.

To complicate things just a bit, the test-makers might require you to calculate r, given either the circle's area or circumference (or vice versa).

In the standard (x,y) coordinate plane, which of the following equations describes the circle that has center $(4,-2)$ and whose enclosed area, expressed in square coordinate units, is 9π ?

F. $(x - 4)^2 + (y + 2)^2 = 9$
G. $(x - 4)^2 + (y + 2)^2 = 3$
H. $(x - 4)^2 + (y - 2)^2 = 9$
J. $(x + 4)^2 + (y + 2)^2 = 9$
K. $(x - 4)^2 + (y - 2)^2 = 3$

The correct answer is F. In the standard form $(x - h)^2 + (y - k)^2 = r^2$, $h = 4$ and $k = -2$. Eliminate choices **H, J,** and **K.** Find r^2 by applying the area formula: $A = \pi r^2$; $9\pi = \pi r^2$; $9 = r^2$, as choice **F** provides.

Alert!

In questions like the preceding one, pay close attention to plus and minus signs in the answer choices. When either h or k (or both) are negative numbers, it's especially easy to overlook that subtracting a negative number is the same as adding a positive one.

In a tougher circle graph question, you might need to supply the equation. You might also need to solve for either x or y—in which case two solutions, or roots, are possible. Here's an example that incorporates both complications:

In the standard (x,y) coordinate plane, the point $(t,-1)$ lies on the circumference of a circle that has center $(4,2)$ and radius 5. Possible values of t include:

I. 0
II. 2
III. 8

A. II only
B. III only
C. I and III only
D. I and II only
E. II and III only

The correct answer is C. In the equation for a graph of a circle, let $x = t$, $y = -1$, and $r = 5$. Solve for t:

$$(t-4)^2 + (-1-2)^2 = 5^2$$
$$t^2 - 8t + 16 + 9 = 25$$
$$t^2 - 8t = 0$$
$$t(t-8) = 0$$
$$t = 0,8$$

Unless a line that passes through a circle is tangent to the circle, the line will cross the circle's circumference at exactly *two* points. That's why, in the equation for the graph of a circle on the (x,y) plane, for every value of x, two values for y are possible (and vice versa).

Equations and Graphs of Ellipses

The general equation for the graph of an ellipse is

$$\frac{(x-h)^2}{a^2} + \frac{(y-k)^2}{b^2} = 1$$

or,

$$\frac{(x-h)^2}{b^2} + \frac{(y-k)^2}{a^2} = 1$$

where h and k are the (x,y) coordinates of the ellipse's center, and where the ellipse's major (longer) axis equals $2a$ and its minor (shorter) axis equals $2b$. If the larger denominator is under the variable x, then the ellipse is horizontally oriented (and the first equation applies), whereas if it is under the variable y, then the ellipse is vertically oriented (and the second equation applies instead).

In the next figure, the left-hand ellipse, which is horizontally oriented, has center (0,0), so you can easily see the lengths of the major axis ($2a$) and minor axis ($2b$). In the right-hand ellipse, which is vertically oriented, the center is in Quadrant I at point (h,k). The value of $2a$ is 4, which is the distance from (2,2) to (6,2). The value of $2b$ is 6, which is the distance from (4,5) to (4,−1). Accordingly, $a^2 = 4$ and $b^2 = 9$.

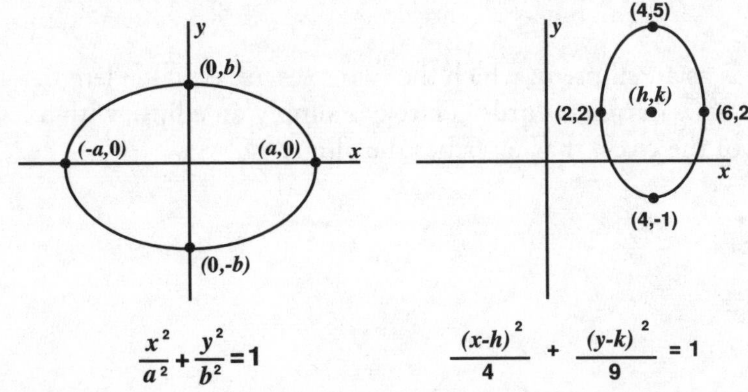

$$\frac{x^2}{a^2} + \frac{y^2}{b^2} = 1 \qquad \frac{(x-h)^2}{4} + \frac{(y-k)^2}{9} = 1$$

Take It to the Next Level

On the ACT, a question might provide an equation for an ellipse in standard form, then ask you to identify one of the ellipse's features—its center or the length of either its major or minor axis. Or, a question might provide an ellipse's graph and ask you to match the graph with its equation. As long as you know the standard form of the equation for an ellipse, you can handle questions like these.

To complicate things a bit, the test-makers might require you to manipulate the equation for an ellipse in order to put it in standard form. For instance, it's easy to see that the center of the ellipse defined by the equation $3(x + 3)^2 + 5(y - 4)^2 = 15$ is $(-3,4)$. But, the values of *a* and *b*—and therefore what the ellipse's graph looks like—aren't so obvious. You need to divide both sides of the equation by 15, so that the right side equals 1:

$$\frac{3(x+3)^2}{15} + \frac{5(y-4)^2}{15} = \frac{15}{15}$$

$$\frac{(x+3)^2}{5} + \frac{(y-4)^2}{3} = 1$$

Now you can see that $a = \sqrt{5}$ and $b = \sqrt{3}$, and that, accordingly, the length of the ellipse's horizontal and vertical axes are $2\sqrt{5}$ and $2\sqrt{3}$, respectively.

An especially challenging ellipse question might require you to recognize the relationship between a circle and an ellipse (and between their equations).

An ellipse defined by the equation $9(x + 2)^2 + 4(y - 2)^2 = 36$ is inscribed in a circle, so that the ellipse is tangent to the circle at exactly two points. Which of the following is the equation of the circle?

F. $x^2 + y^2 = 4$
G. $x^2 + y^2 = 36$
H. $(x + 2)^2 + (y - 2)^2 = 6$
J. $(x + 2)^2 + (y - 2)^2 = 9$
K. $(x - 4)^2 + (y - 9)^2 = 6$

The correct answer is J. First, rewrite the ellipse's equation in standard form:

$$\frac{(x+2)^2}{4} + \frac{(y-2)^2}{9} = 1$$

One way of defining a circle is as an ellipse in which the two axes are equal in length—that is, in the equation for an ellipse, $a = b$. In other words, a circle is simply an ellipse with axes of equal length. Hence, the equation of the circle that inscribes the ellipse is

$$\frac{(x+2)^2}{9} + \frac{(y-2)^2}{9} = 1$$

or $(x + 2)^2 + (y - 2)^2 = 9$.

Equations and Graphs of Parabolas

In the standard (x,y) coordinate plane, the general equation for a *parabola* is one of the following two (depending on the parabola's orientation, either vertical or horizontal):

$y - k = a(x - h)^2$	The parabola extends either up or down, depending on whether the function (the relation between the equation's two sides) is positive or negative.
$x - h = a(y - k)^2$	The parabola extends either right or left, depending on whether the function (the relation between the equation's two sides) is positive or negative.

In these equations, point (h,k) is the parabola's vertex and the constant a determines the parabola's shape (the larger the value of a, the "steeper" and "narrower" the curve). To understand the relationship between a parabola's equation and its graph, examine the following two graphs and their corresponding equations:

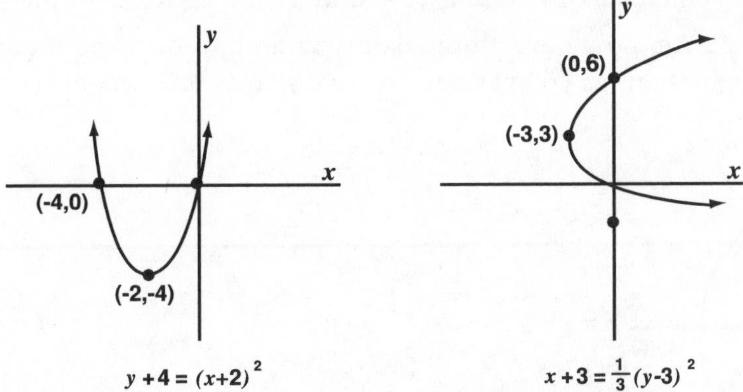

Notice that the right-hand parabola (where $a = \frac{1}{3}$) is "wider" than the left-hand parabola (where $a = 1$).

Tip

To confirm the two x-intercepts (0,0) and (−4,0) shown in the left-hand parabola, let $y = 0$ and find the two roots of the equation $0 = (x + 2)^2 - 4$. Similarly, to confirm the two y-intercepts (0,6) and (0,0) shown in the right-hand parabola, let $x = 0$ and find the two roots of the equation $0 = \frac{1}{3}(y - 3)^2 - 3$.

To answer an ACT parabola question, you might need to match the graph of a parabola to its equation by identifying the parabola's vertex and/or its direction (up, down, left, or right). To complicate this type of question just a bit, the test-makers might give an equation in nonstandard form. For instance, the equations of the two parabolas in the preceding graph might be expressed instead as $y = (x + 2)^2 - 4$ and $x = \frac{1}{3}(y - 3)^2 - 3$. Rewriting the equation in standard form will help you identify the parabola's vertex and direction.

To answer a more difficult parabola question, you might need to do one of the following:

- Draw the graph of a parabola's equation (in order to analyze the question).
- Recognize a relationship between two parabolas, or between a parabola and another shape, such as a circle.

At how many points does the parabola $y = x^2 - 5$ intersect the circle $x^2 + y^2 = 25$?

A. 4
B. 3
C. 2
D. 1
E. 0

The correct answer is B. One way to approach this question is by drawing both shapes on the same coordinate plane. The circle has radius 5 and center (0,0). Rewriting the parabola's equation as $y + 5 = (x - 0)^2$ tells you that the parabola is vertically oriented opening upward and has vertex (0,−5). Plot the two *x*-intercepts by letting $y = 0$ and solving for x in the parabola's equation: $x^2 = 5$; $x = \pm\sqrt{5}$. You now have all the data you need to draw both graphs accurately enough to answer the question (as you can see, the two shapes intersect at three points):

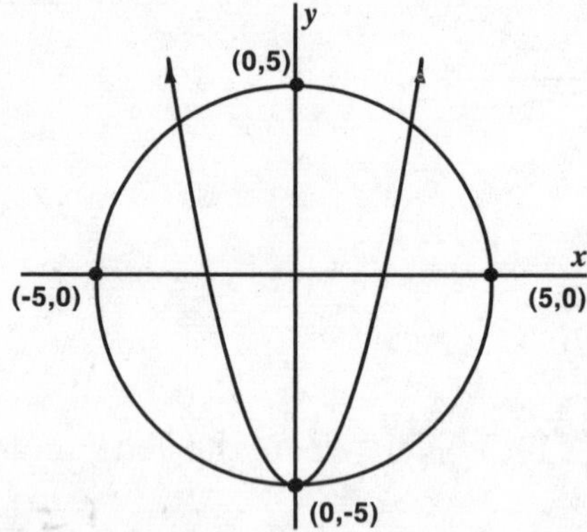

Another, less efficient, way to approach this question is by algebraic substitution. For instance, you can substitute $(y + 5)$ for x^2 (based on the parabola's equation) in the circle's equation, then solve for y:

$$x^2 + y^2 = 25$$
$$(y + 5) + y^2 = 25$$
$$y^2 + y - 20 = 0$$
$$(y + 5)(y - 4) = 0$$
$$y = -5, 4$$

Then, plug in each value for y in both equations. On either curve, $y = -5$ at, and *only* at, point (0,−5). In either equation, letting $y = 4$ yields $x^2 = 9$, or $x = \pm 3$ (two solutions); that is, on either curve, $y = 4$ at points (3,4) and (−3,4). Hence, there are three points of intersection altogether: (0,−5), (3,4), and (−3,4).

Equations and Graphs of Hyperbolas

A *hyperbola* actually consists of two parabolas that "open up" in opposite directions and are symmetrical about the same line, called the *transverse axis* (the *y*-axis in the left-hand graph below and the *x*-axis in the right-hand graph below) and are *asymptotic* about the same two lines, which means that they approach but never meet the two lines (the dotted lines, called the *asymptotes*, in the following two graphs).

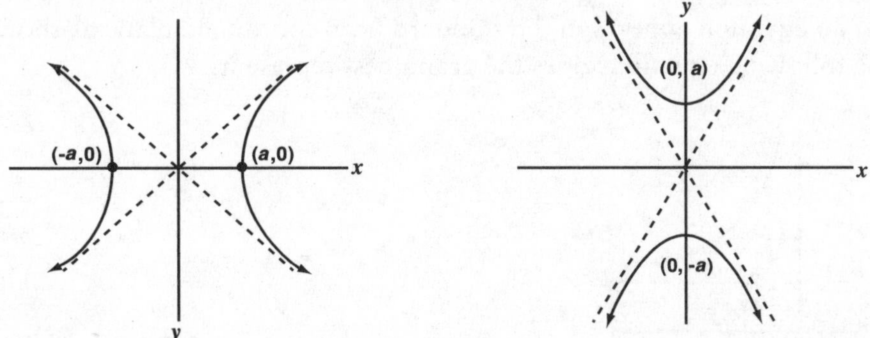

The general equation for the graph of a hyperbola can be either of the following two, depending on the hyperbola's orientation (horizontal or vertical). In these equations, *h* and *k* are the (*x*,*y*) coordinates of the hyperbola's center, which is the midpoint between the two vertices, along the transverse axis:

$\frac{(x-h)^2}{a^2} - \frac{(y-k)^2}{b^2} = 1$	The transverse axis is horizontal, and the hyperbola "opens up" to the left as well as to the right.
$\frac{(y-k)^2}{a^2} - \frac{(x-h)^2}{b^2} = 1$	The transverse axis is vertical, and the hyperbola "opens up" in upward and downward directions.

The distance between the two vertices (along the transverse axis) equals $2a$.

Note

The line perpendicular to the transverse axis is called the *conjugate axis*. The value of *b* is calculated as a segment length along this axis. But, for the ACT, you won't need to determine *b*.

The equations for the asymptotes of a hyperbola whose center is at (0,0) and whose axes are the *x*-axis and *y*-axis, as in the two preceding graphs, are as follows:

$\frac{x}{a} - \frac{y}{b} = 0$ and $\frac{x}{a} + \frac{y}{b} = 0$ (left graph) $\frac{x}{b} - \frac{y}{a} = 0$ and $\frac{x}{b} + \frac{y}{a} = 0$ (right graph)

If you find all these equations a bit confusing, you're not alone. Adding to the confusion is the fact that a hyperbola can be oriented at any angle—that is, the transverse axis need not be either vertical or horizontal. The test-makers realize that hyperbolas are more complex than the other

Take It to the Next Level

curves that the ACT covers, and that you've learned about in this chapter. So, they tend to keep their hyperbola questions simple.

To handle a typical hyperbola question, which will probably ask you to match an equation to its graph, just tabulate and plot a few sample (x,y) pairs. Or, if the asymptotes happen to be vertical and horizontal, you might also be able to handle the question by determining the unique values for x and y that lead to undefined solutions, which the two asymptotes represent graphically.

> The graph of an equation appears in the standard (x,y) coordinate plane as shown below. Which of the following equations does the graph best represent?

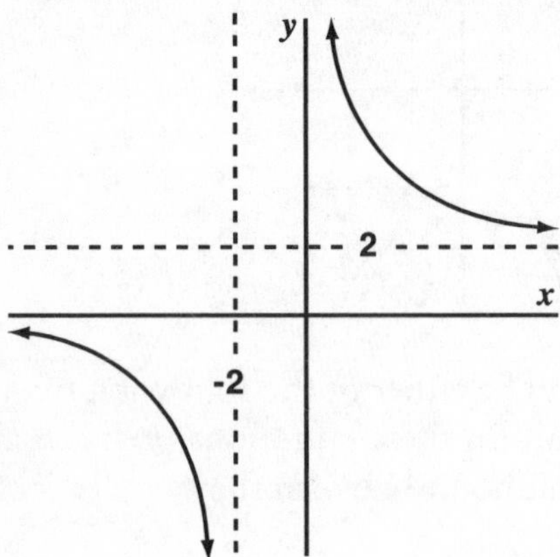

F. $y = \frac{1}{x} + 2$

G. $x = \frac{1}{y} + 2$

H. $y = \frac{1}{x + 2} + 2$

J. $x = \frac{1}{y + 2} + 2$

K. $y = \frac{1}{x + 2} - 2$

The correct answer is H. The graph shows the hyperbola asymptotic at $x = -2$ and at $y = 2$. Hence, in the graph's equation, if $x = -2$, then y is not a real number and, conversely, if $y = 2$, then x is not a real number. Of the five answer choices, only in **H** and **K** is y undefined for $x = -2$. Of these two choices, only in **H** is x undefined for $y = 2$ as well. By elimination, then, choice **H** must be the correct answer.

In all likelihood, any ACT hyperbola question you run across won't be any trickier than the preceding one, and you won't need to resort to the standard equation forms you saw a bit earlier. But you should keep these equations in your "pocket," anyway, just in case the ACT deals you a tough question.

The Reading Test

Chapter 11

Strategies for Effective Reading

In this chapter, you'll learn:

- Why it's important to read ACT Reading passages "interactively"
- A step-by-step approach to handling an ACT Reading set
- Techniques for reading more effectively and efficiently
- Success keys for the ACT Reading Test
- To *Take It to the Next Level*

"*Interactive*" Reading: The Key to the ACT Reading Test

If you're like most ACT test-takers, you'll experience at least one of the following problems as you tackle the Reading passages, at least to some degree:

- Your concentration is poor, perhaps due to your lack of familiarity with or interest in the topic, or perhaps due to general test anxiety.
- Your reading pace is slow, so you have trouble finishing the Reading Test in time.
- To answer each question, you need to search the passage again and again to find the information you need.
- You have trouble narrowing down the answer choices to one that's clearly the best.

Believe it or not, all of these problems are due to the same bad habit: *passive reading*, which means that you simply read the passage from start to finish, giving equal time and attention to every sentence, without thought as to what particular information might be key in answering the questions. You might call this approach the "osmosis strategy," since you're hoping to absorb what you need to know simply by allowing your eyes to glaze over the words.

What's the likely result of this osmosis strategy? You might remember some scattered facts and ideas, which will help you answer some questions. But, the passive mind-set won't take you very far when it comes to keeping all the passage's details straight in your mind or in truly *understanding* the ideas of the passage, both of which require a highly *active* frame of mind—one in which you constantly *interact* with the text as you read, asking yourself questions such as these:

- What's the passage's main idea and overall concern or purpose?
- What does each part of the passage relate to the passage's main idea and overall purpose?
- What's the author's purpose in mentioning each of the various details?
- What's the author's line of reasoning—or so-called "train of thought"—from paragraph to paragraph?
- What's the author's attitude, or viewpoint, on the subject?

Interactive reading is the key to success on the ACT Reading Test, and that's what this chapter is primarily about!

The ACT Reading Test—Your 7-Step Game Plan

The first task in this chapter is to learn the following seven basic steps for handling an ACT Reading passage and question set:

1. Read all 10 question stems (but *not* the answer choices).
2. Earmark spots in the passage where you'll find answers to certain questions.
3. Read the passage; annotate and make margin notes as you go.
4. Recap the passage, focusing on how its ideas connect.
5. For each question, try to "prephrase" the answer; then scan the choices for that answer.
6. Look again at any questions you had trouble with, rereading the passage as needed.
7. On your answer sheet, mark your selections for all 10 questions.

In the following pages, you'll learn what each step involves, and you'll apply the steps to a sample passage and set of 10 questions.

Step 1: Read all 10 question stems (but *not* the answer choices).

Your goal during Step 1 is to anticipate, or predict, the passage's overall topic and main idea, the author's point of view (if any), and the specific areas of discussion. Then read the 10 question stems that follow the passage.

You might ask, "Isn't this step putting the proverbial cart before the horse?" Not for the ACT. Reading the question stems first will give you a leg-up on the test-taker who jumps head-first into the passage without so much as one reflective moment. Step 1 will:

- Help you figure out what the passage is all about, giving you immediate focus and concentration.
- Provide huge clues about the passage's main ideas, supporting ideas, and details.
- Tell you what particular information you'll need to pay special attention to as you read the passage.

Just before each passage you'll find a reference to its source, which also might include when it was written and by whom. Be sure to read the reference; it provides additional clues as to what the passage as a whole is about.

Here are the 10 question stems for a certain Social Studies passage. Go ahead and read them now. As you do so, ask yourself what clues they provide about the passage:

Questions 1–10

1. According to the passage, in traditional Fijian society, individual property was often:
2. A contract from a traditional Fijian would most likely take the form of:
3. In the fourth paragraph (lines 19–25), the author of the passage presents the anecdote about King Taneo's nephew in order to illustrate the principle that:
4. The author of the passage appears to feel that the answer to the question, "What does modern civilization mean for the people of Fiji?" is best answered by asserting that:
5. The author of the passage suggests that "the 'ideals of modern progress' did not take hold at all in Fijian culture until well into the twentieth century" (line 31) due to a lack of:
6. As it is used in the passage, the word *compliance* (line 15) most nearly means:
7. According to the passage, Chief Thakombau was granted this name because he:
8. The passage does NOT strongly support the assertion that an observer of traditional Fijian culture might expect to witness the:
9. According to the information in the second paragraph (lines 5–11), a Fijian chief did not have the right to:
10. One of the main points made in the fifth and sixth paragraphs (lines 26–37) is that although traditional Fijians did not have strong ambitions to acquire personal wealth, one benefit of this lack of ambition was the:

Now, let's try to answer some general questions about the passage, based just on these question stems.

What's the passage's topic? The general topic is the traditional culture of Fiji—that much is pretty obvious. But, we can probably be even more specific. Based on questions 1, 2, and 10, it looks like the passage will focus on certain aspects of that culture, especially customs and attitudes regarding property and wealth.

What's the main idea, point, or message that the passage's author is trying to convey? Of course, we can't know for sure based just on the question stems; but they do provide clues. Look again at questions 4, 5, and 10. Consider them together. It appears that Fijians retained their traditional culture up until recently, and that recent modernization of the culture (or at least certain aspects of it) might not be entirely good for Fijians. Question 10 suggests that a lack of ambition, probably a characteristic of traditional Fijian culture, was actually beneficial—in other words, it was a good thing. Now look at question 5. The passage places the phrase 'ideals of modern progress' within quotes, which are often used to suggest irony. It's possible that the author doesn't think so highly of modern ideals (such as "ambition," perhaps), or doesn't think that the modern world is actually making progress (at least the way the modern world defines progress). Question 4 reinforces what we've predicted to be the passage's main idea. Question 4 strongly suggests that the author has a clear point of view about whether much good has come from modernization of Fiji culture—and so do the Fijians. (Would you guess that the Fijians and the author share the same general viewpoint?)

What subtopics, areas of discussion, or details (example and reasons) will the passage use to support its main idea? Based on the 10 questions, we can list several:

- Questions 1, 2, and 10 tell you that the passage will probably describe certain customs involving contracts, property rights, and property ownership.
- Question 3 tells you that the passage will talk specifically about a Fijian king, perhaps as an illustration of one of these customs, or perhaps to explain how the custom came about.
- Questions 7 and 9 tell you that the passage will deal specifically with the right (or lack of rights) of Fijian chiefs, perhaps to illustrate the customs concerning contracts, property rights, and property ownership.

Just from the questions, we've learned a lot about the passage, haven't we? Some of our predictions about the passage might turn out accurate; others might not. The passage will probably contain at least a few surprises or unexpected twists and turns. That's okay. What's important is that we're already thinking actively about the topic, anticipating what we'll need to know to answer the questions. So, we've already done a lot of the work needed to answer the 10 questions.

Alert!

Don't get us wrong. We're not suggesting you try to answer any question, or even read any answer choice, before reading at least some portion of the passage. The point is: Just by previewing the questions, you're already well on your way to answering the questions correctly.

Step 2: Earmark spots in the passage where you'll find answers to certain questions.

Some question stems will tell you exactly where to go—to which specific paragraph or lines. Other questions might mention proper nouns (specific people, places, and events), which are always capitalized; these words are easy to spot just by scanning the passage.

In the set of 10 questions given, no fewer than five (questions 3, 5, 6, 9, and 10) tell you where to go—which specific paragraph or lines; and two of the questions contain proper nouns—King Taneo (question 3) and Chief Thakombau (question 7)—that you can locate quickly in the passage.

Step 3: Read the passage; annotate and make margin notes as you go.

Read the passage's first logical "chunk," which might be one or two paragraphs, or perhaps a bit more. In your mind, compare what you're reading with what you anticipated after Step 1. Don't stop to answer any questions—even the ones for which you've earmarked the passage (Step 2). Try not to reread any sentence, and don't stop to memorize details (lists of examples, dates, and so forth).

As you read each paragraph, interact with it. Ask yourself, "What are the key ideas the passage's author (or the narrator) is trying to convey here?" Circle or underline words and phrases that will remind you of these ideas, or at least remind you what the paragraph is basically about. Also, earmark key words and phrases that suggest the author's viewpoint (if any) on the subject.

After reading a few paragraphs, pause to recap what you've read so far. Reviewing the words and phrases you marked will help. Then, jot down a few key words and ideas in the left-hand margin; think of these margin notes as an informal outline.

Repeat this process until you've finished reading the passage. To show you what your annotations and margin notes might look like, here's the passage that goes with the 10 questions on pages 272. Also, notice the earmarks from Step 2, which flag passage areas we know are covered in certain questions.

Note

In every ACT Reading passage, every fifth line will be numbered (just as they are here), to help you locate specific lines and paragraphs referenced in the questions. Also, preceding each passage, the test-makers indicate the passage's type along with its source (just like here).

Social Science

This passage is adapted from a sociological study of traditional Fiji culture conducted by Dr. Alfred Goldsborough Mayer.

Even a casual examination of the socio-economic aspects of traditional Fijian culture provides valuable insights into the predominant culture of today's Western World. One can see certain similarities between the two but, more importantly, disquieting differences as well.

As for land rights, in traditional Fijian society, a tribal chief could sell no land without the consent of his tribe. Cultivated land belonged to the man who originally farmed it, and it was passed undivided to all his heirs. Waste land was held in common. Native settlers who were taken into the tribes from time to time were permitted to farm some of the waste land, and for this privilege they and their heirs paid a yearly tribute to the chief either in produce or in service. In essence, this amounted to paying rent to the chief.

Fijians appear never to have been wholly without a medium of exchange. A sperm whale's teeth, for instance, always had a recognized purchasing power. Moreover, they were especially regarded as a means of expressing good will and honesty of purpose. A whale's tooth was as effective to secure compliance with the terms of a bargain in ancient Fiji as a signed contract is with modern Americans. Given Americans' penchant for wiggling their way out of contracts, a whale's tooth from a Fijian probably generated much more trust that the agreement would be fulfilled.

As in all societies, including our own, an individual's wealth consisted not only of what he possessed but even more so of the number of people from whom he could beg or borrow. One anthropologist observed that a rifle and other costly items he had presented to King Tanoa as gifts were being seized by Tanoa's nephew, who had the right to take whatever he might select from the king's possessions. In fact, in order to keep his property in sight, Tanoa was forced to give it to his own sons, thus escaping the rapacity of his nephew.

In a traditional Fiji tribe, an individual as such could hardly be said to own property, for nearly all things belonged to the individual's family or clan, even distant cousins. This custom is partially responsible for the culture's absence of personal ambition. This absence might strike Westerners as illogical, but it was nevertheless the dominant feature of the social fabric of traditional Polynesians and in fact explains why the "ideals of modern progress" did not take hold at all in the Fijian culture until well into the twentieth century.

The Fijians, for much of the last few centuries, were relatively happy; why should they work when every reasonable want was already supplied? None were rich in material things, but none were beggars except in the sense that all were such. No one could be a miser, a capitalist, a banker, or a promoter in such a community, and thieves were almost unknown.

Indeed, the honesty of the Fijians was one of the virtues about which travelers in previous centuries most often commented. During Professor Alexander Agassiz's cruises in the late 1800s, Fijian natives came on board by the hundreds, and not a single object was stolen, although things almost priceless in native estimation lay loosely upon the deck.

In fact, once, when the deck was deserted by all except the Professor, he observed one native gazing wistfully for half an hour at a bottle which lay on a table. Somehow, the man managed to acquire a shilling, a substantial sum of money in Fiji at the time, and this he offered in exchange for the coveted bottle. As Agassiz tells us: "One can never forget his shout of joy and the radiance of his honest face as he leaped into his canoe after having received the bottle as a gift instead."

Hoarded wealth inspired no respect in the Fiji of previous centuries, and indeed, were it discovered, its possession would have justified immediate confiscation. Perhaps because respect for property was so low, reverence for certain members of society was especially high. Tribal chiefs were so greatly revered that, for tribe members, the chiefs' names themselves held more power than any worldly goods.

Names in traditional Fijian culture could change throughout one's life, depending on any important events that occurred. For instance, Chief Thankombau began life as "seru," then after the civil war in which he overcame his father's enemies and reestablished Tanoa's rule in Mbau he was called "Thkombau" (evil to Mbau). At that time, he also received another name, "Thikinovu" (centipede), an allusion to his stealth in approaching his enemy; but this designation, as well as his given Christian name "Ebenezer," (he was converted by British missionaries), did not survive the test of usage.

But all this was the Fiji of the past, when life was an evanescent thing, and only as real as the murmur of the surf when the sea breeze comes in the morning. This was Fiji before capitalism took hold, before the forests were slashed and burned to make more land available for farming, and before the young people began to leave for "a better life"—a life that usually entails hoarding wealth and becoming enmeshed in the rat race of modern civilization. Sadly, this race rarely has a happy ending.

Step 4: Recap the passage, focusing on how its ideas connect.

Take a few seconds to review your annotations and margin notes, then pretend to explain the passage to someone who hasn't read it. To make sure you really "get" the passage's ideas, express them in your own way and in your own words to your fictitious friend. As in Step 3, use a broad brush. It's okay to remind yourself of key examples, but gloss over minor details. Focus instead on identifying the passage's main points and how they flow from one to the next. Your recap should also reveal the author's viewpoint on the subject.

Let's try recapping the passage about Fijian culture, based on our annotations and notes from Step 3. What follows might mirror your thought process as well.

Paragraph 1 clued us in on the author's viewpoint—we're warned of "disquieting" differences between Fijian and modern culture.

Paragraphs 2–4 describe Fijian attitudes toward land ownership, contracts, wealth, and possessions—the basic point is that Fijians shared property freely, at least among clan members.

Paragraph 5 defines Fijian wealth as not what you own but what you have access to (the example about King Tanoa's nephew illustrates this point).

Paragraphs 5–6 explain the outcome of these attitudes: Fijians lack ambition, they're content, and they don't steal (sounds like ideal communal life).

Paragraphs 7–8 provide an example of their honesty (the Professor's ship).

Paragraphs 9–10 tell us that the focus was on who a person is (and what he's done), not the things he possesses (example: Chief Thankombau's name changes).

Paragraph 11 spells out the author's viewpoint: Traditional Fiji beats rat-race capitalism.

Note

A typical ACT Reading passage includes a generous number of paragraph breaks. The sample passage given here has eleven paragraphs altogether, which is typical of ACT Social Studies, Humanities, and Natural Science passages. Prose Fiction passages, which almost always include dialogue, often contain even more paragraphs.

Step 5: For each question, try to "prephrase" the answer; then scan the choices for that answer.

As you read each question stem, try to answer the question *before* looking at the answer choices, and *before* you look back at the passage. In other words, try to predict what you might expect the correct answer would say. If you read the passage actively, you should be able to prephase an answer to *most* of the 10 questions. (For some questions, this technique won't work; but for most questions it will.)

You might ask, "Why go to the trouble of conjuring up an answer in my head, when the correct one is already right in front of me?" Prephrasing the answer is the best way to zero in on the correct choice and, just as important, to avoid those tempting, confusing, and generally distracting wrong-answer choices—in other words, to keep from second-guessing yourself.

Let's walk through the 10 questions you first saw during Step 1. This time around, we'll prephrase an answer to as many as possible, then scan the choices for our homegrown responses. Let's keep in mind, though, that this technique probably won't get us all the way home. We might need to consult the passage to answer certain questions, and we might decide to skip one or two toughies (and then return to them during Step 6). Let's start with question 1:

1. According to the passage, in traditional Fijian society, individual property was often:

Your recap of the passage, especially Paragraphs 2 and 5, tell you that the Fijians shared their property, at least among members of the same clan. So, that's the sort of answer you're looking for among the following four choices:

A. considered by Western explorers to be worthless.
B. collectively owned by the family or clan.
C. owned solely by the chief of the tribe.
D. valued according to the owner's rank in society.

Bingo! Choice **C** expresses exactly what you already knew a good best answer would look like. Circle choice **C** in your test booklet, then move on to question 2.

2. A contract from a traditional Fijian would most likely take the form of:

Your margin notes tell you that this question involves what's in Paragraph 3. Unless you missed something as you read the passage, your notes tell you the answer: a whale's tooth. Now here are the four answer choices:

F. a burnt offering to the gods.
G. a semiprecious stone.
H. the granting of a Fijian name.
J. a whale's tooth.

You can see at a glance that the correct answer is choice **J**. Circle choice **J** in your test booklet, then move on to question 3.

3. In the fourth paragraph (lines 19–25), the author of the passage presents the anecdote about King Taneo's nephew in order to illustrate the principle that:

Check your margin notes for the answer to this question. The anecdote illustrates the point, made early in the paragraph, that a Fijian's wealth is measured not so much by what he owned as by what he had rightful access to. Now, check the answer choices for a statement to this effect.

A. Western civilization has decimated traditional Fijian values.
B. the right to take or borrow from another was a notable indication of wealth in Fijian culture.
C. all communities that value personal property levy heavy sanctions against theft.
D. trust was not easily gained among Fijian tribes.

Notice that choice **B** leaps off the page as the correct one. Circle choice **B** in your test booklet, then move on to question 4.

4. The author of the passage appears to feel that the answer to the question "what does modern civilization mean for the people of Fiji?" is best answered by asserting that:

You won't find an explicit answer to this question in one spot of the passage. Instead, to answer the question, you need to have a sense of the author's viewpoint on the subject. Your recap of the passage tells you that the author seems critical of modern Western culture, and seems to think that Fijians were better off in their traditional culture than by embracing Western ways. Now, scan the answer choices for one that reflects this viewpoint.

F. Fiji, like most island civilizations, must give up its insular culture in order to compete in world markets.
G. capitalism will help the people of Fiji profit from their traditional values of honesty and egalitarianism.
H. modern civilization will not make the people of Fiji any happier than they previously were.
J. there is little chance that modern civilization will ever have an impact on the way of life enjoyed by most Fijians.

Choice **H** is the only one that comes close to expressing the author's viewpoint. It may not hit the bull's-eye, but it's more or less on target, especially compared with the other choices. Circle choice **H** in your test booklet, then move on to question 5.

5. The author of the passage suggests that "the 'ideals of modern progress' did not take hold at all in Fijian culture until well into the twentieth century" (line 31) due to a lack of:

During Step 2, you earmarked the lines quoted in this question, so you should have paid close attention as you read them. Your margin notes remind you that the Fijians were not quick to embrace modern capitalism because it ran so contrary to their established views toward property, with which they seemed perfectly content. Now, scan the answer choices for one that expresses this idea (try not to let other answers distract you):

A. a sense of personal ownership.
B. personal ambition.
C. codified land laws.
D. Western cultural indoctrination.

Choice **A** reflects what we predicted about the Fijian attitude toward property: that it was owned in common rather than by individuals. Circle choice **A** in your test booklet, then move on to question 6.

6. As it is used in the passage, the word *compliance* (line 15) most nearly means:

You earmarked the word *compliance* during Step 2, so you should have been paying close attention when you read the sentence containing it. But, go back and read the sentence again, anyway. Now, check the answer choices, substituting each one for *compliance*.

- **F.** agreement.
- **G.** introduction.
- **H.** withdrawal.
- **J.** inconsistency.

Maybe you already knew the meaning of the word *compliance*: To comply is to be submissive or agreeable to. So, *agreement,* choice **F**, is a good synonym for compliance. Even if you don't have a clue what *compliance* means, you can still zero in on the correct choice. *Agreement* is the only word among the four choices that makes sense as a substitute for compliance in the context of a contractual arrangement. That's a huge clue that choice **F** is the correct answer. Circle choice **F** in your test booklet, then move on to question 7.

Note

Question 6 is an example of what the test-makers call a vocabulary-in-context question. Expect nearly every ACT Reading passage to include at least one such question.

7. According to the passage, Chief Thakombau was granted this name because he:

During Step 2, you earmarked the part of the passage relevant to this question, so you should have paid close attention as you read about Chief Thakombau. But, the passage mentioned numerous name changes, each one for its own reason; so, to make sure you don't confuse the details, go back and read paragraph 10. Lines 55–60 indicate that the chief was granted this name because he defeated Tanoa's enemies and reestablished Tanoa's rule. Now, scan the answers for one that essentially provides this reason.

- **A.** was very stealthy in approaching his enemies.
- **B.** hoarded a large amount of wealth.
- **C.** was converted by British missionaries.
- **D.** restored Tanoa's rule in Mbau.

Just as predicted, our answer is among the four choices. Circle choice **D** in your test booklet, then move on to question 8.

8. The passage does NOT strongly support the assertion that an observer of traditional Fijian culture might expect to witness the:

For this question, it's not possible to predict what the correct answer will look like. (Always expect at least one or two such questions in each set.) Instead, consider each answer choice in turn, and eliminate any that you recall as being a feature of traditional Fijian culture. Here are the four choices:

- **F.** borrowing of a tribe member's name by a member of another tribe.
- **G.** confiscation of personal property taken by a greedy clan member.
- **H.** use of bartering, or exchanging goods and services, instead of the use of currency.
- **J.** free use of common land by some Fijians but not by others.

They all look somewhat familiar, don't they? As you read each answer, you might be thinking, "I recall reading something about that in the passage." And, since the four answers all deal with small details, you might very well have glossed over exactly what you need to know to help narrow down the choices to the best one. These features combine to make this question a relatively tough one by ACT standards. Maybe you know the correct answer. But, we're going to skip this question for now. Put a conspicuous question mark ("?") next to the question number, then move on to question 9. (We'll come back to question 8 during Step 6.)

9. According to the information in the second paragraph (lines 5–11), a Fijian chief did not have the right to:

You might be able to predict the answer to this question based on your margin notes and recap for the second paragraph. The main point of the paragraph was that land ownership was communal. This might be all you need to know to zero in on the best choice. Let's see:

A. declare war.
B. start a new community on the same island.
C. cultivate land.
D. sell tribal land without the tribe's permission.

Sure enough, choice **D** reflects the basic gist of the paragraph. In case you didn't predict what the correct answer might look like, check the first sentence of the paragraph. Circle choice **D** in your test booklet, then move on to question 10.

10. One of the main points made in the fifth and sixth paragraphs (lines 34–48) is that although traditional Fijians did not have strong ambitions to acquire personal wealth, one benefit of this lack of ambition was the:

Your annotations for Paragraph 6 might tell you what you need to predict the answer to this question. The words we circled in Paragraph 6 suggest the culture was characterized by happiness, a lack of theft, and honesty. So, scan the answer choices for any one of these.

F. low level of unemployment among Fijians.
G. greater availability of land for farming.
H. scarcity of theft in Fijian society.
J. growth of friendship between Fijian chiefs.

Choice **H** provides one of those three features. (If you aren't sure about the answer, the fifth and sixth paragraphs are brief enough that you can easily go back and read them again, during Step 6.) Circle choice **H** in your test booklet, then move on to Step 6.

Note

The difficulty level of these 10 questions, as a whole, is typical of what you can expect on the ACT Reading Test. Just as with these questions, some are easier than others, and later questions tend to be more challenging than earlier ones.

Step 6: Look again at any questions you had trouble with, rereading the passage as needed.

Go back to the questions you earmarked to come back to, and try them again. If you need to consult the passage, your annotations and notes should tell you where to find the information you need. Of the ten questions based on the Fiji passage, 8 and 10 are the ones we weren't 100% sure about. Now, let's go back to those questions, and to the passage.

8. The passage does NOT strongly support the assertion that an observer of traditional Fijian culture might expect to witness the:

F. borrowing by one clan member of another clan member's name.
G. confiscation of personal property taken by a greedy clan member.
H. use of bartering, or exchanging goods and services, instead of the use of currency.
J. free use of common land by some Fijians but not by others.

For this question, you need to eliminate any choice that the passage strongly supports. Consider the choices one at a time, starting with choice F: Paragraph 4 discussed the borrowing habits of Fijians (remember the story about King Tanoa?), but that paragraph had to do with borrowing property, not a name. It was much later in the passage, Paragraphs 9 and 10, that the author talks about names, and nothing was mentioned there about borrowing names. (If you're not sure, go ahead and reread that portion of the passage.) So, it looks like choice F combines details from different portions of the passage in a way that doesn't add up. **F** is probably the best choice. But, it's a good idea to compare choice **F** with the other answer choices, just to make sure.

Choice **G** involves information from Paragraph 9. Remember the statement that hoarded property would have been subject to confiscation? If not, go ahead and find that part of the paragraph, and read the statement again. Although you don't see the word "greedy" there, choice **G** expresses the basic idea behind these lines, so **G** is supported well enough to eliminate it.

Choice **H** mentions the concept of bartering, a word not mentioned anywhere in the passage. But, choice **H** defines the word, so ask yourself whether the passage describes an activity that would be considered bartering. Where might you find such a description? Probably early in the passage, where transactions involving property are discussed. Check your annotations and margin notes. At the end of the second paragraph, the passage mentions that native settlers exchanged produce or services for the right to live on tribal land. This matches the definition of bartering given in choice **H**, doesn't it? Since the passage strongly supports **H**, you can eliminate this choice.

Choice **J** also involves activities that you'd most likely find early in the paragraph. In fact, Paragraph 2 is the only one that talks about land ownership. If you quickly read the paragraph again, you'll notice that it indicates that waste land was owned in common by tribal members but that native settlers were required to pay "rent" to use such land. These ideas match what choice **H** says—it's just that **J** states these ideas a bit differently. So, you can eliminate **H**.

You've now confirmed your initial guess: The correct answer to question 8 is choice **F**.

Tip Answer choices, even ones about a passage's minor details, often paraphrase what's in the passage rather than restate the details word-for-word. Evaluate answer choices based on the ideas they convey, not on whether they match the passage verbatim.

The other question we earmarked as one to come back to is question 10. Here it is again:

10. One of the main points made in the fifth and sixth paragraphs (lines 26–37) is that although traditional Fijians did not have strong ambitions to acquire personal wealth, one benefit of this lack of ambition was the:

F. low level of unemployment among Fijians.
G. greater availability of land for farming.
H. scarcity of theft in Fijian society.
J. growth of friendship between Fijian chiefs.

Quickly reread the two paragraphs to confirm **H** as the best choice. The passage tells you that "thieves were almost unknown" (line 37)—essentially what choice **H** indicates.

Step 7: On your answer sheet, mark your selections for all 10 questions.

During a question set, don't interrupt your brainwork to fill in your answer sheet. Wait until after answering all 10 questions, then fill in the corresponding ten ovals on the answer sheet. If you're still uncertain about the correct answer to certain questions, earmark them in your test booklet. You can come back to them if you have enough time remaining after answering all 40 questions on the Reading Test.

Techniques for Interactive Reading

During Step 4 of the 7-step approach you just learned, you annotated, took margin notes, then recapped the passage, all of which worked together to reveal the passage's structure and how its ideas flowed from one to the next. In this section, we'll focus more closely on this step, which lies at the heart of handling ACT Reading passages.

Think of any ACT Reading passage as a structure of ideas. Each passage is designed to convey a number of ideas that are connected to one another in some way. If you understand these ideas *and* the connections between them, then you truly understand the passage as a whole. Focusing on structure helps you in several ways:

- It makes it easy to see the "big picture"—what the passage is about as a whole.
- It tells you the purpose of the supporting details.
- The logical structure organizes all the information in the passage, making it easy to locate any detail to which a particular question might refer.
- The structure explains how the author's main points are related to one another.

It's no coincidence that the preceding list covers what you'll need to know to answer most of the questions the test deals you!

Note

All but the last strategy you'll learn in this section apply mainly to Social Science, Humanities, and Natural Science passages. The fourth passage type, Prose Fiction (excerpts from novels and short stories), is a unique animal; the last strategic tip in this section applies specifically to this passage type.

Focus on the Passage's Logical Structure

Although ACT passages don't invariably have clear-cut, logical structures, a structure of some kind is almost always present. Here's a list of the most common types of logical structures found in ACT passages. Either alone or in combination, these structures underlie most of the passages you'll encounter on the exam:

- A theory or idea illustrated by two (or more) detailed examples or illustrations or supported by two (or more) arguments (The passage might also critique the theory based on the examples or arguments.)
- Two (or more) alternative theories, each of which seek to explain a certain phenomenon (The passage might also argue for one theory over another.)
- Pro and con arguments presented for both sides of a single issue
- A comparison and/or contrast between two (or more) events, ideas, phenomena, or people
- A cause-and-effect sequence showing how one event led to another (presented either in chronological order or via "flashback," with later events described *before* earlier ones)
- Two or three basic types, categories, or classes of a phenomenon identified and distinguished, beginning with main classes, and then possibly branching out to subclasses (This structure is most common in passages involving the natural sciences.)

Alert!

Each structure listed here screams out for paragraph breaks—to turn from one theory, reason, example, or class to another, or to separate pros from cons or similarities from differences. But, don't assume a passage's structure will reveal itself so neatly. Use paragraph breaks as structural clues, but don't rely on them as crutches.

The Art of Annotating

Selective annotating (for example, circling and underlining key words and phrases) serves three important purposes:

1. It helps you maintain an active frame of mind because what you're essentially doing is shopping for the ideas and information that you think are sufficiently important to earmark.
2. It provides a prewritten outline. After you read (and annotate) the entire passage, reviewing the annotated words and phrases can be an effective way to recap the passage for yourself.

3. If you need to refer to the passage as you answer the questions, effective annotating will help you quickly locate the information you need.

What sort of information should you annotate? If you under-annotate, you won't be able to effectively recap the passage by reviewing your annotations. On the other hand, if you over-annotate, your annotations lose their meaning, and you might as well not have annotated at all. Here are some suggestions for finding just the right balance:

- Mark areas of discussion that you may need to locate again to answer one or more of the questions.
- Instead of underlining complete sentences, select key words or phrases that "trigger" for you the idea or point that is made in a sentence or paragraph.
- Mark structural connectors—key words that connect the logical building blocks of the passage.
- In chronological passages, mark historical benchmarks and divisions—centuries, years, decades, or historical periods—that help to form the structure of the author's discussion.
- Use arrows to physically connect words that signify related ideas; for example:
    - to clarify cause and effect in the natural sciences or in the context of historical events
    - to indicate who was influenced by whom in literature, music, psychology, and so on
    - to connect names (philosophers, scientists, authors, and so on) with dates, events, other names, theories, or schools of thought, works, and so on
    - to indicate the chronological order in which historical events occurred
- Create your own visual cues to earmark possible thesis statements, major supporting points, and words that indicate the author's viewpoint.

Look for Structural Clues, or "Triggers"

Triggers are key words and phrases that provide clues as to the structure and organization of the passage and the direction in which the discussion is flowing. The lists below contain many common trigger words and phrases. Be on the lookout for trigger words as you read the passage. They'll help you see the passage's structure and follow the author's train of thought.

These words precede an item in a list (such as examples, classes, reasons, or characteristics):

- first, second (and so on)
- in addition, also, another

These words signal that the author is contrasting two phenomena:

- alternatively, by contrast, however, on the other hand, rather than, while, yet

These words signal a logical conclusion based upon preceding material:

- consequently, in conclusion, then, thus, therefore, as a result, accordingly

These words signal that the author is comparing (identifying similarities between) two phenomena:

- similarly, in the same way, analogous, parallel, likewise, just as, also, as

These words signal evidence (factual information) used to support the author's argument:

- because, since, in light of

These words signal an example of a phenomenon:

- for instance, for example, such as, . . . is an illustration of

To Outline—or Not to Outline

You learned earlier in this chapter that, as you're reading, you should make shorthand notes in the margins to summarize paragraphs and to indicate the flow of the passage's discussion. Margin notes can also help you locate details more quickly and recap the passage more effectively. You also learned to keep your notes as brief as possible—two or three words are enough in most cases to indicate a particular idea or component of the passage.

But what about constructing an outline on your scratch paper? For complicated or high-density passages, an outline might be a good way to organize information and to keep particular details straight in your mind. The following situations are ideal for an informal outline (you might call them "organized notes"):

- If the passage categorizes or classifies various things, use an informal outline to help you keep track of which belong in each category.
- If the passage mentions numerous individual names (for example, of authors, artists, political figures, and so on), take organized notes to link them according to influence, agreement or disagreement, and so forth.
- If the passage describes a sequence of events, construct a simple time-line outline to keep track of the major features of each event in the sequence.

To Preview—or Not to Preview

Many ACT prep books recommend that, before reading a passage straight through from beginning to end, you *preview* the passage by reading the first (and perhaps last) sentence of each paragraph. This technique supposedly provides clues about the scope of the passage, the author's thesis or major conclusions, and the structure and flow of the passage. Although these techniques make sense *in theory,* there are several reasons why *in practice* they are rarely helpful on the ACT:

- Once immersed in the passage itself, you'll quickly forget most, if not all, of what you learned from previewing.
- These techniques call for you to read the same material twice. Does that sound efficient to you?
- Previewing can take more time than you might think. After all, the average ACT Reading passage contains about 10 paragraphs. The time needed to preview even the first sentence

of each paragraph is time (and a lot of it!) that you might not be able to afford under timed testing conditions.

- While reading the beginning and end of each paragraph may be helpful for some passages, for others this technique will be of little or no help—and there's no way to know whether you're wasting your time until you've already wasted it.

Tip

The only situation in which you should preview is if you're running out of time. Some questions, especially ones that refer to particular line numbers, you can answer quickly by reading just one paragraph, or perhaps just a few sentences. And a quick scan of the first and last few sentences of the passage might provide clues about the passage's main idea or primary purpose, so you can at least take educated guesses at certain questions.

What to Look for in Prose Fiction Passages

Prose Fiction passages (excerpts from novels and short stories), in contrast to the three other passage types, don't focus on "concepts," they aren't analytical in nature, and how they're organized is irrelevant. Nor is there any main idea or thesis to look for. ACT Prose Fiction passages almost always contain dialogue between characters. In reading a Prose Fiction passage:

relationships...

- Pay attention not just to what each character is thinking and saying, but also to what their thoughts, words, and behavior suggest about their attitudes, feelings, and motives—any of which might be the focus of a test question.
- Be sure not to confuse the thoughts, words, and actions of one character with those of another character. Making brief notes can help you keep straight who said or did what.
- If the voice of the narrator is that of the author (rather than one of the characters), then the narration provides a point of view that is distinct from those of the characters. Pay close attention to how the narrator describes the characters' thoughts, words, and actions.

Success Keys for the ACT Reading Test

We've covered a lot of ground so far. To help you assimilate it all, here's a checklist of the salient, and sage, points of advice for improving your reading efficiency and comprehension as you read ACT Reading passages. Apply them to the practice tests in Part VI, and then review them again, just before test day.

Use Your Pencil as You Read the Passage

Annotating key words and phrases in the passage, along with making margin notes, helps keep you in an interactive mode, and helps you find information in the passage you need as you answer the questions. Some organized notes on your scratch paper can also help you keep the details of a passage straight.

Focus on the Flow of Ideas

Understanding the structure of a passage's ideas—how they flow from one to another—will help you understand the passage's main ideas as well as the author's overall concern and purpose in mentioning various details, all of which in turn will help you answer the questions. Recognizing structural clues, or trigger words, can help you see the structure.

Don't Get Bogged Down in Details

ACT Reading passages are packed with details: lists, statistics and other numbers, dates, titles, and so forth. If you try to absorb all of the details as you read, you'll not only lose sight of the ideas behind the details, but also lose reading speed. Don't get bogged down in the details; gloss over them. Note where particular examples, lists, and other details are located. Then, if a particular question involving those details is included, you can quickly and easily locate them and read them more carefully.

Sum up the Passage after You Read It

After reading the entire passage, take a few seconds to recap it. What was the author's main point and what were the major supporting points? Remind yourself about the flow of the discussion without thinking about all the details. Chances are you'll be able to answer at least half the questions based just on your recap.

Prephrase an Answer before You Read a Question's Answer Choices

For each question, try to formulate your own response to it, then scan the choices for something resembling your homegrown response. Prephrasing the answers will keep you from becoming confused and distracted by wrong-answer choices. (Keep in mind, though, that some question stems might not give you enough to go on.)

Try to Minimize Rereading

There's nothing wrong with going back to the passage for information you need to answer certain questions. But, you shouldn't need to read the passage more than once all the way through. Rereading the passage uses up valuable time, and adds to eyestrain and mental fatigue. The best way to minimize rereading is to annotate, make good margin notes, and recap after you finish the passage.

Practice, Practice, Practice

During the real ACT is *not* the time to experiment with the methods you learned in this chapter for the first time. You'll need to practice applying them beforehand.

Find Your Optimal Pace and Stick to It

Remember: You've got 35 minutes to handle four Reading sets, each one including 10 questions. That's about 9 minutes per set. As you practice, stick to a 9-minute time limit per set—and do the same during the actual test. Nine minutes is enough time to follow all the steps you learned in this chapter, so relax.

Take It to the Next Level

At this next level, you'll learn:

- How to recognize and handle each of the basic, and most common, types of Reading questions
- Success keys for answering Reading questions
- How the test-makers design wrong-answer choices for each of the following question types (and how to recognize these red herrings when you see them):
    - Simple recall
    - Restatement
    - Inference
    - Recap
    - Method
    - Vocabulary-in-context

Note

Since you're at *Take It to the Next Level*, don't expect to encounter easy reading or "gimme" questions in this level. Everything here is tougher than average.

Sample Reading Passages

Most of the sample questions you'll analyze at this level are based on the following two reading passages. Go ahead and read both passages now. Also, earmark this page, since you'll refer back to it throughout this section.

> **Note**
>
> We want you to focus on answering test questions, not on wading through long passages. So, we've kept these two passages brief—about one third the average length of the ones you'll see on the ACT.

Passage I

When a species of plant or animal becomes established in a place other than where it originated, it's understandable to ask questions such as "How did it get here?"; "Where could it go next?"; and, if the species is unwanted, "How can we stop it from spreading further?"

The arrival of a non-indigenous species in a new location may be either intentional or unintentional. Rates of species movement driven by human transformations of natural environments as well as by human mobility—through commerce, tourism, and travel—dwarf natural rates by comparison. Although the size of the geographic area where species are found naturally expands and contracts over historical time intervals (tens to hundreds of years), geographic ranges rarely expand thousands of miles or across physical barriers such as oceans or mountains.

Preventing an unwelcome species from entering a country can be problematic. A number of factors make it difficult to quantitatively calculate how important one pathway of entry is compared to another. Time lags often occur between establishment of non-indigenous species and their detection, and tracing the pathway for a long-established species is difficult. For instance, experts estimate that non-indigenous weeds are usually detected only after having been in the country for thirty years or having spread to at least ten thousand acres. In addition, federal port inspection, although a major source of information on non-indigenous species pathways, especially for agricultural pests, provides data only when such species enter via scrutinized routes. Finally, some comparisons between pathways defy quantitative analysis—for example, which is more "important": the entry pathway of one very harmful species or one by which many but less harmful species enter the country?

Passage II

Scientists have long claimed that, in order to flourish and progress, their discipline requires freedom from ideological and geographic boundaries, including the freedom to share new scientific knowledge with scientists throughout the world. In the twentieth century, however, increasingly close links between science and national life undermined these ideals. Although the connection facilitated large and expensive projects, such as the particle-accelerator program, that would have been difficult to fund through private sources, it also channeled the direction of scientific research increasingly toward national security (military defense).

For example, scientists in the post-1917 Soviet Union found themselves in an ambiguous position. While the government encouraged and generally supported scientific research, it simultaneously imposed significant restrictions on science and scientists. A strong nationalistic emphasis on science led at times to the dismissal of all non-Russian scientific work as irrelevant to Soviet science. A 1973 article in *Literatunaya Gazeta*, a Soviet publication, insisted: "World science is based upon national schools, so the weakening of one or another national school inevitably leads to stagnation in the development of world science." According to the Soviet regime, socialist science was to be consistent with, and in fact grow out of, the Marxism-Leninism political ideology.

Toward this end, some scientific theories or fields, such as relativity and genetics, were abolished. Where scientific work conflicted with political criteria, the work was often disrupted. During the Stalinist purges of the 1930s, many Soviet scientists simply disappeared. In the 1970s, Soviet scientists who were part of the refusenik movement lost their jobs and were barred from access to scientific resources. Nazi Germany during the 1930s and, more recently, Argentina imposed strikingly similar, though briefer, constraints on scientific research.

"Simple Recall" Questions

For these questions, your job is to identify which answer choice provides information that appears in the passage and that the question asks about. The question stem might look something like one of these:

"Which of the following does the author mention as an example of . . .?"

"According to the passage, . . . is caused by . . .?"

This is the most common question type, and it's the easiest type because all that's required to handle it is to either remember or find the appropriate information in the passage. Here's a good example, based on Passage I (page 289):

According to the passage, the rate at which plant or animal species move naturally across land:

A. might depend on the prevalence of animals that feed on the species.
B. is hindered by federal port inspectors.
C. is often slower than the rate at which they move across water.
D. is slower than human-assisted rates.

The correct answer is D. Only the first paragraph talks about the rate of species movement, so it's there where you'll find the answer to this question. In line 8, the author states that rates of species movement driven by human transformations and mobility "dwarf natural rates by comparison." In other words, natural rates are slower than human-assisted rates, just as choice **D** provides.

Choice **A** might be true in the "real world," but the passage mentions nothing about predators, let alone about their affect on movement rates. So, you can easily eliminate it.

Choice **B** confuses the passage's details. It refers to information in the second paragraph, which discusses problems in determining entry pathways. This paragraph has nothing to do with the rate of species movement. Also, did you notice that choice **B** is a bit nonsensical? How could port inspectors, who are located where ocean meets land, affect the rate at which a species moves *naturally* across land?

Choice **C** involves relevant information from the passage, but it distorts that information. The first paragraph's last sentence indicates that oceans and mountains are barriers that typically prevent species movement. But choice **C** implies that mountains pose a greater barrier than oceans. Nowhere in the passage does the author seek to compare rates across land with rates across water.

Alert!

In handling a Simple Recall question, don't expect the correct answer choice to quote the passage verbatim. That's generally not how the test-makers write them. Instead, they prefer to paraphrase what's in the passage. In the preceding question, for instance, the precise phrase, "human-assisted movement" doesn't appear in the passage, does it? But, that's no reason to eliminate choice **D**, which turned out to be the correct answer choice.

Notice the types of wrong-answer ploys built into the preceding question:

- bringing in *irrelevant details* from elsewhere in the passage
- *distorting* what the passage says
- bringing in *outside information* (not found anywhere in the passage)
- providing a *nonsensical* response to the question at hand

These are the wrong-answer ploys you should always look for in a Simple Recall question.

To complicate a Simple Recall question a bit, the test-makers might turn the question around by asking you to identify an exception to what the passage provides (with a word such as "except" or "least" in upper-case letters):

"The passage mentions all of the following as examples of . . . EXCEPT:"

"According to the passage, . . . could be caused by any of the following EXCEPT:"

To handle this variation, just eliminate all choices that the passage covers and that are relevant to the question, and you'll be left with one choice—the correct one. The following question, also based on Passage I (page 289), is a typical example. Although this question is about as tough a Simple Recall question as you'll find on the ACT, you'll probably agree that it's pretty easy. Here it is again, along with an explanatory answer:

Whether the entry pathway for a particular non-indigenous species can be determined is LEAST likely to depend upon which of the following?

F. Whether the species is considered to be a pest (agr. pest)
G. The size of the average member of the species
H. How long the species has been established
J. Whether the species gains entry through a scrutinized route

The correct answer is G. Nowhere in the passage does the author either state or imply that the physical size of a species' members affects whether the entry pathway for the species can be determined.

You can easily eliminate choices H and J. Both are mentioned explicitly in the third paragraph as factors affecting how precisely the entry pathway(s) of a species can be determined.

Choice F is a bit trickier, and it's the runner-up choice. Unlike the other incorrect choices, choice F is not *explicitly* supported by the passage. However, the final paragraph indicates that federal port inspection is "a major source of information on non-indigenous species pathways, especially for agricultural pests." Accordingly, whether a species is an agricultural pest might have some bearing upon whether or not its entry is detected (by port inspectors). Hence, choice F is not so good a choice as G, which finds no support in the passage whatsoever.

Alert!

In a tougher Simple Recall question (let's call it "less easy"), one wrong-answer choice will be more tempting than the others because the passage will implicitly support it. Don't be fooled; you will find a better choice among the four.

"Restatement" Questions

In handling a Restatement question, your job is to understand a specific idea the author is trying to convey in the passage. These questions are different from Simple Recall questions in that you won't find the answer explicitly in the text. And it's this feature that makes them more difficult. A Restatement question stem might look something like one of the following:

"The passage most strongly supports the assertion that:"

"The author of the passage would probably agree that:"

"Which of the following best characterizes . . . as viewed by . . .?"

Here's a good example of a moderately difficult Restatement question, based on Passage I (page 289). Notice that the wrong-answer choices are designed to confuse you by combining details from the passage that relate to the question—but that don't add up.

Which of the following statements about species movement is best supported by the passage?

A. Species movement is affected more by habitat modifications than by human mobility.

B. Human-driven factors affect the rate at which species move more than they affect the long-term amount of such movements.

C. Movement of a species within a continent depends largely upon the geographic extent of human mobility within the continent.

D. Natural environments created by commerce, tourism, and travel contribute significantly to species movement.

The correct answer is C. This choice restates the point in the second paragraph that rates of species movement driven by human transformation of the natural environment and by human mobility dwarf natural rates by comparison.

Choice **A** is the most tempting wrong-answer choice. Based on the passage, habitat modifications and human mobility can both affect species movement, as choice **A** implies. Also, the passage does make a comparison involving human-driven species movement; so, choice **A** looks appealing. However, the comparison made in the passage is between natural species movement and human-driven movement, not between human modification of habitats and human mobility. So, choice **A** *confuses the details* of the passage.

Choice **B** is easier to eliminate because it is completely *unsupported* by the passage, which makes no attempt to compare rate (interpreted either as frequency or speed) of species movement to total amounts of movement (distance).

Choice **D** is the easiest one to eliminate. You don't even need to read the passage to recognize that choice **D** is a *nonsensical* statement. Human mobility (commerce, tourism, and travel) do not create "natural" environments. It is human mobility itself, not the "natural environment" created by it, that contributes significantly to species movement.

Tip

In ACT Reading questions, many answer choices simply won't make much sense, as with the nonsensical choice **D** in the preceding question. Don't be fooled into second-guessing yourself just because you don't understand what the answer choice means.

This next question, based on Passage II (pages 289–290), is a good example of how the test-makers might boost the difficulty level of a Restatement question. As you read it again here, along with the explanatory answer, notice that some of the wrong-answer choices appear to respond to the question because they describe an "ambiguous position." What's more, at least one of the wrong-answer choices contains information that the passage supports. The use of these two wrong-answer ploys makes this question tougher than average.

Which of the following best characterizes the "ambiguous position" (line 10) in which Soviet scientists were placed after 1917?

F. The Soviet government demanded that their research result in scientific progress, although funding was insufficient to accomplish this goal.

G. They were encouraged to strive toward scientific advancements, while at the same time the freedoms necessary to make such advancements were restricted.

H. While they were required to direct research entirely toward military defense, most advancements in this field were being made by non-Soviet scientists with whom the Soviet scientists were prohibited contact.

J. They were encouraged to collaborate with Soviet colleagues but were prohibited from any discourse with scientists from other countries.

The correct answer is G. According to the passage, the ambiguous position of Soviet scientists was that the Soviet government encouraged and generally supported scientific research, while at the same time it imposed significant restrictions upon its scientists (lines 9–12). Choice **G** restates this idea.

Choice **F** is *unsupported* by the passage. The author neither states nor suggests that the Soviets lacked sufficient funding. Although if true, choice **F** would indicate an ambiguous position for scientists, that ambiguity is not the kind referred to in the passage.

Choice **H** is the easiest one to eliminate. Not only is choice **H** wholly *unsupported* by the passage, which neither states nor suggests either assertion made in choice **H**, this choice does not describe an ambiguous situation.

Choice **J** is the most tempting wrong-answer choice. It's a better choice than choice **F** because the passage supports it, at least implicitly. What's more, if true, choice **J** would present an ambiguous position for Soviet scientists. However, as with choice **F**, the ambiguity that choice **J** describes doesn't reflect the nature of the ambiguity referred to in the passage.

Alert!

Don't panic when you come across a lengthy question or lengthy answer choices, as in the preceding question. Although more reading usually makes for a tougher question, don't assume you're up against as difficult a question as the preceding one. Otherwise, you might decide to give up too soon on what turns out to be an easier question!

"Inference" Questions

Inference questions test your ability to recognize what the author implies, or infers, but does not come right out and state explicitly—in other words, your ability to "read between the lines." To make the inference, you'll need to see a logical connection between two bits of information in the passage (often in two consecutive sentences) and draw a reasonable conclusion from them.

Look for two basic types of Inference questions on the ACT. One type focuses just on the passage's ideas themselves. Your job is to infer a specific idea from what's stated. The question stem will probably contain some form of the word *infer*, *imply*, or *suggest*, as in these examples:

"It can be reasonably inferred from the passage that the reason for . . . is that:"

"In the discussion about . . . (lines X–X), the author of the passage seems to infer that:"

"In the fourth paragraph (lines X–X), the author of the passage suggests that:"

"The passage implies that:"

A second type of Inference question asks you to infer the *author's purpose* in mentioning a specific idea. Look for a question stem that looks like one of these:

"The author mentions . . . (lines X–X) most probably in order to:"

"The example discussed in lines X–X is probably intended to illustrate:"

In designing either type of Inference question, the test-makers will often include a runner-up answer choice in which the inference is a bit more *speculative* than the inference in the best choice. Both of the next two questions, which are based on Passage II (page 289–290), incorporate this wrong-answer ploy.

It can be most reasonably inferred from the passage's first paragraph (lines 1–8) that:

A. expensive research projects such as the particle accelerator program apply technology that can also be applied toward projects relating to national security.
B. scientific knowledge had become so closely linked with national security that it could no longer be communicated to scientific colleagues without restriction.
C. without free access to new scientific knowledge, scientists in different countries are less able to communicate with one another.
D. government funding of scientific research undermines the ideal of scientific freedom to a greater extent than private funding.

The correct answer is B. The first two sentences establish that the link between science and national life undermined scientists' freedom to communicate with other scientists. The next sentence points to the channeling of scientific research toward protecting national security as a manifestation of that link. Notice the almost unavoidable inference here—that national security concerns were part of the "national life" that took precedence over scientific freedoms.

Choice **D** is the runner-up. An argument can be made from the information in the first paragraph that government-funded research is more likely than privately-funded research to relate to matters affecting the national security (that is, military defense). However, this inference is hardly so unavoidable as the one that choice **B** provides. To compete with choice **B**, the inference would need additional supporting evidence.

Choice **A** is unsupported. The author implies no connection between the particle-accelerator program and national security.

Choice **C** is nonsensical. Ready access to new scientific knowledge would require ready communication among scientists, not the other way around.

The author of the passage quotes an article from *Literatunaya Gazeta* (line 14) most probably in order to:

F. illustrate the general sentiment among members of the international scientific community during the time period.
G. support the point that only those notions about science that conformed to the Marxist-Leninist ideal were sanctioned by the Soviet government.
H. point out the Soviet government's emphasis on the notion of a national science.
J. support the author's assertion that the Marxist-Leninist impact on Soviet scientific freedom continued through the decade of the 1970s.

The correct answer is H. This part of the passage is concerned exclusively with pointing out evidence of the Soviet emphasis on a national science. Given the content of the excerpt from *Literatunaya Gazeta*, you can *reasonably infer* that the author is quoting this article as one such piece of evidence.

Choice **F** is easy to rule out because it *distorts* the nature of the quoted article and runs *contrary* to the passage. The article illustrates the official Soviet position and possibly the sentiment among some members of the Soviet intellectual or scientific community. However, the article does not necessarily reflect the views of scientists from other countries.

Choice J is a bit tempting because it might in fact be true and because it is indeed supported by the information in the passage. But the author gives no indication as to when the article was written or published; thus, the article itself lends no support to choice J.

Choice G is the runner-up choice that helps make this question tougher than it would be otherwise. The quoted article does indeed reflect the Marxist-Leninist ideal (at least as interpreted and promulgated by the government) and may in fact have been published only because it was sanctioned (approved) by the Soviet government. However, since this conclusion would require *speculation* and since the quoted excerpt makes no mention of government approval or disapproval of certain scientific notions, it is not likely that choice G expresses the author's purpose in quoting the article.

When handling Inference questions, you need to know the difference between a reasonable inference, which no rational person could dispute based on the passage's information, and mere speculation, which requires additional information to hold water.

"Recap" Questions

For these questions, your job is to recognize either the main idea, or thesis, of the passage (or a particular paragraph) *as a whole*, or the author's primary purpose or concern in the passage (or in a particular paragraph) *as a whole*. In other words, your job is to *recap* what the passage or paragraph is about generally. The question stem will look a lot like one of these:

"The main idea of the passage [or *the final paragraph*] is that:"

"Among the following characterizations, the passage is best viewed as:"

"The author's primary purpose in the passage [or *in the third paragraph*] is to:"

"The passage [or *The first paragraph*] is primarily concerned with:"

To handle this question type, you'll need to recognize the passage's (or paragraph's) overall scope and its main emphasis. Most of the wrong-answer choices will fall into these categories:

- Too broad (embracing ideas outside the scope of the passage or paragraph)
- Too narrow (focusing on only a certain portion or aspect of the discussion)
- Distorted (an inaccurate reflection of the passage's ideas or the author's perspective on the topic)

The test-makers often include a runner-up answer choice that's just a bit off the mark. Here's a moderately difficult question, based on Passage II (pages 289–290), that illustrates this tactic.

The author's primary purpose in the passage is to:

A. examine the events leading up to the suppression of the Soviet refusenik movement of the 1970s.

B. define and dispel the notion of a national science as promulgated by the post-revolution Soviet regime.

C. describe specific attempts by the modern Soviet regime to suppress scientific freedom.

D. examine the major twentieth-century challenges to the assumption that science requires freedom and that it is inherently international.

The correct answer is C. Notice that, with the sole exception of the very last sentence, the passage is entirely concerned with describing Soviet attempts to suppress scientific freedom. In the order mentioned, the attempts include thwarting science's ideals, emphasizing a national science, controlling scientific literature, and threatening and punishing renegade scientists. Choice **C** aptly expresses this overall concern.

Choice **D** is the runner-up. Admittedly, the passage does mention, in the final sentence, two other twentieth-century attempts to suppress scientific freedom. Had the passage continued by describing these two other attempts, choice **D** would probably have been the best answer choice. But since it doesn't, choice **D** is a bit *too broad*.

Choice **A** *distorts* the author's primary purpose. The author does not actually discuss any specific events that might have caused the suppression of the refusenik movement; rather, this historical phenomenon is mentioned simply as another example of the Soviet regime's long-term pattern of suppression.

Choice **B** also *distorts* the author's perspective on the topic. Although the author does define the concept of national science, nowhere does the author attempt to dispel or disprove the concept.

Now here's a Recap question about Passage I (page 289) that focuses on just one paragraph. An easier question would provide wrong-answer choices that refer to information in the *first* paragraph. But this question is a bit tougher—it doesn't allow you such an easy way to rule out wrong choices.

Considered as a whole, the passage's third paragraph (lines 12–23) is concerned with:

F. identifying the problems in assessing the relative significance of various entry pathways for non-indigenous species.

G. discussing the role that time lags and geographic expansion of non-indigenous species play in species detection.

H. pointing out the inadequacy of the federal port inspection system in detecting the entry of non-indigenous species.

J. explaining why it is difficult to trace the entry pathways for long-established non-indigenous species.

Take It to the Next Level

The correct answer is F. In the second sentence of the third paragraph, the author claims that "[a] number of factors confound quantitative evaluation of the relative importance of various entry pathways." In the remainder of the paragraph, the author identifies three such problems: (1) the difficulty of early detection, (2) the inadequacy of port inspection, and (3) the inherent subjectivity in determining the "importance" of a pathway. Choice **F** provides a good "recap" of what the paragraph accomplishes.

Choice **G** is a *distortion*. Although the author mentions these factors, they are not "discussed" in any detail, as choice **G** suggests. Also, the primary concern of the second paragraph is not with identifying the factors affecting species detection, but rather with identifying the problems in quantifying the relative importance of various entry pathways.

Choice **H** is *too narrow*. The author is concerned with identifying other problems as well as in determining the relative importance of various entry pathways.

Choice **J** is a *distortion*. Although the author asserts that it is difficult to trace an entry pathway once a species is well established, the author does not explain why this is so.

The best answer to a Recap question must embrace the whole passage (or paragraph) better than any other choice, while not extending beyond the passage's scope or concerns. Look for at least one red-herring answer choice that is too narrow, and at least one other that is too broad.

Method Questions

Method questions ask you to recognize *how* the author goes about making his or her points, rather than focus on the points themselves. Some Method questions ask for the author's overall approach in the passage, while others ask about how a specific point is made or about the structure of a particular paragraph. In Method questions, the answer choices are usually stated very generally, and it's up to you to connect the general wording of the choices with what's going on in the passage.

A Method question can come in any one of many different forms. Here are just some examples of what the question stem might look like:

"In making the case that . . . , the author's method can be described as:"

"In the last paragraph (lines X–X), the author proceeds by:"

"How does the second paragraph function in relation to the first paragraph?"

"Which of the following most accurately describes the organization of the second paragraph (lines X–X)?"

"Which of the following techniques is used in the second paragraph (lines X–X)?"

When you see a Method question, first let the question guide you to the appropriate area of the passage. Your annotations or notes might suffice to determine how the author proceeds in making his or her points there. If not, reread that section carefully. Focus on what the author is doing; don't get bogged down in details. Again, Method questions concern how the author makes his or her points, not what those points are.

Here's the last paragraph of a passage about Francis Bacon, a sixteenth-century philosopher of science. (As a whole, the passage explores the link between his thinking and the modern-day scientific establishment.) Read the paragraph, then answer the Method question based on it.

> No one questions the immense benefits already conferred by science's efficient methodology. However, since individual scientists must now choose between improving standards of living and obtaining financial support for their research, there is cause for concern. In light of current circumstances, we must ask certain questions about science that Francis Bacon, from a sixteenth-century perspective, could not possibly have put to himself.

Which of the following most accurately describes the technique that the author of the passage uses in the last paragraph?

A. An assertion is made and is backed up by evidence.
B. A viewpoint is expressed and an opposing viewpoint is stated and countered.
C. An admission is offered and is followed by a warning and recommendation.
D. Contradictory claims are presented and then reconciled.

The correct answer is C. The notion that no one questions the benefits of science does qualify as an admission in the context of the paragraph; that is, the author admits that science has given humankind enormous benefits. The author then goes on to voice his concern regarding the current state of the scientific enterprise. Note how the contrast signal word "however" screams at us that some kind of change must come after the author admits that science has conferred immense benefits—and indeed, what comes next is, as choice **C** puts it, a warning: there is cause for concern. A recommendation appears in the final sentence, highlighted by the words "we must ask certain questions. . . ." Every element in choice **C** is present and accounted for, so choice **C** aptly describes the technique used in the paragraph.

Choice **A** indicates that the paragraph begins with an assertion, and we can surely accept that: the assertion that no one questions the benefits of science. Is this then backed up by evidence? No. The contrast signal word "however" tells us that some kind of change is coming, not evidence for the statement in the first sentence. And indeed, the paragraph does go in a different direction.

Choice **B** doesn't reflect what's going on in the paragraph. Choice **B** claims that the final paragraph begins with a viewpoint, which it does. But does an opposing viewpoint follow—that is, an argument against the benefits of science? No; instead he expresses concern about the way science is now conducted.

Choice **D** is incorrect because there are no contradictory claims here. The author admits that science has given humankind enormous benefits, but then goes on to voice his concern regarding the current state of the scientific enterprise. These things aren't contradictory, and nothing in the paragraph reconciles them, so **D** can't be the best choice.

Vocabulary-in-Context Questions

In this question type, the test-maker is gauging your vocabulary and your ability to understand how a word is intended to be used in the context of a sentence (or series of sentences). A Vocabulary-in-Context question stem is easy to spot; it'll look essentially like this (except with a specific line number and vocabulary word):

"As it is used in the passage, the word *[word]* most nearly means:"

In dealing with Vocabulary-in-Context questions:

- You can probably eliminate at least one answer choice that's not even close to the word's meaning (assuming you have at least a general sense of what the word means).
- Be on the lookout for wrong-answer choices that indicate another acceptable or a "close" meaning of the word, but one that doesn't make so much sense in context as the best answer.
- If you don't have a clue what the word means out of context, read around it, then try each answer choice as a substitute for the word. The one that makes the most sense is probably your best bet.

Now, let's take a look at an example, so you get a handle on these questions. Here's an excerpt from a passage about a certain naval warship built by the Union during the U.S. Civil War.

> The *U.S.S. Monitor* was designed by John Ericson, who had already made substantial contributions to marine engineering. The *Monitor* looked like no other ship afloat. With a wooden hull covered with iron plating, the ship had a flat deck with perpendicular sides that went below the waterline and protected the propeller and other important machinery. Even more innovative, the ship had a round, revolving turret that carried two large guns.

As it is used in the passage, the word *innovative* (line 6) most nearly means:

F. dangerous.
G. unusual.
H. revolutionary.
J. clever.

The correct answer is H. The word *innovative* means "new and unique in an inventive way." If you already know this definition, the correct answer should be obvious to you. If you're not sure, examine the context. The answer choice that's easiest to eliminate is F. The revolving turret and guns might be dangerous (to their targets—or even to their operators); but, the phrase "even more innovative" tells you that what preceded this sentence also described something innovative, and there's nothing intrinsically "dangerous" about the shape of the ship as described in that sentence. To the contrary, the sentence implies that the features described helped make the ship *safe*. So, how do you choose between choices G, H, and J? First, let's consider choice J: The author seems concerned here with how the *Monitor* was different from any other ship ever built, not with how "clever" its features (or its designer) were. So, choice J doesn't make much sense in context, even though something "innovative" is usually thought to be "clever" as well. As for the two remaining choices, **G** and **H**, as used in the passage, "innovative" refers to the design choices, made by John Ericson, that made the *Monitor* a remarkably new type of vessel—not just "unusual." So, choice **H** seems a better choice than **G**.

> **Note**
>
> The SAT (that other college admissions test) measures vocabulary directly through *antonym* questions, which are widely criticized as culturally biased and as rewarding rote memorization. The folks who designed the ACT had a better idea: put vocabulary in context to figure out what it means in case you didn't already know.

The Test-Makers' Top 10 Wrong-Answer Ploys

If you read the analysis of each sample question in the Next Level carefully, you learned a lot about how the test-makers design wrong-answer choices. Here's a review list of the types they resort to most often:

1. **The response distorts the information in the passage.** It might understate, overstate, or twist the passage's information or the author's point in presenting that information.
2. **The response uses information in the passage but does not answer the question.** It includes information found in the passage but that isn't useful to respond to the question at hand.
3. **The response relies on speculation or an unsupported inference.** It calls for some measure of speculation in that the statement is not readily inferable from the information given.
4. **The response is contrary to what the passage says.** It contradicts the passage's information or runs contrary to what the passage infers.
5. **The response gets something in the passage backward.** It reverses the logic of an idea in the passage, confuses cause with effect, or otherwise turns information in the passage around.
6. **The response confuses one opinion or position with another.** It incorrectly represents the viewpoint of one person (or group) as that of another.
7. **The response is too narrow or specific.** It focuses on particular information in the passage that is too specific or narrowly focused in terms of the question posed.
8. **The response is too broad (general).** It embraces information or ideas that are too general or widely focused in terms of the question posed.
9. **The response relies on information that the passage does not mention.** It brings in information not found anywhere in the passage.
10. **The response is utter nonsense.** It makes almost no logical sense in the context of the question; it's essentially gibberish.

Final Tips for Answering ACT Reading Questions

Now, here's a checklist of tips for answering Reading questions. Some of these tips reiterate suggestions made earlier in this chapter, suggestions that are worth underscoring. Others are new here. Apply these points of advice to the practice tests in Part VI, and then review them again, just before exam day.

Don't Second-Guess the Test-Maker

The directions for the ACT Reading Test instruct you to choose the "best" answer among the four choices. Isn't this awfully subjective? True, there is an element of subjective judgment involved in interpreting prose. However, these questions are reviewed, tested, and revised several times before they appear as scored questions on an actual ACT. If you think there are two or more viable "best" responses, *you* (not the test-maker) have either misread or misinterpreted the passage, the question, or the answer choices.

Don't Over-Analyze Questions or Second-Guess Yourself

If you believe you understood the passage fairly well but a particular answer choice seems confusing or a bit nonsensical, do not assume that it's your fault. Many wrong-answer choices simply don't make much sense. If an answer choice strikes you this way, don't examine it further; eliminate it. Similarly, if you've read and considered all four choices, and one response strikes you as the best one, more often than not, your initial response will be the correct one.

Don't Overlook the Obvious

ACT Reading Test questions vary in difficulty level, which means that many of the questions are really pretty easy. If a particular answer choice strikes you as obviously correct (or incorrect), don't assume that you're missing something. You might simply be up against a relatively easy question.

Use Two Routes to the Correct Answer

One route is to try to formulate your own answer to a question before even reading the answer choices, then filter out any choice that doesn't resemble what you're looking for as a best answer. Try using this route first. If it doesn't work, go to the second route: process of elimination. In this chapter, you familiarized yourself with the test-maker's favorite wrong-answer ploys to help you in this process.

Keep in Mind the Big Ideas, Even When Answering Questions about Small Details

Always keep in mind the passage's main ideas. No matter what the question is, you can eliminate any answer choice that doesn't jive with the "big picture."

Be Ever-Alert to the Test-Makers' Top 10 Wrong-Answer Ploys

Keep a mental list of the wrong-answer types or ploys you learned about in the Next Level. When you have trouble narrowing down the answer choices, review this list in your mind, and the remaining wrong answers should reveal themselves.

The Science Test

Chapter 12

Strategies for the Science Test

In this chapter, you'll learn:

- What is—and is *not*—covered on the ACT Science Test
- How to read and analyze scientific data presented in graphical form (tables, charts, and graphs)
- A step-by-step approach to handling an ACT Data Representation set
- How scientific experiments are designed
- A step-by-step approach to handling an ACT Research Summary
- Success keys for handling ACT Data Representation and Research Summaries
- To *Take It to the Next Level*

The ACT Science Test Is a Science Reasoning Test

The ACT Science Test includes passages drawn from four broad disciplines:

- *Biology*—including cell biology, botany, zoology, microbiology, ecology, genetics, and evolution
- *Earth/Space Sciences*—including geology, meteorology, oceanography, astronomy, and environmental sciences
- *Chemistry*—including atomic theory, inorganic chemical reactions, chemical bonding, reaction rates, solutions, equilibriums, gas laws, electrochemistry, organic chemistry, biochemistry, and properties and states of matter
- *Physics*—including mechanics, energy, thermodynamics, electromagnetism, fluids, solids, and light waves

For the ACT, it's helpful to know at least the very basics covered in introductory high school coursework in the four broad areas listed above. However, information beyond what's very basic will be provided. For example, in a passage dealing with the life cycle of bacteria (biology), the test-makers would assume that you know that the cell is the basic building block of life, but they *won't* assume that you know specifically how bacteria reproduce. That's because the ACT Science Test is not really a "science" test. It doesn't test you on your *knowledge* of science; rather, it tests your ability to understand the scientific *approach* to a problem, which involves certain ways of *reasoning*. Luckily, this approach (or way of reasoning) is just a special form of common sense.

Let's briefly review the three different formats the test uses to gauge your ability to reason like a good scientist:

- A *Data Representation* set gauges your ability to read, interpret, and draw conclusions from graphical data (tables, charts, and graphs).
- A *Research Summary* set (which provides an account of one or more scientific experiments) tests your ability to understand or critique the design of the experiment(s) and to interpret their results. Research Summaries almost always contain graphical data as well, which you need to read, interpret, and draw conclusions from.
- A *Conflicting Viewpoints* set presents two or more conflicting hypotheses or viewpoints, each based on the same premises or data. The questions measure your ability to understand, compare, and evaluate the hypotheses or viewpoints.

Note

Remember, the Science Test is organized into seven separate sets: three Data Representation sets, three Research Summary sets, and one Conflicting Viewpoints set.

Data Representation—Ways of Presenting Data

Before examining an ACT-style Data Representation set, let's take a detailed look at the various ways that scientists display data in graphical form. Here are the four forms you'll examine in this section:

- Tables
- Line graphs
- Bar graphs
- Scatter plots

Alert!

The four types of displays listed above might not be the only ones you'll encounter during the ACT Science Test, but they're the most likely ones you'll run across.

Tables

The *table* is the form of presenting data that appears most frequently in ACT Science. You'll encounter tables not just in Data Representation sets but also in Research Summary sets. Tables are generally divided into horizontal rows and vertical columns. The values for the *independent* variable usually appear in the leftmost column, while the values for the *dependent* variable(s) appear in columnar form to the right.

So, to analyze a simple two-column table, you might fill in the blank for yourself in this sentence: "As the number in the left column increases, the number in the right column ______." You'd do the same for a table showing multiple dependent variables. For instance, in analyzing Table 1, you might say to yourself: "As Jolt concentration (the independent variable) increases, plant growth, in inches, and the number of observed buds (the two dependent variables) both decrease."

Table 1

The Effect on Plant Growth and Budding of Watering with Varying Concentrations of Jolt Cola Solution

Jolt Concentration (%)	Growth in Inches	Buds Observed
0.0	10	32
0.5	8	16
1.0	6	8
1.5	4	4
2.0	2	2
2.5	0	0

The test-makers' favorite way of "tricking up" a table is to subdivide dependent variables. In Table 2, for instance, each of two dependent variables—industrial environment and rural environment—is divided by sub-environment—either indoor or outdoor. So, the table shows a total of four dependent variables.

Table 2

	NJ Industrial ($\mu g/m^3$)		Maine Rural Township ($\mu g/m^3$)	
Volatile Chemical	Indoor	Outdoor	Indoor	Outdoor
Trichloroethane	21	4	14	3
Tetrachloroethylene	9	3	8	1
Chloroform	5	0.2	2	0.1
O-oxylene	5	3	3	2
Styrene	5	0.5	1	0.2

Table 2 is different from Table 1 in another respect as well. In Table 2, notice that the independent variable (leftmost column) is not a number but rather a chemical type. So, to analyze the table, you wouldn't look for increases or decreases in the values for each dependent variable. Instead, you'd compare numbers *horizontally*—that is, across the four columns. In so doing, you should notice that in each row (for each chemical) the outdoor values are lower than the indoor values.

Line Graphs

A *line graph* plots value pairs on an *xy*-coordinate plane rather than in a table. By convention, a line graph's horizontal axis (*x*-axis) tracks the independent variable, and its vertical axis (*y*-axis) tracks the dependent variable. To analyze a line graph that contains a single line, you might fill in the blank for yourself in the following sentence: "As the value of *x* increases, the value of *y* ____." Or, to simply "look up" information in the graph, fill in the blanks in this sentence: "When *x* equals ___, *y* equals ___."

Not exactly rocket science, is it—especially compared to Chapter 10's coordinate geometry problems? Of course, ACT line graphs can get a bit more complex than this. But not much.

For instance, look at the graph in Figure 1, which shows the effect of temperature (the independent variable) on a substance's solubility (the dependent variable). As you can see, the graph includes four lines, representing four different solutes.

Figure 1

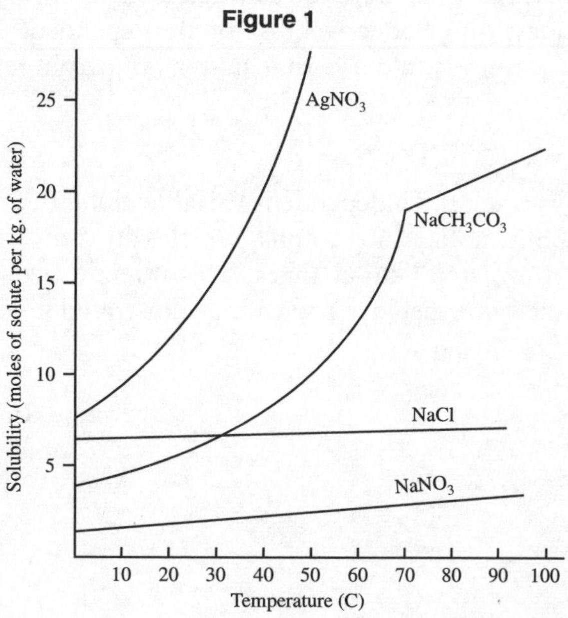

In this graph, to analyze the relationship between temperature and solubility for $NaNO_3$, for instance, you'd fill in the blank in the first sentence you read earlier as follows: "As temperature (the value of *x*) increases, the solubility of $NaNO_3$ (the value of *y*) *increases gradually but steadily*." Or, to simply "look up" information for $NaNO_3$: "When temperature (*x*) equals 60, *y* equals *approximately 3*."

Note

Notice the italicized word *approximately* in the preceding sentence. In reading ACT line graphs, you won't need to determine precise values, for the obvious reason that it's difficult to determine the precise coordinates of a point along an angled line on a line graph. The test-makers aren't interested in testing your visual acuity; so, in defining points on ACT line graphs, rest assured that approximations will suffice to answer the questions.

A trickier aspect of line has to do with the *shapes* and *slopes* of lines. Keep in mind these insights:

- A line moving *upward* from left to right (for example, $NaNO_3$ in Figure 1) indicates a *direct* relationship (as the value of the independent variable increases, so does the value of the dependent variable). The steeper the slope, the larger the increase in the value of the dependent variable for a given increase in the independent variable. (If the line is straight, as in the line for $NaNO_3$ in Figure 1, those increases stay in the same proportion.) A line that curves upward (for example, the lines for $AgNO_3$ and $NaCH_3CO_3$ in Figure 1) indicates the independent variable's increasing "effectiveness" on the dependent variable as the value of the former increases. Conversely, a curve that flattens out from left to right indicates decreasing effectiveness.
- A line moving *downward* from left to right indicates an *inverse* relationship (as the value of the independent variable increases, the value of the dependent variable decreases). The steeper the slope, the larger the decrease in the value of the dependent variable for a given increase in the independent variable. A line that curves downward from left to right would indicate the independent variable's increasing "effectiveness" on the dependent variable as the value of the former increases. Conversely, a curve that flattens out from left to right indicates decreasing effectiveness.

Bar Graphs

Bar graphs, like line graphs, almost always track the independent variable along the *x*-axis and the dependent variable along the *y*-axis. But, unlike line graphs, which can show continuous changes, bar graphs can show only quantum (step-like) changes. This doesn't mean that you can't plot a line graph and bar graph on the same display. You can, as illustrated in Figure 2.

Figure 2

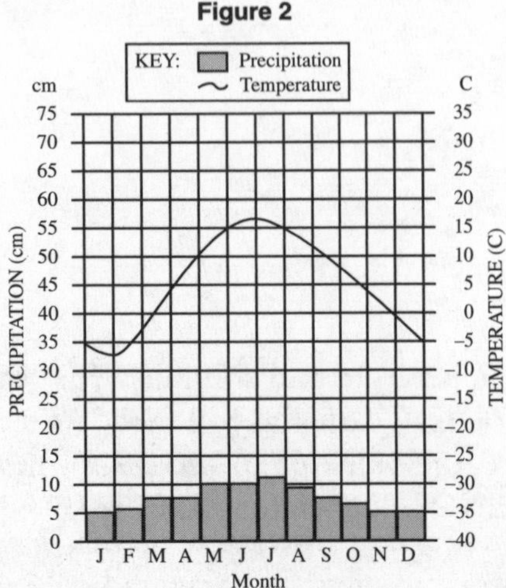

In Figure 2, notice that the bar graph and line graph track the same independent variable (month) but different dependent variables. (The bar graph tracks monthly precipitation totals while the line graph tracks temperature.)

To track temperature, a bar graph could have been used instead of a line graph. But, the bar graph could only show average monthly temperature, not continuous changes. Can you picture what that bar graph might look like? For each month, you would see a second bar overlapping and extending higher than the precipitation bar. From January up to June, the temperature bars would rise in height, peaking in June and July, then decrease in height.

Scatter Plots

A *scatter plot* is useful when the points on an *xy*-graph cannot be connected to form a smooth line, perhaps because the relationship between the independent and dependent variables is complex or influenced by other, secondary factors. For example, a person's height and weight tend to vary together (their relationship is direct). But, other factors, such as diet, play a role as well, and there are certainly exceptions to the general relationship. Thus, a graph depicting the height and weight of twenty randomly selected people would probably not yield dots that could be connected to form a neat, smooth line. Instead, it would probably yield a scattering of points reflecting the general relationship between the two variables *only roughly.* In Figure 3, notice that the thirteen discrete points imply a smooth line, which suggests the general relationship between the two variables, but doesn't attempt to "connect the dots":

Figure 3

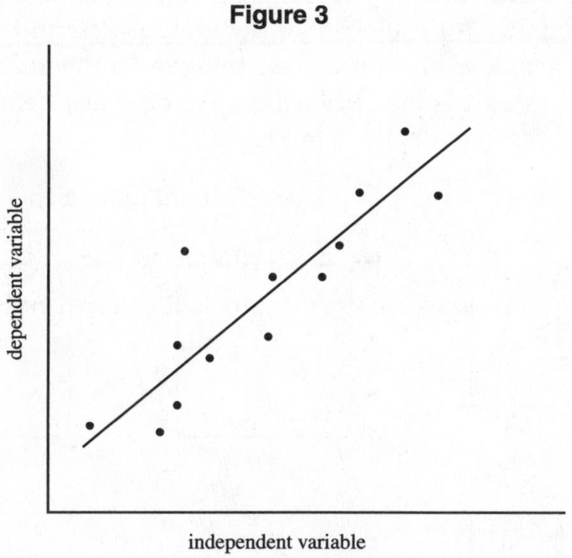

Scatter graph c̄ best fit line

By their nature, scatter plots lend themselves to certain unique types of test questions. For example, a question might ask for a reasonable explanation for an anomalous point—one that's at a distance from the implied line that shows the general pattern. In Figure 3, any point significantly above and to the left of the line might be explained by a secondary factor, such as overeating. Conversely, any point significantly below and to the right of the line might be explained by a health problem that resulted in abnormal weight loss in the individual.

Or, a scatter-plot question might provide additional data—data that diverges from the implied line and suggests that the line needs revising—then ask for a hypothesis or theory to explain the divergence. For instance, if additional data points imply a curved line that becomes flatter as height increases, it would be reasonable to conclude that tall people tend to be proportionately thinner than shorter people.

Data Representation—Your 7-Step Game Plan

On the ACT, you'll encounter *three* Data Representation sets, each of which will contain 5–7 questions. (The most common number of questions is five.) Your task now is to learn a step-by-step approach to ACT Data Representation, using the following passage as an illustration. Go ahead and read the passage and examine the graphical data.

Sample Passage I

Phytoplankton are tiny aquatic plants that are an important food source for larger animals and may be an important source of carbon (the element that is a building block of all living organisms). Phytoplankton abundance is dependent on the presence of warm surface waters. Consequently, changes in phytoplankton abundance can be used as an indicator of changes in surface water temperature.

A system for documenting phytoplankton abundance has been developed using filtering silk towed by merchant ships. The organisms color the silk green, and the intensity of the color is correlated with their abundance. Figure 1 shows data on the average monthly phytoplankton abundance for each of four decades, as determined by the color index system. For each decade, averages are shown beginning in October and ending in September. Data is given for two ocean areas in the Northern Atlantic just below the arctic circle. The boundaries of these areas are depicted in Figure 2.

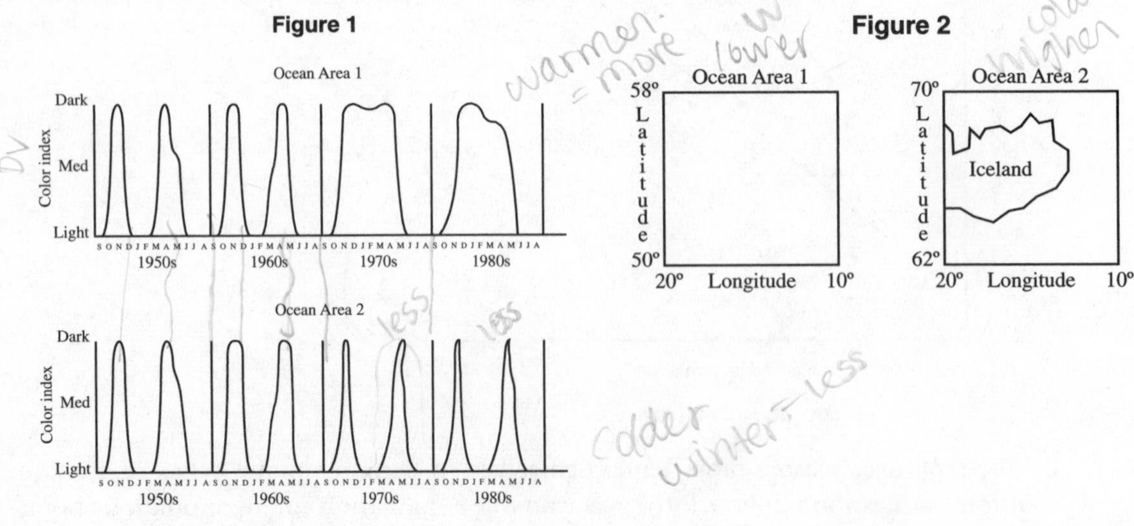

The 7-Step Plan

Here's a 7-step approach that will help you to handle any Data Representation question set:

Step 1: Briefly size up the passage.

Step 2: Read the passage and data again—this time carefully and "actively."

Step 3: Look for patterns, trends, and discrepancies among the data.

Step 4: Hypothesize by asking yourself what might explain patterns, trends, or discrepancies among the data.

Step 5: Answer the questions. For each question, try to formulate an answer before you read the four choices.

Step 6: Look again at any questions you had trouble with, if you have time.

Step 7: On your answer sheet, mark your selections for all the questions in the set.

In the following pages, you'll learn what each step involves, and you'll apply the steps to Passage I and a set of 5 questions.

Step 1: Briefly size up the passage.

First of all, you need to determine which type of passage you're dealing with. Once you see that you're dealing with a set of Data Representation questions, quickly skim the passage and glance at the graphical display(s), just to get a feel for the passage's overall topic and the kinds of data under examination. Some Data Representation passages are easier than others. Try to quickly assess overall difficulty level. If the passage or graphical data confuse or intimidate you, now's the time to cut and run—in other words, to shop around for an easier passage. (You can always come back to the passage later if you have time.)

Let's apply Step 1 to Passage I. As you read the passage and glanced at the two figures, were you able to get the gist of the subject as a whole—and of what the figures are intended to display? If so, this would *not* be a question set you'd skip. On the other hand, if you were left a bit dazed and clueless, you'd probably want to skip to the next question set in the hope that it's a bit easier.

Step 2: Read the passage and data again—this time carefully and "actively."

When you read actively, you ask (and answer) certain questions for yourself as you read and recap. During Step 2, ask yourself:

- What relationships are described in the background information preceding the graphical data?
- In each table or graph, what are the *variables*? In other words, what is it that varies in type, quality, amount, or quantity—variations that the table or graph provides a record of? Any table or graph will involve at least two variables—a *dependent* variable and *independent* variable. During Step 2 is the time to make sure you understand what these variables are.

Let's apply Step 2 to Passage I. The background information describes two important relationships:

- Between water temperature and pH abundance—warmer water is needed for pH abundance.
- Between color intensity of the silk and pH abundance—the more intense the silk color, the more abundant the pH.

In each of the two graphs in Figure 1:

- The *independent* variable is time period, and it's shown along the horizontal axis. Four, one-decade periods are shown. For each decade, the 12 months of a year are indicated—from September through August (not January through December). For each decade, individual years are not shown.
- The *dependent* variable is pH color intensity, and it's shown along the vertical axis. How do we know pH color intensity is the dependent variable? Because it varies according to, or depends on, the month of the year as well as the decade. (Besides, it's shown on the vertical axis, which is where dependent variables are generally shown.)

The two graphs in Figure 2 each shows a specific geographic area. Look carefully at what's shown on each axis. The longitude is the same, but the latitude of area 2 is further north than area 1. (The latitude is greater.) Picture area 2 (the one containing part of Iceland) just above area 1 on a map.

Step 3: Look for patterns, trends, and discrepancies among the data.

Once you understand the function of each chart and graph, your next step is to analyze the data in each one to see what patterns or trends emerge. For each chart or graph, ask yourself:

- What relationship (general pattern or trend) is shown between the variables? For example, as the value of one variable increases, what happens to the value of the other one? Does it always increase? Always decrease? Increase to a certain point, then level off or decrease?

Let's apply Step 3 to Passage I, Figure 1. In each graph, the vertical axis tells us that a higher point on the graph means darker color, which in turn means greater pH abundance. Look first at the graph for Ocean Area 1. It appears that during the two decades of the 1950s and 1960s, there were two distinct "seasons" of pH abundance during the year. Throughout both decades, pH abundance peaked around November, then again around April. Contrast this pattern with the one for the 1970s and 1980s, during which there appeared to be one long season of pH abundance—from November through April.

Now, look at the graph of Ocean Area 2 in Figure 1. During the 1950s and 1960s, the pattern of pH abundance shows the same seasonal pattern as in Ocean Area 1. But, during the 1970s and 1980s, Ocean Area 2 continues to show the same seasonal pattern, except that the "peak" season appears a bit briefer than during the 1950s and 1960s.

In sum, Figure 1 reveals three patterns or trends from the 1960s to the 1970s:

- Something significant happened that effected the annual "seasons" of pH abundance in both Areas 1 and 2.
- In Area 1, two distinct brief seasons grew into one longer extended season.
- In Area 2, two distinct brief seasons each became slightly briefer.

Figure 2 doesn't reveal any patterns or trends in itself—it merely shows a pair of maps.

Step 4: Hypothesize by asking yourself what might explain patterns, trends, or discrepenices among the data.

Once you're sure that you understand the function of each table and graph, and that you've identified any clear patterns or trends in the data, it's time to go one step further. Ask yourself what might explain the trends, patterns, or relationships among the data. What you're doing here is developing a theory, or *hypothesis,* about a possible cause-and-effect relationship. Apply your commonsense understanding of the physical world to theorize about what force might be creating the patterns or trends seen in the data.

If there's more than one table or graph, ask yourself what relationship or connection there is, if any, between the data in the different tables or graphs. Seeing a possible connection might help you develop an hypothesis.

Let's apply Step 4 to Passage I. What do you suppose might have happened from the 1960s to the 1970s to alter the pH "seasons" in both Areas 1 and 2—but in contrary ways? Perhaps Figure 2 provides the clue you need to formulate a hypothesis. Area 2 is just north of Area 1, so the water temperatures are probably colder there. (And, since part of Iceland is located in Area 2, you know that area is pretty far north—at the arctic circle.) The passage told you that warmer water-surface temperatures are needed for pH to thrive. Thus, it appears that, from the 1960s to the 1970s, water-surface temperatures in Area 1 increased during the winter months, while they decreased in Area 2. We're not sure why.

Step 5: Answer the questions. For each question, try to formulate an answer before you read the four choices.

Now it's time to move ahead to the questions themselves. As you read each question stem, try to answer the question *before* looking at the answer choices, by applying your understanding of the data, the patterns and trends you identified, and your hypothesis (if any) from steps 2–4. In other words, try to predict what you might expect the correct answer would say. If you followed steps 2–4, you should be able to prephrase an answer to *most* of the questions. (For some questions, this technique won't work; but for most questions it will.)

Just as for the Reading Test, prephrasing the answer to a Data Representation question is the best way to zero in on the correct choice and, just as important, to avoid those tempting, confusing, and generally distracting wrong-answer choices—in other words, to keep from second-guessing yourself.

Let's walk through 5 ACT-style questions based on Passage I. As we do so, you'll discover that, during steps 2–4, we did most of the brainwork needed to answer nearly every question without breaking a sweat.

1. Figure 1 indicates that significant changes in phytoplankton abundance:

A. occurred evenly over the course of the four decades.
B. occurred over the course of about a decade.
C. occurred over the course of about a year.
D. were apparent in area 1 earlier than in area 2.

The correct answer is B. During Step 2, we determined that, for both ocean areas, there's no significant change in the general shape of the annual phytoplankton abundance graphs from the 1950s to the 1960s, nor is there much change from the 1970s to the 1980s, but that, from the 1960s to the 1970s, the graphs for both ocean areas change quite a bit. (In area 1, the two "humps" merge into one "fat" one, while in area 2 the two humps each become noticeably "skinnier.") Choice **B** tells the essential story: During the course of the 1970s, significant changes in phytoplankton changes occurred in both areas. Of course, we don't know whether the changes during the 1970s were gradual or sudden (perhaps taking place mainly during the final few years of the decade). But, for the purpose of answering the question, it doesn't matter, does it?

Note

Question 1 is a relatively easy one, for two reasons. First, it involves only one of the two figures. Second, you can literally "see" the answer to this question merely by glancing at the graphs in the figure.

2. Certain species of whales migrate annually in order to take advantage of abundant blooms of phytoplankton, one of their principal food sources. During which of the following months would a whale-watching tour in Ocean Area 1 be LEAST likely to encounter phytoplankton-eating whales?

F. January
G. April
H. May
J. August

The correct answer is H. Despite the length of this question, it is probably the simplest of the 5 in this set because it focuses only on Figure 1 and just on one of the two graphs in that figure. Of course, you do need to understand that, in Figure 1, the darker the phytoplankton color (the higher along the vertical axis), the more abundant it is. You also need to understand that, for each decade, the horizontal axis charts phytoplankton levels from September through October (not from January through December). Of course, since we read the passage carefully and analyzed Figure 1 during Step 2, we already know all this.

To answer question 2, aside from understanding what the top graph in Figure 1 shows, all you need to recognize is that, during each decade, the curve is at a very high point (on the vertical scale) during the month of April. (Again, we recognized this during Step 2.) None of the other months listed among the answer choices (January, May, and August) show consistently high levels of phytoplankton abundance across *all four* decades. That's why the correct answer is **H.**

Alert!

Don't assume that a lengthy question is necessarily a tough one—a case in point is question 2 here, which is probably the easiest of the 5 in this set. Conversely, brief questions sometimes can be very challenging. The moral is simple: Don't judge a Science question solely by its length.

3. Based on the information in Figure 1, which of the following statements concerning phytoplankton abundance in the four decades of the study is most accurate?

- **A.** There was no discernible change in patterns of phytoplankton abundance in Ocean Area 1.
- **B.** Annual phytoplankton abundance increased in Ocean Area 2.
- **C.** Annual phytoplankton abundance increased in Ocean Area 1 and decreased in Ocean Area 2.
- **D.** The season of high phytoplankton abundance increased in length in both Ocean Areas.

The correct answer is C. We essentially answered this question during Step 3. In Ocean Area 1, the two annual periods of phytoplankton abundance were so much longer during the 1970s and 1980s than the 1950s and 1960s that they had merged into a single long period of abundance lasting half the year. By contrast, in Ocean Area 2, the two peaks are noticeably "thinner" for the last two decades than the first two, indicating a marked decrease in the phytoplankton population from the start of the four-decade period to the end of it.

4. Assuming that the changes in phytoplankton abundance seen in the study occurred solely because of surface-water temperature variations, the information in the figures indicates that which of the following statements is true?

- **F.** Surface ocean waters above latitude 62° North in the map areas cooled during the study.
- **G.** Surface ocean waters above latitude 50° North in the map areas cooled during the study.
- **H.** Surface ocean waters east of longitude 10° in the map areas warmed during the study.
- **J.** Surface ocean waters west of longitude 10° in the map areas cooled during the study.

The correct answer is F. This question is more challenging than either question 1, 2, or 3, for two reasons. First, it involves information in both figures as well as a key portion of the textual information. Second, to handle it, you need to not only "read" and interpret the graphical and textual information, but also apply it to a given scenario (the hypothetical situation that the question poses). Nevertheless, during Step 4 we did most of the brainwork needed to answer this questions. Only choice **F** provides information consistent with the data in the graphs. Ocean Area 2 is north of latitude 62°; if the waters there got cooler, it would make sense that phytoplankton abundance would decrease. (See the second sentence of the passage.)

5. Some researchers hypothesize that the changes in phytoplankton abundance reflect an increase in global temperature over the last century (global warming). Which of the following findings would support this hypothesis and fit the data seen in the first figure?

A. A greater abundance of fresh water from melted ice and permafrost has begun flowing south to north from the Antarctic during the last century.
B. A greater abundance of fresh water from melted ice and permafrost has begun flowing north to south from the Arctic during the last century.
C. Warmer temperatures have been recorded in and around Iceland during the last century.
D. Barring a few exceptions, phytoplankton numbers have begun to decrease dramatically in ocean areas around the globe during the last century.

The correct answer is B. The question is the toughest and trickiest of the 5 in this set. As with question 4, you need to understand both figures in order to handle it. What's more, the passage's textual and graphical information say nothing about global warming, ice, or melted ice. Nevertheless, performing Step 4 prepared us well for this question! Choice **B** fits both the global warming hypothesis and the data shown in the graphs in several ways. First, the graphs for Ocean Area 1, showing an increase in phytoplankton, certainly fit the notion of global warming. Second, the idea that arctic ice is melting would fit that idea as well. Finally, the abundance of fresh water newly melted from ice appearing in the northern reaches of the Atlantic could help to explain why phytoplankton has actually declined around Iceland: the water temperature there has gone down slightly as a result of the melting ice.

Step 6: Look again at any questions you had trouble with, if you have time.

Go back to the questions you earmarked to come back to, and try them again. Later questions are typically more complex and challenging than earlier ones. Check the time remaining for the Science Reasoning Test. Remember: Your goal is to devote 6 minutes, on average, to each question set. If you're ahead of schedule, go back and look again at the questions you weren't sure about. Otherwise, move on to Step 7.

Step 7: On your answer sheet, mark your selections for all the questions in the set.

During a question set, don't interrupt your brainwork to fill in your answer sheet. Wait until you've answered all the questions, then fill in the corresponding ovals on the answer sheet. After Step 7, if you're still uncertain about the correct answer to certain questions, earmark them in your test booklet. You can come back to them if you have enough time remaining after you've attempted all seven question sets.

Note

You just looked at a very typical Data Representation set—at least half the questions tested you simply on how well you understood what the graphs showed, while the remaining questions (4 and 5) went a bit further, requiring you to apply or hypothesize from the data. Later questions were more challenging than earlier ones, which is also typical of ACT Data Representation.

Research Summaries—Understanding How Scientists Conduct Research

The remainder of this level involves the Research Summary format. (On the ACT, three of the seven Science sets will appear in this format.) Before plunging into a sample passage or question set, let's first examine the key principles of scientific experimentation. You learned these concepts in your high school science coursework, but they're worth reviewing because they form the basis of ACT Research Summary passages and questions.

Inductive and Deductive Reasoning

Scientists employ two types of logic to explain the natural and physical world: *inductive* and *deductive* reasoning. Inductive reasoning moves from the specific to the general. Scientists do this when they use data from experiments or observations as the basis for a more general theory. Deductive reasoning, on the other hand, involves applying general laws to specific cases. Scientists do this when they use existing theories to explain experimental results or observations.

Induction and deduction, in combination, form the underpinnings of the scientific method. Both processes are involved in the development of a scientific theory. Although ACT Research Summaries involve both, the decided emphasis, in the passages as well as in the questions, is on *inductive* reasoning.

Starting with a Hypothesis

The scientific method, in simple terms, involves first forming a *hypothesis* and then testing that hypothesis through observation, experimentation, and/or prediction. A hypothesis is a tentative explanation for some natural phenomenon, one that has not been tested or verified in any way. Think of a hypothesis as an educated guess about why something happens or about the nature of the relationship between two or more variables. Nearly all scientific research, and most (not all) ACT Research Summary experiments, starts with a hypothesis.

The Design of a Scientific Experiment

The crucial objectives in the design of all scientific experimentation are *objectivity* and *reproducibility*. Objectivity refers to the need to design an experiment so as to eliminate the effects of personal bias, either intentional or unintentional, on the part of any experimenter or of anyone who participates in analyzing the resulting data. Reproducibility means that it must be possible to duplicate the procedures in the experiment so as to test the validity of the results. Since these objectives are both aspects of experimental design, they're fair game for the ACT. However, the ACT does not commonly test on these two objectives.

Independent and Dependent Variables

Nearly all experiments are designed with certain elements in common. Two of these basic elements are the *independent* and *dependent variables*. The independent variable is so named because it is adjusted independently of other factors. Usually, independent variables are controlled by the experimenter—they're part of the experiment's design—while dependent variables are what the experimenter observes and what "depend" on the independent variables.

For instance, in a simple experiment designed to determine how time of day affects temperature, the independent variable would be the time of day, while the dependent variable would be the temperature.

In any case, it's desirable to have one and only one independent variable in a given experiment. Experiments with two or more variables are harder to reproduce, and it's difficult to draw reliable conclusions from them since it's usually impossible to determine with certainty the relative importance of each variable—or the unpredictable ways that two or more variables may affect each other. Ideally, scientists need to be able to account for all the phenomena they observe, or else they cannot say for sure why changes occur.

The Control

Another element used in nearly all experiments is the *control*. The control is an experimental subject for which all the relevant variables, including the independent variable, are held constant. Because the independent variable is held constant, any changes observed in the control must be caused by other factors. These changes can then be accounted for throughout the rest of the experiment.

For example, in testing a new experimental therapy for AIDS, researchers might study two groups of patients: a group receiving the new treatment and a control group that is not receiving the new treatment. It would be important to match the two groups as closely as possible in every other way: the average age, the severity of AIDS symptoms, and the nature of any other health problems suffered, among other characteristics. If this is done, and if the experimental group shows a markedly better rate of recovery than the control group, it would be reasonably good evidence that the improvement is due to the new therapy rather than any other factor.

Research Summaries—Your 7-Step Game Plan

On the ACT, you'll encounter *three* Research Summary sets, each of which will contain 5–7 questions. (The most common number of questions is 6.) In this section, you'll learn a step-by-step approach to ACT Research Summaries, using the following passage as an illustration. Go ahead and read the passage and examine the graphical data now.

Sample Passage II

Enzymes are special proteins that act as catalysts to speed up chemical reactions in cells. Enzymes catalyze reactions by first having their active site bind to its *substrate*, usually the molecule that is undergoing reaction. The ability of an enzyme to bind to its substrate is called its *activity*. Thus, activity is also a measure of how well an enzyme catalyzes a reaction. The active site of an enzyme is very specific for its substrate. This specificity is created by the three-dimensional shape of the enzyme. However, this three-dimensional shape is dependent upon environmental factors, such as temperature and pH, a measure of acidity.

If the shape of the enzyme is changed, the enzyme may no longer be able to bind to its substrate. In this case, the enzyme is said to be *denatured*. Extremes of either temperature or pH can cause enzymes to denature.

A scientist isolated three enzymes from a mammalian cell. These enzymes will be denoted Enzyme A, Enzyme B, and Enzyme C.

Experiment 1

A scientist placed samples of Enzyme A into twelve different tubes. Each tube contained a buffer solution at a different pH such that the first tube was at pH = 1, the second tube at pH = 2, the third tube at pH = 3, and so on up to the twelfth tube, which was at pH = 12. The scientist then added an indicator that would turn the solution yellow if bound by the enzyme. Thus, the solution would turn more yellow when more indicator was bound. The temperature for all the tubes was 25°C. This procedure was repeated for Enzyme B and Enzyme C. The scientist was then able to create the graph shown in the following figure.

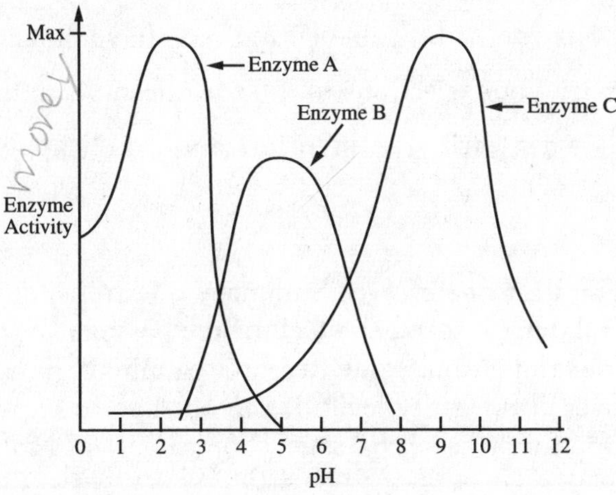

Experiment 2

A sample of Enzyme A was placed into a single tube containing a buffer solution at the pH that gave the greatest activity in Experiment 1. The tube was then brought to near freezing, and a sample was taken and tested for activity by addition of the same indicator above. The tube was then gradually warmed, with samples taken every five degrees and tested for activity. The process was repeated for Enzyme B and Enzyme C. The scientist was then able to make the graph shown in the following figure.

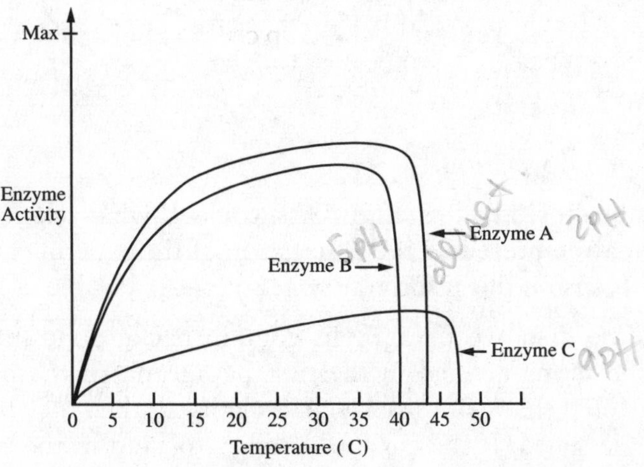

The 7-Step Plan

Here's a 7-step approach that will help you to handle any Research Summary question set:

Step 1: Briefly size up the passage.

Step 2: Understand the background information.

Step 3: Understand the experiments.

Step 4: Identify patterns, trends, and conflicts among the experimental results.

Step 5: Answer the questions. For each question, try to formulate an answer before you read the four choices.

Step 6: Look again at any questions you had trouble with, if you have time.

Step 7: On your answer sheet, mark your selections for all the questions in the set.

In the following pages, you'll learn what each step involves, and you'll apply the steps to Passage II and a set of 6 questions.

Step 1: Briefly size up the passage.

Once you see that you're dealing with a set of Research Summary questions, quickly skim the passage and glance at the experimental data, just to get a feel for the passage's overall topic and the kinds of experimental data under examination. Some Research Summary passages are easier than others. Try to quickly assess overall difficulty level. If the passage or experimental data confuse or intimidate you, shop around for an easier passage. (You can always come back to the passage later if you have time.)

Let's apply Step 1 to Passage II. As you read the passage and glanced at the two figures, you probably noticed that this Research Summary involves biochemistry. If you're comfortable with this general topic, what you see in the passage might look familiar and "easy." And, if you're adept at interpreting line graphs, the two figures probably won't intimidate you. If these reactions describe you, then this would *not* be a question set you'd skip. Otherwise, you might want to skip to the next question set in the hope that it's a bit easier.

Note

The textual information and the figures in Passage II are average in difficulty compared with what you'll see on the ACT. Passage II would be one that most test-takers would *not* skip.

Step 2: Understand the background information.

Once you've sized up the passage, begin reading carefully. Ask yourself what relationships are described in the background information preceding the description of the experiments. At least one of the questions will probably focus on this information.

Let's apply Step 2 to Passage II. The first two paragraphs contain background information. Certain relationships among all the terms defined in the first paragraph of the passage are described there. If the three-dimensional shape of the enzyme is changed, then the ability of the enzyme to bind to the substrate is lessened. If the enzyme's ability to bind to the substrate is lessened, then its ability to catalyze the reaction (that is, activity) is lessened. Therefore, there is a relationship between the three-dimensional shape of the enzyme and its activity. Furthermore, in certain circumstances, there is a relationship between the three-dimensional shape and temperature and between the three-dimensional shape and pH.

Step 3: Understand the experiments.

At least two test questions will focus on the purpose, design, and procedural aspects of the experiments. To be ready for them, you should ask (and answer) the following questions as you read the description of the experiments and look at how the experimental results are presented. (Notice that many of these questions focus on the principles you reviewed in the previous section.)

- In each experiment, what are the *independent* and *dependent variables*?
- In each experiment, what are the *controls* (factors that are kept stable, or constant, during an experiment, and possibly from one experiment to another as well)?
- In each experiment, what is the *hypothesis* that is being tested, if any?

Let's apply Step 3 to Passage II. Since this step involves asking and answering several questions, the following Q&A indicates your thought process during this step.

Question

What are the independent and dependent variables in Experiment 1? In Experiment 2?

Answer

In Experiment 1, the independent variable is pH. In Experiment 2, the independent variable is temperature. For both experiments, the scientist is observing the enzyme's activity. You know this by combining the information in the first paragraph of the passage with the description of the two experimental protocols. Activity, you've seen, is defined as the ability to bind substrate. In both experiments, the degree of yellow in the solution is used to measure how much enzyme binds the indicator; thus, the degree of yellow indicates the enzyme's activity. The activity, then, is the dependent variable.

Question

What factor(s) are kept stable in Experiment 1? In Experiment 2? In both experiments?

Answer

In Experiment 1, temperature is kept stable (so as to highlight the effects of varying pH levels in the twelve tubes). In Experiment 2, pH is kept stable (to highlight the effects of varying temperatures). In both experiments, the same solution and cell types were used, and the same three enzymes were used.

Question

In each experiment, what is the hypothesis that is being tested?

Answer

In Experiment 1, since the scientist is measuring the effect of varying levels of pH on enzyme activity, we can infer that the hypothesis being tested is the following: *The activity of Enzymes A, B, and C is dependent to a greater or lesser extent upon the pH level of the surrounding solution.* In Experiment 2, the scientist is hypothesizing as follows: *The activity of Enzymes A, B, and C is dependent to a greater or lesser extent upon the temperature of the surrounding solution.*

Step 4: Identify patterns, trends, and conflicts among the experimental results.

Now that you understand the essential purpose and design of the experiments, the next step is to interpret and analyze the results. Ask and answer the following questions during Step 4:

- In each table or graph, what relationship (general pattern or trend) is shown between the variables?
- What relationship, if any, is there between the data resulting from the experiments? Do the data from one experiment support the data from the other? Or, is there a conflict?

Let's apply Step 4 to Passage II. The following Q&A reveals your thought process during this step.

Question

In each graph, what relationship is shown between the variables on the axes for each of the three enzymes (A, B, and C)?

Answer

In the first figure, each enzyme shows the tendency first to increase in activity as pH rises, then to decrease in activity as pH rises further. Thus, each enzyme has a pH at which it displays maximum activity. This level differs for each enzyme. For Enzyme A, the pH at which maximum activity occurs is around 2; for Enzyme B, it is around 6; for Enzyme C, it is around 10. In the second figure, each enzyme shows the tendency to slowly increase in activity as temperature rises. This increase eventually levels out, and the enzyme activity is stable over a range of temperatures. Then, it suddenly drops off, quickly falling to no activity. The temperatures at which the enzyme activity rises and (suddenly) falls differ from enzyme to enzyme. In addition, Enzymes A and B attain a markedly higher level of activity than Enzyme C.

Question

How are the two graphs similar and different? What relationship, if any, is there between the data in the two graphs?

Answer

The graphs are similar in that they both present data regarding the activity levels of the same three enzymes (A, B, and C). There's another similarity as well. Notice that Enzyme C's activity level doesn't reach a peak at higher levels of pH and temperature than Enzymes A and B. However, this may just be a coincidence. Since the independent variable is different in each, there probably isn't any direct relationship between the two graphs; each shows the effect on enzyme activity of a different key variable.

Alert!

The questions you should ask (and answer) during steps 2–4 needn't be exactly the same as the ones here. Keep in mind: Research Summaries vary. In some, the tables or graphs are closely related to one other, while in others they're not. Also, in some, you'll find a different hypothesis for each experiment, while in others you won't. (You might find one hypothesis for all experiments, or you might not find any stated hypothesis.) The bottom line: Tailor your Q&A to the specific passage at hand.

Step 5: Answer the questions. For each question, try to formulate an answer before you read the four choices.

Next, move on to the questions themselves. As you read each question stem, try to answer the question *before* looking at the answer choices, by applying what you learned during steps 2–4. In other words, try to predict what you might expect the correct answer would say. If you followed steps 2–4, you should be able to prephrase an answer to *most* of the questions. (For some questions, this technique won't work; but, for most questions it will.)

Let's walk through 6 ACT-style questions based on Passage II. We'll try to answer each question before looking at the answer choices. As we do so, you'll see that, during steps 2–4, we did most of the brainwork needed to anticipate the questions and predict the essence of the correct answers! (The 6 questions generally get tougher as you go.)

1. At which of the following pH levels would you expect the greatest chemical reaction in Enzyme A?

From Step 2, you know that the greatest chemical reaction is also the one that exhibits the most activity; and, from Step 3, you know that the level of activity is the dependent variable, measured along the vertical axes. So, answering this question should be a cinch. Check the curve in Figure 1 (the one for Enzyme A), then match the highest point on that curve to the pH level along the horizontal axis. The peak occurs at a pH level of about 2.0. Now, scan the answer choices for a number close to 2.0:

A. 1.9
B. 3.2
C. 4.9
D. 9.3

Aha! Choice **A** is the only one that comes close to our approximation. (It's the correct answer.)

Tip

The test-makers aren't trying to measure your eyesight. So, in reading line charts, approximations will suffice. (In question 1, for instance, the test-makers wouldn't ask you to choose between 1.9 and 2.0.) One choice will be close enough to what the graph shows to set it apart from the other three.

2. Which of the following was a control in both experiments?

From Step 3, you already know that the correct answer might be either the buffer solution or the type of cell (mammalian) used in the experiments. Among the incorrect answers would be the independent variables—pH level, temperature, and the enzyme—as well as the dependent variable: the color of the solution, chemical reaction, or activity (all three are essentially the same variable). Now, check the answer choices:

F. The enzyme
G. The temperature
H. The buffer solution
J. The pH level

Voila! Choice **H** jumps out at you as the correct one.

3. Which of the following hypotheses do the experimenters appear to be testing?

From Step 3, you know that Experiment 1 appears to test the hypothesis that the activity of Enzymes A, B, and C is dependant on pH levels. Experiment 2 appears to test the hypothesis that the activity of Enzymes A, B, and C is dependent on temperature. (Either hypothesis would be a correct answer.) An incorrect answer might confuse independent with dependent variables. Another incorrect answer might provide a hypothesis that is too general. Now, let's check the answer choices:

A. Chemical reactions in mammalian cells increase in speed when an enzyme is used as a catalyst for the reaction.
B. pH levels of an enzyme are dependent on the enzyme's level of activity.
C. Temperatures of an enzyme are dependent on the enzyme's level of activity.
D. The activity of Enzymes A, B, and C is dependent on temperature.

The correct answer, choice **D**, is one of the two possible ones we predicted. Choice **A** is too general, and choices **B** and **C** each confuses an independent variable with a dependent one.

4. At pH levels where Enzyme C is exhibiting high activity, which of the following observations about Enzymes A and B is best supported by the data?

This question involves the results of Experiment 1 only. In the first figure, look at the point where Enzyme C activity is highest. At that point, check to see whether Enzymes A and B share a common characteristic. Indeed, they do! Both curves have already declined to an activity level of 0. So, you're looking for an answer choice that, in essence, states this. Now, let's check the choices:

F. Enzyme A exhibits higher levels of activity than Enzyme B.
G. Neither Enzyme A nor Enzyme B is able to bind to its substrate.
H. The activity levels of Enzyme A and Enzyme B are about the same as the activity level of Enzyme C.
J. The activity level of Enzyme A is increasing, while the activity level of Enzyme B is declining.

Ouch! None of the answer choices provide the answer we predicted. Does this mean we're wrong? No. You just need to remember what you learned from Step 2: A pH that's too high can cause an enzyme to "denature"—that is, it can no longer bind to its substrate. That's exactly what choice **G** provides. So what if you didn't understand that part of the passage? (After all, it was a bit technical and confusing.) It shouldn't matter! You could zero in on the correct answer by process of elimination. Just looking at Figure 1 tells you that the curves for Enzymes A and B have both already declined to 0. So, neither choice **F**, **H**, nor **J** can possibly be accurate.

5. Based on the experimental data, at which of the following combinations of pH and temperature could you expect the highest activity for Enzyme B?

The vertical axes of both graphs indicate activity. No units of activity are indicated in either graph, so you cannot necessarily make a direct comparison of levels between the two graphs. So, a correct answer to this question must provide a pH-temperature pair that are each near the peak for Enzyme B. You're looking for a pH of about 5 and a temperature of anywhere from 30 to 35. Let's check the choices:

A. A pH of 7.0 and a temperature of 35
B. A pH of 5.5 and a temperature of 40
C. A pH of 5.5 and a temperature of 30
D. A pH of 9.0 and a temperature of 45

As you can see, we were able to predict the answer: choice **C**. Notice that choices **A** and **B** are each partly correct. Also, notice that choice **D** would have been correct if the question had referred to Enzyme A rather than Enzyme B.

Alert!

The preceding question illustrates two of the test-maker's favorite wrong-answer ploys: the choice that's only *partly* correct and the choice that provides a correct answer, but to a slightly *different* question. Careless test-takers often fall prey to these ploys; don't be among them!

6. Which of the following conclusions about enzyme activity is best supported by the data?

This is probably going to be a relatively difficult question, partly because it's difficult to predict what the correct answer might say. But, the key to open-ended questions such as this one usually lies in recognizing the trends and patterns that the data reveal—which you identified during Step 4. Let's go ahead and read the four choices:

F. Enzymes respond more predictably to changes in temperature than to changes in pH level.
G. The pH levels at which different enzymes become denatured vary more widely than the temperatures at which they become denatured.
H. Among the three enzymes, Enzyme A exhibits a chemical reaction to the highest temperature.
J. Enzyme activity is more sensitive to pH level than to temperature.

This is a tough question, no doubt about it! But, from Steps 2–4, you should recognize that choice G provides an unavoidable conclusion. The passage tells us that an enzyme is said to become "denatured" when it no longer binds to its substrate, which means that there is no enzyme activity. The two figures show that point to occur when a curve declines to 0 on the vertical scale. Notice that, according to Figure 2, the temperature at which the three enzymes become denatured varies only slightly (from 40–47 degrees). But, according to Figure 1, the pH level at which the three enzymes become denatured appears to vary widely—from 5 to greater than 12. Thus, based on the results of these two experiments, it seems reasonable to conclude exactly what choice G provides. Of course, this conclusion is not airtight, since only three enzymes were tested. But this doesn't mean choice G isn't the correct answer. It is—because it's better than any of the others.

Step 6: Look again at any questions you had trouble with, if you have time.

Go back to the questions you earmarked to come back to, and try them again. Just as with Data Representation sets, later questions in a Research Summary set are typically more complex and challenging than earlier ones. Check the time remaining for the Science Reasoning Test. Remember: Your goal is to devote 6 minutes, on average, to each question set. If you're ahead of schedule, go back and look again at the questions you weren't sure about. Otherwise, move on to Step 7.

Step 7: On your answer sheet, mark your selections for all the questions in the set.

Wait until after answering all the questions in the set, then fill in the corresponding ovals on the answers sheet. After Step 6, if you're still uncertain about the correct answer to certain questions, earmark them in your test booklet. You can come back to them if you have enough time remaining after attempting all seven question sets.

Note

The preceding Research Summary set is typical of the ACT. The easier questions focused on only one or two aspects of the background information or on one experiment, while tougher questions required you to compare and contrast the results of different experiments and to "read between the lines"—in other words, to recognize the cause-and-effect forces at work in the experiments. Later questions were more challenging than earlier ones, which is also typical of ACT Research Summaries.

Success Keys for Handling Data Representation and Research Summaries

In walking through the sample Data Representation and Research Summary sets in this level, you picked up a variety of tips and techniques for answering these types of questions. Here's a checklist to help you review what you've learned. Apply these strategies to the practice tests in Part VI, and then review them again, just before test day.

Identify and Distinguish between Dependent Variables, Independent Variables, and Controls

In any table, chart, or graph of scientific data, there will be at least one dependent variable and one independent variable. Be sure you know which is which, and why, as well as what relationship is shown between the two. When it comes to Research Summary passages, it's crucial that you also distinguish between controls and variables. (A *control* is a factor that is kept unchanged, or constant, during an experiment, while a *variable* is a factor that is changed.)

Note

The ACT will assume that you know what these terms mean. (The test won't define them or explain them.)

Focus on *Trends* and *Patterns* When Analyzing Graphical Data

The key to understanding ACT tables and graphs is to look primarily for *trends* and *patterns* in the graphical data. Why? Because it's the proverbial "forest" (trends and patterns) rather than the "trees" (all the specific numbers) that most of the questions will focus on.

Don't Get Bogged Down in All the Details, Especially the Numbers

You learned in Chapter 11 that every passage on the ACT Reading Test is made up of two kinds of elements: main ideas and details. The same division between main ideas and details applies to Science Reasoning passages, most of which include dozens of details: the individual data points on each graph; the specific numbers that fill the grid of a table or chart; the readings or values obtained in each experiment described. There's no way you can master or memorize all of them. And you don't need to. Remember, of the 5–7 questions for each passage, only a few will focus on specific details. And you can always look them up as needed.

Tip

Each passage will include some irrelevant information, unrelated to any of the questions. It may appear in the introductory paragraphs or in the body of the passage, including any graphs, tables, or charts. Don't let this confuse you. Focus on the main ideas of the passage, skim the details, and then tackle the questions. If some—perhaps most!—of the details turn out to be unnecessary, so be it.

Don't Get Bogged Down in Scientific Jargon

No matter how big a science nerd you are, some of the passages *will* deal with topics that are unfamiliar to you, and many will use terms, abbreviations, symbols, and phrases you haven't seen before. Don't worry about this. All the information you need to answer the questions is included in the passage, and you can safely ignore the unfamiliar terms.

Recap Each Passage after Reading It

If this sounds more like advice for the ACT Reading Test, it should. This same principle applies to Science Reasoning passages, but with a slight slant. After reading the passage, spend a final 30 seconds to solidify in your mind your understanding of how the pieces of information fit together. For example, for a Research Summary passage, remind yourself of the objective with which the experiments were originally designed. Reviewing will also help you to recall where within the passage various details can be found, in the event certain questions ask about them.

Try Note-Taking—It Can Help

Many ACT test-takers don't annotate Science passages because they don't consider them "reading" passages. But they are! In fact, annotating, and especially note-taking, are even more useful for the ACT Science Test than for the ACT Reading Test. That's because the science passages, by their nature, generally involve classifications, categories, causes-and-effects, and other logical relationships that good note-taking can help organize.

Here are some suggestions for annotating and note-taking that will help you master Data Representation and Research Summaries:

- Circle key features of graphs and tables. If a graph or table shows a trend or pattern, make a brief note of it beside the data, in the margin.
- For Research Summaries, make a note that identifies the *controls* and the *variables* in each experiment and as the passage progresses from one experiment to the next.
- Make simple flow charts of key cause-and-effect relationships that seem to emerge from the data (or the experiments).

Formulate an Answer before You Read a Question's Answer Choices

For each question, try to formulate your own response to it, then scan the choices for something resembling your homegrown response. Prephrasing the answers will keep you from becoming confused and distracted by wrong-answer choices. (Keep in mind, though, that some question stems might not give you enough to go on.)

Find Your Optimal Pace and Stick to It

On the Science Test, you've got 35 minutes to handle seven sets of questions. That's 5 minutes per set, on average. As you take the practice tests in Part VI of this book, try to stick to the 5-minute time limit per set. If you have trouble finishing in 35 minutes, try either skipping one entire set or skipping one question in each set. Once you've determined your optimal pacing plan, stick to it.

Take It to the Next Level

At this level, you'll:

- Read a typical Data Representation passage, and survey the common question types for this format.
- Read a typical Research Summary passage and question set, and survey the common question types for this format.
- Read a typical Conflicting Viewpoints passage and question set, and survey the common question types for this format.

Along the way, you'll learn a variety of strategies, tips, and warnings to give you a leg up on your ACT competition.

Take It to the Next Level consists of two sections. In this first section, we'll walk you through three ACT-style passages and question sets, one in each format. As we go, we'll highlight a variety of strategies, tips, and warnings. We'll also point out the test-makers' favorite wrong-answer tricks and traps as we encounter examples. Most of these highlights reinforce what we covered earlier in this chapter.

Then, in Chapter 13, you'll focus exclusively on the following question types, which are the toughest you'll come across on the Science Test.

Data Representation

Distinguishing meaningful patterns from random data

"Piecing together" separate graphs or tables

Theorizing from the data

Research Summaries

Analyzing, then hypothesizing from, the data

Evaluating a hypothesis

Drawing general conclusions from the data

Assessing the effect of new information

Conflicting Viewpoints

Identifying a theory's hidden assumptions

Assessing the effect of additional evidence

Recognizing implicit points of agreement

For each question type, you'll also learn how the test-makers design wrong-answer choices—and how to recognize these red herrings when you see them.

Note

Don't expect to encounter easy questions in Chapter 13. Everything there is at least average in difficulty—and many questions are tougher than average.

Data Representation

On the ACT, you'll encounter *three* Data Representation sets, each of which will contain 5–7 questions. (The most common number of questions is 5.) In this section, we'll walk you through a typical passage and set of 6 questions. As we go, we'll encounter all the broad question types and all levels of difficulty.

Let's get started. Read the following passage, and then examine the two figures that accompany it. Be sure to read actively, as explained earlier in this chapter.

Passage I

In small communities, infectious organisms such as *Varicella-zoster* virus, which causes chickenpox, occasionally become extinct. The threshold at which such extinctions occur is known as the *critical community size*. Extinctions are followed by a period in which there are no infections until the virus is reintroduced from an outside source.

Researchers collected data on these extinctions, or *fadeouts*, in various communities before a fadeout was defined as a period of three or more weeks in which there were no new reported cases of the infection. They then attempted to develop computer models of the patterns of fadeouts seen, using information about the dynamics of the infection. Figure 1 shows the real data on chickenpox versus the data generated by two different computer models. Figure 2 demonstrates the different assumptions made by the two models concerning the duration of the *infectious period* (the period in which an individual can transmit the infection to another individual). This was the only difference between the two models.

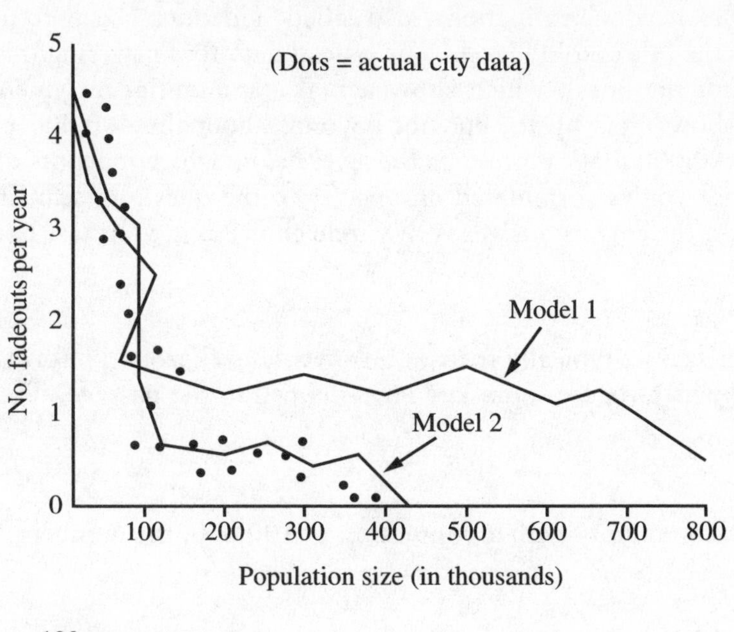

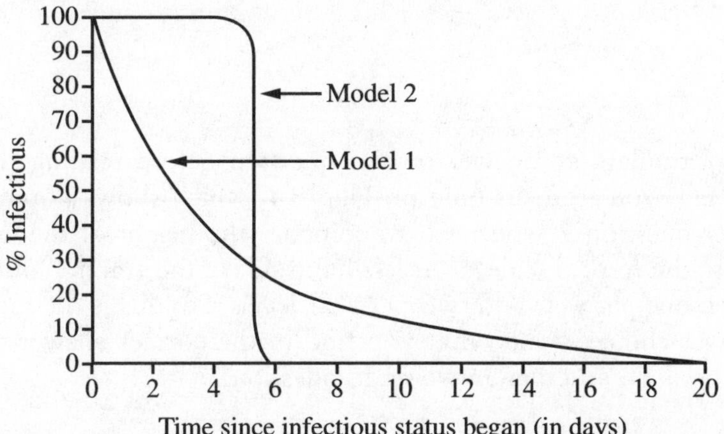

Now, let's tackle 6 questions based on Passage I. Questions 1 and 2 are the simplest ones; each one deals with only one of the graphs, and asks you to essentially "read" certain quantitative data in that graph.

1. The critical community size for chickenpox is:

A. under 100,000.
B. about 400,000.
C. about 700,000.
D. over 1 million.

Try to formulate an answer to this question before reading the answer choices. To answer the question, you need to understand the definition of "critical community size," and then apply this definition to chickenpox based on the data in Figure 1. The passage defines critical community size as the population level *below* which extinctions, also called "fadeouts," begin to occur. (The passage refers to this size as the "threshold" level.) The crucial data for answering this question are the dots in Figure 1 (not the lines), which show actual communities in which fadeouts occurred. Since the graph shows dots up to, but not beyond, about the 400,000 population mark, we can see that this 400,000 mark represents the level *below* which fadeouts of the virus are likely to occur. Now that you've formulated an answer to the question, scan the answer choices for it. As you can see, the correct answer is **B**. Circle choice **B** in your test booklet, and then move on to question 2.

Note

The first question in a Science set typically focuses on specific background information in the passage. Question 1, which focuses on a key term defined in the passage, is a perfect example.

2. Based on the data, in a community with a population of 100,000, the number of fadeouts per year ranges from:

F. 0 to 1.
G. 1 to 2.
H. 2 to 3.
J. 3 to 4.

As with question 1, try to formulate an answer to this question before reading the answer choices. The question itself tells you to focus only on Figure 1, which shows population and fadeout numbers. To answer question 2, you need to compare the height of the dots at the 100,000 population level with the vertical scale at the left-hand side of the graph. Notice that the dots appear to range between one-per-year and two-per-year levels. So, this is the range you're looking for among the answer choices—and what you find in the correct answer choice, **G**. Circle choice **G** in your test booklet, and then move on to question 3.

Tip

In determining quantities shown graphically by lines and points on graphs, it's okay to estimate and "fudge" just a bit. Be assured: To zero in on the correct answer, you won't need to strain your eyes or split hairs. Question 2 is a good example. Notice that there are no dots that line up precisely with the 100,000 population mark. That's okay, though. The graph shows enough dots near that mark so you can figure out which of the four choices best answers the question.

Questions 3 and 4 are each a bit more advanced than questions 1 and 2 because they're *qualitative*, not quantitative. What do we mean? To handle the question, instead of simply "farming" a graph for numerical data, you need to *interpret* or *analyze* the graph as a whole—to determine the relationships between variables, and the patterns or trends in the data.

3. Which of the following is a difference between models 1 and 2?

A. Compared with model 2, model 1 predicts that fewer individuals will be infectious after six days.
B. Compared with model 2, model 1 predicts a more concentrated infectious period.
C. Compared with model 1, model 2 predicts that a greater percentage of individuals in communities with populations under 200,000 will become infected.
D. Compared with model 1, model 2 predicts a greater number of infected individuals during the early days of the infectious period.

Question 3 is a bit tougher than questions 1 and 2, in more than one way. First, the question itself doesn't tell which of the two graphs provides the data you need to answer it. So, you can't formulate an answer until you read the answer choices. Second, to answer the question, rather than simply "reading" the graphical data, you need to *interpret* the data—in other words, to recognize a general relationship shown in the graph. Let's analyze each answer choice, in turn.

Choice **A** gets the relationship between the two models backward. Figure 2 shows that model 1 (not model 2) predicts an infectious period extending up to 20 days, whereas model 2 predicts an infectious period lasting no longer than 6 days.

Choice **B** also gets the relationship between the two models backward. It is model 2 (not model 1) that shows a concentrated infectious period of 6 days.

Choice **C** confuses the information provided in Figure 1. Although Figure 1 involves community population, the relationship is between population and the number of fadeouts, not the percent of residents in a community becoming infected in the first place.

Process of elimination leaves choice **D** as the one that must be correct. Of course, you should read and evaluate choice **D**, anyway, to confirm that it's correct! In Figure 2, notice that, up to day 6, the graph of model 2 shows more infections than the graph of model 1, which is exactly what choice **D** provides. The correct answer is **D**; circle it in your test booklet, then proceed to question 4.

Alert!

Question 3 illustrates one of the test-makers' favorite wrong-answer ploys. Choices **A** and **B** each provide just the opposite, or reverse, of what would be a correct answer to the question. This ploy can easily trip up the nonattentive test-taker.

4. Which of the following statements is best supported by Figure 1?

F. As the number of viruses increases toward one million, the number of fadeouts per year declines.
G. Model 1 is a better predictor of fadeouts for communities under 300,000, while model 2 is a better predictor of annual fadeouts for communities over 300,000.
H. As a community population increases, the discrepancy between the predictive abilities of the two models increases.
J. Both models overestimate the number of annual fadeouts for chickenpox.

As with question 3, it's not possible to formulate an answer to question 4 without reading the answer choices. So, let's analyze each one, in turn.

Choice **F** gets one of the variables in Figure 1 completely wrong. The graph shows community population, not the number of viruses, along the horizontal axis. So, you can easily eliminate choice **F**.

Analyzing choice **G** requires a visual inspection of the two solid lines in Figure 1 as compared to the scatter plot (the pattern of dots) in Figure 1. Notice that at community sizes under 100,000 (the left end of the graph), the two curves of model 1 and model 2 track each other closely. Also notice that the two models are both quite accurate in tracing the "dots," which indicate actual fadeouts. Beyond the 100,000 population level, however, the curves gradually diverge—model 2 tracking actual fadeouts more and more closely than model 1. Choice **G** provides an inaccurate description of this relationship.

As you read choice **H**, you should realize that you've already done the brainwork to handle it—when you analyzed choice **G**. The graph in Figure 1 shows that models 1 and 2 are equally accurate predictors for communities up to 100,000 but that model 2 is a more accurate predictor for larger communities, which is essentially what choice **C** states. So, choice **H** is probably the correct answer. But, you should check choice **J** anyway, just to be sure.

Having analyzed choices **G** and **H**, you can see right away that choice **J** is wrong because model 2 is quite accurate in tracking actual fadeouts (tracing the dots) at all population levels.

The correct answer is **H**; circle it in your test booklet, and move on to question 5.

Alert!

Question 4 illustrates two more of the test-makers' favorite wrong-answer ploys. Choices **G** and **J** are each partly right, but partly wrong. If you're not paying close attention, you might notice only what's right and become lured by the trap. Choice **F** sets another common trap: It indicates the wrong variable for the graph that applies to the question. A careless test-taker might focus just on the numbers—in this case, 300,000—overlooking the trap that the test-makers have set.

Questions 5 and 6 are the most advanced of the 6 questions in this set. To handle them, you need to tie together the textual information and the information in both graphs. What's more, you need to go beyond what the data shows—to either *explain*, or hypothesize about, the patterns and relationships shown or to *apply* what the data reveal to different circumstances or to additional data.

5. Which of the following statements might explain the difference in the abilities of models 1 and 2 to predict the actual number of annual fadeouts of chickenpox?

- **A.** Model 2 predicts that there will be more individuals spreading infection in the early infectious period, resulting in a lower number of predicted fadeouts, compared with model 1.
- **B.** Model 1 predicts that there will be some individuals spreading infection in the late infectious period, reducing the number of predicted fadeouts, compared with model 2.
- **C.** Model 2 predicts that there will be a longer infectious period in larger communities, increasing the number of predicted fadeouts, compared with model 1.
- **D.** Model 2 predicts a more constant rate of movement from an infectious to a noninfectious status.

Question 5 requires you to evaluate the data as a whole—to explain the general patterns shown in both graphs. If you had trouble handling earlier questions, you'd surely have trouble with this one. Before reading the answer choices, try to formulate an answer to question 5. You need to ask (and answer) two questions for yourself. First, what is the difference in the predictive abilities of the two models? In a nutshell, the answer is that model 1 overstated the number of fadeouts for populations above 100,000. Second, what might explain this difference? The only information we have to go on are the assumptions made, as shown in Figure 2. So, you're looking for an answer choice that says essentially that model 1 assumes a longer infection period that tapers off more gradually, compared with model 2, and that the result was that model 1 overstated the number of predicted fadeouts. Now, read each of the four choices with an eye out for your answer.

Right away, you should notice that choice **A** provides essentially what we're looking for—just in a vice versa way. Model 2 does in fact predict a greater number of people spreading infection early in the infectious period, and it also predicts a smaller number of fadeouts. So, **A** is probably the correct answer. But, before moving on to question 6, check the other three answer choices:

Choice **B** is partly accurate, but partly inaccurate. Figure 2 does show model 1 predicts a longer infectious period, but Figure 1 shows that model 1 predicts a higher number of fadeouts than model 2—just the opposite of what choice **B** says.

Choice **C** gets things backward. Figure 1 shows us that it is model 1, not model 2, that predicts longer infectious periods in larger communities.

Choice **D** also gets things backward. Figure 2 shows us that it is model 1, not model 2, that predicts a more gradual, constant, decline in infections as the days pass.

We've confirmed that choice **A** is the correct answer. Circle **A** in your test booklet, and then proceed to the final question in the set, question 6.

Note

Complex Science questions typically involve more than one graph or table, and they often involve two or more steps in the reasoning process. Question 5 is a good example.

6. If researchers applied another computer model for chickenpox using the assumption about the infectious period depicted below (see the following figure, model 3), what could you expect this model to predict?

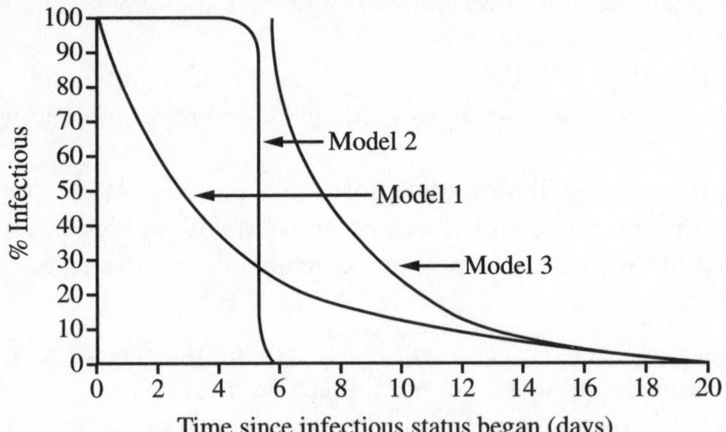

F. Model 3 would predict more annual fadeouts than model 1.

G. Model 3 would predict more annual fadeouts than model 2, but fewer than model 1.

H. Model 3 would underestimate the number of annual fadeouts.

J. Model 3 would predict a better correlation between fadeouts and population size than models 1 or 2.

Question 6 is the final question in this set, and most test-takers would find it to be the toughest one. But, don't turn this question into a tougher one than it needs to be. Simply build on what you know from answering earlier questions to formulate an answer to the question before reading the four choices. Since the new model 3 predicts both a high number of infectious individuals in the early days (as does model 2), while also extending their recovery period over a long period of time (as does model 1), both factors would tend to reduce the number of predicted fadeouts. As a result, model 3 would probably be less accurate than model 2, erring on the side of predicting fewer fadeouts than would actually occur. Now, scan the four choices for one resembling the answer we just formulated. As you can see, choice **H** essentially provides our conclusion. Just to make sure we're thinking straight, let's check the other answer choices:

Choice **F** gets it backward; model 3 would predict fewer (not more) fadeouts than model 1. If our thinking is straight, we must rule out choice **F**. Choice **G** is partly right, but partly wrong; model 3 would predict fewer (not more) fadeouts than model 2. Choice **J** is the easiest one to eliminate. Model 2 accurately predicts fadeouts while model 1 does not. Accordingly, model 3, which resembles model 1 far more than model 2, should also be an inaccurate fadeout predictor.

Don't make Science questions, even relatively complex ones, more difficult than they need be. Forecast the answer before you read the answer choices, and then find the choice that's most consistent with your forecast. And, when all else fails, eliminate obvious wrong-answer choices—such as choice **J** in question 6.

Research Summaries

On the ACT, you'll encounter *three* Research Summary sets, each of which will contain 5–7 questions. In this section, we'll walk you through a typical passage and set of 7 questions. As we go, we'll encounter all the broad question types and all levels of difficulty. Read the following passage, and then examine the two figures that accompany it. Be sure to read actively, as explained earlier in this chapter.

Passage II

Seychelles warblers are insect-eating birds that usually lay one egg a year. Young warblers, particularly the females, often remain with their parents for several years helping them prepare and care for the next *hatchlings* (newly hatched birds), rather than mating themselves. A *breeding pair* (mating male and female) stays in the same territory from year to year.

Two experiments regarding the breeding behavior of the Seychelles warblers were performed.

Experiment 1

Biologists rated the territories of Seychelles warblers based on the density of insects available. They followed 100 breeding pairs in high- and low-quality territories over one breeding season, recording the breeding success (determined by the survival of a hatchling to the point of leaving the nest) for pairs with various numbers of helpers (previous offspring remaining with the mating pair). The results are seen in Table 1.

Table 1

Helper No.	Reproductive Success (%)
High-Quality Territory	
0	86%
1	94%
2	95%
3	79%
Low-Quality Territory	
0	75%
1	65%
2	66%
3	64%

Experiment 2

The researchers hypothesized that Seychelles warblers might be able to adjust the sex ratio (number of males versus number of females) of their hatchlings depending on territory quality or number of helpers present. They again looked at 100 breeding pairs with

Take It to the Next Level

various numbers of helpers in high- and low-quality territories and recorded the sex of their offspring for one breeding season. The results appear in Table 2.

Table 2

Helper No.	Male Hatchlings (%)	Female Hatchlings (%)
	High-Quality Territory	
0	15%	85%
1	13%	87%
2	78%	22%
3	76%	24%
	Low-Quality Territory	
0	75%	25%
1	80%	20%
2	79%	21%
3	74%	26%

Now, let's move on to the test questions. The simplest questions in a Research Summary set will test your *understanding* of the basic purpose, design, and method of the experiments or will ask you to simply "read" the experimental data (usually presented in tables), like you did in the easier Data Representation questions. These questions usually come early in a set. Question 1, based on Passage II, typifies the first of these two types.

1. Which of the following was a control in both experiments?

A. The number of helpers
B. The number of eggs laid by a breeding pair
C. The number of breeding pairs studied
D. The density of insects

The correct answer is C. If you read Passage II actively, you already identified the controls and variables in both experiments and were ready for this question. In both experiments, the number of breeding pairs studied was kept constant at 100 in high-quality territory and 100 in a low-quality territory. In other words, the number of breeding pairs was a *control* in both experiments. The correct answer is **C**. Just for the record, let's look at the other three choices. The number of helpers, choice **A**, and density of insects, choice **D**, were independent variables. As for choice **B**, although the passage's first sentence indicates that warblers usually lay one egg per year, the number of eggs laid was not accounted for at all in the design of either experiment—either as a control or as a variable. Circle choice **C** in your test booklet, and then proceed to question 3.

Note

On the ACT, don't expect a direct question about controls or variables in every one of the three Research Summary sets. Nevertheless, at least one set will include this question type.

Moderately difficult Research Summary questions typically test you on your ability to:

- *Analyze* the experimental results, especially to recognize trends, patterns, and anomalies (specific data that don't fit a general trend or pattern).
- *Draw inferences or conclusions* from the experimental results and recognize conclusions that you *cannot* reasonably draw from the results.

These questions usually occur in the middle of a Research Summary set. Questions 2, 3, and 4, based on Passage II, are typical. Let's tackle them now.

2. Which of the following is the most reasonable conclusion from the results of Experiment 1?

F. The number of helpers has a greater effect on reproductive success than the density of insects available.

G. Breeding pairs generally need at least one helper to achieve the highest possible reproductive success.

H. The density of insects available has a greater effect on reproductive success than the number of helpers.

J. The number of hatchlings that become helpers is greater in low-quality territories than in high-quality territories.

The correct answer is H. Question 2 is designed partly to test you on a basic definition that's part of the experimental design. But, unlike question 1, it goes beyond the background information and design of the experiments to deal with actual experimental results. Notice that it involves only one experiment, and that it tests you on recognizing what is probably the most obvious pattern in the results of that experiment. These features combine to make question 2 a relatively easy one.

The quality of a territory is defined by the density of insects available. Table 1 tells us that, given any number of helpers 0–3, reproductive success was greater in the high-quality territory than in the low-quality territory. Scan the answer choices for this essential idea, and you'll find that choice **H** fits the bill. The correct answer is **H**; circle it in your test booklet, then move on to question 2.

Tip

Before reading any of the questions, analyze the results of each experiment. Check for obvious patterns or trends in the numbers; be sure to compare numbers in different categories. If you spot a clear pattern or trend, you can be sure that at least one test question will focus directly on it.

3. In a high-quality territory, the reproductive success of a breeding pair is best assured:

A. with no helpers.
B. with one or two helpers.
C. with three helpers.
D. when both parents care for their hatchlings.

The correct answer is B. Question 3 has a lot in common with question 2; it covers only the results of Experiment 1, and it focuses on a pattern or trend. However, the trend you need to spot for question 3 is not quite so apparent as the one for question 2, so question 3 is a bit tougher. A quick glance at the answer choices tells you that there's a relationship between reproductive success and number of breeding pairs. The right-hand column of Table 1 provides the reproductive success rates, which in a high-quality territory peak at 94–95%, when one or two helpers are available. Thus, the correct answer is **B**.

4. Which of the following statements is best supported by the experimental data?

F. Warblers in a low-quality territory have the greatest number of male hatchlings when either two or three helpers are present.
G. The sex ratio among hatchlings in a high-quality territory is not affected by the number of helpers present.
H. Warblers in a high-quality territory have the greatest number of female hatchlings when either two or three helpers are present.
J. The sex ratio among hatchlings in a low-quality territory is not affected by the number of helpers present.

The correct answer is J. Question 4 is the most challenging one so far. One feature that makes it tougher is that the question stem provides no clues whatsoever. It's impossible to formulate an answer before reading the choices or to even know which experiment to focus on. To overcome this obstacle, skim the answer choices for clues. Notice that they all involve the sex of the hatchlings, which tells you that you'll focus on the results of experiment 2 to answer the question.

Referring to Table 2, in a low-quality territory, the male-female hatchling ratio varies so slightly as to be insignificant; thus, there is no clear relationship between helper number and sex ratio in a low-quality territory.

What the answer choices all have in common can provide a good clue as to how you should analyze the test question at hand, as questions 3 and 4 based on Passage II both illustrate.

The final questions in a Research Summary set usually require you to perform these two tasks:

Extrapolate from or *apply* the experimental results—to predict what additional data are likely or what an additional or altered experiment might produce.

Theorize or *hypothesize* from the experimental results—in other words, to go well beyond the passage and the data to formulate a reasonable explanation for the patterns and trends seen in the experiments.

Expect questions in the second category above to be the most challenging among all the questions. Let's look at some questions based on Passage II. Question 5 illustrates the first type.

5. Assume that, in a third experiment, 100 warbler breeding pairs are moved after one year in a high-quality territory to a low-quality territory. Which of the following would be the most likely result?

A. The proportion of female hatchlings would decrease where one helper is present.
B. The proportion of male hatchlings would decrease where two helpers are present.
C. The survival rate of warbler hatchlings would increase where no helpers are present.
D. The number of available helpers would decrease.

The correct answer is A. Question 5 itself doesn't tell you which experiment you need to focus on. So, before reading the answer choices, try to formulate *two* plausible answers to the question—one based on each of the two experiments. First, Experiment 1: You know from answering question 2 that reproductive success was greater in the high-quality territory than in the low-quality territory, regardless of the number of helpers. So, one possible answer to question 5 is that the reproductive rate would decrease after the move. But, scanning question 5's answer choices shows that only choice **C** deals with reproductive success (survival rate), and this choice provides an inaccurate statement. That means that the key to question 5 lies in Experiment 2 instead. Table 2 shows that moving from a high- to a low-quality territory would dramatically increase the male-female hatchling ratio where the helper number is either zero or one. Now, scan the answer choices. Aha! Choice **A** matches the answer we've just formulated. Circle **A** in your test booklet, and then move on to the final question in the set, question 6.

In a set of Science questions, later questions sometimes build on earlier ones. Question 5, based on Passage II, is a good example. Our brainwork for questions 2 and 4 helped us analyze question 5.

Take It to the Next Level

Now, let's examine two questions (questions 6 and 7 below) that ask you to formulate a theory based on the experimental results. Keep in mind: To handle these questions, you'll need to go beyond the sure, safe conclusions we drew in earlier questions.

6. Which of the following theories best fits the data collected by the researchers?

F. Warblers have evolved to produce more female than male hatchlings in order to ensure survival of their species.

G. Insect scarcity can create competition among warbler helpers and hatchlings for food resources.

H. Warblers stay on to help their parents care for hatchlings in order to ensure themselves a food supply.

J. Warbler breeding pairs tend to stay in the same territory from year to year in order to ensure that their young stay with them as helpers.

The correct answer is G. Since the question stem doesn't give you any information to formulate your own answer, there's no shortcut to analyzing each answer choice in turn.

First, choice **F**: Did this choice tempt you because it seems to affirm the hypothesis stated in the description of Experiment 2? If so, you weren't alone. Yet, is what choice **F** says—that warblers produce more female than male hatchlings—actually supported by the data? Not for low-quality territories. So, you can eliminate choice **F**.

Next, choice **G**: Experiment 1 showed that fewer hatchlings survive where insect density is low (that is, in a low-quality territory) than where it is high, and that, where insect density is low, helpers actually reduce the rate of hatchling survival. Choice **G** provides a logical explanation for both of these phenomena, so it's probably the correct answer. But, let's check **H** and **J** to be sure there's no better answer.

Next, choice **H**: Does the idea that a child would stay on as a helper in order to ensure themselves a food supply make sense? Perhaps if they're in a high-quality territory, where food is plentiful, and the only other choice is to move to a low-quality territory. But, otherwise, the idea makes little sense; after all, the helper who stays around must compete with the parents, other helpers, and the hatchlings! So, choice **H** is nonsense, and you can rule it out.

Finally, choice **J**: This theory does provide an accurate statement—that warbler pairs tend to stay in the same territory from year to year. And the reason given makes some sense. But is this reason supported by any of the experimental data? No! Read the question again; it asks which theory is best supported by the data. For this reason, choice **G** is better than choice **J**.

Alert!

In theory-formulation questions, answers that don't make much sense, ironically, are most likely to trip up insecure test-takers who assume their failure to understand the answer choice is their own fault. Other wrong answers might tempt you because they make "real-world" sense; but they won't be supported by the data—for example, choices **F** and **J** in question 6. Be on the lookout for either type of wrong-answer trap!

7. Which of the following statements provides the most reasonable explanation for the data collected by the researchers?
   A. In high-quality areas, since more than two helpers will put a drain on resources, breeding pairs with several helpers will adjust the sex ratios of their hatchlings to favor males.
   B. Breeding pairs in low-quality territories need the most help in raising their hatchling and will adjust the sex-ratios of their hatchlings in an attempt to gain more males.
   C. All breeding pairs benefit from at least one helper and will adjust the sex ratios of their hatchlings to favor females if they have no helpers.
   D. Male hatchlings require more resources than female hatchlings, so only birds in high-quality territories with several helpers will adjust the sex ratios of their hatchlings to favor males.

The correct answer is A. Question 7 is another theory-formulation question, and this one is even tougher than question 6. Let's cut to the chase: Choice **A** provides the only theory that even begins to explain the curious data in Table 2, in which all warbler pairs except low-helper pairs in high-quality territories produce more male offspring than female. If we assume that a shortage of resources favors male hatchlings (who perhaps have some different behavior from females; greater aggressiveness in pursuit of food, for example), then the pattern in Table 2 becomes at least understandable and consistent.

Note

On the ACT, you're unlikely to encounter more than one theory-formulation question based on the same passage. We've shown you two examples here (questions 6 and 7) just to give you additional insight into this tough question type.

Conflicting Viewpoints

On the ACT, you'll encounter *one* Conflicting Viewpoints set, which will contain 6–7 questions. We'll walk you through a typical passage and a set of 6 questions. As we go, we'll encounter all the broad question types and all levels of difficulty. Read the following passage, and then examine the two figures that accompany it. Be sure to read actively, as explained in this chapter.

Passage III

Schizophrenia is a mental illness that involves the dissociation of reason and emotion, resulting in symptoms including hallucinations, hearing voices, intense withdrawal, delusions, and paranoia. The average age at which schizophrenia is diagnosed is 18 years for men and 23 years for women. It has been observed to run in families.

The cause remains a mystery, but there are several competing theories. These theories are based in part on findings from twin studies, which look at identical twins in which one or both have the disease. (Identical twins share 100% of their genetic material, while nonidentical twins share about 50%.) In 50% of the cases, when one identical twin is affected, the other will also suffer from schizophrenia. Identical twin pairs in which one individual is ill and the other is well are referred to as *discordant twins*.

genetic

Genetic Theory

One school of thought is that schizophrenia is a *genetic disorder* (one passed through the genes from parents to children). This theory gained support from the fact that schizophrenia runs in families. While it was originally believed that it was the family environment that caused this, a study has shown that children of schizophrenics adopted by families without the disease have the same risk of developing the illness as those raised by their birth parents. A final piece of evidence is the fact that the children of discordant identical twins all have the same chance of developing the illness: 17%. This indicates that even the healthy twin is somehow carrying the agent of the disease, presumably in the genes.

Infection Theory

Another school of thought is that schizophrenia arises because of a viral infection of the brain. Studies have shown that a class of viruses called "slow viruses" can linger in the brain for 20 years or longer before the infected person shows symptoms. Brain infections with viruses such as the common cold-sore virus and herpes simplex type 1 can cause symptoms that resemble schizophrenia. Schizophrenia is also more common in children born in the winter, the season when viral infections are more common. Also, one study looking at families with a history of schizophrenia showed a 70% increase in the rate of schizophrenia among children whose mothers had the flu during the second trimester of pregnancy.

In handling a Conflicting Viewpoints passage, don't rely completely on your memory. Brief, but organized, notes that list supporting points for each hypothesis help keep the details straight in your mind and save time you'd otherwise spend re-reading the passage. Here's an outline of the key ideas you should have gleaned from Passage III:

EVIDENCE FOR GENETIC THEORY:

- runs in families
- adoption makes no difference
- discordant twins each have same chance

EVIDENCE FOR INFECTION THEORY:

- slow viruses linger 20 years before showing (so onset at age 18–23 makes sense)
- symptoms similar to disorders known to be viral
- winter births (flu season) → schiz. more likely
- virus during pregnancy → schiz. more likely

Now, let's move on to the test questions. At least one or two questions in a Conflicting Viewpoints set will cover basic ground:

- The scientific issue that the different viewpoints address
- Areas of agreement (similarities) between the viewpoints

These questions tend to appear early in a set. Question 1, the easiest one in the set based on Passage III, is a good example of the second type.

1. The schizophrenia theories are similar in that both:

- **A.** postulate that the foundation of the illness may be laid before birth.
- **B.** postulate that the family environment plays some role.
- **C.** predict that the children of schizophrenics are not at greater risk than other individuals.
- **D.** show that identical twins are at greater risk for schizophrenia than other individuals.

The correct answer is A. Neither of the two viewpoints expressed come right out and say: "I agree with the other viewpoint in the following respect: . . . ." But that doesn't mean there's no common ground. Both the genetic theory and the infection theory attribute schizophrenia to prenatal events: in one theory, to a genetic disorder; in the other, to a prenatal infection that affects the brain of a developing infant.

Note

As the term "Conflicting Viewpoints" tells you, the different theories that the test presents will be at great odds with one another. But they'll also agree on certain points, usually on certain indisputable facts and findings. Expect at least one test question to focus on some point of agreement.

Some questions will test you on whether you understand the essence of one viewpoint or another—in other words, the essential argument or claim that's made. These questions appear in a variety of forms and are usually moderate in difficulty. Let's look at two examples based on Passage III. Question 2 deals directly with the Infection Theory, while question 3 focuses more on the Genetic Theory.

2. Which of the following additional studies would be most useful in determining the soundness of the Infection Theory?

- **F.** A study that looks for scarring in the brains of schizophrenic individuals, which might be a sign of an early injury or infection
- **G.** A study that looks at the home environments of discordant twins, one of whom is schizophrenic
- **H.** A study that looks for finger abnormalities in the parents and grandparents of schizophrenic children
- **J.** A study that looks for differences in the chromosomes (which hold the genes) of schizophrenic individuals and healthy individuals

The correct answer is F. The essence of the Infection Theory is that schizophrenia is caused by a viral infection of the brain, probably occurring during the mother's pregnancy. So, you should look for an answer choice that relates directly to this essential claim. Choice **F** describes a study that proponents of the Infection Theory would be more interested in conducting next, because evidence of early infection would relate *directly* to that theory. Notice that choices **H** and **J** both relate to the Genetic Theory, while choice **G** relates to neither theory.

Tip

Different tables call for different analytic approaches. To analyze some tables, the key is to compare *numerical trends* (increases and decreases) as you scan *down* the different columns. For other tables, the key is to compare the *sizes of numbers* in the different columns as you scan *across* columns.

3. Which of the following findings would lend the greatest support to the Genetic Theory?

A. In identical twins, the average age at which either twin first shows symptoms of schizophrenia is lower than among the general population.

B. Among pairs of discordant identical twins, it is common that the healthy twin and the ill twin both suffer from at least one other specific illness known to be environmentally caused.

C. Schizophrenia is more common among identical twins than among the general population.

D. Among parents of schizophrenics, less than 50% are schizophrenic themselves.

The correct answer is C. The essence of the Genetic Theory is that schizophrenia is an inherited trait, passed genetically from parent to child. The fact provided in choice C—that the incidence of schizophrenia is greater between identical twins than among the general population—supports the idea that shared genetic material is a major factor in the development of the disorder. Notice that choices **B** and **D** both tend to weaken the Genetic Theory, while choice **A** would provide just as much support for the Infection Theory as for the Genetic Theory.

Expect at least one test question to provide additional evidence, then ask about its impact on both *theories*. These questions also tend to be moderate in difficulty. Question 4 based on Passage III is a typical example.

4. If parents of discordant twins report that the behavior of the twins begins to diverge at about five years of age, on average, these reports would:

F. lend greater support to the genetic theory than the Infection Theory.

G. lend greater support to the Infection Theory than the Genetic Theory.

H. lend equal support to the Infection Theory and the Genetic Theory.

J. tend to weaken both the Genetic Theory and the Infection Theory.

The correct answer is H. The four choices presented in question 4 are basically the same as for any question of this type. Your job is to determine whether the additional evidence favors one viewpoint over the other, or whether it strengthens or weakens both viewpoints. The reports cited in question 4 would provide further evidence against the claim that family environment is the cause of the disorder. In so doing, the reports would lend equal support to the Genetic Theory and the Infection Theory.

At least one Conflicting Viewpoints question will probably ask you to critique one of the viewpoints, which you might be able to do in one of several different ways:

- Identify a logical inconsistency or contradiction in the argument made by the viewpoint's proponents.
- Identify a hidden assumption upon which the viewpoint depends but for which it provides no substantiating evidence (evidence showing that the assumption is true as a matter of fact).
- Point out that it ignores certain evidence that strongly supports an opposing viewpoint.

These questions are often tougher than average and thus tend to appear later in a question set. Try to identify which method is used in question 5 based on Passage III.

5. Which of the following would proponents of the Genetic Theory most likely point out in criticizing the Infection Theory?

A. For mothers who give birth during the winter months, the second trimester of pregnancy occurs prior to those months.
B. The average age at which schizophrenia is usually diagnosed is 18 years for men and 23 years for women.
C. When one identical twin has schizophrenia, there is a 50% chance that the other twin will also have the illness.
D. Symptoms of other illnesses are similar to those of schizophrenia.

The correct answer is A. In support of the Infection Theory, its proponents point out that more schizophrenics are born during the winter months, when flu viruses are most common, than during other months. But, they also cite the fact that children of mothers who had the flu during the second trimester of pregnancy are by far most likely to be schizophrenic. This second fact actually helps show that the first fact is meaningless in showing that the illness can be caused by a flu virus, for the reason that choice **A** cites. In other words, choice **A** points out an inconsistency or contradiction in the Infection Theory—the first method of critique listed earlier.

In the "real world" of science, sometimes what appear to be conflicting theories are actually just different pieces of a puzzle—pieces that, when put together, show the complete explanation for a certain phenomenon. So, the theories turn out not to conflict; instead, they complement each other. The same is often true with ACT Conflicting Viewpoints. A test question might explicitly ask you to explain the discrepancies or conflicts between two theories, or it might pose the question indirectly, as question 6 illustrates.

6. Which of the following hypotheses is LEAST likely to find support among proponents of both the Genetic Theory and the Infection Theory?

F. Individuals with schizophrenia have certain genes that predispose them to viral infections of the brain.

G. Individuals with schizophrenia have certain genes that predispose them to the disease, but require some kind of environmental trigger to turn on the disease.

H. Schizophrenia is not one disease but a collection of diseases.

J. Certain infections occurring in the brains of unborn, embryonic individuals alter the genetic structure within these individuals.

The correct answer is G. Notice that the hypotheses in choices **F**, **H**, and **J** each allow for the possibility that both genetic factors and infection play important roles in the development of schizophrenia. In other words, each hypothesis reconciles the two viewpoints, showing how together they supply a full explanation of what causes schizophrenia. It doesn't matter which one is most plausible. What matters is that neither proponents of the Genetic Theory nor proponents of the Infection Theory are likely to vehemently disagree with any of these hypotheses. However, choice **G** lends support to the Genetic Theory, but not the Infection Theory. Thus, proponents of the Infection Theory are far less likely than proponents of the Infection Theory to agree with this hypothesis.

Alert!

The most advanced type of Conflicting Viewpoints question requires you not only to understand the viewpoints' essential claims and conflicts, but also to reconcile those differences—in other words, to explain how seemingly opposing viewpoints can both be correct.

Chapter 13

Conflicting Viewpoints

In this chapter, you'll learn:

- A step-by-step approach to handling a set of Conflicting Viewpoints questions
- Success keys for handling ACT Conflicting Viewpoints
- To *Take It to the Next Level*

How Conflicting Viewpoints Sets Are Designed

Conflicting Viewpoints passages are a completely different animal than Data Representation and Research Summaries. You won't see any graphical data—only textual information—and the emphasis is much more on understanding scientific theories than on analyzing and interpreting scientific data. (Expect to see very few numbers, if any.) A Conflicting Viewpoints passage begins with a paragraph briefly outlining some scientific problem. It's usually a phenomenon that must be explained somehow—for example:

- A disease whose cause must be determined
- A geological process whose workings must be described
- An astronomical observation that doesn't seem to fit with other known facts about the universe and that must be explained

Then, two or three alternative explanations are offered, each under its own heading. (The heading might refer to them as "theories," hypotheses," "viewpoints," or by some other similar label.) The viewpoints might flatly *contradict* one another; if you accept one, you must reject the other. More likely, however, the viewpoints will be *independent* of one another or even *complementary*; either theory, neither, or **both** could be true—at least in part.

As you read a Conflicting Viewpoints passage, look for the answers to the following questions:

- What is the observed scientific phenomenon that needs to be explained?
- What is the essential claim of each theory?
- On what evidence does each theory rely? Do the theories rely on the same evidence or on different evidence?

- On what points do the theories agree (either explicitly or implicitly)?
- On what points do the theories most fundamentally disagree?
- What weaknesses, or problems, do you see with each theory?

Why ask yourself these particular questions? Simple: The answers to these questions are what you'll need to know to handle the test questions. Next, we'll show you a systematic way of going about all this.

Conflicting Viewpoints—Your 7-Step Game Plan

On the ACT, you'll encounter just *one* Conflicting Viewpoints set, which will contain either 6 or 7 questions. Here you'll learn a step-by-step approach to ACT Conflicting Viewpoints, using the following passage as an illustration. Go ahead and read the passage now.

Sample Passage I

Geologists have continued to engage in debate over the cause of major periods of glaciation, or Ice Ages, during the history of Earth. Although the mechanics of glacier formation are well understood in a general sense, the causes of the alternating periods of global-scale glaciation and intervening periods of glacial retreat have been the subject of some controversy. Below two geologists present two different viewpoints on the issue.

Geologist 1

The dramatic long-term cooling trends leading to widespread terrestrial glaciation depend upon the physics of Earth's motion around the sun and around its own axis of rotation. The generally elliptical orbit of Earth varies in shape, tending sometimes to a form that appears more circular, other times to a shape that has a more pronounced elliptical quality. This cycle of varying between a circular and elliptical trend is repeated on an average of about once every 100,000 years. When Earth's orbit is more elliptical, Earth receives less heat energy from the Sun.

Also, the axis of Earth's rotation fluctuates from a tilt of 21.5 degrees to 24.5 degrees, which influences the amount of heat the planet receives from the Sun. Furthermore, there is a precession, or kind of "wobbling," of the axis itself, which further contributes to fluctuations that must affect the global temperature on a scale that would lead to growth and retreat of the terrestrial ice caps. The precession of Earth's axis operates on a 41,000-year cycle. Research to this date has provided ample evidence of glaciation and warming matching the cycles with cooling trends evident on both the 100,000-year and 41,000-year scales.

Geologist 2

It is now generally accepted that one of the larger mass extinctions to occur on Earth, the K-T boundary event of 65 million years ago, was the result of a massive asteroid or comet impact that caused a kind of "nuclear winter." It makes much sense then, if we keep in mind how common space junk is in our solar system, to infer Earth's contact with dust and debris of a smaller and more plentiful nature would contribute to other cycles of cooling and warming. It is likely that these dustloadings may be random in nature, but not so random and rare as killer impacts on the scale of the K-T boundary event. These dustloadings are simply fluctuations in gross amounts of interplanetary dust in our region that may be affected by gravitational forces and other cosmic interactions that ebb and flow around us.

Furthermore, the planets orbit the Sun in a plane—imagine a plane with the nine orbits drawn concentrically upon its surface. This angle changes ever so slightly, subtly altering the regions of space through which our Earth travels. So, it is the change in position relative to clouds of cosmic dust, gas, and meteoroids that limit the amount of solar energy reaching our planet. The scale in which this occurs is a better match to our evidence of 100,000-year cycles of glaciation and warming.

The 7-Step Plan

Here's a 7-step approach that will help you to handle any Conflicting Viewpoints question set:

Step 1: Briefly size up the passage.

Step 2: Understand the background information and anticipate what will follow.

Step 3: Understand the reasoning and evidence behind each viewpoint; jot down the key points of each one.

Step 4: Look for common ground, that is, points of agreement (explicit and implicit) between the viewpoints.

Step 5: Take note of each viewpoint's weaknesses.

Step 6: Answer the questions. For each question, try to formulate an answer before you read the four choices.

Step 7: Look again at any questions you had trouble with, then mark your final selections on your answer sheet.

In the following pages, you'll learn what each step involves, and you'll apply the steps to Passage I and a set of 6 questions.

> **Note**
>
> From now on, we'll refer to the viewpoints presented in Science Reasoning passages as "theories." Keep in mind, however, that a passage might instead refer to the viewpoints at hand as "hypotheses," "arguments," or "positions." Which term is used makes no difference in analyzing the passage and answering the questions.

Step 1: Briefly size up the passage.

You can tell at a glance that you're dealing with a Conflicting Viewpoints set: After an introductory paragraph, the different viewpoints, or theories, will be presented one at a time, each one under a separate heading that identifies it. Also, Conflicting Viewpoints passages don't contain any tables, charts, or graphs, whereas Data Representation passages and Research Summaries do.

In contrast to the recommended approach to Data Representation and Research Summaries, there's little point in skimming a Conflicting Viewpoints passage to get a feel for the topic or to try and assess its overall difficulty level. Once you know you're dealing with Conflicting Viewpoints, decide to either tackle it or skip it. Which strategy should you adopt? If you find analyzing graphical data easy, tackle all three Data Representation sets and all three Research Summary sets before you attempt the Conflicting Viewpoints set. On the other hand, if you're less "data" oriented and more "verbally inclined," then you'll probably have a relatively easy time with Conflicting Viewpoints, and you should definitely *not* skip this set.

Step 2: Understand the background information and anticipate what will follow.

Read the introductory paragraph carefully. It will describe the particular phenomenon or observation that the theories will attempt to explain. Also, it might, but won't necessarily, indicate the essential claim of each theory. Don't expect any of the questions to test you solely on this background information. The introduction simply sets the stage, or establishes the framework, for the debate that follows.

Let's apply Step 2 to Passage I. The first paragraph tells you that the observed phenomenon at hand is the advancement-retreat cycle of Earth's glaciers. At issue is the cause of these cycles.

Alert!

Conflicting Viewpoints passages always involve either two or three distinct theories. Passage I involves two theories. Passages involving three theories are usually more challenging.

Step 3: Understand the reasoning and evidence behind each viewpoint; jot down the key points of each one.

During Step 3, first read about each theory. As you do so, ask (and answer) for yourself the following questions:

- What is the essence of the theory?
- What reasons are provided in support of the theory?
- What evidence is provided in support of the theory?

Don't evaluate or critique the theories yet—just try to understand each one. Read about it, and then recap it in a way that makes sense to you, like you would for an ACT Reading Test passage. In your own words, explain the theory to yourself as if you were helping a friend understand it. Then, jot down the key points of each viewpoint to help you keep them straight in your mind as you answer the questions.

Let's apply Step 3 to Passage I. Here's the basic gist of the two viewpoints, as we see it (as you read the passage, perhaps your thought process was much like ours):

Viewpoint of Geologist 1 (Recap): It is the fluctuating distance of Earth's ice caps from the Sun that causes these glaciation cycles. (As distance increases, Earth cools near the poles, and so glaciers advance.) There are three distinct, and cyclical, forces causing the fluctuation: Earth's orbit, the angle of its axis, and the amount of axis "wobble." Geological evidence shows two glaciation cycles—a 41,000-year cycle and a 100,000-year cycle—which coincide with these forces.

Viewpoint of Geologist 2 (Recap): The main cause of Earth's cooling phases (and, in turn, glacial advance) is a certain dustloading. Whenever Earth passes through it, the Sun becomes obscured (like during the K-T boundary event, but less dramatic). Earth's orbital plane fluctuates in cycles on the scale of 100,000 years, so it makes sense that, at a certain orbital tilt, Earth passes through this same dense patch of cosmic debris.

Perhaps you found the viewpoint of Geologist 1 more convincing than that of Geologist 2. That's okay. But, both theories should have made at least *some* sense to you, providing at least a partial explanation for the observed phenomenon. That's how the test-makers design Conflicting Viewpoints passages. In other words, don't expect one viewpoint to be clearly the "correct" one while another is obviously complete balderdash. Instead, expect that each viewpoint will have its own merits, yet each one will provide an incomplete explanation of the observed phenomenon. (Again, that's how the test-makers design these passages.)

Next, find some blank space on the test-booklet page, and make some shorthand notes—a bullet list of key arguments and points of evidence supporting each theory. Here's an outline of the key ideas you should have gleaned from the passage:

In handling Conflicting Viewpoints sets, don't rely completely on memory. Brief, organized notes that list supporting points for each theory help keep the details straight and save time you'd otherwise spend rereading the passage.

ISSUE: What causes glacial advance-retreat cycles?

GEOLOGIST 1

3 contributing causes:

(1) shape of orbit varies → ellipse increases distance from Sun (100K-year cycle)

(2) axis shifts → Sun-pole angle varies in cycles

(3) axis wobbles (precession) → Sun-pole angle varies (41K-year cycles)

Geo. evidence supports 100K-year and 41K-year cycles.

GEOLOGIST 2

Main cause is cosmic dustloadings.

3-point argument:

(1) K-T event shows collisions cause cold spell (Sun obscured)

(2) dustloadings must have smaller but similar effect (Sun obscured)

(3) plane of orbit varies in 100K-year cycles

Conclusion: Earth passes through major dustloading every 100K-years.

Step 4: Look for common ground, that is, points of agreement (explicit and implicit) between the viewpoints.

The viewpoints presented will strike you more for their conflicts than their similarities. (After all, the test-makers call them "Conflicting Viewpoints," not "Shared Viewpoints.") But, that doesn't mean they won't have at least something in common. They will! And, expect at least one or two questions to test you on whether you recognize their common ground.

Before you answer the questions, we recommend that you identify these points. If you understood each viewpoint and took organized notes, you shouldn't have any trouble with this step. In your notes, try signaling points of agreement by writing "AGREE" next to them, or jot them down below your other notes.

Let's apply Step 4 to Passage I. There's only one, limited point of agreement between the two geologists: Glaciation cycles are caused at least partly by fluctuations in Earth's orbit that cycle once every 100,000 years. (However, the geologists disagree as to what *type* of fluctuation causes glaciation cycles.) Aside from this limited point of agreement, the two geologists cite entirely different evidence and provide different explanations.

Step 5: Take note of each viewpoint's weaknesses.

At least one test question will require you to "punch holes" in one of the viewpoints—in other words, to recognize one or more of its weaknesses. On the ACT, expect nearly any viewpoint to be vulnerable to the following criticisms (that's how that test-makers write them):

- It fails to back up an explicit claim with hard evidence.
- It relies on a key assumption but provides no evidence that what's assumed is in fact true.
- It ignores evidence that clearly tends to disprove it or that provides greater support for the opposing viewpoint.

Does either viewpoint presented in Passage I suffer from these problems? Yes, indeed. Here are some you might have noticed:

- Geologist 1 ignores the K-T boundary event and fails to explain why dustloadings could not have caused our glaciation cycles.
- Geologist 1 fails to indicate the length of the cycle for Earth's axis tilt. (If it turns out to conflict with the geological evidence about glaciation cycles, this would weaken Geologist 1's argument, at least in part.)
- Geologist 2's viewpoint relies on the assumption that the dustloading remains in about the same area of space in relation to Earth's fluctuating orbital plane. (If the dustloading moves, then there would be no reason to expect Earth to encounter it in predictable, regular intervals.)
- Geologist 2 ignores the obvious effect that the three types of fluctuations—orbital, axis tilt, and wobbling—cited by Geologist 1 would have on the poles' distance from the Sun and, in turn, Earth's temperatures.
- Geologist 2 ignores the 41,000-year glaciation cycle that Geologist 1 points out in support of her own viewpoint.

Any of these weaknesses would make great fodder for an ACT question.

Step 6: Answer the questions. For each question, try to formulate an answer before you read the four choices.

Now that you've essentially figured out what you need to know to handle the questions, it's time to answer them. Just as with Data Representation passages and Research Summaries, as you read each question stem, try to answer the question *before* looking at the answer choices, by applying what you learned during steps 2–5. (This technique will work for most, but not all, of the questions.)

Let's walk through 6 ACT-style questions based on Passage I. We'll try to answer each question before looking at the answer choices. As we do so, you'll see that, during steps 2–5, we did most of the brainwork needed to anticipate the questions and predict the essence of the correct answers.

1. Geologist 1 and Geologist 2 agree that one factor in global glaciation and retreat is the:

During Step 4, we determined that both geologists agree on one limited point: Fluctuations in Earth's orbit have some bearing on glaciation cycles. Now, scan the answer choices for this idea:

A. position of Earth relative to dense areas of interplanetary dust.
B. tilt of Earth's axis relative to the Sun.
C. shape, or curvature, of Earth's axis.
D. specific orbit of Earth.

Viola! Choice **D** jumps out at you as the correct one. Notice that choice **A** provides a factor that only Geologist 2 claims is a factor, and that choices **B** and **C** each provide a factor that only Geologist 1 claims is a factor. So, even if you overlooked the point of agreement—choice D—during Step 4, your notes from Step 3 should tell you by process of elimination that **A** is the only viable choice.

2. Geologist 2 might argue that Geologist 1 does not account for:

During Step 5, you learned that a shortcoming of both geologists is that each ignores the evidence provided by the other. So, Geologist 2 would be quick to point out that Geologist 1 ignores the effect that asteroid and meteorite collisions, and especially dustloadings, would have on Earth's temperature and, in turn, on glaciation. Let's check the answer choices for this essential criticism:

F. all cycles of Earth's glaciation.
G. the impact that cosmic debris has on the temperature of the Earth.
H. the effect that precession of Earth has on the amount of heat the earth receives.
J. the change in the amount of energy Earth receives based on its distance from the Sun.

Choice **G** expresses the same essential criticism, so it's the correct answer. Our notes from Step 3 tell us exactly what's wrong with the other three choices. Choice **F** would be a criticism of Geologist 2's viewpoint, which ignores the 41,000-year cycle that Geologist 1 cites as further evidence for her viewpoint. Choices **H** and **J** each provides a factor that Geologist 1 points out in support of her own viewpoint. So, neither **H** nor **J** respond properly to the question.

3. Assuming the "nuclear winter" that occurred during the K-T boundary event, more so than any other event in Earth's history, operated to cool the Earth by interfering with the Sun's warming of the Earth, this fact would:

What this question is getting at is the effect this fact would have on the two viewpoints. Whose case would it help (if either), and whose would it hurt (if either)? (A quick glance at the first few words of the answer choices tell you what the question is driving at.) Geologist 2's position relies partly on the theory that Earth's passing through dense areas of meteoroids contributes to glaciation—presumably, by creating a cloudy atmosphere that blocks the warmth of the Sun. The K-T boundary event, if substantiated, would lend support to this theory and therefore to Geologist 2's position. The event lends no support to Geologist 1's position, which ignores the possibility that meteoric events played a significant role in global glaciation. So, the correct answer should indicate that it strengthens Geologist 2's viewpoint and/or weakens Geologist 1's viewpoint. Let's scan the four choices for our answer:

A. lend greater support to the position of Geologist 1 than the position of Geologist 2.
B. lend greater support to the position of Geologist 2 than the position of Geologist 1.
C. lend equal support to the positions of Geologist 1 and Geologist 2.
D. serve to refute the position of Geologist 1 and of Geologist 2.

Bingo! The correct answer is **B.**

4. With which of the following statements would Geologist 1 most probably agree?

Okay, this is one of those questions you can't expect to answer without reading the choices. So, let's read them now:

F. About every 100,000 years, the tilt of Earth's axis changes from 21.5 degrees to 24.5 degrees and back to 21.5 degrees.
G. About every 41,000 years, the shape of Earth's orbit changes from nearly circular to more elliptical and back to nearly circular.
H. About every 100,000 years, Earth experiences a complete cycle of global glaciation and retreat that is unmatched in extent by other such cycles.
J. About every 200,000 years, Earth experiences at least five cycles of global glaciation and retreat.

Your notes from Step 3 should help you sort out the wrong answers. Geologist 1 never told us the length of the cycle for Earth's axis tilt, so you can easily eliminate choice **F.** Choice **G** confuses the facts; the length of the orbital fluctuation cycle is 100,000 (not 41,000) years. Choice **H** accurately states what Geologist 1 provides as the length of one of the cycles of global glaciation. But, does Geologist 1 say that this cycle is "unmatched in extent" by other such cycles? No! Nor does Geologist 1 even imply such a claim. So, you can rule out choice **H,** which means that, by elimination, choice **J** must be the correct answer. For the record, let's confirm our choice. According to Geologist 1, Earth's precession cycle (which we inferred affects temperatures at the ice caps) is 41,000 years in length. Thus, five such cycles would occur in just over 200,000 years. So, Geologist 1 would clearly agree with what choice **J** states.

5. Which of the following findings, assuming it is substantiated, would Geologist 1 probably point out in criticizing the position of Geologist 2?

During Step 5, you identified some of the problems with the two theories. To refresh your memory, Geologist 2:

- Assumed that the dustloading remains in about the same area of space in relation to Earth's fluctuating orbital plane.
- Ignored the obvious effect that the three types of fluctuations—orbital, axis tilt, and wobbling—cited by Geologist 1 would have on the poles' distance from the Sun and, in turn, Earth's temperatures.
- Ignored the 41,000-year glaciation cycle that Geologist 1 points out in support of her own viewpoint.

Any of these problems could appear in the correct answer to this question. Now, let's scan the answer choices (move quickly past ones that are confusing to you):

A. The various dustloadings in our solar system are scattered randomly throughout it rather than in any pattern.
B. The evidence indicates that a major cycle of global glaciation occurs every 100,000 years.
C. Earth cools as it moves away from the Sun and warms as it moves toward the Sun.
D. A meteoric event on the scale of the K-T boundary event has only occurred once in the history of Earth.

If you had trouble with this question, don't worry—it's a toughie. Did choice **C** jump off the page at you? Perhaps not. But, look again. It essentially restates the second weakness listed above, doesn't it? The fact that Earth travels in an elliptical orbit means that its distance from the Sun is in continual flux, which in turn means that it cools as it moves farther from the Sun and warms as it moves nearer the Sun. Geologist 2 ignores this dynamic, which is obviously a factor in the advancement and retreat of Earth's glaciers.

If you had predicted what the correct answer might look like, you probably would not have been tempted by any of the other choices. Just for the record, though, let's look at the wrong-answer choices:

Choice **A** is very tempting. But think about it carefully. It does nothing to weaken Geologist 2's viewpoint. So what if dustloadings are scattered randomly? All it takes is one "randomly" positioned dustloading in Earth's path once every cycle of orbital tilt to help prove Geologist 2's theory. Choice **B** lends support to the viewpoints of *both* geologists, so you can easily eliminate it. Choice **D**, like choice **A**, is tempting because it appears to minimize an item of evidence Geologist 2 points out. But, it really doesn't. So what if a dramatic "nuclear winter" on the scale of the K-T boundary event only happened once in Earth's history? That doesn't mean that similar, although less dramatic, events have not occurred repeatedly, and on a regular schedule.

Alert!

Nonsensical answers, like choices **A** and **D** in the preceding question, can be the most tempting ones. Insecure test-takers often assume wrongly that confusing answer choices are more likely to be correct ones, simply because it's difficult to think them through properly. Don't fall into this mind-set!

6. Assuming the evidence shows that a global glacial retreat began about 25,000 years ago, Geologist 2 might conclude that:

Ask yourself: What might Geologist 2 predict based on this evidence? Your notes from Step 3 tell you that, according to Geologist 2, the glaciation cycle caused by a dustloading is 100,000 years long. That means that, 75,000 years from now, Earth will be in the same part of the cycle as it was 25,000 years ago. So, perhaps the correct answer will indicate that a global glacial retreat will begin in 75,000 years. Let's check:

F. Earth will pass through an area of space relatively free of cosmic dust, gas, and meteoroids about 75,000 years from now.
G. Earth will emerge from a dense area of cosmic dustloadings about 75,000 years from now.
H. the tilt of Earth's axis reached either 21.5 degrees or 24.5 degrees about 25,000 years ago.
J. Earth's orbital plane departed from the plane on which the other planets orbit about 25,000 years ago.

Hmm . . . the answer we predicted doesn't appear among the choices. Does that mean we weren't thinking straight? Not at all! We were on the right track. It just didn't occur to us to take the next logical step—which is to realize that, 75,000 years from now, if a glacial retreat has just begun, Geologist 2 would assert that it's because Earth is just emerging from a dustloading (which obscures sunlight and cools the planet). That's exactly what choice **G** provides! Let's be more specific. Geologist 2 suggests that every 100,000 years Earth passes through a significant amount of cosmic dust, gas, and meteoroids (which limit the amount of sunlight reaching the planet)—probably a greater gross amount than at any other time during Earth's orbital trip around the Sun. If so, then when Earth finally emerges from the cosmic dust, more sunlight will begin to warm the surface again—and begin to melt Earth's glaciers. Given a global glacial retreat began 25,000 years ago, the next one should begin in about 75,000 years, in accordance with the 100,000-year cycle.

Even if you didn't recognize choice **H** as what Geologist 2 would conclude, your notes from Step 3 tell you that you can at least eliminate **H** and **J**. Choice **H** is easy to rule out, since it is Geologist 1, not Geologist 2, who cites the tilt of Earth's axis as a factor in glaciation cycles. Choice **J** is also easy to rule out—it's utter nonsense! Nothing in the passage suggested that Earth ever leaves the orbital plane on which our solar system's planets orbit. As for choice **F**, it provides the complete opposite of what Geologist 2 would predict based on her viewpoint. Given a 100,000-year glaciation cycle, then in 25,000 years Earth will be at the same stage in the cycle (the start of a glacial retreat, when Earth is just beginning to emerge from the densest dustloading) as 25,000 years ago.

Note

The preceding series of 6 Conflicting Viewpoints questions provided just the sort of "mix" of question types you'll find on the ACT. Some questions focused on one viewpoint; other questions asked you to identify points of disagreement or agreement; still others required you to recognize a viewpoint's vulnerabilities or to assess the effect of additional evidence on one or both viewpoints. Later questions were tougher than earlier ones, which is also typical.

Step 7: Look again at any questions you had trouble with, then mark your final selections on your answer sheet.

If you have time, revisit questions you had trouble with. (Remember: You have only 5 minutes per question set, on average; try to stay on pace.) Then, fill in the corresponding ovals on the answer sheet. Earmark questions you're still unsure about, so you can come back to them if there's time toward the end of your 35-minute test.

Success Keys for Handling Conflicting Viewpoints

In walking through the sample Conflicting Viewpoints set in this first level, you picked up a variety of tips and techniques for answering these types of questions. To help you assimilate it all, here's a checklist. Apply these strategies to the practice tests in Part VI, and then review them again, just before test day.

A Good Outline Can Make All the Difference

Note-taking is especially helpful for Conflicting Viewpoints sets. Don't trust your memory to keep straight what hypothesis is associated with what details. Set up two columns on your scratch paper—one for each theory—and jot down the key points that are unique to each hypothesis. Once you have an outline of each viewpoint, make a note of the key similarities. (Whatever you haven't earmarked as points of agreement you know are points of disagreement.) Also, make a note of any glaring weaknesses of a viewpoint. Your notes should be all you need to answer the questions.

Focus Not Just on Differences but Also on Similarities

To answer the questions, you'll need to understand the differences as well as similarities between the viewpoints presented. So, keep track of both.

Keep Your Eye on the Big Picture

Focus on the essence of each viewpoint and on how they fundamentally conflict. Armed only with this "big picture," you can at least make a reasoned guess for any question!

Keep in Mind: There's Possible Agreement Wherever There's No Conflict

Where two viewpoints conflict, that's a point of clear disagreement. But, any other point is a potential area of agreement. Thus, any aspect of one viewpoint that is *not inconsistent* with the other is a possible point of agreement. Also, if each viewpoint cites the same evidence, then there's agreement that the evidence is important.

Remember That the Main Vice of Each Viewpoint Is That It Ignores the Other's Virtues

Each viewpoint will probably ignore whatever evidence most strongly supports the opposing viewpoint. (That's how the test-makers design Conflicting Viewpoints passages.) This is the essential flaw to look for in the best among the answer choices for questions asking you to criticize one of the viewpoints.

Bear in Mind: The "Best" Viewpoint Might Be a Hybrid

Most likely, each viewpoint will provide part, and only part, of the full explanation for what's been observed—in other words, one piece of the puzzle. That's how Conflicting Viewpoints passages are usually (but not always) designed. Proponents of both viewpoints are most likely to agree with a hypothesis that accounts for both viewpoints and that completes the puzzle.

Take It to the Next Level

In this level, you'll:

- Learn to recognize and handle the toughest kinds of Data Representation questions.
- Learn to recognize and handle the most challenging Research Summary questions.
- Learn to recognize and handle the trickiest Conflicting Viewpoints questions.

Mastering the Toughest Data Representation Questions

On the ACT, you'll encounter *three* Data Representation sets, each of which will contain 5–7 questions. (The most common number of questions is 5.) In this section, you'll learn how to handle the most challenging Data Representation questions. First, however, read the following passage, and then examine the table and figure that accompany it.

Passage I

By studying rock samples, geologists can reconstruct much of an area's geologic history. Table 1 lists rock samplings taken along the shoreline, in 20-mile intervals. The sampled rock found at each distance is shown, and crystallization temperature and ages typical of each type of rock are listed. Figure 1 shows the cross-sectional area of measurement and the altitude corresponding to each rock sampling indicated in Table 1.

Table 1

Distance East (miles)	Type of Rock in Sample	Crystalization Temp* (°C)	Estimated Age (millions of years)
0 (shoreline)	Rhyolite	750°	10.0
20	Diorite	850°	250.0
40	Periodtite	1,200°	200.0
60	Shale	750°	0.1
80	Limestone	800°	6.0
100	Breccia	750°	0.5
120	Andesite	950°	3.6
140	Andesite	900°	4.0
160	Gabbro	1,100°	300.0
180	Granite	700°	400.0

*(Crystallization temperature is based on the mineral composition of the rock)

Figure 1

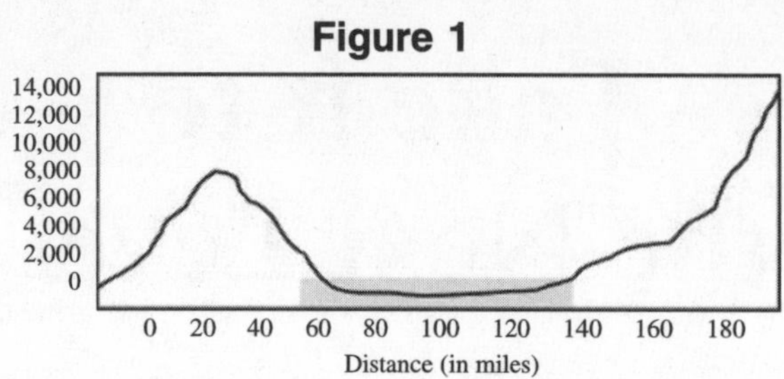

In a typical ACT Data Representation set, about half the questions will ask you to "look up" information in a table, graph, or other display, or to recognize an obvious trend or pattern in the data. As you might expect, questions that call for these basic skills tend to be easier than average. For instance, referring to Passage I:

- An easy question about Table 1 on page 361 might ask you to determine the value of one variable—either distance, rock type, crystallization temperature, or age—given the value of another one of those variables (in other words, to "look up" information in the table). Another easy question might ask you to recognize an obvious pattern in the data—for instance, that the samples' ages decrease as you move inland from the shoreline, then begin to increase as you move even farther inland.
- An easy question about Figure 1 above might ask you what type of measurement is shown on the vertical (or horizontal) axis. Another easy question might ask you to determine the altitude where a sample was collected, given the distance from shore where it was collected.

Since you're at this Next Level, we won't dwell on simple questions like the ones just described. Instead, let's focus on the test-makers' favorite tough question types:

- Questions requiring you to distinguish meaningful patterns from random data
- Questions requiring you to piece together separate graphs or tables, logically speaking
- Questions requiring you to theorize from the data

Distinguishing Meaningful Patterns from Random Data

As you read and recap a Data Representation passage, always be on the lookout for strong patterns or trends in the data—for example, the tendency for the value of a certain dependent variable to increase (or decrease) with any increase (or decrease) in the value of a certain independent variable.

Your ability to recognize such patterns and trends is a big part of what Data Representation questions test on. But, you'll also be tested on distinguishing significant, meaningful patterns from mere coincidences—random data that, by mere happenstance, appear to form a pattern. In a tougher question, you might encounter a "quasi-trend" or "mini-trend," one that only *some* of the data support. Such trends make great fodder for wrong-answer choices. Here's a good example, based on Passage I, that tests your ability to make this kind of distinction:

The data best supports which of the following statements?

A. Rocks more than 100 miles inland generally have higher crystallization temperatures than those closer to shore.
B. Rocks found at high altitudes generally have higher crystallization temperatures than those found at lower altitudes.
C. Rocks having high crystallization temperatures are generally older than those having lower crystallization temperatures.
D. Rocks found at high altitudes are generally older than those found at lower altitudes.

The correct answer is D. Table 1 and Figure 1, considered together, show a definite correlation (a pattern) between altitude and rock age. Generally, the higher the altitude at which a sample was collected, the older the sample's age. Choice **A** is not supported by the data. The relationship between the two variables appears to be random. Choice **B** finds support from only part of the data—specifically, up to 160 miles from shore. Notice that farther inland, the altitude at which samples were collected increases sharply, while the crystallization temperature *decreases* markedly (from 1,100° at about 3,500 feet to 700° at about 13,000 feet). Since choice **B** is not supported by the totality of the data, it is not so good an answer choice as **D.** Choice **C,** like choice **B,** finds support from some of the data, but conflicts with other data. If you focus on the two highest recorded temperatures—1,200° and 1,100°—you'll see that the estimated ages of those samples were high in comparison to most. But, the oldest sample, the one collected 180 feet inland, has a relatively low temperature—lower than the youngest sample among the group! Hence, choice **C** is wrong for essentially the same reason as choice **B.**

Alert!

There's a tendency among ACT test-takers (and among scientists as well) to want to find patterns and trends in scientific data, because it is patterns and trends that allow you to formulate and prove scientific theories. But, keep in mind: In science, and on the ACT, sometimes the data won't show any pattern or trend. So, be careful not to invent a pattern where none exists!

"Piecing Together" Separate Graphs or Tables

If a Data Representation passage includes more than one data display (table, graph, or chart), chances are that at least one question will require you to connect the two displays, logically speaking. To handle this question type, you'll need to recognize where they connect. In Passage I, you should have noticed that distance from shore is shown on both displays. This connection allows you to match either the rock type, crystallization temperature, or rock age to the corresponding altitude where the sample was collected.

An even tougher question of this type, and based on Passage I, might also require one or more of the following tasks:

- Recognize a *pattern* or *trend* in the relationship between altitude (the dependent variable in Figure 1) and one of the three dependent variables (rock type, temperature, or age) in Table 1.

- Recognize *more than one possible value pair* when matching a given altitude to one of the dependent variables in Table 1.
- *Interpolate* from known data points to estimate a value between them.

Here's a question that incorporates all three requirements:

Based on the data, a sample collected at an altitude of 4,000 feet could have an estimated age of about:

F. 125 million years or 200 million years only.
G. 125 million years or 300 million years only.
H. 200 million years or 300 million years only.
J. 125 million years, 200 million years, or 300 million years.

The correct answer is J. Notice in Figure 1 that you attain an altitude of 4,000 feet at *three* different distances from the shore. Those distances are approximately 10, 40, and 160 miles. (Approximations suffice for determining these three corresponding distances in Figure 1, since the question doesn't require precisely measured values.) Accordingly, you need to "look up" the estimated age corresponding to all three distances in Table 1. The ages corresponding to 40 and 160 miles are 200 million and 300 million years, respectively. However, Table 1 does not provide data for a distance of 10 miles from the shore. But, you can *interpolate* from the data provided for the nearest distances less and greater than 10 miles. Since a distance of 10 miles is midway between the shore (0 miles) and 20 miles, it's reasonable to expect an age midway between 10 million and 250 million years; 125 million years is a close enough number. Hence, at an altitude of 4,000 feet, you might expect to find a rock of any of three approximate ages—125, 200, and 300 million years.

Theorizing from the Data

Questions of this type ask essentially: "What theory (among the ones listed) does the data best support?" These questions can be tough because the data will typically provide *some* support for more than one listed theory. What's more, any general statement that is *not inconsistent* with the data and is relevant to it could be a potentially correct answer. So, you might need to make a close judgment call between two or more viable answer choices. To make things even trickier, the question might incorporate one or more of the following:

- Additional information, which you need to assimilate and combine with what's already provided
- Tempting theories (wrong answers) that make perfect "real world" sense but that aren't supported by the specific data provided
- A theory (wrong answer) that gets the data backward (if you're not paying close attention, you might not catch the reversal)

Here's a question based on Passage I that incorporates all three features:

Limestone is sedimentary rock that develops from the accumulated deposits of sea organisms with shells. Andesite is igneous rock deposited by lava flows from volcanoes. Which of the following is the best hypothesis about the geologic record of the shaded area?

A. Lava flows from volcanoes isolated the shaded area from the body of water west of the shoreline.
B. Volcanic activity created a valley west of the volcanoes, then a sea formed in the valley.
C. Volcanoes erupted to the east of an existing sea, located in the shaded area.
D. Lava flows from volcanoes flowed westward into a sea, resulting in the sea's eventual disappearance.

The correct answer is C. Limestone is found 80 miles inland, and andesite is found 120 and 140 miles inland. The andesite is farther east than the limestone. The limestone is 6.0 million years old. The andesite is 3.6 to 4.0 million years old. Andesite from volcanoes would have had to erupt *after* the deposit of the limestone—that is, after the sea existed. Choice **C** is consistent with this chronology and with the location of limestone and andesite. You can easily eliminate choice **B** because it gets the chronology backwards. Choice **A** is consistent with the chronology, but not with the location of the andesite. Choice **A** would be viable only if andesite were found *west* of the shaded area (rather than east of it). Choice **D** is consistent with the chronology and with the location of andesite to the west of the limestone. However, if lava had flowed into the sea, you would expect to find limestone and andesite together in the shaded area. Since the data does not show both types in the same sample, the assertion that lava actually flowed *into the sea* amounts to mere speculation.

Alert!

When you have to evaluate the theories based on graphical data, look out for theories that the data only partially support. Also, be wary of theories that make real-world sense but that don't really "go" with the data.

Tackling the Trickiest Research Summary Questions

On the ACT, you'll encounter *three* Research Summary sets, each of which will contain 5–7 questions. (The most common number of questions is 6.) In this section, you'll learn how to handle the most challenging Research Summary questions. First, however, read the following passage, and then examine the accompanying table.

Passage II

Industrial melanism, the spread of darkly colored moths and butterflies near polluted, industrial centers, was observed in the late 1840s in England. Before the 1840s, tree trunks throughout Britain were a whitish color due to the growth of lichens in trees. These lichens are sensitive to airborne pollutants and are unable to survive near major industrial centers.

In the polluted areas, the lack of lichens on the trees results in the trees being darker than in the unpolluted areas.

The peppered moth *(Biston betularia)* began to appear more and more in its melanic form in the polluted areas. In certain areas, the darker moths constituted 98% of the population. Scientists hypothesized that the comparative decline in the light-colored moths might be due to predation by birds and not a result of the pollution itself.

Scientists performed two experiments to determine the selective force that caused the predominance of the darker moths. In one experiment, they distributed light and melanic moths in a polluted area. In the second experiment, they distributed light and melanic moths in a nonpolluted area. For the two experiments, they recorded the results shown in the table below.

	Light	**Melanic**
Dorset, England		
Woodland (light background)		
Released	496	473
Recaptured	62	30
Percent Recaptured	12.5	6.3
Birmingham, England		
Woodland (dark background)		
Released	137	447
Recaptured	18	123
Percent Recaptured	13.1	27.5

On the ACT, about half the questions in a typical Research Summary set will test you on your ability to *understand* the basic purpose, design, and method of the experiments and to "read" the experimental data, which is usually presented in the form of tables. For instance, referring to Passage II, an easy question might:

- Ask you to distinguish between a control (in this case, the background) and a variable (for example, the type of moth).
- Ask *how many* melanic (or light) moths were recaptured from the polluted (or nonpolluted) region.
- Ask for a numerical or percent difference between the polluted and nonpolluted regions.
- Ask whether the percent (or number) of light (or melanic) moths increased or decreased.

These questions are usually easy because the skills they cover are fairly basic. Since you're at this Next Level, you'll focus instead on the following, more challenging, types of Research Summary questions:

- Questions requiring you to *analyze* the experimental results (especially, recognize trends, patterns, and anomalies), then *hypothesize* from them

- Questions requiring you to *evaluate* a stated hypothesis in light of the experimental data
- Questions requiring you to *draw inferences and general conclusions* from the experimental data (especially, formulate hypotheses or theories) and recognize what conclusions *cannot* be drawn from the data
- Questions requiring you to *assess the effect of new information* from the data to predict what additional data are likely or what additional experiments might produce

Analyzing, Then Hypothesizing from, the Data

In this question type, your job is to decide which hypothesis (among four answer choices) is best supported by the experimental data. What makes this question type tough is that it requires you to recognize key trends or patterns in the various data but also recognize reasonable (and unreasonable) conclusions based on the data.

Here's the key to handling this type of question: The correct answer choice need not provide a completely convincing, bulletproof hypothesis—one that is proven with 100-percent certainty by the data. In fact, the correct answer need only provide a plausible hypothesis, one that is *not inconsistent* with the experimental data. Each of the wrong-answer choices will either be *inconsistent* with the data (or with the passage's textual information) or will call for an unwarranted inference, or *speculation*—a conclusion beyond what a reasonable person (read: a good scientist) would infer from the data.

To make these questions even tougher, the test-makers might incorporate one or more of the following features:

- Analyze a table in both directions—across different rows as well as down different columns.
- Analyze data from more than one experiment.
- Analyze key information from the text as well.

Here's a question about the moth experiments that incorporates all three features:

The passage and experimental data best support which of the following hypotheses?

F. The presence of pollution negatively affects the survival of melanic moths.
G. The existence of lichens on trees generally increases the chances of a moth's survival.
H. Birds eat more moths that differ in color from their background trees than moths that do not.
J. The existence of lichens on trees generally decreases the chances of a moth's survival.

The correct answer is H. Notice that, to analyze this question, you need to analyze the table two ways—across rows and down columns. In other words, you need to look at the background (light/dark) as well as moth color (light/melanic). The table shows that where trees provide a light background, a greater percentage of dark moths disappear (that is, are *not* recaptured) than light moths. And, conversely, where the tree color is dark, a greater percentage of light moths disappear. One plausible explanation for this phenomenon is that birds tend to eat moths that differ in color from their background. Hence, choice **H** is consistent with the tabular data.

Now, look at the wrong-answer choices. Choice **F** contradicts the passage information, which indicates that darker (melanic) moths became more predominant in polluted areas. Therefore, to eliminate choice **F**, you need to recall specific passage information. The data does not support choice **G**, which makes no distinction between light and melanic moths. The table shows that, where lichens grow on trees, light-colored moths have about an *equal* (not greater) chance of survival and that dark-colored moths actually have a *smaller* chance of survival (a 6.3% versus 27.5% recapture rate). Just like choice **G**, choice **J** makes no distinction between light and melanic moths. Although the table does suggest that, where lichens grow on trees, dark-colored moths have a greater chance of survival (a 27.5% versus 6.3% recapture rate), light-colored moths appear to have about an *equal* (not greater) chance of survival against either a light or dark background.

In the previous question, notice that choices **G** and **J** are opposites of each other, but they both over-generalize from a small amount of data about what might be true for *all* moths. Also, notice that choice **J** is only partly accurate. These types of wrong answers are typical in Science Reasoning questions.

Now, try an even tougher question of this type. Remember: Any explanation (hypothesis) that is *not inconsistent* with the data would be considered plausible and hence a viable hypothesis.

Assuming that, in both experiments, birds captured the same percentage of both light and melanic moths, which of the following is the LEAST plausible explanation for the results of the two experiments?

A. The pollution itself causes the light moth's difficulty with survival as compared to the dark moth.

B. Another selective force selects against the melanic moths in the unpolluted area and light moths in the polluted area.

C. Too few light moths were released in the polluted areas to make a valid comparison.

D. The moths were released at a time of year when light moths have a greater chance of survival than melanic moths.

The correct answer is D. Choice **D** might explain the fact that a greater percentage of light-colored moths than melanic moths were captured in Dorset. But, choice **D** ignores the data collected in Birmingham, which show just the opposite. Since **D** is clearly inconsistent with the results of the second experiment, it is the best answer choice.

Now, let's examine each of the wrong-answer choices. Choice **A** is incorrect. The whole purpose of the experiment is to determine the reason for the predominance of dark-colored over light-colored moths in polluted areas. One possible explanation (and probably the most obvious one) is that the pollution *directly*, and adversely, affects the light moth's ability to thrive. Choice **B** is incorrect. The passage does not define *selective force*. However, common sense should tell you that this term refers to an external factor that discriminates between light and dark moths. If there is such a force at work here, the passage information and tabular data clearly suggest that the force discriminates against *melanic* moths in unpolluted areas but against *light* moths in polluted areas. In other words, choice **B** is consistent with the passage information and tabular data. Choice **C** is testing you on a basic assumption upon which all scientific experiments depend—namely, that the number of samples (or amount of data gathered) is sufficiently large to draw reliable conclusions based on those samples (or data). For example, if only *one* light moth had been released in Birmingham (dark background), whether that moth had been recaptured wouldn't provide convincing support for any hypothesis, simply because the sample size of 1 is so small. In the table, notice the small number of light moths released in Birmingham (137) compared with the other three numbers of moths released (496, 473, and 447). Choice **C** essentially points out that this low number renders any conclusions based on it somewhat unreliable.

Alert!

You can draw reliable conclusions from experimental data only if the sample group from which the data is drawn is *representative* of the overall population about which the conclusion is drawn. The larger the sample group, the more likely it represents the overall population—and the more reliable the conclusion based on data about the sample group.

Evaluating a Hypothesis

When you read and recap a Research Summary passage, notice if certain data (results of the experiment) conflict with the hypothesis being tested—in other words, the data tend to disprove the hypothesis. If it does, make a note of it. It's a sure bet that you'll encounter a question that focuses on the discrepancy.

In an easier question of this type, the data might blatantly contradict the hypothesis. In a tougher question, the conflict will be less obvious. You might see mixed results among the data—some supporting the hypothesis, some not. Here's a good example based on the moth passage:

Alert!

Look out for wrong-answer choices that provide accurate but irrelevant information, as well as choices that confuse percentages with raw numbers.

A critic of the experiment would point out that the scientists have NOT adequately accounted for which of the following?

F. Over both trials, the percentage of melanic moths that survived was about twice the percentage of light moths that survived.

G. With a light background, the percentage of melanic moths recaptured was only about one fourth the percentage of melanic moths recaptured where there was a dark background.

H. Light moths were recaptured in approximately the same percentage regardless of background color.

J. With a light background, the number of melanic moths recaptured was nearly twice the number of light moths recaptured where the background was dark.

The correct answer is H. Choice H makes an accurate observation: In both trials, light moths were recaptured in almost equal percentages. Hence, you could conclude that the light moths survive at the same levels regardless of pollution and presence of lichen. This conclusion runs contrary to the rest of the passage information, which suggests that light moths are less likely to survive against a dark background than a light background.

Now, look at the wrong-answer choices. Choice **F** is accurate with respect to a dark background, but when it comes to a light background, **F** gets it backward. (The percentage of melanic moths recaptured is *half* that of light moths.) Choice **G** provides an accurate observation. However, this observation is additional evidence that melanic moths survive better against a dark background than a light one—a basic premise of the scientists' hypothesis and reason for the experiment in the first place. Hence, choice **G** is hardly one that a critic of the experiment would be quick to point out. Choice **J** provides an accurate statement, but so what? The number of moths recaptured, in itself, is not important. What's key is a comparison of percentages.

Drawing General Conclusions from the Data

Questions of this type ask essentially: "What general statements do the experimental data best support?" These questions can be tough because the data will typically provide some support for more than one listed statement. What's more, as with the other question types you've encountered in this section, any general statement that is *not inconsistent* with the data and is relevant to it could be a correct answer.

To handle these questions, you need to be comfortable with going outside the passage information and with statements that are not proven beyond any doubt. To toughen up these questions, the test-makers might turn the question around, asking you to identify the weakest among four generalizations. Here's a good example:

The increase in the percentage of melanic moths recaptured in polluted areas is LEAST consistent with which of the following?

A. A selective force can be strong enough to nearly complete a color change in a species over a short time period.

B. Melanic moths do not depend on lichen for survival to so great an extent as light moths do.

C. Pollution is a force that affects the survival rate of light moths but not of melanic moths.

D. Bird prey can escape detection by predator birds if they blend in with their immediate environment.

The correct answer is C. The increase in the number of melanic moths in polluted areas appears to go hand-in-hand with the decrease of light moths. Based on the information in the passage, pollution seems to be the indirect cause of both. Hence, C is the correct choice.

Now, look at the wrong-answer choices (remember: you can eliminate any choice that is *not inconsistent* with the data). First, choice **A**: The passage points out a phenomenon that occurred "in the late 1840s"; hence, it's reasonable to characterize the increase of dark moths to 98% of the moth population as a "nearly complete" color change in the species "over a short time period." Choice **B** provides one plausible explanation for the predominance of melanic moths in polluted areas. (It might not be the most convincing explanation, but it is nevertheless plausible, and it's not inconsistent with the passage.) Choice **D** provides a plausible explanation for the increase cited in the question. Specifically, given a dark background, it's easier for birds to detect light moths than darker, melanic moths.

Assessing the Effect of New Information

A question of this type will provide a new finding or other fact, then ask about its impact on either the stated hypothesis (if any) or a previously unstated argument based on the original data. Potentially, any additional piece of information might support, weaken, or have no effect on an argument.

A simpler question of this type might provide new evidence that blatantly conflicts with a stated hypothesis. A more complicated question will incorporate other, previously unstated arguments or possible explanations for the original data.

> Assume that the change in color of the *Biston betularia* is due to a genetic mutation and that, once the mutation occurs, the new coloration is dominant and can therefore more successfully be passed to a greater percentage of offspring. This finding in itself would:
>
> **F.** support the argument that pollution was responsible for the increase in melanic moths in polluted areas.
>
> **G.** lend support to the hypothesis that bird predation was the cause of the comparative decline in light-colored moths.
>
> **H.** help explain why darker moths constituted as much as 98% of the moth population in polluted areas.
>
> **J.** help establish that light-colored *Biston betularia* are in danger of extinction.

The correct answer is H. Based on the finding, it is logical to infer that the dominant coloration becomes more and more dominant with each successive generation of moths. This trend would help explain how the dark-colored moths could virtually take over the moth population in polluted areas.

Now, let's find out why the other three answer choices are wrong. Choices F and G are wrong for essentially the same reason: the finding provides a reasonable explanation for the relative decline in light-colored moths, thereby helping to *disprove* (not support) the explanations provided in choices F and G. Choice J requires far more support than what's given in the passage and the question. It assumes that the population of light-colored *Biston betularia* outside industrial England is also declining. But, no evidence is provided to substantiate this crucial assumption. Thus, to assert generally that these moths are "endangered" amounts to little more than speculation.

Alert!

In real life and on the ACT, people often draw conclusions based on assumptions rather than strictly on facts. If an argument relies on a hidden assumption that is not substantiated by evidence, then the argument's conclusion is weak. Answer choice J in the previous question is a perfect example.

Handling the Most Challenging Conflicting Viewpoints Questions

On the ACT, you'll encounter *one* Conflicting Viewpoints set, which will contain 5–7 questions (probably 6). In this section, you'll learn how to handle the most challenging Conflicting Viewpoints questions. First, however, read the following ACT-style passage.

Passage III

The apparent bird-dinosaur evolutionary connection has been a source of considerable debate among paleontologists since early in the second half of the twentieth century. This connection was proposed on the basis of numerous anatomical similarities, and has been supported by the discovery of fossils of a small number of seeming transitional forma uncovered in Europe and Asia. Yet scientists differ in their interpretation of the significance of these similarities and the nature of the fossil evidence as well.

Paleontologist A

The discovery of fossil reptiles equipped with feathers, wings, and beak-like snouts may be significant, but more likely provides only limited support for the dinosaur-into-birds hypothesis. Convergent evolution often provides animals very distant in lineage with similar appendages—witness, for example, the similarities in the body shape and presence of fins in fish and cetaceans such as whales and dolphins. We would never put forth the idea that orcas evolved from sharks based on the morphological similarities of these creatures; it would be immediately deemed absurd.

It is more likely the case that birds and dinosaurs share a very different common ancestor, perhaps from among the thecodonts. These prototypical reptiles of the late Permian Age survived the largest mass extinction recorded in the planet's history to bring forth many more recent lines; crocodiles, dinosaurs, pterosaurs, and birds are the most notable among these.

Paleontologist B

In our studies of numerous dinosaur fossils, it has become obvious that the lifestyles of dinosaurs were amazingly varied. No longer is it acceptable to view dinosaurs only as lumbering, cold-blooded monsters; indeed, the most frightening dinosaurs did not lumber at all. They were agile, swift, and some even possessed limited flying capabilities. Lightweight muscular body structure would be crucial to the success of this type of predator.

Based upon this observation, along with a number of obvious physical similarities and evidence from the fossil record, we are convinced that birds evolved from small, carnivorous dinosaurs called theropods. A mere examination of the forelimb, hindlimb, and feet of a theropod fossil, and a comparison to one of the five available specimens of *Archaeopteryx** will bear this out. In addition, more recent discoveries of fossil dinosaurs with birdlike traits and habits, particularly the finds uncovered in the Liaoning province of China, lend further credible support for our position that birds are for all intents and purposes actual members of the lineage Dinosauria living and thriving in our midst.

**Archaeopteryx* was a feathered reptile of the late Jurassic Era thought to represent an intermediate form between dinosaurs and birds.

In a typical ACT Conflicting Viewpoints set, about half the questions will test you on the following fundamental skills:

- Identifying the basic scientific issue that the different viewpoints seek to address
- Understanding the essence of each viewpoint on the issue
- Recognizing similarities (explicit points of agreement) between viewpoints
- Recognizing key dissimilarities (explicit points of disagreement) between viewpoints

Questions that call only for these basic skills tend to be easier than average. Tougher question types—the ones you'll focus on here—include these three:

- Questions requiring you to *critique* a theory by identifying its hidden assumptions
- Questions requiring you to assess the effect of *additional evidence* on one or more of the theories presented
- Questions requiring you to recognize *implicit* points of agreement between the theories presented

Identifying a Theory's Hidden Assumptions

Any theory presented in a Conflicting Viewpoints passage will rely on one or more unstated, or "hidden," assumptions. What this means is that certain facts that aren't provided must in fact be true in order for the theory to be convincing. Don't expect a theory's proponent to come right out and list the various assumptions on which the theory relies. You'll need to figure out for yourself what crucial assumptions underlie the theory, which is what can make these questions difficult.

The key to handling these questions is to understand that ACT Conflicting Viewpoints provide, in essence, alternative explanations for what *causes* certain observed scientific phenomenon. And, in almost every case, each theory will ignore or overlook other possible causes. Accordingly, a key assumption underlying a typical ACT viewpoint is that there are no other plausible explanations for the observed phenomenon. Here's a question based on Passage III that tests you on this kind of assumption:

> Which of the following is a criticism that Paleontologist A would make of the evolutionary hypothesis of Paleontologist B?
>
> **A.** It ignores the possibility of the existence of transitional forms.
> **B.** It ignores the impact of a very large mass extinction.
> **C.** It assumes that morphological similarities are a result of direct lineage.
> **D.** It proposes that the lineage from which dinosaurs arose is quite distinct from the one from which birds arose.

The correct answer is C. The hypothesis of Paleontologist B relies on the crucial assumption that there's no possible explanation for the body similarities between dinosaurs and early birds other than that birds descended directly from dinosaurs. Choice A contradicts the position of Paleontologist B, whose argument not just acknowledges, but actually relies upon, the possible existence of transitional forms. Choice **B** provides an accurate statement, but so what? The large mass extinction that Paleontologist A mentions is irrelevant to Paleontologist B's argument. Choice **D** provides the essential hypothesis of Paleontologist A, not Paleontologist B.

Assessing the Effect of Additional Evidence

A question of this type will provide a new finding or other fact, then ask about its impact on one or more of the conflicting theories. Potentially, any additional piece of information might do one of the following:

- Support one viewpoint, but weaken another
- Weaken both viewpoints
- Support one viewpoint, but have no effect on the other viewpoint
- Weaken one viewpoint, but have no effect on the other viewpoint
- Have no effect on either viewpoint

What makes these questions more complex than average is that they require you to assimilate the whole passage—to understand all the viewpoints, as well as to recognize their similarities and differences. A less complex question of this type might provide new evidence that blatantly conflicts with one viewpoint and, just as blatantly, supports another.

> If genetic evidence were established to date the lineage of birds 85 million years prior to the rise of *Archaeopteryx*, this finding would tend to:
>
> F. support the theory of Paleontologist A.
> G. support the theory of Paleontologist B.
> H. support the theories of both paleontologists.
> J. refute the theories of both paleontologists.

The correct answer is F. Choice F contradicts the theory of Paleontologist B because Paleontologist B suggests that birds arose from dinosaurs. Paleontologist A suggested that the two arose from an extremely distant ancestor, and the theory of convergent evolution is not inconsistent with birds appearing before dinosaurs.

A tougher question of this sort might provide evidence that either strengthens or weakens one theory but has no effect on the other. Here's a good example:

> Which of the following types of evidence, if found, would lend support to the position of Paleontologist A?
>
> **A.** Discovery of thecodont fossils with characteristics of modern birds and existing dinosaur fossils
> **B.** Discovery of another possible intermediate form between dinosaurs and birds from the Jurassic era
> **C.** Discovery of a bird prototype dating back to before the beginning of the era of dinosaur dominance
> **D.** Discovery of a fossil reptile equipped with a beak-like snout, wings, and feathers

The correct answer is A. Paleontologist A believes that dinosaurs and birds share a common ancestor. A fossil find from before the age of the dinosaurs with common features would support this view. The evidence cited in choice **B** would actually support the position of Paleontologist B, by providing further evidence of an evolutionary link between birds and dinosaurs. The evidence cited in choice **C** would tend to weaken the position of Paleontologist A, who believes that dinosaurs and birds share a common ancestor. A fossil find with features like those of modern birds but unlike those of dinosaurs would tend to show that the lineage of birds is distinct from that of dinosaurs. Choice **D** simply reiterates what Paleontologist A already admits—that the discovery of fossil reptiles equipped with beak-like snouts, wings, and feathers lends support for the dinosaur-into-birds hypothesis.

Alert!

Just because evidence tends to weaken one theory does not necessarily mean that the evidence supports an opposing theory. For example, in the preceding question, the evidence provided in choice **C** would tend to weaken the positions of *both* paleontologists.

The most difficult type of question involving additional facts or findings might *appear* to make a theory airtight. But, if you're paying close attention, you'll realize that whether the evidence proves the theory depends on whether certain *assumptions* can be substantiated.

If Paleontologist B could confirm that birds appeared much later in evolutionary history than any dinosaurs, which of the following statements would reconcile this fact with the theory of Paleontologist A?

F. The ancestors of birds and the ancestors of dinosaurs were exposed to specific environmental conditions at the same time, and this caused the development of similar characteristics.

G. The ancestors of birds and the ancestors of dinosaurs were exposed to specific environmental conditions that caused the development of similar characteristics, but the dinosaur ancestors were exposed to these environmental conditions later than the bird ancestors were.

H. The rate of evolutionary change from the thecodont ancestor was much slower for the lineage that resulted in birds than for the lineage that resulted in dinosaurs.

J. The rate of evolutionary change from the thecodont ancestor was much faster for the lineage that resulted in birds than for the lineage that resulted in dinosaurs.

The correct answer is H. Paleontologist A postulates the existence of a very distant common ancestor for birds and dinosaurs. The development of birds much later than that of dinosaurs might seem to refute this argument. However, the rate of evolutionary change is not constant across different lineages. Dinosaurs may have developed relatively rapidly from thecodonts, for example, whereas birds did not evolve until much later.

Recognizing Implicit Points of Agreement

In handling Conflicting Viewpoints sets, one of your basic tasks is to understand the similarities between the viewpoints presented. Think of these similarities as points of agreement between the proponents of the different theories. Some points of agreement will be explicit in the passage. You'll find them in the background information as well as in the opening sentences of each viewpoint. But, other points of agreement might be implied rather than expressed. These points make for tougher test questions because you need to do more than just "look up" the information in the passage.

Questions of this type are not likely to ask about "agreement" or "similarities." Instead, look for a question stem that asks what is "consistent" with more than one of the viewpoints presented. Here's the key to handling these questions: Whatever is *not inconsistent* with a theory or viewpoint is a point that the viewpoint's proponent might agree with. Here's an ACT-style example based on Passage III that illustrates this key point:

> Which of the following perspectives would be consistent with the views of both paleontologists?
>
> **A.** Convergent evolution produces similar forms in diverse lineages.
> **B.** Dinosaurs and birds may have evolved from the same ancestor.
> **C.** Birds and dinosaurs arose out of completely separate lineages.
> **D.** Birds arose out of a lineage of dinosaurs.

The correct answer is B. Neither Paleontologist B's belief that birds arose out of a lineage of dinosaurs, nor Paleontologist A's belief that they did not, is inconsistent with the view expressed in choice **B**. Choices **A** and **C** are consistent with Paleontologist A's hypothesis but inconsistent with Paleontologist B's. Choice **D** provides the essence of Paleontologist B's hypothesis but is opposite that of Paleontologist A's.

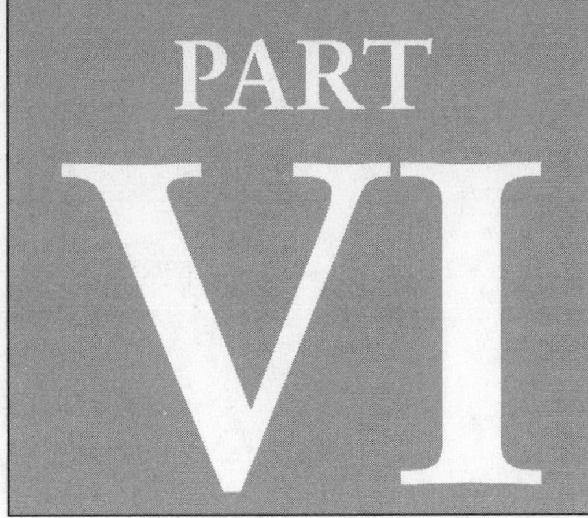

Three Practice ACTs

ANSWER SHEET FOR PRACTICE TEST 1

Name: ______________________________

Date: ____/____/____

School: ______________________________

Class: ______________________________

Completely darken ovals with a No. 2 pencil. If you make a mistake, be sure to erase mark completely. Erase all stray marks.

Start with number 1 for each new section. If a section has fewer questions than answer spaces, leave the extra answer spaces blank.

PART 1

No.	Choices	No.	Choices	No.	Choices	No.	Choices
1	A B C D E	20	F G H J K	39	A B C D E	58	F G H J K
2	F G H J K	21	A B C D E	40	F G H J K	59	A B C D E
3	A B C D E	22	F G H J K	41	A B C D E	60	F G H J K
4	F G H J K	23	A B C D E	42	F G H J K	61	A B C D E
5	A B C D E	24	F G H J K	43	A B C D E	62	F G H J K
6	F G H J K	25	A B C D E	44	F G H J K	63	A B C D E
7	A B C D E	26	F G H J K	45	A B C D E	64	F G H J K
8	F G H J K	27	A B C D E	46	F G H J K	65	A B C D E
9	A B C D E	28	F G H J K	47	A B C D E	66	F G H J K
10	F G H J K	29	A B C D E	48	F G H J K	67	A B C D E
11	A B C D E	30	F G H J K	49	A B C D E	68	F G H J K
12	F G H J K	31	A B C D E	50	F G H J K	69	A B C D E
13	A B C D E	32	F G H J K	51	A B C D E	70	F G H J K
14	F G H J K	33	A B C D E	52	F G H J K	71	A B C D E
15	A B C D E	34	F G H J K	53	A B C D E	72	F G H J K
16	F G H J K	35	A B C D E	54	F G H J K	73	A B C D E
17	A B C D E	36	F G H J K	55	A B C D E	74	F G H J K
18	F G H J K	37	A B C D E	56	F G H J K	75	A B C D E
19	A B C D E	38	F G H J K	57	A B C D E	76	F G H J K

PART 2

No.	Choices	No.	Choices	No.	Choices	No.	Choices
1	A B C D E	16	F G H J K	31	A B C D E	46	F G H J K
2	F G H J K	17	A B C D E	32	F G H J K	47	A B C D E
3	A B C D E	18	F G H J K	33	A B C D E	48	F G H J K
4	F G H J K	19	A B C D E	34	F G H J K	49	A B C D E
5	A B C D E	20	F G H J K	35	A B C D E	50	F G H J K
6	F G H J K	21	A B C D E	36	F G H J K	51	A B C D E
7	A B C D E	22	F G H J K	37	A B C D E	52	F G H J K
8	F G H J K	23	A B C D E	38	F G H J K	53	A B C D E
9	A B C D E	24	F G H J K	39	A B C D E	54	F G H J K
10	F G H J K	25	A B C D E	40	F G H J K	55	A B C D E
11	A B C D E	26	F G H J K	41	A B C D E	56	F G H J K
12	F G H J K	27	A B C D E	42	F G H J K	57	A B C D E
13	A B C D E	28	F G H J K	43	A B C D E	58	F G H J K
14	F G H J K	29	A B C D E	44	F G H J K	59	A B C D E
15	A B C D E	30	F G H J K	45	A B C D E	60	F G H J K

BE SURE TO ERASE ANY ERRORS OR STRAY MARKS COMPLETELY.

DO NOT MARK IN THIS AREA

Use a No. 2 pencil only. Be sure each mark is dark and completely fills the intended oval. Completely erase any errors or stray marks.

Start with number 1 for each new section. If a section has fewer questions than answer spaces, leave the extra answer spaces blank.

PART 3

1	⊂A⊃ ⊂B⊃ ⊂C⊃ ⊂D⊃ ⊂E⊃	11	⊂A⊃ ⊂B⊃ ⊂C⊃ ⊂D⊃ ⊂E⊃	21	⊂A⊃ ⊂B⊃ ⊂C⊃ ⊂D⊃ ⊂E⊃	31	⊂A⊃ ⊂B⊃ ⊂C⊃ ⊂D⊃ ⊂E⊃
2	⊂F⊃ ⊂G⊃ ⊂H⊃ ⊂J⊃ ⊂K⊃	12	⊂F⊃ ⊂G⊃ ⊂H⊃ ⊂J⊃ ⊂K⊃	22	⊂F⊃ ⊂G⊃ ⊂H⊃ ⊂J⊃ ⊂K⊃	32	⊂F⊃ ⊂G⊃ ⊂H⊃ ⊂J⊃ ⊂K⊃
3	⊂A⊃ ⊂B⊃ ⊂C⊃ ⊂D⊃ ⊂E⊃	13	⊂A⊃ ⊂B⊃ ⊂C⊃ ⊂D⊃ ⊂E⊃	23	⊂A⊃ ⊂B⊃ ⊂C⊃ ⊂D⊃ ⊂E⊃	33	⊂A⊃ ⊂B⊃ ⊂C⊃ ⊂D⊃ ⊂E⊃
4	⊂F⊃ ⊂G⊃ ⊂H⊃ ⊂J⊃ ⊂K⊃	14	⊂F⊃ ⊂G⊃ ⊂H⊃ ⊂J⊃ ⊂K⊃	24	⊂F⊃ ⊂G⊃ ⊂H⊃ ⊂J⊃ ⊂K⊃	34	⊂F⊃ ⊂G⊃ ⊂H⊃ ⊂J⊃ ⊂K⊃
5	⊂A⊃ ⊂B⊃ ⊂C⊃ ⊂D⊃ ⊂E⊃	15	⊂A⊃ ⊂B⊃ ⊂C⊃ ⊂D⊃ ⊂E⊃	25	⊂A⊃ ⊂B⊃ ⊂C⊃ ⊂D⊃ ⊂E⊃	35	⊂A⊃ ⊂B⊃ ⊂C⊃ ⊂D⊃ ⊂E⊃
6	⊂F⊃ ⊂G⊃ ⊂H⊃ ⊂J⊃ ⊂K⊃	16	⊂F⊃ ⊂G⊃ ⊂H⊃ ⊂J⊃ ⊂K⊃	26	⊂F⊃ ⊂G⊃ ⊂H⊃ ⊂J⊃ ⊂K⊃	36	⊂F⊃ ⊂G⊃ ⊂H⊃ ⊂J⊃ ⊂K⊃
7	⊂A⊃ ⊂B⊃ ⊂C⊃ ⊂D⊃ ⊂E⊃	17	⊂A⊃ ⊂B⊃ ⊂C⊃ ⊂D⊃ ⊂E⊃	27	⊂A⊃ ⊂B⊃ ⊂C⊃ ⊂D⊃ ⊂E⊃	37	⊂A⊃ ⊂B⊃ ⊂C⊃ ⊂D⊃ ⊂E⊃
8	⊂F⊃ ⊂G⊃ ⊂H⊃ ⊂J⊃ ⊂K⊃	18	⊂F⊃ ⊂G⊃ ⊂H⊃ ⊂J⊃ ⊂K⊃	28	⊂F⊃ ⊂G⊃ ⊂H⊃ ⊂J⊃ ⊂K⊃	38	⊂F⊃ ⊂G⊃ ⊂H⊃ ⊂J⊃ ⊂K⊃
9	⊂A⊃ ⊂B⊃ ⊂C⊃ ⊂D⊃ ⊂E⊃	19	⊂A⊃ ⊂B⊃ ⊂C⊃ ⊂D⊃ ⊂E⊃	29	⊂A⊃ ⊂B⊃ ⊂C⊃ ⊂D⊃ ⊂E⊃	39	⊂A⊃ ⊂B⊃ ⊂C⊃ ⊂D⊃ ⊂E⊃
10	⊂F⊃ ⊂G⊃ ⊂H⊃ ⊂J⊃ ⊂K⊃	20	⊂F⊃ ⊂G⊃ ⊂H⊃ ⊂J⊃ ⊂K⊃	30	⊂F⊃ ⊂G⊃ ⊂H⊃ ⊂J⊃ ⊂K⊃	40	⊂F⊃ ⊂G⊃ ⊂H⊃ ⊂J⊃ ⊂K⊃

PART 4

1	⊂A⊃ ⊂B⊃ ⊂C⊃ ⊂D⊃ ⊂E⊃	11	⊂A⊃ ⊂B⊃ ⊂C⊃ ⊂D⊃ ⊂E⊃	21	⊂A⊃ ⊂B⊃ ⊂C⊃ ⊂D⊃ ⊂E⊃	31	⊂A⊃ ⊂B⊃ ⊂C⊃ ⊂D⊃ ⊂E⊃
2	⊂F⊃ ⊂G⊃ ⊂H⊃ ⊂J⊃ ⊂K⊃	12	⊂F⊃ ⊂G⊃ ⊂H⊃ ⊂J⊃ ⊂K⊃	22	⊂F⊃ ⊂G⊃ ⊂H⊃ ⊂J⊃ ⊂K⊃	32	⊂F⊃ ⊂G⊃ ⊂H⊃ ⊂J⊃ ⊂K⊃
3	⊂A⊃ ⊂B⊃ ⊂C⊃ ⊂D⊃ ⊂E⊃	13	⊂A⊃ ⊂B⊃ ⊂C⊃ ⊂D⊃ ⊂E⊃	23	⊂A⊃ ⊂B⊃ ⊂C⊃ ⊂D⊃ ⊂E⊃	33	⊂A⊃ ⊂B⊃ ⊂C⊃ ⊂D⊃ ⊂E⊃
4	⊂F⊃ ⊂G⊃ ⊂H⊃ ⊂J⊃ ⊂K⊃	14	⊂F⊃ ⊂G⊃ ⊂H⊃ ⊂J⊃ ⊂K⊃	24	⊂F⊃ ⊂G⊃ ⊂H⊃ ⊂J⊃ ⊂K⊃	34	⊂F⊃ ⊂G⊃ ⊂H⊃ ⊂J⊃ ⊂K⊃
5	⊂A⊃ ⊂B⊃ ⊂C⊃ ⊂D⊃ ⊂E⊃	15	⊂A⊃ ⊂B⊃ ⊂C⊃ ⊂D⊃ ⊂E⊃	25	⊂A⊃ ⊂B⊃ ⊂C⊃ ⊂D⊃ ⊂E⊃	35	⊂A⊃ ⊂B⊃ ⊂C⊃ ⊂D⊃ ⊂E⊃
6	⊂F⊃ ⊂G⊃ ⊂H⊃ ⊂J⊃ ⊂K⊃	16	⊂F⊃ ⊂G⊃ ⊂H⊃ ⊂J⊃ ⊂K⊃	26	⊂F⊃ ⊂G⊃ ⊂H⊃ ⊂J⊃ ⊂K⊃	36	⊂F⊃ ⊂G⊃ ⊂H⊃ ⊂J⊃ ⊂K⊃
7	⊂A⊃ ⊂B⊃ ⊂C⊃ ⊂D⊃ ⊂E⊃	17	⊂A⊃ ⊂B⊃ ⊂C⊃ ⊂D⊃ ⊂E⊃	27	⊂A⊃ ⊂B⊃ ⊂C⊃ ⊂D⊃ ⊂E⊃	37	⊂A⊃ ⊂B⊃ ⊂C⊃ ⊂D⊃ ⊂E⊃
8	⊂F⊃ ⊂G⊃ ⊂H⊃ ⊂J⊃ ⊂K⊃	18	⊂F⊃ ⊂G⊃ ⊂H⊃ ⊂J⊃ ⊂K⊃	28	⊂F⊃ ⊂G⊃ ⊂H⊃ ⊂J⊃ ⊂K⊃	38	⊂F⊃ ⊂G⊃ ⊂H⊃ ⊂J⊃ ⊂K⊃
9	⊂A⊃ ⊂B⊃ ⊂C⊃ ⊂D⊃ ⊂E⊃	19	⊂A⊃ ⊂B⊃ ⊂C⊃ ⊂D⊃ ⊂E⊃	29	⊂A⊃ ⊂B⊃ ⊂C⊃ ⊂D⊃ ⊂E⊃	39	⊂A⊃ ⊂B⊃ ⊂C⊃ ⊂D⊃ ⊂E⊃
10	⊂F⊃ ⊂G⊃ ⊂H⊃ ⊂J⊃ ⊂K⊃	20	⊂F⊃ ⊂G⊃ ⊂H⊃ ⊂J⊃ ⊂K⊃	30	⊂F⊃ ⊂G⊃ ⊂H⊃ ⊂J⊃ ⊂K⊃	40	⊂F⊃ ⊂G⊃ ⊂H⊃ ⊂J⊃ ⊂K⊃

BE SURE TO ERASE ANY ERRORS OR STRAY MARKS COMPLETELY.

Practice Test 1

English

75 Questions ■ Time—45 Minutes

Directions: This test consists of five passages in which particular words or phrases are underlined and numbered. Alongside the passage, you will see alternative words and phrases that could be substituted for the underlined part. Select the alternative that expresses the idea most clearly and correctly or that best fits the style and tone of the entire passage. If the original version is best, select "No Change."

The test also includes questions about entire paragraphs and the passage as a whole. These questions are identified by a number in a box.

After you select the correct answer for each question, on your answer sheet, mark the oval corresponding to the correct answer.

Passage I

The Girls Choir of Harlem

It is rare to hear of choirs composed of <u>just girls.</u> (1) In fact, for every girls' choir in the United States, <u>there are ten choirs that are boys' or mixed.</u> (2) But, in 1977, the Girls Choir of Harlem was founded to complement <u>the already existing</u> (3) and justly renowned Boys Choir.

To this day, the Boys Choir of Harlem has always shadowed the Girls Choir. It <u>had been</u> (4) around <u>longer since 1968 and</u> (5) has received the attention needed to gain funding and performance opportunities. The boys have appeared in some of the world's most prestigious musical settings. <u>Performing</u> (6) a sunrise concert for the Pope on the Great Lawn in New York's Central Park, and they have traveled to Washington,

D.C. where in front of the reflecting pool they sung (7) in front of the Washington monument.

[8] During the 1980s, when funds dried up, the Girls Choir temporarily disbanded. However, in 1989, the choir reassembled, and in November of 1997, they made their debut at Alice Tully Hall at Lincoln Center, performing music by Schumann and Pergolesi toward the (9) audience of dignitaries, including the mayor's wife and (10) thousands of music lovers.

Giving (11) kids from broken families and poverty-stricken homes new confidence and hope for their future, the Boys Choir of Harlem acts as a haven for inner-city children. The boys in the choir still attend the Choir Academy. The 500-student public school strongly emphasizes singing. [12] It's a fine learning environment that has given the girls ambitions most of them never before considered. The choir members speak confidently of someday becoming lawyers, doctors, and politicians—jobs appearing (13) out of reach to them.

Since the Girls Choir of Harlem has received some of the recognition that the boys have long enjoyed, perhaps corporations and wealthy individuals will be motivated to give generously to bring the choir back and ensure it will never again be canceled (14) for lack of money.

1. A. NO CHANGE
B. only just girls.
C. girls alone.
D. girls and no boys.

2. F. NO CHANGE
G. ten are either boys' or mixed choirs.
H. each of ten choirs are either boys' or mixed.
J. there are ten that are either boys' or mixed choirs.

3. A. NO CHANGE
B. what already existed
C. the existing
D. already existing

4. F. NO CHANGE
G. was
H. has been
J. being

5. A. NO CHANGE
B. longer, since 1968 and
C. longer since 1968, and
D. longer (since 1968) and

6. F. NO CHANGE
   G. They have performed
   H. A performance of
   J. The choir performs

7. A. NO CHANGE
   B. they sung in front of the reflecting pool
   C. before the reflecting pool they sung
   D. they sung at the reflecting pool

8. Which of the following sentences provides the most effective transition from the previous paragraph to this one?
   F. Such glorious moments eluded their female counterparts, at least at first.
   G. The Boys Choir and Girls Choir both have performed mainly in the Northeastern part of the U.S.
   H. The Girls Choir, though not so experienced as the Boys Choir, is considered equally talented.
   J. The Boys Choir was able to attract more funding than the Girls Choir.

9. A. NO CHANGE
   B. before an
   C. in front of the
   D. at an

10. F. NO CHANGE
    G. wife, and
    H. wife as well as
    J. wife with

11. A. NO CHANGE
    B. They give
    C. By giving
    D. As they give

12. Which of the following sentences, if inserted at this point in the passage, would be most logical and appropriate?
    F. Nevertheless, it provides a well-rounded education that helps prepare students for a variety of careers.
    G. Classes in vocal technique, sight reading, and even music theory are all part of the regular curriculum.
    H. The student body is carefully selected from a much larger pool of applicants.
    J. Students are admitted based on financial need as well as their musical abilities, especially their singing ability.

13. A. NO CHANGE
    B. appeared
    C. that once appeared
    D. that would have appeared

14. F. NO CHANGE
    G. close its doors
    H. stop what they do
    J. go silent

GO ON TO THE NEXT PAGE

Question 15 poses a question about the passage as a whole.

15. Suppose the writer had been assigned to write an essay describing the musical achievements of the Girls Choir of Harlem. Would this essay successfully fulfill the assignment?

- **A.** Yes, because the essay makes it clear that the girls in the choir are talented performers.
- **B.** Yes, because the concert at Alice Tully Hall is explained in some detail.
- **C.** No, because the music performed by the choir is scarcely discussed in the essay.
- **D.** No, because the essay discusses the Boys Choir as extensively as the Girls Choir.

Passage II

[*The following paragraphs may or may not be arranged in the best possible order. The last question will ask you to choose the most effective order for the paragraphs as numbered.*]

Tunnel Vision: The Bane of Business

[1]

Sometimes a business leader stumbles into a kind of trap by waiting and seeing [16] what new technologies develop instead of anticipating them: [17] trading time for the prospect of more information and a decrease in uncertainty. Sometimes the leader is simply so afraid to lose that he or she is [18] incapable of the bold action required for success. Regardless of the reason for inaction, the leader is operating with limited vision, and the company suffers as a result.

[2]

By the early 1980s, Wang Corporation had developed the preeminent office automation capability in the world. In many offices, [19] the name "Wang" had become synonymous with "office automation." Having had gained [20] a reputation for quality and with proprietary hardware and software that guaranteed the uniqueness of its product, Wang had built a market position that seemingly was [21] unassailable. Yet, in less than a decade, Wang faded to near obscurity. [22]

[3]

In place of Wang's specialized computer systems, versatile personal computers linked together in networks had become [23] the dominant office tools. The new personal computers first transformed the market for office automation networks then wiping out the old market. Wang shrank dramatically, surviving only by transforming itself—exploiting its software (24) and engineering strengths in completely different ways.

[4]

Wang had seen itself as a special kind of computer company, one that used large machines to serve entire companies. (25) Its excellence and leadership in innovation was highly respected, and it was important to Wang not to slip up. (26) That view led Wang to continue with its familiar business until it was too late. It failed to see the opportunity that the personal computer presented. Eventually, Wang did attempt to move into personal computers, but by the time that happened. (27) Wang's opportunity to move forward was gone. [28]

[5]

Businesses don't always get into trouble because they are badly run or inefficient. Sometimes, a well-managed company fails (29) because its leaders simply don't understand how the world is changing around them. What happened to Wang, the office automation company, is a classic example.

16. F. NO CHANGE
G. for
H. on
J. to see

17. A. NO CHANGE
B. it,
C. them—
D. them and

18. F. NO CHANGE
G. that they are
H. so as to be
J. that the leaders are

19. A. NO CHANGE
B. In fact, in many offices,
C. In many offices, however,
D. Also, in many offices,

20. F. NO CHANGE
G. Gaining
H. In order to gain
J. With

21. A. NO CHANGE
B. that seemed
C. that was seeming
D. seemingly

22. Which of the following courses of action involving the underlined sentence would organize the information in Paragraphs 2 and 3 in the most logical manner?
F. NO CHANGE
G. Start a new paragraph with the sentence, and omit the paragraph break after the sentence.
H. Move the sentence to the end of Paragraph 3.
J. Omit the sentence.

GO ON TO THE NEXT PAGE

23. **A.** NO CHANGE
B. will become
C. were to become
D. soon became

24. **F.** NO CHANGE
G. by its transformation
H. by means of transforming
J. to transform itself

25. **A.** NO CHANGE
B. a company that used large machines to serve entire companies
C. whose machines served entire companies because of their large size
D. using large machines allowing it to serve entire companies

26. **F.** NO CHANGE
G. to not lose it
H. to maintain that position
J. to avoid slip ups

27. **A.** NO CHANGE
B. it was too late;
C. by that time
D. when time ran out

28. Which of the following sentences, if inserted at this point in the passage, would be most relevant and effective?

F. Wang had been badly outmaneuvered and was left essentially with no market.
G. The company failed to foresee the day that personal computers would appear on millions of desktops.
H. Ultimate responsibility for this lack of foresight rested on the shoulders of the company's leaders.
J. Apparently, Wang was not the excellent computer company everyone in the computer industry had always assumed it was.

29. **A.** NO CHANGE
B. A well-managed company might fail
C. When a well-managed company fails, it's
D. A company that is well-managed fails

Question 30 poses a question about the passage as a whole.

30. Which of the following proposals for the order of the passage's paragraphs, if implemented, would provide the most logical and effective beginning and ending for the passage?

F. NO CHANGE (Don't make any changes in the sequence of paragraphs.)
G. Move Paragraph 5 to the beginning of the passage.
H. Move Paragraph 1 to the end of the passage.
J. Move Paragraph 5 to the beginning of the passage, and move Paragraph 1 to the end of the passage.

Passage III

An Oboist's Quest

[1]

I started playing the oboe because I heard it was a challenging instrument. That was four years ago, and I've enjoyed learning to play the oboe <u>like I</u> [31] expected. However, it was not until recently that I realized what an oboist's real challenge <u>is: finding</u> [32] good oboe reeds.

[2]

Though the reed is a small part of the instrument, mainly it is what the quality of the oboe's sound is determined by (33). Professional oboists make their own reeds. Students (34) like me must buy reeds from either their teachers or from (35) mail-order companies.

[3]

My troubles began when my teacher stopped making reeds, sending all of her students on a wild goose chase for the perfect reed. The problem is there's (36) no such thing as a perfect reed, though oboists like to daydream about it. There is also no such thing as a perfect reed supplier. Reed makers are much in demand, and the reeds are often very expensive. [37] What's more, the reed makers tend to take their time in sending reeds to you. For example, (38) I usually have to wait three to six weeks after they've received my check in the mail. This wouldn't be a problem if I always ordered my reeds well before the time I need it, (39) but oboe reeds are temperamental and often crack or break without warning. Thus, I need to have several back-up reeds available at all times.

[4]

I first tried buying reeds from a reed maker in Massachusetts. They were pretty good at first, but they became progressively lower and lower (40) in quality the longer I bought them from him. It got to the point where none of the reeds he supplied worked, so I had to move on.

[5]

My next source was a company in California. However, they're (41) reeds sounded like ducks quacking, so I dropped that source from my list. Desperate, the next person I called was an oboist friend of my parents (42). She helped me fix a few salvageable reeds I owned, and soon I had several that played in tune and that created a good tone. It seemed my reed troubles were over. However, within two weeks, those precious reeds were all played out, and I needed more.

GO ON TO THE NEXT PAGE

[6]

Recently, however, a friend recommended a reed maker from New York City who made reeds that, according to him, were rather good. I called him immediately, and he asked me questions about my playing so that he could cater to my oboe needs. He promised to send out a supply of reeds within a week. Imagine my disappointment when the reeds he sent turned out to be poorly made, with unstable tones and a thin, unpleasant sound. [45]

(Underlined portions: "Recently, however," = 43; "according to him" = 44)

31. A. NO CHANGE
B. as
C. as much as I
D. to the degree in which I

32. F. NO CHANGE
G. is—it's finding
H is which is finding
J. is finding

33. A. NO CHANGE
B. it is mainly what determines the quality of the oboe's sound
C. it is the main component of the oboe that determines the quality of its sound
D. mainly the quality of the oboe's sound is determined by the reed

34. F. NO CHANGE
G. reeds, but
H. reeds, so
J. reeds. And, students

35. A. NO CHANGE
B. from their teachers or
C. either from their teachers or
D. either from their teachers or from

36. F. NO CHANGE
G. is that there's
H. was there's
J. is, there's

37. At this point, the writer wants to provide an additional remark about the expense of oboe reeds. Which of the following sentences would be most relevant and most consistent with the information in the paragraph as a whole?
A. In addition, if you purchase a reed by mail order, you're charged a shipping fee, making the total expense even greater.
B. In my opinion, reed makers often charge twice what I consider a fair price for an oboe reed.
C. Students, most of whom are on a limited budget, find it difficult to afford expensive reeds.
D. However, since professional reed makers produce the best possible reeds, the high price is well worth it.

38. F. NO CHANGE
G. Typically,
H. In fact,
J. OMIT the underlined portion.

39. A. NO CHANGE
B. need them,
C. plan to use it,
D. need,

40. F. NO CHANGE
G. less and less
H. poor
J. lower

41. A. NO CHANGE
B. it's
C. their
D. its

42. F. NO CHANGE
G. I next called an oboist friend of my parents
H. an oboist friend of my parents was the next person I called
J. I called a person next who was an oboist friend of my parents

43. Among the following alternatives involving the underlined portion, which provides the most logical and effective transition from Paragraph 5 to Paragraph 6?

A. NO CHANGE
B. However,
C. Recently,
D. Also,

44. F. NO CHANGE
G. he claimed
H. my friend told me
J. according to my friend

Question 45 poses a question about the passage as a whole.

45. Which of the following sentences, if inserted at this point, would provide an ending for the passage that best ties together the entire passage?

A. My search for the perfect reed continues and may never come to an end until I learn to make reeds myself.
B. With all the oboists in the New York City area, you'd think that this reed maker's product would be far better than it was.
C. Obviously, I'll never buy another reed from the reed maker that my friend recommended—or from any of the reed makers with whom I've already dealt.
D. When I first began playing the oboe, I never imagined that finding reeds would be more challenging than actually learning to play the instrument.

Passage IV

The First Thanksgiving: Turkey Day and a Whole Lot More

[1]

Every autumn, <u>when Thanksgiving occurs,</u> (46) anxiety and stress levels in millions of American families rise. It's not an easy job <u>to host</u> (47) friends and relatives from all over the <u>country then</u> (48) preparing one of the largest meals of the year. But when the typical Thanksgiving dinner of today is compared with the celebration of the first Thanksgiving, it doesn't seem like such a feat.

[2]

First, consider the menu. At a typical modern-day Thanksgiving dinner, there is a [49] roast turkey, baked yams, stuffing, cranberry sauce, gravy, and some sort of dessert—perhaps ice cream and either pie or cake. Of course, you can fix everything yourself from scratch, if you like; but if you prefer, all the food can be purchased [50] at a local supermarket. In just one trip, you have all you need for your dinner.

[3]

(1) Today's menu seems stingy by comparison [51] to the Pilgrims' meal [52] enjoyed on the first Thanksgiving in 1621. (2) According to contemporary records, the list of foods included five deer; wild turkeys, geese, and duck; eels, lobsters, clams, and mussels fished from the ocean; pumpkin; an assortment of biscuits; hoe and ash cakes; popcorn balls; pudding; berries of several kinds; plums, cherries, and bogbeans; beer made from barley; and wine spiked with brandy. [53] (3) Just in case [54] this weren't enough, the Pilgrims could fill in the corners with "flint corn," a rock-hard corn ground into a mush. (4) And once the dinner was served, the meal lasted not a few hours but rather a few days [55]—and with no football on television to distract the Pilgrims and their friends from the serious business of eating.

[4]

[56] Nowadays, in many households, the whole family comes for Thanksgiving. Statistics show that the average Thanksgiving dinner today boasts twenty-three guests total [57]— no tiny gathering. Both family and friends are included in this number. [58] At the first Thanksgiving, when Squanto, the Indian-in-residence, decided to invite Massasoit, the leader of the Wampanoag tribe, the Pilgrims weren't expecting him to bring along another ninety Wampanoags to a little pot-luck supper [59]. With the Pilgrims, that made a 140-person guest list. [60]

46. F. NO CHANGE
G. when it's Thanksgiving
H. during Thanksgiving
J. whenever Thanksgiving rolls around

47. A. NO CHANGE
B. hosting
C. as a host to
D. of hosting

48. F. NO CHANGE
G. country. Then
H. country; then
J. country, and then

49. A. NO CHANGE
B. it's common to eat
C. you'll dine on
D. the menu consists of

50. F. NO CHANGE
G. you can purchase all the food
H. all the food is purchasable
J. the food you need you can purchase

51. A. NO CHANGE
B. when it is being compared
C. comparing it
D. OMIT the underlined portion.

52. F. NO CHANGE
G. Pilgrim's meal
H. meal the Pilgrims
J. Pilgrims' meal that they

53. Is the repeated use of a semicolon in sentence 2 correct and appropriate?

A. Yes, because the sentence lists more than three distinct items of food.
B. Yes, because the sentence lists different categories as well as specific category items.
C. No, because the resulting sentence is so long that it is not easily understood.
D. No, because a semicolon should be used only to separate clauses that can stand alone as complete sentences.

54. F. NO CHANGE
G. If
H. As if
J. In the case that

55. A. NO CHANGE
B. so many hours that it lasted for a few days
C. not just a few hours but rather a few days
D. a few days and not a few hours

56. Which of the following sentences, if inserted at the beginning of Paragraph 4, would provide the best transition from Paragraph 3?

F. With none of our modern conveniences, such as gas and electric stoves, the Pilgrims needed far more time to prepare Thanksgiving dinner.
G. With so much food and such an extensive menu, it made sense for a Pilgrim host to invite as many guests as possible for Thanksgiving dinner.
H. At a Pilgrim's typical Thanksgiving dinner, the number of guests was often very large.
J. The other major difference between our Thanksgiving and the Pilgrims' Thanksgiving involves the guest list.

GO ON TO THE NEXT PAGE

57. A. NO CHANGE
B. guests in total
C. guests
D. guests altogether

58. Which of the following proposals for the underlined sentence would be most appropriate in the context of Paragraph 4 as a whole?
F. Revise the sentence as follows: *This number includes friends as well as family.*
G. Replace the sentence with the following: *As it turns out, this number is actually comparatively low.*
H. Move the sentence to the end of Paragraph 4.
J. Delete the sentence. (Do not replace it with any other sentence.)

59. A. NO CHANGE
B. the Pilgrims weren't expecting him to bring along to a little pot-luck supper another ninety Wampanoags
C. to a little pot-luck supper, the Pilgrims weren't expecting him to bring along another ninety Wampanoags
D. he wasn't expected by the Pilgrims to bring another ninety Wampanoags to a little pot-luck supper

Question 60 poses a question about the passage as a whole.

60. The writer wants to add a sentence that links the passage's opening and ending. If inserted at the end of the passage, which of the following sentences best achieves this objective?
F. So, instead of complaining about your duties as a Thanksgiving host, be thankful you aren't hosting the first Thanksgiving.
G. As it turns out, then, the dinner menu for the first Thanksgiving was not too extensive after all.
H. Compared to today's Thanksgiving hosts, the Pilgrims certainly had their hands full with the large number of guests for their first Thanksgiving.
J. The unexpected turnout for the first Thanksgiving makes today's typical Thanksgiving dinner look like an intimate gathering.

Passage V

A People's Art, for Good and Ill

[1]

During movies early years, [61] from about 1910 to 1940, the greatness of film as an art form is in [62] its own ingenuity and invention. And this greatness was not lost on the general public, as the numbers of avid moviegoers grew and grew during this time period. Between 1920 and 1930, a generation of filmmakers emerged [63] who were not failed novelists or unsuccessful playwrights but rather moviemakers—through and through. Their essential vision belonged to no other medium with the exception of the cinema, 64 and this is what made the early days of filmmaking so vital and exciting.

[2]

[65] Their public was a universal audience of ordinary people, spread across the world. Like the first dramas of Shakespeare, their art was not a product for the palace or the mansion, but rather for 66 the common playhouse where working people sat shoulder to shoulder with the middle class and the well-to-do. This is what gave the early movie makers the strength and freshness still perceived by us in their art. 67

[3]

(1) Today, movies are more popular than ever, and 68 box-office receipts for the great international hit films running into hundreds of millions of dollars. (2) Movies are becoming more and more conventional, unimaginative, and staler. 69 (3) However, there is a price to be paid for this democratic appeal to the common person. (4) The freshness of the early movie makers has been lost. [70]

[4]

The artist who serves an elite audience has 71 a known patron, or group of patrons, to satisfy. If he is strong enough, he can, like the painters of the Renaissance, mold their taste in the image of his own. This is 72 true of the greater and more resolute artists of the cinema, from Chaplin in the 1920s to Bergman and Antonioni in the 1960s. [73] The larger an audience 74 and the more costly the movies are to produce, the greater become the pressures brought to bear on the less conventional creator to make his work conform to the pattern of the more conventional creator.

61. A. NO CHANGE
B. During movies' early years,
C. During movie's early years,
D. During the early years of movies,

62. F. NO CHANGE
G. was
H. lay in
J. is

GO ON TO THE NEXT PAGE

63. A. NO CHANGE
B. Between 1920 and 1930 emerged a generation of filmmakers
C. Between 1920 and 1930, the emergence of a generation of filmmakers
D. A generation of filmmakers emerged between 1920 and 1930

64. F. NO CHANGE
G. other medium but the cinema,
H. medium with the exception of the cinema,
J. medium other than the cinema,

65. Which of the following clauses, if added to the beginning of the first sentence in Paragraph 2, would provide the most effective transition from Paragraph 1 to Paragraph 2?

A. First of all,
B. However,
C. Furthermore,
D. Without a doubt,

66. F. NO CHANGE
G. but of
H. but instead for
J. it was for

67. A. NO CHANGE
B. we still perceive in their art
C. still perceived in their art today
D. still perceived in their art by us

68. F. NO CHANGE
G. ever;
H. ever, but
J. ever, with

69. A. NO CHANGE
B. more stale
C. stale
D. even stale

70. Which of the following is the best order for the sentences in Paragraph 3?

F. 2, 1, 4, 3
G. 1, 2, 3, 4
H. 3, 1, 4, 2
J. 1, 3, 2, 4

71. A. NO CHANGE
B. has only
C. has had
D. only has

72. F. NO CHANGE
G. This can also be
H. Such an ability is
J. This image is

73. An editor has suggested that the writer insert a sentence at this point in order to provide a logical and effective connection between the sentence that would precede it and the sentence that would follow it. Which of the following sentences would best accomplish this objective?

A. These aren't the only cinematic artists who have been able to accomplish this; but, they are probably the most notable ones.
B. All three of these artists were able to satisfy the quirky tastes of their patrons while satisfying their own creative urges as well.
C. But, these artists were interested mainly in achieving artistic excellence, not in appealing to a mass audience.
D. The films of these artists were eventually seen by millions of people worldwide.

74. F. NO CHANGE
G. For large audiences
H. If the audiences are large
J. A larger audience

Question 75 poses a question about the passage as a whole.

75. An editor has commented that the writer has not ended the passage effectively. Considering the passage's overall structure and flow of information, which of the following would be the most effective course of action?

A. Switch the position of Paragraph 3 with the position of Paragraph 4.
B. Delete the sentence that is currently the last sentence of the passage.
C. Add the following sentence to the end of the passage: *The early years of moviemaking were indeed the best—for both the makers of films and their audiences.*
D. Replace the final sentence with the following: *Nevertheless, some of today's filmmakers have managed to produce movies with great mass appeal and that are highly creative.*

STOP

Math

60 Questions ■ Time—60 Minutes

Directions: Solve each problem; then, on your answer sheet, mark the oval corresponding to the correct answer.

Be careful not to spend too much time on any one question. Instead, solve as many problems as possible, and then use the remaining time to return to those questions you were unable to answer at first.

You may use a calculator on any problem in this test. However, some problems can best be solved without use of a calculator.

Note: Unless otherwise stated, you can assume that:

1. Diagrams that accompany problems are not necessarily drawn to scale.
2. All figures lie in the same plane.
3. The word "line" refers to a straight line (and lines that appear straight are straight).
4. The word "average" refers to arithmetic mean.

1. The number 40.5 is 1,000 times greater than which of the following numbers?

A. 0.405
B. 0.0405
C. 0.0450
D. 0.00405
E. 0.000405

2. Lyle's current age is 23 years, and Melanie's current age is 15 years. How many years ago was Lyle's age twice Melanie's age?

F. 16
G. 9
H. 8
J. 7
K. 5

3. If x is a real number, and if $x^3 = 100$, then x lies between which two consecutive integers?

A. 1 and 2
B. 2 and 3
C. 3 and 4
D. 4 and 5
E. 5 and 6

4. In the standard (x,y) coordinate plane below, which point has the coordinates $(4,-5)$?

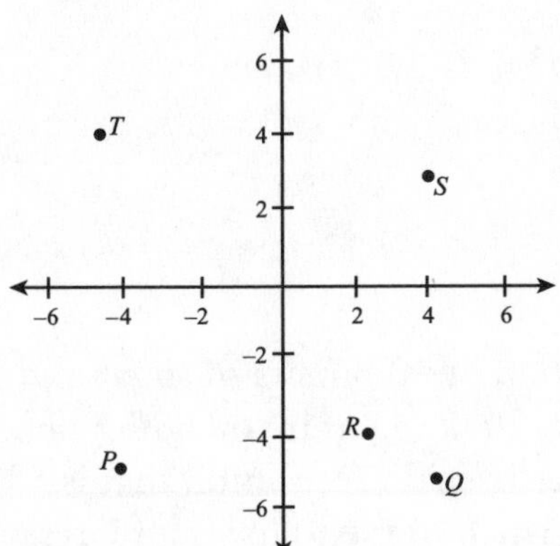

F. P
G. Q
H. R
J. S
K. T

5. A certain zoo charges exactly twice as much for an adult admission ticket as for a child's admission ticket. If the total admission price for the family of two adults and two children is $12.60, what is the price of a child's ticket?

A. $1.60
B. $2.10
C. $3.20
D. $3.30
E. $4.20

6. One marble is to be drawn randomly from a bag that contains three red marbles, two blue marbles, and one green marble. What is the probability of drawing a blue marble?

F. $\frac{1}{6}$
G. $\frac{1}{5}$
H. $\frac{2}{7}$
J. $\frac{1}{3}$
K. $\frac{2}{5}$

7. Point A bisects line segment $\overline{BC}$, and point D bisects line segment $\overline{BA}$. Which of the following congruencies holds?

A. $\overline{DC} \cong \overline{CB}$
B. $\overline{BA} \cong \overline{CB}$
C. $\overline{DC} \cong \overline{DA}$
D. $\overline{AD} \cong \overline{DB}$
E. $\overline{CA} \cong \overline{BC}$

8. If $\frac{2y}{9} = \frac{y-1}{3}$, then $y =$

F. $\frac{1}{3}$
G. $\frac{3}{5}$
H. $\frac{4}{9}$
J. $\frac{9}{4}$
K. 3

GO ON TO THE NEXT PAGE

9. $4\frac{1}{2} + 3\frac{3}{4} - 2\frac{2}{5} =$

A. $\frac{57}{10}$
B. $\frac{231}{40}$
C. $\frac{117}{20}$
D. $\frac{23}{4}$
E. $\frac{29}{5}$

10. If $a = 3$, $b = -3$, and $c = \frac{1}{3}$, then $ab^2c =$

F. -27
G. -1
H. 3
J. 9
K. 27

11. M is P% of what number?

A. $\frac{100M}{P}$
B. $\frac{100P}{M}$
C. $\frac{M}{100P}$
D. $\frac{P}{100M}$
E. $\frac{MP}{100}$

12. In the figure below, lines a and b are parallel, and lines c and d are parallel. What is the measure of $\angle x$?

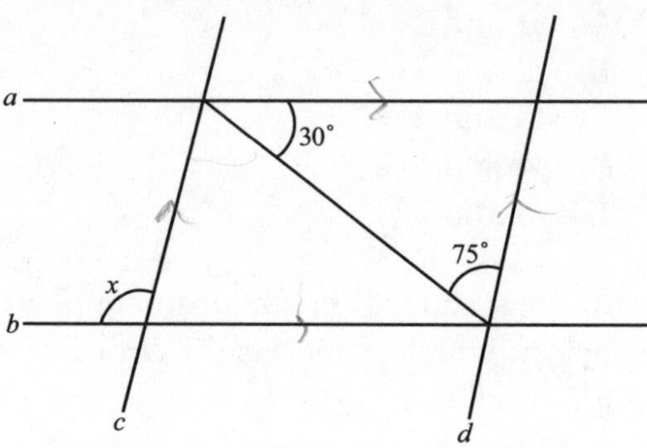

F. 75°
G. 95°
H. 100°
J. 105°
K. 115°

13. A solution of 60 ounces of sugar and water is 20% sugar. If you add x ounces of water to make a solution that is 5% sugar, which of the following represents the amount of sugar in the solution after adding water?

A. $60 - 40x$
B. $0.05(60x - 20)$
C. $0.05(60 + x)$
D. $0.20(60 + x)$
E. $60(0.05 + x)$

14. In the standard (x,y) coordinate plane, lines a and b intersect at point $(5,-2)$ and lines b and c intersect at point $(-3,3)$. What is the slope of line b?

F. $\frac{1}{2}$

G. $-\frac{5}{2}$

H. $-\frac{2}{5}$

J. $-\frac{5}{8}$

K. It cannot be determined from the information given.

15. In the figure below, M is the midpoint of $\overline{RS}$. What is the area of ΔMOP?

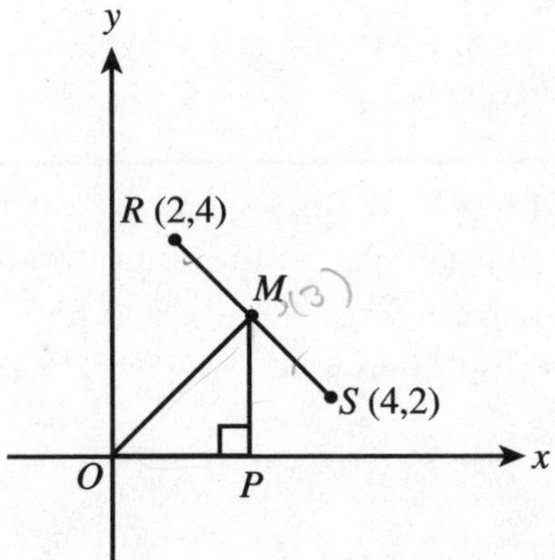

A. 4.5
B. 4
C. 3.5
D. 3
E. $2\sqrt{2}$

16. A photographic negative measures $1\frac{7}{8}$ inches by $2\frac{1}{2}$ inches. If the longer side of the printed picture is to be 4 inches, what will be the length of the shorter side of the printed picture?

F. $3\frac{1}{8}$ inches

G. 3 inches

H. $2\frac{3}{4}$ inches

J. $2\frac{1}{2}$ inches

K. $2\frac{3}{8}$ inches

17. Which of the following is the equation of a straight line that has y-intercept 3 and is perpendicular to the line $4x - 2y = 6$?

A. $2y + 3x = -3$
B. $y + 3x = 2$
C. $2y - x = 6$
D. $y - 2x = 4$
E. $2y + x = 6$

18. Of 60 pairs of socks in a drawer, 40% are blue, while the remaining socks are all gray. If 4 blue socks are removed from the drawer, what is the ratio of gray socks to blue socks?

F. 1:2
G. 5:9
H. 3:5
J. 9:5
K. 2:1

GO ON TO THE NEXT PAGE

19. On the (x,y) coordinate plane, what is the distance from the point defined by (5,4) and the point defined by (1,−2)?

A. $2\sqrt{5}$
B. $4\sqrt{3}$
C. $5\sqrt{2}$
D. $2\sqrt{13}$
E. $3\sqrt{6}$

20. Which of the following is NOT a member of the solution set for the equation $2x(3x - 1)(2x - 2)(x - 3) = 0$?

F. 3
G. 2
H. 1
J. $\frac{1}{3}$
K. 0

21. Which of the following best describes the graph on the number line below?

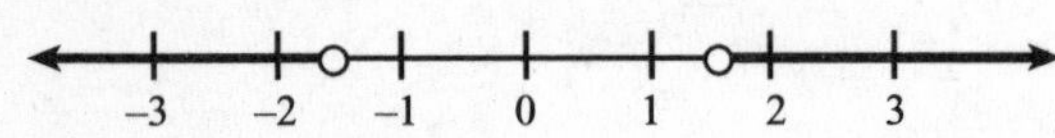

A. $|x| > 1.5$
B. $|x| < -1.5$
C. $-1.5 < |x| < 1.5$
D. $|x| > -1.5$
E. $|x| < 1.5$

22. $\sqrt{\frac{y^2}{2} - \frac{y^2}{18}} =$

F. 0
G. $\frac{10y}{3}$
H. $\frac{2y}{3}$
J. $\frac{y\sqrt{3}}{6}$
K. $\frac{y\sqrt{5}}{3}$

23. If $x + y = a$, and if $x - y = b$, then $x =$

A. $\frac{1}{2}(a + b)$
B. $a + b$
C. $a - b$
D. $\frac{1}{2}ab$
E. $\frac{1}{2}(a - b)$

24. If the equation $x^2 + 8x + s = 0$ has only one solution, then $s =$

F. −4
G. 0
H. 4
J. 8
K. 16

25. On the xy-coordinate plane, a point defined by the (x,y) pair $(m,2)$ lies on a circle with center (3,−1) and radius 5. Which of the following is a possible value of m?

A. 8
B. 6
C. −1
D. −2
E. −7

26. If the sides of a triangle are 8, 15, and 17 units long, what is the measure of the angle formed by the two shortest sides?

F. 30°
G. 45°
H. 60°
J. 75°
K. 90°

27. How many different ways can you add four positive odd integers together for a sum of 10, without considering the sequence of the integers?

A. Five
B. Four
C. Three
D. Two
E. One

28. The figure below shows right triangle *PQR*. What is the length of $\overline{QR}$?

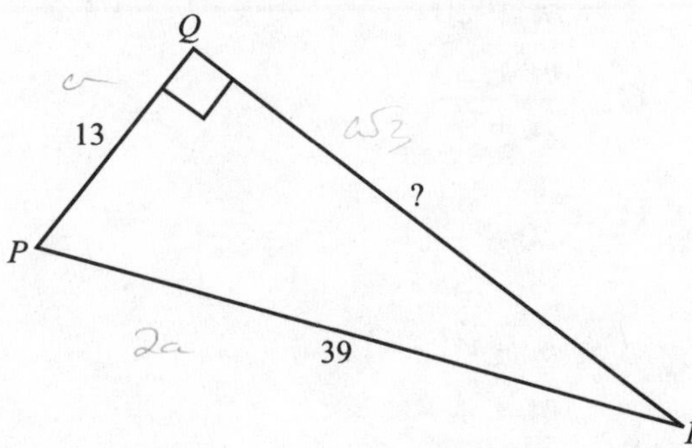

F. $13\sqrt{3}$

G. $\frac{39\sqrt{2}}{2}$

H. 26

J. 30

K. $26\sqrt{2}$

29. The average of five numbers is *A*. If a sixth number *n* is added, which of the following represents the average of all six numbers?

A. $\frac{6A - n}{5}$

B. $6A$

C. $A + \frac{n}{6}$

D. $\frac{5A + n}{6}$

E. $\frac{A \times n}{6}$

30. If two sides of a triangle are 6.5 and 8.5 inches long, which of the following cannot be the length of the third side?

F. 15 inches
G. 12 inches
H. 9.5 inches
J. 6.5 inches
K. 5.5 inches

31. Referring to the graph below, what was the greatest dollar amount by which the share price of ABC common stock exceeded the share price of XYZ common stock during Year X?

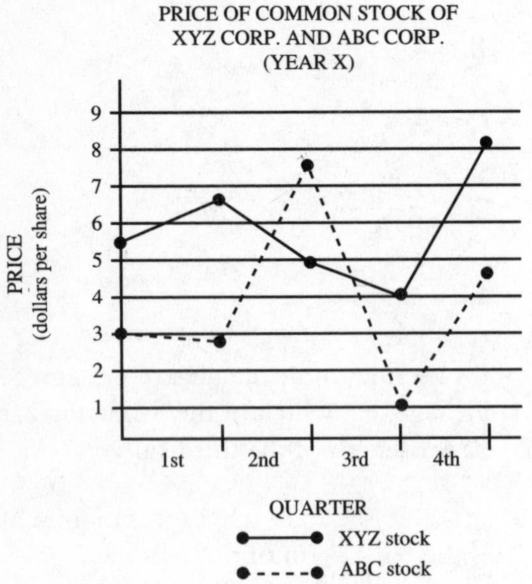

PRICE OF COMMON STOCK OF
XYZ CORP. AND ABC CORP.
(YEAR X)

PRICE
(dollars per share)

9
8
7
6
5
4
3
2
1

1st 2nd 3rd 4th

QUARTER

XYZ stock
ABC stock

A. \$1.80
B. \$2.60
C. \$3.00
D. \$3.60
E. It cannot be determined from the information given.

32. If x and y are negative integers, and if $x - y = 1$, what is the least possible value of xy?

F. 2
G. 1
H. 0
J. -1
K. -2

33. If $\sqrt{4x} = \sqrt{y}$, then in terms of y, $x =$

A. $2y$
B. $\frac{\sqrt{y}}{2}$
C. $\sqrt{y}$
D. y^2
E. $\frac{y}{4}$

34. The distance a moving object travels can be determined as the product of the object's rate of motion (r), or speed, and the amount of time (t) traveling. If a boat travels m miles in 4 hours, then an additional 20 miles in t hours, which of the following represents the boat's average speed, in miles per hour, over the total distance?

F. $\frac{t + 4}{m + 20}$
G. $\frac{m + 20}{t + 4}$
H. $\frac{tm}{20}$
J. $\frac{t + 20}{m + 4}$
K. $\frac{4tm}{5}$

35. In the figure below, if $\overline{AB} \parallel \overline{DC}$ and $\overline{AD} \parallel \overline{BC}$, what is the measure of $\angle ABD$?

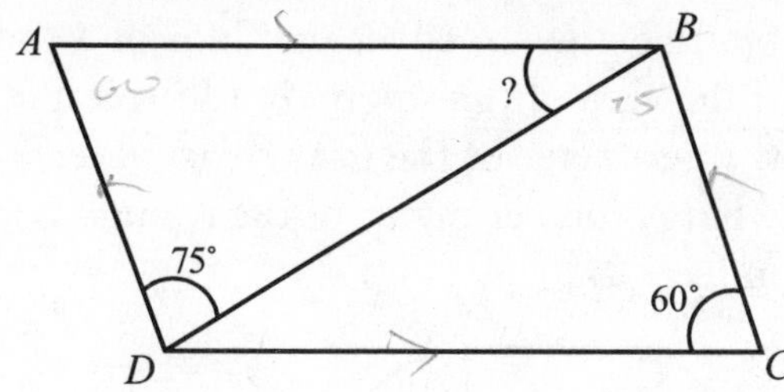

A. 40°
B. 45°
C. 50°
D. 55°
E. 60°

36. What is the value of m in the following system of two equations?

$4m = 12 - 3n$

$\frac{3}{4}n = 3 - m$

F. −6
G. −3
H. 2
J. 8
K. Any real number

37. If $A = \begin{bmatrix} -3 & 5 \\ 3 & 7 \end{bmatrix}$ and $B = \begin{bmatrix} 3 & 2 \\ -1 & 1 \end{bmatrix}$, then $2A - B =$

A. $\begin{bmatrix} -3 & 12 \\ 5 & 15 \end{bmatrix}$

B. $\begin{bmatrix} -9 & 8 \\ 5 & 13 \end{bmatrix}$

C. $\begin{bmatrix} -9 & 8 \\ 7 & 13 \end{bmatrix}$

D. $\begin{bmatrix} -6 & 3 \\ 4 & 6 \end{bmatrix}$

E. $\begin{bmatrix} -3 & 8 \\ 7 & 13 \end{bmatrix}$

38. In an arithmetic sequence, each successive term is either greater than or less than the preceding term by the same amount. What is the tenth term of the arithmetic sequence 30, 27, 24, . . . ?

F. 10
G. 3
H. 0
J. −3
K. −30

39. If $f(x) = 6^x$ and $g(x) = \log_6 x$, which of the following expressions is equal to $f(2g(M))$?

A. $2M$
B. 6^M
C. M^2
D. M^6
E. 6^{2M}

GO ON TO THE NEXT PAGE

40. The figure below shows a rectangular solid with the following unit dimensions: $\overline{QR} = 3$, $\overline{QS} = 4$, and $\overline{ST} = 5$. How many units long is $\overline{RT}$?

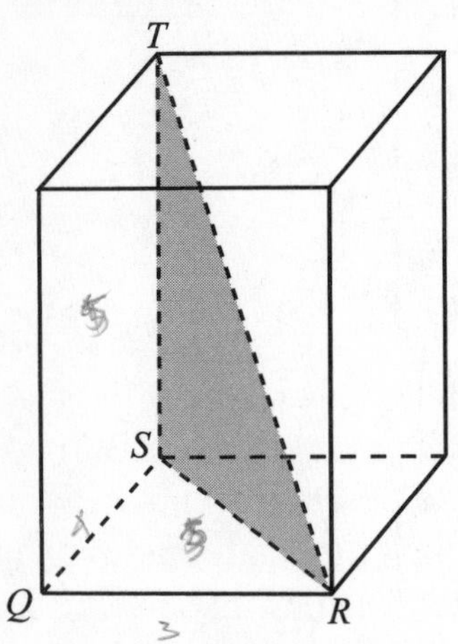

F. $4\sqrt{2}$
G. 6
H. $4\sqrt{3}$
J. 7
K. $5\sqrt{2}$

41. Two competitors battle each other in each match of a tournament with six participants. What is the minimum number of matches that must occur for every competitor to battle every other competitor?

A. 21
B. 18
C. 16
D. 15
E. 12

42. Three carpet pieces—in the shapes of a square, a triangle, and a semicircle—are attached to one another, as shown in the figure below, to cover the floor of a room. If the area of the square is 144 feet and the perimeter of the triangle is 28 feet, what is the perimeter of the room's floor, in feet?

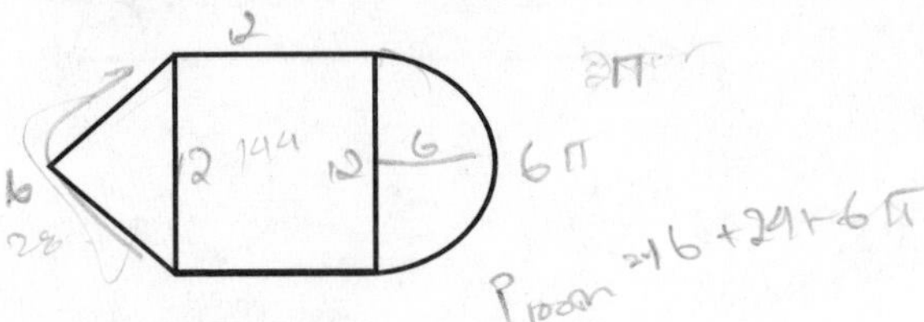

F. $32 + 12\pi$
G. $40 + 6\pi$
H. $34 + 12\pi$
J. $52 + 6\pi$
K. $52 + 12\pi$

43. ΔPQR below has angle measures 90, θ, and β degrees as shown. Which of the following is true for all possible values of θ and β?

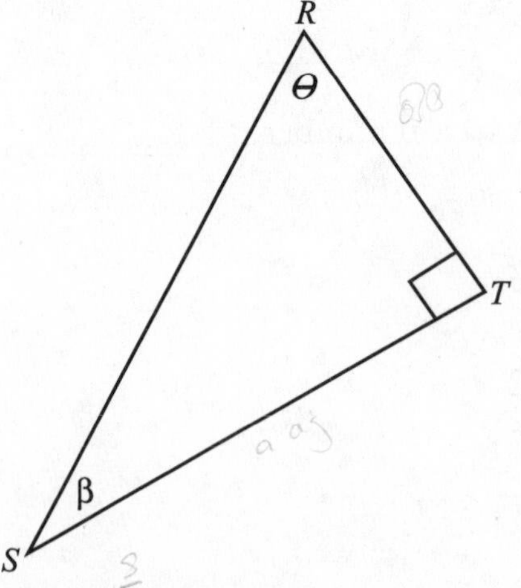

A. $\tan\theta = \tan\beta$
B. $\sin\theta + \cos\beta = 1$
C. $\sin\theta \times \cos\beta = 1$
D. $\tan\theta \times \tan\beta = 1$
E. $\sin\theta \tan\beta = \cos\beta$

44. Two ships leave from the same port at 11:30 a.m. If one sails due east at 24 miles per hour and the other due south at 10 miles per hour, how many miles apart are the ships at 2:30 p.m.?

F. 45
G. 62
H. 68
J. 78
K. 84

45. If the circumference of the circle pictured below is 16π units, what is the unit length of $\overline{AC}$?

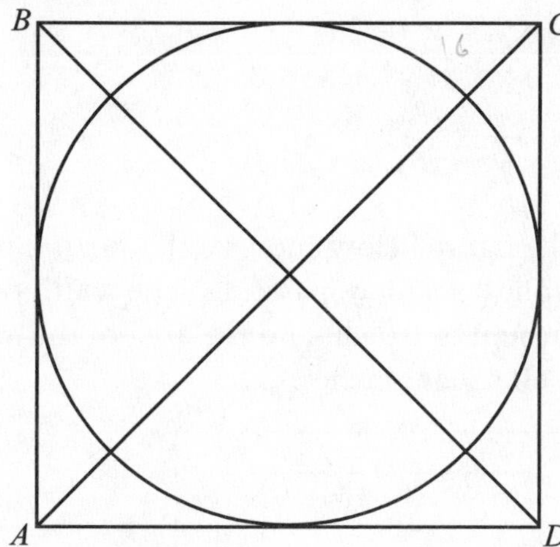

A. $4\sqrt{2}$
B. 16
C. $16\sqrt{2}$
D. 32
E. 16π

46. If $\sqrt{3x} = 6i$, then $x =$

F. 12
G. 6
H. 3
J. 2
K. -12

47. For all $x > 2$, $\dfrac{x^2 - 4}{x^2 - 2x} =$

A. $x - \dfrac{4}{x}$
B. $\dfrac{1}{2x}$
C. $1 + \dfrac{2}{x}$
D. $2 - x$
E. $2x - 1$

48. Events A, B, and C occur every 5 days, 3 days, and 8 days, respectively. What is the number of days after events A, B, and C all occur on the same day that they all occur again for the first time on the same day?

F. 45
G. 65
H. 80
J. 90
K. 120

49. If two of the angles of the polygon shown below are congruent, then $x =$

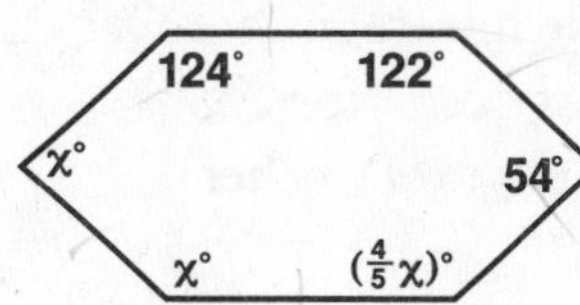

A. 78
B. 84
C. 120
D. 150
E. 174

50. If $x^2 + 2 = -4x$, what are the possible values of x?

F. $-4 \pm \sqrt{2}$
G. $-2 \pm \sqrt{2}$
H. $2 \pm \sqrt{2}$
J. $4 \pm \sqrt{2}$
K. $4 \pm 2\sqrt{2}$

51. A certain cube contains 125 cubic inches. What is the surface area, in square inches, of each square face of the cube?

A. 5
B. 10
C. 15
D. 20
E. 25

52. A certain clock runs 48 minutes slow every 12 hours. Four hours after the clock is set correctly, the correct time is 4:00. In how many minutes, to the nearest minute, will the clock show 4:00?

F. 13
G. 14
H. 15
J. 16
K. 17

53. The figure below shows a parabola in the standard (x,y) coordinate plane.

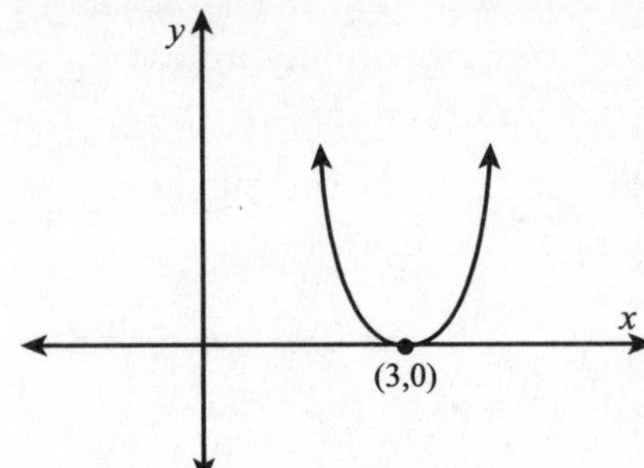

Which of the following equations does the graph best represent?

A. $y = x^2 + 3x + 9$
B. $y = x^2 - 2x + 6$
C. $y = -x^2 + x - 3$
D. $y = x^2 - 6x + 9$
E. $y = x^2 + 2x + 3$

54. The figure below shows a flat picture mat around a square painting. The width of the mat is 1 inch, and the area of the mat is 60 square inches.

What is the length, in inches, of one side of the painting?

F. 30
G. 24
H. 18
J. 14
K. 12

55. The altitude of a triangle is the distance from its base to the vertex opposite the base. If the length of the base (b) of a triangle and the triangle's altitude are equal in length, which of the following represents the area of the triangle?

A. $\frac{b^2}{2}$

B. $\frac{2b^2}{3}$

C. b^2

D. $4b$

E. $2b^2$

56. The graph of the equation $x = \frac{2}{y-2}$ is shown below.

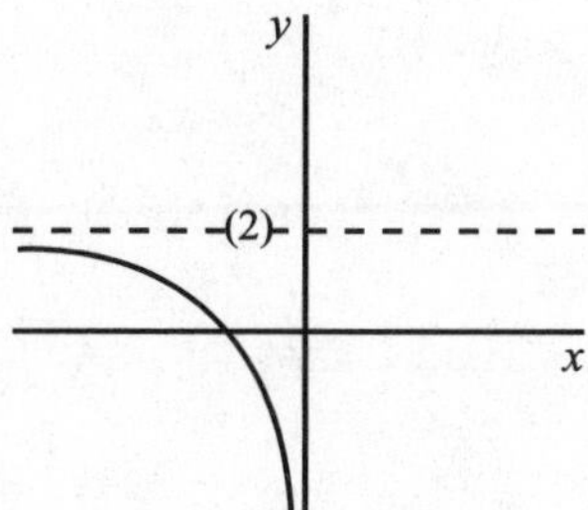

Which of the following best represents the equation $x = \left|\frac{2}{y-2}\right|$?

F.

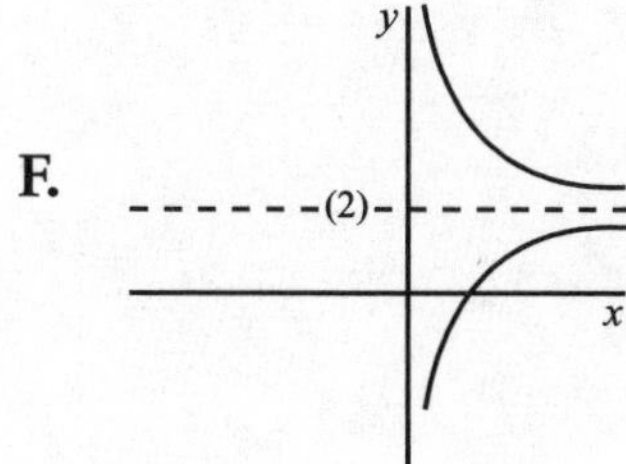

G.

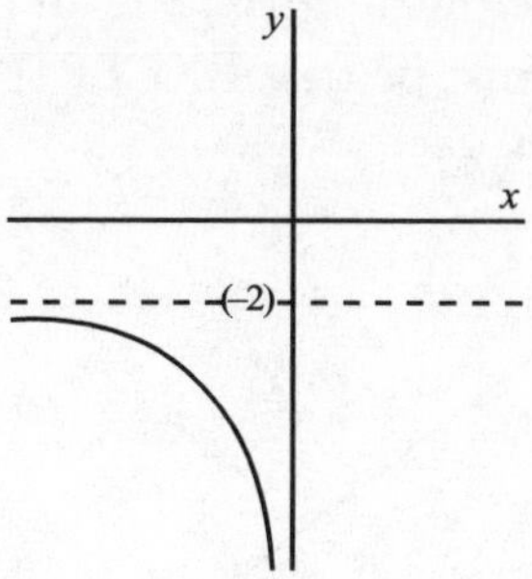

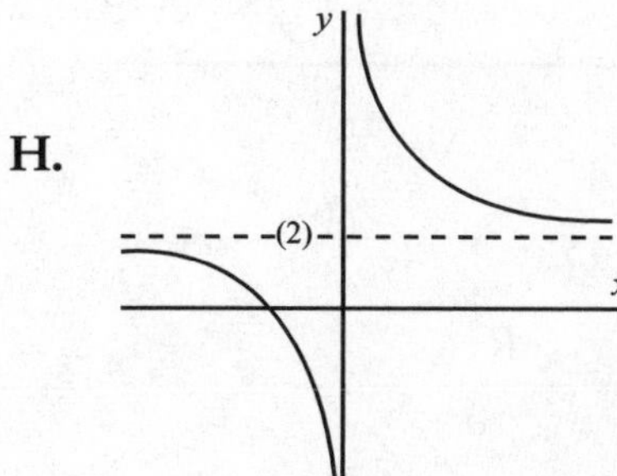

H.

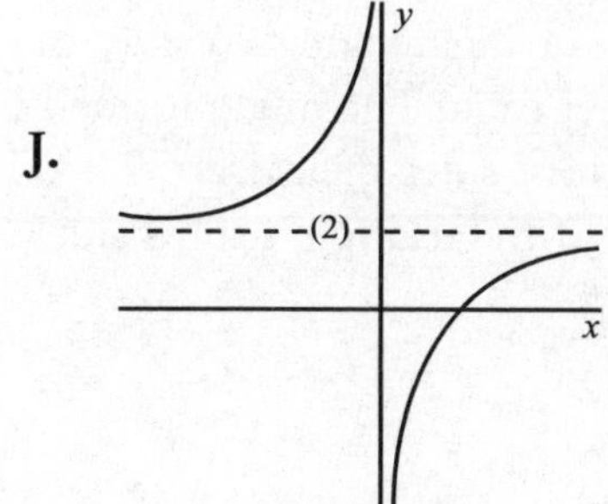

J.

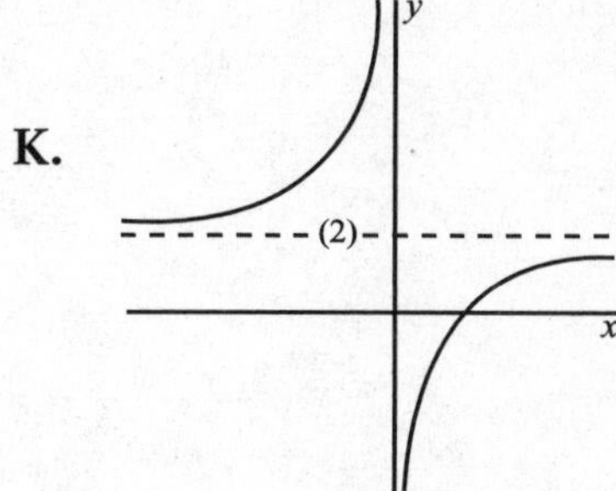

K.

57. In ΔPQR below, if $\tan x > 1$, all of the following must be true EXCEPT:

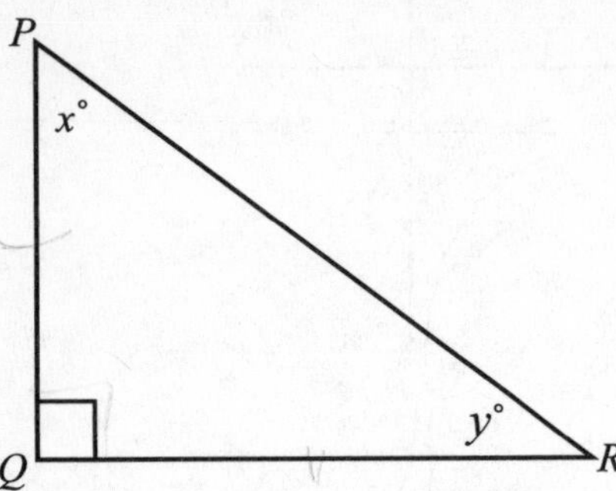

A. $x > 45$
B. $y > 45$
C. $\overline{PQ} \neq \overline{QR}$
D. $x + y = 90$
E. $x \neq y$

58. An isosceles triangle has two sides of length 3 feet each. The angle formed by the two 3-foot sides measures 32°. What is the length of the triangle's third side?

F. 3cos32°
G. 3sin32°
H. 3sin16°
J. 6tan16°
K. 6sin16°

59. If $m = n$ and $p > q$, then which of the following inequalities holds true in all cases?

A. $m - p > n - q$
B. $p - m < q - n$
C. $m - p < n - q$
D. $mp > nq$
E. $m + q > n + p$

60. In the standard (x,y) coordinate plane, the amplitude of a graph is half the distance between the graph's minimum and maximum y-values. What is the amplitude of the graph of the equation $y - 1 = 2\cos 3\theta$?

F. 6
G. 3
H. 2
J. $\frac{3}{2}$
K. 1

STOP

Reading

40 Questions ■ Time—35 Minutes

Directions: This test consists of four passages, each followed by several questions. Read each passage and select the best answer for each question following the passage. Then, on your answer sheet, mark the oval corresponding to the best answer.

Passage I—Prose Fiction

Although Bertha Young was thirty, she still had moments like this when she wanted to run instead of walk, to take dancing steps on and off the pavement, to bowl a hoop, to throw something up in the air and catch it again, or to stand still and laugh at—nothing—at nothing, simply.

What can you do if you are thirty and, turning the corner of your own street, you are overcome, suddenly, by a feeling of bliss—absolute bliss!—as though you'd suddenly swallowed a bright piece of that late afternoon sun and it burned in your bosom, sending out a little shower of sparks into every particle, into every finger and toe. . . ?

Oh, is there no way you can express it without being "drunk and disorderly?" How idiotic civilization is! Why be given a body if you have to keep it shut up in a case like a rare, rare fiddle?

"No, that about the fiddle is not quite what I mean," she thought, running up the steps and feeling in her bag for the key—she'd forgotten it, as usual—and rattling the letter-box. "It's not what I mean, because—Thank you, Mary"—she went into the hall. "Is nurse back?"

"Yes, M'm."

"I'll go upstairs." And she ran upstairs to the nursery.

Nurse sat at a low table giving Little B her supper after her bath. The baby had on a white flannel gown and a blue woolen jacket, and her dark, fine hair was brushed up into a funny little peak. She looked up when she saw her mother and began to jump.

"Now, my lovey, eat it up like a good girl," said Nurse, setting her lips in a way that Bertha knew, and that meant she had come into the nursery at another wrong moment.

"Has she been good, Nanny?"

"She's been a little sweet all the afternoon," whispered Nanny. "We went to the park and I sat down on a chair and took her out of the carriage and a big dog came along and put its head on my knee and she clutched its ear, tugged it. Oh, you should have seen her."

Bertha wanted to ask if it wasn't rather dangerous to let her clutch at a strange dog's ear. But she did not dare to. She stood watching them, her hands by her side, like the poor little girl in front of the rich little girl with the doll.

The baby looked up at her again, stared, and then smiled so charmingly that Bertha couldn't help crying:

"Oh, Nanny, do let me finish giving her supper while you put the bath things away."

"Well, M'm, she oughtn't to be changed hands while she's eating," said Nanny, still whispering. "It unsettles her; it's very likely to upset her."

How absurd it was. Why have a baby if it has to be kept—not in a case like a rare, rare fiddle—but in another woman's arms?

"Oh, I must!" said she.

Very offended, Nanny handed her over.

"Now, don't excite her after her supper. You know you do, M'm. And I have such a time with her after!"

Thank heaven! Nanny went out of the room with the bath towels.

"Now I've got you to myself, my little precious," said Bertha, as the baby leaned against her.

She ate delightfully, holding up her lips for the spoon and then waving her hands. Sometimes she wouldn't let the spoon go; and sometimes, just as Bertha had filled it, she waved it away to the four winds.

When the soup was finished Bertha turned round to the fire.

"You're nice—you're very nice!" said she, kissing her warm baby. "I'm fond of you. I like you."

And, indeed, she loved Little B so much—her neck as she bent forward, her exquisite toes as they shone transparent in the firelight—that all her feeling of bliss came back again, and again she didn't know how to express it—what to do with it.

"You're wanted on the telephone," said Nanny, coming back in triumph and seizing *her* Little B.

1. Based on the passage, Bertha can reasonably be considered to be all of the following EXCEPT:

- **A.** imaginative.
- **B.** affectionate.
- **C.** timid.
- **D.** arrogant.

2. Nanny's facial expression upon seeing Bertha's arrival in the nursery suggests:

- **F.** relief as she can at last eat her supper.
- **G.** a vain attempt to suppress her joy at seeing Bertha.
- **H.** dislike for Bertha's ill-timed visits to the nursery.
- **J.** fear of dismissal from her job because the nursery is untidy.

3. Bertha uses the metaphor of a "rare, rare fiddle" (line 22) to suggest that:

- **A.** she considers her baby girl an extraordinary child.
- **B.** she is frustrated by not feeling free to express her musical talents.
- **C.** people of a certain age are expected to follow a certain code of behavior.
- **D.** wealthy mothers are not allowed to look after their children.

4. Nanny would most likely agree with which of the following characterizations of Bertha?
   F. She is a thoughtless person and an inexperienced mother.
   G. She is a kind employer but a strict mother.
   H. She is forgetful and has no sense of class distinctions in society.
   J. She is giddy and is always lost in her overactive imaginings.

5. Which of the following statements about the relationship between Bertha and Nanny do the details in the passage best support?
   A. Nanny is tired of working for Bertha and would like to find other employment.
   B. Bertha feels that Nanny is a competent nurse and would do anything to keep her on.
   C. Nanny considers herself the baby's primary caregiver and Bertha just an occasional visitor in the baby's life.
   D. Bertha prefers to give over control of the child to Nanny so that she is able to fulfill her inappropriate youthful fantasies.

6. It can most reasonably be inferred that the word *absurd*, as it is used in line 69, refers to:
   F. Nanny's overly possessive attitude towards the baby.
   G. the fact that women over 30 cannot be impulsive in behavior.
   H. Bertha's not being able to question Nanny's decision to let Little B play with a dog.
   J. the fact that Bertha is obligated to have a nanny to take care of her child.

7. In comparing Bertha to a "poor little girl" (line 57), the narrator is suggesting that Bertha:
   A. lacks emotional and psychological strength.
   B. is deprived of care-giving time with her baby.
   C. suffers from an unrealistic hope of having more babies.
   D. desires a closer relationship with Nanny.

8. It can be reasonably inferred from the passage that the central characteristic of Nanny is:
   F. kindness.
   G. disrespectfulness.
   H. jealousy.
   J. possessiveness.

9. Based on the passage, the kind of bliss that Bertha experienced, as described in the first three paragraphs, can best be described as a(n):
   A. emotion brought forth by a walk in the park.
   B. pleasant feeling caused by nothing specific.
   C. overwhelming feeling of maternal love.
   D. tingling feeling in one's fingers and toes.

10. From the use of the word "triumph" in the last paragraph, it is reasonable to infer that Nanny is:
   F. happy to have Little B and the nursery to herself again.
   G. glad that Little B has been able to spend some time with her mother.
   H. feeling justified in her total control of all matters pertaining to the nursery.
   J. glad because the phone call was about another baby being put under her charge.

Passage II—Social Studies

After the opening of the Erie Canal in 1825, the Legislature of New York directed a land survey for a state railroad that was to be constructed, at public expense, through the southern tier of counties from the Hudson River to Lake Erie. The unfavorable profile that the survey indicated apparently prompted the legislature to abandon the project.

But, the notion of an east-to-west railroad spanning nearly the entire breadth of the state continued to hold sway over the minds of many New Yorkers, and the significant benefits that the Erie Canal had brought to the Mohawk Valley and surrounding country led the southern counties to demand a rail route that would work similar wonders in that region. This growing sentiment finally persuaded the legislature to charter, in April 1832, the New York and Erie Railroad Company, and to give it authority to construct tracks and regulate its own charges for transportation.

During the following summer, a partial survey of the route was made by Colonel De Witt Clinton Jr., and in 1834 a second survey was made of the whole of the proposed route. When the probable cost was estimated, opposition to the project grew. Many detractors asserted that the undertaking was "chimerical, impractical, and useless." The road, they declared, could never be built and, if built, would never be used; the southern counties were mountainous, sterile, and worthless, and afforded no products requiring a market; and, in any case, these counties should find their natural outlet in the valley of the Mohawk. Despite this opposition, in 1836, construction of the railroad began.

The Panic of 1837, which precipitated a major economic depression in the U.S., interfered with the work, but in 1838 the state legislature provided a construction loan of $3 million, and the first section of line, extending from Piermont on the Hudson to Goshen, was put in operation in September of 1841. In the following year, however, the company became insolvent and was placed by the courts in the hands of government receivers. This financial disaster delayed further progress for several years, and it was not until 1846 that sufficient new capital was raised to continue the work.

The original estimate for building the entire line of 485 miles had been $3 million, but already the road had cost over $6 million, and only a small portion had been completed. The final estimate now rose to $15 million, and, although some money was raised from time to time and new sections were built, whether the entire road would ever be competed was far from certain.

Ultimately, however, the courts allowed the company's assets out of receivership, and the company soon secured new subscriptions of some millions of dollars, while raising additional money by mortgaging the sections of railroad already finished. Finally, in 1851, after eighteen years of effort, the line was opened to Lake Erie. Various feeders, or branches, were also added, providing rail entry into Scranton, Pennsylvania, as well as Geneva and Buffalo, New York. The railroad's western terminus, at Lake Erie, was at Dunkirk, while its eastern terminus was at Piermont, near Nyack on the Hudson, about 25 miles by boat from New York City.

In the end, even the highest cost estimate of $15 million, made during construction, turned out far too low. The company started its operations in 1851 with capital obligations of no less than $26 million—an outrageously large sum for those days. When the Erie Railroad began operations, the heavy burden of these initial obligations soon became apparent. Freight rates were so high that indignant shippers began banning together in mutual support, and en masse appealed to the state for legislative relief. And, although the company had raised a substantial amount of money for improvements after 1849, the condition of the railway, and the reputation of the company, steadily declined. The Erie Railroad soon became notorious for its many accidents, some due to carelessness in the running of trains, others due to the breaking of the brittle iron rails.

In spite of these problems, the business of the Erie grew. In 1852, it acquired the Ramapo, Paterson, and Hudson River Railroads, thereby securing a more direct connection with New York City.

11. It can be inferred from the passage that the Erie Railroad cost approximately:

A. $36 million.
B. $26 million.
C. $15 million.
D. $3 million.

12. As it is used in the passage, the word *subscriptions* (line 72) most nearly means:

F. an agreement to order a specified number of issues of a newspaper.
G. receiving discounted tickets for a series of railway trips.
H. contributions of a specified amount to a project.
J. a membership fee paid regularly.

13. Which of the following statements best describes the author's method and purpose for addressing his subject?

A. Presenting a comparative history of railroads to justify the success story of the Erie Railroad
B. Constructing an argument for the construction of the Erie Railroad based on the sentiment of the people of the state of New York
C. Presenting the author's own personal experience in the field of railway construction in order to acquaint the reader with the financial hurdles faced by the Erie Railroad project
D. Presenting a series of researched facts in order to provide a detailed chronological history of the Erie Railroad

14. Based on the passage, it can be reasonably inferred that the most remote connecting points of the Erie Railroad were at:

F. Lake Erie and New York City.
G. Lake Erie and Piermont on the Hudson.
H. the cities of Geneva and Buffalo.
J. Mohawk Valley and Lake Erie.

15. Opponents of the Erie Railroad project provided all of the following reasons in arguing against constructing the Erie Railroad EXCEPT:

A. cost estimates were too high.
B. the proposed route was through extremely rough terrain.
C. there weren't enough marketable products along the proposed route.
D. interest in a connection to Lake Erie was insufficient.

16. How long after construction of the Erie Railroad began did it take for the railroad to first reach Lake Erie?

F. 3 years
G. 10 years
H. 18 years
J. 30 years

17. In the context of the passage, the word *insolvent* (line 53) most nearly means:

A. incapable of being solved.
B. unable to pay debts.
C. unable to distribute.
D. incapable of showing profit.

18. The fact that construction of the railroad continued despite the Panic of 1837 was due primarily to:

F. the raising of additional money by the Erie Railroad Company.
G. a loan from the Legislature of New York.
H. the acquisition of feeders to the main line.
J. a court order allowing construction to proceed.

19. It can be reasonably inferred from the passage that the Erie Railroad Company developed an unfavorable reputation because of its:

A. many accidents.
B. high freight rates.
C. bankruptcy.
D. lack of connecting lines.

20. The passage provides clearest support for which of the following statements?

F. Constructing the Erie Railroad is a remarkable feat of engineering.
G. The construction of the Erie Railroad was a disaster of unimaginable proportions.
H. Subsequent surveys changed the planned route during construction.
J. The proposed route for the railroad was successfully completed and expanded upon.

Passage III—Humanities

On July 1, 1882, a brief notice appeared in the *Portsmouth* (England) *Evening News*. It read simply, "Dr. Doyle begs to notify that he has removed to 1, Bush Villas, Elm Grove, next to the Bush Hotel." So was announced the newly formed medical practice of a 23-year-old graduate of Edinburgh University—Arthur Conan Doyle. But the town of Southsea, the Portsmouth suburb in which Doyle had opened his office, already had several well-established physicians, and while he waited for patients the young Dr. Doyle found himself with a great deal of time on his hands.

To fill it, he began writing—short stories, historical novels, whatever would keep him busy and, hopefully, bring additional funds into his sparsely filled coffers. By the beginning of 1886, his practice had grown to the point of providing him with a respectable if not munificent income, and he had managed to have a few pieces published. Although literary success still eluded him, he had developed an idea for a new book, a detective story, and in March he began writing the tale that would give birth to one of literature's most enduring figures.

Although he was familiar with and impressed by the fictional detectives created by Edgar Allan Poe, Emile Gaboriau, and Wilkie Collins, Doyle believed he could create a different kind of detective, one for whom detection was a science rather than an art. As a model, he used one of his medical school professors, Dr. Joseph Bell. As Bell's assistant, Doyle had seen how, by exercising his powers of observation and deduction and asking a few questions, Bell had been able not only to diagnose his patients' complaints but also to accurately determine their professions and backgrounds. A detective who applied similar intellectual powers to the solving of criminal mysteries could be a compelling figure, Doyle felt.

At first titled *A Tangled Skein*, the story was to be told by his detective's companion, a Dr. Ormand Sacker, and the detective himself was to be named Sherrinford Holmes. But by April, 1886, when Doyle finished the manuscript, the title had become *A Study in Scarlet*, the narrator Dr. John H. Watson, and the detective Mr. Sherlock Holmes.

A tale of revenge, in which Holmes is able to determine that two Mormons visiting England from Utah have been killed by Jefferson Hope, an American working as a London hansom cab driver, *A Study in Scarlet* was rejected by several publishers before being accepted that fall for publication by Ward, Lock & Company as part of *Beeton's Christmas Annual* in 1887. Although the author asked to be paid a royalty based on sale of the book, his publisher offered instead only a flat fee of £25 for the copyright (the equivalent of approximately $50 today). Doyle reluctantly accepted.

A handful of reviewers commented kindly on the story, but the reading public as a whole was unimpressed. Ward, Lock published *A Study in Scarlet* in book form the following year, while the disappointed author returned to his historical novels, with which he had finally achieved some modest success. Fictional detection, Doyle thought, was behind him. In August, 1889, however, he was approached by the editor of the American *Lippincott's Monthly Magazine*, published in Philadelphia and London, to write another Sherlock Holmes story. Although he had little interest in continuing Holmes's adventures, Doyle was still in need of money and accepted the offer.

Published in *Lippincott's* in February, 1890, and in book form later that year, *The Sign of the Four* chronicled Holmes's investigation of the murder of Bartholomew Sholto and his search for Jonathan Small and a treasure stolen by British soldiers in India. It too, however, met with little enthusiasm from the public. In the meantime, however, Doyle's other small literary successes had enabled him to move to London, where he became a consulting physician. Fortunately, even this new London practice did not keep him very busy,

GO ON TO THE NEXT PAGE

leaving him time to concentrate on his writing.

In April, 1891, he submitted a short Sherlock Holmes story, "A Scandal in Bohemia," to a new magazine called *The Strand*. It was with the publication of this story, and the series of Holmes tales which followed, that the public finally took an interest in Dr. Doyle's detective, enabling him to give up his practice and turn to writing full time. Despite his own continuing lack of enthusiasm for his protagonist—he considered the Holmes stories insignificant compared to his "serious" historical novels—spurred by the public clamor for more Sherlock Holmes, Doyle eventually wrote 56 short stories and four novels in the series, and in the process created what may be the best-known character in all of English literature.

21. As it is used in the passage, the word *munificent* (line 24) most nearly means:

A. noble.
B. sparse.
C. bountiful.
D. extra.

22. According to the passage, the public finally expressed an interest in Dr. Doyle's detective fiction stories after they were published in:

F. *Beeton's Christmas Annual.*
G. *Portsmouth Evening News.*
H. *The Strand.*
J. *Lippincott's Monthly Magazine.*

23. It can be inferred from the passage that Dr. Doyle could be appropriately described as any of the following EXCEPT a(n):

A. doctor who was less than fully devoted to a career in medical.
B. writer passionate about his fictional detective Sherlock Holmes.
C. writer who considered his historical novels to be of some importance.
D. author who was open-minded to publication of his works in America.

24. What set Dr. Doyle's detective fiction apart from previously published detective fiction?

F. His fictional detection was firmly based on scientific methodology.
G. He always based his protagonists on the exploits of Americans living abroad.
H. Most of his fictional detection was based on the solving of real mysteries.
J. His detective stories were based primarily on medical mysteries.

25. Among the following, who was Doyle's biggest influence in the creation of his fictional detective Sherlock Holmes?

A. Doyle's publicist
B. A police detective in Southsea
C. Dr. Joseph Bell
D. Edgar Allan Poe

26. According to the passage, Doyle started writing because:

- **F.** he had always been fascinated by murder mysteries.
- **G.** he hoped to stay occupied and make extra money.
- **H.** he had always aspired to be a famous author.
- **J.** there were too many physicians in Southsea.

27. The author of the passage uses the word *fortunately* in line 104 in order to suggest that:

- **A.** consulting physicians in London are typically too busy to engage in hobbies such as writing.
- **B.** it would have been in Doyle's best interest at the time to concentrate on his medical practice.
- **C.** Doyle was convinced at that time that his literary career was destined for success.
- **D.** Doyle's literary career was more important than his medical career.

28. Based on the passage, it can be most reasonably inferred that Doyle moved to London because:

- **F.** he could finally afford to reside there.
- **G.** he wanted to practice medicine in a larger town with more opportunities.
- **H.** of the many opportunities there to earn supplemental income.
- **J.** his publisher was based in London.

29. It can be inferred from the passage that Doyle abandoned his medical career primarily because of the:

- **A.** success of his historical novels.
- **B.** increase in demand for more of Holmes's adventures.
- **C.** large number of medical practitioners in London.
- **D.** lack of interest in medical journals among publishers.

30. At a minimum, about how long had Doyle been writing fictional stories before the public began to take a strong interest in any of his stories?

- **F.** Two years
- **G.** Five years
- **H.** Seven years
- **J.** Nine years

Passage IV—Natural Science

[*The following passage discusses the difficulties involved in identifying common causes for community cancer clusters.*]

Line Community cancer clusters are localized patterns of excessive cancer occurrence. They are viewed quite differently by citizen activists than by epidemiologists. Environmentalists and concerned local residents, for instance, might immediately suspect environmental radiation as the culprit when a high incidence of cancer cases occurs near a nuclear facility. Epidemiologists, in contrast, would be more likely to say that the incidences were "inconclusive" or the result of pure chance. And when a breast cancer survivor, Lorraine Pace, mapped twenty breast cancer cases occurring in her West Islip, Long Island, community, her rudimentary research efforts were guided more by hope—that a specific environmental agent could be correlated with the cancers—than by scientific method.

When epidemiologists study clusters of cancer cases and other noncontagious conditions such as birth defects or miscarriage, they take several variables into account, such as background rate (the number of people affected in the general population), cluster size, and specificity (any notable characteristics of the individual affected in each case). If a cluster is both large and specific, it is easier for epidemiologists to assign blame. Not only must each variable be considered on its own, but it must also be combined with others. Lung cancer is very common in the general population. Yet when a huge number of cases turned up among World War II shipbuilders who had all worked with asbestos, the size of the cluster and the fact that the men had had similar occupational asbestos exposures enabled epidemiologists to assign blame to the fibrous mineral.

Furthermore, even if a cluster seems too small to be analyzed conclusively, it may still yield important data if the background rate of the condition is low enough. This was the case when cervical cancer turned up almost simultaneously in a half-dozen young women. While six would seem to be too small a cluster for meaningful study, the cancer had been reported only once or twice before in the entire medical literature. Researchers eventually found that the mothers of all the afflicted women had taken the drug diethylstilbestrol (DES) while pregnant.

Although several known carcinogens have been discovered through these kinds of occupational or medical clusters, only one community cancer cluster has ever been traced to an environmental cause.

Health officials often discount a community's suspicion of a common environmental cause because citizens tend to include cases that were diagnosed before the afflicted individuals moved into the neighborhood. Add to this the problem of cancer's latency. Unlike an infectious disease like cholera, which is caused by a recent exposure to food or water contaminated with the cholera bacterium, cancer may have its roots in an exposure that occurred ten to twenty years earlier. Citizens also conduct what one epidemiologist calls "epidemiological gerrymandering": finding cancer cases, drawing a boundary around them, and then mapping this as a cluster.

Do all these caveats mean that the hard work of Lorraine Pace and other community activists is for naught? Not necessarily. Together with many other reports of breast cancer clusters on Long Island, the West Islip situation highlighted by Pace has helped epidemiologists lay the groundwork for a well-designed scientific study.

31. It can be inferred from the passage that community cancer clusters refer to cancer patterns existing in a:

A. particular religious community.
B. communal living environment.
C. particular geographic location.
D. specific part of the human body.

32. As it is used in the passage, the word *rudimentary* (line 17) most nearly means:

F. healthy.
G. basic.
H. scientific.
J. rigorous.

33. What led the epidemiologists to conclude that asbestos exposure causes lung cancer (lines 41–42) was a combination of all of the following EXCEPT:

A. the number of cases of lung cancer was large.
B. all the people affected were World War II shipbuilders.
C. spouses of asbestos workers did not typically develop lung cancer.
D. all the case subjects were men who had worked with asbestos.

34. The case of six young women with cervical cancer (lines 47–49) is an example of a cluster that has a:

F. high background rate and small size.
G. low background rate and is nonspecific.
H. high background rate and is fairly specific.
J. low background rate and is fairly specific.

35. Based on the information in the second paragraph (lines 21–43), which of the following can most reasonably be inferred about cancer and birth defects?

A. The size of the cluster of people affected is similar in both.
B. Both are caused by the same virus.
C. Cancer victims and people with birth defects have similar backgrounds.
D. Both are impossible to transmit by contact.

36. Which of the following would be most similar to "epidemiological gerrymandering," which the author describes in the fourth paragraph (lines 76–77)?

F. A politician's changing voting district boundaries to gain advantage for elections
G. A census report's correlating statistical data according to gender and race
H. A school's redistributing students according to their academic qualifications to different grades
J. A professor's declaring the result of her student's research "inconclusive" due to lack of sufficient environmental variables

37. Health officials tend to discount the work of citizens involved in mapping cancer clusters partly because citizens often:

A. fail to investigate the background of individual case subjects.
B. fail to gather data from a broad enough geographical area.
C. overemphasize individual characteristics of the cases.
D. discount occupational hazards specific to each case.

38. It can be reasonably inferred from the information in the second paragraph (lines 21–43) that one of the highest background rates in cancer studies is for:

F. cervical cancer.
G. lung cancer.
H. breast cancer.
J. bone cancer.

GO ON TO THE NEXT PAGE

39. The author's main objective in the passage is to:

- **A.** discuss the response of epidemiologists to a cancer threat in a community.
- **B.** inform the reader of Lorraine Pace's activism in West Islip.
- **C.** discuss the difficulties involved in identifying common causes of community cancer clusters.
- **D.** explain the relevance of environmental agents in the study of community cancer clusters.

40. At the end of the passage, the author concludes that:

- **F.** community cancer clusters are viewed differently by citizen activists, who are hindered by preconceptions, than by health officials.
- **G.** the efforts of ordinary citizens can help scientists determine the causes of community cancer clusters.
- **H.** health officials need the help of concerned citizens in order to determine the causes of community cancer clusters.
- **J.** local residents sometimes hinder the progress of scientific research by pushing for a quick resolution.

STOP

Science

40 Questions ■ Time—35 Minutes

Directions: This test consists of seven passages, each followed by several questions. Read each passage and select the best answer for each question following the passage. Then, on your answer sheet, mark the oval corresponding to the best answer. You may NOT use a calculator on this test.

Passage I

Lake ecosystems are highly sensitive to changes in acid-base balance, also referred to as *pH level*. Growing concern over the last few decades about increases in lake sulfate concentrations and pH has led to an environmental campaign to reduce the amount of sulfates released into the atmosphere from industrial sources. To determine the impact of sulfates on some lake ecosystems, ecologists conducted two experiments in a particular alpine area.

In order to take into account changing climatic parameters in the study area, the researchers first looked at rainfall and temperature since 1900. The results appear in Figure 1.

Figure 1

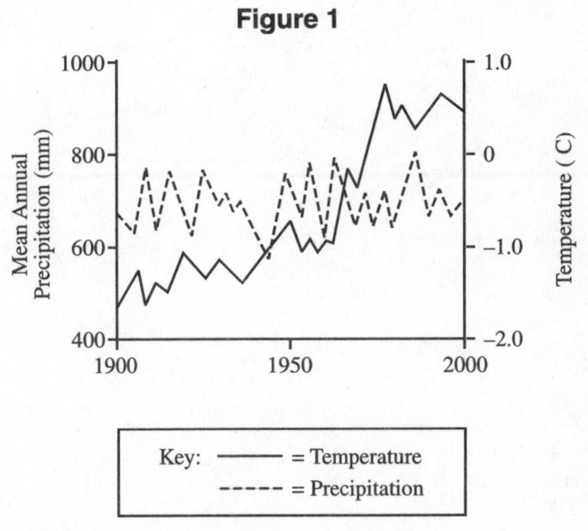

Experiment 1

Ecologists measured the terrestrial deposition (land deposits) of sulfate at five alpine stations located adjacent to five particular lakes annually from 1993 to 2000. Sulfate was measured in soil and rock samples. The averages for two-year sampling periods appear in Table 1 on page 422.

Table 1

Lakes	Sulphate Concentration (Mg/L) 1993–94	1995–96	1997–98	1999–2000
1	0.65	0.60	0.60	0.59
2	0.60	0.59	0.58	0.50
3	0.82	0.82	0.80	0.69
4	0.89	0.69	0.66	0.66
5	0.68	0.65	0.67	0.69

Experiment 2

In 2000, researchers looked at the sulfate concentrations (in equivalents/L) and pH in the lakes adjacent to the alpine stations and compared them to concentrations recorded in the same lakes in 1993. Results appear in Figure 2.

Figure 2

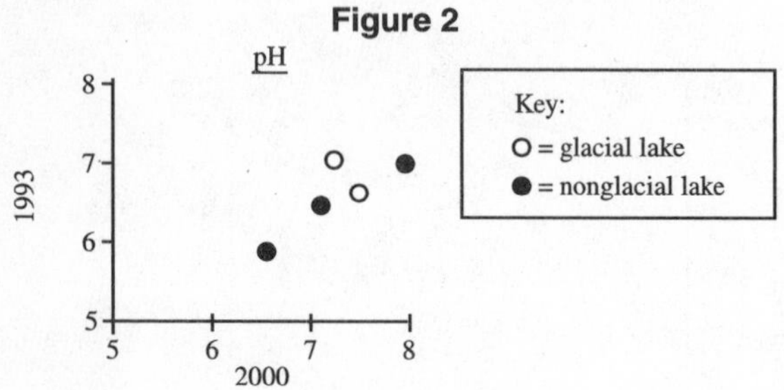

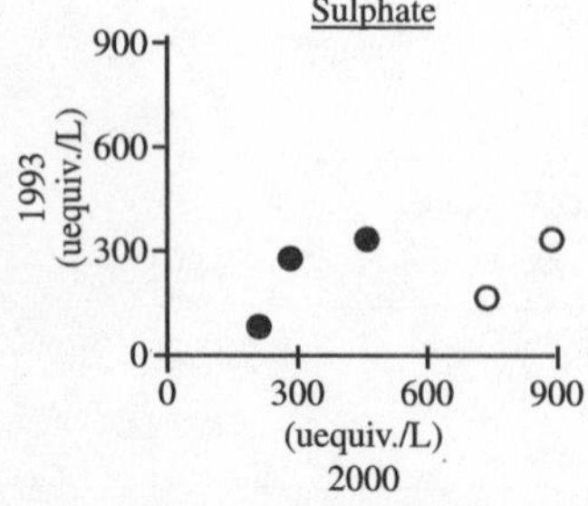

1. At which alpine station did terrestrial sulfate concentration remain the most stable over the study period?

A. The station adjacent to lake 1
B. The station adjacent to lake 3
C. The station adjacent to lake 4
D. The station adjacent to lake 5

2. The results of experiment 2 show that, from 1993 to 2000, pH levels:

F. remained stable in the non-glacial lakes but increased in the glacial lakes.
G. decreased in the glacial lakes but decreased in the non-glacial lakes.
H. increased in the non-glacial lakes but decreased in the glacial lakes.
J. increased in the non-glacial lakes while remaining relatively stable in the glacial lakes.

3. The data collected from Experiments 1 and 2 show:

A. no clear trend in sulfate concentration among terrestrial deposits, but increasing sulfate concentrations in the lakes.
B. increasing sulfate concentration among terrestrial deposits, but decreasing sulfate concentrations in the lakes.
C. no clear trend in sulfate-concentration levels either among terrestrial deposits or among the lakes.
D. increasing sulfate concentrations among terrestrial deposits, but no clear trend in sulfate-concentration levels in the lakes.

4. Which of the following hypotheses do the experimental data best support?

F. Increasing precipitation levels bring increasing amounts of airborne sulfate emissions into the lakes.
G. Increasing air temperatures have the effect of increasing pH levels in the lakes, which in turn increase sulfate-concentration levels in the lakes.
H. The melting of glacial ice due to gradually increasing air temperatures increases the amount of sulfates in lake water.
J. Wide variations in precipitation levels contribute to wide variations among the lakes in both pH and sulfate-concentration levels.

5. Based on the experimental data, which of the following conclusions is the most reasonable one?

A. Industrial sulfate affects pH levels to a greater extent than naturally occurring sulfate.
B. Sufficiently warm water temperatures are needed in order for sulfate to affect the pH levels in lake water.
C. In lake water, pH levels are sensitive to sulfate concentration levels.
D. In lake water, sulfate concentration levels have little or no impact on pH levels.

Passage II

Spacecraft such as the Mariner 10 in the 1970s and the Voyagers in the 1990s successfully passed at close range to nearly all the known planets in our Solar System, providing new information about them that we otherwise would not know. Table 1 shows data collected during these missions as well as other data already known about the planets. Some of the numbers are approximations only. A planet's *rotational period* is the time it takes to turn

Table 1

Terrestrial Bodies	Average Density (water =1)	Average Distance From Sun (millions of miles)	Rotational Period (Earth days)	Orbital Eccentricity	Mean Surface Temp. (°C)	Description
Mercury	5.4	36	59	.206	179	Rocky, ferrous
Venus	5.2	67	243	.007	480	Rocky, ferrous
Earth	5.5	93	24 hrs	.017	22	Rocky, ferrous
Mars	3.9	142	25 hrs	.093	−23	Rocky
Jupiter	1.3	484	9 hrs	.048	−150	Gaseous
Saturn	0.7	887	10 hrs	.056	−180	Gaseous
Uranus	1.2	1,783	11 hrs	.047	−210	Icy, gaseous
Neptune	1.7	2,794	16 hrs	.009	−220	Icy, gaseous
Pluto	1	3,600	6	.25	−230	Icy, rocky, gaseous

GO ON TO THE NEXT PAGE

once on its axis, completing one planetary day. A planet's *orbital eccentricity* is the percent difference between an elliptical path's longest axis and shortest axis. A perfectly circular orbit would have an orbital eccentricity of zero (0).

The following figure is a plot of the densities and diameters of the terrestrial (nongaseous) planets.

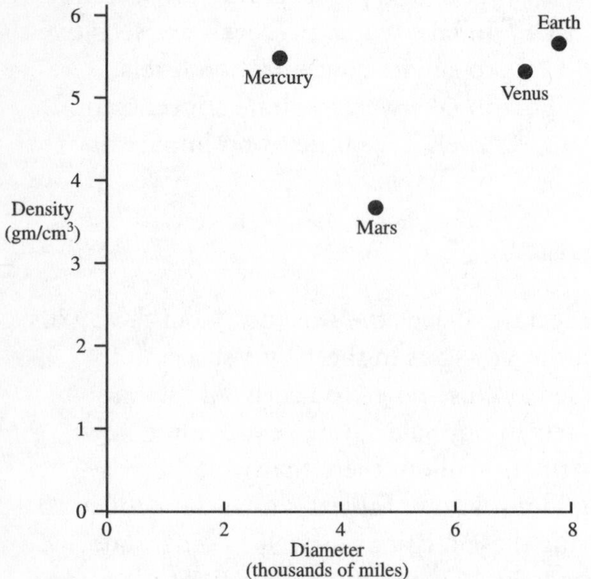

6. Which of the following statements is best supported by the data in Table 1 on page 423?

- **F.** Gaseous planets tend to have higher orbital eccentricities than non-gaseous planets.
- **G.** Planets that rotate slowly tend to have higher surface temperatures than other planets.
- **H.** Planets with low densities tend to rotate more slowly than high-density planets.
- **J.** The gravity of the Sun operates to reduce orbital eccentricity.

7. The data provided in Table 1 on page 423 show that:

- **A.** Jupiter has the shortest rotational period and the third highest orbital eccentricity.
- **B.** Pluto has the lowest average density and the highest orbital eccentricity.
- **C.** Earth has the highest average density and the fifth longest rotational period.
- **D.** Mercury has the highest average density and the highest orbital eccentricity.

8. The planet with an average density closest to that of water is:

- **F.** Uranus.
- **G.** Saturn.
- **H.** Pluto.
- **J.** Mercury.

9. On Mercury, one year (the time it takes to orbit once around the sun) is about 88 Earth days. How many full rotations does Mercury complete in one Mercury year?

- **A.** 1
- **B.** 6
- **C.** 59
- **D.** It cannot be determined from the information given.

10. The data presented suggest that there is:

F. a direct linear relationship between density and diameter among all of the terrestrial planets except Mercury.
G. a direct linear relationship between density and diameter among all of the terrestrial planets.
H. a direct linear relationship between density and diameter among the terrestrial planets but not among the gaseous planets.
J. no clear relationship between density and diameter among the terrestrial planets.

11. Although Venus has a higher mean surface temperature than Mercury, the average high temperatures on the surface of Venus are less than those on Mercury. Which of the following is the most reasonable explanation for this apparent contradiction?

A. Mercury's average density is greater than that of Venus.
B. Mercury is closer to the Sun than Venus.
C. Mercury's rotational period is less than that of Venus.
D. Mercury's orbital eccentricity is greater than that of Venus.

Passage III

The state forestry commission engaged a group of ecologists to study the nutrient flow in a forest on federal lands that was being considered for lease to a logging company. They were also asked to study the effects of clear-cutting in selected areas to predict what the long-term effects on the nutrient budget might be. The scientists selected several small sections of the forest for observation and experiment.

Table 1
Average Concentrations of Dissolved Substances in Bulk Precipitation and Stream Water in 6 Undisturbed Experimental Watersheds

Substance	Precipitation	Stream Water	Percent Change
Calcium	0.21	1.51	−619%
Magnesium	0.05	0.37	−640%
Potassium	0.10	0.23	−130%
Sodium	0.12	0.94	−683%
Aluminum	0.01	0.24	−2,300%
Ammonium	0.22	0.05	340%
Sulfate	3.10	6.20	−100%
Nitrate	1.30	1.14	12%
Chloride	0.42	0.64	−52%
Dissolved Silica	0.03	4.59	−15,300%

Notes: Data is given in kilograms per dry weight of materials per hectar of the watershed. Basin-caught materials are coarse, net-caught materials are fine, and filter-caught materials are super-fine.

The first task was to estimate the average nutrient flow within the entire forest area. Table 1 above shows their estimate based on six experimental areas chosen within the forest. Nutrients enter the forest ecosystem via precipitation, so rain gauges were set up in various locations in the study areas. Nutrients exit the ecosystem through runoff from streams and rivers, so the ecologists measured stream flows in the designated areas.

After estimating the overall nutrient flow in this forest, the ecologists had one 15-hectare* area cleared of trees in order to determine the amount of increase that would occur in runoff. The trees were removed from the area, but nothing else was disturbed. For the first two

*A hectare is a metric unit of measure equal to 2.471 acres.

GO ON TO THE NEXT PAGE

Table 2
Annual Losses of Particulate Matter

		Watershed 1 Undisturbed Area		Watershed 2 Deforested Area	
Source of Output	Year	Organic	Inorganic	Organic	Inorganic
Ponding Basin	1	4.62	8.30	35.41	158.32
Net	1	0.43	0.02	0.26	0.01
Filter	1	2.64	2.80	4.23	4.80
Ponding Basin	2	11.39	31.00	45.13	321.88
Net	2	0.43	0.02	0.25	0.03
Filter	2	3.32	3.70	6.24	7.10
Ponding Basin	3	3.83	5.78	53.72	540.32
Net	3	0.42	0.01	0.27	0.04
Filter	3	2.61	2.97	8.73	12.98

Notes: Data is given in kilograms per dry weight of materials per hectar of the watershed. Basin-caught materials are coarse, net-caught materials are fine, and filter-caught materials are super-fine.

years after the logging, an herbicide was applied so that no vegetation would grow back. The ecologists then compared this cleared watershed with one of the intact watersheds under study. They measured the stream flow for the first three years after the logging took place. Table 2 above summarizes the amounts of organic and inorganic matter found at the watershed basin. A net and filter system was utilized to catch finer matter as the runoff exited the watershed area.

12. Based on the experimental data collected, the forest appears to be experiencing a net:

F. loss in all measured nutrients.
G. loss in all but two measured nutrients.
H. gain in all but two measured nutrients.
J. gain in all measured nutrients.

13. The data provide LEAST support for which of the following hypotheses about the impact of clear-cutting a forest ecosystem during the first three years after deforestation?

A. Clear-cutting has the effect of increasing the amount of coarse particulate matter that exits the ecosystem.
B. Clear-cutting has the effect of increasing the loss of super-fine particulate matter that exits the ecosystem.
C. Clear-cutting has little effect on the amount of fine particulate matter that exits the ecosystem.
D. Clear-cutting has the effect of increasing the loss of organic matter but not inorganic matter.

14. Which of the following claims is best supported by the data in Table 2 on page 426?

F. The undisturbed watershed area received more precipitation during Year 2 than during either Year 1 or Year 3.
G. The deforested watershed area contains a greater amount of organic matter than inorganic matter.
H. The herbicide applied to the deforested area did not effect the amount of organic matter exiting that area.
J. Before the removal of any trees, the undisturbed watershed area contained less inorganic matter than the area where the trees were cleared.

15. Assuming that sodium is naturally found primarily as a fine material rather than either a coarse or super-fine material, which of the following conclusions is best supported by the data?

A. In the deforested area, less sodium was lost during Year 2 than during Year 3.
B. In the deforested area, less sodium was lost during Year 1 than during Year 2.
C. In the undisturbed area, about the same amount of sodium was lost during all three years.
D. In the undisturbed area, less sodium was lost during Year 2 than during Year 3.

16. Which of the following forecasts for the longer-term nutrient budget in the two 15-hectare areas compared in Table 2 on page 426 is most reasonable?

F. Nutrient losses in the deforested area will slowly decline while nutrient losses in the undisturbed area will increase.
G. Both the undisturbed and deforested areas will experience increasing losses of nutrients.
H. Nutrient losses in the deforested area will slowly increase while nutrient losses in the undisturbed area will slowly decrease.
J. Nutrient losses in the undisturbed area will remain stable over the longer term while nutrient losses in the deforested area will slowly decline.

17. Which of the following, if true, would most seriously call into question any conclusions about the entire forest's nutrient budget based on the data in Table 1 on page 425?

A. The total precipitation in the six experimental areas is significantly less than the total precipitation in the remaining areas of the forest.
B. The average precipitation per hectare is less in the six experimental areas than in the remaining areas of the forest.
C. The forest's streams and rivers run mainly through the six experimental areas.
D. In the experimental areas, soil nutrients are found in proportions that differ from their proportions in other areas of the forest.

GO ON TO THE NEXT PAGE

Passage IV

Biologists have discovered certain genes (the basic unit of genetic material found on the chromosomes) that behave very differently depending on whether they are passed down to offspring from the father or the mother. These genes, called imprinted genes, are chemically altered in cells that give rise to eggs and sperm. These alterations result in dramatically different properties. In the imprinted genes that have been most fully studied, the female alters the gene so that certain proteins are not produced. The protein remains active in the father's genes. Researchers have posed numerous theories to explain the evolution of imprinted genes. Three of the theories are presented below.

Competing Parental Interest Theory

Some biologists think that imprinted genes evolved in a battle between the sexes to determine the size of offspring. It is to the genetic advantage of the female to rear a number of offspring, all of which will pass along her genetic material. Consequently, while she wants each offspring to be healthy, she does not want them to be so large that the strain of feeding and/or delivering them would jeopardize her ability to bear future babies.

Conversely, it is to the genetic advantage of males in non-monogamous species (species that do not always mate for life) to have the mother expend as much of her resources as possible to ensure the health of his offspring. He is not concerned with her ability to bear future offspring, since these will not necessarily be fathered by him (and, therefore, will not be transmitting his genetic material). Hence, imprinted genes have developed in this parental tug-of-war. Normally, each offspring receives one copy of an imprinted gene from the father and one from the mother. The changes that the parents make in their genes result in an offspring that is smaller than the male would like and larger than the female would like.

Anti-Cancer Theory

This theory holds that imprinted genes evolved to prevent cancer. The genes have been found in the placenta (an organ that develops to nourish a growing fetus). Placental tissue grows and burrows into the uterus, where the fetus develops. The ability to grow and invade tissues is also seen in aggressive cancers. Imprinted genes might have developed to ensure that the potentially dangerous placenta will not develop if there is no fetus to nourish. The female might inactivate certain growth genes in her eggs, while the sperm kept them turned on. If no fertilization took place, the growth would not occur. If a sperm did join the egg, the male's gene would ensure that the protein developed.

Protein Control Theory

A third group of biologists holds that imprinted genes developed to ensure the precise regulation of certain proteins. Genes do their work by initiating the production of different proteins. Some proteins involved in the growth of embryos may need to be regulated with great precision to ensure the healthy development of the offspring. Proponents of the protein control theory suggest that this careful regulation might be easier if only one parent is involved. Thus, one parent might turn off such genes, leaving the regulation to the other.

18. Which of the following experimental findings poses the most serious difficulties for proponents of the anti-cancer theory?

- **F.** When a mouse was genetically engineered so that it contained two copies of every gene from its mother only, the embryo was unable to develop.
- **G.** Research in animals that lay eggs has never turned up an imprinted gene.
- **H.** Imprinted genes have been found in plants, which have no placentas.
- **J.** Research has shown that imprinted genes have not evolved rapidly as they usually do in competitive situations.

19. Supporters of the protein control theory believe that:

- **A.** imprinted genes are used to regulate crucial proteins.
- **B.** imprinted genes are active only in females.
- **C.** imprinted genes should not be found in monogamous species (ones that mate for life).
- **D.** only the male passes down imprinted genes to the offspring.

20. Supporters of the competing parental interest theory assume that:

- **F.** only females have an interest in regulating the size of their offspring.
- **G.** only males have an interest in ensuring the health and survival of their offspring.
- **H.** both males and females have an interest in producing as many offspring of their own sex as possible.
- **J.** both males and females have an interest in transmitting their genetic material to as many offspring as possible.

21. Supporters of all three theories would agree that:

- **A.** imprinted genes evolved as a means of regulating reproduction-related events.
- **B.** imprinted genes should be absent in non-placental animals (animals whose offspring develop without a placenta).
- **C.** if an embryo is formed without female-imprinted genes, the future ability of the mother to bear off-spring will be jeopardized.
- **D.** imprinted genes should always be turned off in the mother.

22. Which of the following findings is best explained by the competing parental interest theory?

F. An imprinted gene has been discovered in humans that appears to influence a child's social skills.
G. In the imprinted genes that have been most fully studied, the female turns the gene off, while the male's gene remains active.
H. Studies with a monogamous mouse species indicate that imprinted genes are not active.
J. One of the imprinted genes studied is known to control a growth-stimulating hormone.

23. In a rare pregnancy disorder called hydatidiform mole, an abnormal cluster of cells grows in place of the placenta. This cluster grows so large that there is no room for the development of the fetus. The embryo in such pregnancies has been found to carry only the father's genes. This fact could be used to support:

I. The competing parental interest theory
II. The anti-cancer theory
III. The protein control theory

A. I only
B. II only
C. II and III only
D. I, II, and III

24. Researchers conducted breeding studies with two species of mice. Species A was monogamous, while Species B was not. Supporters of the competing parental interest theory hypothesized that the monogamous species was unlikely to have active imprinted genes (since the fathers would have the same genetic stake in all the offspring born). Which of the following experimental results would they expect?

F. When females from Species A were bred with males from Species B, the resulting offspring were extremely small.
G. When females from Species A were bred with males from Species B, the resulting offspring were extremely large.
H. When females from Species B were bred with males from Species A, the resulting offspring were extremely large.
J. The offspring of Species B mice were consistently smaller than the offspring of Species A mice.

Passage V

Electrical circuits that allow electrical signals with some *frequencies* (number of waves per second) to pass while suppressing others are called *filters*. They are used in nearly every electronic device, from computers to VCRs. They may contain *resistors*, which resist the flow of current through a wire, *inductors*, which resist change in the current, and *capacitors*, which store electric charge. The following figure shows the design of three types of filters.

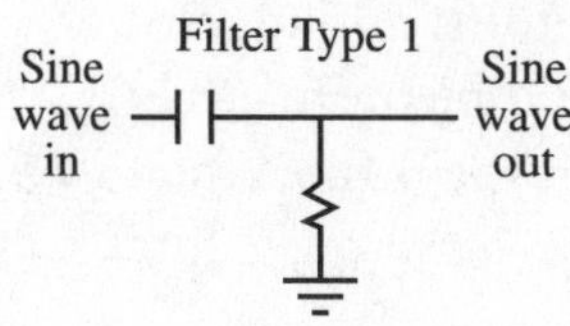

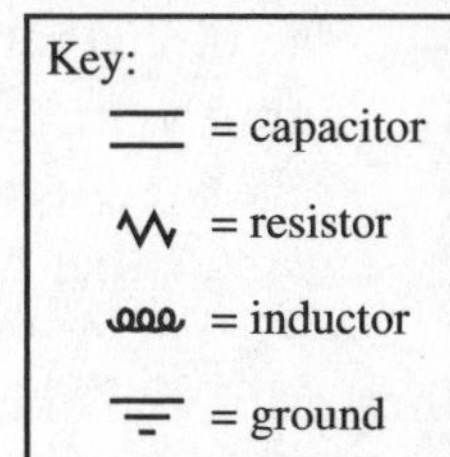

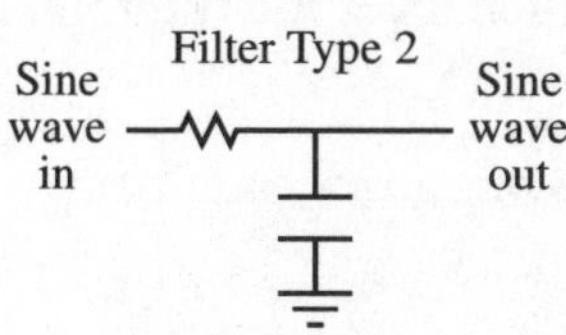

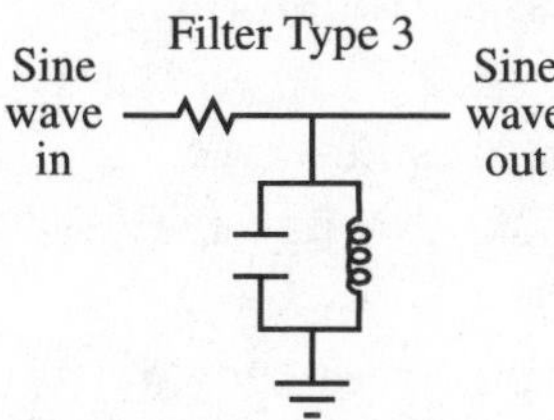

The effects of a filter can be demonstrated with a *frequency response curve*. Such a curve depicts the *amplitude* (wave height) of the output (vertical axis) as one varies the input frequency (horizontal axis), while keeping the input amplitude constant. Several experiments were conducted to test the effects of some filters.

Experiment 1

Researchers fed *sine waves* (oscillating voltage) into an electrical circuit containing the three filters depicted in the figure above. The input amplitude was fixed at 2.0 volts. The amplitude of the resulting waves was measured, and the frequency response curves in the following figure were obtained.

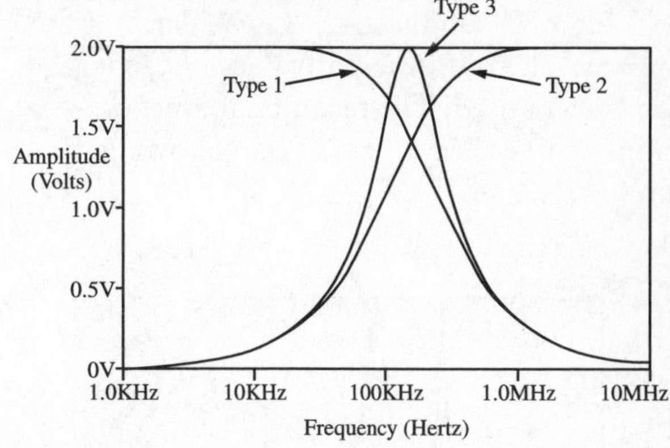

K=1000

M=1 Million

Experiment 2

A sine wave with an amplitude fixed at 2.0 volts was fed into a circuit with a type 3 filter, but in this experiment the researchers used four different values for the inductance (L). The resulting frequency response curves are shown in the following figure.

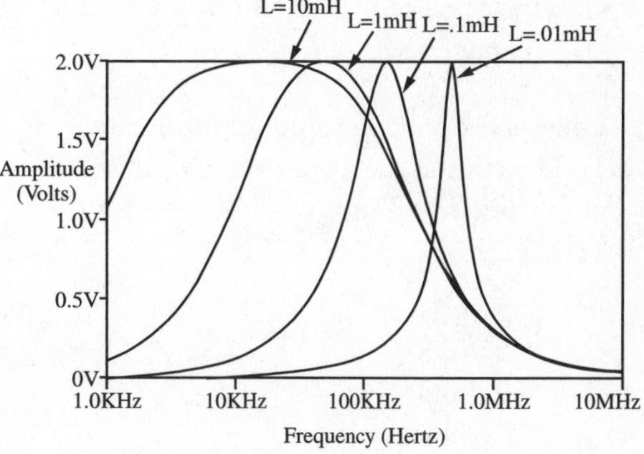

GO ON TO THE NEXT PAGE

Experiment 3

Again, the researchers fed a sine wave with an amplitude fixed at 2.0 volts into a circuit with a type 3 filter. The inductance was held at 0.1mH, while four different values of capacitance C were used. The resulting frequency response curves are shown in the following figure.

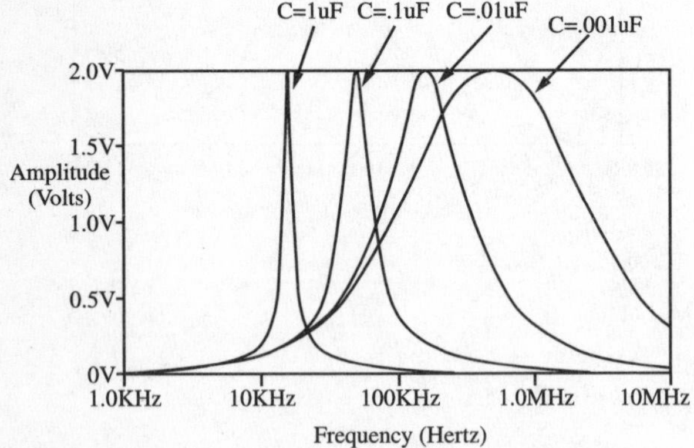

25. Which of the following was a control in all three experiments?

A. Input frequency
B. Input amplitude
C. Inductance
D. Capacitance

26. Using a type 3 filter and an inductance of 1mH, what is the approximate output amplitude at an input frequency of 100KHz?

F. 1.9 volts
G. 1.5 volts
H. 1.0 volts
J. 75 volts

27. Which of the following best explains why a type 3 filter was selected for experiments 2 and 3?

A. The frequency response varied more widely when filter type 3 was used than when either Filter type 1 or Filter type 2 was used.
B. Filter type 3 contains a ground and was therefore the safest of the three types of filters to experiment with.
C. Filter type 3 is the only one among the three that contains an inductor.
D. Input voltage could be more easily regulated using a type 3 filter than using either a type 1 or type 2 filter.

28. Increasing the inductance level for filter type 3 has the effect of:

F. increasing the output amplitude of the electrical circuit.
G. decreasing the average frequency of sine waves that pass through the circuit.
H. reducing the range of sine-wave frequencies that pass through the circuit.
J. increasing the output frequency of the electrical circuit.

29. Based on information given in the three experiments, which of the following can we assume to be true?

   A. The higher the capacitance, the wider the peak in the frequency response curve.
   B. The lower the capacitance, the narrower the peak in the frequency response curve.
   C. The higher the inductance, the narrower the peak in the frequency response curve.
   D. The higher the capacitance, the narrower the peak in the frequency response curve.

30. In the design of a radio receiver containing a type 3 filter, a low capacitance level and a high inductance level would be most useful for the purpose of:

   F. enhancing radio reception across the frequency spectrum.
   G. tuning out signals at high and low frequencies.
   H. tuning in a radio station at a fixed frequency.
   J. minimizing unwanted audio noise at middle frequencies.

Passage VI

Individuals usually have two copies of each gene (the basic unit of genetic material, found on the *chromosomes*), one from their mother and one from their father. Genetic or inherited diseases are those that can be passed down to the next generation through the genes. These diseases follow a number of patterns. Two of the basic ones are *dominant* and *recessive* inheritance.

In a genetic disease with a recessive inheritance pattern, an individual will not be affected by the disease unless he or she is passed two copies of the disease gene, one from each parent. An individual who is passed one copy of the disease gene is called a *healthy carrier*. He or she will not have the disease, but can still pass the gene on to an offspring. Figure 1 shows a family with this type of genetic disease.

Figure 1

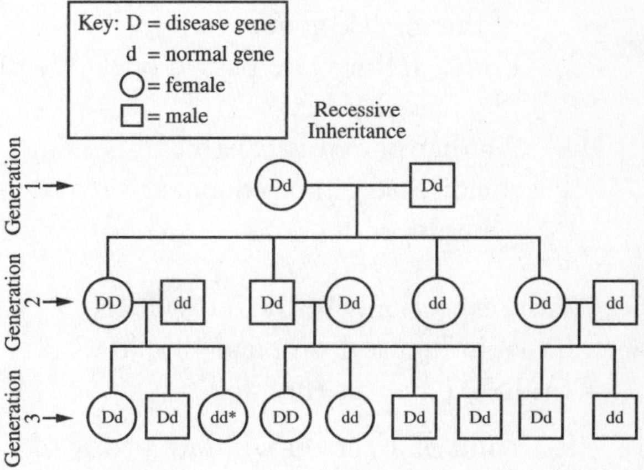

In a disease with a dominant inheritance pattern, any individual with a copy of the disease gene will have the disease. (Depending on the disease, individuals with two copies may have an accelerated or more severe disease course, or may be unable to survive.) There is no such thing as a healthy carrier with this type of disease. Figure 2 shows a family with this type of genetic disease.

Figure 2

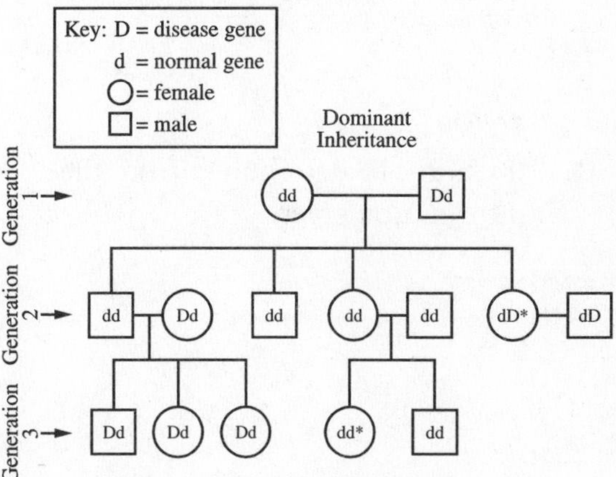

31. In Figure 1 on page 433, which shows a recessive inheritance pattern, which of the following about the parents of generation 2 is true?

A. Neither parent was passed a copy of the disease gene.
B. Both parents were passed two copies of the disease gene.
C. Both parents were passed one copy of the disease gene.
D. Neither parent is capable of passing the disease gene to the next generation.

32. With respect only to the individuals shown in Figure 1 on page 433, it CANNOT be true that a:

F. child of a person without a copy of the disease gene has the disease.
G. child of a person with the disease gene will never contract the disease.
H. child of two healthy carriers has the disease.
J. parent of a healthy carrier is also a healthy carrier.

33. In Figure 2 on page 433, what is the probability that the female marked with an asterisk in generation 3 will pass the disease on to her child?

A. 0%
B. 25%
C. 50%
D. It cannot be determined from the information given.

34. In Figure 2 on page 433, among all the children and grandchildren of the male and female at generation 1, how many have the disease?

F. Three
G. Four
H. Six
J. It cannot be determined from the information given.

35. Pamela is a young mother whose parents are both deceased. Assuming that disease X is a genetic disorder with either a dominant or a recessive inheritance pattern, which of the following statements is accurate?

A. If neither of Pamela's parents ever had disease X, then Pamela does not and never will have disease X.
B. If neither Pamela nor the father of Pamela's child has disease X, then that child will never have disease X.
C. If both of Pamela's parents had at least one copy of the disease X gene, then Pamela also has at least one copy of the disease X gene.
D. If neither of Pamela's parents ever had disease X, but Pamela has disease X, then disease X is not a dominantly inherited genetic disorder.

	Winter	Spring	Summer	Fall
Chemist: Seawater Salinity/Temperature (°C) (Seasonal Average)				
Surface	0/−1°	25/1°	32/12°	15/2°
5 meters deep	0/−1°	29/5°	32/7°	26/7°
20 meters deep (ocean floor)	39/4°	32/5°	32/6°	34/5°
Biologist: Population Counts (Seasonal Average)				
Bay (free-swimming)				
Fur seals (number successfully hunted)	6.3	3.0	5.4	2.2
Salmon (tonnage caught)	0	122.5	1,152.6	4,259.5
Gray whales (number observed)	0	29.8	32.4	1.4
Bay (bottom-dwelling amphipods)				
Gammarus duebeni (sample count in one gallon of seawater)	50	25	15	60
Gammarus locusta (sample count in one gallon of seawater)				
Land species				
Kodiak Bears (number observed)	0	4	22	21
Humans (number counted)	63	66	85	117
Doctor: Number of Medical Complaints (Seasonal Average)				
Dehydration-related illnesses	0.0	0.0	3.4	0.9
Bear attacks	0.0	0.2	1.1	2.2
Protein deficiency-related illnesses	10.4	4.1	1.0	0.0

Passage VII

A chemist, a biologist, and a doctor spent several years studying and measuring their respective populations in an Alaskan fishing community. Some of their observations are recorded above.

36. Which of the following statements about the water in the bay does the chemist's salinity and temperature readings best support?

- **F.** The deeper the water, the lower the temperature.
- **G.** The greater the water temperature, the higher the salinity.
- **H.** The shallower the water, the lower the salinity.
- **J.** The lower the water temperature, the lower the salinity.

GO ON TO THE NEXT PAGE

37. An animal species is said to be thriving if its population is increasing. Assuming that free-swimming water animals are generally found at the surface or within 5 meters from the surface of the bay's waters, the chemist's and the biologist's measurements provide some support for all of the following hypotheses EXCEPT:

A. fur seals thrive as water temperatures decrease.

B. gray whales thrive as salinity levels increase.

C. gray whales thrive as water temperatures increase.

D. salmon thrive as salinity levels increase.

38. Among the following, which is LEAST likely to be a contributing cause of the protein deficiency-related diseases observed by the doctor?

F. The local human population depends primarily on seal meat for their protein consumption.

G. Virtually all of the bay's salmon are caught by commercial fishermen who transport the salmon elsewhere for sale.

H. It is difficult to catch a gray whale in waters hidden beneath ice.

J. Local religious customs prohibit the consumption of bear meat unless the meat is fresh.

39. Which of the following statements is best supported by the evidence?

A. *Gammarus locusta* are more sensitive to salinity changes than *gammarus duebent.*

B. *Gammarus locusta* and *gammarus duebent* are equally sensitive to water temperature changes.

C. *Gammarus duebent* are more sensitive to water temperature changes than *gammarus locusta.*

D. *Gammarus locusta* are more sensitive to salinity changes but less sensitive to water temperature changes than *gammarus duebent.*

40. The doctor wants to reduce the number of protein deficiency-related illnesses among the village's human population. Which of the following would probably be the doctor's best course of action?

F. Stock the bay with more salmon to compensate for the absence of gray whales during the winter.

G. Introduce methods of preserving meat and fish for later consumption.

H. Remove the bears from the area to reduce the local villagers' competition for food.

J. Introduce modern fishing methods to the local fishermen.

Answers and Explanations

English

1. A The original phrasing is a proper way to express the idea of a choir consisting of girls but no boys. In choice **B**, *only* and *just* are redundant. Choice **C** is confusing, while choice **D** uses *and* where *but* would be appropriate.

2. J The idiom *for every (one) . . . there are (ten)* is perfectly appropriate here. However, the word *boys'* sounds awkward without the word *choirs* after it. Choice **J** supplies this word and adds the word *either*, which makes the sentence's meaning even clearer.

3. A The underlined phrase is grammatically correct and clearly conveys the idea that the Boys Choir already existed in 1977, when the Girls Choir was founded.

4. H The present-perfect tense should be used here, to match the clause following the comma and because the time frame involves not just the past but also the present.

5. D The phrase *since 1968* should be set off because the sentence can stand alone without it. One way to set off the phrase is with parentheses.

6. G If you read the sentence as a whole, you see that it lists two distinct performances. Each one should receive similar grammatical and rhetorical emphasis. But, the underlined portion subordinates the first clause to what follows the comma. Choice **G** fixes the problem.

7. D In the original sentence, the phrase *they sung* awkwardly splits the description of the location. Also, the phrase *in front* is used twice in the description, which sounds repetitive. Choice **D** solves both problems.

8. F At the end of the preceding paragraph, the writer notes two of the grand venues where the Boys Choir has performed. The sentence in choice **F** alludes to that point while deftly transitioning to the discussion of the Girls Choir that follows.

9. B A choir is said to perform either *to*, *in front of*, or *before* an audience, not *toward* or *at* an audience. Choice **B** provides one of the idioms that works here.

10. G Without a comma between the two underlined words, the sentence suggests that the thousands of music lovers were also dignitaries, which in all likelihood is not what the writer intended to suggest. Choice **G** supplies the comma that sets off *the mayor's wife*, identifying her (but not the music lovers) as one of the dignitaries.

11. C If you switch the sentence's two clauses, you can see that the sentence boils down to this: The choirs act as havens *by giving* kids new confidence and hope.

12. F The preceding sentence indicates that the school strongly emphasizes singing, while the following sentences suggest that the school sparks student interest in various non-music professional careers. Choice **F** provides a nice transition from one idea to the other.

13. C As it stands, the sentence contradicts itself. The writer is trying to say that these jobs now appear in reach, whereas earlier they seemed out of reach—as choice **C** indicates.

14. J The underlined portion refers to the Girls Choir, not to its performances. It's inappropriate to talk about a choir as either being canceled, choice **F**, or closing its doors, choice **G**. On the other hand, it makes perfect sense to say that a choir might *go silent* without sufficient funding. Although the phrase *stop what they do* also makes sense, *go silent* is a more artful, graceful phrase.

15. C The writer has been asked to describe the choir's musical achievements. The passage explains a bit about the choir's history and its importance in the lives of its members, but it really doesn't describe their musical achievements.

16. J The correct idiomatic expression here is *waiting to see*.

17. C The clause following the underlined portion elucidates, or explains, what is meant by the trap described in the first part of the sentence. A dash, and not a colon, is the appropriate mark for this purpose. (A comma would also be appropriate.) The pronoun *them* is correct here because it refers to the plural noun *technologies*.

18. F The phrase *he or she* is singular, matching the singular subject *leader*. Choices **G** and **J** are wrong because they use plural noun forms. Choice **H** is awkward and confusing.

19. B The purpose of the sentence in which the underlined portion appears is to underscore and support the idea in the previous sentence. The connecting phrase that choice **B** provides (*In fact,*) helps the reader understand the connection between the two sentences.

20. J In this sentence, the first clause and the second clause (following the comma) both employ the past-perfect tense. The result is that it's impossible to tell which event came first—the one described in the first clause or the one described in the second clause. Only choice **J** clears up the ambiguity.

21. B The adverb *seemingly* should not be separated from the adjective it modifies (*unassailable*). One way to fix this problem is to simply reverse the words *seemingly* and *was*. Another way is to replace the underlined phrase with the one that choice **B** provides.

22. G The underlined sentence would be the ideal topic sentence for Paragraph 3 and therefore should begin that paragraph rather than end Paragraph 2.

23. D The simple past tense (*became*) makes the most sense here in light of the next two sentences, which provide details—using the simple past tense—about the development described in the first sentence.

24. F The reflexive verb *itself* is appropriately used here to indicate how Wang survived. Choice **J** retains the reflexive *itself*, but the use of the infinitive *to transform* distorts the meaning of the sentence.

25. A The underlined clause clearly and properly modifies *computer company* and is grammatically correct. Choice **B** is an awkward juxtaposition of *company* and *a company*. Choice **C** contains a pronoun reference problem: To what does the noun *their* refer—Wang or the companies Wang served? Choice **D** is very awkward.

26. H The phrase *slip up* is slang and does not fit the overall style of this passage. Of the three alternatives, choice **H** makes the most sense in the context of the entire sentence.

27. C The underlined portion is unnecessarily wordy; choice **C** provides the same idea, but more concisely.

28. F The sentence in choice **F** explains why Wang had lost its chance to move forward, fleshing out the point the writer makes in the previous sentence.

29. B The underlined phrase is an awkward way of saying that well-managed companies sometimes fail for the reason cited in the sentence. Choice **B** provides a clearer way of making the point.

30. J Each of the two paragraphs—1 and 5—makes either a suitable introductory or concluding paragraph for this passage. However, Paragraph 5 provides a far more effective transition to Paragraph 2. Thus, the passage would be more effective if Paragraphs 1 and 5 were switched.

31. C The word *like* is improperly used here; the writer is not seeking to compare learning the oboe to the experience of expecting. Choice **C** provides the correct idiom. Choice **B** and **D** are correct in usage and grammar, but neither is so effective as choice **C**.

32. F The colon is correctly used here to signal that what's ahead essentially defines what was just described.

33. B The underlined portion employs the passive voice, which is very awkward and confusing here. Choice **B** recasts the clause in the active voice.

34. G In the two sentences, there's a contrast of ideas that the writer seeks but fails to convey. Choice **G** supplies a connecting word that points out that contrast effectively.

35. D What follows *either* should parallel what follows *or*, but it doesn't (*their teachers* and *from mail order companies* are not grammatically parallel). Choice **D** fixes the faulty parallelism. Choice **B** also fixes the problem, but it isn't as precise as choice **D**.

36. G The word *that* is needed between *is* and *there's* to transform the portion of the sentence beginning with *there's no such thing* into a dependent clause. (*The problem is that there's. . . .*)

37. A The point of the sentence that immediately precedes the proposed remark is that oboe reeds are very expensive. Choice **A** provides objective, direct support for that point. It also relates directly to the next sentence. (Both sentences involve a problem with purchasing reeds by mail order.)

38. H The underlined phrase—*For example*—contributes nothing to the sentence. However, simply omitting the phrase isn't so effective as replacing it with the phrase *In fact*, which connects the ideas in the two sentences together by underscoring the point that reed makers take their time sending reeds to their customers.

39. B The plural pronoun *them* should be used instead of the singular form *it* because the writer is referring here to the plural noun *reeds*.

40. J The word *progressively* already conveys the idea that the quality of the reeds worsened in a series of steps. Repeating the word *lower* is unnecessary. Choice **G** fails to eliminate the redundancy, while choice **H** supplies the adjective *poor* where the comparative form (*poorer*) would be needed.

41. D The contraction *they're* (they are) makes no sense here, and should be replaced with *its*, which matches the singular *source* used elsewhere in the sentence to refer to the company in California.

42. G The juxtaposition of the modifier *Desperate* and the sentence's subject (*the next person*) implies that it was the next person who was desperate, when in fact it was the writer who was desperate. Choice **G** solves this misplaced-modifier problem by reconstructing the main clause, positioning *I* (the writer) immediately after the modifier, as the sentence's subject. The clause in choice **J** accomplishes the same thing, but the position of the word *next* creates confusion. (To whom or what does *next* refer?)

43. C The word *however* makes for an illogical and confusing connection between the last sentence of Paragraph 5 and the first sentence of Paragraph 6. Without the word *however*, the transition is smooth and logical.

44. J In the original sentence, the pronoun reference is ambiguous. (Does *him* refer to the friend or the reed maker?) Choice **J** replaces the pronoun with the noun to which the writer probably intends to refer (*my friend*). Although choice **H** also eliminates the ambiguity, it sounds awkward at this point in the sentence.

45. A The writer's persistence in searching for good reeds, along with the enjoyment the writer indicated he gets out of playing the oboe, strongly supports the idea that the writer does not plan to give up. The sentence in choice **A** is consistent with this idea and nicely ties together all the information in the passage. Neither choice **B** nor choice **C** is so successful in embracing the entire passage. Choice **D** does nothing more than essentially repeat one of the statements in Paragraph 1 and thus is less effective than choice **A**, which provides an additional insight: the writer's evaluation of the whole experience.

46. H The purpose of the underlined clause is to identify the specific time of autumn that the events described later in the sentence occur. Choice **H** makes it clear that the writer is concerned only with Thanksgiving, and not with autumn generally.

47. B The two phrases *to host friends* . . . and *preparing one of the* . . . are not grammatically parallel. One solution is to replace the infinitive *to host* with the gerund *hosting*—as choice **B** provides.

48. J A comma is needed here to separate the two distinct tasks discussed in the sentence. The word *and* following the comma is optional.

49. C The underlined portion contains the awkward and vague phrase *there is*. Also, the article *a*, although acceptable here, is best omitted because the list that follows contains both plural and singular nouns. Choice **C** solves both problems and is consistent with the rest of the paragraph, in which the writer uses the second-person *you*.

50. G The passive voice is used in the underlined portion, but the active voice is used throughout the rest of the sentence. Choice **G** recasts the phrase in the active voice, thereby avoiding the awkward shift from active to passive voice, then back to active voice.

51. A The writer uses the idiom *by comparison to* appropriately and effectively here. Choice **B** is acceptable, but it is not as concise as the original version.

52. H The underlined portion is grammatically correct but leaves it a bit unclear as to who enjoyed the meal. Choice **H** makes it clearer that it was the Pilgrims who enjoyed the meal.

53. B If commas were used in the place of semicolons, it would be difficult to distinguish between categories such as fowl and seafood.

54. H With the past tense *wasn't*, either the underlined phrase or choices **G** or **J** would be correct. But, the verb form *weren't* (were not) establishes the subjunctive mood, which calls for an idiom such as *As if*.

55. A The writer has chosen a phrase here that is idiomatic and, by way of its style and structure, very effective in making the point that the Pilgrims' Thanksgiving meal carried on much, much longer than the typical modern-day Thanksgiving dinner.

56. J At the end of the first paragraph, the passage indicates that there were significant differences between the Pilgrims' Thanksgiving and today's typical Thanksgiving. Then, the passage's second paragraph begins with the following sentence: *First, consider the menu.* This sentence is a clue that another major difference will be discussed later in the passage. In the paragraph at hand, the passage finally turns from the menu to another aspect of Thanksgiving dinner: the guest list. Choice **J** provides a sentence that signals the transition from one to the other.

57. D Adding a word such as *total* helps underscore the point that the guest list includes not just immediate family but extended family as well. However, the underlined portion is awkward and should be replaced with either *total guests* or *guests altogether*, as choice **D** provides.

58. G The first part of Paragraph 4 (preceding the underlined sentence) notes the many guests who show up at today's typical Thanksgiving dinner, while the portion of the paragraph following the underlined sentence notes how many more guests there were at the first Thanksgiving. The sentence in choice **G** deftly links the two ideas.

59. C The indirect object of *invite* is the phrase *to a little pot-luck supper.* (Squanto invited Massasoit to a pot-luck supper.) For clarity, these two elements should be placed nearer to each other. Choice **C** fixes the problem.

60. F The concluding remark should underscore the passage's main idea—that the first Thanksgiving was a much greater feat than today's typical Thanksgiving—as well as tying together both main areas of discussion: the extensive menu and the number of guests. Only choice **F** accomplishes all this.

61. D Although replacing *movies* with the possessive *movies'* (as in *their* movies) would correct the underlined portion's only grammatical error, the phrase is still awkward. Choice **D** provides a clearer, more idiomatic alternative.

62. H Since the sentence involves past events, you can eliminate choices **F** and **J**, each of which uses the present-tense verb form *is*. Choice **H** fixes the error by replacing *is* with the past-tense form of the verb *lies*. (It is idiomatic to say that the greatness of something *lies in* a certain characteristic of that thing.)

63. B In the original sentence, *emerged* separates the sentence's subject (*a generation of filmmakers*) from its modifier *who were not. . . .* Choice **B** fixes the problem by reconstructing the underlined portion.

64. J In the original sentence, *no other* and *with the exception of* are redundant. Choices **H** and **J** both solve the problem, but choice **J** is clearer and more concise than choice **H**.

65. C Paragraph 1 ends by indicating one reason for the vitality and excitement surrounding the early days of moviemaking. Paragraph 2 takes up a second reason. The word *Furthermore* signals that another reason is coming, so it provides a good link between the two paragraphs.

66. F The sentence employs the idiomatic correlative pair *not for . . . but rather for. . . .* What follows *not only* is grammatically parallel to what follows *but rather for*.

67. B The passive voice sounds awkward here. Choice **B**, which employs the active voice, sounds more graceful.

68. J The connecting word *and* would be correct here only if what followed it were an independent clause. But, it's a dependent clause. (Notice the use of the gerund *running* rather than *are running* or *run*.). The preposition *with* renders the sentence grammatically correct.

69. C The word *more* is already supplied—immediately preceding the series of three adjectives—so, all that's needed here is the word *stale*.

70. J Sentence 3 refers to the phenomenon described in sentence 1 and thus should immediately follow that sentence. Sentences 2 and 4 provide details that support the assertion in sentence 3, so they should follow sentence 3. Sentences 2 and 4 might work in either order, but choice **J** is the only one in which the sentences are otherwise arranged correctly.

71. B The underlined word is grammatically correct here. The problem is that the sentence doesn't make its point effectively. Adding the word *only* is needed to make the point that the artist whose audience is limited to the elite need not be concerned with satisfying the tastes of a wide variety of people.

72. G In the preceding sentence, the writer points out what strong painters can do. In the sentence at hand, the writer seeks to compare great artists of the cinema to these painters. Choice **G** provides a phrase that makes it clear that the comparison is being made.

73. C From the paragraph's first two sentences, you can infer that artists such as the ones listed were able to create films that were uncompromising in their artistry because they were not pressured to appeal to the masses. To link this idea to the following sentence, this point should be made explicit, which is precisely what the sentence in choice **C** accomplishes.

74. F The writer uses the parallel construction *The larger . . . the greater. . .* , which is idiomatic and perfectly appropriate for conveying the idea here.

75. A Since Paragraph 3 offers a conclusion based on the existence of financial pressures in today's movie industry, it's logical to put that paragraph after paragraph 4, in which those pressures are described.

Math

1. B To find the solution, divide 40.5 by 1,000 by moving the decimal point 3 places to the left.

2. J You can solve the problem algebraically as follows:

$$\begin{aligned} 23 - x &= 2(15 - x) \\ 23 - x &= 30 - 2x \\ x &= 7 \end{aligned}$$

An alternative method is to subtract the number given in each answer choice, in turn, from both Lyle's age and Melanie's age.

3. D $4 \times 4 \times 4 = 64$, and $5 \times 5 \times 5 = 125$. Thus, x must lie between 4 and 5.

4. G The first coordinate in the (x,y) pair $(4,-5)$ is the point's horizontal position (along the x-axis), while the second coordinate in the pair is the point's vertical position (along the y-axis). Point Q matches both coordinates.

5. B The price of two children's tickets together equals the price of one adult ticket. The total admission price is therefore equivalent to the price of three adult tickets.

$$\begin{aligned} 3a &= \$12.60 \\ a &= \$4.20 \end{aligned}$$

Child's ticket price $= \frac{1}{2}(\$4.20) = \$2.10$

6. J Of six marbles altogether, two are blue. Hence, the chances of drawing a blue marble are 2 in 6, or 1 in 3, which can be expressed as the fraction $\frac{1}{3}$.

7. D Given that point D bisects $\overline{BA}$, the length of $\overline{AD}$ must be equal to the length of $\overline{DB}$, as shown in this figure:

B D A C

8. K Cross-multiply to solve for y:

$$\begin{aligned} (9)(y - 1) &= (2y)(3) \\ 9y - 9 &= 6y \\ 3y &= 9 \\ y &= 3 \end{aligned}$$

9. C Your first step is to rename mixed numbers as fractions:

$$\frac{9}{2} + \frac{15}{4} - \frac{12}{5}$$

The least common denominator is 20. Rename each fraction, then combine:

$$\frac{9}{2} + \frac{15}{4} - \frac{12}{5} = \frac{90 + 75 - 48}{20} = \frac{117}{20}$$

10. J $ab^2c = (3)(9)\left(\frac{1}{3}\right) = \frac{27}{3} = 9$

11. A Rewrite the question as an algebraic equation, and solve for x:

$$M = \frac{P}{100}(x)$$
$$100M = Px$$
$$\frac{100M}{P} = x$$

12. J The sum of the measures of any triangle's interior angles is 180°. Accordingly, the third interior angle of the triangle with angles measuring 30° and 75° measures 75°. Since the quadrilateral formed by the two pairs of parallel lines is a parallelogram, the vertex opposite that 75° angle also measures 75°. Since $\angle x$ is the supplement of that 75° angle, $\angle x$ measures 105°.

13. C You can express the amount of sugar after you add water as $0.05(60 + x)$, where $0.05 = 5\%$ and $(60 + x)$ represents the total amount of solution after you add the additional water.

14. J Points (5, −2) and (−3, 3) are two points on line b. The slope of b is the change in the y-coordinates divided by the corresponding change in the x-coordinate:

$$m_b = \frac{3-(-2)}{-3-5} = \frac{5}{-8}, \text{ or } -\frac{5}{8}$$

15. A Applying the midpoint formula, the coordinates of M are $\left(\frac{4+2}{2}, \frac{4+2}{2}\right)$, or (3, 3). The triangle's height and base are both 3, and its area $= \frac{1}{2}bh = \frac{1}{2}(3)(3) = 4.5$.

16. G Equate the proportions of the negative with those of the printed picture:

$$\frac{2\frac{1}{2}}{4} = \frac{1\frac{7}{8}}{x}$$
$$\frac{\frac{5}{2}}{4} = \frac{\frac{15}{8}}{x}$$
$$\frac{5}{2}x = \frac{15}{2}$$
$$5x = 15$$
$$x = 3$$

17. E Put the equation given in the question into the form $y = mx + b$:

$$4x - 2y = 6$$
$$2y = 4x - 6$$
$$y = 2x - 3$$

The line's slope (m) is 2. Accordingly, the slope of a line perpendicular to this line is $-\frac{1}{2}$. Given a y-intercept of 3, the equation of the perpendicular line is $y = -\frac{1}{2}x + 3$. Reworking this equation to match the form of the answer choices yields $2y + x = 6$.

18. J Before 4 socks were removed, the drawer contained 24 blue socks ($60 \times 40\% = 24$) and 36 gray socks ($24 + 36 = 60$.) After removing 4 blue socks, the drawer contained 20 blue socks and 36 gray socks. The ratio of gray to blue socks is 36:20, or 9:5.

19. D To determine the distance between the two points, apply the distance formula:

$$d = \sqrt{(x_1 - x_2)^2 + (y_1 - y_2)^2}$$
$$= \sqrt{(5 - 1)^2 + (4 - [-2])^2}$$
$$= \sqrt{4^2 + 6^2}$$
$$= \sqrt{52}, \text{ or } 2\sqrt{13}$$

20. G Set each of the four expressions, in turn, equal to 0, then solve for x in each equation. Given $2x = 0, x = 0$. Given $3x - 1 = 0, x = \frac{1}{3}$. Given $2x - 2 = 0, x = 1$. Given $x - 3 = 0, x = 3$. The solution set, then, contains $0, \frac{1}{3}$, 1, and 3.

21. A The graph shows all x-values less than -1.5 and all x-values greater than 1.5. Choice A describes all x-values.

22. H Combine the terms under the radical into one fraction:

$$\sqrt{\frac{y^2}{2} - \frac{y^2}{18}} = \sqrt{\frac{9y^2 - y^2}{18}}$$
$$= \sqrt{\frac{8y^2}{18}}$$
$$= \sqrt{\frac{4y^2}{9}}$$

Then factor out "perfect squares" from both numerator and denominator:

$$\sqrt{\frac{4y^2}{9}} = \frac{2y}{3}$$

23. A Add the two equations:

$$\begin{array}{r} x + y = a \\ x - y = b \\ \hline 2x + 0 = a + b \\ x = \frac{1}{2}(a + b) \end{array}$$

24. K Given that the equation has only one solution, the two binomial factors of the trinomial $x^2 + 8x + s = 0$ must be the same: $(x + \sqrt{s})$. Rewrite in unfactored form:

$$(x + \sqrt{s})(x + \sqrt{s}) = 0$$
$$x^2 + (2\sqrt{s})x + s = 0$$

$2\sqrt{s} = 8$. Therefore, $\sqrt{s} = 4$, and $s = 16$.

25. C Apply the formula for the equation of a circle: $(x - h)^2 + (y - k)^2 = r^2$. Given that the circle's center (h,k) is $(3,-1)$, its radius (r) is 5, and the y-coordinate of one point on the circle is 2, you can solve for x (m) as follows:

$$(m - 3)^2 + (2 - [-1])^2 = 5^2$$
$$(m - 3)^2 + 9 = 25$$
$$(m - 3)^2 = 16$$
$$m - 3 = \pm 4$$
$$m = 7, -1$$

One of these two values, -1, appears among the answer choices.

26. K The triangle's three sides are in the ratio 8:15:17, which is one of the Pythagorean side triplets ($8^2 + 15^2 = 17^2$). Thus, the triangle must be a right triangle in which the two shortest sides form the right (90°) angle.

27. C To determine the answer quantity, work systematically, beginning with the greatest possible integer:

$7 + 1 + 1 + 1 = 10$
$5 + 3 + 1 + 1 = 10$
$3 + 3 + 3 + 1 = 10$

As you can see, there are three different ways.

28. K Letting x = the unknown length, by the Pythagorean theorem: $13^2 + x^2 = 39^2$. Solving for x:

$$x^2 = 39^2 - 13^2$$
$$x = \sqrt{39^2 - 13^2}$$
$$= \sqrt{(13)^2(3)^2 - 13^2}$$
$$= \sqrt{13^2(3^2 - 1)}$$
$$= 13\sqrt{8}$$
$$= 26\sqrt{2}$$

29. D Given that the average of the first five numbers is A, their sum must be $5A$. Thus, the sum of all six numbers is $5A + n$. To find the average of all six numbers, divide their sum by the number of terms (6): $\frac{5A + n}{6}$.

30. F The sum of the lengths of any two sides of a triangle must be greater than the length of the third side. Thus, in the triangle at hand, the length of the third side must be less than 15 inches.

31. B You're looking for the point at which the dotted line (ABC's stock price) is furthest above the solid line (XYZ's stock price). The dotted line lies above the solid line only during the second half of the 2nd quarter and the first half of the 3rd quarter; the end of the 2nd quarter marks the greatest difference between prices during that period. At that time, ABC stock was priced at approximately \$7.60, while XYZ stock was priced at approximately \$5 per share. The difference between those two prices is \$2.60.

32. F Solve this problem using the rules for signs and with a bit of logical reasoning. Using negative integers approaching zero (0) will yield the least product. Start with −1, then decrease the values of x and y if necessary. The first two values that satisfy the equation are: $y = -2, x = -1$ $[-1 - (-2) = 1]$. Accordingly, $xy = 2$.

33. E Square both sides of the equation, then solve for x: $4x = y$; $x = \frac{y}{4}$

34. G The question provides the formula: *distance* = *rate* × *time*. The boat's total distance = $m + 20$, while its total traveling time = $t + 4$. Accordingly:

$$m + 20 = (r)(t + 4)$$
$$\frac{m + 20}{t + 4} = r$$

35. B Quadrilateral $ABCD$ is a parallelogram. In any parallelogram, opposite vertices have the same angle measures. Thus, $m\angle DAB = 60°$. The sum of the measures of the 3 interior angles of $\Delta ABD = 180°$. Thus, $m\angle ABD = 45°$.

36. K If you multiply the second equation by 4, and then isolate the m-term, this reveals that the two equations are the same:

$$4\left(\frac{3}{4}n\right) = 4(3 - m)$$

$$3n = 12 - 4m$$

$$4m = 12 - 3n$$

Given one linear equation in two variables, there are an infinite number of possible values for each variable.

37. C First, multiply matrix A by the scalar 2. To do so, multiply each term in matrix A by 2:

$$2A = \begin{bmatrix} -3 & 5 \\ 3 & 7 \end{bmatrix} = \begin{bmatrix} -6 & 10 \\ 6 & 14 \end{bmatrix}$$

Then, subtract matrix B from matrix $2A$. To do so, subtract each term in matrix B by the corresponding term in matrix $2A$:

$$2A - B = \begin{bmatrix} -6 & 10 \\ 6 & 14 \end{bmatrix} - \begin{bmatrix} 3 & 2 \\ -1 & 1 \end{bmatrix}$$

$$= \begin{bmatrix} -9 & 8 \\ 7 & 13 \end{bmatrix}$$

38. G Each successive term is 3 less than the preceding term. Here's the sequence of ten terms: {30, 27, 24, 21, 18, 15, 12, 9, 6, 3}. Including the first term (30), the tenth term in the sequence is 3.

39. C $2g(M) = 2\log_6 M = \log_6 M^2$. Hence, $f(2(g(M)) = M^2$.

40. K ΔQRS is a right triangle in which the length of the sides are in the ratio 3:4:5. The length of $\overline{RS}$ (the hypotenuse) is 5 units. Given that $\overline{ST}$ is also 5 units long, ΔRST is an isosceles right triangle, in which the length of the sides are in the ratio $1:1:\sqrt{2}$. The length of $\overline{RT}$ (the hypotenuse) must be $5\sqrt{2}$ units.

41. D Competitor 1 must engage in 5 matches. Competitor 2 must engage in 4 matches not already accounted for. (The match between competitors 1 and 2 has already been tabulated.) Similarly, competitor 3 must engage in 3 matches other than those accounted for, and so on. The minimum number of total matches = 5 + 4 + 3 + 2 + 1 = 15.

42. G The length of each side of the square is 12 feet. The length of the remaining two sides of the triangle totals 16 feet. The perimeter of the semicircle $= \frac{1}{2}\pi d = \frac{1}{2}\pi(12) = 6\pi$. The length of the two sides of the square included in the overall perimeter totals 24. The total perimeter of the floor $= 16 + 6\pi + 24 = 40 + 6\pi$.

43. D For any right triangle, by definition, the tangent of one acute angle is the reciprocal of the tangent of the other acute angle. Thus, their product is 1.

44. J In 3 hours, one ship traveled 72 miles, while the other traveled 30 miles. The ratio of these two distances is 30:72 or 5:12, suggesting a 5:12:13 triangle in which the hypotenuse is the distance between the two ships at 2:30 p.m. That distance is 78 miles.

45. C $\overline{AC}$ is a diagonal of the square $ABCD$. To find the length of any square's diagonal, multiply the length of any side by $\sqrt{2}$. So first you need to find the length of a side here. Half the length of a side equals the circle's radius, and the perimeter of any circle equals $2\pi r$, where r is the radius. Thus, the radius here is 8, and the length of each of the square's sides is 16. Therefore, diagonal $AC = 16\sqrt{2}$.

46. K The square root of (3)(12), or 36, = 6. However, since $\sqrt{3x} = 6i$ rather than 6, $x = -12$.

47. C Factor the numerator and the denominator. (The numerator provides a difference of two squares.) Simplify, then distribute the resulting denominator to both terms in the numerator:

$$\frac{x^2 - 4}{x^2 - 2x} = \frac{(x + 2)(x - 2)}{x(x - 2)}$$

$$= \frac{x + 2}{x}$$

$$= \frac{x}{x} + \frac{2}{x}$$

$$= 1 + \frac{2}{x}$$

48. K Your task is to determine the least common multiple of all three numbers. The least number of days until events A, B, and C all occur again on the same day is the product of the three numbers (3, 5, and 8), which is 120.

49. D The figure shows a hexagon. The sum of the measures of the six angles = 720°. Subtracting the three known angles from 720 leaves 420°, which is the sum of the measures of the three unknown angles. Set up an equation, then solve for x:

$$x + x + \frac{4}{5}x = 420$$

$$\frac{14}{5}x = 420$$

$$x = (420)\frac{5}{14} = (30)(5) = 150$$

50. G First, express the equation in the quadratic form: ($x^2 + 4x + 2 = 0$) [$a = 1, b = 4, c = 2$]. Then, apply the quadratic formula:

$$x = \frac{-4 \pm \sqrt{4^2 - 4(1)(2)}}{2(1)}$$
$$= \frac{-4 \pm \sqrt{8}}{2}$$
$$= \frac{-4 \pm 2\sqrt{2}}{2}$$
$$= \frac{-4}{2} \pm \frac{2\sqrt{2}}{2}$$
$$= -2 \pm \sqrt{2}$$

51. E First, determine the length of each edge of the cube: $\sqrt[3]{125} = 5$. The surface area of each square face of the cube $= 5 \times 5 = 25$.

52. K After 4 hours, the clock will run behind the actual time by 16 minutes. Accordingly, at 4:00 the clock will show 3:44. It will take 16 minutes *plus* about one additional minute (because the clock runs 1 minute slow every quarter-hour) for the clock to advance to 4:00.

53. D The graph shows a vertically oriented parabola. Thus, the general form for parabola's equation is $y - k = a(x - h)^2$. Since the vertex is at (3,0), $h = 3$ and $k = 0$, and the parabola's equation is $y = a(x - 3)^2$. Each answer choice expresses an equation in unfactored form. Accordingly, rewrite the equation $y = a(x - 3)^2$ in the same manner (to identify the best equation among the five choices, you don't need to know the value of a, which defines the parabola's "width"):

$$y = (x - 3)(x - 3)$$
$$y = x^2 - 6x + 9$$

54. J Letting x = the length of one side of the painting, the painting's area $= x^2$, and the entire area, including the picture and mat, is $(x + 2)^2$. The difference is the area of the mat. Thus:

$$(x + 2)^2 - x^2 = 60$$
$$x^2 + 4x + 4 - x^2 = 60$$
$$4x = 56$$
$$x = 14$$

55. A The area of any triangle $= \frac{1}{2}ba$, where b is its base and a is its altitude. In the triangle in question, $b = a$. Substitute this value for b in the area formula:

$$A = \left(\frac{1}{2}\right)(b)(b) = \frac{b^2}{2}$$

56. F The denominator $|y - 2|$, and hence the value of x, is always positive, even for negative y-values. The graph of the equation is asymptotic at $y = 2$, just like the original equation. Choice **F** provides the appropriate graph.

57. B In ΔPQR, $\tan x = \frac{\overline{QR}}{\overline{PQ}}$. Given $\tan x > 1$, $\overline{PQ} < \overline{QR}$ and, accordingly, $y < x$. Since the sum of x and y must be 90, $x > 45$ and $y < 45$—which choice **B** contradicts. Each of the other four choices must be *true*.

58. K As you can see from the figure below, letting x = half the length of the base, $\sin 16° = \frac{x}{3}$; $x = 3\sin 16°$; and the length of the entire base $= 6\sin 16°$.

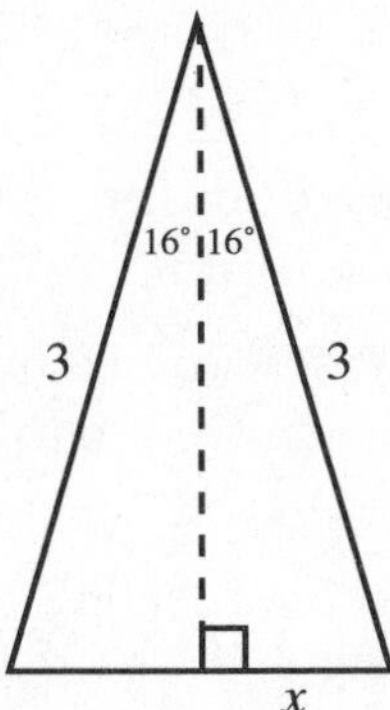

59. C In choice **C**, unequal quantities are subtracted from equal quantities. The differences are unequal, but the inequality is reversed because unequal numbers are being subtracted from rather than added to the equal numbers.

60. H The standard form for the equation of a cosine curve is $y = A\cos kx$, where A is the curve's amplitude. The value of A in the given equation is 2.

Reading

1. D In lines 12–17, Bertha describes her feeling of bliss as swallowing the afternoon sun and it sending a shower of sparks through her whole body—a description that is clear evidence of an imaginative mind. [Eliminate choice **A**.] Later in the passage, Bertha demonstrates affection toward her baby. We are informed in line 55 that Bertha wanted to question the Nanny's judgment, but "she did not dare to." This line indicates her timid nature. However, nowhere in the passage does either the narrator or Bertha herself suggest that Bertha is arrogant.

2. H Upon seeing Bertha arrive at the nursery, Nanny "set her lips in a way that Bertha knew, and that meant she had come into the nursery at another wrong moment." It is reasonable to infer that Nanny dislikes Bertha's visits to the nursery during certain times.

3. C In the paragraph preceding the use of the metaphor, we are told that "although Bertha Young was thirty," she had youthful emotions that she cannot express by such means as "dancing steps on and off the pavement." From this, we can infer that people of a certain age are expected to follow a certain code of behavior by not doing what they feel like doing.

4. F Nanny tells Bertha (in lines 76–78) that Bertha unthinkingly excites the baby, conveniently leaving Nanny to deal with the consequences. From this statement, we can surmise that Nanny considers Bertha a thoughtless person. By Nanny's repeated admonitions to Bertha about the baby's care, we can infer that she would agree that Bertha is inexperienced as a mother.

5. C We know from the details in the passage that Nanny feeds, bathes and grooms the baby, and also takes her out to the park. So, she no doubt considers herself the baby's primary caregiver. Even when Bertha occasionally visits with the baby, Nanny tries to treat Bertha as merely a "visitor"—by criticizing Bertha's behavior vis-à-vis the baby.

6. J The use of the word "absurd" is explained in the sentence that follows, where Bertha (through the narrator) questions the point of having a baby if "it has to be kept . . . in another woman's arms."

7. B Bertha stands watching Nanny with Bertha's baby. Bertha wishes she could be in Nanny's place, taking care of her baby herself. In this way, Bertha is like a poor little girl who wishes she had the doll that she sees the rich girl with, but she cannot afford it.

8. J The passage provides ample evidence of Nanny's possessive nature—for example, the use of "my" lovey (line 40) and the last sentence of the passage, in which we are told that Nanny came back into the nursery and seized "*her* Little B."

9. B In the second paragraph, we are informed that Bertha's "bliss" is a feeling brought about "suddenly"; we are not told of any specific event as the cause of it.

10. F We can infer from details provided by much of the passage that Nanny and Bertha continually compete for Little B and how her time is spent in the nursery. By the use of the word "triumph," we can infer that this round was in Nanny's favor—since Bertha had to not only relinquish the baby but leave the nursery as well.

11. B In the seventh paragraph, the passage states clearly that the company started its operations with capital obligations of "no less than $26 million."

12. H The word *subscriptions* is used in the context of raising money for a project involving the completion of the railway line.

13. D The author presents a chronological (time sequential) account of the history of the Erie Railroad—beginning with the first survey of the proposed construction line and ending with the final stage of construction. The author cites what appear to be carefully researched facts regarding the project's financing, the condition of the completed railroad, and the expansion of the railroad.

14. F In the last paragraph, the author suggests that, in its final expansion, the company's railroad connected Lake Erie with New York City. It is reasonably inferable that this "final expansion" connects the two most remote points.

15. D From the second paragraph, we know that, contrary to choice **D** it was the desire to be connected to Lake Erie by the southern counties that provided the initial impetus to the plan. Hence, it would make no sense to cite insufficient interest in this connection as an argument against the proposed Erie Railroad project.

16. H As stated in the sixth paragraph, "after eighteen years of effort, the line was opened to Lake Erie."

17. B The word *insolvent* refers to the company's monetary (money) problems as explained in the following sentence, which mentions the delay in further progress until sufficient new capital was raised.

18. G In the fourth paragraph, the passage informs us that the Panic of 1837 and the depression that followed did interfere with the construction, but that a year later "the state legislature provided a construction loan." We can surmise that the money loaned was used to continue the construction of the railroad.

19. A In lines 104–105, the author states that the railroad "soon became notorious for its many accidents. . . ." The word *notorious* means having an unfavorable reputation. Thus, we can infer that the company's ill repute was due to the frequent accidents involving its railroad.

20. J The first sentence of the passage tells us that the original plan was for the railroad to connect the Hudson River to Lake Erie. In the sixth paragraph, the passage indicates that the west terminus of the constructed railroad was on Lake Erie while the east terminus was on the Hudson. It is reasonable to infer, then, that the railroad was indeed completed according to the original plan. In the sixth paragraph, the passage indicates that various feeders (branches) were added to the railroad. Then, in the final paragraph, the author tells us of further expansion, via acquisition of other railroads.

21. C The sentence in which the word *munificent* appears tells us that Dr. Doyle's income was quite respectable "if not *munificent.*" The strong implication here is that Doyle's income was ample to lead a comfortable life. The word *bountiful* is consistent with this idea.

22. H The final paragraph tells us that it was only after the publication of a series of Holmes tales in a new magazine called *The Strand* that the "public finally took an interest in Dr. Doyle's detective."

23. B The passage provides ample information that runs contrary to the description in choice B—especially lines 88–91 in which Doyle comes across as a reluctant chronicler of Sherlock's fictional adventures. Also of special note are lines 117–118, in which we are informed of Doyle's "lack of enthusiasm for his protagonist" and how Doyle considered the Holmes stories insignificant compared to Doyle's other novels. It was the public's passion for Holmes stories, not Doyle's, that was the main reason Doyle wrote more Sherlock Holmes adventures.

24. F The third paragraph clearly states that Dr. Doyle believed "he could create a different kind of detective, one for whom detection was a science rather than art." And, nowhere in the passage does the author state or imply that Doyle was unsuccessful in doing so.

25. C The third paragraph tells us that the creator of Sherlock Holmes (Doyle) used one of his medical school professors, Dr. Joseph Bell, as a model for creating a detective "who applied similar intellectual powers to the solving of criminal mysteries."

26. G In lines 18–20 we learn that Doyle started writing because he felt that it "would keep him busy" and "hopefully bring additional funds."

27. D The author considers it fortunate that Doyle had time to concentrate on his writing. The implication here is that, in the author's view, Doyle's literary career was of more significance than his medical one.

28. F In the sixth paragraph, we're told that Doyle's move to London was enabled by "other small literary successes." One reasonable inference is that his successes allowed him to finally afford to live in London.

29. B In the final paragraph, we're told that Doyle was able to give up his practice and turn to writing full time mainly because of the public clamor for more Sherlock Holmes stories.

30. J The first paragraph tells us that Doyle moved to Portsmouth to begin a medical practice in 1882, and that since there were several well established physicians there, Doyle found himself with a great deal of spare time. Then, in the first sentence of the next paragraph, we learn that, to fill this time, "he began writing" stories—presumably, shortly after his arrival in Portsmouth in 1882. The final paragraph tells us that it wasn't until 1891, when *The Strand* begin publishing his Sherlock Holmes tales, that "the public finally took interest in Doyle's detective."

31. C The passage cites instances involving local residents and activists in particular geographic locations.

32. G The first paragraph informs us that Pace's "rudimentary research efforts were guided by hope" rather "than by scientific method." A research effort guided more by hope than by scientific method would be more basic than the other one. In this context, it makes sense that *rudimentary* might mean "basic." Besides, none of the other answer choices make sense in this context.

33. C The passage makes no mention of the spouses of abestos workers. All other choices indicated factors explicitly mentioned in the passage (lines 36–42) as factors leading to the conclusion that asbestos exposure causes cancer.

34. J The second paragraph defines "background rate" as "the number of people affected in the general population." The fourth paragraph indicates that the type of cancer afflicting the six young women "had been reported only once or twice before." This low incidence meets the definition of a "low background rate." The second paragraph defines "specificity" as "any notable characteristics of the individual affected in each case." The fact that the six young women suffered from "a certain vaginal cancer" suggests that what these women shared was a very specific, and unusual, symptom.

35. D The first sentence of the second paragraph refers to "cancer cases and other non-contagious conditions such as birth defects . . . ." This statement infers that cancer and birth defects fall into the same category—noncontagious conditions—meaning that neither type of condition can be transmitted by contact.

36. F To convey the meaning of the phrase "epidemiological gerrymandering," the author cites the case of citizens drawing boundaries around certain cancer cases and labeling it a cluster, thereby giving undue advantage to their cause. The activity that choice **F** describes is most analogous to this activity.

37. A According to the information in the fourth paragraph, the citizens might include cases of cancer that were either diagnosed before they moved into the locality in consideration or might have been exposed to a carcinogen in their previous domicile.

38. G The passage informs us, in lines 34–35, that "lung cancer is very common in the general population"—from which we can reasonably infer that the background rate for lung cancer is very high.

39. C The first paragraph of the passage, along with the passages final sentence, conveys this objective.

40. G In the last paragraph, the author cites the example of the Long Island cancer cluster, brought to light by a basic study conducted by a citizen. This study, combined with reports of other clusters in the community, helped "lay the groundwork" for the scientists to set up a well-designed study to determine the reason for the cancer cluster.

Science

1. D In the station adjacent to lake 5, the sulfate-concentration levels varied only from 0.65 to 0.68 Mg/L—a variation of 0.03 Mg/L, the smallest among the five stations.

2. J The top cluster chart in Figure 2 shows pH levels in one of the two non-glacial lakes (denoted by hollow circles) slightly higher in 2000 than in 1993 (the x-value is slightly greater than the y-value), while for the other non-glacial lake there appears to have been little or no change (the level is just over 7 in both years). In contrast, the chart shows pH levels in all three glacial lakes (denoted by solid circles) to be significantly higher in 2000 than in 1993. (For each one, the x-value is significantly greater than the y-value.)

3. A Table 1 shows that, over the study period (1993–2000), sulfate-concentration levels increased slightly in lake 5 and decreased slightly in lakes 1–4; also, over the time period, decreases as well as increases were seen in all lakes. Hence, the data shows no clear trend in either direction. However, sulfate concentration in all lakes but one of the non-glacial lakes (in which the level was the same, about 300, in 1993 as well as in 2000) increased significantly over the study period.

4. H The rainfall-temperature chart (Figure 1) shows that, over the most recent century, air temperature has been rising steadily—perhaps to a critical point, around 1993, when the glaciers at the two glacial lakes began melting into the lakes, which are frozen over during fewer and fewer days each year. One possible consequence is that more industrial sulfate emissions are finding their way into lake water—by means of precipitation or glacial runoff, or both. The results of Experiment 2, which show the that the most dramatic increase in sulfate-concentration levels have occurred in the two glacial lakes, further support this hypothesis.

5. B Experiment 2 showed that, while sulfate-concentration levels in the two glacial lakes increased from 1993 to 2000, pH levels did not. On the other hand, in the non-glacial lakes, where the water is presumably warmer, levels of both sulfate-concentration and pH increased over the same time period. Choice **B** provides a possible explanation for this distinction between glacial and non-glacial lakes.

6. B The higher the rotational period, the more slowly a planet rotates. Table 1 shows that, in general, there is a direct relationship between surface temperature and rotational period. Mercury and Venus have by far the greatest surface temperatures *and* rotational periods. Surface temperatures and rotational periods for Earth and Mars are similar to each other but significantly less than the ones for Mercury and Venus. The next four planets show similar levels for each, but less than the levels for Earth and Mars. (Pluto presents the only significant exception to the general relationship between surface temperature and rotational period.)

7. C Earth's average density is 5.5 times that of water, the highest among the nine planets shown. Earth's rotational period, 24 hours, is fifth longest. (Mercury, Venus, Mars, and Pluto all have longer rotational periods, while the remaining four planets all have shorter periods.)

8. H In Table 1, average densities are relative to the density of water. Pluto's average density is given as 1.0—which by definition is the density of water.

9. A Mercury's rotational period is 59 Earth days. Thus, in 88 Earth days, Mercury rotates about 1.3 times.

10. F The figure showing density and diameter of the four terrestrial planets reveals a direct linear relationship between density and diameter for Mars, Earth, and Venus (for each planet, the density-diameter ratio is about the same), but not for Mercury (for which the density-diameter ratio is much higher).

11. D Notice that Mercury's orbital eccentricity is far greater than that of Venus (whose orbit is nearly circular). Accordingly, Mercury's surface temperatures will vary greatly as it orbits the Sun— increasing when its distance from the Sun grows smaller, then decreasing as its distance increases.

12. G In Table 1, a positive percent change indicates a net gain, while a negative percent change indicates a net loss. For all but two nutrients—ammonium and nitrate—the percent change is negative.

13. D Table 2 shows that, in each year (1–3) losses of both organic and inorganic matter were generally higher in deforested areas than in undisturbed areas.

14. F Table 2 shows that for two of the three sources of output (basin and filter), the loss of particulate matter in the undisturbed area increased significantly from Year 1 to Year 2, then decreased significantly from Year 2 to Year 3. In an undisturbed area, the most plausible reason for a substantial increase in runoff is an increase in precipitation.

15. C In both experiments, fine material was caught by using a net. Hence, from the information given in the question we can conclude that sodium is primarily a net-caught material. Table 2 shows that losses of net-caught materials changed very little during the three-year period. Nothing in the passage or in the tables suggests that changes in sodium losses were any greater or less than the overall changes shown in the table.

16. J Table 2 shows no clear trend in the undisturbed area; thus it is reasonable to forecast no marked change over the longer term. Although the table shows increasing losses in nutrient matter in the deforested area over the three-year period of the study, no evidence is given suggesting that this trend will continue indefinitely. To the contrary, the fact that the ecologists applied herbicide to the deforested area to prevent organic matter from growing there strongly suggests that, over time, organic matter will reappear in the area, thereby slowly reducing the net losses of nutrients in that area.

17. B If the six experimental areas receive less rainfall per hectare than the forest as a whole, then the amount of nutrients entering each hectare would, on average, be greater than the table suggests. If this is the case, then unless the average runoff from other areas of the forest is also greater, net losses of nutrients would be less (and net gains would be greater) than the table suggests.

18. H Since the anti-cancer theory is based on the idea that gene imprinting evolved as a reaction to the possibility that the placenta might develop in a cancerous fashion, the theory would be severely undermined if it were true that plants, which have no placentas, had also developed the imprinting mechanism.

19. A The first sentence of the paragraph defining the protein control theory states this point succinctly.

20. J The competing parental interest theory assumes that both males and females seek to maximize the chances that their genes will be passed along to the next generation through a large number of healthy offspring. (It then postulates that, because males and females have different reproductive patterns, they have evolved different strategies for pursuing this result.) This assumption is stated in choice J.

21. A All three theories relate to reproduction in one way or another: the parental interest theory in regard to the transmission of genetic material through reproduction; the anti-cancer theory in relation to the development of the placenta, in which the fetus grows; and the protein control theory in relation to the healthy development of the embryo.

22. H Notice that the competing parental interest theory makes sense only if non-monogamous species are involved (since it is the differing reproductive habits of males and females that drives them to handle their genetic material differently). The finding described in choice **H** fits that theory because it suggests that imprinting is an unnecessary strategy in a monogamous species.

23. D This disorder supports the competing parental interest theory because the father's genetic material in that theory is associated with excessive growth, as here; it supports the anti-cancer theory because that theory associates imprinting with the need to control excessive growth of the placenta, as here; and it supports the protein control theory because, if the mother's genes are absent when the disorder occurs, this could explain the abnormal development found.

24. G This result would be consistent with the theory, since the female genes from Species A would not be imprinted for small size, while the male genes from Species B would be imprinted for large size. The combination would produce very large offspring.

25. B In all three experiments, the input amplitude was fixed at 2.0 volts.

26. F Only Experiment 2 shows the effect of a 1mH inductance using filter type 3. In the graph of Experiment 2, an input frequency of 100KHz (measured by the horizontal axis) corresponds roughly to a 1.9 volt output amplitude (measured by the vertical axis).

27. C The graphical representations of the three filters show that filter type 3 is the only one that contains an inductor. Experiment 2 was designed with inductance as the variable. It would make sense to conduct such as experiment only with a filter containing an inductor. Also, Experiment 3 was designed explicitly with inductance as a control; again, the description and methodology of the experiment makes sense only when a filter that contains an inductor is used.

28. G Based on the graph of Experiment 2, the higher the inductance level, the earlier a frequency response curve peaks. This means that at lower frequencies, sine waves are more likely to pass through the filter, contributing to a higher output amplitude.

29. D Only in Experiment 3 is capacitance a variable. The graphical results of that experiment show that, as the value of the capacitance increases, the frequency response curve narrows.

30. F Experiment 2 shows that a high inductance level results in the broadest peak, which is through the lower portion of the frequency spectrum. Conversely, Experiment 3 shows that a low capacitance level results in the broadest peak, which is through the higher portion of the frequency spectrum. Thus, it makes sense to combine both features in order to attain a high level of reception throughout the entire frequency spectrum.

31. C The question refers to generation 1 in Figure 1. The male and the female (the parents of generation 2) each have one copy of the disease gene (denoted by an uppercase "D").

32. F The only person in the figure who might contract the disease is the female in generation 3 identified as "DD." Both of her parents were healthy carriers—that is, they both had one copy of the disease gene. Thus, choice **F** cannot be true.

33. D Figure 2 does not provide any information about the father of her child. If the father has no copy of the disease gene, then the probability of their passing the disease onto their child would be zero (0%). Otherwise (if he has either one or two copies of the disease gene), that probability would be greater than zero.

34. G Figure 2 shows a total of nine children and grandchildren of the two individuals in generation 1. (Do not count the individuals in generation 2 who are parents but are not descended from generation 1.) Of these nine descendants, a total of four (one child and three grandchildren) have a copy of the disease gene (marked by an uppercase "D").

35. D In the case of a disease with a dominant inheritance pattern, if a person has at least one disease gene, that person will definitely have the disease. Since neither of Pamela's parents had disease X, the disease must have a recessive (and *not* a dominant) inheritance pattern.

36. H In every season except summer, salinity is lower at 5 meters than at 20 meters, and even lower at the surface. In summer, salinity is the same at all levels, which at least does not run contrary to the pattern in all other seasons.

37. D Seasonal increases and decreases in the number of salmon caught do not correspond to seasonal increases and decreases in water temperature at the surface and at 5 meters below the surface. As summer turns to fall, salinity levels decrease dramatically while the number of salmon caught, which is one indication of the level of the salmon population in the bay, increases dramatically.

38. G Choice G tells us that the local human population does not depend at all on salmon as a source of protein. But, complaints of protein deficiency-related diseases vary dramatically from season to season. Thus, it makes no sense that salmon availability has anything to do with protein deficiency-related illnesses.

39. A Seasonal changes in salinity at the ocean floor vary directly with the sample count of *Gammarus locusta*. What's more, percent changes in the sample count of *Gammarus locusta* in response to salinity changes are far greater than percent changes in the sample count *Gammarus duebent* in response to salinity changes. From winter to spring, for example, compare the 98% decrease in the *locusta* count (from 340 to 5) to the mere 50% decrease in the *duebent* count (from 50 to 25). Thus, it appears that *locusta* are more sensitive to salinity changes than *duebent*.

40. G The fact that these illnesses occur mainly in the winter and spring, considered together with the comparatively high number of salmon caught and bears observed during the fall, suggest that the local villagers consume salmon and bear meat (if they hunt bears for food) shortly after killing it. By preserving the fish and meat for consumption during the winter and spring, the villagers might very well avoid these types of illnesses.

ANSWER SHEET FOR PRACTICE TEST 2

Name: ______________________________

Date: ____/____/____

School: ______________________________

Class: ______________________________

Completely darken ovals with a No. 2 pencil. If you make a mistake, be sure to erase mark completely. Erase all stray marks.

Start with number 1 for each new section. If a section has fewer questions than answer spaces, leave the extra answer spaces blank.

PART 1

1 ⊂A⊃ ⊂B⊃ ⊂C⊃ ⊂D⊃ ⊂E⊃	20 ⊂F⊃ ⊂G⊃ ⊂H⊃ ⊂J⊃ ⊂K⊃	39 ⊂A⊃ ⊂B⊃ ⊂C⊃ ⊂D⊃ ⊂E⊃	58 ⊂F⊃ ⊂G⊃ ⊂H⊃ ⊂J⊃ ⊂K⊃
2 ⊂F⊃ ⊂G⊃ ⊂H⊃ ⊂J⊃ ⊂K⊃	21 ⊂A⊃ ⊂B⊃ ⊂C⊃ ⊂D⊃ ⊂E⊃	40 ⊂F⊃ ⊂G⊃ ⊂H⊃ ⊂J⊃ ⊂K⊃	59 ⊂A⊃ ⊂B⊃ ⊂C⊃ ⊂D⊃ ⊂E⊃
3 ⊂A⊃ ⊂B⊃ ⊂C⊃ ⊂D⊃ ⊂E⊃	22 ⊂F⊃ ⊂G⊃ ⊂H⊃ ⊂J⊃ ⊂K⊃	41 ⊂A⊃ ⊂B⊃ ⊂C⊃ ⊂D⊃ ⊂E⊃	60 ⊂F⊃ ⊂G⊃ ⊂H⊃ ⊂J⊃ ⊂K⊃
4 ⊂F⊃ ⊂G⊃ ⊂H⊃ ⊂J⊃ ⊂K⊃	23 ⊂A⊃ ⊂B⊃ ⊂C⊃ ⊂D⊃ ⊂E⊃	42 ⊂F⊃ ⊂G⊃ ⊂H⊃ ⊂J⊃ ⊂K⊃	61 ⊂A⊃ ⊂B⊃ ⊂C⊃ ⊂D⊃ ⊂E⊃
5 ⊂A⊃ ⊂B⊃ ⊂C⊃ ⊂D⊃ ⊂E⊃	24 ⊂F⊃ ⊂G⊃ ⊂H⊃ ⊂J⊃ ⊂K⊃	43 ⊂A⊃ ⊂B⊃ ⊂C⊃ ⊂D⊃ ⊂E⊃	62 ⊂F⊃ ⊂G⊃ ⊂H⊃ ⊂J⊃ ⊂K⊃
6 ⊂F⊃ ⊂G⊃ ⊂H⊃ ⊂J⊃ ⊂K⊃	25 ⊂A⊃ ⊂B⊃ ⊂C⊃ ⊂D⊃ ⊂E⊃	44 ⊂F⊃ ⊂G⊃ ⊂H⊃ ⊂J⊃ ⊂K⊃	63 ⊂A⊃ ⊂B⊃ ⊂C⊃ ⊂D⊃ ⊂E⊃
7 ⊂A⊃ ⊂B⊃ ⊂C⊃ ⊂D⊃ ⊂E⊃	26 ⊂F⊃ ⊂G⊃ ⊂H⊃ ⊂J⊃ ⊂K⊃	45 ⊂A⊃ ⊂B⊃ ⊂C⊃ ⊂D⊃ ⊂E⊃	64 ⊂F⊃ ⊂G⊃ ⊂H⊃ ⊂J⊃ ⊂K⊃
8 ⊂F⊃ ⊂G⊃ ⊂H⊃ ⊂J⊃ ⊂K⊃	27 ⊂A⊃ ⊂B⊃ ⊂C⊃ ⊂D⊃ ⊂E⊃	46 ⊂F⊃ ⊂G⊃ ⊂H⊃ ⊂J⊃ ⊂K⊃	65 ⊂A⊃ ⊂B⊃ ⊂C⊃ ⊂D⊃ ⊂E⊃
9 ⊂A⊃ ⊂B⊃ ⊂C⊃ ⊂D⊃ ⊂E⊃	28 ⊂F⊃ ⊂G⊃ ⊂H⊃ ⊂J⊃ ⊂K⊃	47 ⊂A⊃ ⊂B⊃ ⊂C⊃ ⊂D⊃ ⊂E⊃	66 ⊂F⊃ ⊂G⊃ ⊂H⊃ ⊂J⊃ ⊂K⊃
10 ⊂F⊃ ⊂G⊃ ⊂H⊃ ⊂J⊃ ⊂K⊃	29 ⊂A⊃ ⊂B⊃ ⊂C⊃ ⊂D⊃ ⊂E⊃	48 ⊂F⊃ ⊂G⊃ ⊂H⊃ ⊂J⊃ ⊂K⊃	67 ⊂A⊃ ⊂B⊃ ⊂C⊃ ⊂D⊃ ⊂E⊃
11 ⊂A⊃ ⊂B⊃ ⊂C⊃ ⊂D⊃ ⊂E⊃	30 ⊂F⊃ ⊂G⊃ ⊂H⊃ ⊂J⊃ ⊂K⊃	49 ⊂A⊃ ⊂B⊃ ⊂C⊃ ⊂D⊃ ⊂E⊃	68 ⊂F⊃ ⊂G⊃ ⊂H⊃ ⊂J⊃ ⊂K⊃
12 ⊂F⊃ ⊂G⊃ ⊂H⊃ ⊂J⊃ ⊂K⊃	31 ⊂A⊃ ⊂B⊃ ⊂C⊃ ⊂D⊃ ⊂E⊃	50 ⊂F⊃ ⊂G⊃ ⊂H⊃ ⊂J⊃ ⊂K⊃	69 ⊂A⊃ ⊂B⊃ ⊂C⊃ ⊂D⊃ ⊂E⊃
13 ⊂A⊃ ⊂B⊃ ⊂C⊃ ⊂D⊃ ⊂E⊃	32 ⊂F⊃ ⊂G⊃ ⊂H⊃ ⊂J⊃ ⊂K⊃	51 ⊂A⊃ ⊂B⊃ ⊂C⊃ ⊂D⊃ ⊂E⊃	70 ⊂F⊃ ⊂G⊃ ⊂H⊃ ⊂J⊃ ⊂K⊃
14 ⊂F⊃ ⊂G⊃ ⊂H⊃ ⊂J⊃ ⊂K⊃	33 ⊂A⊃ ⊂B⊃ ⊂C⊃ ⊂D⊃ ⊂E⊃	52 ⊂F⊃ ⊂G⊃ ⊂H⊃ ⊂J⊃ ⊂K⊃	71 ⊂A⊃ ⊂B⊃ ⊂C⊃ ⊂D⊃ ⊂E⊃
15 ⊂A⊃ ⊂B⊃ ⊂C⊃ ⊂D⊃ ⊂E⊃	34 ⊂F⊃ ⊂G⊃ ⊂H⊃ ⊂J⊃ ⊂K⊃	53 ⊂A⊃ ⊂B⊃ ⊂C⊃ ⊂D⊃ ⊂E⊃	72 ⊂F⊃ ⊂G⊃ ⊂H⊃ ⊂J⊃ ⊂K⊃
16 ⊂F⊃ ⊂G⊃ ⊂H⊃ ⊂J⊃ ⊂K⊃	35 ⊂A⊃ ⊂B⊃ ⊂C⊃ ⊂D⊃ ⊂E⊃	54 ⊂F⊃ ⊂G⊃ ⊂H⊃ ⊂J⊃ ⊂K⊃	73 ⊂A⊃ ⊂B⊃ ⊂C⊃ ⊂D⊃ ⊂E⊃
17 ⊂A⊃ ⊂B⊃ ⊂C⊃ ⊂D⊃ ⊂E⊃	36 ⊂F⊃ ⊂G⊃ ⊂H⊃ ⊂J⊃ ⊂K⊃	55 ⊂A⊃ ⊂B⊃ ⊂C⊃ ⊂D⊃ ⊂E⊃	74 ⊂F⊃ ⊂G⊃ ⊂H⊃ ⊂J⊃ ⊂K⊃
18 ⊂F⊃ ⊂G⊃ ⊂H⊃ ⊂J⊃ ⊂K⊃	37 ⊂A⊃ ⊂B⊃ ⊂C⊃ ⊂D⊃ ⊂E⊃	56 ⊂F⊃ ⊂G⊃ ⊂H⊃ ⊂J⊃ ⊂K⊃	75 ⊂A⊃ ⊂B⊃ ⊂C⊃ ⊂D⊃ ⊂E⊃
19 ⊂A⊃ ⊂B⊃ ⊂C⊃ ⊂D⊃ ⊂E⊃	38 ⊂F⊃ ⊂G⊃ ⊂H⊃ ⊂J⊃ ⊂K⊃	57 ⊂A⊃ ⊂B⊃ ⊂C⊃ ⊂D⊃ ⊂E⊃	76 ⊂F⊃ ⊂G⊃ ⊂H⊃ ⊂J⊃ ⊂K⊃

PART 2

1 ⊂A⊃ ⊂B⊃ ⊂C⊃ ⊂D⊃ ⊂E⊃	16 ⊂F⊃ ⊂G⊃ ⊂H⊃ ⊂J⊃ ⊂K⊃	31 ⊂A⊃ ⊂B⊃ ⊂C⊃ ⊂D⊃ ⊂E⊃	46 ⊂F⊃ ⊂G⊃ ⊂H⊃ ⊂J⊃ ⊂K⊃
2 ⊂F⊃ ⊂G⊃ ⊂H⊃ ⊂J⊃ ⊂K⊃	17 ⊂A⊃ ⊂B⊃ ⊂C⊃ ⊂D⊃ ⊂E⊃	32 ⊂F⊃ ⊂G⊃ ⊂H⊃ ⊂J⊃ ⊂K⊃	47 ⊂A⊃ ⊂B⊃ ⊂C⊃ ⊂D⊃ ⊂E⊃
3 ⊂A⊃ ⊂B⊃ ⊂C⊃ ⊂D⊃ ⊂E⊃	18 ⊂F⊃ ⊂G⊃ ⊂H⊃ ⊂J⊃ ⊂K⊃	33 ⊂A⊃ ⊂B⊃ ⊂C⊃ ⊂D⊃ ⊂E⊃	48 ⊂F⊃ ⊂G⊃ ⊂H⊃ ⊂J⊃ ⊂K⊃
4 ⊂F⊃ ⊂G⊃ ⊂H⊃ ⊂J⊃ ⊂K⊃	19 ⊂A⊃ ⊂B⊃ ⊂C⊃ ⊂D⊃ ⊂E⊃	34 ⊂F⊃ ⊂G⊃ ⊂H⊃ ⊂J⊃ ⊂K⊃	49 ⊂A⊃ ⊂B⊃ ⊂C⊃ ⊂D⊃ ⊂E⊃
5 ⊂A⊃ ⊂B⊃ ⊂C⊃ ⊂D⊃ ⊂E⊃	20 ⊂F⊃ ⊂G⊃ ⊂H⊃ ⊂J⊃ ⊂K⊃	35 ⊂A⊃ ⊂B⊃ ⊂C⊃ ⊂D⊃ ⊂E⊃	50 ⊂F⊃ ⊂G⊃ ⊂H⊃ ⊂J⊃ ⊂K⊃
6 ⊂F⊃ ⊂G⊃ ⊂H⊃ ⊂J⊃ ⊂K⊃	21 ⊂A⊃ ⊂B⊃ ⊂C⊃ ⊂D⊃ ⊂E⊃	36 ⊂F⊃ ⊂G⊃ ⊂H⊃ ⊂J⊃ ⊂K⊃	51 ⊂A⊃ ⊂B⊃ ⊂C⊃ ⊂D⊃ ⊂E⊃
7 ⊂A⊃ ⊂B⊃ ⊂C⊃ ⊂D⊃ ⊂E⊃	22 ⊂F⊃ ⊂G⊃ ⊂H⊃ ⊂J⊃ ⊂K⊃	37 ⊂A⊃ ⊂B⊃ ⊂C⊃ ⊂D⊃ ⊂E⊃	52 ⊂F⊃ ⊂G⊃ ⊂H⊃ ⊂J⊃ ⊂K⊃
8 ⊂F⊃ ⊂G⊃ ⊂H⊃ ⊂J⊃ ⊂K⊃	23 ⊂A⊃ ⊂B⊃ ⊂C⊃ ⊂D⊃ ⊂E⊃	38 ⊂F⊃ ⊂G⊃ ⊂H⊃ ⊂J⊃ ⊂K⊃	53 ⊂A⊃ ⊂B⊃ ⊂C⊃ ⊂D⊃ ⊂E⊃
9 ⊂A⊃ ⊂B⊃ ⊂C⊃ ⊂D⊃ ⊂E⊃	24 ⊂F⊃ ⊂G⊃ ⊂H⊃ ⊂J⊃ ⊂K⊃	39 ⊂A⊃ ⊂B⊃ ⊂C⊃ ⊂D⊃ ⊂E⊃	54 ⊂F⊃ ⊂G⊃ ⊂H⊃ ⊂J⊃ ⊂K⊃
10 ⊂F⊃ ⊂G⊃ ⊂H⊃ ⊂J⊃ ⊂K⊃	25 ⊂A⊃ ⊂B⊃ ⊂C⊃ ⊂D⊃ ⊂E⊃	40 ⊂F⊃ ⊂G⊃ ⊂H⊃ ⊂J⊃ ⊂K⊃	55 ⊂A⊃ ⊂B⊃ ⊂C⊃ ⊂D⊃ ⊂E⊃
11 ⊂A⊃ ⊂B⊃ ⊂C⊃ ⊂D⊃ ⊂E⊃	26 ⊂F⊃ ⊂G⊃ ⊂H⊃ ⊂J⊃ ⊂K⊃	41 ⊂A⊃ ⊂B⊃ ⊂C⊃ ⊂D⊃ ⊂E⊃	56 ⊂F⊃ ⊂G⊃ ⊂H⊃ ⊂J⊃ ⊂K⊃
12 ⊂F⊃ ⊂G⊃ ⊂H⊃ ⊂J⊃ ⊂K⊃	27 ⊂A⊃ ⊂B⊃ ⊂C⊃ ⊂D⊃ ⊂E⊃	42 ⊂F⊃ ⊂G⊃ ⊂H⊃ ⊂J⊃ ⊂K⊃	57 ⊂A⊃ ⊂B⊃ ⊂C⊃ ⊂D⊃ ⊂E⊃
13 ⊂A⊃ ⊂B⊃ ⊂C⊃ ⊂D⊃ ⊂E⊃	28 ⊂F⊃ ⊂G⊃ ⊂H⊃ ⊂J⊃ ⊂K⊃	43 ⊂A⊃ ⊂B⊃ ⊂C⊃ ⊂D⊃ ⊂E⊃	58 ⊂F⊃ ⊂G⊃ ⊂H⊃ ⊂J⊃ ⊂K⊃
14 ⊂F⊃ ⊂G⊃ ⊂H⊃ ⊂J⊃ ⊂K⊃	29 ⊂A⊃ ⊂B⊃ ⊂C⊃ ⊂D⊃ ⊂E⊃	44 ⊂F⊃ ⊂G⊃ ⊂H⊃ ⊂J⊃ ⊂K⊃	59 ⊂A⊃ ⊂B⊃ ⊂C⊃ ⊂D⊃ ⊂E⊃
15 ⊂A⊃ ⊂B⊃ ⊂C⊃ ⊂D⊃ ⊂E⊃	30 ⊂F⊃ ⊂G⊃ ⊂H⊃ ⊂J⊃ ⊂K⊃	45 ⊂A⊃ ⊂B⊃ ⊂C⊃ ⊂D⊃ ⊂E⊃	60 ⊂F⊃ ⊂G⊃ ⊂H⊃ ⊂J⊃ ⊂K⊃

BE SURE TO ERASE ANY ERRORS OR STRAY MARKS COMPLETELY.

DO NOT MARK IN THIS AREA

Use a No. 2 pencil only. Be sure each mark is dark and completely fills the intended oval. Completely erase any errors or stray marks.

Start with number 1 for each new section. If a section has fewer questions than answer spaces, leave the extra answer spaces blank.

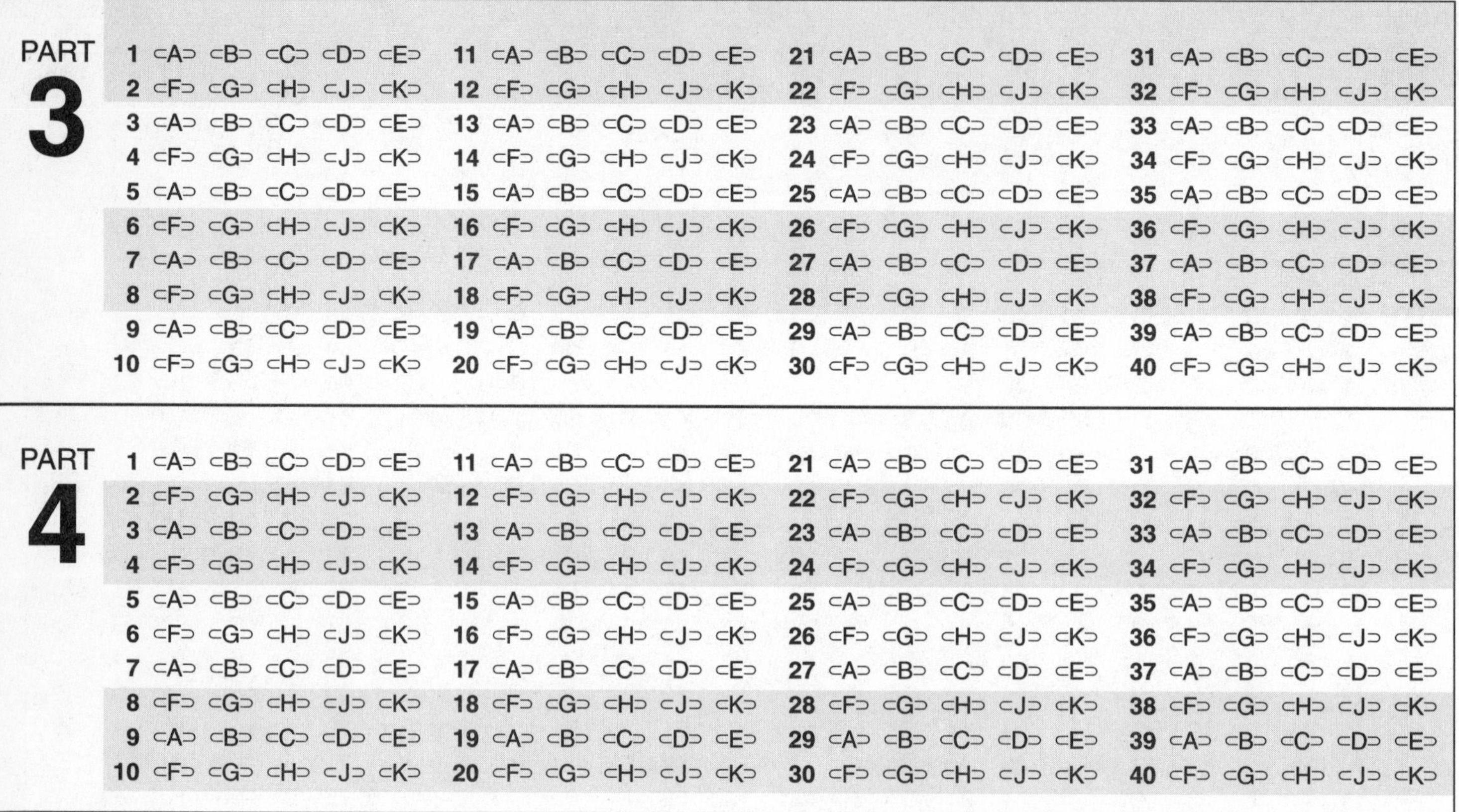

PART 3

1 A B C D E	11 A B C D E	21 A B C D E	31 A B C D E
2 F G H J K	12 F G H J K	22 F G H J K	32 F G H J K
3 A B C D E	13 A B C D E	23 A B C D E	33 A B C D E
4 F G H J K	14 F G H J K	24 F G H J K	34 F G H J K
5 A B C D E	15 A B C D E	25 A B C D E	35 A B C D E
6 F G H J K	16 F G H J K	26 F G H J K	36 F G H J K
7 A B C D E	17 A B C D E	27 A B C D E	37 A B C D E
8 F G H J K	18 F G H J K	28 F G H J K	38 F G H J K
9 A B C D E	19 A B C D E	29 A B C D E	39 A B C D E
10 F G H J K	20 F G H J K	30 F G H J K	40 F G H J K

PART 4

1 A B C D E	11 A B C D E	21 A B C D E	31 A B C D E
2 F G H J K	12 F G H J K	22 F G H J K	32 F G H J K
3 A B C D E	13 A B C D E	23 A B C D E	33 A B C D E
4 F G H J K	14 F G H J K	24 F G H J K	34 F G H J K
5 A B C D E	15 A B C D E	25 A B C D E	35 A B C D E
6 F G H J K	16 F G H J K	26 F G H J K	36 F G H J K
7 A B C D E	17 A B C D E	27 A B C D E	37 A B C D E
8 F G H J K	18 F G H J K	28 F G H J K	38 F G H J K
9 A B C D E	19 A B C D E	29 A B C D E	39 A B C D E
10 F G H J K	20 F G H J K	30 F G H J K	40 F G H J K

BE SURE TO ERASE ANY ERRORS OR STRAY MARKS COMPLETELY.

Practice Test 2

English

75 Questions ■ Time—45 Minutes

Directions: This test consists of five passages in which particular words or phrases are underlined and numbered. Alongside the passage, you will see alternative words and phrases that could be substituted for the underlined part. Select the alternative that expresses the idea most clearly and correctly or that best fits the style and tone of the entire passage. If the original version is best, select "No Change."

The test also includes questions about entire paragraphs and the passage as a whole. These questions are identified by a number in a box.

After you select the correct answer for each question, on your answer sheet, mark the oval corresponding to the correct answer.

Passage I

My Day with Monet at Giverny

[1]

One of my most memorable trips I went on [1] was to Claude Monet's garden at Giverny, about an hour and a half from Paris. Although a [2] chilly, late autumn day, the garden was still in bloom. Gardeners [3] rotate flower plantings by season from spring through the end of fall.

[2]

On the day my companion and I [4] were there, dahlias were everywhere, in a multitude of colors and shades—red, pink, yellow, orange, purple, lavender. Leggy pink and magenta cosmos waved in the cool breeze. The last roses of the season were so massive they could hardly hold their heads up.

[3]

(1) A trellis rises up from the railing around the front porch, [5] frames the house in greenery. (2) Inside and out, [6] Monet's house is simply a marvel. Painted pink ivy covers large swaths of the facade. (3) The day I visited, the trellis was not in bloom, but in summer little red blooms peak from the green leaves. [7]

[4]

The house itself is [8] filled with light and color. Every room has several large windows. Walls are painted light blue, see green, tan, and pale yellow. The kitchen walls are covered with blue and white tiles. Monet was a collector of Japanese prints, which are displayed through [9] the house. Monet's interest in Japanese art is further reflected [10] in the sparseness of the furnishings and the use of wicker for some of the chairs.

[5]

But the most amazing element is the Japanese water garden. I have long been [11] a lover of Monet's series of water lily paintings, I had expected to see a huge pond. Well, first I had expected that Monet's house would be set on a large estate, but it's right in the village of Giverny. [12] The water garden is across the street from Monet's house and is about the size of an Olympic swimming pool.

[6]

(1) Even on a cloudy day in autumn, the garden was beautiful. (2) Willows hung over the water and were reflected in its stillness. (3) Feathery dried grasses were all that lined the shore. (4) Gray vines, all that is left [13] of the wisteria at this time of year, entwined the railings of the Japanese footbridge. (5) Only a few fading wisteria blooms dotted the scattered water lily pads. (6) Above all, there was a quietness. [14]

1. **A.** NO CHANGE
B. in my life
C. of mine
D. OMIT the underlined portion.

2. **F.** NO CHANGE
G. Although it was a
H. Although the day was a
J. It was a

3. A. NO CHANGE
   B. bloom, although
   C. bloom because the gardeners
   D. bloom, and the gardeners

4. F. NO CHANGE
   G. I and my companion
   H. me and my companion
   J. my companion and me

5. A. NO CHANGE
   B. porch and
   C. porch; and it
   D. porch: the trellis

6. F. NO CHANGE
   G. In and out,
   H. Both on the inside and the outside,
   J. OMIT the underlined portion.

7. Which of the following is the most logical order for the sentences of Paragraph 3?
   A. NO CHANGE
   B. 2, 1, 3
   C. 3, 2, 1
   D. 3, 1, 2

8. F. NO CHANGE
   G. inside is
   H. house
   J. house is itself

9. A. NO CHANGE
   B. around
   C. in
   D. throughout

10. F. NO CHANGE
    G. further reflects
    H. also is reflected
    J. is reflected

11. A. NO CHANGE
    B. Long
    C. For a long time I've been
    D. I admit that I am

12. Which of the following proposals for the underlined sentence makes most sense in the context of Paragraph 5 as a whole?
    F. NO CHANGE
    G. Move it to the beginning of the paragraph.
    H. Move it to the end of the paragraph.
    J. Delete the sentence.

13. A. NO CHANGE
    B. all that was
    C. all that's
    D. which were all that was

14. The writer wishes to incorporate the following sentence into Paragraph 6:

    In summer, the sight of the footbridge draped with long purple clusters of wisteria blooms must be dazzling.

    Where would be the best place for this sentence?
    F. At the beginning of Paragraph 6
    G. Between sentence 1 and sentence 2
    H. Between sentence 4 and sentence 5
    J. Between sentence 5 and sentence 6

Question 15 poses a question about the passage as a whole.

15. Suppose the writer were to eliminate Paragraph 4. This omission would cause the passage as a whole to lose primarily:

A. relevant details about Monet's tastes and preferences in art.
B. irrelevant details about the Japanese influence on Monet.
C. a digression from the passage's central concern about Monet's garden.
D. information that establishes the setting for what's described in the other paragraphs.

Passage II

Globalization

The 1990s saw the rise of the concept of globalization, which is the idea that the economies of the world are becoming ever more interrelated. In reality, the process has been at work for several decades.

A number of factors accounts [16] for this interconnectedness: the [17] reduction or elimination of trade barriers in the form of tariffs, the rise of multinationals, and the free flow of capital and workers.

A major cause of globalization has been the reduction or elimination of trade barriers in the form of tariffs. [18] Tariffs are taxes added to the cost of imports, which raises their price to consumers. [19] By decreasing or eliminating tariffs, the price of imported goods is allowed to seek its own level, which may be lower than a similarly domestically produced good.

Another factor that has impacted how and where companies do business is the growth of the multinationals. Thousands of U.S. companies have offices in other nations. Thousands [20] of other nations' companies have presences [21] in the United States. In fact, many companies that Americans typically think of as U.S. in origin are actually owned by corporations in other nations. This is true from publishing companies to food manufacturers to music producers. [22]

The free flow of money and workers from nation to nation is another aspect of globalization. [23] The European Union has eliminated the need for passports and visas for traveling between member nations. Before developing it's own economic problems, the Japanese were heavy investors in foreign businesses such as real estate and entertainment companies in the United States. [26]

The question is whether all this globalization is a good thing or a bad thing for the people of the world. As the recession in the U.S. in 2001 and 2002 showed, the interconnectedness of economies can depress activity across many nations when a high-flying economy begins to lose economic steam. Often, it's the low-level factory worker who is hurt. As economies slow, the demand for goods decline, and people lose their jobs. Economists note that international trade theory is not based on reality but on the ideal. In the ideal world, any worker who loses a job because low-priced imports force his or her company to lay off employees will immediately find a new job in an industry that competes better in the marketplace. [30]

16. F. NO CHANGE
G. Some factors are accounting
H. The number of factors accounts
J. Numerous factors account

17. A. NO CHANGE
B. interconnectedness, the
C. interconnectedness; the
D. interconnectedness. The

18. Which of the following proposals regarding the underlined sentence provides the best transition from the first paragraph to the second paragraph?
F. NO CHANGE
G. At the end of the sentence, add a comma followed by the clause *the first factor identified above.*
H. Replace the sentence with the following: *One major cause of globalization involves tariffs.*
J. Delete the underlined sentence.

19. A. NO CHANGE
B. thereby raising prices consumers pay for imports.
C. which increases prices to consumers.
D. and then consumers pay more for them.

20. F. NO CHANGE
G. nations, but thousands
H. nations; in contrast, thousands
J. nations. Similarly,

21. A. NO CHANGE
B. have presence
C. maintain a presence
D. are present

22. Which of the following proposals for the underlined sentence would be most effective in achieving a smooth flow of ideas in the paragraph?

F. NO CHANGE
G. Delete the phrase *This is true*, and insert the remainder between *origin* and *are* in the preceding sentence, set off by commas.
H. Switch the position of this sentence with the position of the preceding one.
J. Insert this sentence between the paragraph's first and second sentences.

23. A. NO CHANGE
B. Money and workers, flow freely from nation to nation—another aspect of globalization.
C. Another aspect of globalization is that, from nation to nation, money and workers flow freely.
D. Yet another aspect of globalization involves the free flow of money and workers from nation to nation.

24. F. NO CHANGE
G. its
H. they're
J. their

25. A. NO CHANGE
B. businesses, for example
C. business such as
D. businesses in

26. At this point in the passage, the writer is considering adding the following sentence:

Multinationals in the U.S. are now pouring large amounts of capital into China, hoping to reap huge profits from China's market of six billion people.

Would adding this sentence contribute to the understanding of the passage?

F. Yes, because this paragraph's primary concern is with the rise of multinational corporations as a factor in globalization.
G. Yes, because this sentence provides a present-day example of the free flow of money from nation to nation.
H. No, because the sentence provides a poor transition to the next paragraph, which never discusses either U.S. multinationals or China.
J. No, because the writer has already supplied ample evidence of the free flow of money today from nation to nation.

27. A. NO CHANGE
B. either good or bad
C. good or it's bad
D. a good or a bad thing

28. F. NO CHANGE
G. declines
H. will decline
J. might decline

29. A. NO CHANGE
B. based on the ideal that is not reality.
C. based on the ideal rather than on reality.
D. not based on reality. It is based on the ideal.

Question 30 poses a question about the passage as a whole.

30. An editor has commented that the writer has not ended the passage properly. Considering the passage's overall structure and flow of information, which of the following would be most effective as an additional, and final, sentence of the passge?

- **F.** The unavoidable conclusion is that economists, as a group, are more concerned with theoretical macroeconomic models than with the real concerns and problems of the world's people.
- **G.** Therefore, globalization holds strong promise for improved living standards around the world, as well as a greater variety of lower-cost products and services for all its people.
- **H.** In the real world, however, the evidence appears to show that, inevitable as globalization might be at this point, the world's peoples might have been better off, on balance, without it.
- **J.** A number of economists believe that free trade will force industries to modernize, thereby becoming more efficient and producing goods at lower cost to the consumer.

Passage III

[The following paragraphs may or may not be arranged in the best possible order. The last question will ask you to choose the most effective order for the paragraphs as numbered.]

The Magic of Special Effects

[1]

The movies are one place where magic can come true. Sights are seen in movies [31] that you might never hope to see in real life like [32] ocean liners sinking, earthquakes swallowing cities, planets exploding. The movies are also the only place outside your imagination where you can see things that never and might never exist at all [33], including rampaging monsters, battles in outer space, and sky-high cities of the future, to list just a few.

[2]

Effects artists have developed many tricks and techniques over the years. [34] Working closely with movie directors, producers, and actors, effects artists play a growing role in movie making today. Special-effects techniques are useful to movie makers in several ways.

Some movie scenes would be prohibitively costly to produce using ordinary methods, so they can be used to save money. (35) For example, to (36) show an imaginary city, it would cost many millions of dollars to build real buildings, roads, and so on. The clever using of (37) special effects can cut those costs dramatically.

[3]

All these are examples of the movie magic known as special effects, and they're the work of an elite group of amazingly clever (38) and skilled effects artists. The (39) real magic lies in how their able (40) to make a man in a gorilla suit into King Kong, or transform tiny plastic models into huge space ships, or turn instructions in a computer into images of a world that no one has ever imagined before.

[4]

Most important, special effects allow moviemakers to film scenes that would otherwise be impossible. They let movies show non-existent, even impossible worlds. Special effects are the tools of the moviemaker (41) for communicating a unique imaginative experience. And, after all, that's one of the reasons why (42) we all go to the movies.

[5]

(1) Battle or disaster scenes involving explosions, floods, or avalanches can be very dangerous to film. (2) Effects artists can simulate disaster scenes in ways that gives (43) audiences the thrill of witnessing a dangerous event without exposing actors to real hazards. (3) Special effects can also make moviemaking safer. (4) Even in comedies, sometimes characters are placed in harm's way. [44]

31. **A.** NO CHANGE
B. In movies, sights are seen
C. A person sees sights
D. You can see sights

32. **F.** NO CHANGE
G. life;
H. life, such as
J. life; examples are

33. **A.** NO CHANGE
B. might never exist at all
C. don't and might never exist
D. never existed and might never exist

34. Which of the following proposals for the underlined sentence, if implemented, would be most effective in achieving a logical flow of ideas in the passage?

F. NO CHANGE
G. Move the sentence to the beginning of Paragraph 5.
H. Move the sentence to the beginning of Paragraph 4.
J. Delete the underlined sentence.

35. A. NO CHANGE
B. Some movie scenes would be prohibitively costly to produce using ordinary methods; special effects are useful to save money.
C. They can be used to save money wherever movie scenes are prohibitively costly to produce using ordinary methods.
D. They can be used wherever movie scenes are prohibitively costly to produce using ordinary methods to save money.

36. F. NO CHANGE
G. for the purpose to
H. if you wanted to
J. Omit the underlined portion.

37. A. NO CHANGE
B. Cleverly using
C. Clever use of
D. Using clever

38. F. NO CHANGE
G. amazing clever
H. amazing and clever
J. cleverly amazing

39. A. NO CHANGE
B. However, the
C. And the
D. OMIT the underlined portion.

40. F. NO CHANGE
G. they have the ability
H. they're able
J. their capable

41. A. NO CHANGE
B. are the moviemaker's tool
C. is the moviemaker's tool
D. are tools that the moviemaker uses

42. F. NO CHANGE
G. one of the reasons
H. one reason why
J. a reason

43. A. NO CHANGE
B. a way that gives
C. ways that give
D. a way giving

44. Which of the following is the most logical order of sentences in Paragraph 5?

F. 3, 1, 2, 4
G. 4, 2, 1, 3
H. 1, 2, 3, 4
J. 2, 4, 1, 3

Question 45 poses a question about the passage as a whole.

45. For the sake of unity and coherence of the passage, which of the following provides the most effective ordering of the paragraphs?

A. 1, 2, 3, 4, 5
B. 2, 1, 3, 1, 4
C. 2, 4, 1, 3, 5
D. 1, 3, 2, 5, 4

GO ON TO THE NEXT PAGE

Passage IV

[The following paragraphs may or may not be arranged in the best possible order. The last question will ask you to choose the most effective order for the paragraphs as numbered.]

Benjamin Franklin: Unsung Hero

[1]

One of Benjamin Franklin's first acts as minister to France was to request that French troops be sent to the United States to fight alongside Washington's forces. The request was denied, but France did provide money. The American army was badly in need of uniforms, food, weapons, and ammunition. [46] In 1781, the French finally dispatched troops and a contingent of the French navy. It was these ships that blockaded the British at Yorktown, which forced Great Britain to surrender its claim to the former colonies. Lord Cornwallis and his British soldiers marched out of [47] Yorktown between two rows of French and American soldiers.

[2]

When the war ended, Franklin stayed on in France, and [48] negotiated the final peace treaty between the United States and Great Britain. When it was signed, he returned to Pennsylvania, where they elected him [49] President of the Pennsylvania Executive Council. During [50] the Constitutional Convention was convened in 1787, Franklin was among its many [51] illustrious members. At the time of his latest role, he was 81. Franklin died three years later.

[3]

"Benjamin Franklin: Unsung Hero" may seem like a strange title for a biographical sketch of the man, but surprisingly [52] few people realize the important role he played in the American Revolution. When most people think of Franklin, they think of him as [53] the inventor of the lightning rod and perhaps the Franklin stove, overshadowed [54] in history books by Washington, Jefferson, and even the Marquis de Lafayette.

[4]

No one would be more surprised than Franklin at how his role <u>had been</u> 55 overlooked. Franklin spent almost eighteen years in London as an agent for Pennsylvania and several other colonies. His reputation as a serious <u>scientist, philosopher, as well as</u> 56 his wit and charm, gained him entrance to the drawing rooms and studies of many important and politically influential men and women in England and <u>on</u> 57 the continent. When war broke out in 1776, the Continental Congress sent Franklin, then seventy years old, to France to lead a commission to gain France's support. It was through Franklin's efforts that, in 1778, France and the United States signed a treaty <u>pledging its</u> 58 support for American independence. [59] Once diplomatic relations were established, Franklin was named United States minister to France.

46. F. NO CHANGE
G. Although the request was denied, France did provide money to supply the American army with uniforms, food, weapons, and ammunition, all of which were badly needed.
H. The American army, which badly needed uniforms, food, weapons, and ammunition, was denied the request but provided money by France.
J. The request was denied. The American army badly needed uniforms, food, weapons, and ammunition, so France provided money.

47. Which of the following is the most effective in light of the information and ideas conveyed in Paragraph 1 as a whole?
A. NO CHANGE
B. decided to leave
C. ceremoniously left
D. were marched out of

48. F. NO CHANGE
G. France and
H. France; and
J. France and he

49. A. NO CHANGE
B. they elected him as
C. he was elected
D. an election made him

50. F. NO CHANGE
G. Whenever
H. While
J. When

51. A. NO CHANGE
B. many
C. their
D. OMIT the underlined portion.

52. F. NO CHANGE
G. surprising
H. it is a surprise that
J. surprised

53. A. NO CHANGE
B. Most people think of Franklin as
C. Most of the people think that Franklin was
D. Franklin is mostly thought of as

54. Which of the following would be most effective in helping to convey the main point of the Paragraph 3?

F. NO CHANGE
G. stove. He was overshadowed
H. stove. Instead, he was overshadowed
J. stove, as well as a person overshadowed

55. A. NO CHANGE
B. is
C. has been
D. was being

56. F. NO CHANGE
G. scientist and philosopher, as well as
H. scientist, as a philosopher, as well as
J. scientist and philosopher and

57. A. NO CHANGE
B. in
C. through
D. OMIT the underlined portion.

58. F. NO CHANGE
G. which pledged
H. in pledged
J. in which France pledged its

59. At this point in the passage, the writer is considering adding the following sentence:

Had it not been for Franklin's letter of introduction to Washington on Lafayette's behalf, the Marquis de Lafayette would never have served in the war.

Would adding this sentence contribute to the understanding of the passage?

A. Yes, because it helps explain why Franklin would have been surprised that his political career has been largely overlooked.
B. Yes, because it helps show that Franklin's wit served him in influencing politically influential people.
C. No, because the passage provides ample evidence of Franklin's key role in the American Revolution without the additional sentence.
D. No, because the sentence provides no information about Franklin's influence over politically influential people in Europe.

Question 60 poses a question about the passage as a whole.

60. For the sake of unity and coherence of the passage, which of the following provides the most effective sequence of this passage's paragraphs?

F. 1, 2, 3, 4
G. 3, 1, 2, 4
H. 3, 4, 1, 2
J. 1, 2, 4, 3

Passage V

A New Deal for America

[1]

During the Great Depression of the 1930s, relief was much needed. People had no jobs, no food, and (61) were losing their shelter. Franklin D. Roosevelt, president at the time, decided to initiate a much needed system of relief, he called it (62) the "New Deal." There were three stages to the New Deal: relief, recovery, and reform. [63]

[2]

(1) During the first stage, the relief stage, (64) the Civilian Conservation Corps (CCC) and the Federal Emergency Relief Act (FERA) was established. (2) The CCC provided aid in unemployment, (65) mainly for youths from cities. (3) It not only put them to work but the environment was also conserved. (66) (4) They planted forests, fought forest fires, made dams, and created roads and trails. (5) The CCC succeeded in providing jobs for the unemployed youths and protecting the environment. (67) (6) The FERA granted direct financial relief to the needy. It was meant only for short-term relief: Roosevelt (68) did not want the needy to grow dependent on free money.

[3]

During the second, or recovery, stage, the Tennessee Valley Authority (TVA) was created to put legions of people to work building the most extensive electric power system ever devised. Also, new federal laws created minimum wage and maximum work-week laws (69) and prohibited child labor, aiding overworked and underpaid people. Though it (70) helped, Latinos, African Americans, and Asians were not part of the system until decades later.

[4]

During the third, or reform, stage, the Social Security Act was mainly created (71) to aid the elderly, provide pensions funded by taxes, and provide unemployment benefits to protect dependent mothers and children. Another act

safeguarded the rights of workers, providing legal protection against employers which attempted to fire labor organizers, suppress strikes, or stifle unions.
72

[5]

The relief provided by the New Deal's various laws and programs, Roosevelt believed, were part of government's responsibility. [74] If the government had not stepped in, the country might very well have crumbled. While some were given jobs and direct financial aid, others were given hope. With hope, people were able to attempt a better life. The government provided temporary relief, but the rest was up to the individual.
73
75

61. A. NO CHANGE
B. food, and
C. had no food, and
D. no food, and they

62. F. NO CHANGE
G. relief, called
H. relief and he called it
J. relief he called

63. For the sake of unity and coherence, which of the following editorial proposals involving the transition from Paragraph 1 to Paragraph 2 is most effective?

A. NO CHANGE
B. Omit the paragraph break here, and begin Paragraph 2 with what is currently the last sentence of Paragraph 1.
C. Move the last sentence of Paragraph 1 to the beginning of that paragraph.
D. OMIT the paragraph break between Paragraphs 1 and 2.

64. F. NO CHANGE
G. relief stage,
H. first relief stage,
J. stage of relief,

65. A. NO CHANGE
B. unemployment aid,
C. employment,
D. unemployment,

66. F. NO CHANGE
G. but also conserved the environment.
H. and it conserved the environment.
J. as well as conserving the environment.

67. Which of the following proposals for sentence 5 would be most appropriate in the context of the paragraph in which it appears?

A. NO CHANGE
B. Move the sentence so that it immediately follows sentence 1.
C. Replace the sentence with the following: *The CCC succeeded in protecting the environment and in providing jobs for the unemployed youths.*
D. Delete the sentence. (Do not replace it with any other sentence.)

68. F. NO CHANGE
G. relief, Roosevelt
H. relief; Roosevelt
J. relief from Roosevelt who

69. A. NO CHANGE
B. minimum wage laws and maximum work-week laws
C. minimum and maximum wage and work-week requirements
D. a minimum wage and a maximum work week

70. F. NO CHANGE
G. they
H. the laws
J. they were

71. A. NO CHANGE
B. created mainly
C. created—mainly
D. created in the main

72. F. NO CHANGE
G. attempts
H. attempting
J. OMIT the underlined portion.

73. A. NO CHANGE
B. was
C. are
D. is to be

74. Which of the following would be the most relevant and logical sentence to insert at this point in the passage?

F. The American people were hurting, but they had not given up hope.
G. After all, a nation cannot function when its people are starving and homeless.
H. The New Deal was one way that Roosevelt carried out what he saw as that responsibility.
J. A government's main function is to ensure the well being of the citizenry.

75. A. NO CHANGE
B. were capable to live better.
C. could attempt lives that were better.
D. attempted to better their life.

STOP

Math

60 Questions ■ Time—60 Minutes

Directions: Solve each problem; then, on your answer sheet, mark the oval corresponding to the correct answer.

Be careful not to spend too much time on any one question. Instead, solve as many problems as possible, and then use the remaining time to return to those questions you were unable to answer at first.

You may use a calculator on any problem in this test. However, some problems can best be solved without use of a calculator.

Note: Unless otherwise stated, you can assume that:

1. Diagrams that accompany problems are not necessarily drawn to scale.
2. All figures lie in the same plane.
3. The word "line" refers to a straight line (and lines that appear straight are straight).
4. The word "average" refers to arithmetic mean.

1. Of the 120 students enrolled in a certain class, 40 are sophomores, 44 are juniors, and the remainder are seniors. What percentage of the total number of enrolled students are seniors?

A. 42
B. 40
C. 34
D. 30
E. 24

2. In the standard (x,y) coordinate plane, the distance from point A to point B is 6. Which of the following could be the coordinates of the two points?

F. $A(0,3)$ and $B(6,0)$
G. $A(6,3)$ and $B(0,3)$
H. $A(3,0)$ and $B(0,-3)$
J. $A(0,6)$ and $B(3,-3)$
K. $A(3,3)$ and $B(-3,-3)$

3. Which of the following expressions is a simplified form of $(-2x^2)^4$?

A. $16x^8$
B. $8x^6$
C. $-8x^8$
D. $-16x^6$
E. $-16x^8$

4. If $A = 3$, $AB = -9$, and $BC = -6$, then $C =$

F. 9
G. 3
H. 2
J. −2
K. −3

5. If $\frac{ab}{10} + 5 = a - 2$, for what value of a does b equal 5?

A. −12
B. −4
C. 4
D. 9
E. 14

6. The sum of $\sqrt{0.49}$, $\frac{3}{4}$, and 80% =

F. 0.425
G. 1.59
H. 1.62
J. 2.04
K. 2.25

7. What is the perimeter of a rectangle whose length is three times its width and whose area is 12 square centimeters?

A. 18 centimeters
B. 16 centimeters
C. 15 centimeters
D. 8 centimeters
E. 4 centimeters

8. If $0.2t = 2.2 - 0.6s$ and $0.5s = 0.2t + 1.1$, then $s =$

F. 1
G. 3
H. 10
J. 11
K. 30

9. If the value of *XYZ* Company stock drops from \$25 per share to \$21 per share, what is the percent of decrease?

A. 20
B. 16
C. 12
D. 8
E. 4

10. If a portion of \$10,000 is invested at 6% and the remaining portion is invested at 5%, and if x represents the amount invested at 6%, what is the annual income in dollars from the 5% investment?

F. $0.05(10{,}000 - x)$
G. $0.05(x + 10{,}000)$
H. $5(x - 10{,}000)$
J. $5(10{,}000 - x)$
K. $0.05(x - 10{,}000)$

11. If $p = (3)(5)(6)(9)(q)$, and if q is a positive integer, then p must be divisible, with no remainder, by all of the following EXCEPT:

A. 27
B. 36
C. 45
D. 54
E. 90

12. In the figure below, if line k is parallel to line m, which of the following equalities must hold?

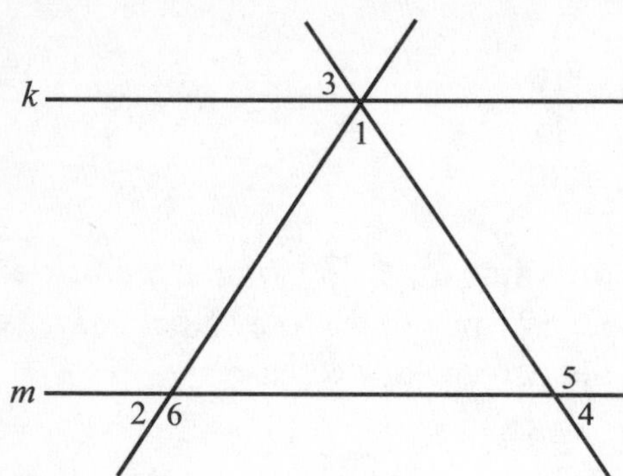

I. $m\angle 1 = m\angle 2$
II. $m\angle 3 = m\angle 4$
III. $m\angle 5 = m\angle 6$

F. I only
G. II only
H. III only
J. I and III only
K. II and III only

13. In which of the following equations does p vary directly as the cube root of q, while q varies inversely as the square root of r?

A. $q = \frac{p^3}{r^2}$

B. $p = \frac{r^3}{\sqrt{q}}$

C. $q = \frac{p^3}{\sqrt{r}}$

D. $r = \frac{\sqrt[3]{p}}{q^2}$

E. $q = \frac{\sqrt{r}}{p^3}$

14. In the standard (x,y) coordinate plane, if a triangle with vertices $(3,-1)$, $(-4,1)$, and $(1,-3)$ is translated 2 units up and 3 units to the right, what are the new coordinates of the triangle's vertices?

F. $(5,2)$; $(-2,4)$; $(3,0)$
G. $(6,1)$; $(-1,4)$; $(4,-6)$
H. $(1,0)$; $(-1,3)$; $(-2,1)$
J. $(5,-2)$; $(1,3)$; $(4,-1)$
K. $(6,1)$; $(-1,3)$; $(4,-1)$

15. In the standard (x,y) coordinate plane below, if the scales on both axes are the same, which of the following could be the equation of l_1?

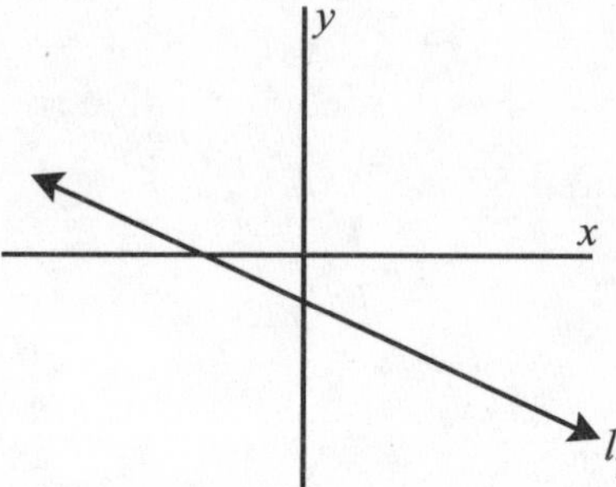

A. $y = \frac{2}{3}x - 3$

B. $y = -2x + 1$

C. $y = x + 3$

D. $y = -3x - \frac{2}{3}$

E. $y = -\frac{2}{3}x - 3$

16. The denominator of a certain fraction is twice as great as the numerator. If 4 were added to both the numerator and denominator, the new fraction would be $\frac{5}{8}$. What is the denominator of the original fraction?

F. 3
G. 6
H. 9
J. 12
K. 13

17. In the standard (x,y) coordinate plane, what is the slope of a line that contains the points $(-1,4)$ and $(3,-6)$?

A. $-\frac{5}{2}$

B. -2

C. $-\frac{1}{2}$

D. 1

E. 2

18. A legislature passed a bill into law by a 5:3 margin. No legislator abstained. What part of the votes cast were cast in favor of the motion?

F. $\frac{5}{8}$

G. $\frac{3}{5}$

H. $\frac{8}{15}$

J. $\frac{2}{5}$

K. $\frac{3}{8}$

19. In the standard (x,y) coordinate plane, the slope of a line segment with endpoints $(7,-2)$ and (p,q) is -1, and the slope of a line segment with endpoints $(1,-4)$ and (p,q) is $\frac{1}{2}$. What is the value of q?

A. $-\frac{3}{2}$

B. $-\frac{4}{3}$

C. $\frac{7}{4}$

D. 4

E. $\frac{19}{3}$

20. When the real number p is multiplied by 3, then the product is decreased by 8, the result is less than 7. Which of the following is the graph of all possible values of p?

F. 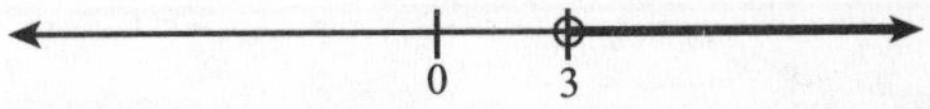

G. 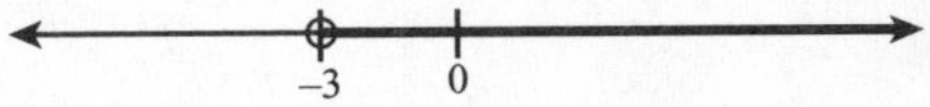

H. 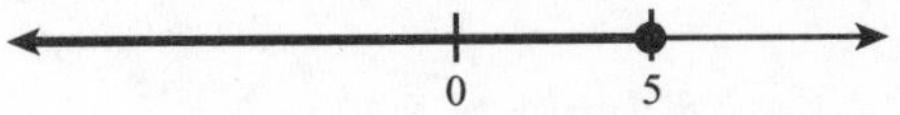

J. 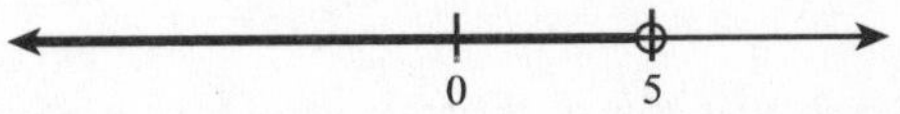

K. 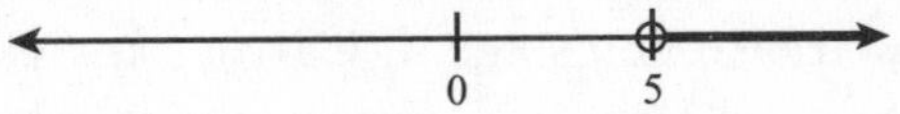

GO ON TO THE NEXT PAGE

21. For what value of q does the equation $4x^2 - \frac{x}{q} + 1 = 0$ have one and only one real-number solution?

A. $\frac{1}{4}$

B. $\frac{1}{2}$

C. 2

D. 4

E. 8

22. If one dollar can buy m pieces of paper, how many dollars are needed to buy p reams of paper? (*Note:* 1 ream = 500 pieces of paper)

F. $\frac{p}{500m}$

G. $\frac{m}{500p}$

H. $\frac{500}{p + m}$

J. $\frac{500p}{m}$

K. $500m(p - m)$

23. Eight years from now, Carrie's age will be twice Ben's age. If Carrie's current age is C and Ben's current age is B, which of the following represents Carrie's current age?

A. B
B. $B + 4$
C. $B + 8$
D. $2B + 8$
E. $3B$

24. If $x^2 - y^2 = 16$, and $x + y = 2$, then $y =$

F. -4
G. -3
H. 2
J. 3
K. 5

25. What is the equation of the line that is the perpendicular bisector of the line segment connecting points $(4,-2)$ and $(-3,5)$ in the standard (x,y) coordinate plane?

A. $y = -x + \frac{3}{2}$

B. $y = x + \frac{1}{2}$

C. $y = \frac{3}{2}x - 1$

D. $y = -x + 2$

E. $y = x + 1$

26. If $x > 0$, and if $x + 3$ is a multiple of 3, which of the following is NOT a multiple of 3?

F. x
G. $x + 6$
H. $3x + 5$
J. $2x + 6$
K. $6x + 18$

27. Which of the following integers is the closest to the value for the unit length of one leg of a triangle with hypotenuse 13, if the other leg is 7 units long?

A. 8
B. 9
C. 10
D. 11
E. 12

28. What is the perimeter of the region shown below, if the curved side is a semicircle?

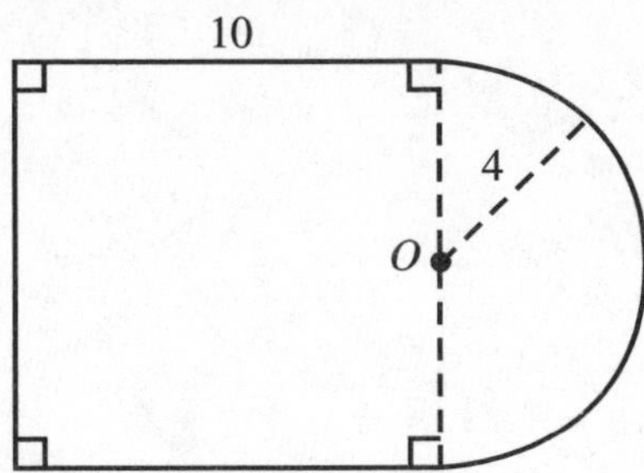

F. $30 + 2\pi$
G. $28 + 4\pi$
H. $30 + 4\pi$
J. $40 + 2\pi$
K. $28 + 8\pi$

29. According to the following chart, during what year was the dollar amount of Country Y's imports approximately twice that of Country X's exports?

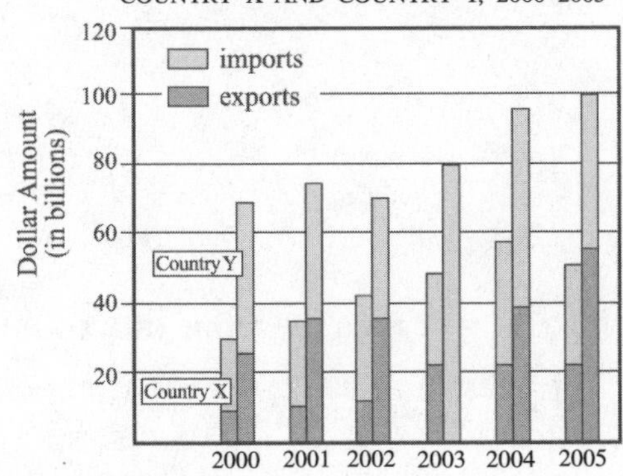

A. 2000
B. 2002
C. 2003
D. 2004
E. 2005

30. In the figure below, if O lies at the center of the larger circle, what is the ratio of the smaller circle's area to the larger circle's area?

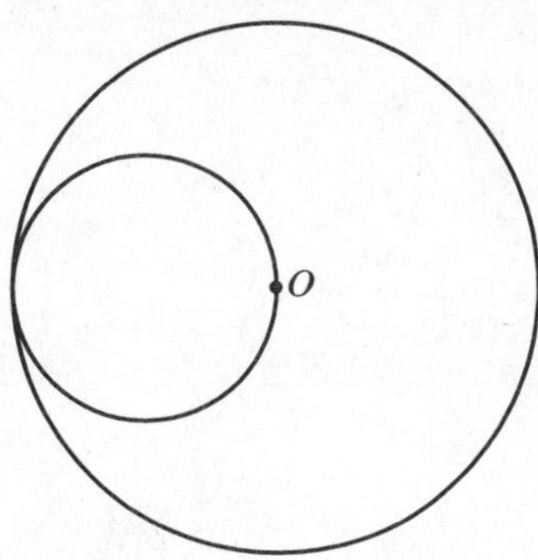

F. π:12
G. 1:4
H. 2:3π
J. π:15
K. 1:5

31. Patrons at a certain restaurant can select two of three appetizers—fruit, soup, and salad—along with two of three vegetables—carrots, squash, and peas. What is the probability that any patron will select fruit, salad, squash, and peas?

A. $\frac{1}{2}$

B. $\frac{1}{3}$

C. $\frac{1}{6}$

D. $\frac{1}{9}$

E. $\frac{1}{12}$

32. If $P = \begin{bmatrix} 1 & 2 \\ 3 & 4 \end{bmatrix}$ and $Q = \begin{bmatrix} -3 \\ -2 \end{bmatrix}$, what is the entry in the second row of the only column of product matrix PQ?

F. 12
G. 6
H. −5
J. −12
K. −17

33. Set R: $\{N + 1, 2N + 2, 3N + 3, \ldots\}$
If $N = 2$, what is the 25th term of Set R?

A. 29
B. 48
C. 50
D. 63
E. 75

34. Cynthia drove for seven hours at an average rate of 50 miles per hour (mph) and for one hour at an average rate of 60 mph. What was her average rate for the entire trip?

F. $51\frac{1}{4}$ mph
G. 52 mph
H. $52\frac{1}{2}$ mph
J. $57\frac{1}{2}$ mph
K. $62\frac{1}{2}$ mph

35. If $x + y < 0$, then which of the following represents a positive number for all possible values of x and y?

A. $y - x$
B. xy
C. $\frac{x}{y}$
D. $x - y$
E. $-y - x$

36. $\sqrt[3]{p + q} + 4 = 0$, then $p + q =$

F. −64
G. −16
H. 4
J. 8
K. 64

37. If P percent of 20 is Q , then $P =$

A. $\frac{Q}{20}$
B. $\frac{Q}{5}$
C. $5Q$
D. $10Q$
E. $20Q$

38. If $\log_x 16 = 4$, then the value of x could be

F. 16
G. 8
H. 4
J. 2
K. −4

39. The length of one rectangular horse corral is exactly two thirds the length of another, but the area of the two corrals is the same. If the shorter corral has a length of L and a width of W, which of the following represents the perimeter of the longer corral?

A. $2L + \frac{4}{3}W$

B. $3L + \frac{2}{3}W$

C. $3L + \frac{4}{3}W$

D. $\frac{3}{2}L + W$

E. $3L + \frac{1}{3}W$

40. If $x = -1$, then $x^{-3} + x^{-2} + x^2 + x^3 =$

F. -2
G. -1
H. 0
J. 1
K. 2

41. In the standard (x,y) coordinate plane, an ellipse is tangent to the x-axis and to the y-axis as shown in the graph below. If $|p| < q$, then which of the following is the equation of the ellipse?

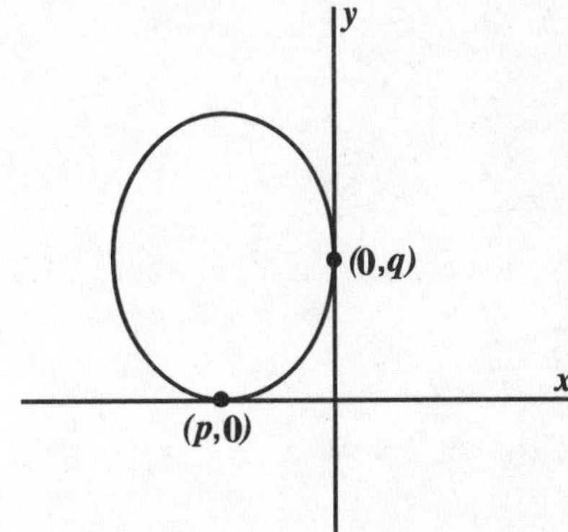

A. $\frac{(x-q)^2}{4q^2} + \frac{(y-p)^2}{4p^2} = 1$

B. $\frac{(x+p)^2}{p^2} + \frac{(y-q)^2}{q^2} = 1$

C. $\frac{(x-p)^2}{p^2} + \frac{(y-q)^2}{q^2} = 1$

D. $\frac{(x-p)^2}{2p^2} + \frac{(y-q)^2}{2q^2} = 1$

E. $\frac{(x-p)^2}{q^2} + \frac{(y-q)^2}{p^2} = 1$

42. If the interior angles of a quadrilateral are in the ratio 1:2:3:4, what is the sum of the degree measures of the two smallest angles?

F. 218°
G. 204°
H. 192°
J. 148°
K. 108°

GO ON TO THE NEXT PAGE

43. An angle is acute if it measures less than 90°. If one angle of a right triangle measures 30°, what is the cosine of the other acute angle?

A. 2
B. $\sqrt{3}$
C. 1
D. $\frac{\sqrt{3}}{2}$
E. $\frac{1}{2}$

44. In the figure below, $x =$

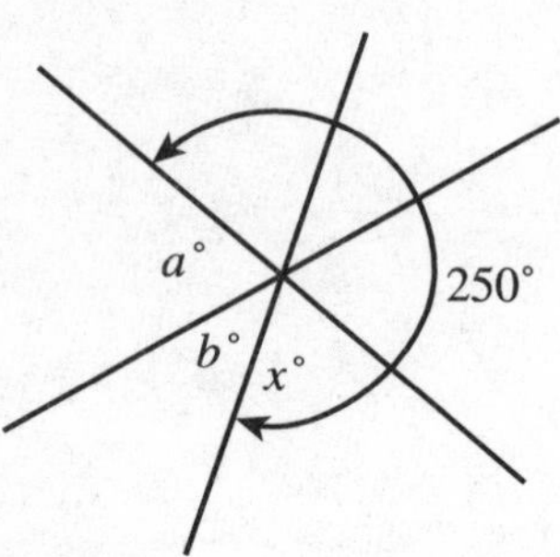

F. 50
G. 55
H. 60
J. 70
K. 80

45. In ΔRST below, A is the midpoint of $\overline{RS}$ and B is the midpoint of $\overline{ST}$. All of the following congruencies hold EXCEPT:

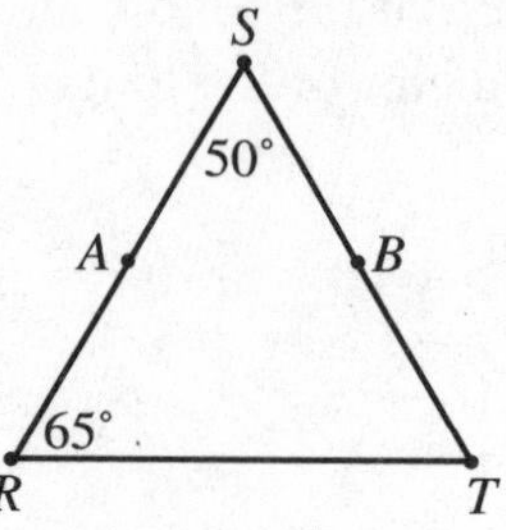

A. $\overline{RS} \cong \overline{TS}$
B. $\overline{AS} \cong \overline{BT}$
C. $\overline{RT} \cong \overline{RS}$
D. $\overline{SB} \cong \overline{AR}$
E. $\overline{AR} \cong \overline{BT}$

46. $\frac{\sqrt{10}}{\sqrt{2}} \times \frac{\sqrt{5}}{\sqrt{2}}$

F. $\frac{\sqrt{10}}{2}$
G. $\frac{5\sqrt{2}}{2}$
H. $2\sqrt{5}$
J. 10
K. $\frac{25}{2}$

47. Which of the following is NOT equal to 4.23×10^{-2}?

A. $4,230 \times 10^{-4}$
B. 0.00423×10^{1}
C. 0.423×10^{-1}
D. 42.3×10^{-3}
E. 0.0423×10^{0}

48. If the average of four numbers is 4, and if the number 6 is added to these four numbers, what is the average of all five numbers?

F. 3

G. $\frac{17}{4}$

H. $\frac{22}{5}$

J. $\frac{9}{2}$

K. 5

49. In the figure below, the centers of all three circles (the three points) lie on the same line. The radius of the middle-sized circle is twice that of the smallest circle. If the radius of the smallest circle is 1, what is the length of the boundary of the shaded region?

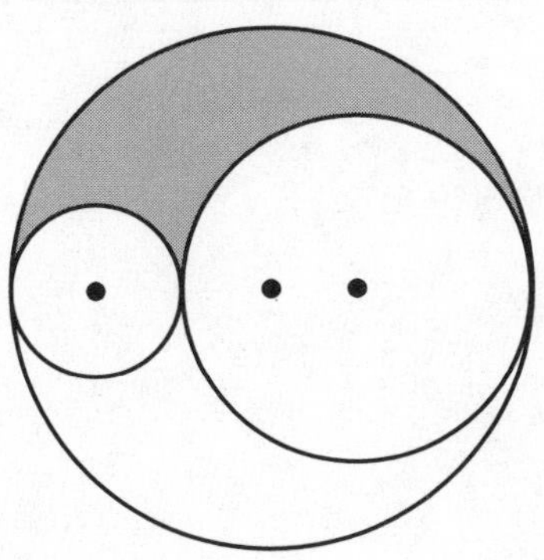

A. 12π
B. 6π
C. 12
D. 3π
E. 9

50. Which of the following is a factor of $x^3 + 3x^2 - 5x - 15$?

F. $(x^2 - 3)$
G. $(x^2 + 5)$
H. $(x^2 - 5)$
J. $(x - 3)$
K. $(x + 5)$

51. All six sides of the polygon shown below are congruent. What is the value of x?

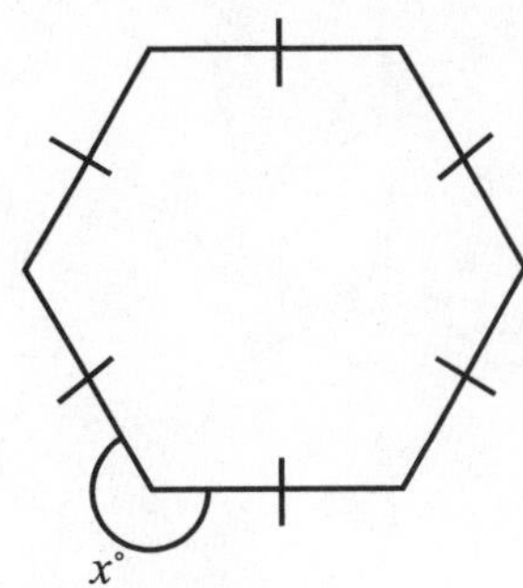

A. 258
B. 240
C. 220
D. 180
E. 165

52. In the figure below, O_1 and O_2 are concentric circles and $\overline{AB}$ is tangent to O_1 at C. If the radius of O_1 is r and the radius of O_2 is twice as long, what is the area of the shaded region?

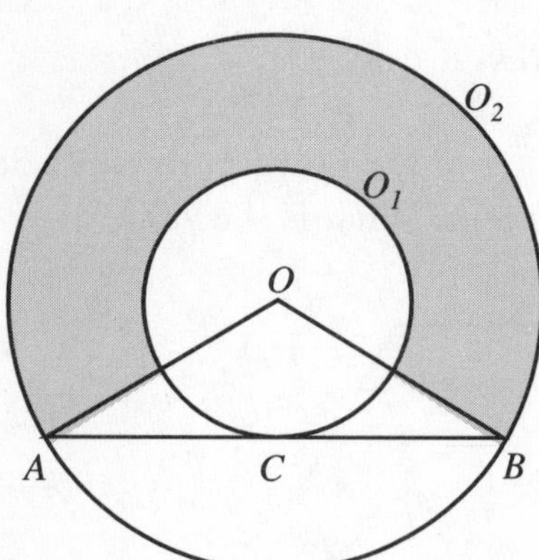

F. $\frac{1}{2}\pi r^2$

G. πr^2

H. $\frac{3}{2}\pi r^2$

J. $2\pi r^2$

K. $3\pi r^2$

53. One x-intercept of the parabola defined by the equation $y = x^2 + 2x - 3$ is within which of the following intervals?

A. $[-6,-4]$
B. $[-2,0]$
C. $[0,2]$
D. $[2,4]$
E. $[3,5]$

54. The figure below shows a solid wooden cube with surface area of 9 square units on each side, except that a 1×1 square hole has been cut through the cube from one side to the opposite side. After the hole is cut, what is the volume of the remaining wood, in cubic units?

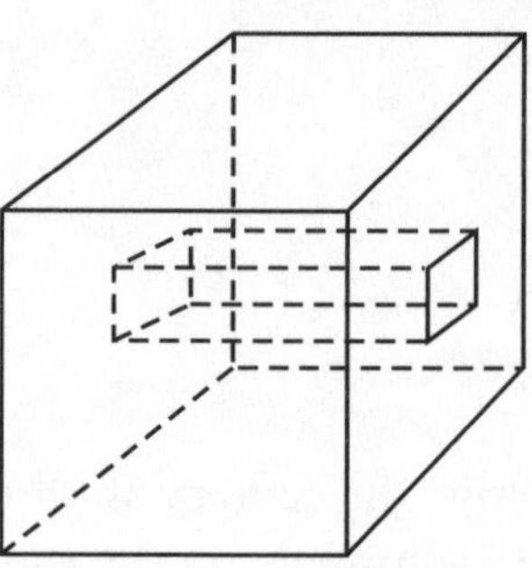

F. 21
G. 24
H. 27
J. 30
K. 33

55. In the figure below, if $\overline{AD} \cong \overline{DC}$, what is the perimeter of the quadrilateral that forms the boundary of the total region shown?

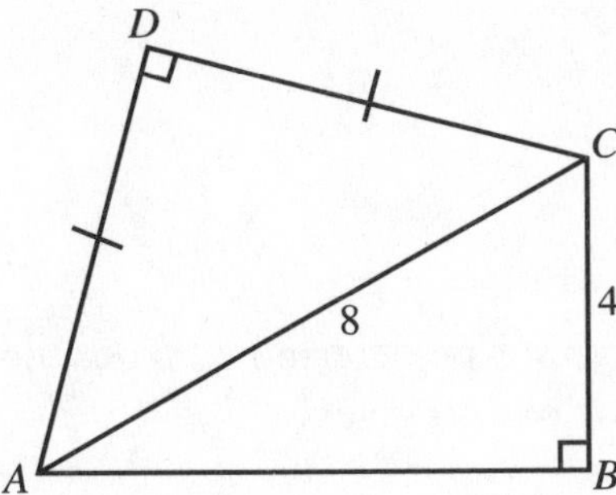

A. 18

B. $10 + 6\sqrt{2}$

C. $4 + 4\sqrt{3} + 8\sqrt{2}$

D. $18\sqrt{2}$

E. $16 + 8\sqrt{3}$

56. In a geometric series, each term is a constant multiple of the preceding one. If x and y are the first two terms in a geometric series, which of the following represents the third term in the series?

F. $\frac{y^2}{x}$

G. $\frac{y}{x}$

H. $\frac{y^2}{x^2}$

J. xy

K. $\frac{x^2}{y}$

57. The figure below shows a wire (represented by the dashed line) connecting the outer edge of a porch roof to the base of the building's wall, creating an angle of θ degrees at the base of the building.

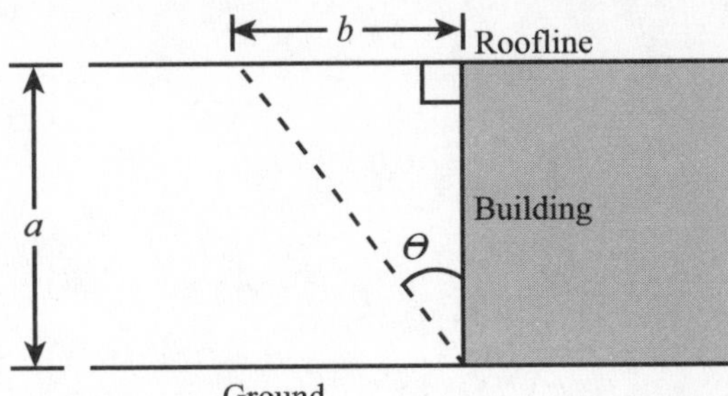

If a and b are the height of the building and width of the porch roof, respectively, which of the following represents the length of wire?

A. $\frac{b}{\cos\theta}$

B. $\frac{b}{\sin\theta}$

C. $\frac{a}{\sin\theta}$

D. $a\cos$

E. $b\sin\theta$

GO ON TO THE NEXT PAGE

58. In the standard (x,y) coordinate plane, the graph of $y = 3\sin 3x$ contains all of the following (x,y) pairs EXCEPT:

F. $\left(\frac{4}{3}\pi, 0\right)$

G. $\left(\frac{5}{6}\pi, 3\right)$

H. $\left(\frac{1}{2}\pi, -3\right)$

J. $\left(\frac{\pi}{3}, 0\right)$

K. $\left(\frac{11}{6}\pi, -\frac{3}{2}\right)$

59. If $f(x) = \frac{x}{2}$, then $f(x^2) \div (f(x))^2 =$

A. x^3
B. 1
C. $2x^2$
D. 2
E. $2x$

60. If $\tan\theta = \frac{5}{12}$, and if $\cos\theta = \frac{12}{13}$, then $\sin\theta =$

F. $\frac{5}{12}$

G. $\frac{5}{13}$

H. $\frac{12}{13}$

J. $\frac{13}{12}$

K. It cannot be determined from the information given.

STOP

Reading

40 Questions ■ Time—35 Minutes

Directions: This test consists of four passages, each followed by several questions. Read each passage and select the best answer for each question following the passage. Then, on your answer sheet, mark the oval corresponding to the best answer.

Passage I—Prose Fiction

Newland Archer was speaking with his fiancée, May Welland. He had failed to stop at his club on the way up from the office where he exercised the profession of the law in the leisurely manner common to well-to-do New Yorkers of his class in the middle of the nineteenth century. He was out of spirits and slightly out of temper, and a haunting horror of doing the same thing every day at the same hour besieged his brain.

"Sameness—sameness!" he muttered, the word running through his head like a persecuting tune as he saw the familiar tall-hatted figures lounging behind the plate glass; and because he usually dropped in at the club at that hour, he had passed by instead. And now he began to talk to May of their own plans, their future, and Mrs. Welland's insistence on a long engagement.

"If you call it long!" May cried. "Isabel Chivers and Reggie were engaged for two years, Grace and Thorley for nearly a year and a half.

"Why aren't we very well off as we are?"

It was the traditional maidenly interrogation, and Archer felt ashamed of himself for finding it childish. No doubt she simply echoed what was said for her, but she was nearing her twenty-second birthday, and he wondered at what age "nice" women like May began to speak for themselves.

"Never, if we won't let them, I suppose," he mused, and recalled his mad outburst to his friend Jackson: "Women ought to be as free as we are—!"

It would soon be his task to take the bandage from this young woman's eyes, and bid her look forth on the world. But how many generations of women before her had descended bandaged to the family vault? He shivered a little, remembering some of the new ideas in his scientific books, and the much-cited instance of the Kentucky cave-fish, which had ceased to develop eyes because they had no use for them. What if, when he had bidden May Welland to open hers,

they could only look out blankly at blankness?

"We might be much better off. We might be truly together—we might travel."

Her face lit up. "That would be lovely," she admitted; she would love to travel. But her mother would not understand their wanting to do things so differently.

"As if the fact that it is different doesn't account for it!" Archer insisted.

"Newland! You're so original!" she exulted.

His heart sank. He saw that he was saying all the things that young men in the same situation were expected to say, and that she was making the answers that instinct and tradition taught her to make—even to the point of calling him original.

"Original! We're all as like each other as those dolls cut out of the same folded paper. We're like patterns stenciled on a wall. Can't you and I strike out for ourselves, May?"

"Goodness—shall we elope?" she laughed.

"If you would—"

"You do love me, Newland! I'm so happy."

"But then—why not be happier?"

"We can't behave like people in novels, though, can we?"

"Why not—why not—why not?"

She looked a little bored by his insistence. She knew very well why they couldn't, but it was troublesome to have to produce a reason. "I'm not clever enough to argue with you. But that kind of thing is rather—vulgar, isn't it?" she suggested, relieved to have hit on a word that would certainly extinguish the whole subject.

"Are you so much afraid, then, of being vulgar?"

She was evidently staggered by this. "Of course I should hate it—and so would you," she rejoined, a trifle irritably.

He stood silent, beating his walking-stick nervously against his shoe-top. Feeling that she had indeed found the right way of closing the discussion, she went on lightheartedly, "Oh, did I tell you that I showed cousin Ellen my engagement ring? She thinks it the most beautiful setting she ever saw. There's nothing like it in Paris, she said. I do love you, Newland, for being so artistic!"

1. It can be inferred from the passage that Newland Archer most yearns for:

   A. a comfortable life.
   B. high social status.
   C. Mrs. Welland's approval.
   D. variety in life.

2. May Welland's comments in the third paragraph (lines 22–25) about her and her friends' engagements suggest that she:

   F. considers the engagement period planned by her mother to be brief.
   G. feels that Newland Archer has insulted her mother.
   H. disagrees with her mother about when she should marry Newland Archer.
   J. believes that her friends Isabel and Grace were engaged for too long a time.

3. The reference to the Kentucky cave-fish (line 49) helps the reader understand:

- **A.** Newland's support of a woman's fundamental right to equality, of which men have robbed her.
- **B.** Newland's fear that May's upbringing might have rendered her incapable of original thought.
- **C.** May Welland's maidenly interrogations which are true to her conventional upbringing.
- **D.** the trauma experienced by women of the mid-nineteenth century who rebelled against the social order of the times.

4. As revealed in the passage, Newland Archer can best be characterized as:

- **F.** a complacent person with little interest in current affairs.
- **G.** a person with curiosity about new ideas who questions conventional ones.
- **H.** a person of leisurely manner and acceptable disposition.
- **J.** adventurous but frustrated by his financial situation.

5. It can be inferred from the passage that, among New York society in mid-nineteenth century, leisure travel was considered:

- **A.** irresponsible.
- **B.** traditional.
- **C.** uncommon.
- **D.** adventurous.

6. May Welland considers Newland Archer to be all of the following EXCEPT:

- **F.** original.
- **G.** amusing.
- **H.** artistic.
- **J.** clever.

7. May Welland puts an end to the discussion that Newland Archer starts by:

- **A.** declaring his points moot because they would find no support from Mrs. Welland.
- **B.** reminding him that agreeing with him would be an invitation to social disaster.
- **C.** denouncing elopement as too vulgar and hateful for both of them.
- **D.** dismissing elopement as romantic but suitable only for protagonists of romance novels.

8. According to the passage, May Welland is of approximately what age?

- **F.** Eighteen years
- **G.** About twenty-four years
- **H.** Approaching thirty
- **J.** Somewhat less than twenty-two years

9. Archer regards May Welland's responses to what he says as excessively influenced by:

- **A.** her educational background.
- **B.** popular romance novels.
- **C.** social mores and cultural expectations.
- **D.** her friends Isabel, Grace, and Ellen.

GO ON TO THE NEXT PAGE

10. It can be most reasonably inferred from the passage that Newland Archer's female contemporaries were:

F. discouraged from thinking for themselves.
G. not so self-confident as women of the previous generation.
H. given too much power in decision making.
J. overly argumentative and bossy.

Passage II—Social Studies

When the framers of the Constitution set to work devising the structure of the United States government, it was natural for them to consider the forms already existing in the several states. The three most basic patterns may be referred to as the Virginia, Pennsylvania, and Massachusetts models.

The Virginia model borrowed its central principal, legislative supremacy, from the thinking of the English philosopher John Locke. Locke had favored making the legislature the dominant focus of government power, and he stressed the importance of preventing a monarch, governor, or other executive from usurping that power. In line with Locke's doctrine, Virginia's constitution provided that the governor be chosen by the assembly rather than by the people directly, as were the members of a special governor's council. The approval of this council was necessary for any action by the governor.

Also derived from Locke was Virginia's bicameral legislature, in which both chambers must concur to pass a bill. Thus dividing the legislative power was supposed to prove its domination by any single faction—the so-called "division of powers" which later became an important feature of the national constitution.

Pennsylvania's constitution was probably the most democratic of any in the former colonies. Pennsylvania extended the right to vote to most adult males. (With the exception of Vermont, the other states allowed only property owners to vote; New Jersey alone extended the privilege to women.) Pennsylvanians elected the members of a single-house legislature, as well as an executive council. These bodies jointly selected the council president, who served as the state's chief executive officer; there was no governor. Neither legislators nor council members could remain in office more than four years out of seven.

The most conservative of the models was found in Massachusetts. The legislature here included two chambers. In the house of representatives, the number of legislators for a given district was based on population; in the "aristocratic" senate, representation was based on taxable wealth. The governor could veto legislature, he appointed most state officials, and he was elected independently of the legislature.

As the delegates to the Constitutional Convention began to debate the merits of these varying models, several fault lines began to appear along which the representatives of the former colonies were divided. One such line was geographic. The economic and social differences between the northern and southern states, which would lead, three generations later, to the cataclysm of the Civil War, were already making themselves felt. Dependent chiefly on the exporting of such raw materials as cotton, tobacco, and rice, the southern states strongly opposed giving Congress the power to regulate international trade, fearing the imposition of onerous taxes or tariffs. Too, the white slaveholders of the south feared federal restrictions on the practice of slavery, which was already a point of controversy between sections of the new nation.

Another dividing line among the states was based on population. The less populous states opposed the notion of allocating political power based on population; they feared having the larger states, especially Virginia, New York, Massachusetts, and Pennsylvania, ride roughshod over their interests. This division to some extent echoed the north-south split, since most of the more populous states were in the north.

The debates over governmental structure quickly focused on the makeup of the legislative branch. The most populous states favored making representation in Congress proportional to population, while the smaller states fought for equality of representation. For a time, it appeared as though the convention might break up over this issue.

The successful resolution was a compromise originally proposed by the delegation from Connecticut, and therefore often referred to as the Connecticut Compromise, or the Great Compromise. According to this plan, which remains in effect to this day, the Congress is a bicameral legislature like those in Virginia and Massachusetts. In the Senate, each state has two representatives, no matter what its size, while seats in the House of Representatives are apportioned by population. Both houses must concur in the passage of legislature, and bills proposing the expenditure of government funds must originate in the House—a precaution demanded by the larger states to protect their financial interests.

The southern states won a series of specific concessions. Although the convention refused to include slaves on a equal basis in the population count for Congressional representation—after all, the slaves were neither citizens nor taxpayers nor voters—it was agreed to count the slave population, a notorious compromise long regarded as a racist blot on the constitution. The north also accepted constitutional clauses forbidding export taxes and preventing Congress from interfering with the slave trade until at least 1808—over twenty years in the future. The sectional differences between north and south, and the simmering issue of slavery, were thus postponed for future generations to face.

11. Based on the passage, under which government model did the governor hold the most extensive powers?

- **A.** Pennsylvania
- **B.** Washington
- **C.** Massachusetts
- **D.** Virginia

12. It can reasonably be inferred that "larger states" (lines 86–87) refers to the states that were:

- **F.** wealthiest.
- **G.** largest in geographic size.
- **H.** most powerful.
- **J.** most populous.

GO ON TO THE NEXT PAGE

13. As it is used in the passage, the word *onerous* (line 76) most nearly means:

A. beneficial.
B. burdensome.
C. unnecessary.
D. useless.

14. Which of the following former colonies mentioned in the passage was most strongly influenced by the philosophy of John Locke?

F. Virginia
G. Pennsylvania
H. Massachusetts
J. New Jersey

15. As a whole, the passage is best viewed as:

A. an account of how former colonizers devised an effective model of self-governance for the newly independent colonies.
B. an explanation of how pre-existing patterns of governance in the original states influenced the constitution of those states newly united as a nation.
C. a study of how the framers of the U.S. Constitution ultimately solved the problems arising from political and economic differences between the Northern and Southern states.
D. a discourse on the influence of diverse political philosophies on the framers of the U.S. Constitution.

16. Based on the passage, which of the following models of a constitution would an adherent of Locke's philosophy most likely prefer?

F. A constitution that calls for a governing body comprised of two chambers and a jointly selected chief executive officer
G. A conservative constitution that provides for a government made up of representatives based on their taxable wealth
H. A constitution requiring the agreement of both chambers to pass any draft of a proposed law
J. A democratic constitution under which the nominated head of the two chambers holds veto power, for the purpose of avoiding dominance by any particular faction

17. It can be inferred from the passage that the representatives of the southern states were concerned with protecting the interests of all of the following EXCEPT:

A. regulators of international trade.
B. owners of cotton-producing plantations.
C. white slaveholders.
D. exporters of tobacco.

18. The northern states strongly supported the constitutional provision that:

F. prohibited export taxes.
G. prohibited Congressional interference in the slave trade.
H. required that all funding bills originate in the House of Representatives.
J. called for equal representation of all states in the Senate.

19. In what way did the constitution of New Jersey differ from those of the other states?

A. It was the only state to confer the right to vote to slaves.
B. It gave women the privilege to vote.
C. It conferred the right to vote exclusively to property holders.
D. Seats in its legislature were given exclusively to taxpayers.

20. The passage supports all of the following ideas EXCEPT:

F. the debate over how Congressional seats should be apportioned nearly resulted in the failure of the Constitutional Convention.
G. the debate over how the new government was to be structured included the issue of how finding bills should be proposed.
H. the question of the legality of slavery in a democracy was left largely unaddressed by the Constitutional Convention.
J. all major differences between the Northern and Southern states were settled by the time the new Constitution was finally adopted.

Passage III—Humanities

[The essay from which this passage is adapted was written in 1909.]

In discussing the value of particular books, I have heard people say—people who were timid about expressing their views of literature in the presence of literary men: "It may be bad from a literary point of view, but there are very good things in it." Or: "I dare say the style is very bad, but really the book is very interesting and suggestive." Or: "I'm not an expert, and so I never bother my head about good style. All I ask for is good matter. And when I have got it, critics may say what they like about the book," and many other similar remarks, all showing that in the minds of the speakers, there existed a notion that style is something supplementary to, and distinguishable from, matter; a sort of notion that a writer who wanted to be classical had first to find and arrange his matter, and then dress it up elegantly in a costume of style, in order to please beings called literary critics.

This is a misapprehension. Style cannot be distinguished from matter. When a writer conceives an idea, he conceives it in a form of words. That form of words constitutes his style, and it is absolutely governed by the idea. The idea can only exist in words, and it can only exist in one form of words. You cannot say exactly the same thing in two different ways. Slightly alter the expression, and you slightly alter the idea. Surely it is obvious that the expression cannot be altered without altering the thing expressed! A writer, having conceived and expressed an idea, may, and probably will, "polish it up." But what does he polish up? To say that he polishes up his style is merely to say that he is polishing up his idea, that he had discovered faults or imperfections in his idea, and is perfecting it. An idea exists in proportion as it is expressed; it exists when it is expressed, and not before. It expresses itself. A clear idea is expressed clearly, and a vague idea vaguely.

You need but take your own case and your own speech. For just as science is the development of common sense, so is literature the development of common daily speech. The difference between science and common sense is simply one of degree; similarly with speech and literature. When you "know what you think," you succeed in saying what you think, in making yourself understood. When you "don't know what you think," your expressive tongue halts. And note how in daily life the characteristics of your style follow your mood; how tender it is when you are tender, how violent when you are violent. You have said to yourself in moments of emotion: "If only I could write—." You were wrong. You ought to have said: "If only I could think on this high plane." When you have thought clearly, you have never had any difficulty in saying what you thought, though you may occasionally have had some difficulty in keeping it to yourself. And when you cannot express yourself, depend upon it that you have nothing precise to express, and that what incommodes you in sot the vain desire to express, but the vain desire to think more clearly. All this just to illustrate how style and matter are co-existent, and inseparable, and alike.

You cannot have good matter with bad style. Examine the point more closely. A man wishes to convey a fine idea to you. He employs a form of words. That form of words is his style. Having read, you say: "Yes, this idea is fine." The writer had therefore achieved his end. But in what imaginable circumstances can you say: "Yes, this idea is fine, but the style is not fine"? The sole medium of communication between you and the author has been the form of words. The fine idea has reached you. How? In the words, by the words. Hence the fineness must be in the words. You may say, superiorly: "He has expressed himself clumsily, but I can see what he means." By what light? By something in the words, in the style. Moreover, if the style is clumsy, are you sure that you can see what he means? The "matter" is what actually reaches you, and it must necessarily be affected by the style.

In judging the style of an author, you must employ the same canons as you use in judging men. If you do this, you will not be tempted to attach importance to trifles that are negligible. There can be no lasting friendship without respect. If an author's style is such that you cannot respect it, then you may be sure that, despite any present pleasure that you may obtain from that author, there is something wrong with his matter, and that the pleasure will soon evaporate.

If you are undecided upon a question of style, whether leaning to the favorable or to the unfavorable, the most prudent course is to forget that literary style exists. For, indeed, as style is understood by most people who have not analyzed their impression under the influence of literature, there is no such thing as literary style. You cannot divide literature into two elements and say: this matter and that style. Further, the significance and the worth of any other phenomenon: by the exercise of common sense.

Common sense will tell you that nobody, not even a genius, can be simultaneously vulgar and distinguished, or beautiful and ugly, or precise and vague, or tender and harsh. And common sense will therefore tell you that to try to set up vital contradictions between matter and style is absurd.

21. When the people whom the author quotes in the first paragraph remark that "critics may say what they like about the book" (lines 13–14), these people probably mean that:

A. literary critics are not reluctant to express their opinions.
B. ordinary readers are just as qualified as literary critics to critique literary works.
C. what literary critics think of the book is not important to these people.
D. literary critics are more likely than these people to find fault with the book.

22. Which of the following best expresses the "sort of notion" (lines 18–19) the author describes in lines 19–23?

F. Critics generally prefer books written in an elegant style.
G. Critics do not generally praise new books written in outdated styles.
H. Many book writers are not daring enough in their writing style.
J. A book is unlikely to become popular unless written in a classic style.

23. Based on the information in the second paragraph (lines 24–48), with which of the following statements would the author of the passage be LEAST likely to agree?

A. An idea cannot exist apart from its expression.
B. The matter and style of a writing are one and the same.
C. Once expressed, an idea cannot actually be polished up.
D. A clear idea cannot develop from any idea expressed vaguely.

24. Based on the information in the third paragraph (lines 49–80), which of the following can we infer is a difference of degree?

F. The difference between scientific writing and literary writing
G. The difference between an idea and the expression of that idea
H. The difference between common sense and literary sense
J. The difference between literature and common speech

25. According to the passage, if you cannot express yourself, the reason for this inability is that:

A. the ideas in your mind at the time are too vague.
B. you have nothing to say at the time.
C. you are feeling too emotional to express yourself clearly.
D. you are too vain about your ideas.

26. As it is used in the passage, the word *canons* (line 105) most nearly means:

F. forms of respect.
G. set of principles.
H. types of judgments.
J. variety of styles.

27. The author states that "there can be no lasting friendship without respect" (lines 108–109) in order to make the point that:

A. a reader cannot remain friends with a writer unless the reader respects that writer.
B. a writer must not insult the reader, or else the reader will not respect the writer's ideas.
C. unless a reader respects a writer's style, the reader will ultimately lose interest in the writer's ideas.
D. two people can remain friends only if there is continued mutual respect between them.

28. The author of the passage recommends that readers:

F. pay no attention to a writer's style.
G. show more respect for matter than for style.
H. read only classic books and other writings.
J. disregard who wrote whatever they are reading.

29. As it is used in the passage, the word *incommodes* (line 76) most nearly means:

A. displeases.
B. troubles.
C. attracts
D. prompts.

30. Based on the information in the passage, if a reader claims that an author's writing style is polished, what this might actually indicate is that the:

F. reader is thinking clearly.
G. writer has used words that sophisticated people use.
H. reader has misinterpreted the author's ideas.
J. writer's ideas are clear.

Passage IV—Natural Science

If you've ever cupped your hand around a blinking firefly or noticed an eerie glow in the ocean at night, you are familiar with the phenomenon of bioluminescence. The ability of certain plants and animals to emit light has long been a source of fascination to humans. Why do certain species of mushrooms glow? Why are midwater squids designed with ornate light-emitting organs underneath their eyes and ink glands? Why do certain particles and biological detritus floating in the depths of the ocean sparkle after a physical disturbance? Are these light displays simply an example of nature in its most flamboyant mode—a case of "if you've got it, flaunt it"—or do they serve any practical purposes?

As it turns out, the manifestations of bioluminescence are as diverse as they are elegant. Yet virtually all of the known or proposed ways in which bioluminescence functions may be classed under three major rubrics: assisting predation, helping escape from predators, and communicating.

Many examples of the first two uses can be observed in the ocean's midwaters, a zone that extends from about 100 meters deep to a few kilometers below the surface. Almost all of the animals that inhabit the murky depths where sunlight barely penetrates are capable of producing light in one way or another. Certain animals, when feeding, are attracted to a spot of light as a possible food source. Hence, other animals use their own luminescence to attract them. Just in front of the angler fish's mouth is a dangling luminescent ball suspended from a structure attached to its head.

What unwitting marine creatures see as food is really a bait to lure them into the angler fish's gaping maw.

The uses of luminescence to elude predators are just as sophisticated and various. Some creatures take advantage of the scant sunlight in their realm by using bioluminescence as a form of camouflage. The glow generated by photophores, light producing organs, on the undersides of some fishes and squids acts to hide them through a phenomenon known as countershading: the weak downward lighting created by the photophores effectively erases the animals' shadows when viewed from below against the (relatively) lighted waters above.

Some marine animals use bioluminescence more actively in their own defense, turning their predators into prey. For instance, there is the so-called "burglar alarm effect," in which an animal coats an advancing predator with sticky glowing tissue that makes the would-be attacker vulnerable to visually cued hunters—like bank robbers marked by exploding dye packets hidden in stolen currency.

Bioluminescence is used not only in such interspecific feeding frays between predators and prey, but also as an intraspecific communication facilitator. The fireflies that seem to blink on and off randomly in the summer woods are actually male and female members signaling each other during courtship. Certain fish use their luminescence as a kind of Morse code in which the female responds to the flashing of a male fish with its own flash exactly two seconds later, which the male recognizes by its timing.

Bioluminescence clearly functions to help certain species ensure their survival, whether it helps them to trick predators or to mate and produce offspring. Yet, when we look at the larger evolutionary picture, bioluminescence as such is generally considered a "nonessential" characteristic. After all, closely related species and even strains of the same species may have both luminous and nonluminous members, and the nonluminous ones appear just as viable and vigorous as their glowing counterparts. For instance, while many of the small marine organisms known as dinoflagellates are luminous, many are not. Yet, on closer inspection, we find that the nonluminous dinoflagellates may benefit from the diversionary flashing tactics of the luminous ones. When the sea is disturbed and light flashes create phosphorescence, the species which flash may provide enough light to serve the entire population. Thus, selection pressure for the development or maintenance of luminescence in additional species is not great if light generated by a part of the population serves the entire community.

There are instances in which bioluminescence seems truly purposeless. What does one make of a creature, such as a newly discovered species of a tomopterid worm, that emits light for no apparent purpose? This agile swimmer with a multitude of paired legs spews a bright yellow bioluminescent fluid from each of its leg pores. While other types of spewers use this strategy to create a visual distraction, this worm's display remains enigmatic, particularly since the light produced is yellow, while most midwater animals have eyes that are

GO ON TO THE NEXT PAGE

sensitive only to blue-green. Perhaps some animal species are simply exploiting their capacity for flamboyance, in the same way that some humans bring a distinctively colorful flair to whatever they do.

31. The author's description of the angler fish in the third paragraph (lines 27–44) most strongly supports the assertion that the angler fish uses bioluminescence:

A. to illuminate its prey.
B. as a means of deterring predators.
C. as a way to attract prey.
D. to blend in with the bright waters near the surface.

32. It can be inferred from the passage that the "burglar alarm effect" (lines 63–64) is an example of:

F. an intraspecific communication facilitator.
G. bioluminescence as a nonessential phenomenon.
H. interspecific use of bioluminescence by predators.
J. luminescence as a defensive tool in interspecific relations.

33. The passage supports all the following statements EXCEPT:

A. most midwater species are sensitive to yellow light.
B. the tomopterid worm is not the oldest known bioluminescent species.
C. strains of the same species can have both nonluminous and luminous members.
D. bioluminescence provides help in ensuring survival of certain species.

34. Based on the information in the seventh paragraph, which of the following would be the best example of "selection pressure" (lines 108–109)?

F. The development of acute eyesight to aid a marine animal in locating its prey in dark or murky waters
G. The survival of an aggressive species of predator at the demise of its less aggressive competitors
H. The habit of one species of fish to scavenge the remains of prey hunted by another species of fish rather than hunt for itself
J. The tendency for a physical characteristic that is attractive to potential mates to become increasingly common among an animal population

35. The author mentions the tomopterid worm most likely in order to:

A. underscore that bioluminescence serves no useful purpose for animals dwelling near the ocean floor.
B. support the argument that bioluminescence is useful primarily in communication among the related species.
C. illustrate the importance of bioluminescence in all midwater inhabitants regardless of their locomotive abilities.
D. illustrate that some examples of bioluminescence in marine organisms cannot be classified according to the known functions of bioluminescence.

36. As it is used in the passage, the word *elude* (line 45) most nearly means:

F. attract.
G. illuminate.
H. challenge.
J. escape.

37. The squid's use of countershading, as it is described in the fourth paragraph (lines 45–59), is most analogous to:

A. a solar eclipse, in which the Earth's moon comes between Earth and the Sun, thereby hiding the Sun from view on Earth.
B. a portrait photographer's use of low-angle lighting to hide the cavernous shadows in a subject's eye sockets.
C. a chameleon's ability to change the pattern and color of its skin to blend in with its immediate environment.
D. an artist's use of contrasting shades to create the illusion that one object in a painting is closer to the viewer than another.

38. Among the following, the author of the passage would most likely agree that bioluminescence is:

F. more common among marine animals than among marine plants.
G. less practical than it is ornamental.
H. most often a nonessential characteristic rather than an essential one.
J. used more commonly for predation than for communication.

39. Which of the following statements, if true, would most seriously weaken the author's claim in the final paragraph that bioluminescence sometimes appears to serve no useful purpose?

A. Male tomopterid worms are sensitive to yellow light, whereas female tomopterid worms are not.
B. Some dinoflagellates can detect countershading, whereas other cannot.
C. The legs of tomopterid worms serve no function other than to emit bioluminescent fluid.
D. Many bioluminescent marine animals are completely blind.

40. The author's primary purpose in the passage is to:

F. provide examples showing that, for some species of marine animals, bioluminescence is essential for survival.
G. examine the manifestations and uses of bioluminescence, especially among inhabitants of ocean midwaters.
H. describe how some marine animals use bioluminescence for the purpose of intraspecific communication.
J. explore the various nonessential purposes that bioluminescence in marine life serves.

STOP

Science

40 Questions ■ Time—35 Minutes

Directions: This test consists of seven passages, each followed by several questions. Read each passage and select the best answer for each question following the passage. Then, on your answer sheet, mark the oval corresponding to the best answer. You may NOT use a calculator on this test.

Passage I

As power is supplied to a circuit, current flows through the circuit. An *ammeter* is the device used to measure the current in milliamps (mA). The *voltage* responsible for the current can be measured by a voltmeter and is measured in volts. When a *resistor* is placed in a circuit, it dampens the current flowing through a circuit at a given voltage.

If there is a linear relationship between current and voltage when a resistor is placed in the circuit, the resistor is considered an *ohmic device*. Some resistors are sensitive to small external temperature changes and will show a change in resistance as a result of these temperature changes. These resistors are called *thermistors*. The change in resistance exhibited by a thermistor can be detected by a change in the observed current at a given voltage.

The following procedure was performed to investigate whether different resistors acted as ohmic devices in a circuit. The circuit was constructed as shown in Figure 1.

Figure 1

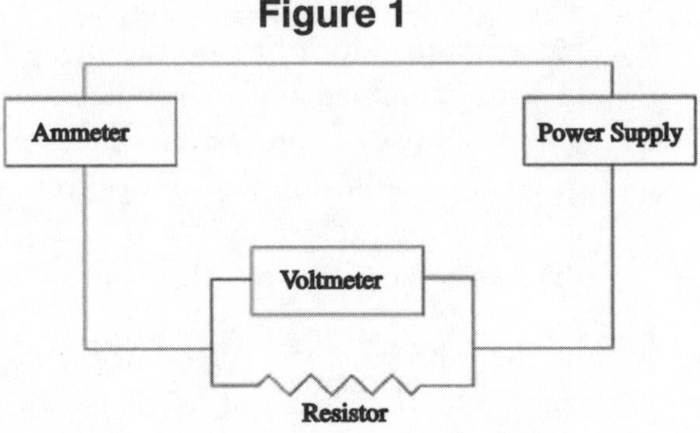

After each resistor was connected to the circuit, the resistor was submerged in water to detect any changes in temperature as well as its sensitivity to different beginning temperatures. The power source was turned on and the voltage of the power source and the resulting current were recorded. The voltage was changed several times and corresponding current was noted.

Table 1 on the following page summarizes the results when three different resistors were tested at two different temperatures. In all cases, no change in water temperature was observed after the resistor was submerged.

Table 1

	Resistor A		Resistor B		Resistor C	
	23°C	25°C	23°C	25°C	23°C	25°C
Voltage (V)	Current (mA)	Current (mA)	Current (mA)	Current (mA)	Current (mA)	Current (mA)
0.25	25	25	150	150	5	4.5
0.50	50	50	195	195	10	9.0
1.00	100	100	230	230	20	18.0
2.00	200	200	295	295	40	36.0
3.00	300	300	345	345	60	54.0
4.00	400	400	405	405	80	72.0
4.50	450	450	420	420	90	81.0
5.00	500	500	445	445	100	90.0

1. During the trials, when the resistor's temperature was 25°C and the current was measured at 100mA, what was the corresponding voltage?

A. 0.50 volts
B. 1.00 volt
C. 1.50 volts
D. 5.00 volts

2. When the voltage was 4.50 volts and the temperature was 23°C, what was the current when Resistor C was used?

F. 72mA
G. 81mA
H. 90mA
J. 420mA

3. Of the three resistors used in the trials, which would be considered an ohmic device but not a thermistor?

A. Resistor A only
B. Resistor B only
C. Resistor C only
D. Resistor A and Resistor B only

4. At a temperature of 25°C, what voltage would produce a current of 126mA if Resistor C is used?

F. 5.50 volts
G. 6.00 volts
H. 7.00 volts
J. 8.00 volts

5. If the water temperature had increased after submerging resistor B, which of the following statements would have been most accurate?

A. The fact that the water temperature increased after submerging Resistor B shows that resistor B is a thermistor.
B. The fact that the water temperature increased after submerging Resistor B shows that resistor B is not an ohmic device.
C. Since the measured current was the same when the initial water temperature was 23°C as when it was 25°C, resistor B is an ohmic device.
D. Since the measured current was the same when the initial water temperature was 23°C as when it was 25°C, resistor B is not a thermistor.

Passage II

Soil is composed of sand, silt, and clay. The relative percentages of each particle type in soil are referred to as its texture. The diagram below is used to identify the soil types for various textures. Soils classified as loams contain organic matter.

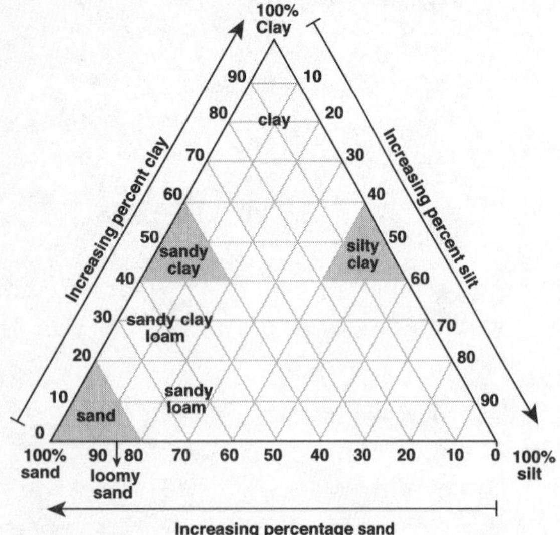

Researchers wished to analyze soil samples from a certain forest and a nearby grassy field and to compare their soil composition and other properties.

Experiment 1

Soil samples were collected from the forest. The samples were dried and then weighed. The dried samples were then separated by particle size. The particles of each size were then weighed and the percentage of each size was calculated. The results are presented in Table 1:

Table 1

Sample No.	% Sand	% Silt	% Clay
Forest 1	45	5	50
Forest 2	20	60	20
Forest 3	43	28	15

Experiment 2

Soil samples were collected from the grassy field. Just as in Experiment 1, the samples were dried and weighed, and then separated by particle size. As in Experiment 1, the particles of each size were then weighed and the percentage of each size was calculated. The results are presented in Table 2:

Table 2

Sample No.	% Sand	% Silt	% Clay
Grass 1	12.5	54.5	33
Grass 2	57	37	6
Grass 3	82	7	11

6. Which of the following soil samples contains the greatest percentage of silt?

F. Soil sample 2 from the grass
G. Soil sample 3 from the grass
H. Soil sample 2 from the forest
J. Soil sample 3 from the forest

7. Which of the following is loam most likely to contain?

A. Sand
B. Clay
C. Silt
D. It cannot be determined from the information given.

8. Assuming all six soil samples contain the same amount of soil, which of the following statements is LEAST accurate?

- **F.** The soil samples from the forest contain about the same amount of silt as the soil samples from the grassy field.
- **G.** The soil samples from the forest contain a smaller amount of clay than the soil samples from the grassy field.
- **H.** The soil samples from the forest contain a smaller amount of sand than the soil samples from the grassy field.
- **J.** The soil samples from the forest contain a larger amount of loam than the soil samples from the grassy field.

9. In both experiments, soil particles in each sample were separated by size in order to:

- **A.** compare sand, silt, and clay to one another according to water content.
- **B.** determine the composition of the soil samples according to particle size.
- **C.** separate forest soil samples with grassy fields samples.
- **D.** compare sand, silt, and clay to one another according to weight.

10. Assume that, in a third experiment, a seventh soil sample is taken from another area, then dried and separated using the same procedure as for the other six samples. If measurements show that the sample contains more silt than either sand or clay, then the sample is probably most similar in texture to either:

- **F.** sample 1 from the forest or sample 3 from the grassy field.
- **G.** sample 1 from the forest or sample 3 from the forest.
- **H.** sample 1 from the grassy filed or sample 3 from the grassy field.
- **J.** sample 2 from the forest or sample 1 from the grassy field.

11. The researchers wished to compare the six soil samples collected during experiments 1 and 2 according to permeability (ability of water to pass through them). A portion of each sample was placed in a separate cup with a filter bottom, and then the same amount of water was added to each cup. After one minute, the amount of water passing through each filter was measured. In order to draw any reliable conclusions about the permeability of the six original samples, all of the following conditions are necessary EXCEPT:

- **A.** one minute is sufficient time for some amount of water to escape at least some of the cups.
- **B.** the same amount of soil was added to all six cups.
- **C.** in each cup, the proportions of sand, silt, and clay were the same as in the original sample.
- **D.** the filters did not allow soil particles to escape through the bottoms of the cups.

Passage III

Airplane wings must be designed *aerodynamically* (with consideration to the airflow over the body of the plane) to ensure efficient flight. Aerodynamic design considers *lift* and *drag*.

Lift is the force acting upwards on the plane. It is generated because the top of a wing is curved, while the bottom is flat. The air moving over the top of the wings must move faster than the air moving over the bottom. This results in a lower pressure area above the wing.

Drag is the air resistance generated by the plane. This is a force acting in opposition to the plane's forward movement. The most efficient planes are those with the highest lift-to-drag ratio.

Researchers testing new wing designs conducted a series of experiments to measure their efficiency.

Experiment 1

Researchers tested aircraft with four wing designs (see the following figure) in a *wind tunnel* (a tunnel in which air is blown over a craft to simulate flight conditions). This test simulated flight at 400 mph. The lift and drag measured for each wing shape are recorded in Table 1.

Figure 1

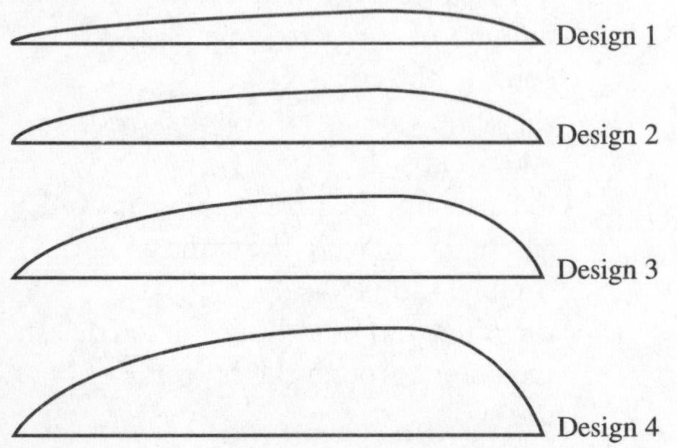

Table 1

Wing Design	Lift (neutrons)	Drag (neutrons)	Efficiency
1	3	.15	20:1
2	8	.2	40:1
3	10	1	10:1
4	18	2	9:1

Experiment 2

Aircraft with the four wing types depicted in figure 1 were tested under similar flight conditions to gauge fuel consumption. After reaching cruising altitude, the planes maintained a speed of 400 mph. The results appear in Table 2.

Table 2

Wing	Fuel consumption (gallons/hr)
1	40
2	20
3	80
4	88

Experiment 3

Lift, drag, and efficiency are dependent on airspeed. The researchers tested wing designs 1 and 2 at different speeds. Efficiency (lift-to-drag ratio) was recorded in Table 3.

Table 3

Airspeed (mph)	Design 1 (Efficiency)	Design 2 (Efficiency)
200	22:1	43:1
300	21:1	42:1
400	20:1	40:1
500	18:1	12:1
600	10:1	8:1

12. The most efficient wing tested in Experiment 1 was:

F. design 1.
G. design 2.
H. design 3.
J. design 4.

13. A passenger plane is able to carry a fixed weight, including passengers and fuel. Which wing design would be best for such a plane?

A. Design 1
B. Design 2
C. Design 3
D. Design 4

14. In cold, damp weather, the buildup of ice on airplane wings can pose significant aerodynamic problems. Which of the following effects would you expect?

F. As ice builds up on the top of the wing, drag increases.
G. As ice builds up on the top of the wing, lift increases.
H. As ice builds up on bottom of the wing, lift decreases.
J. All of the above

15. Which of the following test pairs reflects consistent experimental data?

A. Experiment 1, wing design 2; Experiment 2, airspeed 200
B. Experiment 1, wing design 1; Experiment 2, wing design 2
C. Experiment 1, wing design 3; Experiment 3, airspeed 400
D. Experiment 1, wing design 1; Experiment 3, airspeed 400

16. Which of the following statements about airspeed is supported by the data in Experiment 3?

F. As airspeed increases, the lift-to-drag ratio increases.
G. As airspeed increases, lift and drag increase at about the same rate.
H. As airspeed increases, drag increases faster than lift.
J. As airspeed increases, lift increases faster than drag.

17. New fighter jets are being designed so that the wing is modifiable, depending on the speed at which the plane is going. Which of the following would be a logical adjustment of the wing for such jets?

A. At speeds above 500 mph, the top of the wing would become flatter.
B. At speeds above 500 mph, the top of the wing would become more curved.
C. At speeds above 500 mph, the bottom of the wing would become curved.
D. None of the above

Passage IV

Interstellar objects (objects among the stars) in outer galaxies are often investigated using a method known as spectroscopy. *Spectroscopy* is a method of determining the atomic or molecular makeup of something by observing the object's *spectral lines.* Atoms and molecules have fixed energy levels. When an electron in an atom moves from one of its possible energy states to another, the atom releases light. This light has an energy equal to the difference in the two energy levels through which the electron moved. These energy transitions are observed as a sequence of spectral lines. Spectral lines that are close together indicate transitions in which the change in energy levels is similar.

Figure 1, below, depicts three hypothetical atoms. Energy levels are represented as horizontal segments. The distance between the segments is representative of the energy difference between the various levels. All possible transitions between energy levels are indicated by arrows.

Figure 1

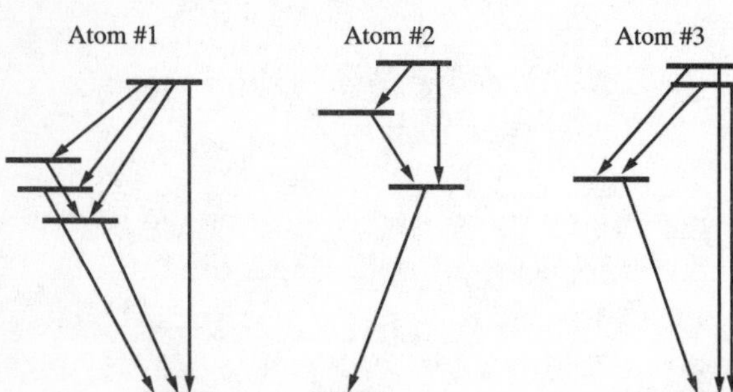

Scientists can observe the spectral lines of atoms that are dominant in far-away galaxies. Due to the speed at which these galaxies are traveling, these lines are shifted, but their pattern remains the same. This allows researchers to use the spectral pattern to determine which atoms they are seeing. Table 1 below shows spectroscopic measurements made by researchers trying to determine the atomic makeup of a particular far-away galaxy. Light energy is not measured directly, but rather is determined from measuring the frequency of light, which is proportional to the energy.

Table 1

Frequencies Measured
868440
880570
879910
856390

18. For each of three hypothetical atoms (Atom 1, Atom 2, and Atom 3), Figure 1 depicts the:

F. number of electrons and the amount of energy the atom contains.
G. distance an electron travels from one part of the atom to another.
H. energy released by the atom as an electron as it moves from one energy state to another.
J. frequency with which the atom's electrons move from one energy state to another.

19. In which of the three hypothetical atoms depicted in Figure 1 does the energy of the light released by the atom vary the least?

A. Atom 1
B. Atom 2
C. Atom 3
D. It is impossible to tell.

20. Scientists observing an actual atom similar to hypothetical Atom 1 in the figure might observe:

F. three spectral lines close together and two other spectral lines close together.
G. light blinking at six different frequencies.
H. a much brighter light emanating from one electron than from any other.
J. four distinct spectral lines emanating from six different electrons.

21. Based on the spectroscopic measurements shown in Table 1 on page 510, which of the atoms in Figure 1 on page 510 (Atom 1, Atom 2, or Atom 3) is most similar to the one the scientists were observing, and why?

A. Atom 2, because it contains four different energy levels.
B. Atom 3, because it contains four different energy levels.
C. Atom 1, because the frequencies listed in Table 1 on page 510 indicate a high level of atomic activity.
D. Atom 3, because there is a comparatively small difference between exactly two of the four frequencies listed in Table 1 on page 510.

22. The laws of atomic physics prohibit electron movements between certain energy states. In atomic physics, these prohibitions are called "forbidden transitions." Based on Figure 1 on page 510, which of the following is most accurate?

F. Atom 2 has the same number of forbidden transitions as Atom 1.
G. Atom 2 has more forbidden transitions than Atom 3.
H. Atom 3 has the same number of forbidden transitions as Atom 1.
J. Atom 1 has fewer forbidden transitions than Atom 2.

Passage V

Tree age is important to researchers for understanding typical life-cycles in the forest and developing sustainable forestry practices. Counting tree rings is the method that is usually used to determine the age of trees, but in tropical rain forests, such as the Amazon, tree rings may be irregular (not annual) or nonexistent.

Carbon-14 dating is another method of determining tree age. Trees take carbon dioxide, which contains some of the radioactive element carbon-14, into their tissues at a known rate. By

Table 1

Tree No.	Tree Species	Tree Diameter (cm)	Tree Age (Years)	Calculated Average Growth Rate (cm/yr)
1	*Cariniana micrantha*	140	200	0.7
2	*Cariniana micrantha*	100	400	0.25
3	*Cariniana micrantha*	140	1,400	0.1
4	*Hymenolobium* species	180	300	0.6
5	*Hymenolobium* species	90	900	0.1
6	*Bagassa guianansis*	120	400	0.3
7	*Bagassa guianansis*	150	300	0.5
8	*Caryocar glabrum*	130	200	0.65
9	*Caryocar vilosum*	120	200	0.6
10	*Iryanthera grandis*	160	800	0.2
11	*Dipteryx odorata*	120	1,200	0.1
12	*Sclerolobium* species	80	200	0.4

measuring the levels of carbon-14 in a plant, scientists can determine its age. Table 1 on page 511 lists the age and other data for 12 trees that have emerged from the canopy in a small Amazon forest plot. The age of the trees was determined by carbon-14 dating.

Historical patterns of forest disturbance are also important to biologists for determining the extent to which the forest is affected and the forest's pattern of recovery. The following figure shows the catastrophic events that are known to have occurred in the area where the trees in Table 1 on page 511 were growing.

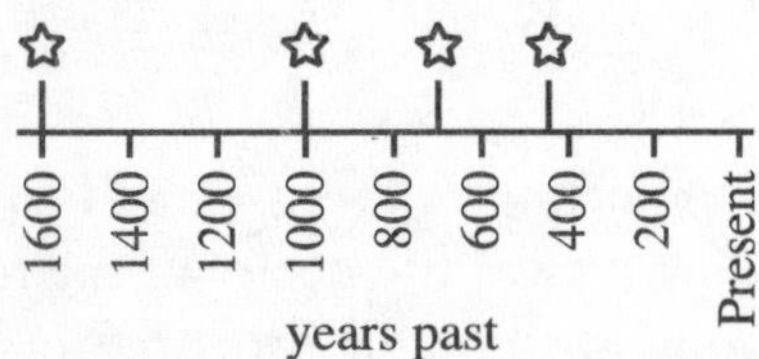

23. Which of the following statements about the trees listed in Table 1 on page 511 is LEAST accurate?

A. The *Caryocar glabrum* specimen is younger than the *Bagassa guianansis* specimens.
B. The *Cariniana micrantha* specimens are larger in diameter than the *Sclerolobium* specimen.
C. The *Bagassa guianansis* specimens have a higher current growth rate than the *Dipteryx odorata* specimen.
D. The *Iryanthera grandis* specimen is older than the *Hymenolobium* specimens.

24. Based on the data and other information given, which of the following is the most accurate way of confirming the hypothesis that one tree is older than another tree of the same species located just a few feet away in a tropical rain forest?

F. Compare the number of rings in the two trees.
G. Compare carbon-14 samples from the two trees.
H. Compare the height of the two trees.
J. Compare the diameters of the two trees.

25. Which of the following general relationships involving trees in tropical rain forests emerges from Table 1 on page 511?

A. An inverse relationship between a tree's growth rate and its age
B. An inverse relationship between the number of trees of a species and the species' general growth rate
C. A direct relationship between a tree's growth rate and its age
D. A direct relationship between a tree's age and its diameter

26. Outside of tropical rain forests, trees almost always increase in diameter with age. Looking just at the species named in each answer choice below, a researcher who has never observed tropical rain forests but knows the general relationship between tree diameter and age might reasonably conclude that it is possible to:

F. compare the ages of different specimens of *Bagassa guianansis* based solely on their diameters.
G. compare the age of a *Sclerolobium* to the age of a *Dipteryx odorata* based solely on their diameters.
H. compare the ages of different *Hymenolobium* specimens based solely on their diameters.
J. compare the age of a *Dipteryx odorata* to the age of an *Iryanthera grandis* based solely on their diameters.

27. Which of the following conclusions is best supported by the data?

A. Three of the trees survived at least three catastrophic events.
B. More than half the trees survived the most recent catastrophic event.
C. Four of the trees survived at least two catastrophic events.
D. One of the trees survived four catastrophic events.

28. Assume a researcher concludes, based on Table 1 on page 511 and the timeline figure on page 512, that *Dipteryx odorata* is better able to survive catastrophic events than *Cariniana micrantha*. Which of the following would be the most effective challenge to the researcher's conclusion?

F. Two of the specimens of *Cariniana micrantha* are larger in diameter than the *Dipteryx odorata* specimen.
G. The growth rate of the *Dipteryx odorata* specimen is greater than two of the three specimens of *Cariniana micrantha*.
H. Only one of the twelve specimens is a *Dipteryx odorata*, while three are of *Cariniana micrantha* species.
J. One of the specimens of *Cariniana micrantha* is older than the *Dipteryx odorata* specimen.

Passage VI

Although astronomers have a general outline for the steps that lead up to the formation of the wide-ranging interplanetary bodies called *comets*, there remain many questions as to where and exactly how comets were formed. The major points of dispute involve the location of their formation and the processes by which the comets were drawn into the Oort Cloud becoming permanent members of our Solar System. Three astronomers describe their views on this process.

Astronomer 1

The flattened, rotating disk of the nebula* out of which our Sun and its companion planets were formed is the ideal place for comets to have been born. The long, slow collapse of a nebula that evolved into a planetary system

*A nebula is a vast cloud of interstellar gas and dust.

included the type of compression that would facilitate the accretion of the key specks of matter into comet pellets. At a certain concentration level, these pellets began to clump into cometesimals and later aggregated into larger bodies. When our solar system was formed, the bodies that formed in the outskirts became the population of comets known as the Oort Cloud. Those comets that formed among the planets likely collided with the giant members of the Sun's family, coalescing into them. There is sufficient evidence of significant disturbance among the outer giant planets and their companion satellites in the early solar system to support this theory.

Astronomer 2

We may reasonably suspect that the nebula out of which our Sun formed was at least twice the mass of the Sun at its current stage. We believe that the processes that formed the inner solar system worked rapidly and were completed within 100,000 years. The remaining, less thoroughly coalesced matter was blown into the outer regions of the infant solar system. The larger masses eventually became the four outer gas giants: Jupiter, Saturn, Uranus, and Neptune. The smaller masses were thrown much farther, forming the Oort Cloud. Here, so distant from the gravitational influence of their parent sun, they were much more subject to the random forces of other nearby stars. Some of them are pushed in towards us, making their periodic and sometimes spectacular visits; others are pushed out to wander unseen in the vast galaxy.

Astronomer 3

The interstellar clouds out of which stars are formed are more vast, cold, and formless than can easily be imagined. In the absence of evidence that all the members of the solar system arose out of the same nebula, it is difficult to explain the birth of the wandering comets. The most likely scenario based on the actual evidence available is that icy grains of matter in these vast gas-molecular clouds slowly grew by aggregation as they wandered in cold, dark space. Eventually, the masses would grow large enough to be deemed cometary. When the Sun compressed and ignited, it possessed enough gravity to capture a large number of these cometary masses, forming a captive population of comets now orbiting far beyond the realm of the other solar companions.

29. Astronomer 1 and Astronomer 3 would both agree with all of the following statements EXCEPT:

A. comets are formed by a process by which they slowly accumulate mass and volume.
B. our solar system was formed as a result of a collapsing nebula.
C. the comets in our solar system were formed in the nebula that became our solar system.
D. some comets collided with newly formed planets during the formation of our solar system.

30. Which of the following is a claim that Astronomer 2 would make and with which both Astronomer 1 and Astronomer 3 would probably disagree?

F. Our solar system was formed by a process of expansion away from a central core.
G. Gravitation forces played a minor role in determining the eventual location and paths of comets in our solar system.
H. Some comets collided with and, as a result, became part of our solar system's larger planets.
J. The formation of our solar system's outer regions took longer than the formation of its inner regions.

31. Astronomer 2 would probably agree with all of the following statements EXCEPT:

A. our inner solar system was formed earlier than our outer solar system.
B. the Oort Cloud was formed by particles arriving from outside the nebula that became our solar system.
C. the planets in our solar system all arose out of the same nebula.
D. the planets in our solar system were all part of a single mass at one time.

32. With which of the following statements would Astronomer 1 most likely agree?

F. The comets in our solar system were formed in both its inner and outer regions.
G. The time needed to complete the formation of our outer solar system was greater than for our inner solar system.
H. Comets that pass near the Earth were not originally part of the nebula out of which our solar system arose.
J. During the formation of our solar system, collisions between comets and the smaller planets close to the Sun were not a common occurrence.

33. The theory of Astronomer 3 allows for the possibility that:

A. the formation of comets occurred inside the nebula that became our solar system.
B. the Oort Cloud was formed earlier than our solar system's sun.
C. some comets coalesced with planets during the formation of our solar system.
D. some comets that strike the Earth were originally part of the Oort Cloud.

GO ON TO THE NEXT PAGE

34. The fact that the four planets nearest to the Sun are much smaller than our solar system's two largest planets lends:

F. equal support to Astronomer 1's theory and Astronomer 3's theory but less support to Astronomer 2's theory.
G. greater support to Astronomer 3's theory than to either Astronomer 1's theory or Astronomer 2's theory.
H. greater support to Astronomer 2's theory than to either Astronomer 1's theory or Astronomer 3's theory.
J. equal support to Astronomer 2's theory and Astronomer 1's theory but less support to Astronomer 3's theory.

Passage VII

Environmental levels of the organic volatile chemical benzene are of concern to public health officials because studies have shown that continual exposure to high concentrations of this compound can cause leukemia. Organic volatile chemicals are carbon-containing compounds that are easily vaporized and therefore are present in the air. Experiments to test for the presence of such chemicals were devised.

Experiment 1

Researchers outfitted individuals in urban, suburban, and rural areas with monitoring instruments that they could wear throughout the day. These instruments recorded the concentrations of benzene they were exposed to as they went about their normal activities. Other monitoring devices were used to record the benzene output of various known sources in the participants' environment. The average percentage of total benzene that participants were exposed to from various sources as well as the average percentage of total output from these sources are given in Table 1.

Table 1

Sources	% of Total Benzene Emissions	% of Total Benzene Exposure
Automobiles	80%	20%
Industry	15%	4%
Household sources (e.g., stored paints and gasoline)	4.5%	35%
Cigarettes	0.5%	41%

Experiment 2

The researchers decided to look at whether other volatile organic compounds were found in greater concentrations indoors or outdoors. Residents from two areas wore monitoring devices that recorded the levels of a number of volatile organic compounds that they were exposed to during outdoor and indoor activities for several days. The first area was a highly industrial New Jersey city and the other was a rural township in Maine. The average exposure levels of residents in these areas are listed in Table 2.

Table 2

Volatile Chemical	NJ Industrial (µg/m^3)		Maine Rural Township (µg/m^3)	
	In-door	Out-door	In-door	Out-door
Trichloroethane	21	4	14	3
Tetrachloroethylene	9	3	8	1
Chloroform	5	0.2	2	0.1
O-oxylene	5	3	3	2
Styrene	5	0.5	1	0.2

Experiment 3

Fine particles in the air, particularly breathable particles (those that are 10 microns or smaller and are able to penetrate into the lungs), are another environmental concern. Large population studies have suggested that elevated outdoor concentrations of fine particles are associated with premature death. Most fine particles form through processes of combustion, such as cooking, burning candles, smoking, or burning firewood.

Researchers wanted to see what the total levels of such particles were indoors and outdoors and how these levels compared with an individual's exposure levels. Monitors that recorded levels of breathable particles were put inside and outside the homes of one individual from both of the communities in Experiment 2. These individuals were also asked to wear monitoring devices for one day and one night. The results from this experiment are shown in Table 3.

35. Experiment 1 was designed to accomplish all of the following EXCEPT:

A. compare benzene emissions from urban sources with benzene emissions from suburban and rural sources.
B. compare sources of benzene emission with levels of benzene exposure.
C. compare benzene emissions from automobiles with benzene emissions from other sources.
D. determine which aspects of people's daily routines exposes them to high levels of benzene.

36. Based on Experiment 1, which of the following two sources, considered together, expose an average individual to the greatest amount of benzene?

F. Automobiles and industry
G. Household sources and automobiles
H. Industry and household sources
J. Cigarettes and automobiles

37. In Experiment 2, with respect to which of the following compounds was the outdoor exposure level lowest overall?

A. O-oxylene
B. Chloroform
C. Styrene
D. Trichloroethane

38. Based on the results of Experiment 3, which of the following conclusions is most reasonable?

Table 3

	Day			Night		
	Personal Exposure µg/m^3	Indoor Levels µg/m^3	Outdoor Levels µg/m^3	Personal Exposure µg/m^3	Indoor Exposure µg/m^3	Outdoor Exposure µg/m^3
NJ Indust. City	152	98	100	75	65	95
Maine Rural Township	149	95	93	73	72	90

GO ON TO THE NEXT PAGE

F. Indoor levels of combustion are similar to outdoor levels of combustion.
G. Nighttime levels of combustion are similar to daytime levels of combustion.
H. Combustion levels in industrial areas are similar to those in rural areas.
J. Daytime levels of personal exposure to combustion particles are similar to nighttime levels.

39. Which of the following best reconciles the results of Experiment 2 and the results of Experiment 3?

A. The compounds whose levels were measured in Experiment 2 become airborne as particles greater than 10 microns in size.
B. Combustion is only one of many human-generated activities that contribute to the emission of volatile organic compounds into the air.
C. The individuals whose activities were monitored in Experiment 3 were not the same individuals who were monitored in Experiment 2.
D. Industrial areas experience higher emission levels of volatile organic compounds than rural areas.

40. In Experiment 3, if one of the study subject's nighttime indoor exposure level was 45 micrograms/meter^3, which of the following would most likely be the level of that subject's nighttime outdoor exposure?

F. 105 micrograms/meter^3
G. 68 micrograms/meter^3
H. 46 micrograms/meter^3
J. 29 micrograms/meter^3

STOP

Answers and Explanations

English

1. D In referring to the trip as *One of my most memorable trips*, the writer has already told us that it was a trip she made; the underlined portion is redundant and can simply be omitted. Choices **B** and **C** are each redundant as well.

2. G In the original sentence, the first phrase (*Although a chilly, late autumn day*) appears to modify, or describe, *the garden*, which makes no sense, of course. Choice **G** clears up the confusion. Although choice **H** accomplishes the same thing, the result is a wordy and repetitive phrase (*the day was a . . . day . . .)*. Choice **J** creates a comma splice—two independent clauses connected only by a comma.

3. C The sentence beginning with *Gardeners* explains why the garden was still in bloom in late autumn. The original version provides no link between this sentence and the preceding one. Choice **C** remedies the problem, by providing a connection (*because*) that tells the reader that an explanation is just ahead.

4. F The underlined portion correctly uses the subject-case pronoun *I*. Although choice **G** also uses the correct pronoun, it is more idiomatic to refer to *my companion and I* than to *I and my companion.*

5. B The clause that follows the comma is vague. Choice **C** makes clear that it is the trellis that frames the house.

6. F The writer seeks to emphasize how wonderful Monet's residence is. The underlined portion, although unnecessary, helps provide this emphasis and fits the admiring and enthusiastic tone the writer has adopted for the passage. Choice **G** suggests movement and is the wrong idiom here. Choice **H** is unnecessarily wordy; the original version supplies more rhetorical punch.

7. B Sentence 2 states a general idea, which the other two sentences support with detail. Thus, sentence 2 should be either the first or the last sentence of the paragraph. Notice that sentence 1 begins with *A trellis*, which suggests that the trellis is being mentioned for the first time. Accordingly, sentence 1 should immediately precede sentence 3, which provides additional information about the trellis.

8. F The writer uses the reflexive pronoun *itself* appropriately and effectively here to emphasize that it is the house, and not some other part of the property, that is being discussed here.

9. D In this sentence, the writer misuses the word *through*. In order to convey the idea that the art is displayed in all the different areas of the house, the writer should use the word *throughout* instead.

10. F In the preceding sentence, the writer points out one way that the house reflects Monet's interest in Japanese art. In the sentence at hand, the writer points out another such way. Using the word *further* is an effective way to indicate that additional evidence is being provided. Choice **H** would be viable if *also* and *is* were reversed *(is also reflected)*; as it stands, however, choice **H** obscures the meaning of the sentence.

11. B As the sentence stands, two independent clauses are improperly connected with only a comma. Choice **B** transforms the first clause into a dependent clause with the use of a concise phrase.

12. J The paragraph's first sentence tells us that this paragraph will explain the amazing features of the water garden. The fact that Monet's property is located in the village is not relevant to this discussion. What's more, the sentence can be omitted without adversely affecting the flow of information in the paragraph.

13. B From the preceding sentences, the writer suddenly shifts tense to the present (all that *is* left), then back to the past (*entwined*). All of the writer's observations occurred in the past, and so the shift to the present tense is unwarranted. Choice **B** corrects the problem.

14. J Sentences 4 and 5 both talk about what autumn brings to the wisteria that entwines the footbridge railings. The best place to contrast these images to what the observer might see during the summer is after sentence 5.

15. C The passage's other paragraphs all discuss Monet's garden. By turning to a brief discussion of Monet's house, the writer departs from the central topic.

16. J The original sentence contains a subject-verb agreement error. The sentence's subject, *number of factors*, is considered plural. Accordingly, *account* should be used instead of *accounts*. Choice **J** corrects this error.

17. A A colon is appropriate here because it signals that what follows is a list that elucidates what has just been described (factors accounting for this interconnectedness).

18. H At the end of the first paragraph, the writer lists three factors in globalization. In the second paragraph, the writer discusses the first of the factors. The underlined sentence essentially repeats a substantial portion of the previous one. Choice **H** provides a more concise, less repetitive alternative. Not only does it tell the reader what to expect in the paragraph, it also provides a clue that subsequent paragraphs will take up the other two factors, each one in turn.

19. B In the original sentence, the word *which* is intended to modify *tariffs*, but its juxtaposition with *imports* creates confusion. Also, it is unclear as to what the pronoun *their* refers. Choice **B** is the only one that eliminates both sources of confusion.

20. J The transition from the second to the third sentence is stilted. Since their ideas are so closely related, an appropriate connector, such as the one choice **J** provides, should be used to link them together and to help get the point across.

21. C It is idiomatic to refer to companies as either having or maintaining *a presence* in a particular location.

22. G The phrase *This is true* is awkward. Choice G suggests a way to eliminate it and to enhance the flow of ideas: *In fact, many companies that Americans typically think of as U.S. in origin, from publishing companies to food manufacturers to music producers, are actually owned by corporations in other nations.*

23. D Notice that the preceding paragraph introduced the second of three factors with a sentence that begins: *Another factor* . . . . An effective way of reinforcing the structure and sequence of ideas in the passage is to begin the third paragraph (which deals with a third factor) using the same structure—which is exactly what choice D accomplishes.

24. J The underlined word refers to *the Japanese*, a plural noun. Thus, the plural possessive form *their* is correct here.

25. A The plural *businesses* is an appropriate reference to more than one business. Also, the phrase *such as* is idiomatic here. Choice B provides an acceptable alternative, but the punctuation is incorrect (*businesses—for example,* would have been correct).

26. G The paragraph's first sentence states the paragraph's topic. The proposed sentence provides an example of the flow of money from one nation to another, and is therefore a fitting addition to the paragraph. What's more, since only one of the two previous examples is current, another current example is especially useful to support the paragraph's main point.

27. A The underlined portion exhibits a parallel grammatical structure. The choice of phrases—"good thing" and "bad thing"—may not be ideal for this passage ("helpful" and "harmful" might arguably convey a more appropriate tone), but the choice is nevertheless acceptable.

28. G The clause immediately following the underlined portion is key here. Notice that both clauses are similar in structure—they're brief and to the point, employing simple present-tense verbs. This is an effective technique for giving two ideas equal rhetorical emphasis. The only problem with the underlined verb *decline* is that it does not agree in number with the singular subject *demand*. Choice B corrects this error and maintains a grammatical structure that parallels the structure of the clause that follows.

29. C The proper idiom is *based not on . . . but rather on* . . . . The underlined portion not only omits *rather* but also suffers from faulty parallelism. (The words *not* and *based* should be switched.) Choice B completely fails to make the intended point. Choice D fails to connect the two ideas; the result is rhetorically ineffective. Choice C, the best of the four, provides an effective, idiomatic alternative and presents no parallelism problem.

30. H In the final paragraph, the writer first poses the question of whether globalization is good or bad for the world's people. The writer then provides evidence suggesting that, on balance, globalization has done more harm than good. Then, the writer remarks that, in the economist's ideal world, globalization is good. The writer should add a final sentence that counters the economist's viewpoint and provides a realistic answer to the question posed in the paragraph's first sentence. Choice H provides just such a sentence.

31. D Following the underlined portion, the writer employs the active voice and refers twice to *you.* But, the underlined portion employs the passive voice. Choice **D** provides for a consistent, active voice throughout. There's no need to refer to movies here; the context is clear enough from the preceding sentence.

32. H For clarity, a punctuation mark is needed between the words *life* and *like.* Also, the phrase *such as* is more appropriate than *like* here, since the writer is providing examples.

33. B Choice **B** provides a more concise, less repetitive alternative to the underlined phrase. The idea that these sights never existed in the past is implied in this phrase. Choices **C** and **D** are both grammatically correct, but they're wordy and awkward.

34. J The sentence is unrelated to any of the ideas in this paragraph or in the following two paragraphs. In fact, nowhere in the passage does the writer describe specific tricks and techniques that effects artists use. The best proposal is to simply omit the sentence.

35. C In the underlined sentence, the pronoun *they* is intended to refer to *special-effects techniques* (in the preceding sentence), but the reference is unclear. Choice **C** clears up the confusion by reconstructing the sentence; with *they* at the beginning, the reference is much clearer.

36. F The original version is idiomatic and gets the point across. Choice **H** is acceptable but unnecessarily wordy.

37. C As the underlined phrase is constructed, the gerund form *using* is not idiomatic. One solution is to replace it with the noun *use.* The word *the* is optional—it can either be kept or omitted. Choice **B** is clumsy, and choice **D** distorts the meaning of the original underlined portion. (*Clever* should refer to *use*, not to *special effects.*)

38. F The adjective *amazing* is intended to modify, or describe, the adjective *clever.* For this purpose, the suffix *-ly* is proper.

39. B With the phrase *the real magic lies in . . .* , the writer is trying to suggest that what follows is even more amazing than the impressive but "less magical" effects described in the previous paragraph. The transition word *However* helps to convey this idea.

40. H The underlined portion contains the possessive pronoun form of *they*, which makes no sense in context since the writer is not referring to something belonging to effects artists. The contraction *they're* (they are) should be used instead. Choice **H** provides a concise alternative that corrects the error and clearly conveys the intended idea.

41. B The subject of the sentence, *special effects*, is plural. Thus, in the underlined portion, the verb *are* is correct. However, the sentence would be clearer if *tools* were juxtaposed with the phrase that modifies it (*for communicating*). Choice **B** reconstructs the phrase in a way that accomplishes this goal. (The singular *tool* is idiomatic here, even though *special effects* is plural.)

42. G The use of *reason* and *why* together is redundant. The word *why* can simply be omitted.

43. C The verb form *give* agrees in number with the plural noun *ways.* In other words, "it" gives, but "they" give. Choices **A** and **D** wrongly suggest that there's only one way to give audiences the thrill described in the sentence. Choice **D** is also clumsy.

44. F Sentence 3 states a general idea that the other three sentences support with detail, so it makes sense to begin the paragraph with this sentence. Notice that sentence 4 begins with *Even in comedies*, which suggests that sentence 4 should follow sentences 2 and 3, both of which involve another movie genre.

45. D Paragraph 1 provides a fitting introduction to the subject of the passage, establishing its framework. In the first sentence of Paragraph 3, the writer refers to "all these examples." The only examples that make sense in context are the ones listed in Paragraph 1. Thus, Paragraph 3 should immediately follow Paragraph 1. Notice that Paragraph 2 states early that effects artists play a growing role in moviemaking. Also, notice that the remainder of Paragraph 2, along with Paragraphs 4 and 5, flesh out this idea with details. So, it makes sense that Paragraph 2 should come third, before Paragraphs 4 and 5. Paragraph 4, which provides apt concluding remarks for the passage, should come last—immediately after Paragraph 5.

46. G The underlined portion fails to make clear why France did not provide troops but did provide money. It also lacks coherence. (What is the point of the second sentence?) Choice **G** reorganizes the ideas into a construction that clearly indicates the purpose of France's monetary support.

47. D In Paragraph 1, the writer seeks to show how cooperation between France and the United States helped defeat the British. Choice **D** provides an image of the British soldiers being forced by the combined presence of French-American soldiers to surrender and leave. This is just the sort of image that reinforces the idea the writer wishes to convey.

48. G The phrase *and negotiate . . .* is not an independent clause and thus should not be preceded by a comma.

49. C The pronoun *they* is a so-called "dangling modifier"; that is, it has no antecedent. (Who are *they*? We're not told.) One solution to the problem is to use the passive voice so that the pronoun is not needed, as in choice C.

50. J The sentence refers to the time at which the convention was convened. In context, the relative pronoun *When* makes the most sense.

51. A The singular pronoun *its* agrees with the singular antecedent *Convention* and is needed to make clear as to what *illustrious members* refers.

52. F The writer's point here is that it should surprise the reader how few people realize that Franklin played a key role in the Revolution. The adjective form with *-ly* is correctly used here to describe the adjective *few* and is more concise than the phrase in choice C.

53. B Although the underlined portion is grammatically correct, it is repetitive. Choice **B** provides a more concise and rhetorically effective alternative.

54. G In the context of the entire sentence, the underlined portion leads the reader to believe that most people think of Franklin as someone overshadowed in history. However, the main thrust of the paragraph is that most people are actually unaware of the fact that he was overshadowed in history—because history has largely overlooked Franklin's political role. The alternative construction that choice **G** provides clears up the confusion.

55. C When the writer tells us in the previous paragraph that few people *realize* Franklin's role and tells us how people *think* of him, the author is speaking of people today (at the present time), not people of the past. In this context, the sentence at issue is clearly intended to refer to people today (not people of the past) who overlook Franklin's role in the Revolution. Also, the idea that the history books have overlooked this role suggests the use of the present-perfect tense—occurring in the past and up to (and including) the present. Accordingly, it is correct to use the present-perfect form *has been* rather than either the past-perfect form *had been* or the simple-present form *is*.

56. G In the sentence, the writer intends to cite Franklin's reputation as a scientist and as a philosopher—along with Franklin's wit and charm—to explain how he gained influence among the powers-that-be in Europe. But, only the first two items in the list should be parallel in construction, as choice G provides.

57. A It is idiomatic to refer to a person's location as *in* a particular country but *on* a particular continent.

58. J In the underlined portion, the antecedent of *its* is unclear. (Does the pronoun refer to France or to the United States?) Choice J clarifies the pronoun reference.

59. A The sentence helps explain why Franklin would have been surprised that history has overlooked his role in the American Revolution—the main point of the passage.

60. H Paragraph 3 provides a fitting introduction to the subject of the passage, establishing its framework and even its thesis. Thus, it should come first. For coherence, the writer should present the events of Franklin's political contributions in chronological order—from his initial efforts to position himself as an international diplomat (Paragraph 4), to his subsequent acts as minister to France (Paragraph 1), to his post-war involvement in the U.S. government until his death (Paragraph 2).

61. C The third problem listed in the sentence is not grammatically parallel to the first two. Reading the sentence as follows reveals the faulty parallelism: *People had no jobs, people had no food, and people were losing their shelter.* Choice C provides one solution to this problem.

62. J In the underlined portion, a comma improperly separates two independent clauses (each of which could stand on its own as a complete sentence). One solution is to add an appropriate connecting word immediately after the comma, such as *which*. Choice J provides another solution: Transform the second clause into a dependent one and omit the object *it*.

63. A Sentence 4 of Paragraph 1 is an effective way to introduce the three topics that the writer takes up in the next three paragraphs—one topic per paragraph. The sentence belongs exactly where is—at the end of Paragraph 1. (Notice that Paragraphs 2, 3, and 4 each begin similarly—a strong clue that the paragraph break between Paragraphs 1 and 2 is appropriate where it is, and it should be neither omitted nor moved.)

64. G The preceding sentence identified the three stages in sequence, so there's no need to immediately remind the reader that the first stage is the relief stage. Even aside from what the preceding sentence indicates, the underlined portion seems repetitive. It suffices to start the sentence with *During the relief stage*—as choice G suggests. (An equally effective starting clause would be *During the first stage*.)

65. C The underlined portion wrongly suggests that the CCC facilitated *un*employment, rather than employment. All that the writer needs to say here is that the Corps provided jobs, or employment—as choice C provides.

66. G The phrase *not only* should be paired with *but also*, and what follows one should be grammatically parallel to what follows the other. Choice G provides the complete correlative pair (*not only . . . but also*) and restructures the underlined phrase so that it parallels the preceding one.

67. D In sentence 3, the writer has already made the essential point made in sentence 5. Nothing would be lost by simply omitting sentence 5.

68. H A colon is inappropriate here because what follows it neither restates what precedes it nor provides a list. What follows the colon is a reason for the short-term relief mentioned before the colon. One way to correct the punctuation problem is to replace the colon with a semicolon, which is appropriately used to signal that an explanation or reason for what precedes it is just ahead.

69. D The underlined portion, together with the preceding portion of the sentence, tells us essentially that laws created laws—a nonsensical idea. What the laws created were a minimum wage and a maximum work week, which is just what choice D indicates.

70. H The pronoun *it* is intended to refer to *new federal laws*, but the reference is unclear. The best way to clear up the confusion is to replace the pronoun with the noun to which it refers.

71. C As it is constructed, the original sentence nonsensically suggests that the SSA might have also been created during another stage. Clearly, the writer's intent is to first point out that the SSA was created during the third stage, and then to list its main purposes. Choice C carries out the writer's intent effectively, by reconstructing the underlined portion and separating the two ideas with an appropriate mark.

72. H The relative pronoun *which* is used improperly here. Choice H solves the problem. Choice G is wrong because the form of the subject *employers* is not possessive (as in *employers' attempts*).

73. B The subject of the sentence is the singular *relief*, which calls for the singular verb form *was*.

74. G The sentence that choice G provides helps explain why providing relief under the New Deal was the responsible thing to do for the good of the nation.

75. A The phrase *attempt a better life* is idiomatic. (Either the singular *a better life* or the plural *better lives* would be acceptable.)

Math

1. D Given a total of 120 enrolled students, 36 of them must be seniors. To determine the percentage, divide 36 by 120, then move the decimal point two places to the right: $36 \div 120 = 0.3$, or 30%.

2. G The line segment connecting the two points $A(6,3)$ and $B(0,3)$ is horizontal because the y-coordinate is the same for both points. Thus, the distance between A and B is simply the difference of their x-coordinates: $6 - 0 = 6$. In addition, by using the distance formula, it can be shown that the distances for choices **F, H, J,** and **K** are $3\sqrt{5}$, $3\sqrt{2}$, $3\sqrt{10}$ and $6\sqrt{2}$, respectively.

3. A Raise both the coefficient -2 and variable x^2 to the power of 4. When raising an exponent to a power, multiply together the exponents:

$$(-2x^2)^4 = (-2)^4x^{(2)(4)} = 16x^8$$

4. H First, substitute 3 for A in the equation $AB = -9$: $3B = -9$, $B = -3$. Then, substitute -3 for B in the equation $BC = -6$: $-3C = -6$, $C = 2$.

5. E Substitute 5 for b in the equation, then solve for a:

$$\frac{a(5)}{10} + 5 = a - 2$$

$$\frac{a}{2} + 5 = a - 2$$

$$\frac{a}{2} - a = -2 - 5$$

$$-\frac{a}{2} = -7$$

$$a = 14$$

6. K Since the answer choices are expressed in decimal terms, rename all three terms in the question as decimals, then add:

$$\sqrt{0.49} = 0.7$$

$$\frac{3}{4} = 0.75$$

$$80\% = 0.8$$

$$0.7 + 0.75 + 0.8 = 2.25$$

7. B Letting w equal the rectangle's width, its length is $3w$ and its area is $(w)(3w) = 3w^2 = 12$. To find the rectangle's perimeter, first solve for w:

$$3w^2 = 12$$

$$w^2 = 4$$

$$w = 2$$

The perimeter is $2l + 2w = 6w + 2w = 8w = (8)(2) = 16$.

8. G Because the t-terms are the same ($.2t$), the quickest way to solve for s here is with the addition-subtraction method. Manipulate both equations so that corresponding terms "line up," then add the two equations:

$$\begin{aligned} 0.2t + 0.6s &= 2.2 \\ -0.2t + 0.5s &= 1.1 \\ \hline 1.1s &= 3.3 \\ s &= 3 \end{aligned}$$

9. B The amount of the decrease is \$4. The percent of the decrease is $\frac{4}{25}$, or $\frac{16}{100}$, or 16%.

10. F The amount invested at 5% is $(10{,}000 - x)$ dollars. Thus, the income from that amount is $0.05(10{,}000 - x)$ dollars.

11. B Multiplying together any combination of the factors of p will result in a product that is also a factor of p. The only number among the choices listed that is not a product of any of these combinations is 36.

12. G $m\angle 3$ corresponds to $m\angle 4$, both of which are formed just by the same transversal of lines k and m. Thus, statement II is always true. However, $m\angle 1$ and $m\angle 2$ are not corresponding angles; $m\angle 1$ is formed by both transversals, but angle two is formed just by one transversal. $m\angle 5$ and $m\angle 6$ are not corresponding angles; they are formed by different transversals. Thus, neither statement I nor statement III need be true.

13. C The relationship between p and q is $p = \sqrt[3]{q}$, or $p^3 = q$. The relationship between q and r is $q = \frac{1}{\sqrt{r}}$. Choice **C** expresses the relationship between q and both p and r in one equation.

14. K Increase the first coordinate (the x-value) in each pair by 3, and increase the second coordinate (the y-value) in each pair by 2. Choice **K** provides the correct translation.

15. E The line shows a negative y-intercept (the point where the line crosses the vertical axis) and a negative slope less than -1 (that is, slightly more horizontal than a 45° angle). In choice (E), $-\frac{2}{3}$ is the slope and -3 is the y-intercept. Thus, choice (E) matches the graph of the line.

16. J One way to solve this problem is to substitute each answer choice in turn into the given fraction. You can also solve the problem algebraically. Let $\frac{x}{2x}$ represent the original fraction. Add 4 to both the numerator and denominator, then cross-multiply to solve for x:

$$\begin{aligned} \frac{x+4}{2x+4} &= \frac{5}{8} \\ 8x + 32 &= 10x + 20 \\ 12 &= 2x \\ 6 &= x \end{aligned}$$

The original denominator is $2x$, or 12.

17. A Apply the formula for determining a line's slope (m):

$$m = \frac{y_2 - y_1}{x_2 - x_1} = \frac{-6 - 4}{3 - (-1)} = \frac{-10}{4} = -\frac{5}{2}$$

18. F You can answer this question without knowing the total number of legislators who voted, because the question involves ratios only. Think of the legislature as containing 8 voters divided into two parts: $\frac{5}{8} + \frac{3}{8} = \frac{8}{8}$. For every 5 votes in favor, 3 were cast against. Thus, 5 out of every 8 votes, or $\frac{5}{8}$, were cast in favor of the motion.

19. B Using the formula for a line's slope, $m = \frac{y_2 - y_1}{x_2 - x_1}$, formulate an equation in variables p and q for each of the two line segments. Given that the slope of a line segment with endpoints (7,−2) and (p,q) is −1:

$$-1 = \frac{q - (-2)}{p - 7}$$

$$-1 = \frac{q + 2}{p - 7}$$

$$7 - p = q + 2$$

$$p = 5 - q$$

Given that the slope of a line segment with endpoints (1,−4) and (p,q) is $\frac{1}{2}$:

$$\frac{1}{2} = \frac{q - (-4)}{p - 1}$$

$$\frac{1}{2} = \frac{q + 4}{p - 1}$$

$$p - 1 = 2q + 8$$

$$p = 2q + 9$$

With two equations in two variables (p and q), you can now solve for q. Using the substitution method:

$$p = 2q + 9$$

$$(5 - q) = 2q + 9$$

$$-3q = 4$$

$$q = -\frac{4}{3}$$

20. J The information in the question indicates the inequality $3p - 8 < 7$. Solve for p: $3p < 15$; $p < 5$. The graph in choice J indicates this inequality.

21. A The question asks essentially for the negative reciprocal of b in the standard form $ax^2 + bx + c = 0$. If the equation is to have one and only one root, the trinomial must be factorable into two identical binomials in which the first term is the square root of $4x^2$ and the second term is a negative-number square root of 1. You can rewrite the equation in factorable form as follows: $(2x - 1)(2x - 1) = 0$. In unfactored form, this equation is $4x^2 - 4x + 1 = 0$. Hence, $4 = \frac{1}{q}$, and $q = \frac{1}{4}$.

22. J The number of dollars increases proportionately with the number of pieces of paper. The question is essentially asking: "1 is to m as what is to p?" First, set up a proportion (equate two ratios, or fractions). Then convert either pieces of paper to reams (divide m by 500) or reams to pieces (multiply p by 500). (The second conversion method is used below.) Cross-multiply to solve for x:

$$\frac{1}{m} = \frac{x}{500p}$$

$$mx = 500p$$

$$x = \frac{500p}{m}$$

23. D Equate C's age eight years from now $(C + 8)$ to twice B's age eight years from now $(B + 8)$, and then solve for C:

$$C + 8 = 2(B + 8)$$

$$C = 2(B + 8) - 8$$

$$C = 2B + 16 - 8$$

$$C = 2B + 8$$

24. G Since $x^2 - y^2$ is the difference of two squares, $x^2 - y^2 = (x + y)(x - y) = 16$. Given $x + y = 2$, solve for x:

$$(x + y)(x - y) = 16$$

$$2(x - y) = 16$$

$$x - y = 8$$

$$x = 8 + y$$

To solve for y, you can substitute $(8 + y)$ for x in the equation $x + y = 2$:

$$x + y = 2$$

$$(8 + y) + y = 2$$

$$2y = -6$$

$$y = -3$$

25. E First, find the midpoint of the line segment, which is where it intersects its perpendicular bisector. The midpoint's x-coordinate is $\frac{4-3}{2}=\frac{1}{2}$, and its y-coordinate is $\frac{-2+5}{2}=\frac{3}{2}$. Next, determine the slope of the line segment: $\frac{5-(-2)}{-3-4}=\frac{7}{-7}=-1$. Since the slope of the line segment is -1, the slope of its perpendicular bisector is 1. Plug the (x,y) pair $\left(\frac{1}{2},\frac{3}{2}\right)$ and slope (m) 1 into the standard form of the equation for a line $(y = mx + b)$, then solve for b (the y-intercept):

$$\frac{3}{2}=(1)\left(\frac{1}{2}\right)+b$$

$$1=b$$

You now know the equation of the line: $y = x + 1$.

26. H $3x$ is a multiple of 3; thus, adding 5 to that number yields a number that is not a multiple of 3. None of the other choices fit the bill. Choice **F** is incorrect because $x > 0$ and therefore must equal 3 or some multiple of 3. Choices **G**, **J**, and **K** are incorrect because any integer multiplied by 3 is a multiple of 3, and any multiple of 3 (such as 6 or 18) added to a multiple of 3 is also a multiple of 3.

27. D Letting x = the length in question, by the Pythagorean theorem:

$x^2 + 7^2 = 13^2$; $x^2 = 169 - 49$; $x^2 = 120$; $x \approx 11$.

28. G The radius of a circle with circumference twice that of the semicircle shown in the figure would be 4 units, and the circle's circumference would be $2\pi r = 2\pi(4) = 8\pi$. Thus, the curved side of the region in the figure is half that circumference, or 4π. The height of the region is twice the radius of that circle, or 8. Thus, the total length of the straight sides of the region = 10 + 8 + 10 = 28. The total perimeter is $28 + 4\pi$.

29. E For each year, visually compare the difference in height between Country X's dark bar and Country Y's light bar. (For each year, the left-hand bars represent data for Country X, while the right-hand bars represent data for Country Y.) A quick inspection reveals that only for the year 2005 is Country Y's light bar approximately twice the height of Country X's dark bar. Although you don't need to determine dollar amounts, during 2005, Country Y's imports totaled about $45 million, while Country X's exports totaled about $22 million.

30. G The area of a circle = πr^2. Letting the radius of the smaller circle = r, the radius of the larger circle = $2r$, and its area $\pi(2r)^2$, or $4\pi r^2$. The ratio of the smaller circle's area to the larger circle's area is $\pi r^2 : 4\pi r^2$, or 1:4.

31. D In each set are three distinct member pairs. Thus the probability of selecting any pair is one in three, or $\frac{1}{3}$. Accordingly, the probability of selecting fruit and salad from the appetizer menu along with squash and peas from the vegetable menu is $\frac{1}{3}\times\frac{1}{3}=\frac{1}{9}$.

32. K To determine the entry for row 2, column 1 of matrix PQ, multiply each term in P's row 2 by each term in Q, then add the products:

$$(3)(-3) + (4)(-2) = -9 + (-8) = -17.$$

33. E Given $N = 2$, the 25th term of Set $R = 25N + 25 = 25(2) + 25 = 75$.

34. F You can eliminate answer choices **J** and **K** immediately, since common sense tells you that Cynthia's average rate is closer to 50 than to 60, and certainly not more than 60. Think of Cynthia's average rate as the average of eight equally weighted one-hour trips. Seven of those trips receive a weight of 50, and one of the trips receives a weight of 60. You can express this algebraically as follows:

$$\frac{7(50) + 60}{8} = \frac{350 + 60}{8} = \frac{410}{8} = 51.25$$

Cynthia's average rate during the entire trip was 51.25 mph.

35. E The question provides that $x + y < 0$. Accordingly, $-(x + y) > 0$. Distributing the minus sign to both x and y gives you the inequality $-x - y > 0$, which is the same as $-y - x > 0$.

36. F Isolate $\sqrt[3]{p + q}$ on one side of the equation, then "cube" both sides:

$$\sqrt[3]{p + q} = -4$$

$$\left(\sqrt[3]{p + q}\right)^3 = (-4)^3$$

$$p + q = -64$$

37. C P percent means $\frac{p}{100}$. Hence, $\frac{p}{100} \times 20 = Q$. To answer the question, solve for P:

$$\frac{p}{100} \times 20 = Q$$

$$\frac{P}{5} = Q$$

$$P = 5Q$$

38. J The function $\log_x 16 = 4$ is equivalent to $x^4 = 16$. Hence, $x = \sqrt[4]{16} = 2$.

39. C Since the two areas both equal $L \times W$, the other (longer) corral must have a length of $\frac{3}{2}L$ and a width of $\frac{2}{3}W$. Accordingly, the perimeter of the longer corral $= (2)\left(\frac{3}{2}L\right) + 2\left(\frac{2}{3}W\right)$, or $3L + \frac{4}{3}W$.

40. H Any term to a negative power is the same as "the reciprocal of" the term, but raised to the *positive* power. In addition, a negative number raised to a power is *negative* if the exponent is *odd*, yet *positive* if the exponent is *even*:

$$[-1]^{(-3)} + [-1]^{(-2)} + [-1]^2 + [-1]^3 = \frac{1}{-1} + \frac{1}{1} + 1 - 1 = 0$$

41. C The ellipse's center is at (p,q); hence, applying the standard form of the equation for an ellipse, in which the ellipse's center is at (h,k), $h = p$ and $k = q$. The length of the ellipse's x-axis is $-2p$, and the length of its y-axis is $2q$. Since $|p| < q$, the ellipse is vertically oriented. Accordingly, in the standard form of the equation for an ellipse, the larger denominator, in this case q^2, is under the variable y:

$$\frac{(x-p)^2}{p^2} + \frac{(y-q)^2}{q^2} = 1$$

42. K Letting x = the degree measure of the smallest angle, $x + 2x + 3x + 4x = 360$; $10x = 360$; $x = 36$. The second smallest angle ($2x°$) measures 72°. The sum of the measures of the two angles is 108° (36° + 72°).

43. E The question describes a 30°-60°-90° triangle. The ratios among the sides opposite those angles, respectively, are $1:\sqrt{3}:2$. The cosine of the 60° angle equals the length of its adjacent leg (1) divided by the length of the hypotenuse (2), or $\frac{1}{2}$.

44. J A complete circle contains 360°. Accordingly, referring to the figure below, the combined measure of all six angles is 360°. Given that the measures of all angles but a and b add up to 250°, $a + b = 110$. Since $a + b + x = 180$ (the three angles combine to form a straight line), $x = 70$.

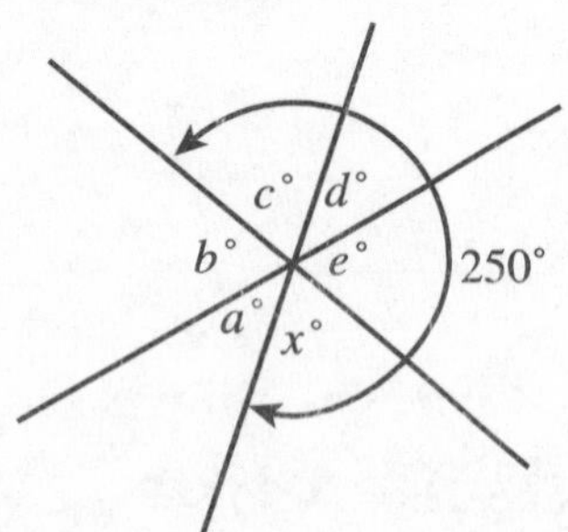

45. C The measures of any triangle's three interior angles total 180°. Thus, $\angle T = 65°$. Since $m\angle T = m\angle R$, the sides opposite these angles are congruent; that is, $\overline{RS} \cong \overline{TS}$. Since A and B bisect their respective sides, $\overline{AS} \cong \overline{AR} \cong \overline{SB} \cong \overline{BT}$. However, $\overline{RT}$ is opposite the triangle's smallest angle. Thus, the length of $\overline{RT}$ must be less than the length of $\overline{RS}$.

46. G Multiply numerators together, and multiply denominators together. When combining, apply the rule $(\sqrt{a})(\sqrt{b}) = \sqrt{ab}$ to the numerators. Then, factor and simplify:

$$\frac{\sqrt{10}}{\sqrt{2}} \times \frac{\sqrt{5}}{\sqrt{2}} = \frac{\sqrt{(10)(5)}}{(\sqrt{2})^2}$$

$$= \frac{\sqrt{50}}{2}$$

$$= \frac{\sqrt{(25)(2)}}{2}$$

$$= \frac{5\sqrt{2}}{2}$$

47. A $4{,}230 \times 10^{-4} = 4.23 \times 10^{-1}$.

48. H Since the average of the four original numbers is 4, their sum must be 16. To calculate the average of all five numbers, divide the new sum (22) by the number of terms (5). The new average is $\frac{22}{5}$.

49. B Since the smallest circle has a radius of 1, the medium circle has a radius of 2, and hence the diameter of the large circle must be 6, which makes its radius 3. The arc of a semicircle is half the circle's circumference—that is, πr. So the length of the boundary of the shaded region is the sum of the arcs of the three semicircles: $\pi + 2\pi + 3\pi = 6\pi$.

50. H The answer choices suggest two binomial factors, one containing the term x^2 and the other containing the term x: $(x^2 + ?)\ (x + ?)$. Since the fourth term of the expression given in the question is -15, the product of the second terms of the two binomials must be -15. A bit of trial and error reveals that the factored form that yields the correct expression is $(x^2 - 5)\ (x + 3)$.

51. B The polygon is a regular hexagon (six-sided polygon). Each interior angle measures $720° \div 6 = 120°$. The angle whose measure is $x°$ combines with its adjacent angle (interior to the hexagon) to total 360°—the total number of degrees in a circle. Thus, $x = 360 - 120 = 240$.

52. J The area of the entire ring between the two circles is the area of the larger circle minus the area of the smaller circle. Letting that area equal A:

$$A = \pi(2r)^2 - \pi r^2$$
$$= 4\pi r^2 - \pi r^2$$
$$= 3\pi r^2$$

Drawing a line segment from C to O forms two right triangles, each with hypotenuse $2r$. Since $\overline{OC} = r$, by the Pythagorean theorem, the ratios among the triangle's sides are $1{:}\sqrt{3}{:}2$, with corresponding angle ratios 30°:60°:90°. $\angle A$ and $\angle B$ each = 30°. Accordingly, interior $\angle AOB$ = 120°, or one third the degree measure of the circle. Hence, the area of the shaded region is two thirds of area A and must equal $2\pi r^2$.

53. C The equation defines a vertically oriented parabola, opening upward. Since the question indicates that the parabola intercepts the x-axis, it must intercept that axis at *two* points. To determine those two values, set $y = 0$, and then solve by the quadratic formula, with $a = 1$, $b = 2$, and $c = -3$:

$$x = \frac{-2 \pm \sqrt{2^2 - 4(1)(-3)}}{2(1)}$$

$$= \frac{-2 \pm \sqrt{4 + 12}}{2}$$

$$= \frac{-2 \pm \sqrt{16}}{2}$$

$$= \frac{-2 \pm 4}{2} = 1, -3$$

One of the two x-intercept values, 1, is within the interval [0,2].

54. G Given a surface area of 9 for each side, each edge of the cube is 3 units long, and the volume of the cube before the hole is cut is $3^3 = 27$. The square hole removed 3 cubic units of material ($1 \times 1 \times 3$), leaving a volume of 24.

55. C ΔADC is a right isosceles triangle, and therefore the ratio of each leg to the hypotenuse is $1{:}\sqrt{2}$. Given a hypotenuse of length 8, the length of each leg ($\overline{AD}$ and $\overline{DC}$) $= \frac{8}{\sqrt{2}} = \frac{8\sqrt{2}}{2} = 4\sqrt{2}$. Since ΔABC has a hypotenuse 8 units long and one leg ($\overline{BC}$) 4 units long, the other leg ($\overline{AB}$) must be $4\sqrt{3}$ units long. (The sides of triangle ΔABC are in the ratio $1{:}\sqrt{3}{:}2$.) You can now determine the perimeter of the quadrilateral:

$$4 + 4\sqrt{3} + 4\sqrt{2} + 4\sqrt{2} = 4 + 4\sqrt{3} + 8\sqrt{2}.$$

56. F You multiply x (the first term) by $\frac{y}{x}$ to obtain y (the second term). Thus, $\frac{y}{x}$ is the constant multiple. To obtain the third term, multiply the second term (y) by this multiple:

$$y \times \frac{y}{x} = \frac{y^2}{x}$$

57. B Either the cosine or sine function can relate the length of wire to the angle of θ degrees. Applying the sine function (let x = the length of the wire):

$$\sin\theta = \frac{b}{x}$$

$$x\sin\theta = b$$

$$x = \frac{b}{\sin\theta}$$

58. K The curve's amplitude and its frequency over period 2π are each 3. Here's the curve's graph:

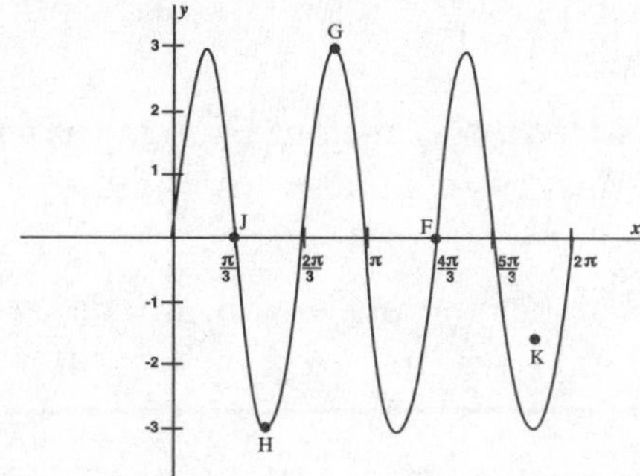

Observation reveals that the graph intercepts the x-axis in regular $\frac{1}{3}\pi$ intervals beginning at $x = \frac{1}{3}\pi$, and that it attains its positive as well as negative amplitude at regular $\frac{1}{3}\pi$ intervals as well. Choices **J** and **K** are the only two that provide points between an amplitude point and x-intercept. The point $\left(\frac{\pi}{3}, 0\right)$, which is choice **J**, is a point on the curve. However, at $x = \frac{11}{6}\pi$, the curve is at negative amplitude -3. Hence, $\left(\frac{11}{6}\pi, -\frac{3}{2}\right)$, which is choice **K**, cannot be a point on the curve.

59. D $f(x^2) = \frac{x^2}{2}$, and $(f(x))^2 = \left(\frac{x}{2}\right)^2$. Accordingly, $f(x^2) \div (f(x))^2 = \frac{x^2}{2} \div \frac{x^2}{4} = \frac{x^2}{2} \times \frac{4}{x^2} = 2$.

60. G In right-triangle trigonometry, given $\tan\theta = \frac{5}{12}$, the side opposite $\theta = 5$. Given $\cos\theta = \frac{12}{13}$, the hypotenuse = 13. In general, $\sin\theta = \frac{\text{opposite}}{\text{hypotenuse}}$; thus, $\sin\theta = \frac{5}{13}$.

Reading

1. D From the first paragraph, we understand that Newland is afraid his life is becoming overly routine and that he has developed a "horror of doing the same thing every day." The point is further reiterated in the next paragraph—by the repeated mention of "sameness," which he obviously abhors. Conversely, his longing for variety reveals itself in almost every aspect of his life, from the change in his daily routine to his suggesting that he and May strike out on their own simply because it would be something different from what is expected of them.

2. F May's response—"If you call it long"—strongly suggests that she considers her mother's proposed engagement period to be short, especially compared to the engagement periods of some of her acquaintances.

3. B In lines 41–54, Newland is contemplating his upcoming task of removing the metaphorical bandages from May's eyes, which in turn reminds him of the incidence of the cave-fish and how they had ceased to develop eyes because of the uselessness of eyes in the dark. Newland extends the metaphor to how the development of May's eyes (a metaphor for the mind) might have been stultified by the dark (metaphor for unenlightened upbringing), thus robbing her mind of newer, original thoughts.

4. G The passage informs us that Newland is a lawyer who is curious enough to read about new ideas put forth in scientific books, which in turn fosters questions about everything traditionally accepted—from travel to the situation of women in society.

5. C In lines 60–62, we're told of May's belief that her mother—who, in context, symbolizes "society"—would consider May's and Newland's wanting to travel as different—in other words, not too common during the time.

6. G May calls Newland "original" (line 65) and "artistic" (line 110). In line 91, May declared that she is "not clever enough" to argue with Newland; we can infer from this statement that she considers him more clever than her. However, the passage cites no evidence of Newland being amusing, either in word or in action.

7. C In line 93, May states that Newland's ideas are "rather vulgar." Then, speaking for both of them, she says, ". . . I should hate it—and so would you." This declaration marks the end of the discussion since May proceeds to a new topic.

8. J Lines 32–33 indicate that "she was nearing her twenty-second birthday."

9. C Archer concludes, in lines 70–71, that May was "making the answers that instinct and tradition taught her to make." In context, it is reasonable to infer that tradition means the conventional behaviors, attitudes, and values of a culture.

10. F The passage makes us privy to Newland's understanding that his fiancée, who is typical of young women of the time, was spouting responses that simply parrot what she has been taught. The clear inference here is that she, like most young women of that time, had not been encouraged to think for herself or to speak her own mind.

11. C The fifth paragraph informs us that, in Massachusetts, the governor not only appointed most state officials but also had the ultimate power to veto legislature. Contrast the Massachusetts model to the Virginia model (described in the second paragraph), under which the legislature was supreme and under which the approval of a special council was necessary for any action by the governor. In Pennsylvania, there was no governor, and the passage never mentioned Washington; thus, choices **A** and **D** cannot be correct.

12. J The paragraph in which the term "larger states" appears involves the debate about the allocation of power based on population. If you substitute "more populous states" for "larger states," the paragraph makes perfect sense.

13. B The sentence in which the word *onerous* appears informs us that the southern states feared "the imposition of onerous taxes or tariffs." The rest of the sentence tells us the reason for that fear—that these states depended economically on the exporting of certain raw materials. In this context, it makes sense that taxes or tariffs (on exported goods) would impose an economic burden on the southern states.

14. F The first sentence of the second paragraph informs us that the Virginia model borrowed its central principle from the thinking of the English philosopher John Locke.

15. B The first five paragraphs describe three distinct patterns (models) of governance used in three of the original states. The rest of the passage explains how the framers of the Constitution set about devising the structure of a newly united government by considering those three different patterns. Choice **B** nicely sums up the gist of the passage.

16. H The third paragraph informs us that Virginia's bicameral legislature, in which both chambers must concur to pass a bill, was "derived from Locke."

17. A The sixth paragraph tells us that the southern states feared the taxes and tariffs that Congress might impose if it were given the power to regulate international trade. Thus, it is reasonable to infer that the southern leaders would not be concerned with protecting the interests of whoever regulated international trade.

18. H The provision requiring that all funding bills originate in the House of Representatives afforded more power to the Northern states, which as a whole were more populous than the Southern states. Moreover, lines 119–121 indicate that the larger (more populous) states demanded this provision as "a precaution . . . to protect their financial interests."

19. B The fourth paragraph informs us that New Jersey *alone* extended the voting privilege to women.

20. J The information in the last paragraph—and especially the last sentence of the passage—is clearly contrary to the idea that choice **J** provides. According to the final paragraph, concessions made by both the North and the South served to postpone sectional difference until the future—in other words, they were not resolved at the time the new Constitution was adopted.

21. C To infer the meaning of this remark, read the entire sentence along with the preceding one. Together, the two quoted sentences seem to suggest that, for these people, all that is important is that the book's matter is good; if it is, then it doesn't matter whether the critics think highly of it or not.

22. F According to lines 20–23, the notion that some people have is that writers who want to be "classical," once they have their content, feel that they must "dress it up elegantly in a costume of style" in order to please the critics. Of the five choices, **F** provides a best restatement of this idea.

23. D The last sentence of the paragraph claims that, by definition: "A clear idea is expressed clearly, and a vague idea vaguely." But, this does not mean that a person with a vague idea (which is expressed vaguely) cannot then develop a similar, clearer idea (which is expressed clearly) from it.

24. J In the third paragraph, the author tells us that "just as science is the development of common sense, so is literature the development of common daily speech. The difference between science and common sense is simply one of degree; similarly with speech and literature."

25. A In lines 74–75, the author tells us that when you cannot express yourself, "depend on it that you have nothing precise to express. . . ."

26. G The word *canon* means "rule or criterion." When you judge something, you evaluate it according to a rule, standard, or *principle*. Hence, "set of principles," choice **B**, makes perfect sense in context.

27. C In this paragraph, the author is making the point that the relationship between a reader and a book (or other writing) is similar to a relationship between two men. Unless you respect a writer's style of writing (as you might respect another person), any pleasure you derive from the writing (or from your acquaintance with the person) will be short-lived. Of the four answer choices, C best expresses this notion.

28. F In the sixth paragraph, the author suggests to any reader who finds herself evaluating a writing based on "style" to "forget that literary style exists"—for the reason that, ultimately, there really is no such thing as literary style.

29. B The word *incommode* means "disturb or trouble." Even if you didn't already know the word's meaning, you can infer its gist, based on the context. The author is saying here that, when you cannot express yourself, what's getting in the way is your desire to think more clearly. Another way of putting it is that this desire is *troubling* you, thereby holding you back from expressing yourself. (Besides, none of the other answer choices provides a word that makes as much sense in context as *troubles*.)

30. J Throughout the passage, the author makes the point repeatedly that what people consider writing "style" is not actually independent of, or distinct from, matter. For example, if a reader thinks a style is clumsy, it is actually the writer's ideas that are clumsy (lines 96–98). Similarly, if a reader thinks a writer's style "polished," it is actually the matter that is polished. [The word *clear* in choice J is a good synonym for *polished*.]

31. C In the third paragraph, the author informs us that the angler fish uses its bioluminescence to bait, or lure, marine creatures attracted to the spot of light as a possible source of food into the angler's gaping maw—in other words, to attract its prey.

32. J At the beginning of the fifth paragraph, the author informs us that "[s]ome marine animals use bioluminescence in their own defense," and then illustrates the point by describing the "burglar alarm effect." Also, notice that the first sentence of the next paragraph (lines 71–74) indicates that bioluminescence "is used not only in such interspecific feeding frays between predators and prey. . . ." It is reasonable to infer that the author is referring here to what is described in the preceding paragraph.

33. A In the final paragraph, the author indicates that most midwater animals have eyes that are sensitive only to blue-green and, by implication, suggests that they are not sensitive to yellow. Choice A contradicts what the author states and what the author infers.

34. F The phrase "selection pressure" refers to environmental forces that pressure a species to develop a specific characteristic—in this instance, acute eyesight.

35. D At the beginning of the final paragraph, the author informs us that there are instances "in which bioluminescence seems to be truly purposeless." Then, the author goes on to discuss the tomopterid worm as a specific case in point. It is reasonable to infer that the author is at a loss as to how to classify the function of the worm's luminescence.

36. J The word *elude* means "to adroitly escape detection or danger." Even if you don't know the word's meaning, you can infer it from its context. After its first sentence, the paragraph goes on to explain how a prey uses luminescence to avoid or escape predators. In context, then, the word *escape* makes perfect sense as a synonym for *elude*.

37. C The squid uses its luminescence as a form of camouflage so that a predator looking up toward the squid cannot identify it against the light background above it—in other words, the squid avoids detection by blending in with its background. (Admittedly, the analogy is not perfect, as the specific mechanisms used by two species differ; nevertheless, the analogy is the closest among the four choices.)

38. H In the seventh paragraph, the author states that, although bioluminescence clearly functions to help some species survive, "when we look at the large evolutionary picture, bioluminescence is generally considered a nonessential characteristic." The author then proceeds to provide details to support this general view and does not refute it.

39. A If it turns out that male tomopterid worms are sensitive to yellow light, then the emission of yellow bioluminescent fluid might very well serve some function, at least among tomopterid worms—perhaps having to do with mating.

40. G Although the author begins by pointing out examples of bioluminescence in fireflies and mushrooms, she soon narrows the discussion to examples of bioluminescence in marine life inhabiting the ocean's midwaters—and to its various essential and nonessential uses. Choice G neatly sums up the overall picture.

Science

1. B Only with Resistor A was the current measured at 100mA when the temperature was 25°C. The corresponding voltage was 1.00.

2. H The question refers you to the column of Table 1 that is second farthest to the right. The current that corresponds to 4.50 volts (in the first column) is 90mA.

3. A With Resistor A, the percent increase from one voltage to the next higher increment results in the same percentage increase in measured current (mA). In other words, with Resistor A there is a linear relationship between voltage and current—which defines Resistor A as an ohmic device. Also, using Resistor A, the measured current at 23°C is the same as at 25°C—at all voltage levels. Thus, Resistor A is not a thermistor.

4. H In Table 1, the rightmost column shows the increase in current resulting from incremental increases in voltage. For each 0.05 volt increase, current increases by exactly 9.0mA. The relationship is linear. (Resistor C is an ohmic device.) Thus, it is possible to extrapolate from the known data. A current measuring 126mA is 36mA greater than 90.0mA, which Table 1 shows to result from 5.0 volts. Since each 18mA increase corresponds to a 1.0 volt increase, the voltage that produces 126mA current must be 7.00 volts.

5. D Resistor B is not considered a thermistor for the reason that it is not sensitive to different water temperatures. This is true regardless of whether the resistor affected the water temperature.

6. H Soil sample 2 from the forest contains 60% silt, the largest percentage of silt among the six samples.

7. A The diagram shows that all of the areas indicated as a type of loam are nearer to the corner that represents 100% sand than either of the other two corners (which represent 100% silt and 100% clay).

8. G Given that the amount of soil is the same in all six samples, you can simply add together percentages, then compare totals. For example, the total percent of clay from the three forest samples is 50% + 20% + 15% = 85%, while the total percent of clay from the three grassy-field samples is 33% + 6% + 11% = 50%. As you can see, the statement in choice G is clearly inaccurate. (Just the opposite is true.)

9. B The description of each experiment provides is that the percentages of each particle size were calculated. Since the tables list separate percentages for sand, silt, and clay, the clear inference here is that these three particle types are distinguishable from one another in their size.

10. J Sample 2 from the forest or sample 1 from the grassy field both contain more silt by percent than either sand or clay.

11. C As long as the particle proportions in each cup are known and the proportions in the cups differ, it is possible to compare sand, silt, and clay according to permeability with this experiment—then rank the six original samples according to permeability based on the data in Tables 1 and 2.

12. G The answer can easily be found in the fourth column of Table 1: the efficiency of design 2 (in terms of lift-to-drag ratio) was 40:1, a higher ratio than for any of the other wings.

13. B To handle the question, you need to infer that the "best" design would be one that is most efficient in terms of its lift-to-drag ratio as well as in terms of fuel consumption. Fortunately, Tables 1 and 2 each show that design 2 is most efficient.

14. J To answer this question, you need to understand the concepts of lift and drag. You also need to recognize that Table 1 provides the data relevant to the question. Ice building up on top of the wing would increase lift, since the higher the curved upper surface of the wing, the greater the difference between the speed of air moving under the wing and above it. It would also increase drag, as suggested by the third column of Table 1: notice how the wings with the higher upper surface also have greater drag. Finally, ice building up under the wing would decrease the speed of air moving under the wing and so reduce lift. Thus, all three effects would occur.

15. D In both experiments that choice **D** identifies, conditions are the same: the same wing design is used, and the airspeed of 400 mph is the same. (Logically enough, the efficiency result is also the same: 20:1.)

16. H Remember that "efficiency" is the same as the lift-to-drag ratio. Since Table 3 indicates that efficiency decreases as speed increases, we can tell that drag must be increasing faster than lift.

17. A Since the question deals with speed, it's a good bet that experiment 3 (Table 3) is the one that's most relevant. In Table 3, notice that wing design 2 is more efficient than design 1 at lower speeds, but once a speed of 500 mph is reached, design 1 outperforms design 2. Thus, it appears that at high speeds a "flatter" wing design is more beneficial.

18. H According to the passage, when an electron moves from one possible energy state to another, the atom emits light whose energy level equals the difference in energy levels between the two states. This difference is seen as a spectral line, which is shown by each arrow in Figure 1.

19. B In Figure 1, the horizontal lines represent the different energy states. The length of an arrow between two horizontal lines represents the energy of the light released by the atom as an electron moves from one energy state to the other. As you can see, the lengths of the arrows vary the least in the depiction of Atom 2.

20. F According to the passage, observed spectral lines that are close together indicate transitions in which the change in energy levels is similar. In Figure 1, the length of an arrow represents the amount of change in that energy. In the depiction of Atom 1, notice that the three arrows in the top left are close in length, and the two arrows at the bottom left are close in length. These relationships depict the spectral lines described in choice **F**.

21. D The frequencies listed in Table 1 indicate measurements of light energy. In the figure, the length of an arrow also indicates an amount of light energy. Thus, if the differences between measurements in Table 1 corresponds to the differences between the lengths of the arrows in one of the three atoms depicted in the figure, this correlation is a strong indication that the scientists are observing an atom like that hypothetical one. In Table 1, the two frequencies 868440 and 880570 are high numbers and very close to each other in value compared to the other two frequencies—just as the two longest arrows in the depiction of Atom 3 are very close in length to each other and significantly longer than the other arrows depicted for Atom 3.

22. G To determine the number of forbidden transitions in any one of the atoms, start at each energy level (horizontal line) and look for an arrow connecting it to each of the other energy levels. Each pair of levels that don't connect indicate a forbidden transition. Atom 1 has a total of two forbidden transitions. Atom 2 has only one forbidden transition. Atom 3 has no forbidden transitions.

23. D The age of the *Iryanthera grandis* is 800 years—greater than one of the two *Hymenolobium* specimens but younger than the other one.

24. G The passage indicates that counting rings can be an unreliable method of dating trees. Table 1 suggests that comparing diameters can be misleading as well. No information about comparing tree height is provided. The carbon-14 dating method appears to be the most reliable one, based on the information given.

25. A Among the 12 trees listed in Table 1, the two oldest (trees 3 and 11) have the two smallest growth rates, while the four youngest (trees 1, 8, 9, and 12) have the highest growth rates. This data strongly suggests that the older the tree, the slower its growth rate.

26. G The *Dipteryx odorata* specimen (tree 11) is older and is larger in diameter than the sclerolobium specimen (tree 12). Looking just at this data, the researcher would reasonably conclude that comparing tree diameter is a reliable way to compare the age of any dipteryx odorata to the age of any sclerolobium.

27. C The two most recent catastrophic events occurred 400 and 700 years ago. Four of the 12 trees are older than 700 years and hence must have survived at least those two events.

28. H A single specimen is probably too small a sample to draw any reliable conclusions about the ages of other *Dipteryx odorata* in the forest. It is entirely possible that tree 11 is just one of many *Dipteryx odorata* specimens in the forest, most of which are very young. If so, this evidence would tend to show that this species is no better able, or perhaps even less able, to survive catastrophic events than the cariniana micrantha species.

29. C Both agree that comets were formed by the process of aggregation; however, Astronomer 3 theorizes that this process occurred as the fledgling comets wandered through "cold dark space"; then, as they entered our nebula, they were captured by our Sun's gravitational force. Astronomer 1 claims, however, that comets were formed by the same compression force that formed the planets in our solar system—inferring that their formation did not occur outside the nebula.

30. F Astronomer 2 theorizes that, during the solar system's formative stage, the inner solar system formed early and quickly, while material that had not coalesced was "blown out" farther away from the Sun. The clear inference here is that the process was an expansion out from a central mass (now our Sun). On the other hand, Astronomer 1 and Astronomer 3 both theorize that our solar system was formed by the collapse of a nebula.

31. B Choice **B** expresses Astronomer 3's viewpoint, while it runs contrary to Astronomer 2's theory that the comets that form the Oort Cloud were originally part of the same mass as our Sun and planets.

32. J According to Astronomer 1, there is good evidence that the giant outer planets of our solar system were disturbed, which supports the theory that comets collided and then became part of those planets. However, Astronomer 1 never mentions any evidence of similar disturbances among the smaller planets nearer the Sun. Moreover, common sense tells us that a moving object is more likely to strike a large object than a small one.

33. C Although it is Astronomer 1, rather than Astronomer 3, who claims that some comets coalesced with planets during the formation of our solar system, the theory of Astronomer 3 (under which our solar system's comets come from elsewhere in space) is not inconsistent with this claim.

34. F Astronomer 2 theorizes that the solar system resulted from a violent expansion from a central core and that larger chunks, which had sufficiently coalesced, remained near the center while the smaller bodies, which had not sufficiently coalesced, were thrown farther from the center. The fact that the two largest planets are farther away from the Sun than several planets that are significantly smaller tends to weaken this theory. This evidence is not inconsistent, however, with the theory of either Astronomer 1 or Astronomer 3.

35. A Table 1, which shows the results of Experiment 1, does not explicitly distinguish between urban, suburban, and rural sources of benzene emissions. Hence, as far as we know, the experiment was not concerned with comparing these three types of areas in terms of their benzene emission levels.

36. J The right-hand column in Table 1 indicates benzene exposure levels to various sources. Cigarettes and automobiles together account for 61% (41% + 20%) of an average individual's benzene exposure—a greater combined percent than any of the other combinations listed among the answer choices.

37. B In both geographic areas, the levels of outdoor exposure to chloroform (0.2 micrograms/meter^3 for industrial New Jersey and 0.1 micrograms/meter^3 for rural Maine) were lower than to any of the other four compounds.

38. H The passage indicates that most of the fine particles measured by Experiment 3 are the result of combustion; hence, it is reasonable to view Table 3 as comparing levels of combustion. Choice **H** compares the levels provided in the top row (NJ Industrial City) with the corresponding numbers in the bottom row (Maine Rural Township). Although some of the corresponding levels differ, the differences are slight, and in neither row are the numbers consistently higher nor lower than the numbers in the other row.

39. A Experiment 3 measured the number of airborne particles 10 microns in size or smaller. This experiment showed no significant difference between the New Jersey industrial area and the rural area in Maine in terms of the number of airborne particles in this size range. However, Experiment 2 showed significantly higher numbers of the five listed airborne compounds in the same industrial area of New Jersey than in the same rural area in Maine. If the compounds listed in Table 2 were 10 microns in size or smaller, then Table 3 should reflect this difference. But it doesn't. The most reasonable explanation for the discrepancy between the two tables is that the compounds listed in Table 2 are at least 10 microns in size and therefore were not measured in Experiment 3.

40. J The *total* level of personal nighttime exposure was 73 or 75 micrograms/meter^3, depending on the individual subject. The information given in the question suggests that only part of that exposure (45 micrograms/meter^3) occurred inside, while the remaining exposure (28–30 micrograms/meter^3) occurred outside.

ANSWER SHEET FOR PRACTICE TEST 3

Name: ______________________________

Date: ____/____/____

School: ______________________________

Class: ______________________________

Completely darken ovals with a No. 2 pencil. If you make a mistake, be sure to erase mark completely. Erase all stray marks.

Start with number 1 for each new section. If a section has fewer questions than answer spaces, leave the extra answer spaces blank.

PART 1

1	(A) (B) (C) (D) (E)	20	(F) (G) (H) (J) (K)	39	(A) (B) (C) (D) (E)	58	(F) (G) (H) (J) (K)
2	(F) (G) (H) (J) (K)	21	(A) (B) (C) (D) (E)	40	(F) (G) (H) (J) (K)	59	(A) (B) (C) (D) (E)
3	(A) (B) (C) (D) (E)	22	(F) (G) (H) (J) (K)	41	(A) (B) (C) (D) (E)	60	(F) (G) (H) (J) (K)
4	(F) (G) (H) (J) (K)	23	(A) (B) (C) (D) (E)	42	(F) (G) (H) (J) (K)	61	(A) (B) (C) (D) (E)
5	(A) (B) (C) (D) (E)	24	(F) (G) (H) (J) (K)	43	(A) (B) (C) (D) (E)	62	(F) (G) (H) (J) (K)
6	(F) (G) (H) (J) (K)	25	(A) (B) (C) (D) (E)	44	(F) (G) (H) (J) (K)	63	(A) (B) (C) (D) (E)
7	(A) (B) (C) (D) (E)	26	(F) (G) (H) (J) (K)	45	(A) (B) (C) (D) (E)	64	(F) (G) (H) (J) (K)
8	(F) (G) (H) (J) (K)	27	(A) (B) (C) (D) (E)	46	(F) (G) (H) (J) (K)	65	(A) (B) (C) (D) (E)
9	(A) (B) (C) (D) (E)	28	(F) (G) (H) (J) (K)	47	(A) (B) (C) (D) (E)	66	(F) (G) (H) (J) (K)
10	(F) (G) (H) (J) (K)	29	(A) (B) (C) (D) (E)	48	(F) (G) (H) (J) (K)	67	(A) (B) (C) (D) (E)
11	(A) (B) (C) (D) (E)	30	(F) (G) (H) (J) (K)	49	(A) (B) (C) (D) (E)	68	(F) (G) (H) (J) (K)
12	(F) (G) (H) (J) (K)	31	(A) (B) (C) (D) (E)	50	(F) (G) (H) (J) (K)	69	(A) (B) (C) (D) (E)
13	(A) (B) (C) (D) (E)	32	(F) (G) (H) (J) (K)	51	(A) (B) (C) (D) (E)	70	(F) (G) (H) (J) (K)
14	(F) (G) (H) (J) (K)	33	(A) (B) (C) (D) (E)	52	(F) (G) (H) (J) (K)	71	(A) (B) (C) (D) (E)
15	(A) (B) (C) (D) (E)	34	(F) (G) (H) (J) (K)	53	(A) (B) (C) (D) (E)	72	(F) (G) (H) (J) (K)
16	(F) (G) (H) (J) (K)	35	(A) (B) (C) (D) (E)	54	(F) (G) (H) (J) (K)	73	(A) (B) (C) (D) (E)
17	(A) (B) (C) (D) (E)	36	(F) (G) (H) (J) (K)	55	(A) (B) (C) (D) (E)	74	(F) (G) (H) (J) (K)
18	(F) (G) (H) (J) (K)	37	(A) (B) (C) (D) (E)	56	(F) (G) (H) (J) (K)	75	(A) (B) (C) (D) (E)
19	(A) (B) (C) (D) (E)	38	(F) (G) (H) (J) (K)	57	(A) (B) (C) (D) (E)	76	(F) (G) (H) (J) (K)

PART 2

1	(A) (B) (C) (D) (E)	16	(F) (G) (H) (J) (K)	31	(A) (B) (C) (D) (E)	46	(F) (G) (H) (J) (K)
2	(F) (G) (H) (J) (K)	17	(A) (B) (C) (D) (E)	32	(F) (G) (H) (J) (K)	47	(A) (B) (C) (D) (E)
3	(A) (B) (C) (D) (E)	18	(F) (G) (H) (J) (K)	33	(A) (B) (C) (D) (E)	48	(F) (G) (H) (J) (K)
4	(F) (G) (H) (J) (K)	19	(A) (B) (C) (D) (E)	34	(F) (G) (H) (J) (K)	49	(A) (B) (C) (D) (E)
5	(A) (B) (C) (D) (E)	20	(F) (G) (H) (J) (K)	35	(A) (B) (C) (D) (E)	50	(F) (G) (H) (J) (K)
6	(F) (G) (H) (J) (K)	21	(A) (B) (C) (D) (E)	36	(F) (G) (H) (J) (K)	51	(A) (B) (C) (D) (E)
7	(A) (B) (C) (D) (E)	22	(F) (G) (H) (J) (K)	37	(A) (B) (C) (D) (E)	52	(F) (G) (H) (J) (K)
8	(F) (G) (H) (J) (K)	23	(A) (B) (C) (D) (E)	38	(F) (G) (H) (J) (K)	53	(A) (B) (C) (D) (E)
9	(A) (B) (C) (D) (E)	24	(F) (G) (H) (J) (K)	39	(A) (B) (C) (D) (E)	54	(F) (G) (H) (J) (K)
10	(F) (G) (H) (J) (K)	25	(A) (B) (C) (D) (E)	40	(F) (G) (H) (J) (K)	55	(A) (B) (C) (D) (E)
11	(A) (B) (C) (D) (E)	26	(F) (G) (H) (J) (K)	41	(A) (B) (C) (D) (E)	56	(F) (G) (H) (J) (K)
12	(F) (G) (H) (J) (K)	27	(A) (B) (C) (D) (E)	42	(F) (G) (H) (J) (K)	57	(A) (B) (C) (D) (E)
13	(A) (B) (C) (D) (E)	28	(F) (G) (H) (J) (K)	43	(A) (B) (C) (D) (E)	58	(F) (G) (H) (J) (K)
14	(F) (G) (H) (J) (K)	29	(A) (B) (C) (D) (E)	44	(F) (G) (H) (J) (K)	59	(A) (B) (C) (D) (E)
15	(A) (B) (C) (D) (E)	30	(F) (G) (H) (J) (K)	45	(A) (B) (C) (D) (E)	60	(F) (G) (H) (J) (K)

BE SURE TO ERASE ANY ERRORS OR STRAY MARKS COMPLETELY.

DO NOT MARK IN THIS AREA

Use a No. 2 pencil only. Be sure each mark is dark and completely fills the intended oval. Completely erase any errors or stray marks.

Start with number 1 for each new section. If a section has fewer questions than answer spaces, leave the extra answer spaces blank.

PART 3

1	A B C D E	11	A B C D E	21	A B C D E	31	A B C D E
2	F G H J K	12	F G H J K	22	F G H J K	32	F G H J K
3	A B C D E	13	A B C D E	23	A B C D E	33	A B C D E
4	F G H J K	14	F G H J K	24	F G H J K	34	F G H J K
5	A B C D E	15	A B C D E	25	A B C D E	35	A B C D E
6	F G H J K	16	F G H J K	26	F G H J K	36	F G H J K
7	A B C D E	17	A B C D E	27	A B C D E	37	A B C D E
8	F G H J K	18	F G H J K	28	F G H J K	38	F G H J K
9	A B C D E	19	A B C D E	29	A B C D E	39	A B C D E
10	F G H J K	20	F G H J K	30	F G H J K	40	F G H J K

PART 4

1	A B C D E	11	A B C D E	21	A B C D E	31	A B C D E
2	F G H J K	12	F G H J K	22	F G H J K	32	F G H J K
3	A B C D E	13	A B C D E	23	A B C D E	33	A B C D E
4	F G H J K	14	F G H J K	24	F G H J K	34	F G H J K
5	A B C D E	15	A B C D E	25	A B C D E	35	A B C D E
6	F G H J K	16	F G H J K	26	F G H J K	36	F G H J K
7	A B C D E	17	A B C D E	27	A B C D E	37	A B C D E
8	F G H J K	18	F G H J K	28	F G H J K	38	F G H J K
9	A B C D E	19	A B C D E	29	A B C D E	39	A B C D E
10	F G H J K	20	F G H J K	30	F G H J K	40	F G H J K

BE SURE TO ERASE ANY ERRORS OR STRAY MARKS COMPLETELY.

Practice Test 3

English

75 Questions ■ Time—45 Minutes

Directions: This test consists of five passages in which particular words or phrases are underlined and numbered. Alongside the passage, you will see alternative words and phrases that could be substituted for the underlined part. Select the alternative that expresses the idea most clearly and correctly or that best fits the style and tone of the entire passage. If the original version is best, select "No Change."

The test also includes questions about entire paragraphs and the passage as a whole. These questions are identified by a number in a box.

After you select the correct answer for each question, on your answer sheet, mark the oval corresponding to the correct answer.

Passage I

[The following paragraphs may or may not be arranged in the best possible order. The last question will ask you to choose the most effective order for the paragraphs as numbered.]

The Not-So-Good Old Days

[1]

Many of us look back at the turn of the century through a haze of nostalgia. Perhaps we do so (1) because we've begun to feel overwhelmed by modern technology—digital media, cell phones, the Internet—long (2) for an era we like to think of as a simpler time. Perhaps certain images, such as glowing coal stoves, the gentle aura of gaslight, the sound of a horse and buggy on the pavement—the images we associate with simple pleasures of the "good old summertime," is what makes (3) that era seem so appealing.

[2]

Although, in [4] our imagination we see the "Gilded Age" as a more genteel time, the reality was less pleasant. In many respects, things were really not so good as we imagined [5] they were in "the good old days."

[3]

Those glowing coal-burning stoves are a good example. [6] They did not provide much heat at all. Coal-burning stoves were best [7] at using [7] up the oxygen in a room and replacing it with enough soot and dust to make a house almost uninhabitable. And early radiators, though cleaner than coal, filled homes with the constant noises of "water hammer" and hissing. By the 1880s, those who could afford [8] two to four thousand dollars—a very considerable sum for the day—might install central heating. [9]

[4]

Then there were those horses in the street. We think nostalgically of the days before automobiles polluted our air, but horses and buggies produced different kinds of pollution. [10] There was so much manure in the streets that the stench was often overwhelming.

[5]

Even worse, perhaps, were those "good old summertimes." There was, of course, no air conditioning, [11] and in the cities, at least, summers were hotter than they are today because then the buildings were shorter than today's buildings. [12] Contemporary clothing also added to the problem—the garments worn by the average person during the 1890s were considerably more bulky than those worn today.

[6]

Much worse could be cited—for example, the condition of the poor, the status of women and children, and the level of health care. The list is almost endless. [13] It's probably true that the pace of life a hundred years ago was slower and, at least in this respect, perhaps more congenial to human sensibilities. The truth is that [14] the "good old days" really weren't so good after all.

1. A. NO CHANGE
   B. the reason is
   C. its
   D. it's

2. F. NO CHANGE
   G. making us long
   H. we long
   J. and long

3. A. NO CHANGE
   B. are what make
   C. makes
   D. are making

4. F. NO CHANGE
   G. Although in
   H. In
   J. Through

5. A. NO CHANGE
   B. than we imagined
   C. as we imagine
   D. as we once thought

6. F. NO CHANGE
   G. good examples of this
   H. good as examples
   J. examples

7. A. NO CHANGE
   B. What they did do was use
   C. They were better at using
   D. Also, they weren't supposed to use

8. F. NO CHANGE
   G. had as much as
   H. afforded
   J. could spend

9. Considering Paragraph 3 as a whole, which of the following sentences, if inserted at this point, would be most relevant and effective?
   A. This relatively new type of heating system did not suffer from any of the problems associated with other systems.
   B. This type of heating system, although expensive, could heat a house far more effectively than either a coal-burning stove or a radiator.
   C. In the meantime, everyone else was left with three options: Live in a sooty house, endure a contain din, or go cold all winter.
   D. Today, we take central heating for granted, but in the "good old days" it was truly a luxury, due to the high cost of installation.

10. F. NO CHANGE
    G. different pollution
    H. pollutions that were different
    J. pollution of a different kind

11. A. NO CHANGE
    B. Without any air conditioning, of course,
    C. Air conditioning did not, of course, exist,
    D. Of course, that era was before air conditioning,

12. F. NO CHANGE
    G. today's buildings are taller than they were then
    H. the buildings were shorter then than today
    J. the buildings were shorter then

13. Is the underlined sentence an appropriate and effective addition at this point in the passage?

- **A.** Yes, because it helps make the main point that life one hundred years ago was not so good overall as it is today.
- **B.** Yes, because the sentence ties together the examples in the preceding sentence and the examples provided earlier in the passage.
- **C.** No, because the writer has already provided enough supporting examples for the point that life then was not so good as it is today.
- **D.** No, because the writer does not explain why the list of examples showing how difficult life used to be is such a long list.

14.
- **F.** NO CHANGE
- **G.** The whole truth, however, is that
- **H.** It is also probably true that
- **J.** OMIT the underlined portion. (Begin the sentence with *The*.)

Question 15 poses a question about the passage as a whole.

15. Which of the following alternatives provides the most logical sequence of paragraphs for the passage?

- **A.** Reverse the order of Paragraphs 1 and 2.
- **B.** Reverse the order of Paragraphs 2 and 3.
- **C.** Reverse the order of Paragraphs 4 and 5.
- **D.** Reverse the order of Paragraphs 2 and 6.

Passage II

Jaguars and the Olmec Culture

The Olmecs are considered as 16 the oldest known people of Mesoamerica thought to live 17 between 1500 B.C.E. and 400 B.C.E. Not much is known about them; all researchers have to go on are artifacts thought to have been Olmec in origin. Their art, by its maturity and style and expressive intensity, 18 ranks among the finest works ever produced in Mesoamerica.

The jaguar, a species of wild cat, is represented frequently 19 in Olmec art. [20] In Olmec art, this large feline is almost always shown with a human face, and sometimes also 21 other human physical features as well. Anthropologists call this part-human, part-jaguar image the "were-jaguar." The face of a were-jaguar is clean-shaven, the head is pear-shaped and too large for the body, and the legs are too short. Their 22 arms are also disproportionately large to the bodies.

Because virtually nothing is known about the Olmecs themselves, we have only theories about why the Olmecs were so fascinated with the jaguar. One such theory is the possible belief among the Olmecs that, as a people, they originated from the mating of either a man and a female jaguar or a woman and a male jaguar. Numerous cave paintings support both variations on this theory. Another theory grew out of the Olmecs' understandable fear and awe of the animal, which is the largest, most powerful member of the cat family, not to mention an excellent climber and swimmer. [27]

23 — the Olmecs themselves,
24 — such theory is
25 — Numerous cave paintings support both variations on this theory.
26 — not to mention

The were-jaguar, whether it represented a creation myth or simple respect for the animal, shows that the Olmecs obviously felt something strongly about the powerful feline, or else it would not have been such an inspiration for them. Regardless of the reason for the Olmecs' preoccupation with the jaguar, their artistic representations of the animal, masterful in detail, clearly reveal a culture that was sophisticated, mature, and aesthetically sensitive. The Olmecs have left an enduring legacy on Mesoamerican art with their representation of the jaguar.

28 — something strongly
29 — reveal a culture that

16. F. NO CHANGE
G. to be
H. as being
J. they are

17. A. NO CHANGE
B. Mesoamerica; people think they have lived
C. Mesoamerica; they are thought to have lived
D. Mesoamerica who we believe lived

18. F. NO CHANGE
G. maturity, style, and expressive intensity,
H. maturity, its style, as well as expressive intensity,
J. maturity and style and its expressive intensity,

19. A. NO CHANGE
B. frequent
C. extensively
D. often

GO ON TO THE NEXT PAGE

20. Which of the following would be the most appropriate and relevant sentence to insert at this point in the passage?

F. The style and expressiveness of these art works is typical of the high level of sophistication seen among Olmec art in general.
G. In fact, the jaguar is found so pervasively throughout Olmec art that researchers speculate that it may be what first tied the culture together.
H. The Olmecs depicted the jaguar in a way that clearly shows their respect and awe for this large, powerful member of the cat family.
J. The jaguar was one of many species of wild cats found in the geographical areas of Mesoamerica where the Olmecs lived.

21. A. NO CHANGE
B. at times it has shown
C. sometimes it shows
D. is sometimes shown with

22. F. NO CHANGE
G. The
H. Were-jaguar's
J. OMIT the underlined portion.

23. A. NO CHANGE
B. them,
C. the people,
D. Olmecs,

24. F. NO CHANGE
G. of these theories is
H. theory is
J. such theory involves

25. A. NO CHANGE
B. Each of the two variations is supported by numerous cave paintings.
C. A number of cave paintings have been found that support both variations.
D. Numerous cave paintings support both of the theory's variations.

26. F. NO CHANGE
G. and besides, is
H. and it is also
J. but also

27. Which of the following sentences, if inserted at this point in the passage, would be LEAST appropriate?

A. Determining the "correct" theory might require looking at the issue from both angles.
B. Perhaps a new theory will emerge, one that disproves the two current theories.
C. Perhaps researchers will find new evidence that helps prove one theory or disprove the other.
D. These are not the only two theories about why the Olmecs were so intrigued by the jaguar.

28. F. NO CHANGE
G. strong
H. strongly
J. that there was something strong

29. A. NO CHANGE
B. reveals that the culture
C. reveal their culture
D. reveals a culture that

Question 30 poses a question about the passage as a whole.

30. For the sake of achieving unity by tying together the passage's ending with the rest of the passage, does the passage's final sentence provide an appropriate and effective ending?

F. Yes, because it provides a good summary of the passage as a whole.
G. Yes, because it reiterates the main point, or thesis, of the passage.
H. No, because it is not central to the passage's theme.
J. No, because it does not mention either of the two theories discussed in the passaye.

Passage III

Cities on the Sea

[1]

(1) Three quarters of the earth surface (31) is covered with water. (2) Many scientists are now looking at these vast watery regions for solutions to some pressing human dilemmas. (3) Hunger has long plagued millions of the world's people, especially in the underdeveloped regions of Africa, Asia, and the Indian subcontinent. (4) The food to feed the world's growing population may come largely from ocean resources. (5) Minerals such as iron, nickel, copper, aluminum, and tin are a limited supply (32) on and below dry land. (6) Undersea mines are expected to yield fresh supplies of many of these resources. [33]

[2]

Some scientists foresee, to take advantage of these ocean-based resources, entire cities on the ocean. (34) At first, they will be built close to the shore. Later, floating cities might be located hundreds of miles on the sea. (35)

[3]

(1) Some of the people living there could harvest fish and sea plants as farmers of the ocean. (2) Also, the floating cities serve (36) as terminals, or stations, for international travel, where (37) ships could stop for refueling or repairs. (3) Others could operate oil and gas wells or work in undersea enclosures mining the ocean floors. (4) These cities could provide many functions and (38) play a variety of roles. [39]

GO ON TO THE NEXT PAGE

[4]

The cities would need to be virtually self-sufficient. Shipping (40) supplies from the mainland would be costly. Each city would be a multi-story structure with room for many kinds of facilities needed by the inhabitants. [41]

[5]

Much of the technology needed to build such (42) cities already developed. (43) Oil drilling on a large scale is already conducted at sea. Rigs as large as small towns built on floating platforms or on platforms anchored into the seabed now serve as homes to scores of workers for months at a time. The same principles used for rigs could be used to create ocean-going cities on a larger scale. (44)

[6]

Many thousands of men, women, and children might inhabit these cities on the sea. They (45) would probably visit the mainland from time to time, but otherwise would spend their lives at sea as ocean-dwelling pioneers.

31. A. NO CHANGE
B. the earth
C. the earth's surface
D. the earths surface

32. F. NO CHANGE
G. are limited
H. are limited in their supply
J. are in limited supply

33. Which of the following is the best editorial suggestion for Paragraph 1, considering the paragraph's assertions, supporting details, and overall flow of information?
A. After sentence 6, add a sentence that explains how scarcity of minerals has created a pressing human dilemma.
B. Begin a new paragraph that starts with sentence 5.
C. Move sentences 1 and 2 to the end of the paragraph (following sentence 6).
D. After sentence 3, add a sentence that assesses the potential impact of population growth on food scarcity in the world's underdeveloped regions.

34. F. NO CHANGE
G. Some scientists foresee entire cities, which take advantage of these ocean-based resources, on the ocean.
H. To take advantage of these ocean-based resources, some scientists foresee entire cities on the ocean.
J. Taking advantage of these ocean-based resources, some scientists foresee entire cities on the ocean.

35. A. NO CHANGE
B. from land
C. in the sea
D. out into the sea

36. F. NO CHANGE
G. have served
H. served
J. could serve

37. A. NO CHANGE
B. travel where
C. travel: where
D. travel. There

38. F. NO CHANGE
G. provide a variety of functions and
H. provide many functions that
J. OMIT the underlined portion.

39. Which of the following is the most logical order of sentences in Paragraph 3?

A. 1, 2, 3, 4
B. 4, 1, 3, 2
C. 3, 1, 2, 4
D. 2, 4, 1, 3

40. F. NO CHANGE
G. self-sufficient because
H. self-sufficient, and
J. self-sufficient, although

41. The writer wishes to add another sentence at this point in Paragraph 4. Which of the following sentences would be best, considering the paragraph's ideas and flow of information?

A. Fish, sea-grown plants, and even foodstuffs synthesized from algae, could all be harvested by ocean-city dwellers for their own consumption.
B. Pollution of the seas has not yet reached levels where ocean cities could not harvest the food they need from the sea.
C. The tides and thermal currents—water movements caused by temperature fluctuations—may be future energy sources.
D. The ocean itself could provide much of the needed food and other raw materials, while solar panels and generators running on water power could provide energy.

42. F. NO CHANGE
G. such as these
H. such a
J. the

43. A. NO CHANGE
B. has already been developed
C. is developed
D. are already developed

44. F. NO CHANGE
G. The same principles they use they could also use to create larger-scale ocean-going cities.
H. The same principles could be used on a larger scale to create ocean-going cities.
J. On a larger scale, the same principles used for rigs could create ocean-going cities.

GO ON TO THE NEXT PAGE

45. A. NO CHANGE
B. These men, women, and children
C. The thousands of inhabitants
D. Those that

Passage IV

The New Globe Theater

The original Globe Theater was built on the south bank of the Thames River in London in 1598. Home to the plays of Shakespeare [46] and other Elizabethan playwrights, the Globe burned down in 1613, was rebuilt the following year, and it [47] was a victim of the Puritan purges of the 1640s. The 1613 blaze was caused by a cannon that caught fire during a performance of Shakespeare's *Henry VIII*.

(1) In 1949, American actor, director, and producer Sam Wanamaker determined to reconstruct the theater. (2) The size and shape of the Globe and even the design of the stage were needed to be [48] gleaned from drawings and archaeological excavations of the original Globe as well as other Elizabethan theaters. (3) It took 47 years to realize Wanamaker's dream, but the new Globe Theater opened in 1996. [49] (4) Letters and diaries of theatergoers also provided clues, as did Shakespeare's plays, in which reference here and there to the theater could be found. (5) Little but the approximate site of the original building was known when Wanamaker began his campaign to reconstruct it. [50]

The Globe was not a perfect circle, but actually a polygon of twenty small sides. The stage jutted out into the center, and three tiers with [51] multiple rows of seats ringed the other three-quarters of the polygon. Between the stage and the first tier of seats was a large open area. This area was the [52] pit where groundlings stood to watch the performance.

The new Globe is as true as possible to an Elizabethan theater, given [53] what scholars have been able to learn and what modern craftworkers could construct. Building techniques from the sixteenth century and [54] building materials with which sixteenth-century workers would have been familiar. The roof is thatch, all the wood supports are oak, and the walls over them are made of a lime plaster mix. [55]

The resemblance of the new Globe to the original also extends to the theater-going experience. The audience may sit on hard benches that ring the theater in three tiers or stand in the pit. Groundlings may find themselves in the way of King Lear's soldiers if they aren't careful. (56) Actors' entrances and exits often take place (57) through the pit. Sword-play, however, is usually confined to the stage.

Originally, performances were to be held in the new Globe only during the day, as was true with the original Globe because electric lighting had not yet been invented. However, England's theaters today typically attract larger audiences in the evening. [58] Rain, however, will cancel a performance, for like the original Globe, the new one has no roof over neither the stage nor (59) the groundlings' pit.

46. F. NO CHANGE
G. Home to Shakespeare's plays
H. It was home to Shakespeare's plays
J. The theater, home to plays by Shakespeare

47. A. NO CHANGE
B. the Globe
C. it then
D. OMIT the underlined portion.

48. F. NO CHANGE
G. had to be
H. was
J. was to be

49. A. NO CHANGE
B. Although the new Globe Theater opened in 1996, it had taken 47 years to realize Wanamaker's dream.
C. The new Globe, after 47 years to realize Wanamaker's dream, opened in 1996.
D. It took 47 years to realize the dream of Wanamaker of the new Globe Theater opening in 1996.

50. Which of the following is the most logical order for the sentences of this paragraph?

F. NO CHANGE
G. 1, 2, 5, 4, 3
H. 1, 5, 2, 4, 3
J. 1, 3, 2, 4, 5

51. A. NO CHANGE
B. with three tiers of
C. having three tiers of
D. but three tiers with

52. F. NO CHANGE
G. area—the
H. area; which was the
J. area, which area was the

GO ON TO THE NEXT PAGE

53. A. NO CHANGE
B. depending on
C. true to
D. OMIT the underlined portion.

54. F. NO CHANGE
G. as well as
H. were used, as were
J. used by the craftworkers

55. At this point in the passage, the writer is considering adding the following sentence:

The end result was what most scholars agree is a close replica of the original Globe.

Would adding this sentence contribute to an understanding of the passage?

A. Yes, because thatch, oak, and lime plaster are all examples of typical sixteenth-century building materials.
B. Yes, because the sentence provides an effective transition to the paragraph that follows.
C. No, because the writer does not describe any specific building techniques that were used for both the original Globe and the new Globe.
D. No, because the writer has already made the point that the building materials used were similar to those used for the original Globe.

56. F. NO CHANGE
G. Groundlings may find themselves, if they aren't careful, in the way of King Lear's soldiers.
H. If they aren't careful, groundlings may find themselves in the way of King Lear's soldiers.
J. Groundlings may, if they aren't careful, find themselves in the way of King Lear's soldiers.

57. A. NO CHANGE
B. An actor will often both enter and exit
C. Often, actors' entrances and exits take place
D. Actors often enter and exit

58. Which of the following sentences would provide the most appropriate and effective addition at this point in the passage?

F. Daytime performances would interfere with the daily life of a typical resident of modern London.
G. Evening performances in the original Globe would have required extensive use of candlelight, which would have been unsafe.
H. As a result, performances at the Globe are now given primarily during evening hours.
J. A covered theater would have allowed for performances in any weather.

59. A. NO CHANGE
B. either the stage or
C. either the stage or over
D. neither the stage or

Question 60 poses a question about the passage as a whole.

60. The writer has realized that the passage needs a closing statement. Which of the following would be most appropriate and most effective in unifying the entire passage?

F. Nevertheless, weather permitting, today we can enjoy the Globe Theater experience in much the same way as audiences of Shakespeare's day.
G. The new Globe Theater is as similar to the original Globe as it could possibly be, given how little we know of its original design.
H. The New Globe has proven to be popular with residents of the surrounding area as well as with tourists from around the world.
J. The New Globe owes its existence to the many talented scholars, designers, and engineers who made Wanamaker's dream a reality.

Passage V

Reflections on My Disability

I enjoyed the use of my legs for 44 years, until a simple misstep on a hiking trail left them (61) paralyzed and useless. Now, two years after the initial shock, I can reflect more calmly on my fate, and what surprises me most are (62) my own reactions to becoming disabled have been easier to live with and adapt to than the ways that able-bodied people in society responded to my disability. (63)

My responses are what I think of as pure and direct. They are (64) grief, rage, self-pity, depression, pride, anger. [65] Yet society's responses to myself (66) and to my disabled peers are far less direct, akin to the averted gaze and sidelong way in which most people look not at us, instead, (67) somewhere to either the left or the right (68) of us. In nine encounters out of ten, an able-bodied person will respond to his or her own supreme discomfort with "the handicapped" and not to me—the reality of who I am and what I am. In a culture that glorifies the body beautiful, in the eyes of most people, a disabled person is somehow viewed as posing a threat to an American ideal. (69)

(1) One way that normal society manages its own discomfort with the abnormal is to classify us. (2) Today, as if the normal cannot get over their own guilt at being normal, we have the euphemistic terms "differently abled" or (70)

"physically challenged"—labels so vague as to describe anyone and no one. (3) First there was the word "cripple": a bald statement of the truth of our situation, yet one suggestive of deviance. (4) Then came the less loaded terms, which are still, however, euphemisms: "handicapped" and "disabled.". [73]

I don't mean to sound so cynical and jaded. After all, I remember normality, and I remember responding to people like me in the same way. [75]

61. A. NO CHANGE
B. when they were left
C. caused them to become
D. resulted in

62. F. NO CHANGE
G. are mostly
H. the most is
J. most is that

63. A. NO CHANGE
B. responded
C. have responded
D. responded to it

64. F. NO CHANGE
G. direct:
H. direct; these responses include
J. direct, including

65. At this point, the writer is considering the addition of the following sentence:

I've since learned that experiencing a wide range of emotions is common among not only disabled adults but also disabled children.

Would this be a logical and relevant addition to the passage?

A. Yes, because the discussion in the paragraph involves not just the writer but the writer's disabled peers as well.
B. Yes, because it shows that the writer has come to grips with the psychological effects of his disability.
C. No, because it is not directly related to the issue of how society treats the disabled.
D. No, because the writer first became disabled as an adult, not as a child.

66. F. NO CHANGE
G. regarding me
H. to me
J. of myself

67. A. NO CHANGE
B. not at us, but rather
C. at not us, but
D. instead of at us,

68. F. NO CHANGE
G. either to the left or the right
H. either left or to the right
J. to one or the other side

69. A. NO CHANGE
B. an American ideal is somehow threatened by a disabled person, in the view of most people
C. in most people's eyes, a disabled person is viewed as somehow threatening an American ideal
D. most people somehow view a disabled person as a threat to an American ideal

70. F. NO CHANGE
G. terms "differently abled" or
H. term "differently abled" or
J. terms "differently abled" and

71. A. NO CHANGE
B. as vague as possible in describing
C. so vague in their description of
D. that vaguely describe almost

72. F. NO CHANGE
G. terms, namely, "handicapped" and "disabled," but still euphemisms, however.
H. terms, the two euphemisms "handicapped" and "disabled," which are still euphemisms.
J. terms—"handicapped" and "disabled"—which nonetheless are still euphemisms.

73. Which of the following is the most logical order for the sentences in this paragraph?

A. 1, 2, 3, 4
B. 1, 3, 4, 2
C. 3, 4, 1, 2
D. 2, 3, 4, 1

74. F. NO CHANGE
G. was also normal,
H. remember being normal,
J. wish I were normal,

Question 75 poses a question about the passage as a whole.

75. The writer wants to add a sentence that provides a better ending for the passage. Considering the passage as a whole, which of the following would be most relevant and effective?

A. I suppose it's true that until you try on someone else's shoes you can't know what it's like to walk in them.
B. A disabled person is a constant reminder of a terrible possibility: "This could happen to me."
C. I admit that society has come far in treating the disabled with dignity and respect; but, we still have a long way to go.
D. Now that I'm disabled, I truly understand what it's like to be treated as something less than what you really are and have always been.

STOP

Math

60 Questions ■ Time—60 Minutes

Directions: Solve each problem; then, on your answer sheet, mark the oval corresponding to the correct answer.

Be careful not to spend too much time on any one question. Instead, solve as many problems as possible, and then use the remaining time to return to those questions you were unable to answer at first.

You may use a calculator on any problem in this test. However, some problems can best be solved without use of a calculator.

Note: Unless otherwise stated, you can assume that:

1. Diagrams that accompany problems are not necessarily drawn to scale.
2. All figures lie in the same plane.
3. The word "line" refers to a straight line (and lines that appear straight are straight).
4. The word "average" refers to arithmetic mean.

1. If $\frac{a}{b} \bullet \frac{b}{c} \bullet \frac{c}{d} \bullet \frac{d}{e} \bullet x = 1$, then $x =$

A. $\frac{a}{e}$

B. $\frac{e}{a}$

C. e

D. $\frac{1}{a}$

E. $\frac{be}{a}$

2. $|7 - 2| - |2 - 7| =$

F. -14
G. -9
H. -5
J. 0
K. 10

3. For all $x \neq 0$ and $y \neq 0$, $\frac{x^6y^3y}{y^6x^3x}$ is equivalent to:

A. $\frac{y^2}{x^2}$

B. xy

C. $\frac{x^2}{y^2}$

D. 1

E. $\frac{x^3}{y^3}$

4. In the standard (x,y) coordinate plane, point $(a,5)$ lies along a line of slope $\frac{1}{3}$ that passes through point $(2,-3)$. What is the value of a?

F. 35
G. 26
H. 3
J. -3
K. -26

5. How many distinct (x,y) pairs satisfy the equation $6x - 4 = 3y$?

A. 0
B. 1
C. 2
D. 3
E. Infinitely many

6. $\dfrac{\frac{3}{5}+\frac{3}{4}}{\frac{3}{4}-\frac{3}{5}} =$

F. 9

G. $\frac{27}{4}$

H. 5

J. $\frac{27}{10}$

K. $-\frac{57}{20}$

7. In the figure below, if $\angle BFD$ measures 90°, what is the measure of $\angle DFE$?

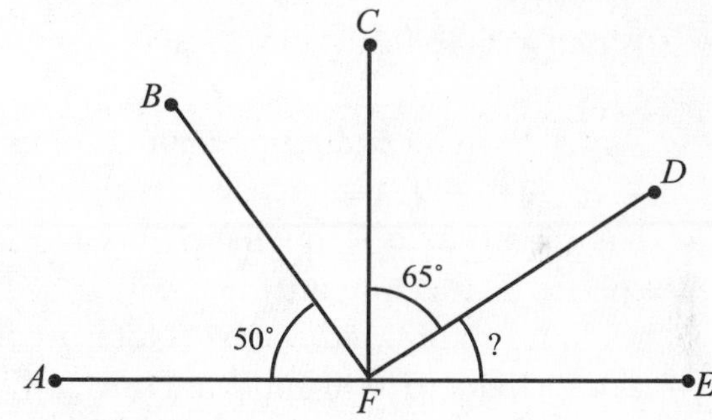

A. 35°
B. 40°
C. 50°
D. 55°
E. 65°

8. If $\sqrt{ab} = 4$, then $a^2b^2 =$

F. -128

G. $\frac{1}{64}$

H. 64

J. 256

K. It cannot be determined from the information given.

9. What value of x satisfies the equation $\frac{x+1}{2} + 2 = x - 1$?

A. -5

B. -2

C. $\frac{1}{2}$

D. 7

E. 11

10. What is 150% of the product of $\frac{1}{8}$ and 0.4?

F. 0.025
G. 0.075
H. 0.25
J. 0.75
K. 2.5

11. Water from a certain pond contains an average of 4.9 specimens of species Z per cubic centimeter. How many specimens of species Z are contained in 3 cubic millimeters of pond water? [Note: 1 cubic centimeter = 1,000 cubic millimeters]

A. 1.47×10^{-1}
B. 4.9×10^{-2}
C. 1.47×10^{-2}
D. 4.9×10^{-3}
E. 1.47×10^{-3}

12. What is the area of a circle with circumference of 6?

F. $\frac{9}{\pi}$

G. 3

H. π

J. $\frac{3\pi}{2}$

K. 6

13. $4^n + 4^n + 4^n + 4^n =$

A. 4^{4n}
B. $4^{(n+1)}$
C. $4^{(n \times n \times n \times n)}$
D. 16^n
E. 16^{4n}

14. In the figure below, what is the perimeter of ΔOPQ?

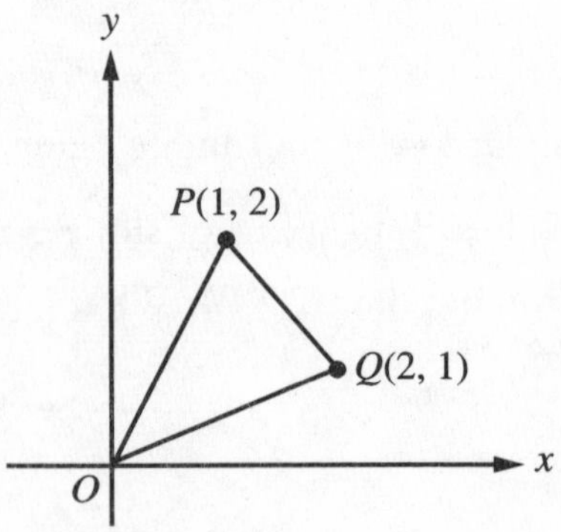

F. $\sqrt{7}$

G. 3

H. $\sqrt{5} + \sqrt{2}$

J. $\sqrt{5} + 2\sqrt{2}$

K. $2\sqrt{5} + \sqrt{2}$

15. The graph below shows the standard (x,y) coordinate plane in which certain regions are shaded.

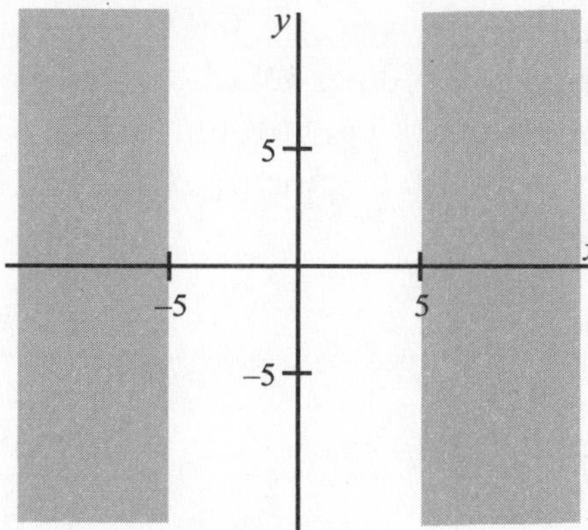

Which of the following inequalities represents the set of all points in the shaded regions?

A. $|x| \le 5$
B. $|x| \ge 5$
C. $|y| \le 5$
D. $|y| \ge 5$
E. $|x| \le 5y$

16. A certain animal shelter houses two different types of animals—dogs and cats. If d represents the number of dogs, and if c represents the number of cats, which of the following expresses the portion of animals at the shelter that are dogs?

F. $\frac{d}{c+d}$

G. $\frac{c}{c+d}$

H. $\frac{d}{c}$

J. $\frac{c}{d}$

K. $d + \frac{c}{d}$

17. In the standard (x,y) coordinate plane, $(-3,4)$ is the midpoint of a line segment connecting the point defined by the coordinate pair $(5,2)$ to the point defined by the coordinate pair:

A. $(8,-3)$
B. $(-10,7)$
C. $(4,1)$
D. $(-8,4)$
E. $(-11,6)$

18. Three of four women—*A*, *B*, *C*, and *D*—are to be selected randomly to serve on a certain committee. Two of three men—*X*, *Y*, and *Z*—are to be selected randomly to serve on the same committee. What is the probability that the committee will consist of *B*, *C*, *D*, *Y*, and *Z*?

F. $\frac{2}{9}$

G. $\frac{3}{16}$

H. $\frac{1}{6}$

J. $\frac{1}{9}$

K. $\frac{1}{12}$

19. If the diameter of a circle increases by 50 percent, by what percent is the circle's area increased?

A. 50
B. 75
C. 100
D. 125
E. 150

20. Which of the following is another form of the expression $(x + 2)(4x - 1)(x - 2)$?

F. $4x^2 - 10x + 4$
G. $8x^3 - 20$
H. $4x^3 + 2x + 8$
J. $4x^3 - x^2 - 16x + 4$
K. $4x^3 + x^2 + 16x - 2$

21. Which of the following is the graph of the solution set for $6 - \frac{x}{2} \leq 4$?

A. 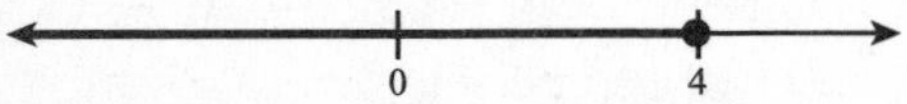

B. 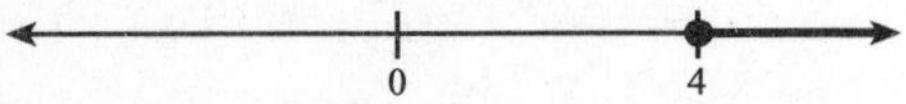

C. 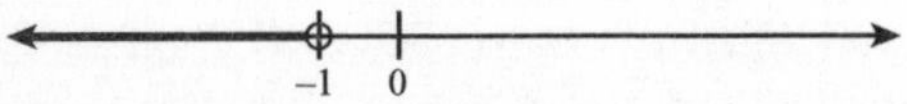

D. 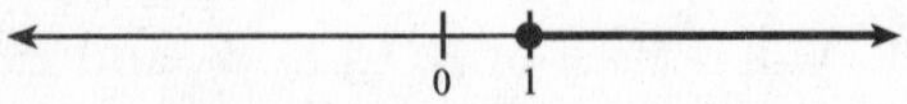

E. 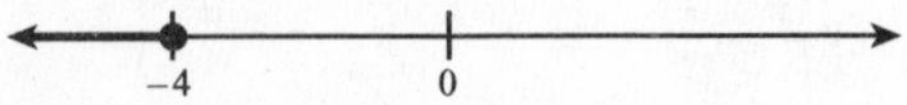

22. The average of seven numbers is 84. Six of the numbers are: 86, 82, 90, 92, 80, and 81. What is the seventh number?

F. 76
G. 77
H. 79
J. 81
K. 85

23. ABC Company pays an average of $140 per vehicle each month in outdoor parking fees for three of its eight vehicles. The company pays garage parking fees for the remaining five vehicles. If ABC pays an average of $240 per vehicle overall each month for parking, how much does ABC pay per month in garage parking fees for its vehicles?

A. $300
B. $420
C. $912
D. $1,420
E. $1,500

24. If $2\sqrt{2x} + t = 4$, then $x =$

F. $2t^2 + \frac{t}{2}$
G. $4 - t^2 + \frac{t}{8}$
H. $2 + t + \frac{t^2}{2}$
J. $2 - t + \frac{t^2}{8}$
K. $8 - t + \frac{t^2}{4}$

25. In the standard (x,y) coordinate plane, what is the perimeter of the quadrilateral $ABCD$, which is formed by connecting the four points $A(-1,-1)$, $B(-1,3)$, $C(2,-1)$, and $D(2,3)$?

A. 10
B. 11
C. 12
D. 13
E. 14

26. Which of the following is the prime factorization of 1,650?

F. $2 \times 5^2 \times 33$
G. $5 \times 23 \times 11$
H. $2 \times 3 \times 5^2 \times 11$
J. $2^2 \times 3^2 \times 5 \times 11$
K. $2 \times 3 \times 5 \times 11$

27. In ΔABC, $m\angle A$ exceeds $m\angle B$ by 20°, and $m\angle B$ exceeds $m\angle C$ by 20°. Which of the following indicates the degree-measure ratio A:B:C?

A. 3:2:1
B. 4:3:2
C. 5:4:3
D. 6:5:4
E. 8:7:6

28. In the figure below, if $\overline{AB} \parallel \overline{CD}$, then $x =$

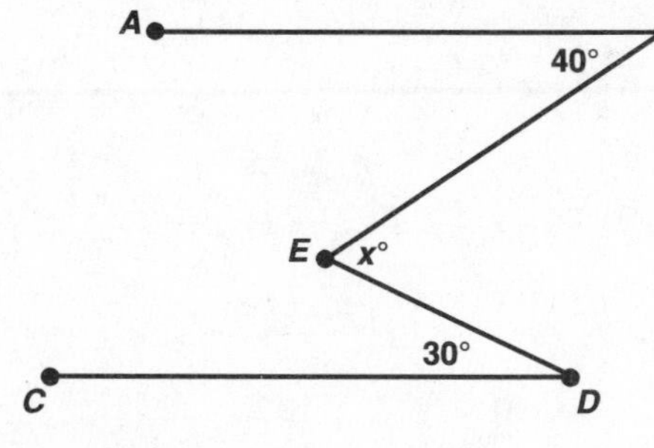

F. 80
G. 70
H. 60
J. 50
K. 40

29. Kirk sent $54 to the newspaper dealer for whom he delivers papers, after deducting a 10% commission for himself. If newspapers sell for 40 cents each, how many papers did Kirk deliver?

A. 600
B. 540
C. 160
D. 150
E. 135

30. The shortest side of a right triangle is 8 units long, and its longest side is 17 units long. What is the area of the triangle, in square units?

F. 68
G. 60
H. $34\sqrt{2}$
J. 40
K. $17\sqrt{5}$

31. A *peck* is a unit of measurement for the volume of grain. One liter is equivalent to 0.113 peck. If the volume of a load of grain is 2.8 pecks, how many liters is the load of grain, to the nearest liter?

A. 40
B. 32
C. 25
D. 21
E. 14

GO ON TO THE NEXT PAGE

32. *M* college students agree to rent an apartment for *D* dollars per month, sharing the rent equally. If the rent is increased by $100, what amount, expressed in terms of *D* and *M*, must each student contribute?

F. $\frac{D + 100}{M}$

G. $\frac{D}{M} + 100$

H. $\frac{D}{M}$

J. $\frac{M}{D + 100}$

K. $\frac{M + 100}{D}$

33. In an arithmetic sequence, the difference between one term and the next is the same for any two successive terms in the sequence. What is the sum of the first 50 terms of the arithmetic sequence 0, 2, 4, . . .?

A. 2,450
B. 2,000
C. 1,950
D. 1,550
E. 1,000

34. $\sqrt{\frac{a^2}{b^2} + \frac{a^2}{b^2}}$

F. $\frac{a^2}{b^2}$

G. $\frac{a}{b}$

H. $\frac{a^4}{b^4}$

J. $\frac{a}{b}\sqrt{\frac{a}{b}}$

K. $\frac{a}{b}\sqrt{2}$

35. What is the perimeter of a rectangle that is twice as long as it is wide and has the same area as a circle of diameter 8?

A. $8\sqrt{2}$
B. 8π
C. $3\pi\sqrt{2}$
D. $12\sqrt{2\pi}$
E. 12π

36. An investor can buy *p* shares of MicroTron stock for a total of $210 and *q* shares of Dynaco stock for a total of $572. Which of the following represents the total cost, in dollars, of 6 shares of MicroTron stock and 11 shares of Dynaco stock?

F. $210\left(\frac{p}{6}\right) + 572\left(\frac{q}{11}\right)$

G. $\frac{210}{p + 6} + \frac{572}{q + 11}$

H. $6\left(\frac{572}{q}\right) + 11\left(\frac{210}{p}\right)$

J. $6\left(\frac{p}{210}\right) + 11\left(\frac{q}{572}\right)$

K. $6\left(\frac{210}{p}\right) + 11\left(\frac{572}{q}\right)$

37. If $R + S = \begin{bmatrix} 5 & -3 \\ -3 & 5 \end{bmatrix}$, then R and S could be:

A. $\begin{bmatrix} 1 & -1 \\ -5 & 2 \end{bmatrix}$ and $\begin{bmatrix} 4 & -2 \\ 2 & 3 \end{bmatrix}$

B. $\begin{bmatrix} 5 & -1 \\ -3 & -1 \end{bmatrix}$ and $\begin{bmatrix} 1 & 3 \\ 1 & -5 \end{bmatrix}$

C. $\begin{bmatrix} 2 & -2 \\ -4 & 1 \end{bmatrix}$ and $\begin{bmatrix} 3 & 12 \\ 1 & 4 \end{bmatrix}$

D. $\begin{bmatrix} 0 & 5 \\ -1 & 6 \end{bmatrix}$ and $\begin{bmatrix} 5 & -8 \\ 3 & -1 \end{bmatrix}$

E. $\begin{bmatrix} 4 & 2 \\ -6 & -1 \end{bmatrix}$ and $\begin{bmatrix} 1 & -4 \\ 3 & 4 \end{bmatrix}$

38. In a room are five chairs to accommodate three people, one person to a chair. How many seating arrangements are possible?

F. 45
G. 60
H. 72
J. 90
K. 120

39. Out of a total of 78 first-year students at a school, 15 are enrolled in both Chemistry and Physics, and 47 are enrolled in Chemistry but not Physics. How many students are enrolled in Physics but not Chemistry? Assume that each student is enrolled in at least one of these two subjects.

A. 15
B. 16
C. 46
D. 62
E. 63

40. The area of a square carpet is x^2. If a rectangular piece of material $(x - 3)$ units long and $(x - 4)$ units wide is removed from the carpet, which of the following represents the area of the remaining material of the carpet, in square units?

F. $7x - 12$

G. $x^2 - \frac{x}{3}$

H. $x(x - 7)$

J. $4x + 3$

K. $12 - 7x$

41. In the standard (x,y) coordinate plane, which of the following equations represents the circle that has center $(-1,5)$ and whose circumference is 4π ?

A. $(x + 1)^2 + (y - 5)^2 = 4$
B. $(x + 1)^2 + (y - 5)^2 = 2$
C. $(x - 5)^2 + (y - 1)^2 = 4$
D. $(x - 1)^2 + (y + 5)^2 = 2$
E. $(x - 5)^2 + (y + 1)^2 = 4$

42. In the figure below, $\overline{AC}$ is tangent to the circle at point B. The length of $\overline{BD}$ equals the diameter of the circle, whose center is O. What is the degree measure of minor arc DE?

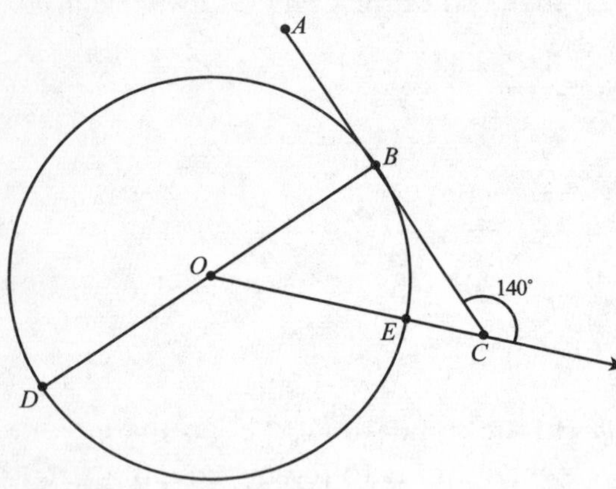

F. 220
G. 130
H. 120
J. 110
K. 40

43. In the triangle below, if $\tan x = 1$, then $\sin y =$

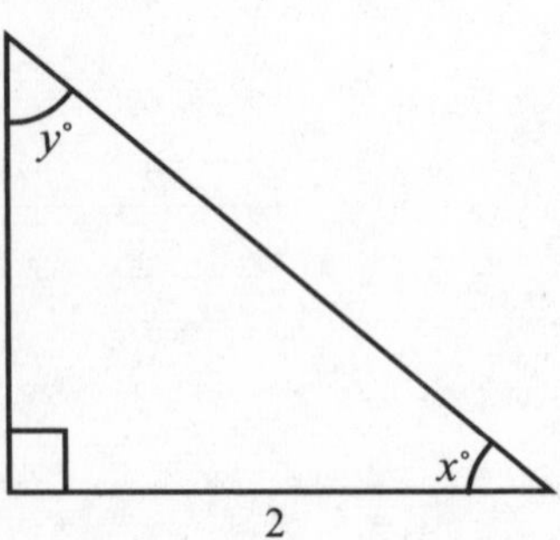

A. $2\sqrt{2}$
B. $\sqrt{2}$
C. 1
D. $\frac{\sqrt{2}}{2}$
E. $\frac{1}{2}$

44. As shown in the figure below, from runway 1 airplanes must turn 120° to the right onto runway 2 and 135° to the left onto runway 3.

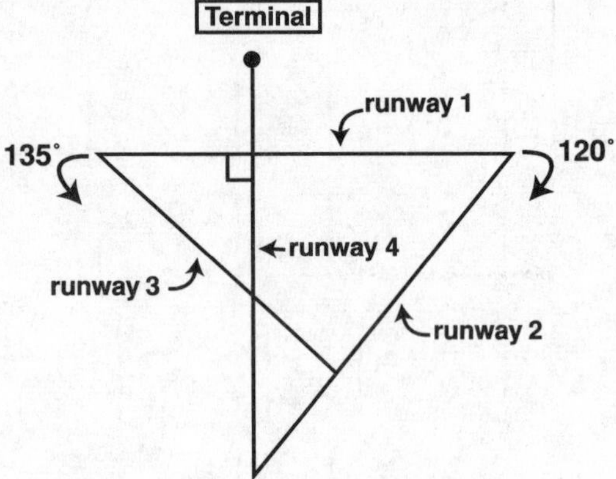

Which of the following does NOT indicate a complete turn from one runway to another?

F. 105°
G. 75°
H. 60°
J. 55°
K. 45°

45. In the figure below, quadrilateral $BCDE$ is a square with an area of 4 square inches, and A is the midpoint of $\overline{DE}$.

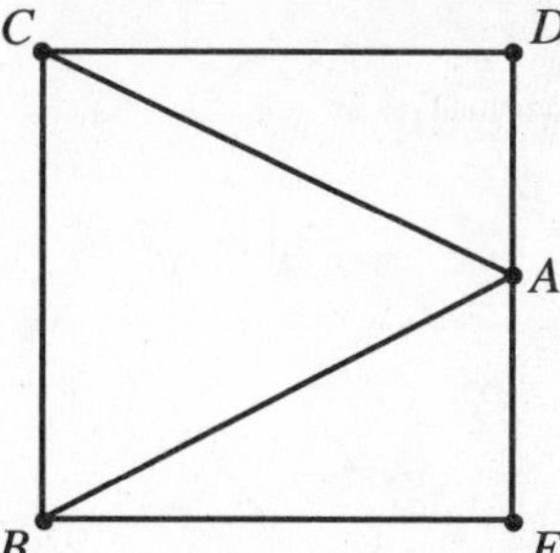

How many inches long is $\overline{AC}$?

A. $\sqrt{5}$
B. 2.5
C. $\frac{3\sqrt{3}}{2}$
D. $2\sqrt{2}$
E. 3

46. Given that $|3x - 4| \geq 8$, which of the following is the largest set of numbers NOT included in the solution set of this inequality?

F. All numbers greater than $-\frac{4}{3}$ that are also less than 4
G. All numbers less than $-\frac{4}{3}$ and all numbers greater than 4
H. All numbers greater than -4 and all numbers less than $-\frac{4}{3}$
J. All numbers less than -4 and all numbers less than $-\frac{4}{3}$
K. All numbers except $-\frac{4}{3}$ and 4

47. If $x = \log 2$ and $y = \log 5$, then $2y - 3x =$

A. $\log\frac{8}{25}$
B. $\log\frac{25}{8}$
C. $\log\frac{25}{4}$
D. $\log 25$
E. $\log 200$

48. If n is a positive integer, and if $n \div 3$ results in a quotient with a remainder of 1, which of the following expressions is NOT divisible by 3?

F. $n + 2$
G. $n + 5$
H. $n - 1$
J. $n \times 2$
K. $n \times 3$

49. If the length, width, and height of a cube measuring 2 centimeters along each edge are each increased by 50%, what is the resulting increase in the cube's volume, expressed in cubic centimeters?

A. 27
B. 24
C. 19
D. 16
E. 12

50. In a geometric series, each term is a constant multiple of the preceding one. If the first three terms in a geometric series are -2, x, and -8, which of the following could be the sixth term in the series?

F. 512
G. 256
H. 64
J. -17
K. -128

51. In the figure below, line segments $\overline{AC}$ and $\overline{AD}$ trisect $\angle BAE$. What is the value of x?

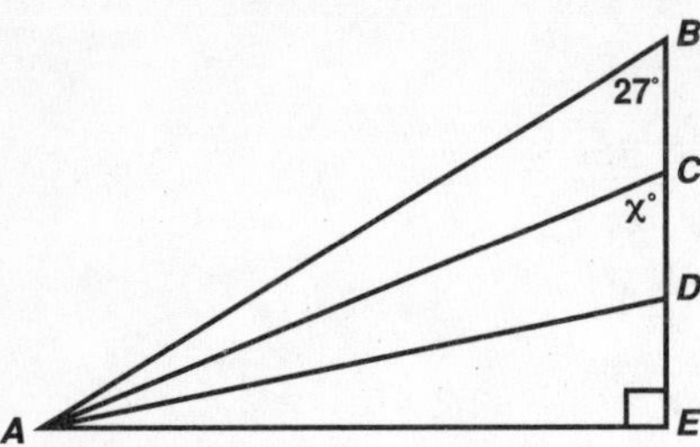

A. 66
B. 58
C. 54
D. 48
E. 42

52. Four of the five interior angles of a pentagon measure 110°, 60°, 120°, and 100°. What is the measure of the fifth interior angle?

F. 150°
G. 135°
H. 125°
J. 110°
K. 100°

53. In the standard (x,y) coordinate plane, the line that contains points (8,3) and (3,8) also contains the point:

A. (0,−11)
B. (−8,−3)
C. (−3,−8)
D. (11,0)
E. (11,−3)

54. In the figure below, the circle's diameter is 6 centimeters long.

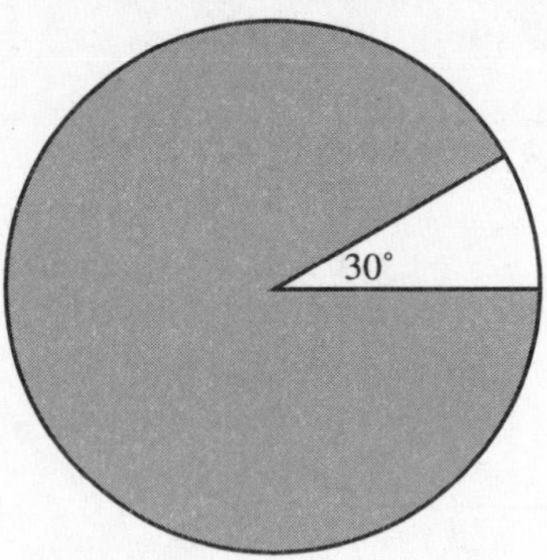

What is the area, in square centimeters, of the shaded region?

F. $\frac{20\pi}{3}$

G. 9π

H. $\frac{33\pi}{4}$

J. 48

K. 12π

55. If $f(x) = x^2 - 2x - 3$, and if $x = a - 3$, then which of the following indicates the entire set of possible real-number values of a, given that $f(x) = 0$?

A. −3 and 1
B. −4 and −2
C. 1 and 3
D. 2 and 6
E. All real numbers

56. Which of the following equations defines a parabola?

F. $(x + 2)^2 + (y - 1)^2 = 16$
G. $(x + 2)^2 + 2(y - 1)^2 = 16$
H. $(x + 2) + 2y^2 = 16$
J. $(x + 2)^2 - (y - 1)^2 = 16$
K. It cannot be determined from the information given.

57. In ΔABC below, the measure of $\angle A$ is 35°, and $\overline{BC}$ is 5 units long. Which of the following most closely approximates the unit length of $\overline{AC}$? (Note: $\sin 35° \approx 0.58$, $\cos 35° \approx 0.82$, and $\tan 35° \approx 0.70$)

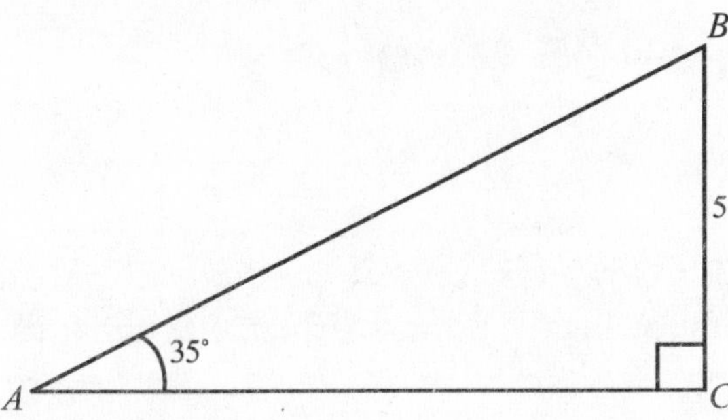

A. 6.10
B. 7.00
C. 7.14
D. 7.78
E. 8.20

58. If $\cos\beta = \frac{5}{7}$, and if β is the degree measure of an acute angle of a right triangle, then $\tan\beta =$

F. $\frac{2\sqrt{6}}{5}$
G. $\frac{7}{5}$
H. $\frac{\sqrt{6}}{2}$
J. $\frac{12}{7}$
K. It cannot be determined from the information given.

59. Which of the following is one root of the equation $x^2 + 13 = 4x$?

A. $4 + i$
B. $3 - 2i$
C. $4 + 3i$
D. $2 - 6i$
E. $2 + 3i$

60. In the graph of the equation $y = 3\cos 2x$, what is the least positive value for x when y is at its minimum value?

F. $\frac{\pi}{4}$
G. $\frac{\pi}{2}$
H. π
J. $\frac{3}{2}\pi$
K. 2π

STOP

Reading

40 Questions ■ Time—35 Minutes

Directions This test consists of four passages, each followed by several questions. Read each passage and select the best answer for each question following the passage. Then, on your answer sheet, mark the oval corresponding to the best answer.

Passage I—Prose Fiction

The nearer the train drew toward La Crosse, the soberer the little group of "vets" became. On the long way from New Orleans they had beguiled tedium with jokes and friendly chaff; or with planning with elaborate detail what they were going to do now, after the war. The journey was long, slow, irregular, yet persistently pushing northward. When they entered Wisconsin Territory, they gave a cheer, and another when they reached Madison, but after that they sank into a dumb expectancy. Comrades dropped off at one or two points beyond, until there were only four or five left who were bound for La Crosse County.

Three of them were gaunt and brown, the fourth was gaunt and pale, with signs of fever and ague on him. One had a great scar down his temple; one limped; and they all had unnaturally large bright eyes, showing emaciation. There were no bands greeting them at the stations, no banks of gaily dressed ladies waving handkerchiefs and shouting "Bravo!" as they came in on the caboose of a freight train into the town that had cheered and blared at them on their way to war. As they looked out or stepped upon the platform for a moment, as the train stood at the station, the loafers looked at them indifferently. Their blue coats, dusty and grimy, were too familiar now to excite notice, much less a friendly word. They were the last of the army to return, and the loafers were surfeited with such sights.

The train jogged forward so slowly that it seemed likely to be midnight before they should reach La Crosse. The little squad of "vets" grumbled and swore, but it was no use, the train would not hurry; as a matter of fact, it was nearly two o'clock when the engine whistled "down brakes."

All of the group were farmers, living in districts several miles out of the town, and all were poor.

"Now boys," said Private Smith, he of the fever and ague, "we are landed in La Crosse in the night. We've got to stay somewhere till mornin'. Now, I ain't got no two dollars to waste on a hotel. I've got a wife and children, so I'm goin' to roost on a bench and take the cost of a bed out of my hide."

"Same here," put in one of the other men. "Hide'll grow on again, dollars come hard. It's goin' to be mighty hot skirmishin' to find a dollar these days."

Smith went on: "Then at daybreak we'll start for home—at least I will."

The station was deserted, chill, and dark, as they came into it at exactly a quarter to two in the morning. Lit by the oil lamps that flared a dull red light over the dingy benches, the waiting room was not an inviting place. The younger man in the group went off to look up a hotel, while the rest remained and prepared to camp down on the floor and benches. Smith was attended to tenderly by the other men, who spread their blankets on the bench for him, and by robbing themselves made quite a comfortable bed, though the narrowness of the bench made his sleeping precarious.

It was chill, though August, and the two men sitting with bowed heads grew stiff with cold and weariness, and were forced to rise now and again, and walk about to warm their stiffened limbs. It didn't occur to them, probably, to contrast their coming home with their going forth, or with the coming home of the generals, colonels, or even captains—but to Private Smith, at any rate, there came a sickness at heart almost deadly, as he lay there on his hard bed and went over his situation.

In the deep of the night, lying on a board in the town where he had enlisted three years ago, all elation and enthusiasm gone out of him, he faced the fact that with the joy of homecoming was mingled the bitter juice of care. He saw himself sick, worn out, taking up the work on his half-cleared farm, the inevitable mortgage standing ready with open jaw to swallow half his earnings. He had given three years of his life for a mere pittance of pay, and now—

Morning dawned at last, slowly, with a pale yellow dome of light rising silently above the bluffs which stand like some huge battlemented castle, just east of the city. Out to the left the great river swept on its massive yet silent way to the south. Blue jays called across the river from hillside to hillside, through the clear, beautiful air, and hawks began to skim the tops of the hills.

The two vets were astir early, but Private Smith had fallen at last into a sleep, and they went out without waking him. He lay on his knapsack, his gaunt face turned toward the ceiling, his hands clasped on his breast, with a curious pathetic effect of weakness and appeal. An engine switching near woke him at last, and he slowly sat up and stared about. He looked out of the window and saw that the sun was lightening the hills across the river. He rose and brushed his hair as well as he could, folded his blankets up, and went out to find his companions.

1. By using the word *soberer* in the first sentence of the passage (line 2), the author implies that the soldiers were:

A. no longer bored with the long journey.
B. recovering from a drinking binge.
C. unaccustomed to train travel.
D. in a relatively subdued mood.

GO ON TO THE NEXT PAGE

2. The passage suggests that the war from which the soldiers were returning took place in:
   - F. the Wisconsin Territory.
   - G. the southern part of Georgia.
   - H. the vicinity of New Orleans.
   - J. La Crosse County.

3. As it is used in the passage, the word *beguiled* (line 4) most nearly means:
   - A. cheated.
   - B. induced.
   - C. provoked.
   - D. begun.

4. Among the following, the "bitter juice" mentioned in line 96 is LEAST likely to involve Smith's:
   - F. untended farm.
   - G. near certainty of unemployment.
   - H. duty to provide for his family.
   - J. outstanding mortgage.

5. Based on the narrator's comments in the second paragraph, it can be most reasonably inferred that a person with "unnaturally large bright eyes" (lines 21–22) is:
   - A. joyful.
   - B. sorrowful.
   - C. fatigued.
   - D. hungry.

6. The dialogue and narration in the passage suggest that Private Smith:
   - F. lived in the town of La Crosse.
   - G. was injured in the war.
   - H. did not have much money.
   - J. was drafted into the army.

7. According to the passage, Private Smith's train did not arrive in La Crosse until:
   - A. nearly midnight.
   - B. almost two o'clock in the morning.
   - C. nearly daybreak.
   - D. after dawn.

8. As it is used in the passage, the phrase *surfeited with* (lines 36–37) most nearly means:
   - F. agreeable to.
   - G. bored of.
   - H. relieved to see.
   - J. deprived of.

9. In the passage, the narrator contrasts the:
   - A. homecoming reception that Private Smith received with the reception that higher-ranking military men received.
   - B. farewell the soldiers received as they left for war with the reception they received upon their return.
   - C. weather in La Crosse with the weather elsewhere in the Wisconsin Territory.
   - D. soldiers' mood as they left for war with their mood as they returned from war.

10. The passage's dialogue and narration suggest that the group of vets:
    - F. are sorry that they volunteered to be army soldiers.
    - G. are disappointed that nobody greeted them at the station.
    - H. consider Smith to be their leader.
    - J. are physically weakened from the war.

Passage II—Social Studies

As the climate in the Middle East changed beginning around 7000 B.C.E., conditions emerged that were conducive to a more complex and advanced form of civilization in both Egypt and Mesopotamia. The process began when the swampy valleys of the Nile in Egypt and of the Tigris and Euphrates rivers in Mesopotamia became drier, producing riverine lands that were both habitable and fertile, and attracting settlers armed with the newly developed techniques of agriculture. This migration was further encouraged by the gradual transformation of the once-hospitable grasslands of these regions into deserts. Human population became increasingly concentrated into pockets of settlement scattered along the banks of the great rivers.

These rivers profoundly shaped the way of life along their banks. In Mesopotamia, the management of water in conditions of unpredictable drought, flood, and storm became the central economic and social challenge. Villagers began early to build simple earthworks, dikes, canals, and ditches to control the waters and reduce the opposing dangers of drought during the dry season (usually the spring) and flooding at harvest time.

Such efforts required a degree of cooperation among large numbers of people that had not previously existed. The individual village, containing only a dozen or so houses and families, was economically vulnerable; but when several villages, probably under the direction of a council of elders, learned to share their human resources in the building of a coordinated network of water-control systems, the safety, stability, and prosperity of all improved. In this new cooperation, the seeds of the great Mesopotamian civilizations were being sown.

Technological and mathematical invention, too, were stimulated by life along the rivers. Such devices as the noria (a primitive waterwheel) and the Archimedean screw (a device for raising water from the low riverbanks to the high ground where it was needed), two forerunners of many more varied and complex machines, were first developed here for use in irrigation systems.

Similarly, the earliest methods of measurement and computation and the first developments in geometry were stimulated by the need to keep track of land holdings and boundaries in fields that were periodically inundated.

The rivers served as high roads of the earliest commerce. Traders used boats made of bundles of rushes to transport grains, fruits, nuts, fibers, and textiles from one village to another, transforming the rivers into the central spines of nascent commercial kingdoms. Mud from the river banks originally served as the region's sole building material, as well as the source of clay for pottery, sculpture, and writing tablets. With the opening of trade, however, non-indigenous materials became available. Building stones such as basalt and sandstone were imported, as was alabaster for sculpture, metals such as bronze, copper, gold, and silver, and precious and semiprecious gemstones for jewelry, art, and decoration.

Eventually, Middle Eastern trade expanded surprisingly widely; we have evidence suggesting that, even before the establishment of the first Egyptian

GO ON TO THE NEXT PAGE

dynasty, goods were being exchanged between villagers in Egypt and others as far away as Iran.

By 3500 B.C.E., Mesopotamian society was flourishing. The major archaeological source from which we derive our knowledge of this period is the city of Uruk, site of the modern Al Warka. Two major structures from the time are the so-called Limestone Temple, an immense structure about the size of an American football field (250 × 99 feet), and the White Temple, built on a high platform some 40 feet above the plain. Associated discoveries include several outstanding stone sculptures, beautifully decorated alabaster vases, clay tablets, and many cylinder seals, which were both artistic expressions and symbols of personal identification used by Mesopotamian rulers. Clearly, a complex and advanced civilization was in place by the time these artifacts were created.

Historians have observed that similar developments were occurring at much the same time along the great river valleys in other parts of the world—for example, along the Indus in India and the Hwang Ho in China. The history of early civilization, it seems, was shaped to a remarkable degree by the relationship between humans and rivers.

11. The passage as a whole is primarily concerned with:

A. describing the importance of rivers in the growth of ancient human civilizations.
B. showing how recent archaeological findings provide insight into how certain ancient civilizations grew and developed.
C. explaining how human civilizations have been affected by changes in climate.
D. describing the relationship between climate changes and ancient Middle Eastern commerce.

12. It can be inferred from the passage that most of the early inhabitants of the Nile valley were previously experienced in:

F. mathematics.
G. warfare.
H. agriculture.
J. commerce.

13. According to the passage, the climate change that begin to occur around 7000 B.C.E. in the Middle East led to:

A. unprecedented cold weather.
B. higher levels of ocean water.
C. an increase in swampy grasslands.
D. an increase in desert land.

14. As used in the passage, the hyphenated word *non-indigenous* (lines 73–74) most nearly means:

A. unavailable locally.
B. of great value.
C. widely used.
D. superior for building.

15. In ancient Mesopotamia, the rivers shaped all of the following aspects of the lives of riverine settlers EXCEPT:

A. measurements and computation.
B. trade and commerce.
C. defense and warfare.
D. building and coordination of water-control systems.

16. The passage contains information useful in answering all of the following questions EXCEPT:

F. Where did the field of geometry originate?
G. What did the Mesopotamian riverine use alabaster for?
H. Why did the Mesopotamian populace first gravitate toward the great rivers?
J. When did the cultural sophistication of Mesopotamian society reach its peak?

17. The author of the passage mentions the Limestone and White Temples (lines 94–97) most probably in order to:

A. illustrate that Mesopotamian society was architecturally sophisticated and rich in resources.
B. underscore the significance of religion in the culture of Mesopotamia.
C. illustrate how the Mesopotamian rivers allowed for the use of building materials found only in Egypt.
D. emphasize that Mesopotamian society flourished despite adverse conditions.

18. Prior to 7000 B.C.E., which of the following building materials was available to the Mesopotamians?

F. Sandstone
G. Mud
H. Alabaster
J. Limestone

19. It can be inferred from the passage that the earliest trade routes in the Middle East served:

A. the Egyptian Dynasty and villages in Iran.
B. the various villages along the rivers.
C. as a link between the various ancient civilizations.
D. all the villages that were open to trading goods.

20. Which of the following describes the most significant social effect that unpredictable river conditions, discussed in the second paragraph (lines 20–30), had on the settlers of the riverines of Mesopotamia?

F. They forced many settlers to move away from the rivers to higher grassland areas.
G. They helped boatsmen who were able to navigate the rivers command unprecedented respect among settlers.
H. They necessitated a high degree of cooperation among the various members of society.
J. They served as catalysts for new inventions and engineering methods for controlling and harnessing rivers.

GO ON TO THE NEXT PAGE

Passage III—Humanities

French impressionism is considered by many art historians the beginning of modernism in painting. The French impressionists of the late nineteenth century—Manet, Degas, Pissarro, Monet, and others—had a far-reaching effect on artists around the world, as much for the philosophy underlying their work as for the new painterly aesthetic they pioneered. For although the impressionists expressly disavowed any interest in philosophy, their new approach to art had significant philosophical implications. The view of matter that the impressionists assumed differed profoundly from the view that had previously prevailed among artists. This view helped to unify the artistic works created in the new style.

The ancient Greeks had conceived of the world in concrete terms, even endowing abstract qualities with bodies. This Greek view of matter persisted, so far as painting was concerned, into the nineteenth century. The impressionists, on the other hand, viewed light, not matter, as the ultimate visual reality.

The philosopher Taine expressed the impressionist view of things when he said, "The chief 'person' in a picture is the light in which everything is bathed." In impressionist painting, solid bodies became mere reflectors of light, and distinctions between one object and another became arbitrary conventions; for by light all things were welded together. The treatment of both color and outline was transformed as well. Color, formerly considered a property inherent in an object, was seen to be merely the result of vibrations of light on the object's colorless surface. And outline, whose function had formerly been to indicate the limits of objects, now marked instead merely the boundary between units of pattern, which often merged into one another.

The impressionist world was composed not of separate objects but of many surfaces on which light struck and was reflected with varying intensity to the eye through the atmosphere, which modified it. It was this process that produced the mosaic of colors that formed an impressionist canvas. "Light becomes the sole subject of the picture," writes one art historian. "The interest of the object upon which it plays is secondary. Painting thus conceived becomes a purely optic art."

From this profoundly revolutionary form of art, then, all ideas—religious, moral, psychological—were excluded, and so were all emotions except certain aesthetic ones. The people, places, and things depicted in an impressionist picture do not tell a story or convey any special meaning; they are, instead, merely parts of a pattern of light drawn from nature and captured on canvas by the artist.

Paradoxically, the impressionists' avowed lack of interest in subject matter made the subject matter of their work particularly important and influential. Prior to the impressionist revolution, particular themes and subjects had been generally deemed more suitable than others for treatment in art. Momentous historic events; crucial incidents in the lives of saints, martyrs, or heroes; the deeds of the Greek and Roman gods; the images of the noble, wealthy, and powerful—these dominated European painting of the eighteenth and early nineteenth centuries.

The impressionists changed all that. If moral significance is drained from art, then any subject will serve as well as any other. The impressionists painted life as they found it close to hand. The bustling boulevards of modern Paris; revelers in smoky cafes, theatres, and nightclubs; working-class families picnicking by the Seine—these are typical of the images chosen by the impressionists. It was not only their formal innovations that surprised and disturbed the academic critics of their day. The fact that they chose to depict the "low life" of contemporary Paris rather than the exalted themes preferred by their predecessors made some wonder whether what the impressionists created was art at all.

In this regard, as in so many others, the impressionists were true precursors of twentieth-century painting. Taking their cue from the impressionists, modernists from the cubists to the pop artists expanded the freedom of the creator to make art from anything and everything. Picasso, Braque, and Juan Gris filled their still lifes with the machine-made detritus of a modern city, even pasting actual printed labels and torn sheets of newsprint into their pictures and so inventing what came to be called collage.

Six decades later, Andy Warhol carried the theme to its logical conclusion with his pictures of Campbell's soup cans, depicted in a style as grandiose and monumental as any king or prophet in a neo-classical painting. Among its other messages, Warhol's work proclaims, "If art is a game of surfaces—an experiment in color and light—then the beauty and importance of a tin can is equal to that of Helen of Troy." In this, he was a true kin—if a distant one—to Degas, Renoir, and Pissarro.

21. Which one of the following was of primary importance to an impressionist painter?

A. Outline
B. Light
C. Color
D. Object

22. As it is used in the passage, the word *precursors* (line 106) most nearly means:

F. rebels.
G. forerunners.
H. followers.
J. philosophers.

23. It can be inferred from the passage that Andy Warhol and the impressionists shared:

A. a similar disregard for the historical, religious, or political importance of a subject.
B. a love of current socio-political subjects.
C. great regard for images of wealthy and powerful people.
D. an irreverent approach to depicting religious themes in art.

24. It is most reasonable to infer from the information in the seventh paragraph (lines 87–104) that "some wondered whether what the impressionists created was art at all" because:

F. impressionists created art with scraps of discarded newsprint and gravel.
G. the works of art created by the impressionists depicted only still life.
H. impressionists made only monochromatic paintings.
J. impressionists depicted common, everyday life subjects.

25. The quote from an art historian in the fourth paragraph (lines 55–60) supports all of the following statements about a typical impressionist picture EXCEPT:

A. the object of interest is of secondary importance.
B. light is the sole subject of the picture.
C. the exalted theme of the painting is as important as the mosaic produced by the light on it.
D. the painting is a purely optic art.

26 The impressionist painter comes across in the passage as a person convinced of the:

F. importance of emotions in art.
G. relevance of structure in a painting.
H. importance of light in a visual.
J. importance of the illustrated story.

27. Of the following subjects, an impressionist painter would most likely choose to depict:

A. a scenic landscape.
B. a busy city street.
C. an architectural wonder.
D. a significant historical event.

28. It can be inferred from the passage that an impressionist painting can best be considered a:

F. mosaic of interconnected outlines of a collection of objects.
G. depiction of abstract poses of the human form.
H. collage of separate objects.
J. pattern of units welded together by light of varying intensity.

29. As it is used in the passage, the word *paradoxically* (line 72) refers to something:

A. pertaining to historical importance.
B. involving mainstream art.
C. self-contradictory in nature.
D. to do with an academic synopsis.

30. The author conveys the main point of the passage by:

F. methodically explaining the pioneering value of the French impressionists' painterly esthetic by way of comparing it to the accepted values of the time and the modernists who followed the path paved by them.

G. explaining the value of the Greek view of art in conceiving the world in concrete terms and paving the way for all artists to follow up until the twentieth century.

H. deconstructing the modernist painting to find its strong roots in impressionist works of art by Manet, Degas, and other French artists of the late nineteenth century.

J. harkening back to times before the impressionist revolution when certain select subjects were deemed worthy of treatment by artists and patrons alike thereby sealing the fate of the scope of art as a static form of expression.

Passage IV—Natural Science

[The article from which this passage is adapted was written in 1986.]

Around the turn of the century, two major innovations in the field of forensic science were added to the repertoire of scientific crime-fighting tools. One was fingerprinting; the other was blood typing. Only in the last ten years, however, have scientists begun to believe that genetic markers in blood and other body fluids may someday prove as useful in crime detection as fingerprints.

The standard ABO blood typing originated in the work of Austrian pathologist Karl Landsteiner. He found in 1901 that four basic blood types existed and that these were transmitted from generation to generation according to the recently rediscovered laws of inheritance developed by Gregor Mendel earlier in the century.

The four blood types classified by Landsteiner are known as A, B, AB, and O. Their names derive from the presence or absence of two substances, designated A and B, found on the surface of some blood cells. Persons with blood type A have red blood cells with substance A on their surface. Their blood also contains an antibody that reacts defensively against blood cells with substance B on their surface. Conversely, persons with blood type B have substance B on the surface of their red blood cells, as well as an antibody against substance A.

When a person of either of these blood types is transfused with blood of the opposite type, the antibodies swing into action, destroying the transfused cells. (Indeed, it was the failure of many blood transfusions that had first led physicians to suspect the existence of mutually incompatible blood groups.)

Blood type AB contains both substances and neither antibody; it can harmlessly receive a transfusion of any blood type. Hence its designation as the "universal recipient." Blood type O contains neither substance and both antibodies; it reacts negatively to blood types A, B, and AB, and can receive only type O blood. However, type O blood may be safely transfused into any recipient, since it lacks any substance that could cause a negative reaction; therefore, type O is the "universal donor."

In addition to their obvious importance in medical treatment, the four basic

GO ON TO THE NEXT PAGE

blood types of the ABO system have long been used by police as a form of negative identification. Testing traces of blood found in or around a crime scene could help rule out suspects who were members of a different blood group. Added sophistication came with the discovery of additional subgroups of genetic markers in blood (such as Rh factor, by which an individual's blood type is generally designated as either positive [+] or negative [−], depending on whether or not the factor is present) and with the discovery that genetic markers are present not only in blood but in other body fluids, such as perspiration and saliva.

These discoveries were still of limited use in crime detection, however, because of the circumstances in which police and scientists must work. Rather than a plentiful sample of blood freshly drawn from a patient, the crime laboratory is likely to receive only a tiny fleck of dried blood of unknown age from an unknown "donor" on a shirt or a scrap of rag that has spent hours or days exposed to air, high temperature, and other contaminants.

Then, British scientists found a method for identifying genetic markers more precisely in small samples. In this process, called electrophoresis, a sample is placed on a tray containing a gel through which an electrical current is then passed. A trained analyst reads the resulting patterns in the gel to determine the presence of various chemical markers.

Electrophoresis made it possible to identify several thousand subgroups of blood types rather than the twelve known before. However, the equipment and special training required were expensive. In addition, the process could lead to the destruction of evidence. For example, repeated tests of a blood-flecked shirt—one for each marker—led to increasing deterioration of the evidence and the cost of a week or more of laboratory time.

It remained for another British researcher, Brian Wrexell, to demonstrate that simultaneous analyses, using inexpensive equipment, could test for ten different genetic markers within a 24-hour period. This development made the study of blood and fluid samples a truly valuable tool for crime detection.

31. According to the passage, blood type O can safely be transfused with which blood type?

A. Type B
B. Type O
C. Type AB
D. Type A

32. It can most reasonably be inferred from the passage that, as a medical procedure, blood transfusions were first performed:

F. during the mid-twentieth century.
G. after the discovery of genetic markers in blood.
H. after pathologist Landstiener's work on blood typing.
J. prior to the twentieth century.

33. All of the following are drawbacks of the process of electrophoresis EXCEPT:

A. the process requires special equipment that is very expensive.
B. the process requires special training that can be expensive.
C. the process is difficult to use for testing small samples of blood.
D. the process often results in the deterioration and ultimate destruction of evidence.

34. According to the passage, a person of blood type B+ has blood cells containing:

F. blood types B and A, both tested positive for Rh factor.
G. Rh factor and antibodies against type A blood.
H. antibodies against type O but no Rh factor.
J. Rh factor and antibodies against blood type B.

35. The author of the passage mentions the expense of conducting electrophoresis (lines 98–100) most likely in order to:

A. underscore the importance of the developments growing out of Brian Wrexell's research.
B. help explain why electrophoresis never gained widespread use among forensic scientists.
C. call into question the motives of the crime laboratories that use the process.
D. support the argument that blood typing is not a practical tool for solving crimes.

36. The author's primary purpose in the passage is to:

F. acquaint the reader with the history of blood typing in the twentieth century.
G. inform the reader of the significance of medical research funded by the special interest groups focused on crime solving.
H. provide a brief chronological history of the advances in the science of blood typing and their usefulness in crime detection.
J. familiarize the reader with the history of the tools and methods used in crime detection, focusing on the comparative importance of blood typing and fingerprinting.

37. Which of the following assertions about fingerprinting and blood typing does the passage best support?

A. They were both discovered at around the same time.
B. They have long been used to identify genetics of individuals present at a crime scene.
C. Both provide a form of negative identification.
D. Both became truly useful in the 1970s.

38. It can be inferred from the passage that electrophoresis can help crime labs determine:

F. the age of the blood sample "donor."
G. the gender and ethnicity of a suspect in a crime.
H. how a spot of dried blood came to be found at a crime scene.
J. whether a blood sample could have come from a certain individual.

GO ON TO THE NEXT PAGE

39. As it is used in the passage, the word *repertoire* (line 3) most nearly means:

A. collection.
B. album.
C. importance.
D. chronology.

40. Among the following, it is most likely that the author sets off the word *donor* (line 82) with quotation marks in order to:

F. give credit to the literary source from which the author is drawing her information.
G. point out that the individual from whom the blood came did not intentionally supply the blood sample.
H. suggest that the quoted word is often used in conversation among forensic scientists.
J. imply that a blood sample amounts to poor evidence that any particular person committed the particular crime.

STOP

Science

40 Questions ■ Time—35 Minutes

Directions: This test consists of seven passages, each followed by several questions. Read each passage and select the best answer for each question following the passage. Then, on your answer sheet, mark the oval corresponding to the best answer. You may NOT use a calculator on this test.

Passage I

The nuclei of atoms consist of protons and neutrons. The total number of protons and neutrons in an atom's nuclei is its mass number. Atoms of the same element can have different mass numbers, depending on the number of neutrons in each atom. Atoms of the same element with different mass numbers are identified by their mass number. The three isotopes of uranium are U-234, U-235, and U-238. Uranium is used to produce energy

Figure 1

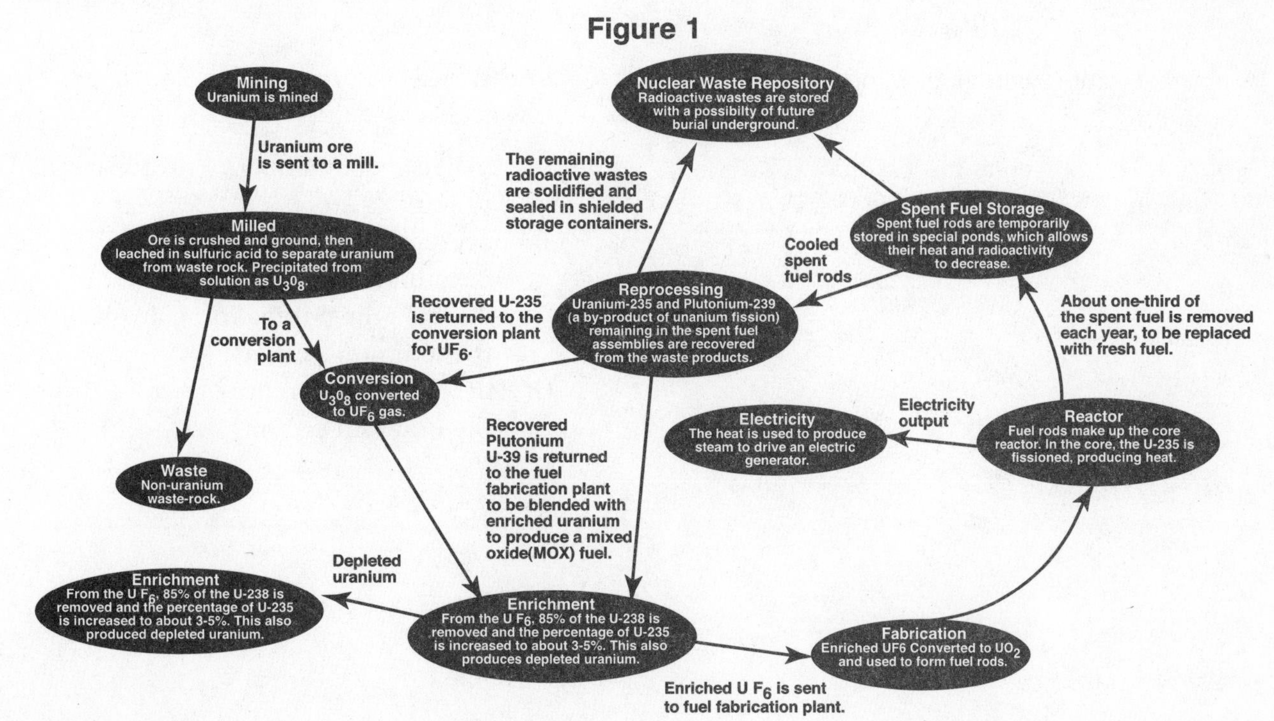

GO ON TO THE NEXT PAGE

through fission, which is the process in which the nuclei of atoms are split to release energy.

Figure 1 on page 587 summarizes the processes of the Nuclear Fuel Cycle in which naturally occurring uranium is converted to usable fuel. Table 1 below explains some of the terms used in the processing of uranium.

Table 1

Term	Definition
UF_6	uranium hexafluoride gas
U_30_8	solid concentrate uranium oxide
UO_2	solid uranium dioxide
Natural Uranium	contains 99.3% U-238 and 0.7% U-235
Low Enriched Uranium	contains U-235 in a concentration higher than 0.7% and less than 20%
Highly Enriched Uranium	contains U-235 in a concentration above 20%
Weapons-Grade Uranium	enriched to more than 90% U-235
Depleted Uranium	contains less than 0.7% of the isotope U-235

1. The uranium-enrichment process summarized in Figure 1 on page 587 results in:

A. solid (U_3O_8) uranium containing isotope U-235 in a concentration of 3–5%.
B. low enriched uranium containing isotope U-235 in a concentration less than 0.7%.
C. enriched uranium in which the percentage of isotope U-238 is less than that of isotope U-235.
D. enriched uranium containing isotope U-238 in a concentration of less than 0.7%.

2. Before uranium is used to generate energy for electric power, raw uranium is converted from:

F. solid to gas form.
G. gas to solid form.
H. solid to gas form, then back to solid form.
J. gas to solid form, then back to gas form.

3. In order to use uranium for electric power, it is necessary to:

A. increase the number of protons in the uranium's atoms.
B. decrease the number of protons in the uranium's atoms.
C. increase the number of neutrons in the uranium's atoms.
D. decrease the number of neutrons in the uranium's atoms.

4. Based on Figure 1 on page 587, which of the following statements is most probably accurate?

   F. Uranium with a high concentration of isotope U-238 U-235 is not reprocessed unless it is depleted of its radioactive isotopes.
   G. Plutonium is reprocessed for nuclear fission but uranium is not.
   H. Uranium with a high concentration of isotope U-238 is reprocessed unless its radioactivity levels are too high.
   J. Uranium with a very high concentration of isotope U-238 is stored at a nuclear waste depository.

5. Based on the information in Figure 1 on page 587 and Table 1 on page 588, it is reasonable to conclude that:

   A. raw uranium can be enriched for use as fuel only if it contains at least 0.7% isotope U-235.
   B. plutonium is of little use as a source of fuel for generating electric power.
   C. uranium and plutonium, when enriched together, provide a more efficient fuel source than either one alone.
   D. highly enriched uranium is prohibitively expensive to produce in large quantities.

Passage II

Researchers are interested in optimizing methods for cooling electronic components such as *semiconductors* (a type of computer chip). Semiconductors generate heat as they operate, but excess levels of heat cause such components to malfunction or may shorten their life span. However, cold objects cannot be applied directly to these components, because they are too sensitive.

One cooling method that has been used is the placement of foam material between the semiconductors and a cooling plate. Foam acts as a *heat conductor*. Heat from the computer chip flows through the foam, toward the cooling plate. As heat is conducted through the foam in this manner, the semiconductor is cooled, and the temperature difference between the cooling plate and the semiconductor becomes smaller. Various experiments were performed to determine more about the heat conduction properties of foam.

Experiment 1

Foam pads that all had a surface area of 1 $inch^2$ but were of various thicknesses were inserted between a semiconductor and a cooling plate. The temperature of the cooling plate was kept constant. The semiconductor was generating 1 watt of heat. The researchers measured the difference in temperature between the semiconductor and the cooling plate. Results appear in Table 1.

Table 1

Trial No.	Thickness of Foam (mm)	Measured Temperature Difference Between Computer Chip and Plate (°C)
1	1	2.2
2	2	3.9
3	4	7.2
4	6	11.0
5	8	14.2
6	10	16.3

Experiment 2

Researchers placed a foam pad between a semiconductor and a cooling plate, but in this experiment the thickness of the pad was 6mm in all cases, while the surface area of the pad varied. The heat generated by the semiconductor remained at 1 watt. Results appear in Table 2.

Table 2

Trial No.	Foam Surface Area (inches^2)	Measured Temperature Difference Between Computer Chip and Plate (°C)
1	0.2	17.4
2	0.4	13.3
3	0.6	11.0
4	0.8	8.3
5	1.0	7.1
6	1.5	5.3

Experiment 3

The researchers were interested in seeing the performance of the foam cooling system when the heat dissipated (released) by the semiconductor was varied. To vary the heat dissipation, they varied the wattage generated by the semiconductors. A foam pad that had a surface area of 1 inch^2 and a thickness of 6mm was used in all of the tests. The results appear in Table 3.

Table 3

Trial No.	Heat Dissipation (watts)	Measured Temperature Difference Between Computer Chip and Plate (°C)
1	.25	4.2
2	.5	6.3
3	1.0	11.3
4	2.0	17.6
5	3.0	22.5
6	5.0	24.0

6. Experiment 1 demonstrated that:

F. foam pads are more effective heat conductors than metal cooling plates.
G. thin foam pads are more effective than thicker foam pads in cooling semiconductors.
H. thick foam pads are more effective than thinner foam pads in cooling semiconductors.
J. metal cooling plates make better heat conductors when used in conjunction with foam pads.

7. Based on Experiments 1 and 2, which of the following types of foam pads would serve as the most effective heat conductor?

A. A pad with a thickness of 4mm and a surface area of 0.4 inches^2
B. A pad with a thickness of 2mm and a surface area of 1.5 inches^2
C. A pad with a thickness of 8mm and a surface area of 0.6 inches^2
D. A pad with a thickness of 1mm and a surface area of 0.2 inches^2

8. If a foam pad 6mm thick and with surface area 1.0 inches^2 is used, and the difference in temperature between the semiconductor and cooling plate is measured at 20°C, then which of the following is probably closest to the number of watts of heat generated by the semiconductor?

F. .75
G. 1.5
H. 2.5
J. 3.5

9. Which of the following, if true, would be the best reason that a semiconductor using a foam-pad and cooling-plate system for cooling might continue to operate properly at very high temperatures?

A. Foam is the most effective material available for drawing heat from semiconductors.
B. Foam pads begin to disintegrate at sufficiently high temperatures.
C. Foam pads expand in surface area at higher temperatures.
D. Foam pads expand in thickness at higher temperatures.

10. The graph below shows the graph of a curved line on an *xy*-plane.

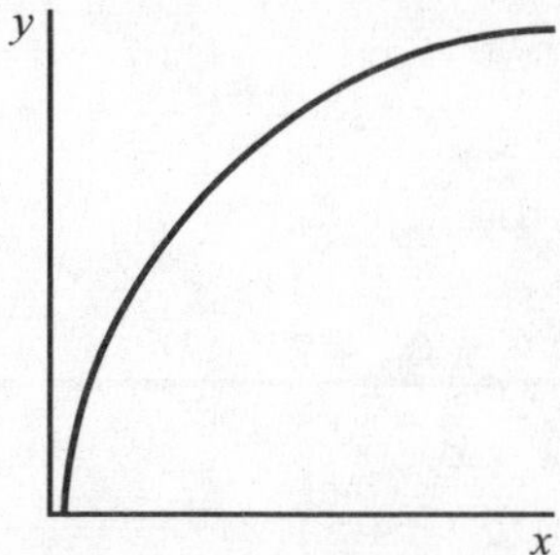

Based on the data collected from the three experiments, which of the following statements about the graph could be accurate?

F. Heat dissipation is shown on the *x*-axis and temperature difference between the computer chip and plate is shown on the *y*-axis.
G. Foam thickness is shown on the *x*-axis and the measured temperature difference between the computer chip and plate is shown on the *y*-axis.
H. Foam surface area is shown on the *x*-axis and the measured temperature difference between the computer chip and plate is shown on the *y*-axis.
J. The measured temperature difference between the computer chip and plate is shown on the *x*-axis and foam surface area is shown on the *y*-axis.

11. A manufacturer must use only foam pads with a thickness of 8mm. Assuming that semiconductor wattage and pad surface area are equally important in affecting the temperature difference between a semiconductor and cooling plate, the optimal cooling design would combine which of the following pairs of specifications?

A. A wattage of 2.0 and a pad with a surface area of 0.4 inches^2
B. A wattage of 1.0 and a pad with a surface area of .6 inches^2
C. A wattage of 3.0 and a pad with a surface area of 0.8 inches^2
D. A wattage of 5.0 and a pad with a surface area of 1.0 inches^2

Passage III

The first graph below shows the number of maternal deaths from 1979 to 1986. The term *maternal death* refers to the deaths of women whose pregnancies ended in live birth. The second graph shows the percentage of pregnancy-related deaths by the number of days from the end of the pregnancy until death. Pregnancy-related deaths include those deaths that occur while a woman is pregnant or up to one year from the end of pregnancy and are from any cause related to or aggravated by the pregnancy, excluding accidental deaths.

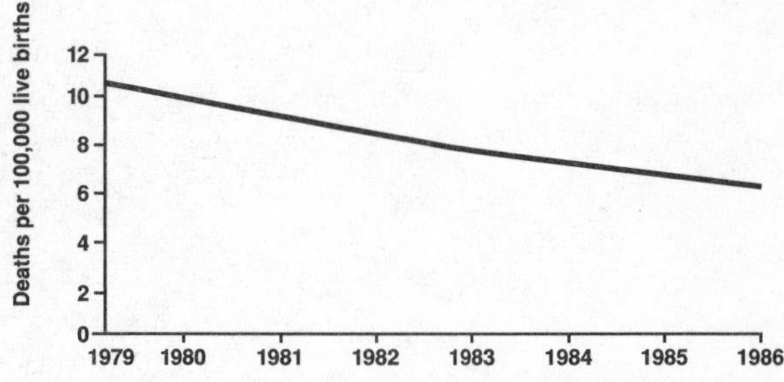

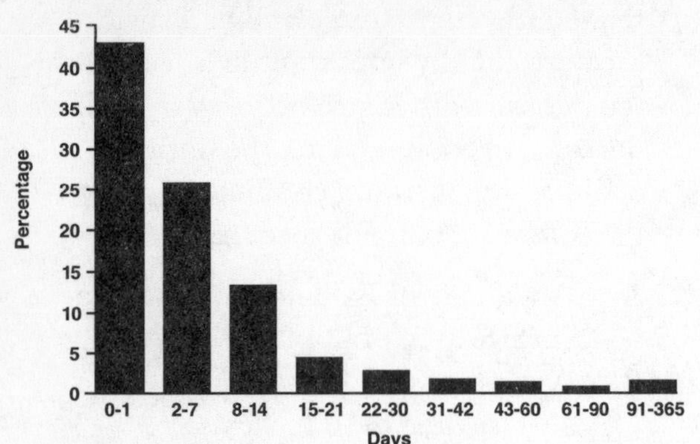

12. From the beginning of the time period measured through the end of the time period measured, the annual number of maternal deaths declined by about:

F. 4 percent.
G. 200,000 live births.
H. 4 per 100,000 live births.
J. 6 per 100,000 live births.

13. During the time period measured, pregnancy-related deaths occurring 8 or more days after birth accounted for about what percent of all such deaths?

A. 10
B. 30
C. 50
D. 70

14. Which of the following graphs best represents the relationship between the percentage of pregnancy-related deaths and the number of days after the end of pregnancy for the period of 31–365 days?

F.

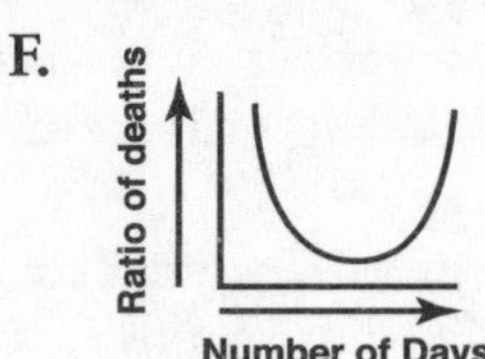

G.

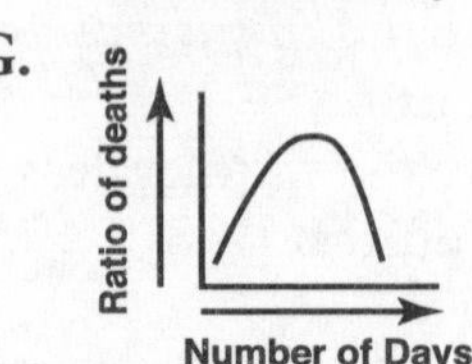

H.

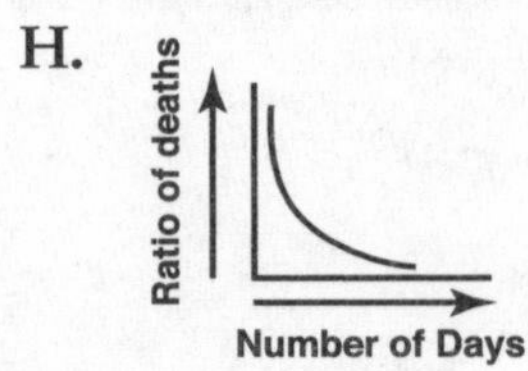

J.

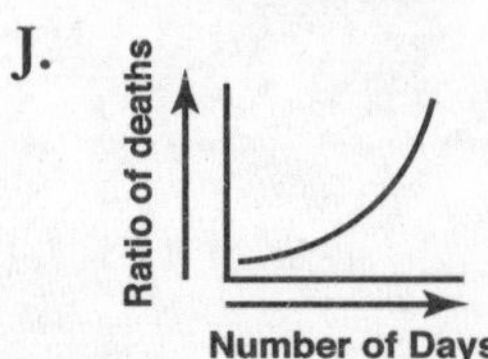

15. Based on the first graph, which of the following conclusions about the 7-year period is most reasonable?

A. The percentage of pregnancies end in live births increased over the 7-year period shown.
B. The percentage of all women giving birth declined over the 7-year period shown.
C. The death rate of women who never gave birth increased over the 7-year period shown.
D. New treatments for extending the lives of cancer patients were developed during the 7-year period shown.

16. Which of the following is the most accurate distinction between the two graphs?

F. The first graph accounts for the deaths of mothers over the entire 7-year period, whereas the second graph accounts only for deaths of mothers occurring during one 365-day portion of that 7-year period.

G. The first graph presents the number of maternal deaths over a time period, whereas the second graph presents percentages of births over a time period that were live.

H. The first graph accounts for all deaths of women who have given live birth, whereas the second graph accounts only for deaths of women occurring within one year after giving live birth.

J. The first graph does not account for pregnancy-related deaths, whereas the second graph does.

Passage IV

Recently, flywheels with magnetic bearings have been designed (see the next figure). These flywheels produce none of the friction associated with mechanical bearings, making them efficient energy-storage devices. One application they may have is in alternative energy cars. In experimental designs, a flywheel is "spun-up" while the car is at rest with the electrical power supplied from a standard electrical outlet. After the flywheel has reached a high rate of rotation, the car can be disconnected from the socket, and the energy can be extracted from the high-speed rotating flywheel.

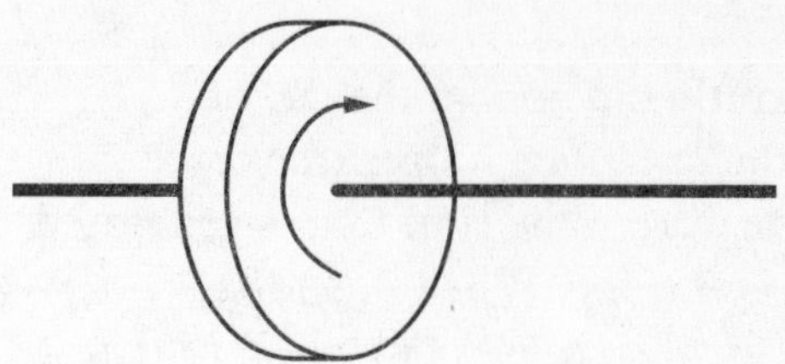

Experiment 1

Researchers looked at flywheels with different radii to gauge the effect of size on the total energy they could store. The wheels were all started at an initial frequency of 50 revolutions per second (rev/sec). All of the flywheels were *disk-type* (they had a uniform thickness along their entire radius), all were made of the same material, and all had the same thickness. After reaching the initial speed, a uniform resisting force was applied to determine how much energy it took to stop the wheel. The results of this experiment appear in Table 1.

Table 1

Radius (cm)	Energy Stored (joules)
10	100
20	1,600
30	8,100
40	25,600

Experiment 2

Next, a disk-type flywheel with a radius of 30 cm was brought up to various initial speeds by an electric motor. The energy stored at each speed was measured. Results appear in Table 2.

Table 2

Frequency (rev/sec)	Energy Stored
40	5,184
60	11,664
80	20,736
100	32,400

Experiment 3

One of the limiting factors in the use of flywheels is the *centrifugal force* (the force pulling outward from the rim) that is generated as the wheel is turning. When this force becomes too great, it causes the wheel to fly apart or explode. The centrifugal force is determined by the frequency and the radius of the wheel. A doubling of the radius results in a doubling of the centrifugal force; a doubling of the frequency results in a quadrupling of the centrifugal force.

Researchers tested three flywheel designs (see figure below). All of the wheels had a radius of 30 cm and the same mass; wheel thicknesses were changed to keep the mass constant. The frequency of each wheel was increased slowly until it exploded. The frequency at which this occurred as well as the energy stored in the wheel at the time was recorded. Results appear in Table 3 below.

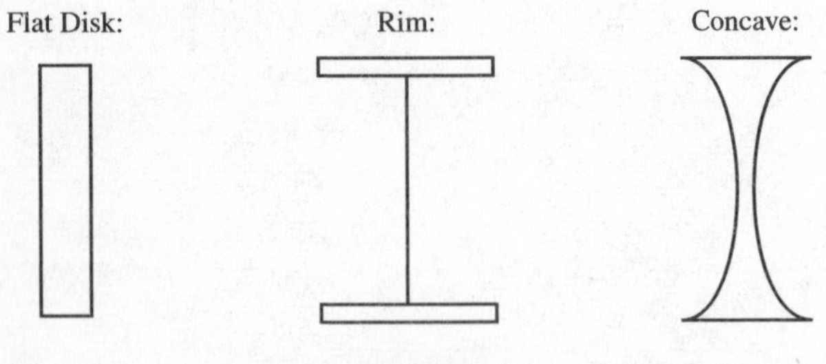

Table 3

Flywheel Type	Energy Stored (joules)	Strength (Maximum Frequency) (rev/sec)
Flat Disk	17,266	73
Rimmed	16,231	42
Concave Disk	19,627	72

17. All of the following were controls in both Experiments 1 and 2 EXCEPT:

- **A.** disk thickness.
- **B.** disk material.
- **C.** initial rate of rotation.
- **D.** flatness of the disk.

18. Based on Experiments 1 and 2, a flywheel with which of the following features would store the greatest amount of energy, assuming that all other characteristics of the flywheels are the same?

- **F.** A radius of 20 cm. and an initial frequency of 40 rev/sec.
- **G.** A radius of 20 cm. and an initial frequency of 50 rev/sec.
- **H.** A radius of 30 cm. and an initial frequency of 40 rev/sec.
- **J.** It cannot be determined without more information.

19. Which of the following is the best reason that a flywheel spun up to a high initial rate of revolution (frequency) might not save electricity in an electric motor?

- **A.** With a flywheel at a high initial frequency, it would take a significant amount of resistant energy to slow down the flywheel and ultimately stop it from rotating.
- **B.** The electrical power needed to bring the flywheel up to an initial frequency might be significantly greater than the amount needed for attaining a lower initial frequency.
- **C.** A high initial frequency requires a small radius, a feature which is not conducive to storing a large amount of energy.
- **D.** The greater the initial frequency of the flywheel, the longer the flywheel continues to rotate.

20. To keep a flywheel's centrifugal force low, the flywheel's designer should consider all of the following designs EXCEPT:

F. a flat disk.
G. a disk with a small radius.
H. a flywheel spun up to a low initial frequency.
J. a disk with a high mass.

21. In designing a flywheel, if the primary objective is to maximize the flywheel's energy storage rather than its strength, which of the following describes the best design for the flywheel?

A. A concave disk with a small radius
B. A flat disk with a large radius
C. A rimmed disk with a large radius
D. The best design cannot be determined without more information.

22. If energy storage and strength are of equal importance in designing a flywheel system, which of the following most likely describes an optimal design of the system, using a given mass of flywheel material?

F. A concave disk with a large radius and spun up to a low initial frequency
G. A rimmed disk with a small radius and spun up to a high initial frequency
H. A flat disk with a small radius and spun up to a low initial frequency
J. A concave disk with a large radius and spun up to a high initial frequency

Passage V

The following diagrams show typical changes in temperature and dissolved oxygen levels in two lakes from season to season. The two lakes have very similar temperature (T) and dissolved oxygen (DO) levels in the spring and the fall, so only one graph is shown for each of these two seasons. One lake is eutrophic, and the other is oligotrophic. A eutrophic lake is one that is rich in nutrients with many microorganisms and fish, as well as algae and other plants. An oligotrophic lake is one that is nutrient-poor with little plant or animal life. The water of oligotrophic lakes is generally quite clear.

The diagrams show the dissolved oxygen (DO; top scale) and temperature (T; bottom scale) of the two lakes during each season.

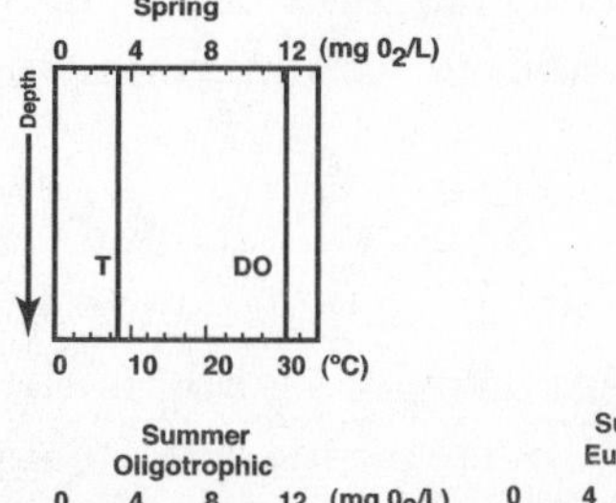

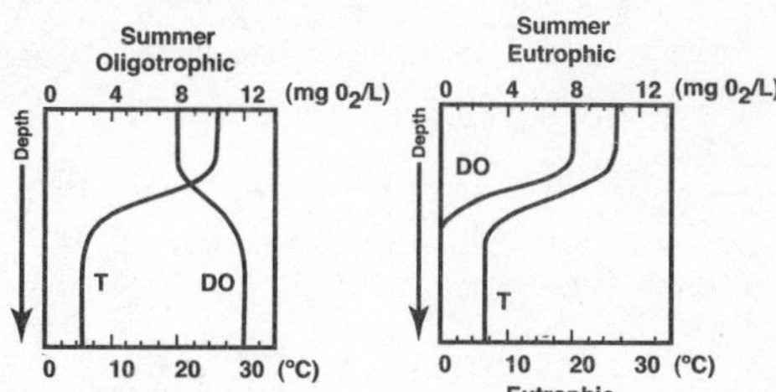

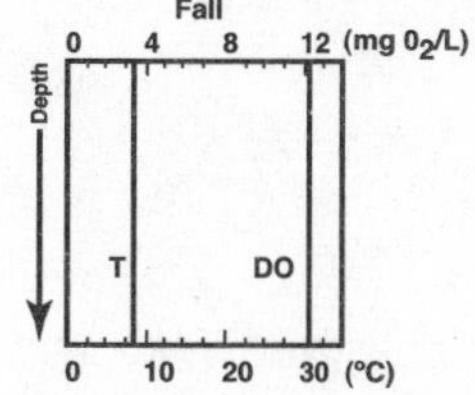

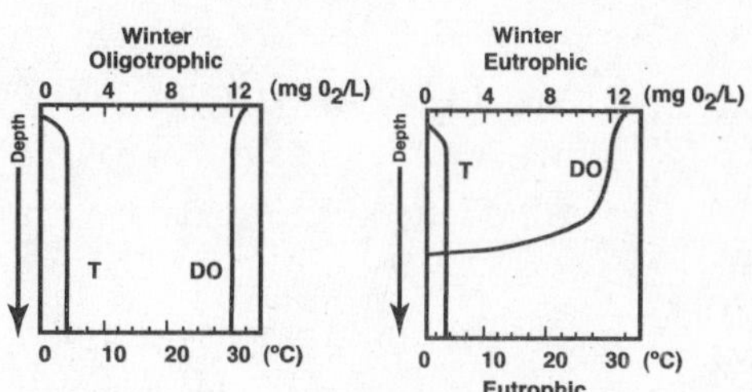

23. During the summer, the water temperature at the surface of either type of lake is approximately:

A. 8°C.
B. 10.5°C.
C. 20°C.
D. 27.5°C.

GO ON TO THE NEXT PAGE

24. In the oligotrophic lake, if the DO level is measured at 10mg O_2/L, then the water temperature where the DO level was measured is approximately:

F. 0°C
G. 5°C
H. 10°C
J. 15°C

25. From summer to fall, how do the dissolved oxygen levels vary in the eutrophic lake?

A. The levels increase in shallow water but remain stable in deeper water.
B. The levels increase slightly in shallow water but increase more dramatically in deeper water.
C. The levels decrease near the lake's surface but remain stable near the lake bottom.
D. The levels remain stable in shallow water but increase in deeper water.

26. Which of the following most likely accounts for the difference in DO levels between the eutrophic lake and the oligotrophic lake during the winter?

F. An increasing level of nutrients in the waters of the oligotrophic lake
G. The warmer waters of the oligotrophic lake as compared with the eutrophic lake
H. The smaller number of microorganisms in the eutrophic lake than in the oligotrophic lake
J. The increasing amount of decomposing algae in deeper waters of the oligotrophic lake

27. What might explain the temperature levels in both lakes during the winter?

A. Plants near the surface might get just enough sunlight to decrease temperatures there.
B. Surface ice cools the shallow waters to lower temperatures than those at deeper levels.
C. When oxygen dissolves in water, the effect is to cool that water.
D. When lakes freeze over, little sunlight can penetrate the surface.

28. Which of the following is the most plausible explanation as to why the DO and temperature levels in the oligotrophic lake are so different during the summer than during the other three seasons?

F. During the summer, warming of the lake's shallower waters allows some plants and animals to live in those waters.
G. During the summer, the warm sun heats not just the oligotrophic lake's shallow waters but also its deep waters.
H. As the weather cools after summer, some animals migrate from deep waters to shallower waters in search of warmth and sunlight.
J. The oligotrophic lacks sufficient nutrients to sustain any plant or animal life.

Passage VI

A greenish, potato-sized meteorite discovered in Antarctica is believed to have originated on Mars. Investigations of the meteorite have revealed a number of unusual features. Some scientists believe that these features are evidence of primitive life on Mars, while other scientists believe that they are more probably the result of nonbiological (nonliving) processes, such as hydrothermal synthesis.

Hydrothermal Synthesis Hypothesis

The meteorite crystallized slowly from *magma* (molten rock) on Mars 4.5 million years ago. About half a million years later, the rock became fractured. This was a time when Mars was much warmer and had abundant water. Deep inside the planet, in a process called *hydrothermal synthesis*, hot water and carbon seeped into the fractured rock and formed new complex *organic compounds* called polycyclic aromatic hydrocarbons (PAHs). (Organic compounds, or those that contain carbon, are formed from life processes, such as bacterial decay, as well as processes that are not associated with life, including hydrothermal synthesis and star formation.)

As the chemical environment of the planet changed over time, crystals of magnetite, iron sulfides, and carbonate formed in the rock. The crystallization of the carbonate resulted in the formation of unusual elongated and egg-shaped structures within the crystals.

Primitive Life Hypothesis

The meteorite crystallized slowly from *magma* (molten rock) on Mars 4.5 million years ago. About half a million years later, the rock became fractured. This was a time when Mars was much warmer and had abundant water. The rock was immersed in water rich in carbon dioxide, which allowed carbon to collect inside the fractured rock, along with primitive bacteria.

The bacteria began to manufacture magnetite and iron sulfide crystals, just as bacteria on Earth do. As generations of bacteria died and began to decay, they created PAHs inside of the meteorite's carbon molecules. Finally, some of the bacteria themselves were preserved as elongated egg-shaped fossils inside of the rock.

29. About which of the following points do the two hypotheses differ?

- **A.** The meteorite's age
- **B.** The origin of the meteorite's organic molecules
- **C.** The conditions on Mars when the meteorite formed
- **D.** The origin of the fractures in the meteorite

30. Proponents of both theories would agree that which of the following statements is true?

- **F.** The meteorite contains some type of fossil.
- **G.** Water was important for the original entry of carbon into the meteorite.
- **H.** The organic compounds seen in the rock were the result of decay.
- **J.** Magnetite crystals from Antarctica seeped into the meteorite.

31. Which of the following represents a difference in opinion between proponents of the two theories?

A. Proponents of the Primitive Life Hypothesis maintain that Mars has changed substantially since the meteorite was formed.
B. Proponents of the Primitive Life Hypothesis dispute the notion that PAHs can occur from processes other than bacterial decay.
C. Proponents of the Hydrothermal Synthesis Hypothesis believe that hot water and carbon formed organic compounds in the rock.
D. Proponents of the Hydrothermal Synthesis Hypothesis believe that the fossils found inside the meteorite were probably the remains of an organism other than a bacteria.

32. Which of the following findings would help to bolster the case of proponents of the Hydrothermal Synthesis Hypothesis?

F. The magnetite found in the meteorite sometimes occurred in chains, similar to those produced by bacteria on Earth.
G. Glass within the meteorite hints that it was probably fractured and launched toward Earth when a meteoroid or comet hit Mars.
H. Recent studies indicate that liquid water, one of life's most fundamental necessities, does not exist on Mars.
J. Minerals can grow into shapes that are similar to the elongated egg-shaped structures seen in the meteorite.

33. Which of the following additional findings would help the case of proponents of the Primitive Life Hypothesis?

A. Researchers analyzing glacial ice found very low concentrations of PAHs.
B. Organic molecules were also discovered in meteorites known to have originated in the asteroid belt (an area that is rich in asteroids and that orbits the Sun).
C. Some of the carbonates in which the PAHs were found had element ratios that are similar to those found on Earth.
D. Experiments with the weathering of rocks have shown that under certain conditions, molecules in the environment can make their way deep within a rock.

34. Which of the following experiments might help to resolve the question of whether the PAHs in the meteorite actually originated on Mars?

F. Examine the ratios of the PAHs found in glacial ice and see if these are similar to those seen in the meteorite.
G. Test for PAHs in meteorites known to have come from the moon.
H. Test for PAHs in meteorites known to have formed on Mars after its era of abundant water ended.
J. All of the above

Passage VII

Interferometry is a highly sensitive method of measuring distances that are close to the wavelength of light. A wave's length is the distance from one peak to the next peak or from one trough to the next trough. An interferometer (depicted in the following figure) uses a *partially reflecting* mirror (one that reflects half the light and allows the other half to continue through) to split a *coherent* light source, such as a laser beam.

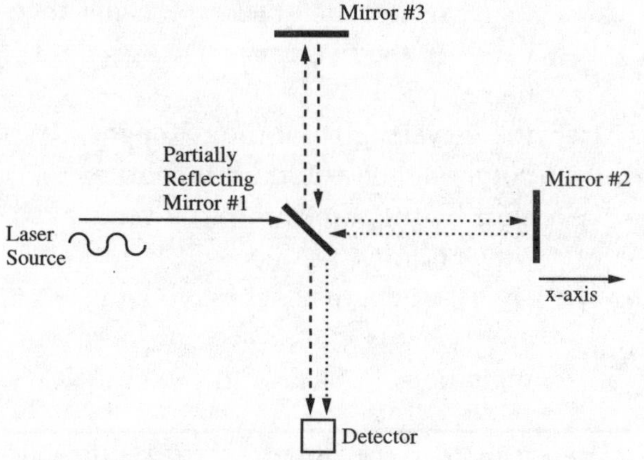

Coherent light consists of a single frequency. After the light is split, the two components will continue until they are reflected backwards by mirrors 2 and 3. After this reflection, they proceed to the partially reflecting mirror again, and each path has a component (about a half) that proceeds to the light detector. The detector receives the sum of the two components of light, each with its own *phase* (position of the wave with respect to a fixed spot).

Two experiments using an interferometer were conducted.

Experiment 1

In Experiment 1, researchers moved mirror 2 slowly away from the partially reflecting mirror (to the right along the diagram's x-axis), thereby lengthening the path that one component of the light travels and changing its phase. The light received by the detector was recorded at a number of positions. The following figure shows some of their findings along with the phase relationship of the waves that they deduced from these results. The deductions are assumed to be correct.

Table 1

Measured Light Intensity (milliwatts)	Mirror Position along x-axis (nanometers)	Phase relationship of the two different light components
1	0	
35	75	
57	150	
35	225	
1	300	

Experiment 2

In Experiment 2, researchers used various light sources with different frequencies (number of waves per second). With each source, they moved mirror 2 slowly away from the partially reflecting mirror (to the right along the diagram's x-axis), *recording the light received by the light detector at each position. The results of this experiment are shown in the following figure.*

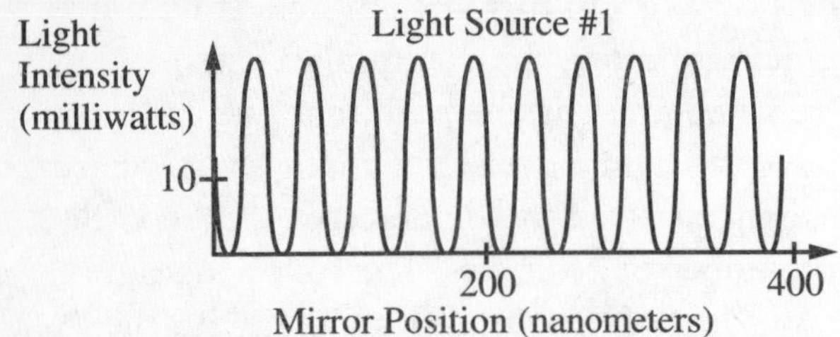

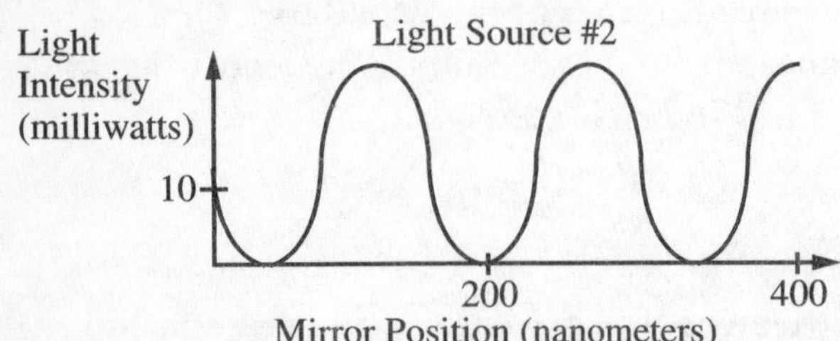

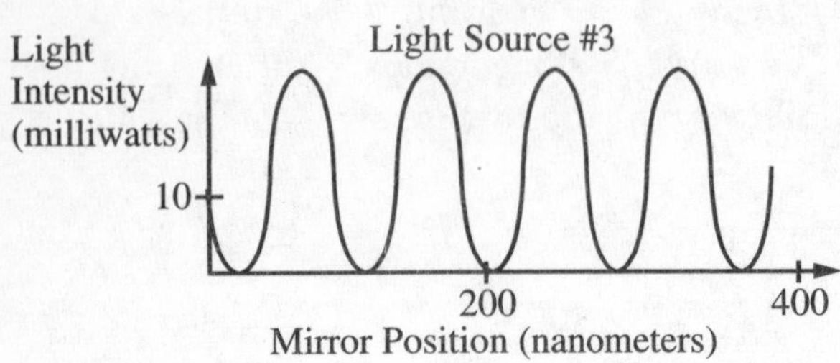

35. During Experiment 1, the two components of the light were in phase (their peaks and troughs all matched) most probably:

A. when mirror 2 and mirror 3 were equal in distance from the partially reflecting mirror.
B. at the measured light's lowest intensity.
C. at all of the measured light's lowest intensity levels.
D. at the measured light's greatest intensity.

36. In Experiment 1, assume that the researchers had continued to move mirror 2 farther away from the partially reflecting mirror. Based on the results of Experiment 1 and the researchers' deductions, it would be most reasonable to expect that:

F. measured light intensity would decrease and then increase as distance between the two mirrors was increased.
G. measured light intensity would increase and then decrease as distance between the two mirrors was increased.
H. the wavelengths of the two light components would both continue to shift by the same amount over a fixed time period.
J. the wavelengths of the two light components would become increasingly out of phase with each other.

37. Referring to Experiment 2, what is the approximate wavelength of the light from source #1?

A. 20 nanometers
B. 40 nanometers
C. 80 nanometers
D. 100 nanometers

38. In Experiment 1, assume that, instead of keeping mirror 3 in a fixed position, the researchers had moved it toward the partially reflecting mirror to match whatever distance by which they moved mirror 2 away from the reflecting mirror. Based on the data provided in Table 1, if mirror 3 were moved 75 nanometers, measured light intensity would be:

F. 70 milliwatts.
G. 57 milliwatts.
H. 35 milliwatts.
J. 1 milliwatt.

39. In Experiment 2, when light source #2 was used, the two components of the light were:

A. in phase when mirror 2 was moved by about 200 nanometers.
B. in phase before mirror 2 was moved.
C. in phase when mirror 2 was moved by about 267 nanometers.
D. out of phase when mirror 2 was moved by about 400 nanometers.

40. Which of the following conclusions do the experimental data most strongly support?

F. The higher a light source's frequency, the greater the light's intensity.
G. The higher a light source's frequency, the greater the light's intensity varies.
H. The higher a light source's frequency, the greater the number of components into which the light can be split.
J. The higher a light source's frequency, the shorter the light's wavelength.

STOP

Answers and Explanations

English

1. A The underlined portion is an idiomatic phrase that works well here. Choice **B** creates redundancy; *the reason is* and *because* convey the same idea, so they should not both be used. As for choices C and D, the contraction *it's* (it is), and not *its*, would be correct here if the pronoun reference were clear. But, in either case, the reference is vague.

2. J The sentence should make sense and be grammatically correct without the phrase set off by dashes. In the original version, *overwhelmed by modern technology . . . long for an era* makes no sense. Choice J works perfectly: *we feel overwhelmed by modern technology . . . and long for an era . . . .*

3. B The sentence's subject is *certain images*, which is plural. Hence, the verb form should also be plural.

4. G The first part of the sentence, through *genteel time*, is a single dependent clause. Interrupting the flow of the clause with a comma is pointless and confusing.

5. C Our imagining is occurring *now*—at the present time—not in the past. Thus, the present-tense *imagine* is the correct verb form here.

6. F The writer uses *glowing stoves* here in the singular sense—as one example of how the "good old days" were not so good. Hence, *a good example* (which is singular) is correct.

7. B This sentence and the preceding one should be considered together because their ideas are closely connected. The writer is trying to point out that coal stoves *didn't* do what they were supposed to and, what's more, caused a lot of problems. Choice **B** provides an effective way of getting this point across.

8. J It is proper to say that a person *can afford a product* or *can afford to buy (spend money on) a product*, but it is improper to say that a person *can afford the money* to buy a product.

9. C The main point of the paragraph is that the sense of nostalgia we associate with an old-fashioned coal heater, or even a radiant heater, ignores the real problems associated with trying to stay warm during the so-called "good old days." Choice C underscores this idea quite effectively.

10. J The point here is that the horse and buggy created a different kind of pollution than the automobile. But, the underlined portion wrongly implies a comparison between horse pollution and buggy pollution. Choice J clears up the confusion.

11. A Of the four alternatives, the original version makes the point most clearly and effectively. Choice **B** fails to make it clear that air conditioning did not exist. The problem with choice **C** is that the grammatical unit *did not exist* is split. Choice **C** draws an illogical comparison between *that era* and *air conditioning*.

12. J In context, the word *then* is clearly intended to refer to the past. But, juxtaposing *because* and *then* creates confusion about the meaning of *then* as used in the sentence. Choices **G**, **H**, and **J** each fix this problem. However, choice **G** creates a pronoun reference problem: The word *they* appears to refer to *today's buildings*, which makes no sense. The problem with choice **H** is that the juxtaposition of *then* and *than* is awkward and confusing. Choice **J** is clear and concise.

13. A The main thrust of the passage is that, contrary to our nostalgic images of the past, life a century ago was not so good overall as it is today. The sentence clearly provides additional support for this assertion.

14. G In the preceding sentence, the writer admits that life a century ago held certain advantages over life today. But, the writer wants to leave the reader with the impression that these advantages tell only part of the story and that, on balance, life was actually worse then. Choice **G** provides an appropriate and effective retort.

15. C In Paragraph 3, the writer talks about the problems associated with heating a cold building. In Paragraph 5, the writer talks about the difficulty of cooling a hot building. It makes sense that one paragraph should immediately follow the other. Paragraph 4 isn't so closely related to either Paragraph 3 or 5 and fits nicely between 5 and 6.

16. G The proper idiom here is *to be*, not *as*.

17. C The original sentence is vague as to who is thought to have lived during the time period indicated. Choice **C** makes it clear that it is the Olmecs, rather than Mesoamericans generally, that are believed to have lived during this period. A semicolon is appropriate here to connect what are now two independent, and closely related, sentences.

18. G The three items in the series are grammatically parallel, but the repeated use of *and* makes the phrase unnecessarily wordy. Choice **G** maintains parallelism while rendering the sentence crisper and more concise.

19. C The words *frequently* and *often* are better used to describe the repeated occurrence of some event in short time intervals. That's not the idea the writer intends to convey in this sentence. The word *extensively*—which means "pervasively throughout"—is a better choice here.

20. F The paragraph is concerned solely with describing the details of these art works. Choice **F** provides a good transition to this discussion. Choices **G** and **J** are off the topic of the passage, while choice **H** involves a specific topic of the following paragraph.

21. D The underlined portion is awkward, and the use of both *also* and *as well* in the sentence is redundant. Choice **D** provides a phrase that parallels the previous clause and solves the redundancy problem. Choices **B** and **C** are very awkward.

22. G The possessive *Their*, although grammatically correct here, is inconsistent with the use of *the* (rather than *their*) in the preceding sentence as well as later in the sentence in question. Since the two sentences are so closely related in their ideas and construction, the same article (*the*) should be used throughout.

23. A The reflexive pronoun *themselves* is appropriate, and effective, here. It emphasizes that a distinction is being made between the people and their art. Each of the three alternatives is grammatically correct; however, none is so effective as the original version.

24. J The phrase *one such theory* is idiomatic. The problem with the underlined portion is that it sets up an illogical comparison between *theory* and *belief*. The theory is not the belief; rather, it *involves* the belief, as choice J correctly indicates.

25. B The underlined sentence is ambiguous; it's not clear whether each cave painting simultaneously supports both variations on the theory, or whether some paintings support one variation while other paintings support the other variation. Only choice B provides a sentence that clears up the ambiguity.

26. F In context, the underlined phrase is idiomatic and rhetorically effective.

27. D The sentence in choice D tells us that there is at least one additional theory, but it supplies no details about that theory (nor does the next paragraph). By itself, then, the sentence provides a truncated, unsatisfying way to conclude the paragraph.

28. H The adverb *strongly* (ending in *-ly*) is correct here because it modifies the adjective *felt*; the intervening word *something* obscures the idea that the Olmecs *felt strongly*, so it should simply be omitted.

29. A The subject of the sentence, *representations*, is plural, calling for the verb *reveal* (as in "they reveal").

30. H In the passage, the writer never talks about what kind of legacy the Olmecs left for Mesoamerican cultures that came after theirs. The passage's central concern is with one aspect of Olmec art (the jaguar theme) and what it might reveal about the Olmecs themselves.

31. C The contraction *earth's* should be used here to indicate possession (as in "its surface").

32. J In the underlined portion, the verb *are* nonsensically suggests that *minerals* and *a limited supply* are the same thing. Choice J remedies this problem. Although choice H also fixes the problem, the word *their* is unnecessary; choice J is more concise.

33. A Sentence 2 provides the main assertion or idea of the paragraph; what follows are supporting examples. The first supporting point is that food from the ocean can help solve world hunger. The second supporting point involves minerals beneath the ocean floor, but the writer never mentions what human dilemma these minerals can help solve. Choice A provides a sentence that supplies this missing information.

34. H The original sentence splits the verb *foresee* and its direct object *entire cities*; the result is awkward and confusing. Choice H reworks the sentence so that it makes more sense and provides a more logical transition from the preceding discussion to the one that follows. Choice G suffers from the same type of problem as the original version, while choice J wrongly suggests that it is the scientists who would take advantage of the new cities.

35. B The writer should use a preposition here that suggests distance—for example, *out to sea* or *from land*—as choice **B** provides.

36. J The writer is referring to possible future events, not present events. The phrase *could serve* establishes the proper time frame as well as the subjunctive mood, which is appropriate here.

37. A A comma is needed to set off the dependent clause that begins with the word *there*. Otherwise, the clause appears to modify (describe) *travel* rather than *terminals*.

38. J The two phrases *provide many functions* and *play a variety of roles* are redundant. (They express the same essential idea.) The writer should omit one or the other.

39. B Sentence 4 provides the topic sentence for the paragraph and thus should come first. Notice that sentence 3 begins with *Others*, a clue as to what should immediately precede it. In the context of the sentence, *Others* probably refers to other people. Thus, sentence 3 should immediately follow sentence 1, which refers to *some of the people*. Since sentence 2 begins with the word *Also* and does not refer to the people living in the ocean cities, sentence 2 should come last in the paragraph.

40. G The sentence following the period explains why ocean cities would need to be self-sufficient. The word *because* provides a needed link in the chain of reasoning.

41. D In the paragraph, the writer stresses the need for self-sufficiency in the ocean cities, then explains how a city would be structured for self-sufficiency. At this point, it would make sense for the writer to provide additional examples of how an ocean city could be self-sufficient. Choices **A** and **D** are the best candidates. Of the two, **D** is the better choice because it addresses two basic needs—food and energy—whereas choice **A** addresses only one (food).

42. F The word *such* is idiomatic and helps make it clear that the writer is referring to the kinds of cities just described.

43. B The original version uses the simple past tense where the present-perfect tense is more appropriate—especially in light of the next sentence.

44. H The underlined sentence is grammatically correct. However, the phrase *used for rigs* is redundant and results in a wordy, repetitive sentence; the phrase can simply be omitted, as in choice **H**. Also, the way the original sentence is constructed unfairly implies that rigs are in fact ocean-going cities, just smaller than the ones planned for the future. Choice **H** rearranges the sentence to make it clear that rigs and the proposed ocean-going cities are two distinct things.

45. A The pronoun reference is clear enough as the sentence stands. There's no need to replace the pronoun *they* with what it is intended to modify, as in choices **B** and **C**.

46. F The first clause of the sentence (up to the comma) is a dependent clause that modifies (describes) the Globe. The underlined portion is grammatically correct, and the reference to the Globe is clear. Choice **G** creates an illogical comparison between plays and playwrights. Choice **H** creates a so-called "comma splice"—two independent clauses connected improperly by only a comma. Choice **J** makes no sense if you remove the modifying clause: *The theater . . . the Globe burned . . . .*

47. D The three phrases that follow *the Globe* should be grammatically parallel to one another. Since the word *it* does not immediately precede the phrase *was rebuilt . . .*, the word *it* should not precede the phrase *was a victim . . .* either. Simply omitting the word achieves proper parallelism.

48. G The underlined portion provides two verbs where only one is needed; the result is an awkward grammatical construction. Choice **G** makes the essential point in a succinct, grammatically correct way. Choices **H** and **J** are wrong because the plural verb form *was* conflicts with the sentence's compound subject (which is considered plural).

49. A The underlined portion is grammatically correct and clearly gets across the point: It took a long time, but Wanamaker's dream was finally realized. Each of the three alternatives are constructed in a way that actually obscures this point. Also, choices **C** and **D** are awkwardly constructed.

50. H In the paragraph, the writer presents a sequence of events from Wanamaker's conceptualizing the new Globe to its eventual opening. Accordingly, it makes sense for the paragraph to begin as it does, with sentence 1, but to end with sentence 3. As for the best sequence for what comes between, sentence 5 informs us of the problem at the outset that needed solving, and so it makes sense that this sentence precedes the two that discuss how the problem was solved. As for these two sentences, the word *also* in sentence 4 tells us that it should come after sentence 2.

51. A In the underlined portion, the conjunction *and* is appropriate to connect the sentence's two ideas, which should be given equal rhetorical emphasis. The preposition *with* is also appropriate here—it is idiomatic to refer to a tier *with* multiple rows.

52. G The underlined portion is grammatically correct but unnecessarily repeats the word *area*. Choice **G** provides a more concise and effective alternative. The dash signals that what follows it elucidates what immediately precedes it.

53. A The writer intends to make the point that, based on what was known about the original Globe, the new Globe was as accurate a replica of the original as possible. The word *given* is idiomatic and is rhetorically effective in making this point.

54. H The sentence in which the underlined portion appears is merely a fragment (not a complete sentence); it contains a compound subject but no predicate. Choice **G** solves the problem by providing the predicate *were used*, then transforming the remainder of the sentence into a dependant clause. Neither choice **G** nor choice **J** solves the problem with the original version.

55. D Although the proposed sentence makes sense in context, it would be redundant because the writer has already made this essential point in the first sentence of the paragraph.

56. H The phrase *if they aren't careful* is intended to modify *groundlings*. Placed at the end of the sentence, however, it appears to modify *soldiers*. Choice **H** clears up the confusion by reconstructing the sentence, positioning the modifier near what it modifies. Although choices **G** and **J** also place the modifier closer to what it modifies, in each case the result is an awkward splitting of a grammatical unit.

57. D The underlined portion is grammatically correct, but it is wordy and awkward. Of the three alternatives, choice **D** provides the clearest, most concise phrase.

58. H In the paragraph's first two sentences, the writer points out what was originally planned, and then suggests that this plan changed. Choice **H** completes the thought—by telling us how the plan was revised.

59. B The original sentence uses the double-negative *no roof over neither* . . . , which is not only awkward and confusing but also makes no sense in context—the writer intends to make the point that the new Globe does *not* have a roof. Choice **B** solves both problems by using the correlative *either* . . . *or*. Choice **C** also solves the problem but results in faulty parallelism (the second *over* should be omitted). Choice **D** improperly mixes *neither* with *or*.

60. F The sentence in choice **F** connects to the idea that immediately precedes it, as well as tying together the passage's main point that the New Globe building itself as well as the New Globe theatergoing experience closely resemble the original.

61. A The original version is concise and grammatically correct. (It is idiomatic to say that an accident *left* someone injured.) The phrase that choice **B** provides should be preceded by a comma. Choice **C** is wordy and awkward. Choice **D** creates a usage error (*resulted in paralysis* would have been correct).

62. J What was surprising to the writer was not his own reactions (as the original version wrongly implies) but rather *the fact that* his own reactions differed from those of able-bodied people. Choice **J** conveys the writer's intended point.

63. C The writer needlessly shifts tense—from the present-perfect tense (*have been easier*) to the simple past tense (*responded*). Presumably, other people are still responding to the writer's disability, so the writer should maintain the present-perfect tense, as choice **C** provides.

64. G *They are* is an awkward way to begin this sentence. Since what follows is a list, omitting *They are* and replacing the period with a colon is perfectly appropriate here.

65. C The theme of the passage is how able-bodied people treat the disabled, and virtually every sentence connects with that theme in some way. The proposed addition, however, does not—and therefore the writer should leave it out.

66. H The reflexive pronoun *myself* is incorrect here because the sentence involves other people's responses to the writer, not the writer's responses. The object-case pronoun *me* should be used instead.

67. B The appropriate idiom is *not . . . but rather* . . . , as choice **B** provides.

68. F The underlined portion uses the correlative pair *either . . . or*. . . . What follows one element of a correlative pair should be grammatically parallel to what follows the other element—which is the case here.

69. D The structure of the original sentence is clumsy and confusing. In particular, the sentence strings together two subordinate clauses, both of which begin with the preposition *in*. Choices **B** and **D** both fix this problem by rearranging the sentence. But in choice **B**, the resulting sentence is just as clumsy in its own way. Choice **D** provides a better solution: Recast the underlined portion in the active voice, with *most people* as the sentence's subject.

70. J Immediately after identifying the two terms, the writer uses the plural word *labels*—which refers to *terms* (plural), not one term or the other.

71. A The underlined portion is idiomatic and is effective in making the point. (An acceptable alternative would be: *so vague that they describe. . .*.) Each of the three other choices distorts the idea that the writer seeks to convey.

72. J The original sentence refers to *less loaded terms* but doesn't identify them until later in the sentence. It makes more sense to list them immediately for the reader, as in choice **J**.

73. B Sentence 1 is a good topic sentence for the paragraph, so it should remain first. Since the rest of the paragraph describes how the use of words to describe the disabled has changed over time, it would be logical to arrange the sentences in time sequence: "First" (sentence 3), "Then" (sentence 4), and finally "Today" (sentence 2).

74. H The original version is too vague. (To whose normality is the writer referring?) Also, though it is a word, *normality* is a bit clumsy in this sentence. Choice **H** solves both problems. Choice **G** is ineffective in making the point. (A better alternative would be: *I was once normal.*) Choice **J** obscures the whole point of the sentence.

75. A In the previous paragraphs, the writer points out how normal people treat people with disabilities. Then, in the final paragraph, the writer recalls what it was like to treat disabled people the way he is treated. Choice **A** provides a reflective concluding remark that nicely ties together the entire discussion.

Math

1. B In combining fractions, you can divide across fractions all variables except *a* (in the numerator) and one *e* (in the denominator), leaving $\frac{a}{e} \bullet x = 1$. Then, to isolate *x* on one side of the equation, multiply both sides by $\frac{e}{a}$:

$$\frac{e}{a} \bullet \frac{a}{e} \bullet x = 1 \bullet \frac{e}{a}$$

$$x = \frac{e}{a}$$

2. J $|7 - 2| - |2 - 7| = |5| - |-5| = 5 - 5 = 0$

3. C Multiply like base numbers by adding exponents, and divide like base numbers by subtracting the denominator exponent from the numerator exponent:

$$\frac{x^6y^3y}{y^6x^3x} = \frac{x^6y^4}{y^6x^4} = \frac{x^2}{y^2}$$

4. G Given any two *xy*-coordinate points, a line's slope $m = \frac{y_1 - y_2}{x_1 - x_2}$. Accordingly, $\frac{1}{3} = \frac{5 - (-3)}{a - 2}$. Simplify, then cross-multiply to solve for *a*:

$$\frac{1}{3} = \frac{8}{a - 2}$$
$$a - 2 = (3)(8)$$
$$a - 2 = 24$$
$$a = 26$$

5. E A linear equation in two variables, regardless of the number of terms or values of coefficients, allows an infinite number of combinations for the two variables.

6. F Rename all four fractions as fractions with the least common denominator, which is 20. Then, add together the two numerator fractions and the two denominator fractions. Then, multiply the resulting numerator fraction by the reciprocal of the resulting denominator fraction:

$$\frac{\frac{3}{5} + \frac{3}{4}}{\frac{3}{4} - \frac{3}{5}} = \frac{\frac{12}{20} + \frac{15}{20}}{\frac{15}{20} - \frac{12}{20}} = \frac{\frac{27}{20}}{\frac{3}{20}} = \left(\frac{27}{20}\right)\left(\frac{20}{3}\right) = \frac{27}{3} = 9$$

7. B $m\angle BFC + m\angle CFD = 90°$, and $m\angle AFB = 50°$. The sum of the measures of those three angles, added to $m\angle DFE$, is 180; that is, $90° + 50° + m\angle DFE = 180°$. Thus, $m\angle DFE = 40°$.

8. J Given $\sqrt{ab} = 4$, $ab = 16$. Although you do not know the individual values of *a* and *b*, $a^2b^2 = (ab)^2$. Accordingly $(ab)^2 = (16)^2 = 256$.

9. D Eliminate the fraction by multiplying each term in the equation by 2. Then isolate *x*:

$$\frac{2(x + 1)}{2} + (2)2 = 2x - (2)1$$
$$x + 1 + 4 = 2x - 2$$
$$7 = x$$

10. G One way to solve the problem is to first express $\frac{1}{8}$ as its decimal equivalent 0.125, then multiply: $0.125 \times 0.4 = 0.05$. Then, express 150% as the decimal number 1.5, and calculate the product: $1.5 \times 0.05 = 0.075$.

11. C Express 4.9 in scientific notation: 4.9×10^0. To express the number of specimens per cubic millimeters, divide by 1,000. To accomplish this in scientific notation, subtract 3 from the exponent: 4.9×10^{-3}. Multiply by 3 to obtain the number of specimens per 3 cubic millimeters: 14.7×10^{-3}, or 1.47×10^{-2}.

12. F A circle's circumference = $2\pi r$. Given a circumference of 6, $r = \frac{3}{\pi}$. The area of a circle with this radius is $\pi\left(\frac{3}{\pi}\right)^2 = \frac{9}{\pi}$.

13. B The expression given in the question is equivalent to 4×4^n. In this expression, base numbers are the same. Since the terms are multiplied together, you can combine exponents by adding them together: $4 \times 4^n .= 4^{(n+1)}$.

14. K The length of OQ and OP are the same: $\sqrt{2^2 + 1^2} = \sqrt{5}$. The length of PQ is $\sqrt{1^2 + 1^2} = \sqrt{2}$. Therefore, the perimeter is $2\sqrt{5} + \sqrt{2}$.

15. B The right-hand shaded region shows all points for which the value of x is 5 or greater—that is, $x \geq 5$. The left-hand shaded region shows all points for which the value of x is, -5 or less—that is $x \leq -5$. If $x \leq -5$, then $|x| \geq 5$, as the inequality in choice **B** provides.

16. F The shelter houses $d + c$ animals altogether. Of these animals, d are dogs. That portion can be expressed as the fraction $\frac{d}{c + d}$.

17. E Given midpoint $(-3,4)$, you can express the midpoint's coordinates using the midpoint formula: $M = \left(\frac{x_1 + x_2}{2}, \frac{y_1 + y_2}{2}\right)$. Solve for x_2 to determine the x-coordinate of the other endpoint:

$$-3 = \frac{5 + x}{2}$$
$$-6 = 5 + x$$
$$-11 = x$$

Similarly, solve for y_2 to determine the y-coordinate of the other endpoint:

$$4 = \frac{2 + y}{2}$$
$$8 = 2 + y$$
$$6 = y$$

18. K Any one of four distinct groups of three women might be selected: ABC, ABD, ACD, or BCD. The probability that the selections will result in any particular one of these groupings is 1 in 4, or $\frac{1}{4}$. Similarly, any one of three distinct pairs of men might be selected: XY, XZ, and YZ. The probability that the selections will result in any particular one of these pairs is 1 in 3, or $\frac{1}{3}$. To determine the combined probability, multiply one individual probability by the other:

$$\frac{1}{4} \times \frac{1}{3} = \frac{1}{12}.$$

19. D Try plugging in a simple number (let $d = 2$ and $r = 1$):

$$A = \pi r^2 = \pi(1)^2 = \pi.$$

The new area $= \pi\left(\frac{3r}{2}\right)^2 = \frac{9}{4}\pi$. The new area is $\frac{9}{4}$ the area of (or 125% greater than) the original one.

20. J Notice that the product of the first and third binomials is the difference of two squares: $(x + 2)(x - 2) = x^2 - 4$. Find the product of $(x^2 - 4)$ and $(4x - 1)$ using the FOIL method: $(x^2 - 4)(4x - 1) = 4x^3 - x^2 - 16x + 4$.

21. B Solve for x in the inequality:

$$6 - \frac{x}{2} \leq 4$$

$$-\frac{x}{2} \leq 4 - 6$$

$$-\frac{x}{2} \leq -2$$

$$-x \leq -4$$

$$x \geq 4$$

The graph in choice **B** indicates this inequality.

22. G You could solve the problem algebraically by using the arithmetic-mean formula (x is the seventh number):

$$84 = \frac{86 + 82 + 90 + 92 + 80 + 81 + x}{7}$$

There's a quicker way, however. 86 is 2 above the 84 average, and 82 is two below. These two numbers "cancel" each other. 90 is 6 above and 92 is 8 above the average (a total of 14 above), while 80 is 4 below and 81 is 3 below the average (a total of 7 below). Thus, the six terms average out to 7 above the average of 84. Accordingly, the seventh number is 7 below the average of 84, or 77.

23. E The total parking fee that ABC pays each month is \$1,920 (\$240 × 8). Of that amount, \$420 is paid for outdoor parking for three cars. The difference (\$1,920 − \$420 = \$1,500) is the total garage parking fee that the company pays for the other five cars.

24. J Solve for x by isolating the x-term, then squaring both sides of the equation:

$$2\sqrt{2x} + t = 4$$

$$2\sqrt{2x} = 4 - t$$

$$\left(2\sqrt{2x}\right)^2 = (4 - t)^2$$

$$(4)(2x) = (4 - t)(4 - t)$$

$$8x = 16 - 8t + t^2$$

$$x = \frac{16 - 8t + t^2}{8}$$

$$x = 2 - t + \frac{t^2}{8}$$

25. E Points $A(-1,-1)$ and $C(2,-1)$ connect to form a horizontal line segment of length 3. Similarly, points $B(-1,3)$ and $D(2,3)$ connect to form a horizontal line segment of length 3. Points $A(-1,-1)$ and $B(-1,3)$ connect to form a vertical line segment of length 4. Similarly, points $C(2,-1)$ and $D(2,3)$ connect to form a vertical line segment of length 4. The total perimeter = 3 + 3 + 4 + 4 = 14.

26. H Divide 1,650 by the least possible prime factor, then divide the quotient by the least possible prime factor, and so forth (prime factors are italicized below):

1,650 ÷ 2 = 825 ÷ *3* = 275 ÷ *5* = 55 ÷ *5* = *11*

The prime factorization of 1,650 is the product of the prime factors (the italicized numbers above): $2 \times 3 \times 5^2 \times 11$.

27. B The sum of the degree measures of the three angles is 180—that is, $m\angle A + m\angle B + m\angle C = 180$. Express $m\angle B$ and $m\angle C$ in terms of $m\angle A$, then find $m\angle A$:

$$A + (A - 20) + (A - 40) = 180$$

$$3A = 240$$

$$A = 80$$

Since $A = 80$, $B = 60$, and $C = 40$. The ratio of $A:B:C$ = 80:60:40, or, in simplest form, 4:3:2.

28. G Extend $\overline{BE}$ to F (as in the diagram below). $m\angle EFD = m\angle ABE = 40°$. $m\angle FED$ must be 110° because a triangle contains a total of 180°. Since $\angle BED$ and $\angle FED$ are supplementary, $m\angle BED = 70°$.

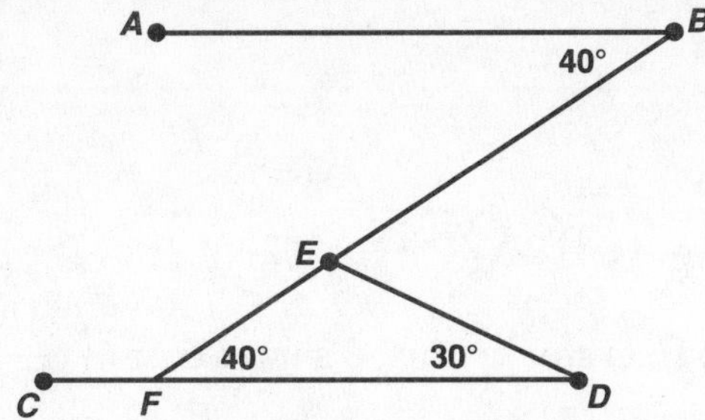

29. D \$54 is 90% of what Kirk collected. Express this as an equation:

$$54 = 0.90x$$
$$540 = 9x$$
$$x = 60$$

Kirk collected \$60. If each paper sells for 40 cents, the number of papers Kirk sold is $\frac{60}{0.40} = \frac{600}{4} = 150$.

30. G Letting x = the unknown length, by the Pythagorean theorem: $8^2 + x^2 = 17^2$. The length of the sides must be in the ratio 8:15:17 (one of the Pythagorean side triplets). The triangle's area $= \frac{1}{2}bh = \frac{1}{2}(8)(15) = 60$.

31. C To answer the question, you need to determine how many times 0.113 goes into 2.8. In other words, divide 2.8 by 0.113. The quotient is approximately 24.8 (or, to the nearest liter, 25).

32. F The total rent is $D + 100$, which must be divided by the number of students (M).

33. A Since 0 (not 2) is the first term, the 50th term is 98. Since the 50 terms are equally spread apart, the mean value of all 50 terms is 49—midway between 0 and 98. The sum of all 50 terms is the product of the mean and the number of terms: $49 \times 50 = 2{,}450$.

34. K First combine the two terms inside the radical, using the common denominator b^2. Then remove perfect squares from the radical:

$$\sqrt{\frac{a^2}{b^2} + \frac{a^2}{b^2}} = \sqrt{\frac{a^2 + a^2}{b^2}} = \sqrt{\frac{2a^2}{b^2}} = \frac{a}{b}\sqrt{2}$$

35. D Letting w equal the rectangle's width, its length is $2w$ and its area is $(w)(2w) = 2w^2$. The area of a circle (πr^2) of diameter 8 is $\pi(4)^2 = 16\pi$. To find the rectangle's perimeter, first solve for w:

$$2w^2 = 16\pi$$
$$w^2 = 8\pi$$
$$w = 2\sqrt{2\pi}$$

The perimeter is $2l + 2w = 4w + 2w = 6w = (6)(2\sqrt{2\pi}) = 12\sqrt{2\pi}$.

36. K It costs $\frac{210}{p}$ dollars to buy one share of MicroTron stock; thus, 6 shares cost $6\left(\frac{210}{p}\right)$ dollars. Similarly, it costs $\frac{572}{q}$ dollars to buy one share of Dynaco stock; thus, 11 shares cost $11\left(\frac{572}{q}\right)$ dollars.

37. A To determine each entry in $R + S$, add together corresponding entries in R and S. Considering choice **A**, adding together the first entry in row 1 of R (1) and the first entry in row 1 of S (4) gives you the first entry in row 1 of $R + S$ (5). The other entries in choice **A** add up correctly as well.

38. G The first person can select any one of 5 chairs, the second person can select any one of the 4 remaining chairs, and the third person can select any one of the 3 remaining chairs. Thus, the number of seating arrangements is $(5)(4)(3) = 60$.

39. B Letting P = the number of students enrolled in Physics only, and letting C equal the number of students enrolled in Chemistry only: $P + C + 15 = 78$. Given that $C = 47$, $P = 16$.

40. F First, determine the area of the rectangular piece removed, which is the product of the piece's length and width:

$$A = (x - 3)(x - 4)$$
$$= x^2 - 7x + 12$$

To find the area of the remaining material, subtract the area of the rectangular piece from x^2 (the original area of the square carpet): $x^2 - (x^2 - 7x + 12) = x^2 - x^2 + 7x - 12 = 7x - 12$.

41. A In the standard form $(x - h)^2 + (y - k)^2 = r^2$, $h = -1$ and $k = 5$. Find r^2 by applying the circumference formula: $C = 2\pi r$; $4\pi = 2\pi r$; $2 = r$; $4 = r^2$. Only choice **A** supplies the correct values for all three variables: h, k, and r.

42. G Since $\overline{AC}$ is tangent to the circle, $m\angle OBC = 90°$. $\angle BCO$ is supplementary to the 140° angle shown; thus, $m\angle BCO = 40°$ and, accordingly, $m\angle BOE = 50°$. Since $\angle BOE$ and $\angle DOE$ are supplementary, $m\angle DOE = 130°$. (This angle measure defines the measure of minor arc DE.)

43. D Given $\tan x = 1$, the triangle's two legs are equal in length (2) and, by the Pythagorean theorem, the length of the hypotenuse $= 2\sqrt{2}$. Accordingly, $\sin y = \frac{2}{2\sqrt{2}} = \frac{1}{\sqrt{2}} = \frac{\sqrt{2}}{2}$.

44. J The key to this problem is in determining the interior angles of the various triangles formed by the runways. The interior angle formed by the 120° turn from runway 1 to 2 is 60° (a 180° turn would reverse the airplane's direction). Similarly, the interior angle formed by the 135° turn from runway 1 to 3 is 45° (180° − 135°). Two triangle "angle triplets" emerge: a 45°-45°-90° triplet and a 30°-60°-90° triplet, as shown in the figure below. Since the sum of any triangle's interior angles is 180°, the remaining angles can also be determined:

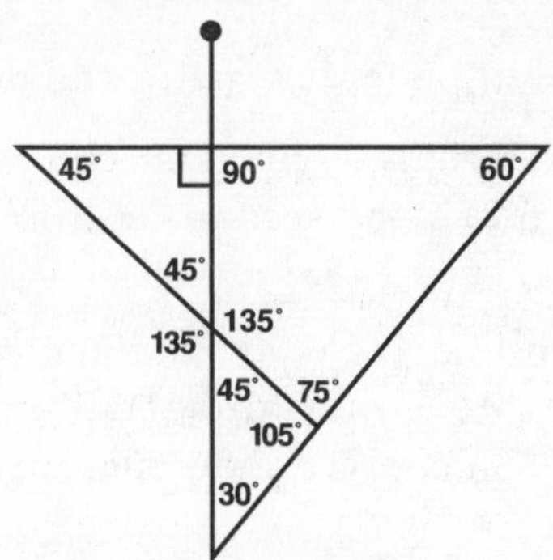

The only answer choice not appearing in the figure above is 55°, choice **J**.

45. A Given that the area of the square is 4, each side is 2 units long. Since *A* bisects $\overline{DE}$, $\overline{DA}$ is 1 inch long. Apply the Pythagorean theorem to find the length of $\overline{AC}$, which is the hypotenuse of ΔACD:

$$1^2 + 2^2 = \left(\overline{AC}\right)^2$$

$$5 = \left(\overline{AC}\right)^2$$

$$\sqrt{5} = \overline{AC}$$

46. F Express $|3x - 4| \geq 8$ as the two distinct inequalities $3x - 4 \geq 8$ and $3x - 4 \leq -8$. Solve for x in each inequality:

$$3x - 4 \geq 8 \qquad 3x - 4 \leq -8$$

$$3x \geq 12 \qquad 3x \leq -4$$

$$x \geq 4 \qquad x \leq -\frac{4}{3}$$

Excluded from the possible values of x is the set $\{-\frac{4}{3} < x < 4\}$. Choice **F** expresses this value set.

47. B Since no base numbers are given, both bases are understood to be 10. Substitute the expressions given for x and y as follows: $2y - 3x = 2\log 5 - 3\log 2$. To combine the two terms, apply the properties of logarithms: $2\log 5 - 3\log 2 = \log 5^2 - \log 2^3 = \log 25 - \log 8 = \log\frac{25}{8}$.

48. J Simply choose a number like 7 for n. $7 \div 3$ leaves a remainder of 1. By substituting 7 for n in each answer choice, we get 9 for choice **F**, 12 for choice **G**, 6 for choice **H**, 14 for choice **J**, and 21 for choice **K**. Of these, only 14 is NOT divisible by 3.

49. C The original volume of the cube $= 2 \times 2 \times 2 = 8$. A 50% increase in each edge increases the volume to $3 \times 3 \times 3 = 27$, an increase of 19 cubic centimeters.

50. H Based on the definition of a geometric series in the question, all pairs of successive terms must have the same ratio. Thus, $\frac{x}{-2} = \frac{-8}{x}$. Cross-multiplying, $x^2 = 16$, and hence $x = \pm 4$. The constant multiple is either 2 or -2. If the second term is +4, then the constant ratio is $+4 \div -2 = -2$; thus, the sixth term is $(-2)(-2)^5 = 64$. If the second term is -4, then the constant ratio is $-4 \div -2 = +2$; thus, the sixth term is $(-2)(2)^5 = -64$.

51. D First, examine ΔABE, which is a right triangle with one angle 90° and another angle 27°. Thus, the third angle, $\angle BAE$, measures 63°. Since $\angle BAC$ is one third of 63°, or 21°, looking at ΔABC, $\angle BCA$ must be $180° - 21° - 27° = 132°$. Since x is the supplement to that angle, $x = 180 - 132 = 48$.

52. F Since the figure has 5 sides, it contains 540°:

$$180(5 - 2) = 540$$

The sum of the measures of the five angles is 540°. Set up an equation, and then solve for x:

$$540 = x + 110 + 60 + 120 + 100$$
$$540 = x + 390$$
$$150 = x$$

53. D First, determine the equation of the line. The line's slope $(m) = \frac{8 - 3}{3 - 8} = \frac{5}{-5} = -1$. Find the y-intercept by substituting either pair of coordinates for x and y in the general equation $y = mx + b$:

$$3 = (-1)(8) + b$$
$$11 = b$$

Since $m = -1$ and $b = 11$, the equation of the line is $y = -x + 11$. For each answer choice, substitute the x-value and y-value for these two variables in the equation. Only choice **D** provides values that satisfy the equation.

54. H The circle's area $= \pi r^2 = \pi(3)^2 = 9\pi$. A 30° segment is $\frac{30}{360}$, or $\frac{1}{12}$, the circle's area. Thus, the area of the shaded region is $\frac{11}{12}$ that of the circle: $\left(\frac{11}{12}\right)(9\pi) = \left(\frac{11}{4}\right)(3\pi) = \frac{33\pi}{4}$.

55. D First, substitute $a - 3$ for x in the function. Rewrite in unfactored form, then factor the resulting trinomial:

$$\begin{aligned} f(a-3) &= (a-3)^2 - 2(a-3) - 3 \\ &= a^2 - 6a + 9 - 2a + 6 - 3 \\ &= a^2 - 8a + 12 \\ &= (a-2)(a-6) \end{aligned}$$

Given that $f(x) = 0$, there are two possible values of a: 2 and 6.

56. H The general equation for the graph of a parabola whose vertex is at (h,k) is either $y - k = a(x - h)^2$ or $x - h = a(y - k)^2$. The equation in choice **H** fits the latter form.

$$\begin{aligned} (x+2) + 2y^2 &= 16 \\ x - 14 &= -2(y-0)^2 \end{aligned}$$

Choice **F** defines a circle, choice **G** defines an ellipse, and choice **J** defines a hyperbola.

57. C To answer the question, the function you need is tan35°, defined as $\frac{\text{opposite side } BC}{\text{adjacent side } AC}$. Set up an equation, then solve for the length of AC:

$$\begin{aligned} \tan 35° &= \frac{5}{AC} \\ (AC)(\tan 35°) &= 5 \\ AC &= \frac{5}{\tan 35°} \\ AC &\approx \frac{5}{0.7}, \text{ or } 7.14 \end{aligned}$$

58. F Given that $\cos\beta = \frac{5}{7}$, the hypotenuse of the right triangle is 7 units long, while the side adjacent to the angle that measures β degrees is 5 units long. To find tanβ, you need to determine the length of the third side by the Pythagorean theorem:

$$\begin{aligned} 5^2 + x^2 &= 7^2 \\ 25 + x^2 &= 49 \\ x^2 &= 24 \\ x &= 2\sqrt{6} \\ \tan\beta &= \frac{\text{opposite}}{\text{adjacent}} = \frac{2\sqrt{6}}{5} \end{aligned}$$

59. E First, express the equation in the quadratic form: $x^2 - 4x + 13 = 0$ [$a = 1, b = -4, c = 13$]. Then, apply the quadratic formula:

$$x = \frac{-(-4) \pm \sqrt{(-4)^2 - 4(1)(13)}}{2(1)}$$

$$= \frac{4 \pm \sqrt{16 - 52}}{2}$$

$$= \frac{4 \pm \sqrt{-36}}{2}$$

$$= \frac{4 \pm 6i}{2}$$

$$= 2 \pm 3i$$

The two roots are $2 + 3i$, choice (E), and $2 - 3i$.

60. G The equation defines a cosine curve that has a frequency of 2 and therefore reaches its minimum (lowest) point *twice* over one 2π period—that is, over the interval $[0, 2\pi]$. The two minimum points are at $x = \frac{\pi}{2}$ and $x = \frac{3}{2}\pi$.

Reading

1. D Immediately following the first sentence, the author describes the jovial mood of the soldiers earlier in the trip by implication. Their "soberer" state later in the trip contrasts with this earlier mood.

2. H The author makes clear throughout the passage that the soldiers are returning from war, and in the passage's second sentence, the author describes how the soldiers passed the time "on the long way from New Orleans." The clear implication here is that the war took place in or near that city.

3. A The word *beguile* means "divert attention pleasantly from toil." So, the soldiers were diverting their own attention from the tedium (monotony) of the long train ride by jokes and lighthearted banter ("they had beguiled tedium with jokes and friendly chaff") (lines 4–5). Although the word *cheated* is not the best possible synonym of *beguiled*, it is the most apt of the four choices, especially considering the context.

4. G In the next sentence (lines 96–100), the narrator refers to Smith's untended farm and mortgage payments. The "bitter juice of care" is a clear reference to these concerns. Earlier in the passage, Smith tells one of the other soldiers, "I've got a wife and children, so I'm goin' to roost on a bench and take the cost of a bed out of my hide." Thus, when Smith arrives home, he also has a duty to provide for his family—which might be viewed as another "bitter pill of care." However, nowhere in the passage does either the narrator or any of the characters mention Smith's employment prospects after returning home. Hence choice **G** is the best among the four choices.

5. D In the second paragraph, the narrator tells us: "The men showed sure signs of near starvation." Then the narrator lists various abnormal physical characteristics of the men, among them their "unnaturally large bright eyes." The clear inference here is that this characteristic is a sign of near starvation. (It's common knowledge that a starving person is someone who's been deprived of food and thus is very hungry.)

6. H In lines 46–48, the narrator tells us: "All of the group were farmers, living in districts several miles out of the town, and *all were poor*."

7. B In lines 63–65, the narrator tells us: "The station was deserted . . . as [the soldiers] came into it at exactly a quarter to two in the morning."

8. G The word *surfeit* is used as a verb here. In this part of speech, the word means "to overfill or fill beyond (in excess of) limit." The previous sentence indicates that the "blue coats, dusty and grimy, were too familiar now to excite notice." In other words, the loafers had already seen many, many soldiers like these. So, it makes sense that the loafers would be "bored of" such sights by now.

9. B The second paragraph provides the contrast indicated in choice **B**. The narrator tells us: "There were no bands greeting them at the stations, no banks of gaily dressed ladies waving handkerchiefs and shouting 'Bravo!' as they came . . . into the town that had cheered and blared at them on their way to war." The narrator then adds that, as the returning soldiers arrived at the train stations, "the loafers looked at them indifferently."

10. J The second paragraph informs us that all four soldiers clearly showed signs of physical wear and tear—obviously from the long war.

11. A The passage devotes itself primarily to explaining how the Mesopotamian rivers attracted settlers, who then exploited the riverways to expand their civilization. The passage concludes by briefly informing us of similar developments in other river valleys of the world. The passage's final sentence provides a good recap of the passage—its main idea. Of the four answer choices, A most closely reflects that main idea.

12. H The first paragraph informs us that the riverine lands (at the banks of the Nile, Euphrates, and Tigris Rivers) attracted "settlers armed with the newly developed techniques of agriculture." The clear inference here is that these settlers already had some experience in agriculture.

13. D The first paragraph begins by telling us that new conditions emerged in the Middle East as a result of the climate change that began around 7000 B.C.E. The paragraph goes on to describe some of the resulting geographic changes, including the gradual transformation of the region's grasslands into deserts.

14. F The word *indigenous* means "native or original to a particular region." Accordingly, something *non-indigenous* would be unavailable locally unless and until it is brought into the locality from elsewhere. Even if you don't know the word's meaning, you can infer it from the context. The passage states that, originally, the region's sole building material was mud, but with the opening of trade, non-indigenous materials became available. In this context, it makes perfect sense that the word *non-indigenous* refers to materials not native to the region—in other words, unavailable locally.

15. C Nowhere in the passage are we informed of the strategic military value of rivers or what role they played in anything related to warfare.

16. J Nowhere in the passage does the author indicate when Mesopotamian culture reached its peak or when it began to decline. Paragraphs 5, 6, and 1 contain information useful in answering the questions in choices F, G, and H, respectively.

17. A In the eighth paragraph (lines 88–107), the author is claiming that, by 3500 B.C.E., Mesopotamian society was flourishing and that a complex and advanced civilization was in place. In all likelihood, then, the author mentions the temples to support this claim. The sheer size and locations of the temples suggests that the society was rich in the resources of physical labor, raw materials, and engineering talent. The temples also suggest a high level of architectural sophistication, which would be required to construct such enormous structures.

18. G The sixth paragraph informs us that mud "originally served as the region's sole building material."

19. B The sixth paragraph informs us that the rivers served as high roads of the earliest commerce. The next paragraph then tells us that goods were eventually exchanged between villagers in Egypt and Iran as well. From these two paragraphs, it is reasonable to infer that the earliest trade routes were between various villages along the rivers.

20. H The third paragraph provides the answer to this question. The efforts to control the waters required a high degree of cooperation among large numbers of people, which meant that people from various villages needed to join together in the effort. The last sentence of the paragraph describes this social phenomenon as a "new cooperation."

21. B The second paragraph points out that impressionists viewed light as the ultimate visual reality. The third paragraph indicates that, for the impressionists, the chief "person" in a picture is light. The fourth paragraph tells us that the subjects of a picture are merely parts of a pattern of light. Clearly, then, light is of primary importance to the impressionist painter.

22. G The rest of the paragraph tells us that the cubists, pop artists, and other modernists took their cue from the impressionists—from which we can surmise that *precursors* means forerunners of the movements that followed.

23. A It can be inferred from the passage that Andy Warhol, by choosing a tin can as a subject, showed his disregard for the importance given to conventional subjects—as did the impressionist who preferred to depict a lowly street scene as his subject, instead of the conventional, accepted subjects of his time.

24. J The impressionists' depiction of the "low life" of contemporary Paris is an example of the kind of subject that made some people doubt the credibility of the impressionist's art.

25. C In the quote, the art historian does not attribute anything with more importance than the use of light on an impressionist canvas. In fact, he calls light the sole subject of the picture.

26. H The passage reveals that the ultimate visual reality for an impressionist is the light and its properties, which supersede even color and drawing.

27. B A busy city street is most similar to the typical impressionist scenes listed in the seventh paragraph (lines 87–104).

28. J As explained in the third paragraph, an impressionist painting is not of any particular object but of the vibrations of light reflected by the objects, which often merge together.

29. C In the sentence beginning with the word *paradoxically*, the author explains that, contrary to the impressionists' claim that subject matter is of no interest to them, it just so happens that it is subject matter that makes their work influential and powerful. Therein lies the contradiction, or paradox.

30. F The author's main concern in the passage is to point out the impressionists' pioneering role in modern art. The author conveys that concern methodically, by pointing out examples of the types of art before and after the advent of impressionism.

31. B Blood type O contains neither substance A nor B, and it contains both antibodies, so a blood transfusion from a person with any blood type other than O would cause a negative reaction.

32. J The fourth paragraph informs us that it was the failure of many blood transfusions that first gave physicians the idea that there might be incompatible blood types. The first paragraph tells us that blood typing was added to the tools of forensic science around the turn of the century (1900). The clear inference is that blood transfusions were already being performed at that time.

33. C The seventh paragraph tells us that the lack of substantial amounts of blood at a typical crime scene makes other blood-typing methods difficult to use for solving crimes. Then, the next paragraph informs us that the major advantage of electrophoresis over other blood-typing methods is that this process can precisely test even small samples of blood. Choice **C** contradicts this information. Each of the other answer choices indicates a problem with electrophoresis that the passage explicitly mentions as such.

34. G Blood is type B if it has antibodies against blood type A. The blood is type B+ if it also tests positive for the presence of Rh factor.

35. A The ninth paragraph lists expense as a major drawback of electrophoresis (lines 98–100). The next (and final) paragraph discusses Wrexell's research, from which a less expensive, and otherwise better, process was developed. According to the author, this development "made the study of blood and fluid samples a truly valuable tool for crime detection." So, mentioning the drawbacks of electrophoresis helps the author make a convincing case for the significance of this later development.

36. H The author introduces the passage by informing us of two major tools added to the crime-fighting arsenal around the turn of the twentieth century: fingerprinting and blood typing. After providing a glimpse into the relative importance of fingerprinting until recently, the author informs us of how all this changed about ten years ago. Specifically, the author describes a series of events, from the origination of blood typing to its refinements, then culminating with Wrexell's analysis of blood and fluid samples and how blood typing then became a valuable tool for crime detection. Choice **H** nicely recaps the entire discussion.

37. A The passage's first sentence states that fingerprinting and blood typing both joined the family of crime-fighting tools around the turn of the century (1900).

38. J The sixth paragraph describes Rh factor as a "genetic marker" that helps narrow down the possibilities when it comes to possible identity of a person from whom a blood sample came. The eighth paragraph then describes electrophoresis as "a method for identifying genetic markers more precisely." The clear inference here is that electrophoresis helps further narrow down the possible identities of the blood "donor."

39. A In the first paragraph, the author alludes to an array of tools used in forensic science. The word *collection* is an apt substitute for the word *repertoire* in this context.

40. G A blood donor voluntarily supplies his or her own blood for medical purposes—especially for blood transfusions. Although a person who leaves his or her own blood at a crime scene is supplying the blood to medical scientists, that person would not be considered a donor. The quotes help make clear that the word is being used here ironically—and that it should not be understood literally.

Science

1. B The enrichment process increases the percentage of isotope U-235 to 3–5%. According to Table 1, at these levels of U-235, uranium is "low enriched." The enrichment process also produces "depleted uranium," which Table 1 defines as uranium with less than 0.7% isotope U-235.

2. H During the conversion stage, U_3O_8 (a solid) is converted to UF_6 (a gas). Then, during the fabrication stage, enriched UF_6 (a gas) is converted to UO_2 (a solid). At this point, the uranium is fissioned to produce the energy used for electric power.

3. D An isotope's mass number refers to the number of neutrons contained in the atom. Accordingly, isotope U-238 is defined by a greater number of neutrons than isotope U-235. Figure 1 and Table 1 both inform us that uranium must be enriched by increasing the concentration of isotope U-235 before it can be fissioned for use in producing electric power. Thus, the number of neutrons in the uranium's atoms must be decreased.

4. J The entire purpose of the enrichment process is to increase the concentration of isotope U-235 relative to isotope U-238. Thus, it would make no sense to reprocess uranium with a very high concentration of isotope U-238. Most likely, this uranium is disposed of (stored at a nuclear waste depository for later burial).

5. A The enrichment stage results not only in low enriched uranium but also in so-called "depleted uranium," which Table 1 defines as uranium with less than 0.7% concentration of isotope U-235. Figure 1 shows that depleted uranium is not used in the fabrication process, but rather is disposed of.

6. G Table 1 shows that the thinner the foam pad, the smaller the temperature difference between the semiconductor and cooling plate—which means that the pad is serving as an effective conductor of heat from the semiconductor into the plate.

7. B The ideal pad for heat conduction is a thin one with a large surface area. Among the four choices, **B** provides the specifications that best match this description.

8. H In Experiment 3, the researchers used a foam pad 6mm thick and with surface area 1.0 inches^2, just as specified in the question. Thus, you can consult Table 3 to answer the question. 20°C lies about midway in value between the values 17.6°C and 22.5°C in Table 3. Thus, a good estimate of the wattage is a value midway between 2.0 and 3.0 watts—the two values that correspond to a 17.6°C and a 22.5°C temperature difference, respectively.

9. C Table 2 suggests that a foam pad with a large surface area is a better heat conductor than one with a smaller surface area. Table 3 suggests that foam becomes a less effective heat conductor as a semiconductor generates higher wattages. But, the foam's expanding surface area at higher temperatures would compensate for this decrease in effectiveness—at least to some extent.

10. F In Table 3, as the wattage increases in equal increments of 1.0 watt, temperature difference continues to increase, but by less and less:

As wattage increases from 1.0 to 2.0, temperature difference increases by 6.3°C.

As wattage increases from 2.0 to 3.0, temperature difference increases by 4.9°C.

As wattage increases from 3.0 to 5.0, temperature difference increases by 1.5°C.

Notice that the wattage increase from 3.0 to 5.0 is twice the amount of either of the previous two incremental increases, but that the corresponding increase in temperature difference is substantially less—suggesting that the curve begins to "flatten" above a certain wattage, as indicated in the graph.

11. B Choice **B** combines a wattage that, under Experiment 2's conditions, results in a temperature difference of 11.3 with a surface area that, under Experiment 3's conditions, results in a temperature difference of 11.0. Assuming that the two specifications have an equal impact on temperature difference (as given in the question), you would average the two numbers to determine their combined effect on temperature difference. Applying the same analysis to each of the three other pairs of specifications shows that choice **B** results in the lowest combined temperature difference, which indicates the most effective cooling design.

12. H In the first year measured, the annual number of maternal deaths was just over 10 per 100,000 live births. In the final year measured, the number is just over 6 per 100,000 live births. Therefore, the number declined by about 4 per 100,000 live births.

13. B To answer the question quickly, combine the levels shown by the first two bars, then subtract the total from 100%. For 0–1 days (the first bar) the percent was about 43, while for 2–7 days (the second bar) the percent was about 27. Their combined percent is about 70. Accordingly, all other pregnancy-related deaths accounted for 30% of such deaths.

14. F Starting with the 31- to 42-day period, bar height (which indicates percentage of pregnancy-related deaths) decreases through the 61- to 90-day period, but then increases for the final (91- to 365-day) period. Choice **F** shows a graph that reflects this decline, then subsequent increase.

15. D The graph shows a declining death rate over the 7-year period among all women who have given live birth. One explanation for the decline might be an increase in the life span of people generally—including women who have given birth at one time or another.

16. H The first graph provides information about *all* "maternal deaths" (over the 7-year period), which is defined as deaths of women who have given live birth. The second graph presents information about the deaths of only some of those women—specifically, the ones who died within one year of giving birth (as well as women who died within one year after the end of their pregnancy but whose pregnancy did not end in a live birth).

17. C In Experiment 1, rotation rate was a control—it was fixed at 50 rev/sec. However, in Experiment 2, rotation rate (rev/sec) was the key variable, as Table 2 shows.

18. H Table 2 tells us the amount of energy stored in the flywheel described by choice **H**: 5184 joules. Table 1 tells us that that there is a direct relationship between a flywheel's radius and the amount of energy it can store. Thus, the flywheel described in choice **F** would store less energy than the one described in choice **H**, which has a larger radius but is otherwise the same as the one described in choice **F**. Table 1 tells us the amount of energy stored in the flywheel described by choice **G**: 1,600 joules, which is less than the flywheel described in choice **H**.

19. B The initial paragraph of the passage indicates that electrical power is required to spin up the flywheel to its initial rate. Common sense tells us that it would take longer (and would take more electrical power) to spin up the flywheel to a high frequency than to a lower one. To some extent, then, the electrical power used to spin up the flywheel offsets the energy that is created. It is theoretically possible that the amount of electrical power used might offset the amount of energy stored in the flywheel.

20. J Experiment 3 is the only one that mentions the mass of flywheels. In this experiment, the three flywheel designs all had the same mass. Thus, there is no way to know from this experiment what effect a higher or lower mass might have on a flywheel's centrifugal force. The description of Experiment 3 tells us of a direct relationship between radius and centrifugal force, as well as between frequency and centrifugal force. Thus, you can eliminate choices **G** and **H**. Table 3 shows us that a flat disk holds together at higher frequencies than the other two designs. Since it is centrifugal force that causes a flywheel to break apart, it is reasonable to conclude that a flat disk design helps lower a spinning disk's centrifugal force.

21. D Table 3 tells us that a concave disk stores more energy than either a flat or rimmed disk. On the other hand, Table 4 tells us that a disk with a large radius stores more energy than a disk with a smaller radius. Thus, which type of disc—the one described in choice **A**, **B**, or **C**—results in optimal energy storage depends on the particular specifications of each disk, which neither the question nor answer choices **A**, **B**, and **C** provide.

22. F As the results of Experiment 3 suggest, a concave shape contributes to strength *and* to a high level of energy storage. A large radius and high initial frequency operate contrary to each other, thereby providing a balance between strength and energy storage. A large radius contributes to a high level of energy storage but a large centrifugal force (which in effect weakens the flywheel), while a low initial frequency contributes to a low level of energy storage but a small centrifugal force (which in effect strengthens the flywheel). None of the other designs provide so reasonable a degree of both strength and energy storage while at the same time ensuring a balance between the two factors.

23. D Water temperature is measured on the bottom scale. For either the eutrophic or oligotrophic lake, the temperature graph at the surface (top of the graph) is between 27°C and 28°C.

24. H The only summer graph of the oligotrophic lake is the one that shows a DO level of 10 mg O_2/L. The temperature that corresponds to that DO level is about 10°C.

25. B From summer to fall, the DO level near the surface increases from about 8 mg O_2/L to about 12 mg O_2/L. However, in deeper water the increase is more dramatic—from 0 mg O_2/L to about 12 mg O_2/L.

26. J The oligotrophic lake has consistently higher DO levels than the eutrophic lake. Based on the information in the passage, the key difference between the two lakes is that plant and animal life are abundant in eutrophic lakes while they are virtually nonexistent in oligotrophic lakes. Thus, a difference in DO levels between the two lakes is best explained by a difference in the amount of either plant or animal life between the two lakes. In the winter, DO levels of the two lakes remain about the same. However, in deeper waters, DO levels in the eutrophic lake decline dramatically, while they remain high in the oligotrophic lake. Based on the information provided, the most logical explanation for this phenomenon is that, during the winter, animal and plant life appear in greater abundance in the eutrophic lake's deep waters than in its shallow waters.

27. B Winter is the only season during which temperatures near or at the surface are lower than temperatures at deeper levels. A logical explanation for this fact is that the water's surface freezes during the winter, making the water near the surface colder than deeper water.

28. F The graphs show that DO levels are consistently lower in the eutrophic lake than in the oligotrophic lake. Since plant and animal life thrive in an eutrophic lake but not in an oligotrophic lake, there must be an inverse relationship between DO levels and the amount of plant and animal life that a lake can support. During the summer, the oligotrophic lake's DO levels decrease while its temperatures increase, suggesting that, even though the lake is highly oligotrophic most of the year, during the summer, the oligotrophic lake's water temperature becomes high enough to support some plant and animal life.

29. B This question calls for you to recognize the essence of the conflict between the two viewpoints. The Hydrothermal Synthesis Hypothesis states that the PAHs (the organic molecules in the meteorite) were formed by hydrothermal synthesis, while the Primitive Life Hypothesis says that they were formed by the decay of bacteria. This difference between the two theories is what the passage is all about: Are the egg-shaped structures within the crystals evidence of an organic process (and therefore of life on Mars) or an inorganic one?

30. G See the fourth sentence of each section describing the two hypotheses. In both cases, seeping water is described as the mechanism that allowed carbon to enter the rock.

31. C This is the only true statement among the four that also names a difference between the proponents of the two theories. Choice A is particularly tricky because the statement is true, based on the passage; however, it describes a belief that is actually *shared* by proponents of both theories.

32. J If it's true that minerals can form "egg-shaped structures" like those found in the meteorite, this would strengthen the Hydrothermal Synthesis Hypothesis by providing an alternative explanation for these forms, which the Primitive Life proponents consider evidence of life on Mars.

33. A This question assumes you know that Antarctica consists primarily of glacial ice—a fact that the passage does not supply but one that the test-makers assume you know. The fact that low concentrations of PAHs were found in glacial ice, choice **A**, strengthens the Primitive Life Hypothesis by tending to *disprove* the notion that the PAHs in the meteorite seeped in after the rock landed in Antarctica.

34. F This test would at least help to eliminate—or confirm—the possibility that the PAHs found in the meteorite actually appeared there as a result of contamination from glacial ice.

35. D The right column of Table 1, which indicates the relationship between the two light components, shows them in phase at the highest measured light intensity (57). Although 57 milliwatts might not have been the greatest intensity between a 0–300 nanometer change in distance from the reflecting mirror to mirror 2, of the five measurements provided, it is. The fact that 150 nanometers is the precise midway point between 0 and 300 further suggests that 57 milliwatts might very well have been the light's greatest intensity during Experiment 2.

36. G Experiment 1 shows that, before mirror 2 is moved, measured light intensity for the two components is minimal. Then, as mirror 2 is moved farther from the partially deflecting mirror, light increases to a peak intensity, then decreases to reach the minimal intensity again. It is reasonable to conclude that this is a cycle, which will repeat itself.

37. B Measuring a wave length from either peak to peak or trough to trough, Experiment 2 measured about 10 waves from light source #1 over the 400-nanometer distance—or 40 nanometers for each wave.

38. G The key to the question is to recognize that it is the distance by which one mirror exceeds the other in relation to the partially reflecting mirror that determines whether the two light components are in phase—which in turn determines light intensity. Moving mirror 2 away from the partially reflecting mirror by 150 nanometers without moving mirror 3 (the results of which are shown in Table 1) is equivalent to moving mirror 2 away from it by 75 nanometers while moving mirror 3 toward it by 75 nanometers. Accordingly, based on the information in Table 1, the expected light intensity would be 57 milliwatts.

39. C The results of Experiment 1, as recorded in the table, tell us that the two components of light are in phase at high light intensity, while they are out of phase at low light intensity. Referring to the graph of the curve for light source #2, notice that, as mirror 2 was slowly moved by 400 nanometers, light intensity peaked three times. The second peak occurred at one-third of the interval from 200 to 400 nanometers. Choice **C** identifies this peak.

40. J The passage indicates that "frequency" of a light source refers to the number of waves per second. Experiment 2 was designed to compare wavelengths (measured in nanometers) of light sources with different frequencies. The three graphs clearly show that the wavelengths differ. A direct relationship between frequency and wavelength makes sense. The statements in answer choices **F** and **G** contradict the results of Experiment 2. Choice **H** provides a nonsensical statement. (In both experiments, the number of light components was fixed at 2.)

Your Practice Test Scores

The results from your practice tests will give you a **general** idea of what you might score if you had to take the ACT today. To convert the number of right answers on your self-evaluation test into an ACT scaled score, do the following:

Refer to the table below. For each subject area, count the number of right answers and find that number in the left-hand column marked "Raw Score." Move to the right until you have the column for the appropriate subject. That is your ACT scaled score for the subject area. For example, if you had 39 right answers on your Math test, you would find the number 39 in the left-hand column, then move right to the Math column and see that you have an ACT scaled score of 23.

After you have found your scaled score for each subject, add all four scaled numbers together and divide by four. Round fractions to the nearest whole number; round upward. This number is your ACT composite score.

Score Conversion Table

Raw Score	English Scaled Score	Math Scaled Score	Reading Scaled Score	Science Scaled Score
75	36			
74	35			
73	34			
72	33			
71	32			
70	31			
69	30			
68	30			
67	29			
66	29			
65	28			
64	28			

Score Conversion Table				
Raw Score	English Scaled Score	Math Scaled Score	Reading Scaled Score	Science Scaled Score
63	27			
62	27			
61	26			
60	26	36		
59	25	35		
58	25	34		
57	24	34		
56	24	33		
55	23	32		
54	23	31		
53	23	30		
52	22	30		
51	22	29		
50	22	29		
49	21	28		
48	21	28		
47	21	27		
46	20	27		
45	20	26		
44	20	26		
43	19	25		
42	19	25		
41	19	24		
40	18	24	36	36
39	18	23	35	34
38	18	23	33	32
37	17	23	32	30
36	17	22	31	29
35	17	22	30	28
34	16	21	29	27

Score Conversion Table				
Raw Score	English Scaled Score	Math Scaled Score	Reading Scaled Score	Science Scaled Score
33	16	21	28	27
32	15	20	27	26
31	15	20	27	25
30	14	19	26	24
29	14	19	25	24
28	14	19	25	23
27	13	18	24	23
26	13	18	23	22
25	13	18	23	22
24	12	17	22	21
23	12	17	21	21
22	12	17	20	20
21	11	16	19	20
20	11	16	18	19
19	11	16	18	19
18	10	15	17	18
17	10	15	16	18
16	10	15	15	17
15	9	14	15	17
14	9	14	14	16
13	9	14	14	16
12	8	13	13	15
11	8	13	13	15
10	7	13	12	14
9	7	12	11	13
8	6	12	10	12
7	6	11	8	11
6	5	11	7	10
5	4	10	6	9
4	3	8	5	8

Score Conversion Table				
Raw Score	English Scaled Score	Math Scaled Score	Reading Scaled Score	Science Scaled Score
3	2	6	4	7
2	2	5	3	5
1	1	3	2	3
0	1	1	1	1

Peterson's Book Satisfaction Survey

Give Us Your Feedback

Thank you for choosing Peterson's as your source for personalized solutions for your education and career achievement. Please take a few minutes to answer the following questions. Your answers will go a long way in helping us to produce the most user-friendly and comprehensive resources to meet your individual needs.

When completed, please tear out this page and mail it to us at:

Publishing Department
Peterson's, a Nelnet company
2000 Lenox Drive
Lawrenceville, NJ 08648

You can also complete this survey online at **www.petersons.com/booksurvey.**

1. What is the ISBN of the book you have purchased? (The ISBN can be found on the book's back cover in the lower right-hand corner.) ____________________

2. Where did you purchase this book?

- ❑ Retailer, such as Barnes & Noble
- ❑ Online reseller, such as Amazon.com
- ❑ Petersons.com
- ❑ Other (please specify) ____________________

3. If you purchased this book on Petersons.com, please rate the following aspects of your online purchasing experience on a scale of 4 to 1 (4 = Excellent and 1 = Poor).

	4	**3**	**2**	**1**
Comprehensiveness of Peterson's Online Bookstore page	❑	❑	❑	❑
Overall online customer experience	❑	❑	❑	❑

4. Which category best describes you?

- ❑ High school student
- ❑ Parent of high school student
- ❑ College student
- ❑ Graduate/professional student
- ❑ Returning adult student
- ❑ Teacher
- ❑ Counselor
- ❑ Working professional/military
- ❑ Other (please specify) ____________________

5. Rate your overall satisfaction with this book.

Extremely Satisfied	Satisfied	Not Satisfied
❑	❑	❑

6. Rate each of the following aspects of this book on a scale of 4 to 1 (4 = Excellent and 1 = Poor).

	4	3	2	1
Comprehensiveness of the information	❑	❑	❑	❑
Accuracy of the information	❑	❑	❑	❑
Usability	❑	❑	❑	❑
Cover design	❑	❑	❑	❑
Book layout	❑	❑	❑	❑
Special features *(e.g., CD, flashcards, charts, etc.)*	❑	❑	❑	❑
Value for the money	❑	❑	❑	❑

7. This book was recommended by:

❑ Guidance counselor
❑ Parent/guardian
❑ Family member/relative
❑ Friend
❑ Teacher
❑ Not recommended by anyone—I found the book on my own
❑ Other (please specify) ______________________________

8. Would you recommend this book to others?

Yes	Not Sure	No
❑	❑	❑

9. Please provide any additional comments.

____

____

____

____

____

Remember, you can tear out this page and mail it to us at:

Publishing Department
Peterson's, a Nelnet company
2000 Lenox Drive
Lawrenceville, NJ 08648

or you can complete the survey online at **www.petersons.com/booksurvey.**

Your feedback is important to us at Peterson's, and we thank you for your time!

If you would like us to keep in touch with you about new products and services, please include your e-mail address here: ______________________________________